DATE DUE

MAY 03 2001			
AUG 1 0 2005	-ILL		
9-6-05-ILL			
JUL 1 8 2012			

THE SONGS OF JOHANNES BRAHMS

THE SONGS OF

JOHANNES BRAHMS

ERIC SAMS

Yale University Press

New Haven and London

Typeset in Adobe Garamond
by Northern Phototypesetting Co. Ltd, Bolton
Printed in Great Britain by Biddles Ltd, Guildford and King's Lynn

Library of Congress Cataloging-in-Publication Data
Sams, Eric.
   The songs of Johannes Brahms / Eric Sams.
      p. cm.
   Includes bibliographical references (p.) and indexes.
   ISBN 0-300-07962-1 (cloth: alk. paper)
   1. Brahms, Johannes, 1833-1897. Songs. 2. Songs—Analysis, appreciation.
   I. Title.
   MT121.B73 S36 2000
   782.42168′092—dc21   99-88597

A catalogue record for this book is available from the British Library.

10 9 8 7 6 5 4 3 2 1

in memory of Gretel

CONTENTS

FOREWORD

This is the most eagerly awaited book on lieder to be published in recent times. For twenty years there have been rumours of a 'Brahms' to complement the Sams *Wolf* and *Schumann*[1]; indeed, it was beginning to seem a chimera as elusive and legendary as Proust's long-promised *chef-d'oeuvre*. There was a tantalizing foretaste in the shape of a *BBC Music Guide* of 1972, but this was a summary of the plot rather than the complete novel. The question '*Aimez-vous Brahms?* Sag an' was left hanging in the air ... Here is the answer at last, a resounding 'yes' from Op. 3 to Op. 121, and well worth the wait. It is enough to say that the book is a fit companion for the others; like those masterpieces (it was Gerald Moore who described *The Songs of Hugo Wolf* as such in his preface of 1961) this study will systematically open up a great composer's song-output to the deeper under-standing of countless music lovers. And the book's long gestation has turned out, in the end, to be for the best. Twenty years ago Brahms still suffered from many an anti-Victorian put-down (I heard Walter Legge refer to him as 'Holy Joe' and Benjamin Britten once called him 'Silly old Brahms'). Since then, new scholarship (one thinks of Malcolm MacDonald and Styra Avins) has given him back his rightful stature in the English speaking world; this book appears as a timely and important part of that continuing re-evaluation.

The writing welcomes the enthusiast without excluding the beginner, a kind-liness which is typical of the author, despite his uncompromising integrity and intellect. These latter qualities, whilst indispensable, have led to many a didactic disquisition on this subject which is dry as dust. Dry is hardly the word for this beautifully flowing and playful prose, ever-allusive because that is what the lied itself is. And dry is not the word for Sams himself who is never ashamed to shed a tear with the music, and who is at one with the public in their amazement at a musical miracle. There is no one-upmanship in Eric Sams the writer on lieder (he reserves his battling for the skirmishes of Shakespeare studies); simultaneously 'Germanist' and English patriot, he is our most knowledgeable guide at the enchanted nineteenth-century crossroads where word intersects with music, but he is not much taken by present-day geography. What he loves, with an affection unsullied by modern-day reality, are the enchanted realms of *Märchen* and yes,

---

[1] *The Songs of Hugo Wolf* with a foreword by Gerald Moore (1961) and *The Songs of Robert Schumann* with a foreword by Gerald Moore (1969).

Lieder. Sams's Germany is untouched by twentieth-century conflicts, and the reputations of his composer-heroes are impervious to the fluctuations of the Frankfurt stock exchange. Thus, despite his fathomless knowledge of another language and literature, his feet remain securely on English-speaking soil; he understands how his fellow music-lovers may be drawn to this music, heart and soul, without being able to quote chapter and verse. And here he helpfully intercedes, never at a loss as a gentleman-prophet with, now, *three* books which constitute the lieder lover's Bible. The wisdom therein is various: it is lucid enough for the layman, and detailed and challenging enough for the most seasoned scholar.

The Songs of Johannes Brahms is cunningly organized so that singers, ever in a hurry, may consult one song at a time for a quick fix, while the serious Brahmsian can explore with relish the notes after each song (these are the fruit of a lifetime's gathering of knowledge), the admirable poets' appendix, or the bibliography. For me, the two prefatory chapters are the purest and most valuable Sams. As in his book on Schumann, he adumbrates a list of motifs – tonal analogues for verbal ideas, which shows how the mind of the composer worked when it came to finding appropriate and apposite music for the poets' imagery. This section may at first seem over-fanciful, or heavy-going; you can ignore it and still learn more here about the Brahms songs than anywhere else. But I am convinced that Sams's reputation as a great song scholar will not rest solely on the felicities of his descriptive prose: here is an ordered attempt to get inside the very mind of a great composer and to understand how the Brahmsian creative process, just like that of his mentor-model Schumann, was governed by the magic of what Schumann, in his *Carnaval,* called 'Lettres dansantes'. This section of the book, and its equivalent in *The Songs of Robert Schumann,* are nothing less than spell-binding: here are the secrets behind the various alchemies (decoded by Sams after decades of thought) used by those masters to help them to release words from the printed page and transform them into tones both golden and significant.

When we listen to the music of Brahms we often hear in it a depth of emotion which seems too profound to explain; it takes the mind of a Sams to lay bare the layers of secret meaning which make up the complex weave of these great songs. The deciphering of each palimpsest in sound is accompanied by a profound and imaginative sympathy for Brahms's own buried feelings; where else but on page twenty of this very book would we read of a documented incident where the composer, in conversation with a friend, identifies the notes on which frogs croak, followed by Sams's observation that those very notes constitute the musical letters of the composer's name, and that in certain works the lonely composer, like the fairy-tale prince, is trying to tell us that he, too, had long croaked unkissed? This scholarship is *fabelhaft* in every sense of the word.

The inter-relationship of word and tone is a discipline that confuses both the musicologists *pur sang,* and the literary scholars. Thus it is that the skills of an Eric Sams or of a Susan Youens, which seem to me outrageously under-rewarded, are hard to place within conventional academe. On the concert platform, however, they are the very breath of life; an understanding of why and how *that* text goes with *this* music releases, like nothing else, the communicative power of singer and pianist. The universities should have given Eric Sams a chair, but their loss has been practical music making's gain. I hereby nominate him for a piano stool, an honorary seat at any concert hall he cares to visit, but even this is not really his milieu. Although he regularly supports his performing friends and colleagues, listening to recitals has never been at the core of Sams's song gathering. Home is where the art is, and the lied began in the home as a domestic form. Countless evenings in Surrey have been spent around the piano playing and singing songs so that his sons (especially the famous Jeremy) have a vast knowledge of everything from Schubert to *The Geisha* and Billy Mayerl. This juxtaposition is typical of the lack of pretentiousness that one only finds in the homes of the greatest experts. And throughout his life Sams has been amiably accessible to anyone who loves the same things – information, advice, translations have poured out of his home, and the enquiries of the great Walter Legge and of the most humble student have been treated with equal courtesy.

In the early 1970s, at a party following a colleague's recital, I found myself talking to a man who seemed to be interested in my views on Wolf. I was a recent enough convert to the lied but counted myself well-informed. He seemed to want to know my opinion on this and that and, to my shame, I gave it. Then he asked me something about Wolf and Wagner, and at last I had to acknowledge my limitations – 'You'd have to ask Eric Sams about that,' I said. 'That's not very helpful' he replied 'You see, I *am* Eric Sams.' It was thus that I first met the man who has shaped my thinking about music as much as Gerald Moore, Peter Pears, Pierre Bernac and other masters at whose feet I have been privileged to sit. This does not mean that Eric and I have talked much over the years about pianistic or vocal technicalities, fingering, arm-weight or breath-control. Instead, we have endlessly discussed the ideas behind the music and the way that a handful of great composers was able to illuminate poetry with a truth and aptness that gives wings to the soul and brings tears to the eyes. We have cried together, and laughed even more, often uproariously. But each time I telephoned him I felt that I was taking him away from his 'Brahms'. I almost certainly was – that is if he was not engaged with Shakespeare who is a Samsian hero, I suspect, because he wrote plays with a mindset similar to that of a great lieder composer. So I (and the hundreds of others who knew they could always 'ask Eric') have an apology to make to the public for the delay of this book, among others. In the absence of a 'Schubert' (the next task, I hope) this 'Brahms' will do more than nicely.

GRAHAM JOHNSON
London, 2000

PREFACE

This book has been delayed by circumstance, Meanwhile, Brahms scholarship has flourished. In particular a minutely detailed catalogue (McCorkle 1984) and two critical biographies (MacDonald 1990, Swafford 1997) have become available, together with a book on the songs (Stark 1995) and a comprehensive collection of letters in English translation (Avins 1997). All five are recommended as sources of further information and commentary.

The present volume, like its predecessors in the same format,[1] gives a date, translation, commentary and notes on points of detail for each of the published songs for voice and piano arranged by opus number if any, or else inserted in order of composition. The eight solo versions of the *Zigeunerlieder* Op. 103 have also been included, bringing the total tally to 212. The heading of each song gives its title in German (with an English equivalent in brackets) together with its opus number if any, the poet or source-book, the date of the setting, and its key and written compass.[2]

Next comes the German text (a novel feature), as set by Brahms and printed in the two main collected editions, the *Gesamtausgabe* or Peters. As in those sources, the contractions have been preserved (thus apostrophes are often omitted); but the older *Gesamtausgabe* spellings have been modernised (e.g. to 'Blüte' from 'Blüthe'). Similarly the poetry is printed without indentation, except where this is required by the verse-form.

It is admittedly not always easy to determine which of the composer's many alterations or variants were deliberate and which inadvertent; nor are they all now reversible. Some may be considered venial or trivial; and not all call for comment. In general, I have refrained from mentioning changes of title or differences of spelling or punctuation (such as the presence or absence of exclamation marks) between the original poems and the text underlay familiar to lieder-lovers. But all

---

[1] *The Songs of Hugo Wolf,* Faber and Faber, 3/1992; *The Songs of Robert Schumann,* Faber and Faber, 3/1993.

[2] In the so-called Helmholtz notation, i.e.

other significant divergences from the known or inferable textual sources, together with any recommendations for restoring the original text, whether in performance or in future editions, are duly recorded in the first note to each song.

The translations are again designed to bring out, if possible without addition or paraphrase, the meaning of the words. Square brackets enclose the composer's textual repetitions, while added indentations (also a novel feature) denote a substantive piano interlude. The commentaries assume no knowledge of German, and all their quotations are duly translated. The detailed notes, however, are intended for performers and students, and here some knowledge of German is assumed.

As a general rule, the notes begin with textual points and end with a reference to any other major settings of the same words. In between come comments on Brahms's use of motivic device and his preferred poetic topics, together with structural analysis where that aspect calls for special mention.

An appendix contains brief biographies of the poets and a listing (another novel feature) of all their settings ever written or sketched by Brahms, in any genre.

The whole is prefaced with general reflections on Brahms as a song-writer. Here I have striven to avoid repetition of my own earlier thoughts (1972) on that subject, while retaining the same general approach, namely that the essential task shared by listeners and performers alike is to appreciate the intimate interconnection between words, music and emotion – the essence of what Brahms called his *Wortausdruck* or musico-verbal expression in the song form.

ACKNOWLEDGEMENTS

I owe most to my family and friends. The London Library was, as ever, indispensable. I am indebted to the scholarship of Kurt Hofmann and his monographs on Brahms's books (1974) and first editions (1975). Thanks are also due to the staff and services of the British Library, the Institute of Germanic Studies, the Wiener Stadt- und Landesbibliothek, Dr Ernst Hilmar, Graham Johnson and Frank Sypher.

BRAHMS AS A SONG-WRITER

Brahms is the most misunderstood and neglected of all the great lied-composers. He was a thorough-going Romantic, who expressed his own feelings. Yet he often chose to conceal or dissemble those feelings. Indeed, his instrumental music sometimes sounds almost ashamed of its own emotivity. This reticence is what anti-Brahmsians such as Wagner, Wolf, Nietzsche, Shaw and Britten heard and hated. In 1886, Wolf outspokenly called it 'die intensivste musikalische Impotenz' (*Kritiken* 244), as more famously echoed by Nietzsche two years later in his much-mistranslated phrase 'Die Melancholie des Unvermögens', the melancholy of inability.

There is some truth in such strictures. The long-flighted melodic lines sometimes tend to tail off. Every music-lover knows how the first symphony's glorious last-movement theme begins, but who recalls exactly how or where it ends? And although Brahms matured early as a composer, he remained a late developer in other respects. His voice was slow to break and slower still to deepen. When his beard grew he hid behind it; the sweet sensitive mouth and chin escaped out of harm's way. Just so in the music; the warm animated features are often covered by the mask of introversion or depression.

So the deep Brahmsian warmth has to be cajoled out, *con amore*. His lieder in particular respond readily to that treatment. Of all the great nineteenth-century German song-writers, he most needs vibrato and rubato. The language of musical emotion is Italian; and it is no coincidence that Brahms spent in Italy all the time (and much of the money) he could spare. Some of that sunshine went into his happier songs, especially those depicting an easy-going Latin attitude to life and love (such as *Serenade*, No. 99, addressed to the delectable Dolores). He never mastered the Italian language, though he loved the sound and sense of it; but he was a master of its grammar. In music too he was devoted to form and structure; and those elements will dominate, to the detriment of expressiveness and appreciation, unless the true depths of feeling are plumbed and exploited.

But here another difficulty supervenes. Schubert, Schumann and Wolf were often inspired by poetry as such. Brahms was better grounded than they in musical techniques and technicality; and he remained a voracious reader all his life. But he had little time, in any sense, for literary criticism. To start with, he was too busy earning his living, and his family's. From the age of fourteen, if not earlier, he spend much time as a public-house pianist, in what have been decorously called 'simple restaurants for respectable people' (Avins 4). But according to Brahms's own account (as attested in Schauffler 224–6; Swafford cites several other sources) some of them at least were more like brothels; and that was when, where and what he learnt about women (see also MacDonald 397). Despite the wealth of great love-poetry so freely accessible to him in the work of Goethe, Heine and Mörike, he far more frequently chose lesser lyrics embodying topics or sentiments that happened to hold a special significance for him personally, and clothed them in matching music. Inside the songs, listeners can sense, and interpreters can reveal, the naked original inspiration, which is very often derived directly from poetic words and ideas that struck personal chords of memory and emotion.

Songs were among Brahms's first works (in 1853); they were among his last (in 1896). All his life, most of his music was associated with words, whether as overt texts or covert allusions. Even the instrumental works often contain printed words, as on all three early piano sonatas Opp. 1, 2 and 5, the Edward-Ballade Op. 10/1 and the late Intermezzo Op. 117/1. The G major sextet Op. 36 declaims the name Agathe in musical notes; and of course Brahms also used special themes and formulae to denote Clara Schumann, the longest, dearest and deepest love of his whole life. In all this he much resembled his revered master Robert Schumann. When the latter's life and works were commemorated in 1873, Brahms was asked to compose a choral piece for the occasion. He replied (Kalbeck ii 430–31) that he could find no suitable words, and in any event felt that the music to be heard should be that of Schumann himself, 'who speaks my language better than I do'. And he added that Schumann would always be his ideal or model.

In other words, Brahms too incorporated his own inward feelings into his art. There is clear evidence about his musical means for achieving this aim, especially in his lieder. He described his desiderata in detail to his only song-writing pupil (Jenner 1905).

Talent for melody, Brahms explained, was of course the first requisite. Next came counterpoint.[1] The combination of melodies was rated essential; an art-song should begin as a vocal line and a bass part. All such technique should be mastered as early as possible. Then musical form should correspond with the poetic text, which the composer should have by heart (a view that colourably confirms some of Brahms's changes as mere memorial errors, which now need correction).

The structure and metre of the poem were major considerations, and errors in translating them into musical terms were to be condemned as defects in understanding. Thus the aptness of musical form, whether strophic, ternary or through-composed, depends on Brahms's appreciation and understanding of the poem as such, which is impossible to establish and hence unrewarding to analyse. It is perhaps enough to know that he always prided himself on his literary appreciation. And there is certainly good evidence, as set forth in the commentaries or notes concerned, that he had studied prosody, both German and

[1] which Brahms also recommended to the young Hugo Wolf (much to the latter's fury) as the essential subject for serious study.

classical. The vital criterion is that Brahms meant his songs to mirror their poems down to the last detail. In particular, he felt that any pauses for emphasis or effect which would be made by a skilled speaker should also be reflected in the music, which had its own phraseology and punctuation. For example, any cadential 6/4 chord should always be carefully positioned. Key relationships and modulations also had their part to play, like every other aspect of rhythm, melody and harmony. Accompaniments were to be independent. A vital detail was 'verbal expressiveness' (*Wortausdruck*), though not to the detriment of the general picture.

These austere prescriptions were not easy to follow, even for Brahms himself. He rejected and destroyed many songs before selecting those he thought suitable for publication. Even then he often failed to indicate the necessary nuances, even in the vital *Wortausdruck*, which he may have assessed as self-evident. As every singing-teacher knows, however, it is not. All his life, Brahms modestly supposed that others were as susceptible to musical meaning as he was. Thus he was always as ready to learn as to teach. In particular he recommended his own practice of studying Schubert, as the greatest of masters and mentors. He would certainly have noticed 'Schubert's composing unconscious . . . in the process of forming a vast vocabulary (sometimes borrowed from other sources, particularly Mozart) of tonal analogues and motifs, a library of words-to-music correspondences' (Johnson, notes to CDJ 33020).

Brahms the great technician also developed his own special expressive vocabulary for song-writing, as Jenner (1905) indicates. But as the same source shows, and the songs confirm, every element of music is available for such purposes, from general structure to the timbre of particular notes. The supposedly classical composer, supreme master of the purely objective sound-pattern, is also an incorrigible Romantic whose music expresses subjective moods and feelings. Hugo Wolf, the finest composer-critic as well as the greatest song-writer of his generation, heard this latter aspect of Brahms with startling clarity, for example in the G major string sextet Op. 36 (*Kritiken* 19, 31) and the 'splendid song' *Von ewiger Liebe* (No. 58; ibid. 362). The latter was 'the best that Brahms has created in this genre', i.e. up to 1887; it was 'deeply-felt and consistently atmospheric', two qualities which Wolf was supremely well placed to identify and appreciate. He ranked the sextet as a fine companion-piece to the F major string quintet Op. 88, in the first movement of which he heard picturesque musical imagery, a component rarely associated with Brahms, least of all in the instrumental music, but detected and analysed in fine detail by the most sensitive of receptors. For certain listeners, therefore, Brahms's song-music must be even more motivic, in its inmost essence.

This book shares that standpoint. But it leads to certain difficulties, even among like-minded advocates and devotees. Firstly, it means that the Brahms lied-genre may often sound undifferentiatedly identical, i.e. abstract and detached, as his instrumental work in general is often described. And indeed many well-informed experts and scholars have heard it thus. Nor is such a reaction by any means mistaken. Brahms was indeed the cerebral introvert that his friends and correspondents, as well as his detractors, so often described. Of all the great composers, he was the foremost musicologist, an eclectic collector and editor of works from all periods and sources. So, secondly, words often seem inessential to him, even foreign to his purposes. Even in the songs, he displays the unity of rhythm and tempo that characterises the master of absolute music. It is no coincidence that his lieder always seem so ready to turn into duo sonatas – sometimes with shared melodies, as when the violin in the sonata Op. 100/1 is heard singing a variant of the vocal line in *Wie Melodien zieht es* (No. 186), composed in the same summer season. Elisabet von Herzogenberg (ii 207) told the composer that his *Auf dem See* (No. 101) sounded better on the fiddle than sung. So much for his painstaking preoccupation with verbal detail; but one can hear what she meant. How much better still, though, to appreciate such all-pervasive expressiveness, which is conceived as quasi-verbal. In such respects, Brahms is an innovator, the creator of a new individual tonal world that has to be explored and mapped before it yields up its full rewarding richness. The language has to be learned, or the message will be misconstrued even by devoted admirers. It was again the outspoken Elisabet (ii 132) who complained that the rootless chords and progressions in *Immer leiser* (No. 187) lacked the usual Brahmsian beauty and indeed positively pained her. She might have heard them differently had she realised that such rootlessness was deliberately designed to express the idea of hovering between life and death. In our own day, a usually perceptive critic has complained that the seeming change from 6/8 to 3/4 at the end of *Von ewiger Liebe* (No. 58) merely wrenched the rhythm awry. On the contrary; those hemiolas are a deep response to the poem's final affirmation that 'our love must for ever, for ever abide'; and they are entirely typical of the Brahms song at its superlative best. The following pages are intended to offer a general (though of course far from complete or definitive) guide to Brahmsian methods of *Wortausdruck*, or verbal expressiveness, in music.

MOTIFS

From its earliest beginnings in Mozart, Beethoven and above all Schubert (see Johnson, CD notes) the lied form is characterised by an intimate interconnection between ideas and music, often at a depth that defies description, let alone analysis. Brahms is a past master of this style, which renders his song-music intimately motivic down to its finest details. These need to be known and studied. The following conspectus aims to help performers to express, and listeners to experience, the meaningful content of each song. It is confined to examples only; there are far too many motifs to mention each time they occur. For the same reason, only those that are especially frequent or manifest, or readily definable, have been allotted a specific serial number, prefixed by M for motif; but many further instances of close correspondence between word and tone are also included in the notes to individual songs. Further, a mass of motivic elements can combine and recombine in hundreds of different compounds; and this is especially true of Brahms, whose motifs range from the physical to the metaphysical.

One such motif-cluster, which unites both those realms, is universally acknowledged as signifying death. Brahms, like Keats, was 'half in love with easeful death', and for far longer; and he met his own end with stoic fortitude. His musical musings on that stern subject, though well known, are still perhaps not always well understood. Thus he has been rebuked (by the poet concerned, among others) for his treatment of the words 'mir ist's als ob ich längst gestorben bin' (I feel as though I had long since passed away) in *Feldeinsamkeit* (No. 157). In its context, this means no more than the poetic sensation of drifting disembodied through space. Yet Brahms supposedly interprets the phrase funereally; his alternating piano octaves audibly descend into darkness, slow step by step. And this interpretation also conforms closely with the separate motivic ideas of which this cluster is composed. Thus, as we shall see, depths and heights on the keyboard correspond to dark and bright, despair and delight. But the music is marked staccato, which implies a light touch in every sense. Nothing is here for tears; the feeling is one of detachment, in the music as in the poem.

Here, as always, each separate component has its own special significance, which varies according to context. Thus the same descending pattern at the words 'der noch nicht ist' (whoever does not yet exist) in *Ich wandte mich* (No. 202) falls by successive minor thirds, creating diminished-seventh harmonies suitable for the mysteries of non-existence, much as in the *Feldeinsamkeit* passage but shorn of its staccato. Also entirely legato is the same pattern in a sadly broken G minor chord at 'da lobte ich die Toten' (then I praised the dead) in the same song. Elsewhere the sombre key of E flat minor darkens the broken octaves still further; thus the keyboard's descent falls pat at the word 'Grab' (grave) in *Lied* (No. 4), while the opening accompaniment of *Es reit ein Herr* (WoO 33 No. 28), even in that ostensibly folk-song setting, sounds so sinister as to presage the murder described in the third verse. Brahms himself, in a letter to Hermine Spies (Avins 647), specifically associates this key with lamentation.

Other motivic clusters and their components (touch, key, register, harmony and so forth) will be described later. But one common element of this multi-faceted 'death' compound can serve as a starting-point for all Brahmsian song-motifs, namely the limping broken octaves that here as elsewhere imply motion and often locomotion. The pianist's fingers walk along the keyboard; motif (hereafter M) 1.

This physical aspect is basic. From the first, the songs are often written in vigorous body-language. The young Brahms was an athlete, as Eugenie Schumann (1925 14–15) remembered all her long life. 'I can clearly picture a crowd of children standing in the hall of a house in Düsseldorf [i.e. the Schumann family home in the 1850s]. They were looking up in amazement at the landing banisters. There a young man with long blond hair was performing all manner of daring gymnastic routines, swinging to left and right, up and down. At last he lifted up both arms, stretched his legs high in the air and leapt down with one swoop, right into the middle of the admiring crowd of children, We were those children, I and my rather older siblings, and the young man was Johannes Brahms.'

The same young man was always a tireless walker who had made a Rhine journey like Siegfried but on foot, with a rucksack (Kalbeck i 69ff). In his experience, country walks were a steady source of inspiration, especially in the early morning (E. Schumann 266); the repetitive bodily movement rendered the creative mind free and receptive. Throughout the songs, relevant poetic imagery is instantly translated into motifs of walking, whether free or fettered, young or old.

Thus when Ludwig Tieck says how slowly time moves in the absence of the beloved, he invokes an image of walking with lead weights on the feet, which Brahms depicts thus in *Wie soll ich die Freude* (No. 48):

Again, when Friedrich Rückert claims in *Mit vierzig Jahren* (No. 164) that life's mountain is climbed at forty, this is no mere figure of speech for Brahms, whose piano accompaniment walks with a palpable effort. The same marching quavers are shifted off the beat, thus, like catches in the breath:

And even if the words never mention walking, the sad belated wanderer envisaged in *An den Mond* (No. 136) is musically characterised as trudging bravely on:

As it happens, each of those passages begins in B minor, which like other keys has its own unique tone of discontent and distress. But essentially each is offered here as an example of M1, the walking movement of feet and legs.

Next, M2, comes the corresponding effortful movement of hands and arms. This clearly occurs in the famous *Der Schmied* (No. 32), when the blacksmith is heard and seen at his forge, wielding his hammer. But the same motif can also be far more metaphorical, indeed perhaps subliminal, as in *Salamander* (No. 197), when a bad girl threw that mythical creature into the fire with a certain finicking distaste, as conveyed by the pianist's right hand at the words 'ins Feuer ihn hinein', thus:

Similarly when the apostle Paul speaks of the faith that can move mountains (No. 204), the music mentally bares its biceps and makes as if to shift those obstacles, this time with both hands:

In a natural corollary (M3) the flight of birds is drawn in the same swift brush-strokes; arms become wings. Again the words offer corroboration. Thus the nightingales happily ply their pinions in the early song *Nachtigallen schwingen* (No. 14); here, as in *Das Mädchen spricht* (No. 198) over thirty years later, the wings fly at the touch of hands on the keyboard, to right and to left. And when a little bird flies over the Rhine at the beginning of *Auf dem Schiffe* (No. 181), the two right-hand semiquaver triplets flutter engagingly in wing-beats of falling seconds or thirds, with a moment's rest for recovery.

Here the scale is smaller; the wings are seen in the distance. The same figuration can also connote the fluttering of leaves (M4), as in *Lied* (No. 6). The apt pattern here is one of alternation; the music fluctuates and flickers. The widening of these intervals indicates that the leaves are being blown further apart; so broken octaves hint at a stiff breeze as the woodlands rustle in *Parole* (No. 16).

Such pulsation is also apt for waves, which when in the distance (as seen far out from the shore in *Treue Liebe*, No. 15) go lapping upwards in broken thirds. But their closer approach is drawn in bolder arpeggio outline, which needs a separate classification (M5); and this in turn is further developed into cascades of broken chords that tell of foaming waves in *Verzweiflung* (No. 52) or *Wie froh und frisch* (No. 56).

All this music is infinitely variable; and the examples so far cited will serve to confirm how such elements as register, compass, texture and pitch continually relate to notional or actual position in space; thus walking (M1) takes place at a lower level than throwing (M2), and this in turn ranks far below flying (M3), which graces the upper reaches of the keyboard. Down below, the left hand signals real or imagined depths, of the ocean or of despair (M6). These concepts naturally entail descent in pitch, as in the death motif already adumbrated, which moves down into darkness; and this is what low left-hand notes or octaves often signify (M7); thus the bass B keynote of the prelude to *Von ewiger Liebe* (No. 58) has already anticipated the opening words of the poem, 'Dunkel, wie dunkel', while in the postlude to *Der Tod, das ist die kühle Nacht* (No. 176) the churchyard bell tolls an ominous C major midnight. Similarly bass notes can also connote deep roots, firm foundations, unshakable faith (M8). All such concepts (M6–M8) are often underlined or sustained by pedal points. From the low notes of darkness also arise the arpeggios of dream (M9), often (again as in No. 176) actually associated with the word 'Traum'. These slow waves rarely aspire to the conscious realms of the right hand but tend to remain within the left-hand realm of night, sleep and reverie. The contrasting heights and highlights in voice or keyboard (M10) stand for such ideas as life and love, zest and exultation. These feelings are surprisingly prevalent; and they light up the melodic lines. Yet they are not always aptly brought out. It is true that even among his intimates, Brahms was often rated much more of a pessimist, or at least a pejorist, than an optimist or a meliorist. But perhaps his real emotions, in his life as in his music, were often well disguised. Certainly many of the motifs here described can also be heard as the merest rudiments of music; ordinary sonorities, with no special significance. For some listeners and performers, however, the words of the vocal music will permit the identification of correspondences, as on the Rosetta stone, from the first published song onwards. In *Liebestreu* (No. 1) the music ascends graphically up the keyboard or the vocal line from darkness into light, despair into hope, to illustrate the poetic idea that stones sink in the sea but love rises on high. Similarly, great differences of pitch in voice or piano can form a composite image of spaciousness or distance, ranging from M6 to M10. At the zenith, just as in Schubert or Wolf, high keyboard notes suggest bright stars (M11), as in *Wie rafft ich mich auf* (No. 34), at the words 'melodischer Wandel der Sterne' (melodious movements of the stars). This too forms part of an unobtrusive Brahmsian image-cluster; the top right-hand notes also make a melody, while the circling triplet quavers in contrary motion modestly illustrate the stars in their courses.

These lieder-devices may sometimes be difficult to detect, because they so often merge into rather than emerge from the purely sonorous surface of the music. It may well at first seem something of an exaggeration to propose for example that a final fermata, i.e. a pause sign written over a song's last note or chord, is in any real sense motivic. But such ideas nevertheless possess audible meaning in many a Brahms song. Listen, reflect on what you have just heard; or, more mundanely, don't clap yet. Picture the scene, identify with the protagonist, wonder what happens next; in a word, wait. Such ideas are quasi-operatic in their evocation of scene and character; and they are admittedly old-fashioned in their unabashedly self-absorbed 19th-century Romanticism. Like the Lost Chord itself, they tremble away into silence as if they were loth to cease. In that context, they even aspire to pitch a Jacob's ladder between heaven and the concert-hall. No doubt the agnostic Brahms never intended, still less articulated, any such feelings. But the fermatas should be observed, in every sense, even though their verbal implications (such as finality, triumph, meditation, and so forth) often defy detailed verbal analysis.

The same applies to other quasi-operatic inflections of the melodic line, such as the turn, mordent or gruppetto, meaning a serene assurance of bel canto utterance, or a sudden upward leap to express emotional expansiveness. Recitative passages put the vocal line in inverted commas, so to speak, while the insertion of a pause between syllables indicates an excited gasping for breath. All this serves to create mood or character. So do such devices as canon, augmentation, diminution, contrary motion or inversion. These were all second nature to Brahms, who was indeed in a sense a classical composer creating highly organised sound-patterns. But such patterns, in the German tradition from Bach onwards, were often charged with quasi-verbal significance. Thus canon (M12) entails two separate but related figures, like the mother and daughter throughout the first published song, *Liebestreu* (No. 1), or the tendrils of convolvulus that twine around the roses in *Liebe und Frühling* (No. 2). So when the opening long-flighted vocal melody of *Mein wundes Herz* (No. 106) instantly recurs in the left hand, in a gentle G major instead of a wounded E minor, the attentive listener hears an image of yearning followed by the desired fulfilment. Meanwhile the same E minor theme has appeared in right-hand quaver-for-crotchet diminution, an indefinable image of increased intensity. Contrary motion (M13) is more readily verbalized; it usually occurs in combination, as with the star-cluster image already mentioned in *Wie rafft ich mich auf* (No. 34), or the wings that nestle closer together in *Das Mädchen spricht* (No. 198).

Other such devices include hemiola (M14) and polyrhythm (M15), which respectively ease or enhance the musical tension, creating images of rest and release or of increased activity and complexity. Similarly the introduction of new rhythms, usually in smaller note-values, into accompaniment figurations already heard, are not just an automatic variation procedure; they express extra excitement (M16).

Melodic lines can also be meaningful in their own right, whether in voice or keyboard or both. Their convergence can constitute a love-motif (M17), as in Hugo Wolf. More usually, two voices sing a love-duet in thirds or sixths, standing for unity in duality, as in opera (M18). Then there is the joyous major alternation 5–6–5–6–5 that Brahms audibly associated with cheerful student songs and serenades (M19). This recurs throughout the *Academic Festival Overture* Op. 80, often in extended sequences:

The minor counterpart occurs less often; but its last two notes, 6♭–5 in any key, is a constant symbol for moans of distress (M20). This idea is often also represented by heavy or light sighs, thus < > written over whole bars or a few notes (M21). The required organ-like swell and fade is often difficult to attain on the piano; but the effect is worth recapturing, because of the verbal significance with which Brahms invested it, as demonstrated at the beginning of a letter in 1865:

'Dearest Clara, $\longrightarrow$ ff $\longrightarrow$ rit. 'Such a big sigh is sent in advance' (Litzmann, i 496).

The downward semitone of distress can on occasion be extended into a chain of major or minor seconds which can become a literal chain, tying or binding, as in *Liebe kam aus fernen Landen* (No. 46) at the moment when that idea is mentioned. A simple scalar descent to the tonic, conversely, connotes the attainment of a goal, such as arrival back home on the first page of *Wir müssen uns trennen* (No. 50) or just going to sleep as throughout *Ruhe, Süssliebchen* (No. 51). Upward movement, conversely, for example towards the mediant, as in the vocal melody that ends *O kühler Wald* (No. 142), implies incompleteness.

As in the German song tradition generally, horn-passages signal the open air, the countryside, the chase (M22), whether literally as in *Vor dem Fenster* (No. 21) where the watchman blows his horn, or allusively as in *Der Jäger* (No. 172), or conceptually as in *Parole* (No. 16) where no such notions are explicitly voiced in the poem. Further, all aspects of harmony are strongly motivic. Thus the flat supertonic of any key, e.g. D flat in C major, whether as single sound or complex chord, always brings the eternal note of sadness in (M23). A dominant chord asks a question, while the dominant seventh goes further and presents a puzzle or poses a problem (M24) which is then resolved both musically and verbally. This idea is often used to increase tension, especially when followed by a meaningful pause that audibly demands and awaits resolution. At the outer limit of this emotional range stands the diminished seventh (M25), the chord built up solely from the sad descending minor thirds so often heard throughout the Brahmsian oeuvre. In the songs, this chord signifies such tragic feelings as despair or calamity. More arcane are the rootless and hovering second inversions that characterise imminent release from earthly bonds in *Immer leiser* (No. 187), or the analogous omission of the third from certain chords to illustrate emptiness, as at the end of *Lied* (No. 6) or to show that hope itself can be hollow, as in *He, Zigeuner* (No. 205).

Similarly, chordal progressions are also verbally significant. Thus the simple undelayed resolution of a dominant seventh on to its tonic at the conclusion of a song, often has the effect of slamming a door or a possibility tight shut, as in *Vergebliches Ständchen* (No. 148) or announcing a firm resolve, as in *Das Mädchen spricht* (No. 198) or *Maienkätzchen* (No. 199), while the Amen cadence IV–I, as in Schumann, expresses piety or nobility.

Other aspects of harmony are also meaningfully expressive, both personally (as in motifs 37–42 below) or more generally. Thus particular keys or tonalities are regularly invested with verbal significance by Brahms, as by other German songwriters. His use of E flat minor, for example, regularly expresses the darkness of death and despair, as in Schumann, while the opposite extreme, A major, is a bright springtime and sunshine key, as in Wolf. Again, a minor triad, especially in a piano prelude, serves as a signpost to melancholy, also as in Schumann. There is external evidence of Brahms's clear key-associations; thus he complained to his publisher Simrock (1917.x.8) that *Herbstgefühl* (No. 78) had been transposed down a semitone, into F sharp minor, without authorisation, whereas 'G minor would have been more relevant to the composer's intention; the effect is quite different'.

In fact, only those with absolute pitch would notice anything amiss, and few of those would feel affronted. But Brahms himself was among that minority, and his views should be respected. Even though he himself sanctioned transposition for practical purposes, each of his songs should be performed in its original key if at all possible, because his tonalities are avowedly motivic. Other examples are the florid melodrama of B minor (*Von ewiger Liebe*, No. 58, or *Verrat*, No. 190), or the floral tributes of B major (*Liebe und Frühling* I–II, Nos, 2–3) depicted in exotic colours. Similarly D major and D minor characterise some of the colloquies between mothers and daughters; such key-relations correspond to the actual kinship and notional contrast between youth and age, innocence and experience.

The diatonic treatment of basic keys expresses simplicity, as in *Sonntag* (No. 69), while complex emotions are clothed in poignant chromatics as on the last page of *Agnes* (No. 104). Both those refined lyrics were conceived in folk-song style, and each setting is adapted accordingly, the former in elementary chords and a drone bass and the latter in the use of two different time-signatures (M26). Another folk-song device is the employment of modal harmonies (M27), as in *Sehnsucht* (No. 28); and their sad sound recreates a mood endemic in Brahms, whose song-music is often in tears (M28). These trickle and splash in large mezzo-staccato drops, as in *Sapphische Ode* (No. 167), which can also represent the sprinkling of dew, as in that same song, or a whole shower of rain, as in *Während des Regens* (No. 93). It takes a special mastery of technique to distinguish this soft wet sound from other equally motivic types of touch, such as the hard dry grains of dust in *Denn es gehet* (No. 201), or the trembling staccato chords in *Heimkehr* (No. 20) which introduce the detached vocal notes at 'du zitterst sehr' (you tremble so). Different again is the mysterious and delicate flitting of soft separate tones, conveying a variety of light touches as in *Blinde Kuh* (No. 92) or *Sommerfäden* (No. 141).

This idea shades into effects of silence, which omit expected sounds (M29). Thus the missing last quaver of three in the piano part at the outset of *Dämmrung senkte sich* (No. 100) indicates the gradual seeping of light from the twilit scene. Similarly the omission of a first beat may imply helplessness or weakness, while the total silence that follows the words 'und der noch nicht ist' in *Ich wandte mich* (No. 202) eerily evokes the non-existence of the unborn.

The converse concept of tight-packed song-space crammed with physical activity in both hands, as at the end of *Heimkehr* (No. 20) means, on the contrary, the prospect of a full and vibrant life (M30). Other examples are the excited alternate-hand hammering of chords for the duel scene in *Verrat* (No. 190) or of octaves as at 'O hört mich' in the *vivace* section of *Sind es Schmerzen* (No. 45) or of mixed notes and chords as throughout *Meine Liebe ist grün* (No. 117).

Such virile or adversarial moods are often expressed in dotted rhythms (M31) as at the interludes and postlude of *Murrays Ermordung* (No. 23) or on the word 'kämpfen' in *Frühlingstrost* (No. 113).

Within this varied motivic vocabulary there is still room for overt onomatopoeia, as in the galloping hoofbeats of the rider's entry in *Es liebt sich so lieblich* (No. 135), the plucked-string sound of the serenading guitar in *Serenade*

(No. 99), the church-organ tones of *Auf dem Kirchhofe* (No. 189) or the rumbustious drumming in *Tambourliedchen* (No. 126).

Brahms also employs a whole conspectus of motifs stemming from the deep-rooted German tradition of musical cryptography (Sams 1980a, etc.) from Bach onwards. This had culminated in the work of Brahms's much-loved friend and mentor Schumann, whose cast of mind Brahms shared and emulated. Thus the commonplace book of favourite quotations that the latter compiled in his youth was called *Des jungen Kreislers Schatzkästlein* (Young Kreisler's Box of Treasures). Old Kreisler was an eccentric musician in the tales of E.T.A. Hoffmann, and there was a surprisingly close affinity between that fictional character and his adventures and those of Brahms (Avins 40). But the earliest allusion was surely to Schumann's use of that name among his many personal sobriquets, e.g. in the piano cycle *Kreisleriana*. As Kalbeck says (i 103), 'there was a spiritual kinship between Kreisler junior and Kreisler senior (Schumann)'. And 'Kreisler junior' was used by Brahms as a sobriquet and pen-name, on music as well as letters, until he was about thirty years old (Avins 13). The power of that kinship is further evidenced by the *Schatzkästlein's* copious preponderance of excerpts from Jean-Paul Richter, Schumann's lifelong favourite writer. That anthology, begun *c.* 1854, draws from many other sources surely supplied or recommended by the older mentor, such as Gottfried Kinkel and Elisabeth Kulmann, who both figured among the poets of Schumann's songs. He himself is quoted (item 490) from an 1833 article that was not reprinted until 1891; prima facie he had brought this to Brahms's attention, together with other aphorisms (items 584–8). Schumann also taught Brahms chess. another fertile source of symbolism. Soon after their first meeting in 1853 the twenty-year-old Brahms was writing a scherzo movement for the so-called F.A.E. violin sonata devised by Schumann and composed by him and others in honour of their friend Joachim. It incorporated deliberate references both musical (in those notes) and verbal (in the superscription 'In *E*rwartung der *A*nkunft des … *F*reundes', in expectation of the arrival of [their] friend) to the acronym or anagram of Joachim's personal motto 'Frei aber Einsam' (free but lonely). Some commentators have contended that Brahms's contribution, the *Sonatensatz* WoO 2, makes no overt use of this F–A–E motif; but it would surely be more sensible to ask how, not whether, those notes are woven into the music. The correct answer will yield clear insights into Brahms's earliest compositional methods. So taken was he by the adoption of F.A.E. as a pseudonym that all his quotations from Joachim in the *Schatzkästlein* are signed thus, whether in musical notes (items 225–6, 228–30) or in letters of the alphabet (items 231, 234–44, 250).

No such motif is detectable in his songs. Nor is F–A–F, an acronym for Brahms's own rejoinder 'Frei aber Froh' (free but happy) expressed by those notes in any inflexion (e.g. as f#'–a'–f#" at the beginning of the *Ballade* Op. 10 No. 2, or of the duet Op. 75 No. 3). The much-debated phrase 'free but happy' surely connotes a cheerful acquiescence in loneliness, or bachelorhood, if that is the price of artistic independence. This is the very voice of creative introversion, over the ages; it would ring true even if the facts had not been vouched for by Brahms's friend and biographer Max Kalbeck (i 98–99), who was well placed to know. Nor can anyone now know better. Nor need it be doubted that Brahms himself had an innately and intensely verbo-musical mind of his own. Thus a letter to Joachim teasingly mentions the 'canonic themes f a e/gis e a': the latter, as Kalbeck explains (i 263), refers to Joachim's young admirer Gisela[1] von Arnim.

So it is no surprise that the young Brahms also spells out the first name of his beloved Agathe von Siebold in the musical notes, A–G–A–H[2]–E, again in a letter to Joachim. Kalbeck helpfully adds (i 331) that 'Brahms preserved a sonorous memento of his Göttingen love-affair [*c.* 1858] in his sweet G major sextet Op. 36, but so secretly that only the initiated know anything about it.' In the second main theme of the first movement, the first violin, in unison with the first viola, calls out three times[3]

A   G   A   H   E

So when the same notes in the same key are freely repeated in the alto and piano parts of *Und gehst du über den Kirchhof* (When you cross the churchyard) Op. 44 No. 10, a threnody for lost love sung by a four-part choir of women's voices, those with ears to hear know its likely date, place and inspiration. And then what of this repetition

on the first violins in bars 14–17 of the first Scherzo of the *Serenade* Op. 11, composed *c.* 1858?

Brahms gave Agathe an engagement ring, which is still kept in her family; and he sent her his manuscripts (now lost) of love-songs she had inspired (Avins 748). The songs have been identified (Kalbeck i 332) as most of those in Opp. 14, 19 and 20; and these are surely very likely to include her name-monogram, in various forms.[4] Such possibilities (foreshadowed in Sams 1971a) may be of especial interest to those musical minds that are most akin to Brahms's own. They are subsumed here under the rubric of M32.

---

[1] gis is G# in German; la is the note A in solmisation.

[2] H means the note B in German.

[3] In fact, as analysis will disclose, the same pattern is discernible in various permutations (beginning on different notes), including inversions, throughout the entire movement; there is no reason to deny, and much reason to affirm, that these effects are deliberate.

[4] for example embroidered with accidentals ad libitum, or written at any pitch. These devices are designed to turn words into music, and their results are therefore musical, not verbal.

The twenty-year-old Brahms first met Clara Schumann in 1853, when she was thirty-four. The age gap between his own parents was greater still; his mother was seventeen years older than his father. Of course Brahms would soon have heard[1] in confidence from Schumann about the existence of a Clara-theme, literally (so to speak) C–B–A–G–A, but with accidentals ad libitum. Like Brahms's own later use of A–G–A–H–E (which it may well have inspired) this theme is music, not a word; so it can begin on any note, in any key, without losing its Clara-evocative significance. It can for example be heard, just as recognisably, a tone higher, like D–C#–B–A#–B in the B minor sections of Schumann's *Davidsbündlertänze* Op. 6, which, according to that composer, included 'many wedding thoughts', or in his opera *Genoveva* at the words 'Meines Weibes nimm dich an' (take care of my wife), a duty that Brahms would later gladly undertake (Sams 1971b). Brahms for his part could clearly hear that name in those notes. As he tells Clara (Litzmann i 18), 'I gaze ever deeper into a pair of wondrously beautiful eyes; now they are looking out at me from the *Davidsbündlertänze* ...'. The same features shine from his own first great work, the early piano trio Op. 8, which, as his friend Max Kalbeck rightly says (i 153), is built from a motto-theme that ends in D–C#–B–A#–B. Those notes, in the key of B minor, are indeed among the main building-blocks of the trio, especially in its first version (which may well have been reckoned too revealing – hence perhaps its revision many years later). There they recur in canon at the B minor fugal section of the first movement; they form the main theme of the second, a B minor scherzo; in the major mode, they are hidden among the opening chords of the succeeding Adagio; the Finale repeatedly sings the tune of 'Nimm sie hin denn, diese Lieder' (accept them, then, these songs) from Beethoven's *An die ferne Geliebte* (To the Distant Beloved) – the same strain that Schumann had himself employed to convey the same loving message to the same woman in his own *Phantasie* Op. 17 among other musical contexts. Thus Brahms too could express his love for her. And he adds his own unhappiness by quoting, in the E major section of the trio's slow movement, the beginning of Schubert's *Am Meer* (D957/12), set about with pizzicato tears in the style of M28. The Heine poem of *Am Meer* is about standing on the shore at Hamburg (Brahms's home town, where Clara had visited him) with a weeping woman. Those tears recur at the end of each verse in *Sapphische Ode* (No. 167), where Brahms despairingly cites the *Am Meer* vocal melody at the words 'vergiftet mit ihren Tränen' (poisoned [me] with her tears). Brahms introduces this quotation with the sung notes C–B♭–A–G#–A. Thus this same C–B–A–G–A motif, with optional inflexions, in any key, at any pitch, evokes Clara Schumann (M33), just as the pattern A–G–A–H–E, with analogous variants (M32) evokes Agathe von Siebold.

The former identification is even better documented than the latter, and over a much longer period. Soon after Brahms met Clara he composed his Op. 9, sixteen variations for piano on a theme by Schumann (itself Clara-thematic, e.g. in bars

---

[1] as had Mendelssohn, to judge from the suave D–C–B–A#–B in the main theme of his Op. 62 No. 1, the first of a set of *Songs without Words* composed in the early 1840s and dedicated to Mme Clara Schumann.

2–4). In one of them, he excitedly explained, 'Clara speaks'. This utterance has been interpreted to allude to his quotation of a phrase from her own variations on the same theme. But the sympathetic listener can see as well as hear the notes C–B–A–G#–A woven into Brahms's Variation XI (e.g. at bars 1–3). This fertile field for Schumann and Brahms research was first identified over thirty years ago (Sams 1965, etc.); but it remains almost entirely untilled, even though 'the general principle of Schumann's and Brahms's employment of such musical ciphers is not now seriously disputed' (MacDonald 34). There are well-documented addenda, such as Schumann's own use of the same motto-theme, F–E–D–C#–D in D minor, to create his own D minor symphony – of which he wrote 'my next symphony shall be called Clara, and in it I shall depict her'. The parallel with Brahms's early piano trio Op. 8 is manifest; these are the first two works to be thus monothematic, and they are both Clara-thematic. Posterity has good cause for gratitude to her; two great composers loved her and enshrined that love in their music. In case there is any doubt about Brahms's feelings for her, here is what he wrote to Joachim in 1854, in words omitted from the published correspondence:

> I believe I admire and honour her no more highly than I love and am in love with her. I often have to restrain myself forcibly just from quietly embracing her and even ——: I don't know, it seems to me so natural, as though she could not take it at all amiss. I think I can't love a young girl any more, at least I have entirely forgotten them; after all, they merely promise us the heaven which Clara shows us unlocked. (Avins 48).

Both her musical worshippers may have felt that their ritual devotions were too public. Like the Brahms trio, the Schumann symphony was radically revised. But Brahms remained wedded to that symphony's first version, and was responsible for its later separate publication. Many Brahmsians, similarly, would be grateful to hear more performances of his trio's first version, with all its own special autobiographical (indeed, confessional) content.

There is further supporting evidence from Clara herself, such as her reference to the Intermezzo of Brahms's piano quartet Op. 25 (Litzmann i 371): 'I think you must already have known as you wrote it down, how delighted I'd be, if you were thinking of me' – as he surely was, accompanying her theme in love-duet sixths (M18 above) with a prolonged C pedal in repeated quavers. The same effect of Clara-theme plus C pedal begins the opening *Allegro non troppo* of the piano quartet Op. 60, which, according to Brahms himself (as cited in many sources, most recently MacDonald 225), was inspired by love for a married woman, as in Goethe's *Werther*. Both movements were written in 1855, long before Schumann's death in the asylum at Endenich.[1] The note C can thus stand for Clara as clearly as her motto-theme, of which it is another aspect (also classified here as M33); and this too is derived from Schumann's own usage, as exemplified in his

---

[1] Cf. also the finale of Op. 60, where the strings play the same theme (e.g. at bars 30–33), ending with a viola repetition of it surrounded by some of the longest top and bottom Cs in musical history; meanwhile they murmur 'frei aber froh' (as F#–A–F# or F) four times.

Davidsbündlertänze Op. 6, mostly in B minor and major but ending on a final repeated left-hand C.

Again, Brahms's early D minor piano concerto Op. 15, also inspired by the Schumanns, contains an Adagio which Brahms described to Clara as 'a soft portrait of you' (Litzmann i 48, 198). This thought may also have inspired the Adagio of his *Serenade* Op. 16, with its C–B–A–G#–A in the second bar. Even earlier, in the A major piano trio (classified as dubious in McCorkle, 687) a Brahmsian Clara motif has been detected 'in the second limb of the Finale's opening theme ... bars 9–10' (MacDonald 476). Some forty years later Brahms sent Clara the piano pieces Op. 119 with the comment 'there are a dozen bars – which are they? – where I seem to see you smile'. The word he uses is 'schmunzeln', which signifies a self-satisfied contentment, like a cat that has been at the cream. The dozen bars in question are surely bars 65–76 of Op. 119 No. 4, in C minor tonality with a C pedal; and when they recur at bars 133–44 they have the Clara-themes E(♭)–D–C–B(♭)–C added as an inner voice at 135–6 and 143–4. Meanwhile Brahms had at last completed his first symphony, Op. 68 in C minor, on which he worked from 1862 (or earlier) to 1876. It was certainly written with Clara much in mind (MacDonald 249), and may well incorporate her theme (Musgrave 117f); it begins with the longest C pedal in orchestral history, namely fifty-one successive strokes on kettledrums doubled by basses. The inference is that this slow introduction was composed, or completed, in 1870, the year of Clara's 51st birthday. Some of the C pedals in the songs sound fully as meaningful in the sense of M33 as the Clara theme itself.

They also occur in earlier vocal music, such as Op. 17 No. 4, about the lament of a widowed woman. It too combines C pedals with Clara-themes, such as 'Wein' an den Felsen' (Weep by the rocks) with the same E♭–D–C–B–C melody as in Op. 25 and Op. 60; and when Brahms sent Clara her copy of that Op. 17 set, for women's voices, harp and horn, he wrote (Litzmann i 318), 'did anything special occur to you?' As he also told her (Litzmann ii 463), 'by rights I should label all my best melodies "in fact by Cl. Sch!"'. Certainly his Clara-themes were no less heartfelt for being enciphered; that was how his mind worked, all his life, just like Schumann's.[1] As he told her (Litzmann i 35), he liked to mystify with names. He added (ibid. 50) that he often saw her, as good as bodily, for example in the trill passage that concludes the slow movement of the C major symphony, and at the pedal points in the great fugues (sic: 'in den grossen Fugen'). The former reference surely identifies Schumann's second symphony, Op. 61; that violin trill ends with E♭–D–C–B–C. The latter may seem harder to place; but it seems significant that Beethoven's *Grosse Fuge* Op. 133 has those very same notes, in the same register (two octaves above middle C) at bars 648–9, just after a repeated C at bars 645–8. These are also the same notes over the same pedal as in Brahms's Op. 25 and Op. 60, duly certified significant, as cited above, by Clara and by the composer

[1] and Elgar's, who doted on Schumann and called Brahms 'my ideal' (Sams 1997 414). The musical name-encipherments used by each of those three great composers are illustrated and discussed in Sams 1989.

respectively. Brahms lovers would profit from a close analysis of his correspondence with Clara, which even in its published selection is replete with significant allusion.

At the outset (Litzmann i 39), he calls her his 'liebe Frau' and compares their relationship to a frankly erotic tale from the *Arabian Nights* (Litzmann i 57) which describes a passionate and secret love-affair.[1] Over forty years later, in 1894, Clara counsels caution in their correspondence (Litzmann ii 558). These years encompass Brahms's song-writing, the most intimate of all his creative outlets; and he says in terms that he enjoys mystifications with names (Litzmann, i 35) and that he can express himself far better in notes of music than in letters of the alphabet. His Clara-themes combine both media.

Max Kalbeck, who had inside information, also suggests (ii 157) that the first movement of Brahms's string sextet Op. 36 not only enciphered Agathe as A–G–A–H–E but used its opening sequence G–D–Es[= E♭, pronounced S in German, as in Schumann's *Carnaval*]–B [= B♭ in German] as an interlinked musical acronym standing for Gathe Siebold, Dein Brahms. This would be entirely compatible with such known usages as his salutation when his friend the violinist Anton Door married Ernestine Groag:

[1] The topic has been much debated. At least there is no doubt that Schumann was dangerously and distressingly ill by the early 1850s, and that the whole family suffered severely in consequence. After a suicide attempt he entered an asylum in March 1854 for fear he might harm his children; his wife never visited him there until the day he died, over two years later. He himself told the physician that '1831 ward ich syphilitisch' (Trautwein 21). Brahms (*pace* Avins 747 and Swafford 642) like all other rational and instructed observers and commentators in the last two centuries, was surely well aware of this sad fact, and of its all too predictable sequelae (as expounded in Sams 1969, 3/1993, 276–80). Hence perhaps his alarmist reactions to the illnesses of Bargiel and Dietrich (Avins 248, 294); and also his admittedly rather gauche reference to Ibsen's *Ghosts* (Litzmann ii 334) as a play that Clara might have appreciated. It is about the mental deterioration of a syphilitic's son, witnessed by his agonized mother, who is in no way to blame; the mentally ill Ludwig Schumann, son of Robert and Clara, spent most of his life in an asylum, to her under-standable deep distress. The intended message from Brahms was that she was in no sense responsible for the sickness and early death among her children; that agony, at least, was spared her. On any analysis it will hardly be mere coincidence that Brahms was racked with remorse as well as regret because of his love for another man's wife (see also Sams 1971b). Thus he was much preoccupied with the Scottish ballad *Edward*, translated by Herder, e.g. in the piano *Ballade* Op. 10 No. 1, which cites that text and ends with a sustained F–E–D–C#–D, the motto-theme of Schumann's 'Clara' symphony. Brahms set that same poem, about a man who kills his father for the sake of his mother, as the duet Op. 75 No. 1 which begins with a dominant C pedal in 19 deep left-hand octaves, 36 left-hand quavers and 90 right-hand semiquavers, all in the first ten bars of common time. Its main vocal melody corresponds almost exactly with the motto-theme discerned by Max Kalbeck in the Brahms piano trio Op. 8.

Thus A. D. is embraced by E. G. in the guise of the violin's open strings. After those notes and slurs Brahms added the words 'with best congratulations on so musical a union!' (Kalbeck iii 212–13). In a parcel of his latest publications, furthermore, sent to Heinrich and Elisabet von Herzogenberg (ii 243) on 27 October 1890, Brahms enclosed a mock invoice to

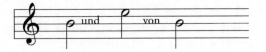

that is to say, H and E von H.

Given also his use of a Clara-theme, and his general devotion to musical letters,[1] it seems reasonable to suppose that Brahms's earlier *tendresse* for his handsome young blonde piano pupil (whose photograph stood on his writing-table until his dying day) would also have been secretly expressed in the songs in terms of her maiden name Elisabet von Stockhausen, as the notes E and E♭ (or D#). Perhaps other women that Brahms loved were paid analogous musical homage. Of course such ideas, even if demonstrably present within the music, will be difficult if not impossible to identify and evaluate; but they are just as surely worth considering. Suggested examples of the E. S. (= E♭ or D#) usage are included here under the heading M35.

In describing the Agathe motif (M32), Max Kalbeck (i 331) adds that in the G major sextet theme already quoted the second A is always followed by a D on second violin and viola. He attributes this D to a notional spelling of Agathe as A–G–A–D–H–E; but he adds that the notes A–D, which as letters form the German word 'Ade' (farewell), are a component of the thought 'Agathe, ade!'; thus the music can be heard as bidding a sad goodbye. Those notes also occur at bars 27–28 of the opening violin theme, in what may well be a deliberate allusion.

There are good grounds for supposing that Brahms used the notes A–D elsewhere to mean 'Ade!'. The opening Maestoso of the first piano concerto Op. 15, as he confided to Joachim, was inspired by the turmoil occasioned by Schumann's attempted suicide in 1853. Its Adagio, as already noted, expresses adoring love for Schumann's wife. Its energetic Finale begins with the notes A–D–E–F–A–D linking on to a Clara-theme in reverse, D–C#–D–E–F, which might well mean a farewell to Robert Schumann (who used E and F as his own musical monograms, as in the *Davidsbündlertänze* Op. 6) and a farewell to Clara (in her retrograde form, again as in Schumann Op. 6). In the Brahmsian context, the interval A–D is used as a ground bass. The same applies to the two *Serenades* Op. 11 and Op. 16; and they both seem to contain musical allusions, e.g. the former's M32 and the latter's M33, as cited above. Max Friedländer (1922, 122) independently calls

---

[1] and indeed all forms of conceptual and symbolic diversions, such as puns and word-play (as confirmed by his letters and note-books) as well as chess.

attention to the same motif in the song *Mit vierzig Jahren* (No. 164), where as he says the falling fifth of farewell A–D regularly recurs in varied harmonisations. It would be wholly Brahmsian to use those notes thus allusively; suggested examples in the songs are classified as M34.

It would also be entirely characteristic of Brahms to use the musical letters of his own name (M36) as a sort of self-portrait, just like Schumann in the A–S(= Es, = E♭)–C–H (= B) ciphers of *Carnaval* Op. 9. Bach had already set the same example, much earlier; and this name too was publicly used by Schumann in his keyboard fugues Op. 60 on the theme B–A–C–H, and also privately by Brahms, in his cadenza to Beethoven's fourth piano concerto, WoO 12. Perhaps it was the Schumann precedent that prompted Brahms to treat his own name in the same way: H (= C♭, or B), B (= B♭), S (=Es = E♭), A, as in his Organ Fugue WoO 8, *c.* 1856, in the amazingly remote and sad key of A♭ minor, in seven flats:

H   B   S   A

Thus the composer himself figures as the fugue subject, as further suggested by the manuscript signature 'Brahms' followed by 'Ganz eigentlich für meine Clara' (McCorkle 523).

This personal interpretation is involuntarily corroborated by Georg Henschel, whose 1878 reminiscences (Kalbeck iii 78f) tell how he and Brahms chatted about women on a woodland walk, and then listened to the mating calls of toads. Brahms reportedly asked 'Is any sound sadder or more melancholy than this music, with its tones that can't ever be pitched exactly and are repeated over and over within the compass of a diminished minor third, mostly like this' – here he sang the falling and rising sequence C♭, A, B♭ – 'as in my latest songs'. And he continued, 'on this spot you can easily imagine how those stories arose about bewitched princesses, and – listen, there's the prince again with his C♭ lament-ation'. Henschel leaves these curious comments unexplained. Of course his readers would know about the king's son who was turned into a toad, from which predicament he could be released only by a kiss from a princess. But no such source stipulates that the victim croaks C♭–A–B♭, i.e. the German letters H–A–B, which together with E flat (Es = S) happen to be the musical letters of Brahms's name. The composer is saying, cryptically but clearly, that he too has long croaked unkissed; and that he writes his own sad-sounding name thus in his love-songs. Of course he meant for example the C♭–A–B♭ in the first interlude of *Dein blaues Auge* (No. 107) with E♭ in the left hand, thus:

The corresponding Brahmsian sense of loneliness or isolation (M37) is regularly expressed in terms of consecutive unisons or octaves between voice and accompaniment, always with the same meaning of individual concern. A similar sense of introversion is expressed by a hidden or inner voice singing within the music (M38). Thus words are underlined and feelings enhanced. Such treatment characterises the nineteenth-century song-writer and his art. The two go together; each expresses the other. Aptly, their main shared medium is harmony. Thus the Schubertian key-relation of major and minor on the same tonic (M39) is invariably meaningful to Brahms, who was the greatest Schubertian of his time, whether as performer, arranger, editor or collector (Pascall 1998). This device indicates the shared duality of joy and pain, good and ill, that stem from the same root – the 'mingled yarn', as Shakespeare calls it, whence life is woven. These two contrasting ideas are often compressed in a tierce de Picardie, where a minor song ends hopefully on a full major chord. Similarly the mingling of sharps and flats, in keys and their notation, is Brahmsian for the same ambivalence (M40). In his own life, as the songs plainly say, pain preponderated; in the melodic line, the sixth or seventh above the keynote is often flattened (M41), or the whole harmony droops flatwards (M42). Deep down in the nature of things, there are tears; and this is not only individual but universal.

This Romantic cast of mind, so characteristic of all German nineteenth-century song-writers,[1] relies on music as its homeland, its nationhood and its language as well as its personal sense of individual identity. So the device of musical cross-reference or allusion is also electively Brahmsian. His quotations, such as the theme from Marschner's *Hans Heiling* in the E flat minor scherzo Op. 4 (MacDonald 62), are surely meant to be heard, even if he later regretted and removed some of them, no doubt as too revealing. Some are deeply meaningful, if mysterious; thus there can be no doubt that the F major symphony Op. 90 begins with an echo of Schumann's *Rhenish* symphony Op. 97, I/459 etc. Others are more manifest, though mainly unmentioned; thus the famous admirer of Johann Strauss and his *Blue Danube* waltz (Swafford 553) cannot refrain from quoting its opening strains at bars 11–13 of the ninth of his own *Liebeslieder* Op. 52, which begins 'Am Donaustrande' (by the banks of the Danube). Brahms had called his next masterpiece, the *Alto Rhapsody* Op. 53, an 'epilogue' to Op. 52, meaning that it too was a love-song (for Julie Schumann); and the final section of

---

[1] including Elgar, a collection of whose songs was published, with German translation, as 'Seven Lieder'.

the *Neue Liebeslieder* Op. 65 begins with a ground-bass that quotes the *Rhapsody's* final 'prayer for heart-healing' (MacDonald 221).

As we have seen (but can all too rarely hear), an early example of quotation appears in the slow movement of the first version of the piano trio Op. 8. Some listeners, then as now, would know about Brahms's habit of using known vocal melodies to signify the words to which they were sung: thus he sometimes accepted invitations by writing the tune of Don Ottavio's 'Wer kann da widerstehn' (who can resist), from the German version of *Don Giovanni*, which the recipient could be relied upon to recognise. Similarly he patched up a quarrel with Hans von Bülow by sending him the melody of Pamina's 'Soll ich dich, Teurer, nicht mehr sehn?' (shall I never see you again, my dear?) from *The Magic Flute*. Those familiar with this practice, or sharing the same cast of mind, could hear Op. 8 saying that Clara had visited Brahms in Hamburg. This (as he would well know) was the town known to Heine as *Die Stadt*, with spectral mists evoked by the diminished-seventh arpeggios in the Schubert setting of that poem; they recur not only in Brahms Op. 8 but also in his piano quartet Op. 26, and his piano trio Op. 87, perhaps in covert allusion to the same sea-side and the same lost love. That desolate shore, another typical Brahmsian topic, was also the scene of another Heine lyric set by Schubert as *Am Meer*. To ears attuned to Brahms, the quotation from that song in *Sapphische Ode* (No. 167) sounds clearer and sadder still. Similarly the allusion to the end of Schubert's *Der Doppelgänger* at the end of *Herbstgefühl* (No. 78) is even more self-evidently a personal allusion, redolent of a composer much given to the expression in music of masochistic nostalgia and of the so-called pathetic fallacy, the identification of nature's changing moods with one's own.

TOPICS

Such allusions are also implicit in the composer's choice and treatment of poems he adjudged suitable for setting. His *Wortausdruck* of course included elements of autobiography. His life, personality and psychology are subjects of special study, first adumbrated by Schauffler (1933) and expounded by MacDonald (1984) and others, with impressive feeling and insight. The songs offer eloquent testimony to the situations and subjects for which Brahms felt a special affinity. Performers and listeners will profit from a measure of sympathy, if not empathy. Apathy is a disqualification.

First and foremost, Brahms is the supreme master of Romantic isolation. He began his emotional life in a triangular tangle; lover of Clara Schumann, devoted admirer yet rival of her husband Robert, who by then was mortally sick in mind and body. Throughout the Brahmsian lied, whether in texts or titles (such as *In Waldeinsamkeit* No. 155 or *Feldeinsamkeit* No. 157), singer and pianist unite in a lament for loneliness, usually because of separation from the loved one. The feeling is so keen and strong that it resembles standing in icy darkness outside a warm lit house, as in *Es hing der Reif* (No. 193). This recurrent predicament is more a real nightmare than a mere imagining or metaphor. Even when the situation is described humorously, or at least good-humouredly, as in *Vergebliches Ständchen* (No. 148), the music shivers and freezes as well as the words. Not only does the artistic expression, as it were, look in yearningly while standing outside in the cold, a Schubertian hybrid between Doppelgänger and Leiermann; it often also looks back from later life through lapsed and lost time towards a remembered past, as in *Heimweh* I (No. 119). Such feelings of nostalgia, coupled with misfortune and lamentation, are among the main Brahmsian themes, not only in his sole song-cycle, the *Magelone-Lieder* (Nos. 43–57) but in all the other songs that he grouped together for publication under his own title, namely *Junge Lieder* (Nos. 117–18), *Heimweh* (Nos. 119–21) and *Klage* (Nos. 122–3). Similarly, in single songs, scenes of erstwhile happiness are often revisited in moods of present despair, cf. *In der Gasse* (No. 97). In such situations the music aims at and often achieves universality, from the first, by habitual identification with deserted and lonely girls. This impulse began with the earliest published song *Liebestreu* (No. 1) and continued into the much later *Mädchenlied* (No. 200). In the latter, as in the early *Anklänge* (No. 17) the damsel sits at her spinning-wheel making her wedding-dress. Here Brahms was certainly influenced by Schubert, who also expressed such feelings in song throughout his creative life, from *Gretchen am Spinnrade* to *Der Doppelgänger*: but the later composer's voice, if no more poignantly intense and concerned, is surely far more personal. Those who relish so direct and immediate an appeal will also appreciate Brahms's obsession with faithfulness in love, as exemplified not only by *Liebestreu* but the famous master-piece *Von ewiger Liebe* (No. 58). Thus the titles (also *Treue Liebe*, No. 15, or *Treue Liebe dauert lange*, No. 57) as well as the texts of his chosen poems resound with such tributes; the idea of undying devotion recurs in his songs as in no one else's. This is no mere general reflection of nineteenth-century German verse; it stems directly from the mind and heart that chose the poems. The same refrain, perhaps a burden in every sense, recurs throughout the letters and other writings, which are vibrant with sincere protestations of his own undying love and loyalty.

His own experience surely sharpened his perceptions and compounded his disappointments. His chosen song-texts often appeal for reassurance; say a word (*Nicht mehr zu dir*, No. 35), give me a sign (*Die Liebende schreibt*, No. 71). His mother was finally separated from his father, who was seventeen years her junior. Clara Schumann herself took a clandestine lover in the early 1860s (Reich 209). In these years Brahms's letters to her fail to figure in the published correspondence; his song-texts and music often cry out with sexual jealousy and rivalry (as in *Murrays Ermordung*, No. 23, or *Verrat*, No. 190) as well as tension and frustration. Again, Frau Brahms must have had many heart-to-heart talks with her daughter Elise, and Frau Schumann with her own daughters; and Brahms loved not only Clara but also her daughter Julie. The mother–daughter colloquy is far more marked and continuous a feature of his song-writing, from 1853 (No. 1) to 1881 (Nos. 145–7), than of anyone else's. Again, many of the song-texts (such as *Dein blaues Auge* No. 107, *Salamander* No. 197) also seem to have been selected for their references to healing coolness as a remedy for the burning of passion, or a refuge from the fires of love; these topics too appear disproportionate to their normal occurrence in German lyric verse, or indeed in any other artistic context. They dwell deep in the Brahmsian psyche, where the outsider's lonely coldness is tragic but his self-sufficient coolness is often blissful; 'frei aber froh', free but happy, in very truth. It is all a question of degree.

There was some light relief, literally. Of all great song-writers, Brahms was the most keenly aware of the flight and song of birds, which form a favourite focus for his most sensitive feelings, from *Nachtigallen schwingen* (No. 14) to *Das Mädchen spricht* (No. 198). He had a penchant for poems on such subjects, or including such ideas; and this pursuit led him naturally to metaphors of birds and brides, nests and homes. Thus Brahms sings electively of the natural world and his own direct physical involvement in it, sometimes with the explicit notion that music mirrors the beauty of nature, as in *Juchhe* (No. 12) or *Auf dem See* (No. 101). As a corollary, Brahms loves visual art and artists, as further evidenced by the unusually high proportion of painters among the poets whose verses he set to music. Hence also his devotion to the work of the artist and sculptor Max Klinger (1857–1920), to whom the *Four Serious Songs* were dedicated.

All this exemplifies one touch of nature above all others: a childlike innocence that celebrates what it sees and feels. The song-music loves to withdraw into its own safe world, a departure no doubt prompted by personal experience of perils elsewhere. In the company of children, for example, Brahms could unfeignedly be his own natural self. This trait is clearly reflected in his folksong arrangements for children, the fifteen *Volkskinderlieder* WoO 31. But great art demands much more than naturalness; and in the songs Brahms never assumes a childlike posture or persona. His closest approach is by way of folksong, a predilection that also embodies his own fierce consciousness of his humble origins. All his life he was preoccupied, not to say obsessed, with folk-melodies and arrangements. Their innate freedom no doubt offered a welcome relief to the strict technician; so they dance and sing as it were in folk costume, free of restraint.

But sadness prevails and night falls. Perhaps Brahms has a special affinity with, and appeal for, older listeners. He lived far longer than other great song-writers, and like them he had a cyclic personality. As he confessed to Clara in his youth (Litzmann i 217), he was almost never at ease with himself but 'alternately elated or sombre'. That disposition mellowed but never changed; it afforded priceless insights into the human condition. Here is the home and the heart of the Brahms song. A song-writer of the autobiographical school is known by the words he chooses, and in particular by those he chooses to repeat. It is no coincidence that the commonest Brahmsian concepts in that category are 'love' and 'heart'. But by far the heaviest weight of emphasis falls on feelings of heartbreak and tears, the outsider left lonely in the cold and dark, often with waves lapping or breaking ominously on the seashore, as in a remembered Hamburg boyhood. There are countervailing metaphors of a musical community, and artistic fellowship, as birds sing and fly in bright sunshine. The journey, of boat or bird, or on foot, whether seaborne, airborne or earthbound, sets out in high hope, rejoicing in the natural beauty of mountains and meadows, and the abiding endurance of true love. But it ends in the comfort or despair of sleep, night, dream, age, death, with no religious consolation, not even in the justly-famed Biblical settings of the *Four Serious Songs*.

Undeniably, many of the feelings thus unwittingly exhibited are obsessive. They will be appreciated best by those who share them. They range from the quasi-cryptographic preoccupations of the verbalising chess-player and composer to those far stranger heights and depths powerfully described by Gerard Manley Hopkins: 'O the mind, mind has mountains; cliffs of fall/Frightful, sheer, no-man-fathomed. Hold them cheap/May who ne'er hung there.' For those lieder-lovers who hold them dear, Brahms is the most perfect – and arguably the greatest – of all song-writers.

THE SONGS

OPUS 3

Six songs for tenor or soprano voice with pianoforte accompaniment, dedicated to Bettina von Arnim, published December 1853, revised 1882.

As the title suggests, Brahms was largely unconcerned at this early stage about the presentation of specific identifiable characters, male or female; and the expression of human emotion in general would always remain his chief concern. This set of songs shows the strong influence of Schumann, who had already set Reinick, Hoffmann and Eichendorff, no doubt from volumes in his own possession; these and the Bodenstedt source may have stood on his own Düsseldorf shelves, to which the young Brahms had free access. On textual evidence, Brahms took the Eichendorff poem *In der Fremde* (see No. 5) from Schumann's own setting, wrong words and all. Here and elsewhere his treatment of the text is also Schumannian in its predilection for voice–piano unisons. Such indebtedness was predictable; these and other early works had been published on Schumann's recommendation.

1. (Op. 3, No. 1) Liebestreu (Faith in love) January 1853
Robert Reinick   E♭ minor e♭′–a♭″

> 'O versenk, o versenk dein Leid, mein Kind,
> In die See, in die tiefe See!'
> Ein Stein wohl bleibt auf des Meeres Grund,
> Mein Leid kommt stets in die Höh.
>
> 'Und die Lieb, die du im Herzen trägst,
> Brich sie ab, brich sie ab, mein Kind!'
> Ob die Blum auch stirbt, wenn man sie bricht,
> Treue Lieb nicht so geschwind.
>
> 'Und die Treu, und die Treu, 's war nur ein Wort,
> In den Wind damit hinaus.'
> O Mutter, und splittert der Fels auch im Wind,
> Meine Treue, die hält ihn aus.

'Oh drown, oh drown your grief, my child, in the sea, in the deep sea!' A stone will surely stay on the sea-bed, but my grief will always rise to the surface.

'And the love that you still bear in your heart, break it off, break it off, my child.' Though a flower will die when plucked, faithful love will not fade so fast.

'And your faith, and your faith, it was only a word, out with it into the wind.' Oh mother, even though a rock may split in the wind, my faith will withstand it [will, will withstand it].

When the young Brahms first left his native Hamburg, he took various early works with him, including this song, which earned him many lifelong admirers including the violin virtuoso Joseph Joachim. Everyone who heard it was impressed by its emotive power and technical mastery; and posterity has never ceased to admire those two components and their intimate interrelation. They would do honour to a practised master of the song form; they continued to characterise all Brahms's best writing; and on this evidence they were both equally innate. They render this debut strikingly mature and original. Yet other songs of the same early period are naïve and derivative in comparison. So these verses must have made some intense personal appeal to which the music is a deep response. That rapport would not have been solely poetic; Reinick at best was hardly more than an accomplished rhymester. But it cannot be mere coincidence that his themes here include no fewer than four of those that obsessed Brahms all his life: a mother-and-daughter colloquy, a deserted and desolate girl, faithfulness in love, and the depths of the sea. That last metaphor is confined to the first verse; but it underlies the whole song down to the last left-hand full-fathom-five keynote, where in the composer's imagination the girl herself as well as her sorrow lie drowned.

The first bar announces the continuous right-hand triplets that will resound throughout, hammering at grief in over four hundred chords. The left hand and the voice have overlapping phrases that convey the sense of colloquy; their canonic discords emphasise the clash of opposed viewpoints. After 'in die tiefe See' (in the deep sea), we hear the well-meant advice instinctively rejected; over the left hand's rising motif the right hand starts to ascend of its own accord, to match the girl's higher vocal register as well as the idea that her grief would soon resurface. She is more musingly melodic and less declamatory than her mother; and those serenely assured tones carry instant conviction. They even sustain and dignify the girl's metamorphosis into the plucked and discarded flower of Romantic convention, in the second ten-bar verse of this strict musico-poetical structure. The third is extended and developed by repetitions in a style that the young Brahms has already completely mastered in this earliest example, and would often exploit for his later song-writing climaxes. The opening left-hand motif now has upward octaves or double octaves of passionate despair; a new top note, the highest in the vocal line, italicises and underlines the key-word 'Treue' (faith); the last words are long drawn out to make a coda and a final postlude, down to the final depths of an imagined death by drowning. And all this is attained by purely musical means, with no hint of conscious artifice. From the outset, the techniques and devices of musical structure are spoken by Brahms as an expressive language of the heart's affections, his own mother tongue.

NOTES. 1. The text is taken from Reinick's *Lieder* (1844), which Brahms owned.

2. In January 1853 Brahms was nineteen and a half years old. He shares with the seventeen-year-old Schubert (in *Gretchen am Spinnrade*, D118) the inauguration of his lieder by empathy with the plight of a deserted girl in a dramatic scene (here a duet) made visually vivid by keyboard motifs. Both composers begin by concentrating operatic depth and scope of feeling into voice and piano, and converting the theatre into a drawing-room. For all this song's originality, therefore, it owes much to the subconscious influence of Schubert, especially *Aufenthalt* D957/5, which has the same insistent quaver triplet chords, canon in voice and piano, an extended final verse with expressive top note and coda, and

a poem about rocks, rivers and eternal grief. There could have been no better ideal or model for the young song-writer than the Schubertian style, by which Brahms must have been deeply imbued and no doubt instructed.

3. The canons are M12; the top notes (M10) on the key words 'Leid', 'Her[zen]', 'Lieb', 'Fais' and above all 'Treue' summarise the story of the song. The final left-hand depths of darkness and death are M6/7 respectively. The soulful unisons of voice and piano as the girl replies are deliberately motivic (M37), and the sombre key of E♭ minor is expressive throughout.

2. (Op. 3, No. 2) Liebe und Frühling I (Love and springtime I) July 1853

Heinrich Hoffmann von Fallersleben   B major d#'–g#''

> Wie sich Rebenranken schwingen
> In der linden Lüfte Hauch,
> Wie sich weisse Winden schlingen
> Luftig um den Rosenstrauch:
>
> Also schmiegen sich und ranken
> Frühlingsselig, still und mild,
> Meine Tag- und Nachtgedanken
> Um ein trautes liebes Bild.

As the tendrils of the vine sway in the breath of the gentle breezes, as white bindweed airily entwines the rosebush, so my thoughts by day and night, blissful with springtime, silent and tender, ever nestle and twine around a dear and lovely picture [my thoughts by day and night around a dear and lovely picture].

Max Kalbeck (i 152) confides that this song and the next contain personal musical allusions to the twenty-year-old composer's fondness for a young singer who had taken the part of Zerlina in Mozart's *Don Giovanni*. So the first appearance of the phrase 'meine Tag- und Nachtgedanken' is sung to the opening melody of Zerlina's F major aria, disguised by the harmonically remotest major key and a shift of stress, thus:

Bat - ti,   bat - ti, o bel   Ma - set - to   Meine   Tag- und   Nachtge - dan - ken

The same heavily-veiled allusion, but beginning at the half-bar as in Mozart, had already appeared in the voice at 'selig, still und mild' (blissful, silent and tender); it serves as a secret symbol of the flowering rosebush around which Brahms's own thoughts were romantically entwining by day and by night. At that phrase, as quoted above, the idea is enhanced by full left-hand chords which sing the melody of the opening words, 'Wie sich Rebenranken schwingen'. That melody (itself an inversion of the Mozart theme, which is designed to pervade and bind the entire song in a fragrant bouquet of music) is announced in bare octaves and unison between voice and piano, so as to attract the audience's attention and intensify the opening statement. Its analogous two-bar answer rises on high with the breath of the breezes at 'Lüfte Hauch'. Here, however, the first strain is treated in right-hand canon to illustrate trailing tendrils of convolvulus. At 'Also schmiegen sich und ranken' (so nestle and twine) the human feeling is deliberately linked with the leaf-and-flower imagery by a further statement of the first theme, so as to parallel in music the poetic use of the word 'ranken', first noun and then verb, in both contexts. After the first 'Bild' (picture) the piano's diminished harmonies drift back into day- and night-dreaming, with the Mozart motif now an octave higher in the right hand and its inversion augmented into minims in the voice. Yet another image of intimate intertwining appears in the consecutive chromatic thirds that ease down into the bass clef during the postlude, like a long love-duet, over a further reprise of the opening theme of 'Wie sich Rebenranken schwingen' which ends in the dark depths of the left hand as the night-dreaming finally prevails and the fermatas send the song to sleep. Once again the combination of intense personal feeling and superlative musical technique is entirely typical.

NOTES. 1.   The text is taken from Hoffmann's *Gedichte* (1834 and 1843), also a Schumann source. The poem has no comma after 'trautes'; so both the *Gesamtausgabe* and the Peters edition might be amended accordingly, to avoid a break in the melodic line.

2.   The histrionic pause on a dominant seventh after 'Rosenstrauch' is M24; the final descent into dreamy darkness is M6/7. The entwining canons are M12; and all the other lavish technical devices of augmentation and inversion are deliberately designed as erotic images of flower-painting. Similarly the converging melodic lines at bars 16–17 represent yet another love-motif (M17).

3.   So intense a feeling seems to transcend the 'young Zerlina' disclosed to Kalbeck, and no doubt reported by him in all good faith. The Schumannian Clara key and motif (D#–C#–B–A#–B, M33, marked 'espressivo' in the right hand after 'also schmiegen') may imply that her own maternal kindness and Brahms's own almost masochistic suffering were the real source of the 'Batti, batti' theme, which would thus allude to its musical context in *Don Giovanni*. If so, some components of this song (of which a copy is dated October 1853; McCorkle 9) could commemorate their first meeting in September, when Clara was still only 34; for Brahms, if not for both, it was love at first sight.

4.   Brahms thought this song worth revising, in various slight details, some years later; the *Gesamtausgabe* prints both versions.

3. (Op. 3, No. 3) Liebe und Frühling II (Love and springtime II) July 1853

Heinrich Hoffmann von Fallersleben

B major, B minor and B♭ minor f#′–g#″

Ich muss hinaus, ich muss zu dir,
Ich muss es selbst dir sagen;
Du bist mein Frühling, du nur mir
In diesen lichten Tagen.

Ich will die Rosen nicht mehr sehn,
Nicht mehr die grünen Matten;
Ich will nicht mehr zu Walde gehn
Nach Duft und Klang und Schatten.

Ich will nicht mehr der Lüfte Zug,
Nicht mehr der Wellen Rauschen,
Ich will nicht mehr der Vögel Flug
Und ihrem Liede lauschen.

Ich will hinaus, ich will zu dir,
Ich will es selbst dir sagen;
Du bist mein Frühling, du nur mir
In diesen lichten Tagen.

I must go forth to find you; I must tell you myself that you and you alone are the only springtime for me in all these bright days. I've no wish to behold the roses or the green meadows any more, I've no wish to go to the forest in search of scent and sound and shade. I've no wish to feel the coolness of the air or to hear the sound of waves any more, nor to see the flight of birds or listen to their song. My sole wish is to go forth to find you and tell you myself that you and you alone are the only springtime for me in all these bright days.

The verses have a certain rhythmic élan, generated by the dancing iambic feet of 'ich muss', 'ich will' and so on. This impetus is converted by Brahms into 𝄴 ♪|♩. first in the right hand alone and then in the voice, to express continuous impatience. From the outset, the going forth is imagined as a bird-like flight, so that the opening vocal melody, buoyed on a flutter of semiquavers, twice soars up an octave. The Mozart quotation from the previous song (No. 2) is repeatedly reused (beginning with 'Ich will nicht mehr zu Walde gehn', I'll to the woods no more), perhaps also with Clara-significance, though without any clear corresponding reference to the sung words. The music, for all its delight in graphic illustration, such as the piano decoration and diminution of the vocal line at 'Lüfte' (breezes) and 'Wellen' (waves), sometimes seems out of phase with the words; thus 'lauschen' (listen to) is set as a long enhanced dominant that strains to catch the faintest bird-call – the opposite of what the poet implies. But at the reprise all such uncertainties are dispelled by the renewed impetus of the initial melodies, this time accompanied by an even more rapid tremolando pulse and an even more sustained and expansive top note. There is no mistaking the true exhilaration that these verses called forth from a young composer who, above all others, was entranced by the coolness of the air and the flight and song of birds, yet still more overjoyed by a new and lasting love.

NOTES. 1. The text is again taken from Hoffmann's *Gedichte* (1834 and 1843), also a Schumann source. Brahms has not only decapitalised the poem's consistent 'Du' and 'Dir', but also omitted the comma after 'gehn', and substituted a full stop both for the long dash at the end of the third verse and for the concluding exclamation mark. But the music as it were incorporates the original typography and punctuation.

2. Schumann, in a letter to Brahms of March 1855 from his Endenich asylum, remarked especially on 'the third song, which begins with a melody for loving girls to yearn at' and reaches a 'marvellous climax', no doubt the bright top G# on the last 'licht[en]'. The erotic content of this lively love-song would not have escaped Schumann even in his tragic decline; its opening outcry 'ich muss zu dir' recalls and indeed all but quotes his own *Mondnacht* (Op. 39, No. 5), also about winging one's way to lasting love.

3. The tremolando wings are M3. The notation in flats instead of sharps at 'sehr zart und innig' (M40) serves to add further distance to that contrasting section; the long enhanced dominant seventh to which it leads, on 'lauschen' is an image of intense listening (M24). The piano's parallel tenths there and earlier are the love-motif M18; the top note on 'Lich[ten]' has the brightness of M10, especially when its shine is sustained and enhanced by a crescendo at the penultimate word.

4. (Op. 3, No, 4) Lied (Song) *c.* July 1853
Friedrich von Bodenstedt   E♭ minor e♭'–g''

Weit über das Feld durch die Lüfte hoch
Nach Beute ein mächtiger Geier flog.

Am Stromesrande, im frischen Gras
Eine junge, weissflüglige Taube sass;

O verstecke dich, Täubchen, im grünen Wald,
Sonst verschlingt dich der lüsterne Geier bald!

Eine Möwe hoch über der Wolga fliegt,
Und Beute spähend im Kreise sich wiegt.

O halte dich, Fischlein, im Wasser versteckt,
Dass dich nicht die spähende Möwe entdeckt!

Und steigst du hinauf, so steigt sie herab,
Und macht dich zur Beute und führt dich zum Grab.

Ach, du grünende feuchte Erde du!
Tu dich auf, leg mein stürmisches Herz zur Ruh!
Blaues Himmelstuch mit der Sternlein Zier,
O trockne vom Auge die Träne mir!
Hilf, Himmel, der armen, der duldenden Maid!
Es bricht mir das Herz vor Weh und Leid!

Far over the fields, high through the air, a mighty vulture flew in quest of prey. By the river bank in the fresh green grass sat a young dove with white wings. Oh hide yourself, little dove, in the green wood, or the lecherous vulture will soon devour you. A seagull flies high over the Volga and weaves gliding circles in its search for prey. Oh keep well hidden in the water, little fish, so that the questing gull cannot find you. If you rise it will swoop down and take you as its prey and bring you to the grave.

*   Oh you green soft earth, open up and lay my stormy heart to rest! Blue cloth of heaven, embroidered with little stars, oh, dry the tears from my eyes! Heaven help the*

poor suffering maiden; my heart is breaking [my heart is breaking] with sorrow and
pain [with sorrow and pain]!

The opening arpeggios in voice and piano surge powerfully upward and fall again, to emulate the vulture's actual launch and lunge. Then its potential lunch appears, in music of dove-like innocence with staccato flutterings in alternate octaves. In a piano interlude, these are metamorphosed into an ominous death motif that falls stricken down the keyboard into deep left-hand darkness, thus:

The same pattern is fittingly repeated for the strong seagull and the frail fish, which also trembles in mortal terror of death and the grave. So far, the word 'Beute' (prey) has been heard thrice, each time on a stressed high note. At the beginning of each verse it is accompanied by an ominous swooping figuration which seems to search the landscape below before rising again for a better view.

Each bird symbolises the human raptor; the vulture's initial description as 'lüstern' (lecherous) gives the game away. In the last verse the innocent victim is unveiled. Here the same music continues though its metaphorical meanings are abandoned, as if to say 'this is my own story'. The girl's 'stürmisches Herz' (stormy heart) is thus portrayed as the cause of her own downfall, with the same soaring and plummeting; the victim trembles in the same flimsy octaves as before, until her final *cri de coeur* is uttered on new top notes accompanied by huge crashing fortissimo chords.

This Victorian melodrama can be finely affecting in a good performance. The imagined Russian background of wide steppe-land lends a special spaciousness to the panorama. The song's themes and symbols were then new-minted, and Brahms would continue to coin them afresh for the whole of his creative life. They always ring true, because they were genuine from the first. The composer's sympathies were deeply engaged by such subjects as death, deserted girls and the flight of birds; and their fortuitous but fortunate conjunction here makes its own music.

NOTES. 1. Bodenstedt has 'herauf' not 'hinauf' in his sixth couplet; the slip is worth correcting. In Brahms's source, the *Gedichte* (1852), the poem is entitled 'Lied aus "Iwan" '. This versified dramatic sketch of 1842 had a Russian background; hence the Volga, also in verse two. Perhaps the young composer sought to introduce a touch of local colour; he has been identified as the 'G. W. Marks' under whose name a piano-duet pot-pourri called 'Souvenir de la Russie' had been published in Hamburg *c.* 1851.

2. This was presumably the song of which Schumann wrote from the Endenich asylum: 'der vierte ganz originell'. It would also have appealed to him as a piano piece with added vocal line, much in his own style.

3. The key of E♭ minor and the bare descending octaves are harbingers of death (in the excerpt cited above the *Gesamtausgabe* fails to notate the one-bar time-change to 2/4). The high-flying vocal line crests at 'hoch' in the second verse; the same top register stands for heightened emotion, again M10, at the first 'Weh und Leid', where the sad falling semitones are M20. The trembling victim's alternating staccato octaves at bar 5f etc. are expressive; so are the full heavy chords of the three vigorous predators (M30). At the meaningful final fermata an ominous emptiness is emphasised by the omitted third, M29.

5. (Op. 3, No. 5) In der Fremde (Far from home) November 1852
Joseph von Eichendorff   F# minor g#'–g''

Aus der Heimat hinter den Blitzen rot,
Da kommen die Wolken her.
Aber Vater und Mutter sind lange tot,
Es kennt mich dort keiner mehr.

Wie bald, ach wie bald kommt die stille Zeit,
Da ruhe ich auch, und über mir
Rauscht die schöne Waldeinsamkeit,
Und keiner kennt mich mehr hier.

From my homeland, behind the red lightning, the clouds are coming. But my father and mother are long since dead and no one there knows me any more [no one there knows me any more].

How soon, oh how soon the silent time will come when I in turn shall sleep, and above me the lovely loneliness of the forest will murmur, and no one will know me here any more [no one will know me here any more].

The song, despite its apparent naïvety and its audible indebtedness to Schumann's setting in the same key and time-signature, has sensitive poetic ideas of its own. The prelude's minor melody with its guitar style of broken chords and parallel sixths, doubled and redoubled in thirds in both hands as the voice enters, suggest a sad love-duet, as if the impending death is due to a broken heart. The accompaniment's echoes of 'Wolken her' (clouds are coming) and 'keiner mehr' (no one any more), with that latter phrase repeated and intoned by the voice as a sonorous left-hand fifth is tolled like a knell, are not mere imitations of Schubert; as in that master's songs, they add extra verbal meanings. Those clouds add an alienating darkness to the mood as to the scene, which is vividly imagined in the sustained high isolated note at 'über' (above) standing for the quiet tree-tops in the lonely forest. Again as in Schubert, the final move into the major mode on the same tonic at that moment mysteriously makes the music even more sad in its quiet resignation.

All this belongs to, and helpfully exemplifies, the autobiographical song-writing style that selects and stresses certain revealing aspects of the text. Brahms was already a nature-lover and a natural loner, from his earliest years; and music was his consolation.

NOTES. I. This song too was sent to Schumann in the Endenich asylum; he replied that the music was beautiful like the poem. His verbal faculties were dimmed by his illness, and he may not have noticed that his own idiosyncratic alterations to Eichendorff's second quatrain had been incorporated into this song, showing that his setting, not the original poem, had served as the source of the lyric. Schumann had found it in the 1843 *Gedichte*, together with its title; but neither that source (which Brahms also owned, perhaps by direct bequest or inheritance) nor the 1833 novella *Viel Lärmen um Nichts* (Much Ado about Nothing) gives any support to the Brahms–Schumann version, which inserts 'ach' after the first 'wie bald', changes 'rauschet' to 'rauscht', and remodels Eichendorff's last line from 'und keiner mehr kennt mich auch hier' to the weaker and less thematic 'und keiner kennt mich mehr hier'.

2. But since Brahms had no doubt read the novella (see next song, note 1), and had a special sympathy with lonely girls, the context may be of interest: 'A beautiful young woman sat in a window-niche holding a guitar and looking out over the landscape, which was lit by flashes of lightning. As [the company] came in they heard her begin to sing.'

3. There is a parallel in Wolf's setting of *Das verlassene Mägdlein*, No. 7 of his Mörike songbook, which (quite exceptionally) takes its text, errors and all, from Schumann's Op. 64 No. 2 and not from the poem. Such examples at least serve to show how powerful an influence Schumann exerted on his successors.

4. The prelude's sad sigh is M21. The love-duetting thirds and sixths are M18, the unisons and octaves M37. The top Gs at 'keiner' and 'kennt' are M10; so is the apt long top E at 'über', showing the height and extent of the forest canopy. The final minor Amen cadence and tierce de Picardie, complete with fermata, mirror the mood of sad resignation. Perhaps the rather unexpected accented A–D left-hand fifth at bar 14 means 'Ade'; M34.

5. A comparison with Schumann's Op. 39 No. 1 is rewarding.

6. (Op. 3, No. 6) Lied (Song) December 1852
Joseph von Eichendorff   A major c#'–f#"

Lindes Rauschen in den Wipfeln,
Vöglein, die ihr fernab fliegt,
Bronnen von den stillen Gipfeln,
Sagt, wo meine Heimat liegt?

Heut im Traum sah ich sie wieder,
Und von allen Bergen ging
Solches Grüssen zu mir nieder,
Dass ich an zu weinen fing.

Ach, hier auf den fremden Gipfeln;
Menschen, Quellen, Fels und Baum,
[Wirres Rauschen in den Wipfeln,]
Alles ist mir wie ein Traum!

Muntre Vögel in den Wipfeln,
Ihr Gesellen dort im Tal,
Grüsst mir von den fremden Gipfeln
Meine Heimat tausendmal!

Soft rustling in the treetops, little birds flying afar, springs flowing from the silent peaks
– tell me, where does my homeland lie [tell me, where does my homeland lie]?

Today in a dream I saw it again, and from all the mountains such a greeting came
down to me that I began to weep [that I began to weep].

Oh, here on these foreign peaks, the people, the springs, rock and tree, all this too
seems like a dream [like a dream]!

Blithe birds in the treetops, you friends down in the valley, give my greeting from
these foreign peaks to my homeland, a thousand times [a thousand times]!

Yet again the chosen theme stresses the romantic artist's exile from homeland and happiness. Brahms knew both those deprivations. As in No. 3 above the alternating major seconds of the right hand prefigure the blurred fluttering of leaves and wings, which combine in a tremulous image of excited longing for home. This takes total precedence over the accentuation; in later years Brahms would have hesitated before setting 'die', 'von' or 'auf' on a strong downbeat. But the recurrent discords on 'Rauschen' (rustling), 'Wipfeln' (tree-tops) etc., and their resolution, assort well with the poem's yearning for fulfilment. At the first 'weinen' (weep) the flattened harmony sheds a passing tear. The middle section's musing open-air recitative effects are memorably made to dwindle into a dream as the following interlude drifts canonically down the keyboard, like half-heard hunting-horns that fade within the German forests. Thence the right-hand flutterings emerge bright in the higher octave as the birds fly out in the reprise, where the final high and sustained cry of 'Heimat' (homeland) is especially heartfelt. Of course the last vocal note should be C#, not the higher alternative E, despite the composer's tacit permission.

NOTES. 1. Again this poem appears in the 1833 novella *Viel Lärmen um Nichts* (Much Ado about Nothing), which is accordingly the likeliest source, especially since the lyric is an actual song in that context (hence no doubt the composer's title), while the Eichendorff *Gedichte* (1843), which Brahms owned, omits the final quatrain. In the novella the verses are introduced thus; 'a marvellous song suddenly resounded across from the forest. They could make out the following words [i.e. the first three verses above]. Then the singer appeared among the trees in the full bright flush of dawn; it was Florentin, a young hunts-man in the entourage of [the hero, Prince] Romano.' After a page of prose conversation and description we learn that 'Florentin once again appeared high up on the cliffs, waved his hat and sang to the departing company' [as in the last verse]. Florentin was a heroine in disguise; so perhaps this is yet another song of an isolated girl.

2. In both sources the third quatrain has a third line, after 'Baum' – 'Wirres Rauschen in den Wipfeln' (a confused murmur in the tree-tops), which the young Brahms simply omits, as if inadvertently, though he may have felt that the first line needed no repetition, even when varied, or that two 'Wipfeln–Gipfeln' rhymes were enough.

3. 'Quite different from the others', wrote Schumann, in proper praise of the diversity already discernible even in this earliest set of songs; and he added, gratifyingly, that the combination of melody and harmony at 'Rauschen' and 'Wipfeln' had pleased him.

4. The semiquaver fluttering is M3; the flattened supertonic chord at the first 'Heimat' has its meaning of sad nostalgia brought out even more clearly when heard again at the first 'weinen'. The open-air hunting horns after the mention of landscape at 'Gipfeln ... Fels und Baum' are M22, and the parallel thirds or tenths in voice and piano *passim* are M18, here signifying love of homeland. The climax on the final high note at 'Heimat' is M10.

7. (No opus no.) Mondnacht (Moonlit night) by 1853
Joseph von Eichendorff   A♭ major g′–g♭″

Es war, als hätt der Himmel
Die Erde still geküsst,
Dass sie im Blütenschimmer
Von ihm nur träumen müsst.

Die Luft ging durch die Felder,
Die Ähren wogten sacht,
Es rauschten leis die Wälder,
So sternklar war die Nacht.

Und meine Seele spannte
Weit ihre Flügel aus,
Flog durch die stillen Räume
Als flöge sie nach Haus.

It was as if the sky had gently kissed the sleeping earth, so that the earth in her bright haze of blossom must now dream only of the sky [only of the sky].

The air moved through the fields and the ears of corn swayed quietly; the woods murmured softly, the night was so starry-clear [so starry-clear].

And my soul spread wide [spread wide] its wings and flew through the silences of space as if it were flying home [home, as if it were flying home].

This early work, now catalogued as WoO 21, was published in an 1854 album of eight songs by various composers, and reissued separately in 1872. But Brahms himself seems to have forgotten or even disowned it, and his devotees will understand why. It fails both *per se* and in comparison with Schumann's justly famous setting. Yet that challenge may have been deliberate; the young Brahms consciously strove to emulate, if not rival, the older master, and he was under the spell of both Schumanns by the time this song was completed.

The prelude, in anticipating the later treatment of 'träumen müsst' (must dream), seems to sing or say that phrase twice, so that the musing mood of reverie is already created before the voice enters. Then its melody is shared with the right hand in the Schumannian style; but the mezzo-staccato bass line in parallel tenths sounds like the voice of the young Brahms sharing in a typically tearful love-song duet. Brahms also follows his mentor's structural pattern of exact verse-repetition followed by a development. As in Eichendorff, and in both settings, two strophes serve to set the scene and the third transcends it. Perhaps Brahms strives over-assiduously for that final apotheosis, enhanced by quasi-operatic devices of recitative with repeated words and pauses for effect, together with a transition to a remote tonal region at 'flog durch die stillen Räume' (flew through the silences of space) and deep dark bass notes at 'als flöge sie nach Haus' (as if flying home), followed by a sustained and dwindling high G flat that disappears into the distance on the second 'nach Haus', as if attempting a guided musical tour of the solar system. But the final contrast of quiet serenity high on an earthly horizon is moving and memorable.

NOTES. 1. As with *In der Fremde* (No. 5), there is some textual evidence that the source was not Eichendorff's *Gedichte* (1843), which Brahms owned, but the Schumann setting. Here the shared error is 'nur' (only) for 'nun' (now) in the first line. The latter correct reading should surely be sung, in both contexts. Brahms adds a mistake of his own, namely 'Räume' (space) instead of the rhyming 'Lande' (lands); it seems permissible to prefer the latter in print and performance.

2. Here, as in the Andante of the piano sonata Op. 5 with its epigraph about two loving hearts, the keyboard's consecutive tenths sing a love-duet (M18), while the mezzo-staccato tells of tears (M28). Like Schumann, Brahms has noted Eichendorff's nuptial symbolism of a masculine sky stooping to kiss a feminine earth holding a profusion of flowers and dreaming of her beloved. Perhaps it was Brahms's own personal association of brides with birds that makes the piano's wings move as it were literally (M3), from the moment the voice enters, even though the poet's soulful flights of fancy remain furled until the last verse, and even then are no more than metaphorical. At that later stage there is also a graphic keyboard union of height and depth, at the words 'nach Haus, nach Haus', where the distance of five octaves from lowest bass note to highest treble (M6, M10) is even greater than in the Schumann setting. The high repeated piano notes at 'Haus' also sound clearly starry (M11); the night was 'so sternenklar'.

3. Perhaps Brahms had already been told of Schumann's comment to Clara that 'E–H–E' (marriage) was 'a very musical word' (E–B–E in German notation). The surprising modulation after 'Flügel aus' at least has the effect, and may well have had the intention, of introducing those actual notes into five consecutive bars while maintaining the original key signature of four flats. The brightness of sharps within the darkness of flats is very Brahmsian (M40). Indeed, much of his most typical motivic writing is here, in its earliest form. So it would be no surprise if the vocal melodic shape of the final 'als flöge sie nach Haus', shared with the piano in the song-writing style of Schumann, may have been meant to say 'Clara' (M33) to initiated ears.

4. Cf. Schumann's Op. 39, No. 5.

8. (No opus no.) Die Müllerin (The mill-girl) by 1853
Adalbert von Chamisso   E♭ minor b♭♭'–g♭''

Die Mühle, die dreht ihre Flügel,
Der Sturm, der saus't darin,
Und unter der Linde am Hügel,
Da weinet die Müllerin.

Lass sausen den Sturm und brausen,
Ich habe gebaut auf den Wind,
Ich habe gebaut auf die Schwüre –
Da war ich ein törichtes Kind.

Noch hat mich der Wind nicht belogen,
Der Wind, der blieb mir treu,
Nun bin ich verarmt und betrogen –
Die Schwüre, die waren nur Spreu.

> Wo ist, der sie geschworen?
> Der Wind nimmt die Klagen nur auf,
> Er hat sich aufs Wandern verloren –
> Es findet der Wind ihn nicht auf.

The mill's sails are whirling, the storm is blowing them round, and under the lime-tree on the hill the mill-girl is weeping.

'Let the storm roar and rage; I have built on the wind, I have built on vows, I was a foolish child.

The wind has never yet lied to me, the wind stayed true to me, now I am left poor and betrayed; the vows were mere chaff.

Where is he who swore them? The wind just absorbs my cries. He is lost on his travels, the wind will not find him'.

The sails turn and the winds whirl in the piano part, with sustained notes and off-beat accents; the vocal direction is 'sehr bestimmt und stark' (very resolute and strong). Brahms might have made a fine song from these metaphors of passion and separation, on his favourite theme of the girl left lonely. But there is little matching melodic impulse, and the verse-repeating form soon becomes over-insistent, not to say oppressive. No wonder that this early sketch was itself abandoned, after only twenty-two bars plus a poetic text, to remain unpublished until 130 years later (Breitkopf 1983, ed. Draheim), and uncatalogued save as an addendum (Anhang III/13 in McCorkle 679–80). But it deserves better; and a powerful and committed performance could help to redeem and re-establish it.

NOTES. 1. The original poetic source is unclear; but Chamisso's finalised text has 'sauset' not 'saus't' in the first verse, 'auf Schwüre' not 'auf die Schwüre' in the second and 'und bin ich' not 'nun bin ich' in the third. Such changes are often found in Brahms, whose later different setting for women's voices in four parts, Op. 44, No. 5, contains two extra discrepancies.

2. The funereal key of E flat minor is thematic, as in *Lied* (No. 4). So are the persistent bass syncopations, not found elsewhere, which suggest the flapping of mill-sails in a wind-storm. The piano's minor 5–6–5 after 'weinet' is M20.

4. Cf. Grieg's setting, Op. 2 No. 1.

OPUS 6

Six songs for a soprano or tenor voice with piano accompaniment, dedicated to Luise and Minna Japha and published (like op. 3) in December 1853.

This time the poets are named on the cover; and the soprano voice comes first, because No. 1 is a woman's song. But the vocal range continues to be high throughout, as if the composer's own singing voice had not quite settled down.

9. (Op. 6, No. 1) Spanisches Lied (Spanish song) April 1852
Anon. Spanish (trans. P. Heyse)   A minor e'–f#"

> In dem Schatten meiner Locken
> Schlief mir mein Geliebter ein;
> Weck ich ihn nun auf? Ach nein!

Sorglich strählt ich meine krausen
Locken täglich in der Frühe,
Doch umsonst ist meine Mühe,
Weil die Winde sie zerzausen;
Lockenschatten, Windessausen
Schläferten den Liebsten ein;
Weck ich ihn nun auf? Ach nein!

Hören muss ich, wie ihn gräme,
Dass er schmachtet schon so lange,
Dass ihm Leben gäb und nähme
Diese meine braune Wange.
Und er nennt mich seine Schlange
Und doch schlief er bei mir ein;
Weck ich ihn nun auf? Ach nein!

In the shadow of my tresses my lover has fallen asleep. Shall I wake him up now? Oh no [oh no, oh no]!

I carefully combed out my curling tresses early this and every morning; but in vain is my labour, for the winds dishevel them.

Shadowing tresses, sighing winds, sent my lover to sleep. Shall I wake him up now? Oh no [oh no, oh no]!

I'll have to hear how grieved he is by his long yearning, how my brown cheek gives him life and takes it away again.

And he calls me his serpent, and yet he fell asleep at my side. Shall I wake him up now? Oh no [oh no, oh no].

As in Nos. 33 and 104, Brahms worthily anticipates Wolf, here with a treatment of the same poem in the same style and basic A–B–A–B–A structure. Not even the detailed word-setting within the three-four Spanish dance-rhythm is significantly different; thus both composers stress such unessential words as 'dass' and 'und' on strong beats. In each song, the coquettish character-sketch is the paramount inspiration. Brahms too offers special felicities and subtleties of his own; and even at this early stage his mastery of craftsmanship is entirely comparable. But his version predictably has less sprightly lilt and more sobriety; his models are his own North German notions of Spanish song (his own title) and dance, guitar and saraband, and the girl herself sounds staider and sturdier. In the opening section, which serves as a repeated refrain, the keyboard's detached downward arpeggios are distinct and deliberate; the beat is measured and sedate. This makes the words sound serious and indeed sad, in the music's minor mode. 'Schlief mir mein Geliebter ein' (my lover has fallen asleep) has a dying fall, enhanced by verbal repetition, each time it occurs; and the piano part unobtrusively echoes that phrase in diminution throughout the song, with only slight shifts of position, like the lover's long uninterrupted sleep. For Brahms, the poem's breezes set the scene in the open air. The lovers are perhaps imagined as gypsies, because of her tanned cheek or 'braune Wange'; hence the horn passages, evocative of the countryside, at 'sorglich strählt' ich' (I carefully combed). But before then, after the first verse's final 'Ach nein!', the piano's arpeggios are heard hinting that the small sighs of affectionate regret have wafted and floated up and away on the soft summer air, as again in the middle section and at the end.

NOTES. 1. The source was the recently-published *Spanisches Liederbuch* (1852) of Heyse and Geibel. Brahms's subjunctives 'gäb und nähme' at bars 41–2 should surely be replaced by the original 'geb und nehme'.

2. Again the chosen topic is the girl left on her own, at least for a time; so the minor 6–5 unisons between voice and right hand in bar 3 may have motivic point (M20). So may the consecutive octaves (M37) between voice and left hand at 'Mühe', '(zer)zausen', 'nähme' and 'Wange'. Brahms later avoided these by changing the falling third E–C# to the falling sixth E–G#, as in the *Gesamtausgabe*; but the popular Peters edition fails to incorporate this typically modest and rather pedantic amendment.

3. The left-hand F# in bar 14 etc. is intended as an acciaccatura touch of local colour. There the dreamy right-hand ascending arpeggios are M9, with a touch of sunlight in the higher register applied with a Schubertian brush of bright A major.

4. Cf. Wolf's far more famous setting, No. 2 of the secular songs in his *Spanisches Liederbuch.*

10. (Op. 6, No. 2) Der Frühling (Springtime) April 1852
Johann Rousseau   E major f#'–f''

Es lockt und säuselt um den Baum;
Wach auf aus deinem Schlaf und Traum,
Der Winter ist zerronnen.
Da schlägt er frisch den Blick empor,
Die Augen sehen hell hervor
Ans goldne Licht der Sonnen.

Es zieht ein Wehen sanft und lau,
Geschaukelt in dem Wolkenbau
Wie Himmelsduft hernieder.
Da werden alle Blumen wach,
Da tönt der Vögel schmelzend Ach,
Da kehrt der Frühling wieder.

Es weht der Wind den Blütenstaub
Von Kelch zu Kelch, von Laub zu Laub,
Durch Tage und durch Nächte.
Flieg auch, mein Herz, und flattre fort,
Such hier ein Herz und such es dort,
Du triffst vielleicht das Rechte.

The breezes murmur enticingly around the tree; awake from your sleep and dreams, winter has melted away [winter has melted away]. Now the tree looks freshly up on high; its eyes shine out brightly towards the golden light of the sun [towards the golden light of the sun].

A soft and balmy stirring among the swaying cloud-shapes descends like heavenly fragrance [descends like heavenly fragrance]. Then all the flowers awaken, the birds' melting lament resounds, and springtime returns again [springtime returns again].

The wind wafts pollen from blossom to blossom, leaf to leaf, through days and through nights [through days and through nights]. You too, my heart, must take wing and flutter away; seek out another heart here and there, and perhaps you'll find the right one [perhaps you'll find the right one].

As in other verses favoured by the young Brahms (in the next song for example) the poetic style is overwrought in every sense. Even its 'schmelzend Ach' (melting lament) is cribbed from the Voss edition of Hölty, as Brahms would soon discover (in *An die Nachtigall.* No. 66). The heavenly fragrance savours of cheap scent, because the essences are over-lavish. Brahms finds his own equivalent in the copious sprinkling of flats within the sharp-key notation. This effect is at least responsive to the words; and the music might have stayed fresh if left a little less hectic. The song is filled with wings-and-winds motifs of fluttering and flight that anticipate the poet's final apostrophe to his heart; and they make that appeal almost persuasive. The prelude's drooping tones and semitones derive from the vocal melody and its accompaniment at 'da kehrt der Frühling wieder' in the second verse, to epitomise the music's message; and that soft sighing recurs at each rhyming word such as as 'Baum' and 'Traum' (tree, dream) in the first verse and each repetition, such as 'zerronnen' (melted), throughout.

NOTES. 1. Brahms's textual source was no doubt Rousseau's *Gedichte* (1832), unchanged save for the omission of the poet's third verse of four, between 'Frühling wieder' and 'Es weht' above.

2. The breeze-and-birds motif of flight from the prelude onwards is M3, heard here as a preliminary study for its more sophisticated use, e.g. in *Botschaft* (No. 67). The prelude's converging melodic lines are M17; the piano's right-hand consecutive thirds throughout are the love-motif M18. So are the parallel tenths with vocal doubling at the beginning of each verse. This last motif entails the difficulty that the syllables 'lockt', 'säu-' etc. cannot be sustained, because of the consequent sharp clash with the right hand; so crotchet rests have to be written instead, to the detriment of the melodic line and the verbal sense alike. But perhaps the gasping effect thus created inspired Brahms to use this device more effectively in later contexts. The sustained dominant seventh at 'hervor' in the first verse is M24; the flats-in-sharps notation at 'der Winter' etc. is M40. The plush Amen cadence in the postlude, as if the right partner has been duly located and led to the altar, is also expressive.

3. Brahms is influenced here by Mendelssohn's piano style in the *Lieder ohne Worte*, where Op. 38 No. 1, for example, contains this song's right-hand combination of melody plus accompaniment figure.

11. (Op. 6, No. 3) Nachwirkung (Aftermath) April 1852
Alfred Meissner   A♭ major e♭'–f''

> Sie ist gegangen, die Wonnen versanken,
> Nun glühen die Wangen, nun rinnen die Tränen,

Es schwanken die kranken,
Die heissen Gedanken,
Es pocht das Herz in Wünschen und Sehnen.

Und hab ich den Tag mit Andacht begonnen,
Tagüber gelebt in stillem Entzücken,
So leb ich jetzt träumend,
Die Arbeit versäumend
Von dem, was sie schenkte in Worten und Blicken.

So hängen noch lang nach dem Scheiden des Tages
In säuselnder Nachtluft, beim säuselnden Winde
Die Bienen wie trunken
Und wonneversunken
An zitternden Blüten der duftigen Linde.

She has gone, my joys have foundered; now my cheeks glow, my tears trickle, my love-sick passionate thoughts swirl, my heart pounds with desire and yearning [my heart pounds with desire and yearning].

Once I began each day with worship and continued it in silent delight; yet now I neglect my work and live in a dream of what she bestowed upon me with her words and looks [of what she bestowed upon me with her words and looks].

Just so, long after the departure of daylight, in the sighing night air among the sighing breezes, the bees still hang as if drunken and drowned in bliss on the trembling blossoms of the fragrant lime [on the trembling blossoms of the fragrant lime].

The verses are deliberately erotic; their persistent dactyls strive to titillate the ear and the mind by an effusion of rhyme and other technical artifice designed to evoke the lingering languor of lost love. But the intended feeling of *fatigue amoureuse* falls rather flat, and so does the young Brahms. For all his responsive ardour, with added verbal repetitions of his own to enhance the effect of incantation, the music remains merely mellifluous. The chordal harmonies are more like a church anthem than a paean of passion, and the strait-laced strophic structure sounds almost prim in its controlled propriety.

NOTES. 1. Brahms found the text in Meissner's *Gedichte* (2/1846), whence he mistranscribed the last verse's 'in schweigender Nachtluft, beim säuselnden Winde' as 'in säuselnder Nachtluft' etc, thus using the second epithet twice. Perhaps he felt that sighs and silence were incompatible. But the resulting repetition jars even more, and should surely be corrected in print and performance. So perhaps should his 'Bienen' for 'Bienlein' in the same verse.

2. In places, the verses evoked a vivid and detailed reaction which identifies the born song-writer. Thus the prelude's consecutive sixths sing a love-duet (M18); the staccato tears ('Tränen') prickle in diminished harmony (M25/28); the heart beats ('pocht') with added staccato in voice and piano (M28).

3. The chordal style and 9/8 time-signature invite comparison with such Mendelssohn songs as *Morgengruss* Op. 47 No. 2 and *Frühlingslied* Op. 71 No. 2.

12. (Op. 6, No. 4) Juchhe! (Hurrah!) April 1852

Robert Reinick   E♭ major d'–a♭''

Wie ist doch die Erde so schön, so schön!
Das wissen die Vögelein;
Sie heben ihr leicht Gefieder,
Und singen so fröhliche Lieder
In den blauen Himmel hinein.

Wie ist doch die Erde so schön, so schön!
Das wissen die Flüss und Seen;
Sie malen im klaren Spiegel
Die Gärten und Städt und Hügel,
Und die Wolken, die drüber gehn!

Und Sänger und Maler wissen es,
Und es wissens viel andre Leut,
Und wers nicht malt, der singt es,
Und wers nicht singt, dem klingt es
Im Herzen vor lauter Freud!

How truly beautiful the world is, how beautiful! The little birds know this [the little birds know this], and they lift their light feathers [they lift their light feathers] and sing such blithe songs [and sing, and sing] up into the blue sky [into the sky, up into the blue sky].

How truly beautiful the world is, how beautiful! The rivers and lakes know this [the rivers and lakes know this] and in their clear mirror they paint gardens and towns and hills [in their clear mirror they paint gardens and hills] and the clouds that pass by above [that pass by above, and the clouds that pass by above].

And poets and painters know this, and many other people know it too [and many other people know it too]! And those who don't paint it, sing it, and those who don't sing it can hear it resounding in their hearts for sheer joy [in their hearts for sheer joy, for sheer joy, hear it resounding in their hearts for sheer, sheer joy].

Brahms's remorseless repetitions can make the banal sentiments sound not just excitingly breathless as intended but distressingly witless. Yet if both performers can feel inspired by mood, message and music alike, the work will take wing and soar. Reinick was a painter, and his verses are at least clear and colourful; his euphoria evokes music of transpicuous brightness, from the staccato of the opening statement through the wide open spaces of widely separated hands to the final rather portentous peroration culminating in a massive Amen from the world at large.

NOTES. 1. Brahms took his text from Reinick's *Lieder* (1844), which he owned. There, as in Reinick's *Lieder eines Malers* (1838), the last verse has the unabbreviated 'andere' and 'in dem Herzen'. Peters has 'Stadt' instead of the plural 'Städt' in line 9, which needs correction.

2. The prelude's flight of ascending arpeggios speaks of springtime uplift, again in the

voice and accents of Mendelssohn as heard in his spring songs *Gruss* Op. 19a No. 5 and *Frühlingslied* Op. 47 No. 3. The staccato accompaniment is bird-like in its lightness; the plunging left-hand is a sketch of looking down in a bird's eye view, much as in No. 4 above. The piano's consecutive thirds (M18) at 'heben ihr leicht Gefieder' etc., expressing the poem's love for Nature, recur in *O liebliche Wangen*, No. 70. The accented octave dominants which introduce that phrase recall similar effects throughout Mendelssohn's *Jagdlied* Op. 84 No. 3; the right-hand semiquaver scales after the last 'Himmel hinein' and 'drüber gehn' echo those in his *Frühlingslied* Op. 8 No. 6. The top notes at 'blauen' and 'Wolken' are M10; the vocal octave leaps that soar heavenward at 'in den blau(en)' are equally expressive. The last seventeen bars are full of convergent love-motifs, M17; the two huge final chords incorporate a full-throated Amen of approval, as it were from massed choirs.

13. (Op. 6, No. 5) Wie die Wolke nach der Sonne (As the cloud strays after the sun), July 1853

Heinrich Hoffmann von Fallersleben   B major and minor e$'$–g#$''$

Wie die Wolke nach der Sonne
Voll Verlangen irrt und bangt,
Und durchglüht von Himmelswonne
Sterbend ihr am Busen hangt:

Wie die Sonnenblume richtet
Auf die Sonn ihr Angesicht
Und nicht eh'r auf sie verzichtet,
Bis ihr eignes Auge bricht:

Wie der Aar auf Wolkenpfade
Sehnend steigt ins Himmelszelt
Und berauscht vom Sonnenbade
Blind zur Erde niederfällt:

So auch muss ich schmachten, bangen,
Spähn und trachten, dich zu sehn,
Will an deinen Blicken hangen,
Und an ihrem Glanz vergehn.

As the cloud, filled with longing, strays fearfully after the sun and hangs dying on its bosom, all aglow with heavenly bliss;
as the sunflower turns its face to the sun and never ceases to gaze until its own eyes close;
as the eagle on its cloudy path soars yearningly into the canopy of heaven, and enraptured by bathing in sunlight falls blindly back to earth;
so I too must yearn, tremble, gaze and strive to see you: I long to hang on your looks and, in their radiance, to pass away [and, in their radiance, to pass away, to pass away].

Here, yet again, is the same high-flown and -blown style of early romantic poetry, filled with the very ecstasy of adolescent love. The first two verses are deliberately designed to glow in five sharps and tremble in broken staccato chords, in a sustained image of sun-worship. The fate of Icarus is not forgotten; each verse has its own bereavement. The cloud and the sunflower both die at the same moment, with the same sad declining motif.

For the eagle, the quaver rhythm expands into triplet wings, with aptly high soaring notes; after 'blind' the great wings stay outstretched as the eagle glides rather than plummets down the sky. Finally the lover is identified with each of the three images, among continuing wing-beats; and his own destiny of dying for love again falls pat at the same point of the strophe as before. The final repetition of 'und an ihren Glanz vergehn' (pass away in their radiance) is first triumphant and then finally fulfilled. Despite the poem's faded rhetoric, the music has a fine freshness and a perfect structure which can still combine most effectively.

NOTES. 1. The Hoffmann source (*Gedichte* 1843) has 'nach der Sonn' again in the second verse, as a parallel to the first; the composer's variant 'auf die Sonn' should perhaps be corrected.

2. The main accompaniment figure hints at horn passages (M22), to set the open-air scene. The idea of death, induced by 'sterbend' in the first verse and 'Auge bricht' in the second, is shadowed by a descending diminuendo in broken octaves, as at the first interlude in *Lied*, No. 4 above. The same idea recurs in the reprise, to match 'vergehn', but this time in a serene major tonality. The triplet wing-beats of 'der Aar' (M16) gradually descend from a top G# on 'blind' (M10).

14. (Op. 6, No. 6) Nachtigallen schwingen (Nightingales ply their plumage) July 1853

Heinrich Hoffmann von Fallersleben   A♭ major f'–g"

> Nachtigallen schwingen
> Lustig ihr Gefieder,
> Nachtigallen singen
> Ihre alten Lieder,
> Und die Blumen alle,
> Sie erwachen wieder
> Bei dem Klang und Schalle
> Aller dieser Lieder.
>
> Und meine Sehnsucht wird zur Nachtigall
> Und fliegt in die blühende Welt hinein,
> Und fragt bei den Blumen überall,
> Wo mag doch mein, mein Blümchen sein?
>
> Und die Nachtigallen
> Schwingen ihren Reigen
> Unter Laubeshallen
> Zwischen Blütenzweigen,
> Von den Blumen allen
> Aber ich muss schweigen,
> Unter ihnen steh ich

Traurig sinnend still;
Eine Blume seh ich,
Die nicht blühen will.

Nightingales joyously ply their plumage, nightingales sing their old songs; and all the flowers reawaken at the tones and sounds of all these songs.

And my longing becomes a nightingale and flies out into the blossoming world and asks each flower everywhere – where then may my [my] own floweret be [where may my floweret be]?

And the nightingales ply their music and their dances under leafy arbours among blossoming boughs. But I must be silent about all the flowers. I stand among them sadly, lost in silent thought. I see a flower that has no wish to bloom.

The poet laments his inability to find and experience love, symbolised here as so often in Brahms by the flight and song of birds. The prelude's consecutive thirds that lift and dip in both hands rehearse the nightingales' flight and song, which bursts out wide-winged and full-throated, *molto staccato e leggiero*, as the voice enters. The music effectively imagines a flock of birds wheeling and singing. After 'aller dieser Lieder' (of all these songs) they poise and settle; the two-handed flight furls and folds into a high repeated right-hand minor third, which after a modulation becomes the blossom that hangs on the bough, to illustrate a world in flower.

For the contrasting second verse, these soft staccato off-beat quavers, later extended into chords, echo the vocal line over a new lefthand melody of love-longing, marked 'äusserst zart' (with the utmost tenderness). The rhythm is relaxed, the voice recites its secret sorrow. In the composer's mind, the perched birds listen in silence. After 'wo mein Blümchen sein?' (where may my floweret be?) it is as if their sympathies are again engaged. As the prelude and the first strain recur at 'und die Nachtigallen' the whole flock seems to fly off, helpfully skimming and swooping among a profusion of flowers in quest of the right one. To illustrate 'ich muss schweigen' (I must be silent) the left-hand quaver triplets turn into crotchets that sound like an instrumental solo, a wordless singing. First they range widely up the keyboard, then turn around as if searching. All this brilliant invention is lavished on verse that cannot sustain the response it has inspired; and if the audience fails to share the poet's predicament the song will sadly sag, especially in its would-be pathetic peroration. But it remains well worth a hearing for its vocal melodies and bravura pianism, which in fine performance can sound both impressive and appealing.

NOTES. 1. In the last verse, Peters amends 'von den Blumen' to 'vor den Blumen', which seems preferable. In the penultimate line, Brahms substituted 'Blume' for the 'Knospe' found in the source (Hoffmann's *Gedichte* 1843). This should surely be corrected; the poet's symbolism requires a bud which (quite unlike a flower) cannot and will not unfold.

2. The beginning and end of the poem strive to convey their excitement by short (trimeter) lines whose rhymes (e.g. 'schwingen/Gefieder/singen/Lieder') need to be brought out. The declamation needs freedom; undue deference to accents and barlines will detrimentally enhance the first-beat dissonances between voice and piano at 'lustig', 'ihre', etc.

3. The pianist's arms work as wings, M3; the middle section's quite different staccato in voice and piano has a touch of tears, M28; the chromatic descents at 'unter ihnen steh' ich' etc. combine the bright top notes of M10 with the sadness of M20.

OPUS 7

Six songs for solo voice with pianoforte accompaniment, dedicated to Albert Dietrich and published in November 1854.

The designation 'for soprano or tenor' is now omitted. There are two new poets, Ferrand and Uhland; but both had already been set by Schumann, and again his library may well have been their original source. The German folksongs however are really new. Schumann had already lamented the difficulty of writing in this vein; but the style came naturally to Brahms, who was by birth and temperament closer to the common man.

Perhaps this opus was designed to tell a story, or at least convey a message; after five successive deserted girls, a young man finally returns home to his sweetheart.

15. (Op. 7, No. 1) Treue Liebe (Faithful love) November 1852
Eduard Ferrand   F# minor d#'–e''

> Ein Mägdlein sass am Meeresstrand
> Und blickte voll Sehnsucht ins Weite:
> 'Wo bleibst du, mein Liebster, wo weilst du so lang?
> Nicht ruhen lässt mich des Herzens Drang.
> Ach, kämst du, mein Liebster, doch heute!'
>
> Der Abend nahte, die Sonne sank
> Am Saum des Himmels darnieder.
> 'So trägt dich die Welle mir nimmer zurück?
> Vergebens späht in die Ferne mein Blick.
> Wo find ich, mein Liebster, dich wieder?'
>
> Die Wasser umspielten ihr schmeichelnd den Fuss,
> Wie Träume von seligen Stunden,
> Es zog sie zur Tiefe mit stiller Gewalt;
> Nie stand mehr am Ufer die holde Gestalt,
> Sie hat den Geliebten gefunden!

A girl sat by the sea-shore and gazed yearningly at the horizon; 'Where are you, my dearest, where do you tarry so long? My heart's desire gives me no peace; oh, my dearest, if only you would come today [if only you would come today].'

Evening neared; the sun sank down to the rim of the sky. 'So the waves will never bring you back to me? In vain my gaze searches the horizon. Where, my dearest, shall I find you again [where, my dearest, shall I find you again]?'

The water rippled playfully around her feet, like dreams of blissful hours. The tide drew her down into the depths, with silent power. Her fair form was never again seen on the shore; she has found her loved one!

The ideas of desertion and the sea-shore engulfed the young Brahms, just as irresistibly. The sentimental poem offers a channel for his music to flow through and fill, often very movingly. The piano's waves begin their sad gentle lapping in the brief prelude. This grey monotonous motion is itself a sea-symbol of change-less sorrow, as the vocal melody confirms; the falling arpeggio at 'Meeresstrand' (sea-shore) is repeated at 'weilst du so lang?' (tarry so long?). This latter phrase, though a question in the poem, is a statement in the music, as if there can be no return; thus the listener, like the singer, is already half-aware that the separation will be final, and why. The sea, like the hand, waves farewell. As in *Liebestreu*, No. 1, the accompaniment moves into a higher register at the first sound of the girl's own voice, and which again sings in unison with the piano (here at 'nicht ruhen', no peace), to emphasise the characterisation and intensify the girl's feeling of isolation. The melody sounds alone, frail and unsupported.

After the second verse, to the same music (again with the question to the waves 'nimmer zurück?' treated as a statement – no, they will never bring him back) Brahms hurries the poem along to its rather too predictable dénouement. The innocuous wavelets of the earlier verses now begin to crest and splash more ominously and purposefully in the accompaniment, with quicker note-values and fuller chords. At 'seligen Stunden' (blissful hours) the keyboard speaks in the accents of passion, which was once as overwhelming as the sea now. That tide gath-ers in both hands, and after 'stiller Gewalt' (silent power) the sudden swell surges and recedes above a tolling left-hand fifth, like a funeral knell. The ensuing recita-tive at 'nie stand mehr' (was never again seen) is quasi-operatic; the staccato along the vocal line means that the syllables are to be enunciated with special intensity, almost spoken. The final phrase 'sie hat den Geliebten gefunden' implies that the singer's lover, as she has long known or suspected, had been lost at sea. The postlude's final bass octaves explain where the two are to be reunited: in the depths.

NOTES. I. The second verse's reading 'Saume' found in the *Gedichte* (1834) of Eduard Schulz alias Ferrand is surely preferable to 'Saum' as printed in the *Gesamtausausgabe* and Peters.

2. Schumann had sketched a Ferrand setting in 1840 from the same source; Brahms may well have inherited that volume, and selected this poem for its theme of tragic separation.

3. The lapping waves are M5; their later arpeggio extensions are M16, crested by the moaning minor seconds of M20. The voice-piano unison at bars 8–11 is motivic (M37) in the sense of isolation, while the left-hand open fifth A–D after 'Gewalt', as the girl disap-pears, may well have the special meaning of 'Ade', farewell (M34). The ominous final octaves are M6.

16. (Op. 7, No. 2) Parole (Password) November 1852
Joseph von Eichendorff   E minor c′–g#″

> Sie stand wohl am Fensterbogen
> Und flocht sich traurig das Haar,
> Der Jäger war fortgezogen,
> Der Jäger ihr Liebster war.

Und als der Frühling gekommen,
Die Welt war von Blüten verschneit,
Da hat sie ein Herz sich genommen
Und ging in die grüne Heid,

Sie legt das Ohr an den Rasen,
Hört ferner Hufe Klang,
Das sind die Rehe, die grasen
Am schattigen Bergeshang.

Und abends die Wälder rauschen,
Von fern nur fällt noch ein Schuss,
Da steht sie stille zu lauschen:
'Das war meines Liebsten Gruss!'

Da sprangen vom Fels die Quellen,
Da flohen die Vöglein ins Tal!
'Und wo ihr ihn trefft, ihr Gesellen,
O grüsst mir ihn tausendmal!'

*She stood at the arched window and sadly braided her hair. The huntsman had trav-
elled far away; the huntsman was her beloved.*

*And when spring came and the world was snowed under with blossom, then she took
fresh heart and went out into the green moorlands.*

*She puts her ear to the turf and hears the sound of distant hooves. That's the deer
grazing on the shaded slopes of the hills [on the shaded slopes of the hills].*

*And at evening the forest rustles, and in the distance one last shot is heard. She stands
still to listen; 'that was my dearest's greeting [that was my dearest's greeting]'!*

*Then the springs leapt from the cliff, and the birds fled down into the valley. 'And
when you meet him, dear friends, oh greet him from me a thousand times [a thousand,
a thousand times]!'*

This time the music, if not the poem, presages a happy ending in joyous reunion,
off-stage. The scene is set with a Mendelssohnian flourish of horn-calls, which
falter away in a yearning sigh as the absent huntsman is remembered and longed
for. The broken chords suggest a zither accompaniment, which instantly echoes
the opening vocal melody as if to imply the answering call of a distant voice.
When the heroine herself goes out into the green moorlands ('ging in die grüne
Heid') there are more horn-calls, and the voice resumes among the Brahmsian
music of the countryside and the chase, with left-hand horn-passages evoking the
missing huntsman more graphically still. The last verse reverts to the opening
mood and music; but the new sense of expectancy is made vivid by a transition to
the major and a bright sustained top note, followed by a hunting-horn postlude
that imagines an exultant meeting, as the two hands converge, with a quiet
embrace on the final chord.

NOTES. 1. Brahms found the poem in Eichendorff's *Gedichte* (1843), which he owned;
there it was entitled *Parole* (Password), presumably in reference to the symbolic signal of

the rifleshot-greeting. Both the *Gesamtausgabe* and Peters have 'flohen' in line 18; but this may be a misreading for the more natural 'flogen', as in all modern editions of Eichendorff. In the last line the composer added 'o' before 'grüsst' for the sake of melodic continuity; but his 'das' instead of the poet's 'ihr' [Haar] in the second line could readily be restored. No doubt the widely-read Brahms also knew the Eichendorff novella *Dichter und ihre Gesellen* (1834), where as in No. 6 above the lyric is sung by a girl in huntsman's guise, this time to zither accompaniment.

2. The piano's opening and closing flourishes are closely paralleled in Mendelssohn's spring song *Gruss* Op. 19a No. 5, an echo perhaps evoked by 'als der Frühling gekommen' here. The ensuing diminished seventh chord in the prelude expresses dismay (M25). As in the previous song, the music moves from a minor tonic to the even sadder minor chord on the flattened supertonic (M23), here in bars 10 and 12, to match the mention of departure. In the middle section, the left-hand horn passages are M22, and the broken octaves of the rustling forest are M4. The exultant top G# is M10; the postlude's converging chords are the love-motif M17.

17. (Op. 7, No. 3) Anklänge (Echoes) March 1853
Joseph von Eichendorff   A minor e′–g″

> Hoch über stillen Höhen
> Stand in dem Wald ein Haus;
> So einsam wars zu sehen,
> Dort übern Wald hinaus.
>
> Ein Mädchen sass darinnen
> Bei stiller Abendzeit,
> Tät seidne Fäden spinnen
> Zu ihrem Hochzeitskleid.

High over silent heights a house stood in the forest; it was so lonely there, looking out over the forest.
Inside, there sat a girl at silent eventide, spinning silken threads for her wedding dress [spinning silken threads for her wedding dress].

The lyric is an evocative sylvan vignette typical of Eichendorff; its seeming naïveté conceals deep art. The wide, wild and high natural scene forms a fitting frame for human feelings; but the latter are presented as transient though tragic, and the former as immutable. The silence and solitude were there before the poem began, and will last long after it ends. The patterns of repetition ('Hoch/Höhen' in the first line, 'Wald' twice in the first quatrain, 'stillen' in the first quatrain and 'stiller' in the second) and position (outside and inside, standing and sitting) create an exalted mood of ritual observance. Brahms preserves and extends this by his own final repetition, like an echoing voice among the high mountains. Indeed, the weaving of the wedding dress may be the only ceremony that will take place; this remote and unattainable fastness, this timeless and undisturbed landscape, are worlds away from the warmth and commitment, the finery and festivity of an actual wedding.

Instead, the words suggest a jilted girl left on a high shelf. The masterly music is also suffused with Brahmsian themes of isolation. The composer seems to pick from the poem the word 'einsam' (lonely). His inner ear hears a woman's voice singing high and far through twilight. Her melody begins on 'hoch' and climbs even higher, like a spiral path uphill. The only sign of companionship lies in the low left-hand consecutive thirds; and they are as it were wishful thinking, far below the surface of consciousness. Otherwise the marriage remains imaginary. The left-hand melody is distantly doubled in voice and piano, like the voices of a man and a woman who never meet. The right hand lingeringly echoes each vocal note; the off-beat right-hand octave knell sounds hopeful but hesitant. In the second verse, at 'Ein Mädchen sass' (a girl sat), the tonal ideas seem to change places; the outdoor scene of the first verse sounded like a girl's sad song to virginal accompaniment, while the indoor scene of the second begins with open-air horn passages which evoke an absent lover. The so-called pathetic fallacy, which equates external nature with human emotion, is made audible. The rising major melody of 'zu ihrem Hochzeitskleid' (for her wedding dress) is forced to fall in the minor mode when those words are repeated to end the song. The piano's repeated pedal note is now an insistently dark tolling bass tonic on the beat instead of the first verse's high and bright off-beat dominant. Thus a question has been asked and answered, as if the future bride is already envisaged as a perpetual spinster, or perhaps an early widow; no happiness for her. But the final major chord may be meant to strike a more optimistic note, leaving the church door open.

NOTES. 1. In the *Gedichte* (1837) this poem (with 'übern' in line 4, not 'überm' as in Peters) forms the central panel of a triptych called *Anklänge* which begins the section *Frühling und Liebe*; its isolation as a song, as well as its sad setting, leaves little doubt about Brahms's motives. As throughout the whole of Op. 7, he is here exemplifying a favourite theme, the girl left lonely; perhaps the linking horn passages for example were a deliberate device of unification. He may well have been familiar with a much longer lyric introduced as a folk ballad sung in the novella *Ahnung und Gegenwart*: this too begins with a spinning-girl in the same scene of isolation, and soon moves into overt tragedy via her love for a huntsman.

2. The indication of right-hand staccato for the first six bars only may be misleading, if the intended effect is to bring out those repeated dominants (M24). The vocal melodies are expressive in their stepwise climb to top notes at 'Höhen' etc.; the keyboard sigh at bars 9–10 is M21. The Schumannian style of voice–piano doubling is characteristic of the young Brahms, who however hears the effect as much more motivic. His consecutive octaves in voice and piano are enhanced in their symbolism of separation (M37) if the singer is a soprano, at two octaves' remove from the bass line instead of the tenor's single octave. The horn passages at 'Mädchen sass darinnen' etc. are quasi-literal (M22), since Brahms was surely well aware of the huntsman lover here as in the previous song. The descending minor 5–4–3–2–1 at 'tät seidne Fäden spinnen' is deliberately contrasted with the ascending major version which scales a hopeful top G (M10) at '–kleid', and is then made to droop and dwindle on the same word at the last vocal note, where the open fifth A–D may again say 'Ade' (M34), as in No. 15.

18. (Op. 7, No. 4) Volkslied (Folksong) August 1852
Anon.   E minor e'–g"

> Die Schwälble ziehet fort, ziehet fort,
> Weit an en andre, Ort;

Und i sitz do in Traurigkeit,
Es isch a böse, schwere Zeit.

Könnt i no fort durch d'Welt, fort durch d'Welt,
Weil mirs hie gar net, gar net g'fällt!
O Schwälble, komm, i bitt, i bitt!
Zeig mir de Weg und nimm mi mit!

The swallow flies away, flies away, far off to another [another] place, and I sit here in sorrow; it is a bad sad time.

If only I too could fly off through the world, off through the world, because I'm so very, so very unhappy here. Oh, swallow, come, I beg, I beg, show me the way and take me with you.

We can instantly hear that the girl is unhappy; and we can soon guess that her far-off lover would still prove elusive and her flight fruitless. Even the envied and longed-for wings beat sadly in the minor, throughout the piano part. The lyric's folk-song style, garnished with dialect, lacks natural freshness, and the heaped helpings of sadness flatten it still further; thus the music's insistence on the E minor mode causes that keynote to resonate in almost every bar, often prolonged with a pedal. But the beginning and end with wing-beats of broken thirds are effective in depicting a wheeling and heavy flight of sorrow, which is lightened by subtler touches, such as when the harmony after 'andre Ort' (another place) or 'hie gar net g'fällt' (so very unhappy here) makes a brief hopeful excursion into the major mode in search of happiness for the first and only time in each verse.

NOTES. 1. The textual source was Georg Scherer's anthology *Deutsche Volkslieder* (1851); Brahms repeats 'andre' for the sake of an expressive top note (M10).

2. The insistent yearning wing-beats are M3, and the parallel thirds and sixths strive to sing a hopeful love-duet, M18; but the octave doublings speak of loneliness (M37) within a tonic minor pedal that expresses unending distress.

19. (Op. 7, No. 5) Die Trauernde (The grieving girl) August 1852
Anon. A minor e′–e″

Mei Mueter mag mi net,
Und kei Schatz han i net,
Ei warum sterb i net,
Was tu i do?

Gestern isch Kirchweih g'wä,
Mi hot mer g'wis net g'seh,
Denn mir ischs gar so weh,
I tanz ja net.

Lasst die drei Rose stehn
Die an dem Kreuzle blühn;
Hent ihr das Mädle kennt,
Die drunter liegt?

*My mother doesn't love me, and I have no sweetheart; I might as well be dead, what
am I doing here?*

   *Yesterday was the parish fair, but I'm sure no one saw me, because I'm so sad, I don't
dance any more.*

   *Leave alone the three roses that bloom on my little cross; did you know the girl who
lies below it?*

Yesterday was the parish fair, for the consecration of the church. The composer
converts the idea of organ- or harmonium-tone into four-part harmonies, an
offertory for repentant sinners. This country lass is a Tess of the d'Urbervilles,
betrayed and deserted, and hence dear to Brahms. The modal music is very affecting in its sedate melodic lament. Its persistent four-bar phrases ending on the
dominant keep on asking the same question: 'was tu i do?' (what am I doing
here?); what is to become of me, in my outcast state? There is no escape; whatever
the frail little tune tries to do, wherever it turns, it falls back hopelessly on the same
lower dominant, like the twelvefold tolling of a passing bell. Thrice in the first
verse and once in the second the voice's lower dominant E coincides with and
reinforces the negation of 'net', a dialect form of 'nicht'. In the last verse, the vocal
line twice lifts and lightens into the tonic major; roses are blooming in a brief
bright tierce de Picardie at 'lass die drei Rose stehn'. But then the tolling resumes
at 'kennt' (know), and the interment is complete at the last low 'liegt' (lies), this
time with low-lying bass chords, after which the left hand solemnly strikes the
keynote of darkness.

   All this is made moving and true by the restraint and sincerity of the music.
Here, as in the previous song, the young Brahms is heard communing with dialect
folk-poetry; his own origins were humble, and such verses, authentic or not,
seemed to him imbued with the true feelings of ordinary humanity and hence especially significant. At least his music, if not the girl's lost lover, can hear and respond.

NOTES. 1.   The text was again taken from *Deutsche Volkslieder*, ed. George Scherer (1851).
   2. The modal harmonies are M27; the recurrent dominants incorporate the questioning of M24. The sighs at bars 10–11 and 12–13 are M21; the low final bass note is M6.
   3. Cf. the admirable Franz setting Op. 17, No. 4.

20. (Op. 7, No. 6) Heimkehr (Homecoming) May 1851
Ludwig Uhland   B minor and major e′–g″

> O brich nicht, Steg, du zitterst sehr,
> O stürz nicht, Fels, du dräuest schwer;
> Welt, geh nicht unter, Himmel, fall nicht ein,
> Bis ich mag bei der Liebsten sein!

*Oh, break not, footbridge, though you tremble so; crash not, cliff, though you ominously
threaten to. World, do not end, sky, do not fall [sky, do not fall] until I'm back with my
best beloved [until I'm back with my best beloved, until I'm, until I'm back with my
best beloved]!*

The lyric's touch is far lighter than the music's. Uhland smiles at his own fears;

Brahms is intensely serious in his youthful rhetoric. His hero is on a journey, from the outset. The prelude strides on stage, striking quasi-operatic attitudes of alarm and despondency. Its right-hand rising strains anticipate the vocal plea of 'break not', 'crash not', as if those same thoughts had just entered the young composer's mind. The left hand is agitated, pulsating, apprehensive yet defiant, as the bridge and the cliff tremble and totter in detached quaver triplet chords. After a loud sustained dominant that seems to cry out 'Shall I ever see her again?', the voice enters; and the motifs of impending calamity are turned upside down and pulled apart. Now the right hand has the staccato chords and the left the rising implorations, with one-bar wedges of ill-boding silence thrust between them. They are soon sent plummeting into the bass at 'du dräuest schwer' (you ominously threaten). The ensuing canons and imitations between voice and piano are further effective devices of fragmentation and separation. Then in the final bars, with insistent verbal repetition, all possible catastrophes are overcome. The impending reunion is also made audible, as if the two lovers are waving to each other from a distance, on the road and at a window. Voice and keyboard join and swell in triumphant unison, with a typical top note; the piano's tonic major chords hammer on the homestead door with both hands, as if shouting 'I'm safe back!'.

This earliest surviving song, for all its melodramatic exaggeration, already shows the consummate artistry of a mature master. The powerful emotion, at least as much personal as poetic, is serviced by technical skill of the highest order. Above all, the rudiments of music are used and heard as expressive song-motifs from the first.

NOTES. 1. Brahms owned the 1839 edition of Uhland's *Gedichte* (1815), where this quatrain figures as the last of nine *Wanderlieder*. The second and third were set as Op. 19, Nos, 2–3 (see Nos, 30–31), which may thus have been sketched at the same early period. In bars 12, 14 and 16 here, Uhland's 'eh' (before) at the beginning of the last line may be preferred to Brahms's repeated 'bis' (until).

2. The prelude's left-hand staccato should continue into bar 2, and the right-hand staccato at the opening words should be extended to 'stürz nicht, Fels', with the same significance of impending collapse in each context. The intense dominant question in bars 4–5 is M24; the small sighs at bars 6 and 8 are M21, with ominous left-hand silences akin to M29. The canons are motivic (M12) in the sense of shifting, slipping and sliding; so is the B minor tonality with its Schubertian relaxation into B major (M39). The exultant top notes on 'ich' and 'Lieb(sten)' are M10, and the final two-handed hammering is M30.

OPUS 14

Songs and romances for solo voice and pianoforte accompaniment, without dedication, published in January 1861.

This opus continues and culminates one of the main original developments within the lied tradition. Each of the eight texts is taken from an actual or putative folk-song source. There had been one-volume settings of folk-poems before, notably Franz's *Sechs Gesänge nach Texten deutscher Volkslieder* Op. 23; but no earlier opus had ever been so concentrated in effect or so authentic in tone.

Brahms had already displayed an expert knowledge of European (not only German) traditional music, in widely contrasting moods and styles; here he benefits from his boyhood pot-pourris of Russian tunes and gypsy airs, his early association with the Hungarian violinist Reményi and consequent composition of Hungarian dances, his folk-song collections including Finnish, French, Irish, Scottish and Swedish melodies, and above all his arrangements of German folk-songs by the hundred, from all areas and eras.

For the first time, the works are described as 'Lieder', not 'Gesänge'. Both words mean 'songs'; but the former category is often less extended in form and easier to assimilate at first hearing. What Brahms or his publisher meant by 'Romanzen' is less clear; but Nos 1, 4 and 7 of Op. 14 are supreme examples of the modern popular love-song for voice and piano, written by a major master of art-music. The world would hear nothing truly comparable until the advent of Gershwin, in a different language and style but engendered by the same uncondescending ethnic and aesthetic approach.

21. (Op. 14, No. 1) Vor dem Fenster (Outside the window) September 1858

Anon.   G minor and major d′–g″

Soll sich der Mond nicht heller scheinen,
Soll sich die Sonn nicht früh aufgehn,
So will ich diese Nacht gehn freien,
Wie ich zuvor auch hab getan.

Als er wohl auf die Gasse trat,
Da fing er an ein Lied und sang,
Er sang aus schöner, aus heller Stimme,
Dass sein feïns Lieb zum Bett aussprang.

Steh still, steh still, mein feines Lieb,
Steh still, steh still und rühr dich nicht,
Sonst weckst du Vater, sonst weckst du Mutter,
Das ist uns Beiden nicht wohl getan.

Was frag ich nach Vater, was frag ich nach Mutter,
Vor deinem Schlaffenster muss ich stehn,
Ich will mein schönes Lieb anschauen,
Um das ich muss so ferne gehn.

Da standen die zwei wohl bei einander
Mit ihren zarten Mündelein,
Der Wächter blies wohl in sein Hörnelein,
Ade, es muss geschieden sein.

Ach Scheiden, Scheiden über Scheiden,
Scheiden tut meinem jungen Herzen weh,
Dass ich mein schön Herzlieb muss meiden,
Das vergess ich nimmermehr.

If the moon shines no brighter, if the sun doesn't rise too early, I'll go a-wooing tonight, as I've done before.

When he stepped into the street he began a song and sang; he sang with a clear bright voice, and his sweetheart leapt from her bed.

Keep quiet, keep quiet, my dear love, keep quiet, keep quiet and don't move, or else you'll wake my father and wake my mother, and that would bode ill for us both.

What care I for your father, what care I for your mother, I must stand outside your bedroom window, I must see my beautiful love for whose sake I must go so far away.

And there they both stood together with their tender lips touching, and the watch-man blew his horn — farewell [farewell], it is time to part.

Parting, parting, always parting; parting hurts my young heart. Having to leave my own dear love, that I shall never forget.

By lavishing every device of his art on this seemingly artless folk-song lyric Brahms creates a rare hybrid of simple words and masterly music. The opening strains tease the ear with unexpected complexities of mode, modulation and rhythm; and their triple repetition through three verses builds up powerful harmonic tensions not found in the German folk-song tradition. But then, at 'was frag ich nach Vater' (what care I for your father), the feelings flow out freely; and their unfeigned simplicity of utterance sounds by contrast as if an actual folk-song is being new-created. The same effect recurs at 'Scheiden' (parting) after the origi-nal minor section is repeated; again the memorable melodies are now in a major mode which somehow sounds sadder still, as the serenader departs diminuendo into the darkness. Thus the listener is drawn into the love-drama, which in fine performance can itself be unforgettable.

NOTES. 1. Brahms seems to have altered his folk-song source, found in various antholo-gies such as Karl Simrock's *Die deutschen Volkslieder* (1851) or Franz Mittler's *Deutsche Volk-slieder* (1855) – perhaps to make it less folksy. But he used the original dialect text unchanged in his arrangements of this poem's folk-song melody for solo voice in WoO 33 No. 35 and for four women's voices in WoO 38 No. 19, as also for the art-song *Die Trauernde* (No. 19); so a case could be made for unchanged retention here too. Further, Brahms's 'aufgehn' instead of 'aufgahn' in the first verse, and 'nimmermehr' instead of 'nimmermeh' at the last word, forfeit the rhyme as well as the dialect. However, his newly-invented melody justifies the repeated 'ade', and 'Hörnelein' instead of 'Hörnlein', in verse five, and the added 'ach' before verse six. In the latter, his 'meinem' instead of 'einem [jungen Herzen]', whether deliberate or not, serves as strong evidence of personal identification with the lover; but there seems no compelling reason to retain the 'aus' between 'schöner' and 'heller' in verse two.

2. The companionable consecutive thirds sing a love-duet, M18; just as clearly, the insistent horn-passages of M22 speak of open-air pursuits. But their relevance to the favourite Brahmsian topic of separation would be clearer still, in this year of his own parting from Agathe von Siebold, if some such formula as this

A   G   A   H   E

had been in and on his mind, as in the G major string sextet (M32). Further, the notes A–D certainly occur, no doubt in deliberate if cryptic allusion, in the right hand at the word 'ade' (M34). The expressive top notes are M10. Although the same 3/8 time-signature and three-quaver or crotchet-quaver rhythm recur throughout, the waywardness of folk-song is attained by the irregular insertion of piano interludes. The minor–major shift on the same keynote mirrors a Schubertian mingling of joy and sorrow (M39); the postlude's sadly flattened seventh (M41) suggests the sadness of separation.

22. (Op. 14, No. 2) Vom verwundeten Knaben (The wounded lad) January 1858

Anon.   A minor e'–f''

Es wollt ein Mädchen früh aufstehn
Und in den grünen Wald spazieren gehn.

Und als sie nun in den grünen Wald kam
Da fand sie einen verwundten Knab'n.

Der Knab, der war von Blut so rot.
Und als sie sich verwandt, war er schon tot.

Wo krieg ich nun zwei Leidfräulein,
Die mein feins Lieb zu Grabe wein'n?

Wo krieg ich nun sechs Reuterknab'n,
Die mein feins Lieb zu Grabe trag'n?

Wie lang soll ich denn trauern gehn?
Bis alle Wasser zusammen gehn?

Ja alle Wasser gehn nicht zusamm'n,
So wird mein Trauern kein Ende han.

A girl thought she'd get up early and walk in the greenwood.
And as she now came into the greenwood she found a wounded lad.
The lad was so red with blood, and as she turned to him he was already dead.
Where shall I find two mourning maidens who'll weep my dear love to his grave?
Where shall I find six young squires who'll carry my dear love to his grave?
How long then must I go on mourning? Until all waters flow together?
Yet all waters will never flow together; and so my mourning will have no end.

We are to understand that the dead young lover has been slain by a jealous husband or rival, off-stage; instead of the duel and the drama we see only the grief-stricken woman and her feeling. Even that is detached, almost remote, as if the music too is in shock. The invariant rhythm, the modal harmonies, the pedal points, and the sparseness of the texture combine to portray the maiden of once upon a time lamenting in the past tense about far away and long ago. Yet the tears are still flowing unstaunched, even now. The mourning will have no end, as the song says.

Thus Clara Schumann mourned her wayward husband for forty years, from his death in 1856 until her own. Of course the song is not telling her story; nor does the lamented lad directly embody either her dead husband or her young adorer. Yet the unspoken inspiration is surely the triangular tragedy that was so poignantly congruent with Brahms's own early experience; and that thought may, for some listeners, make this music all the more moving – especially since the same text had already been set in the same key by Schumann himself, a fact which may help to confirm the background of deliberate personal allusion.

NOTES. 1. This lyric first appeared in Herder's *Volkslieder* (1778–9), later reissued as *Stimmen der Völker* (1807), but it was republished with additions and variants in other collections also available to Brahms (e.g. in Schumann's Düsseldorf library) including *Des Knaben Wunderhorn* (1805–8), and Karl Simrock's *Die deutschen Volkslieder* (1851, a source of No. 21). However, the likeliest single source was the *Stimmen der Völker* volume of Herder's *Sämmtliche Werke* (1827–30), which Brahms owned. If so, he shortened 'verwundeten' in the second couplet and 'feines' in the next two, to preserve his steady flow of even crotchets. But the last two couplets' substitution of 'trauern' for the dialect form 'trauren' (which appears unchanged in No. 61) would be less justifiable and may have been inadvertent; it could now be reversed.

2. The horn-passage falling fifth in the left hand after 'früh aufstehn', 'Wald kam' etc., suggests arrival in the open air (M22); the augmented left-hand echoes of the voice's major third C–E at the end of each verse add to the effect of spaciousness. The prolonged dominant pedal-points on G (bars 16–24) and F (25–33) convey a cortège effect of monkish intoning as well as organ-playing as the body is borne 'zu Grabe'.

3. If there is a Clara-theme here it is shrouded among inner parts and veiled by division between voice and piano; but the sad features of M33 may still be recognisable as

C LA R A

at bars 7–9 for each of the first three verses and again at 40–42 and 53–5. That last passage contains the verbal icon 'So wird mein Trauern kein Ende han'.

4. Cf. Schumann's own choral setting of the same text, Op. 75 No. 5 (which retains 'trauren').

23. (Op. 14, No. 3) Murrays Ermordung (The assassination of Murray) January 1858

Anon., Scottish (trans. J. Herder)   E minor d'–g''

> O Hochland und o Südland!
> Was ist auf euch geschehn!
> Erschlagen der edle Murray,
> Werd nie ihn wiedersehn.
>
> O weh dir! Weh dir, Huntley!
> So untreu, falsch und kühn,

Sollst ihn zurück uns bringen,
Ermordet hast du ihn.

Ein schöner Ritter war er,
In Wett- und Ringelauf;
Allzeit war unsres Murray
Die Krone oben drauf.

Ein schöner Ritter war er,
Bei Waffenspiel und Ball.
Es war der edle Murray
Die Blume überall.

Ein schöner Ritter war er,
In Tanz und Saitenspiel;
Ach, dass der edle Murray
Der Königin gefiel.

O Königin, wirst lange
Sehn über Schlosses Wall,
Eh du den schönen Murray
Siehst reiten in dem Tal.

Oh highlands and oh lowlands, what has happened to you! Slain is the noble Murray, I'll never see him more [never see him more].

Oh woe to you, woe to you, Huntley! so faithless, false and bold; you were told to bring him back to us, and you have murdered him [you have murdered him].

He was a handsome knight in racing and riding at the ring; the crown was always ready to be placed upon our Murray's head.

He was a handsome knight in armed combat and ball-games; the noble Murray was the flower of all everywhere.

He was a handsome knight, in dancing and lute-playing; but alas, noble Murray pleased the queen.

Oh queen, you will long look over the castle rampart before you see the handsome Murray riding in the valley [see him riding in the valley].

The fate of the handsome Murray is movingly set forth in the Scottish ballad cited below. Herder's paraphrase is quite compelling; but the source of its audibly deep appeal to the young Brahms is a matter for conjecture. As in so many other songs, early and late, its theme is triangular tragedy. Here a queen is said to be mourning her illicit lover; and the Herder version plainly inculpates the unnamed king (James VI of Scotland, later James I of England) for his complicity in that killing, because 'der edle Murray der Königin gefiel' (noble Murray pleased the queen). She may even have been imagined by Herder as the speaker of the first three verses. In the music however we seem to hear the voice of the people. This setting is all fiery indignation, displaying the wounded body and demanding vengeance as in an illustrated broadsheet or ballad. Brahms sounds personally involved. His music rages against the injustice of early death and conspiracy; it celebrates the physical strength and prowess of the young victim and denounces his dastardly assailants. The two-handed battering of right-hand chords and left-hand octaves includes a vocal line deliberately written in an uncomfortably high range to exacerbate an already harsh reality. The third verse, at 'Ein schöner Ritter' (a handsome knight) relaxes with recitatives in loving memory; we hear why his accomplishments appealed to the queen. At those words we are as it were reminded of his foul murder. Regrets and sighs are suddenly overwhelmed by recollections of the virile Murray riding through the valley like a knight in armour, with a reprise more evocative of vengeance than of regret. This music has an operatic scope which demands the extremes of tenderness and power from both singer and pianist.

NOTES. 1. Brahms no doubt, took his text from the *Stimmen der Völker* volume of Herder's *Sämmtliche Werke* (1827–30), which he owned. There, the queen in question is wrongly identified as Mary Stuart. Herder's version of the ballad, headed 'Schottisch', is so free that the original stanzas in Bishop Percy's *Reliques of Ancient English Poetry* (1765) are well worth quoting, though they can hardly be sung to this music:

> Ye highlands and ye lawlands,
>   Oh! quhair hae ye been?
> They hae slain the Earl of Murray
>   And hae laid him in the green.
>
> Now wae be to thee, Huntley!
>   And quhairfore did you sae!
> I bade you bring him wi' you
>   But forbade you him to slay.
>
> He was a braw gallant
>   And he rid at the ring;
> And the bonny Earl of Murray,
>   Oh! he might hae been a king.
>
> He was a braw gallant
>   And he played at the ba';
> And the bonny Earl of Murray
>   Was the flower among them a'.
>
> He was a braw gallant
>   And he played at the gluve
> And the bonny Earl of Murray
>   Oh! he was the Queenes luve.
>
> Oh! lang will his lady
>   Luke owre the castle downe
> Ere she see the Earl of Murray
>   Come sounding through the town.

The words and music of this fine traditional ballad are well known in Britten's arrangement.

2. In the Percy source (ii 213) the text is preceded by an explanatory note. 'In December 1591, Francis Stuart, Earl of Bothwell, had made an attempt to seize on the person of his sovereign James VI but being disappointed had retired towards the north. The king

unadvisedly gave a commission to George Gordon Earl of Huntley to pursue Bothwell and his followers with fire and sword. Huntley, under cover of executing that commission, took occasion to revenge a private quarrel he had against James Stewart Earl of Murray, a relation of Bothwell's. In the night of Feb. 7, 1592, he beset Murray's house, burnt it to the ground, and slew Murray himself; a young nobleman of the most promising virtues, and the very darling of the people . . . K. James, who took no care to punish the murtherers, is said by some to have privately countenanced and abetted them, being stimulated by jealousy for some indiscreet praise which his Queen [Anne of Denmark] had too lavishly bestowed on this unfortunate youth.' A further footnote adds that "castle downe" in the last verse above "has been thought to mean the Castle of Downe", a seat belonging to the family of Murray'. In the third verse, 'rid (rode) at the ring' refers to the chivalric sport where riders competed to carry off, on the point of a lance, a metal circlet suspended from a post; hence 'Ringelauf' in the German version.

3. Murray is in armour and on horseback from the first, with virile dotted rhythms (M31) and left-hand descending octaves alternating with cantering triplets (a variant of M1) that echo the voice in canon at bars 5–8 etc. (M12). At bars 11–13 the two strands of the love-motif M18 are as far sundered as the queen from Murray, while the outside voices disperse apart in an added image of separation. In the middle section, physical prowess is embodied in the full chords of M30; the vocal recitative aptly reserves its highest notes (M10) for 'oben drauf' and 'über all'; there the major IV–I progression is an image of nobility.

24. (Op. 14, No. 4) Ein Sonett (A Sonnet) September 1858
Thibault de Champagne (trans. J. Herder)   A flat major e♭'–a♭''

> Ach könnt ich, könnte vergessen sie,
>   Ihr schönes, liebes, liebliches Wesen,
> Den Blick, die freundliche Lippe die!
>   Vielleicht ich möchte genesen!
> Doch ach, mein Herz, mein Herz kann es nie!
> Und doch ists Wahnsinn zu hoffen sie!
>   Und um sie schweben
>   Gibt Mut und Leben,
>   Zu weichen nie.
> Und denn, wie kann ich vergessen sie,
>   Ihr schönes, liebes, liebliches Wesen,
> Den Blick, die freundlich Lippe die?
>   Viel lieber nimmer genesen!

Oh could I, could I but forget her and her fair dear lovely being, her look and her friendly lips, perhaps I might then recover.

But alas, my heart, my heart cannot forget, and yet it is madness to hope for her! And to attend upon her gives me new life and courage never to falter.

And then how can I forget her and her fair dear lovely being, her look and her friendly lips? I would far prefer never to recover.

Here is the very picture of courtly love, drawn from French troubadour sources and coloured with the music of Minnesang. From the first note, a long piano line bows downwards for more than two octaves of devoted enslavement, never venturing to look up or raise its voice above a half-heard inner melody. At 'den Blick' (her look) this long slow obeisance begins all over again, in line with the worshipping words. Thus the music strives to renounce love, in the belief that 'ich möchte genesen' (I might then recover). No sooner are those words out than a moan from the piano explains how hopeless that plan would prove. From the depths of abnegation the accompaniment now involuntarily rises, step by step, not in single notes as before but in parallel thirds and sixths. The heart 'kann es nie', that is, it cannot forget, cannot be suppressed or kept down; it must aspire. Now comes a magical moment; for thirteen bars of dominant pedal the music dances attendance on the loved one, hovering around her in a soft saraband, at 'Und um sie schweben' (And to attend upon her). The high sustained notes on 'nie' (never) stand for the idea and ideal of endless devotion. With the reprise, at 'Und denn' (And then) the singer returns to the notion of renunciation, with the same long declining line as before, and reiterates its utter impossibility, with an even higher top note at 'Viel lieber' and a heartfelt Amen from the piano.

NOTES. 1. Neither the original thirteenth-century French (published in a 1765 Paris anthology, ed. Monier, and there attributed to Thibault, Count of Champagne, King of Navarre) nor Herder's fine German version (no doubt taken by Brahms from the *Stimmen der Völker* volume of the *Sämtliche Werke*, 1827–30, which he owned) is a sonnet in any strict sense; *pace* Friedländer (1922 15), Brahms cannot be rebuked for not adhering to that form.

2. Indeed, he sets the text with unusual respect, without repetition or change, apart from decapitalising 'Sie' (= Her), much as in No. 3; and here too he no doubt felt that his music was already sufficiently respectful. The same Herder source also contains two translations from English which Brahms used for his soprano–alto duets Op. 20 Nos. 1–2, *Weg der Liebe*, written in the same period, which also embody his love for Agathe von Siebold, on whom Brahms bestowed this song in manuscript. Her presence here would explain the apparently gauche left-hand progression at bars 13–15; the notes F–E♭–F–G–C are her sextet theme A–G–A–H–E (M32) transposed.

3. The piano's long descending melodic lines limn a Brahmsian portrayal of self-effacing abasement (M38), culminating in the postlude's prayerful Amen. The loving thirds and sixths are M18; the sad minor 6–5 at 'Herz kann es nie' is M20; the dominant pedal after 'hoffen Sie' is M24; the inner voice is M38; the top notes are M10.

25. (Op. 14, No. 5) Trennung (Separation) November 1858
Anon.   F major f#'–g''

> Wach auf, wach auf, du junger Gesell,
> Du hast so lang geschlafen,
> Da draussen singen die Vögel hell,
> Der Fuhrmann lärmt auf der Strassen!
>
> Wach auf, wach auf, mit heller Stimm
> Hub an der Wächter zu rufen,
> Wo zwei Herzlieben beisammen sind,
> Da müssen sie sein gar kluge.

Der Knabe war verschlafen gar,
Er schlief so lang, so süsse,
Die Jungfrau aber weise war,
Weckt ihn durch ihre Küsse!

Das Scheiden, Scheiden tuet not,
Wie Tod ist es so harte,
Der scheid't auch manches Mündlein rot
Und manche Buhlen zarte.

Der Knabe auf sein Rösslein sprang
Und trabte schnell von dannen,
Die Jungfrau sah ihm lange nach,
Gross Leid tat sie umfangen!

Awake, awake, you young fellow, you have slept so long; outside, the birds are singing brightly, the waggoner makes a noise in the street.

Awake, awake, the watchman began to call out in a clear voice; when two lovers are together they must be very discreet.

The lad was very drowsy, his sleep had been so long and so sweet, but the girl was wise and woke him with her kisses.

Parting, parting is needful; it's as pitiless as death; it has sundered many a rosy lip and many a young sweetheart.

The lad sprang on to his steed and trotted briskly away; the girl watched him for a long time, great grief took hold of her.

Brahms responds to the poem's hints of illicit love, discovery and danger. The alternate two-handed high-speed hammering of left-hand notes and right-hand chords continues unabated throughout the song, in vibrant urgency. 'Awake' is the immediate command, with intervals to match; a falling fifth in the accompaniment and a rising fourth in the voice at 'wach auf', with notes soon echoed four times over in the left hand at 'so lang geschlafen' (slept so long). At the same moment voice and piano unite to dwell reproachfully on the same note, twenty times between them. The fifths continue to fall admonishingly in left hand sequences as the birds sing their warning; the waggoner is heard in a vocal crescendo and top note. The same music serves, though rather less appositely and compellingly, for the next two verses. Then comes an element of change. Within the same excited rhythmic background, new themes and (at 'manche Buhlen zarte', many a young sweetheart) a new modulation are now heard, as the composer or poet is imagined as meditating and commenting on the scene from outside, philosophically, as a detached observer. Then the music returns to the home key and a final reprise, as if to rejoin and indeed identify with the sad story and its repeated exhortations to awake and depart. The postlude relaxes, and settles down to sleep again; this time the rest will remain undisturbed, no doubt for ever. In Brahms's artistic imagination, partings tend to be final, and lovers are unlikely to return. The final grief is taken for granted; there is no overt musical equivalent for the word 'Leid', which should hence be sung with special expression.

NOTES. I. The source was the Kretzschmer–Zuccalmaglio *Deutsche Volkslieder* (1840), which has 'da draussen da singen' in the first quatrain and 'tät sie' in the last. In the fourth, the Peters edition's 'manchen [Buhlen]' should be corrected to 'manche'.

2. The top note at 'lärmt' is M10. A–G–A–E in the left hand at 'Das Scheiden, Scheiden', bars 13–14, may allude to Agathe von Siebold (M32), while the dominant C pedals are so insistent as to suggest Clara's initial (M33); they were both idolised at this time. The use of A–D in the voice at 'der scheid't' may also be intentional (M34). The drooping chromatic descent in the left hand at 'wie Tod ist es so harte' is certainly expressive; so is the postlude's diminuendo of departure.

26. (Op. 14, No. 6) Gang zur Liebsten (Walking to the beloved) December 1858

Anon.   E minor g'–g"

> Des Abends kann ich nicht schlafen gehn,
> Zu meiner Herzliebsten muss ich gehn,
> Zu meiner Herzliebsten muss ich gehn,
> Und sollt ich an der Tür bleiben stehn,
> Ganz heimelig!
>
> Wer ist denn da? Wer klopfet an,
> Der mich so leis aufwecken kann?
> Das ist der Herzallerliebste dein,
> Steh auf, mein Schatz, und lass mich ein,
> Ganz heimelig!
>
> Wenn alle Sterne Schreiber gut,
> Und alle Wolken Papier dazu,
> So sollten sie schreiben der Lieben mein,
> Sie brächten die Lieb in den Brief nicht ein,
> Ganz heimelig!
>
> Ach hätt ich Federn wie ein Hahn
> Und könnt ich schwimmen wie ein Schwan,
> So wollt ich schwimmen wohl über den Rhein,
> Hin zu der Herzallerliebsten mein,
> Ganz heimelig!

I cannot sleep at night, I must go to my dearest love, I must go to my dearest love even though I'd have to wait at her door, in secret.

Who's there, who's knocking, and waking me so gently? It is your own dearest love, arise, my dear and let me in, in secret.

If all the stars were clerks and all the clouds were paper, they should write to my sweetheart, but they'd never get all my love into one letter, in secret.

Oh if I had feathers like a rooster and could swim like a swan then I'd swim right across the Rhine, to be with my dearest love, in secret.

The text juxtaposes homely simplicity and quaint conceit. On any interpretation its mood is surely joyous or passionate, but the minor key and modal harmonies make the music melancholy and mysterious. As in *Vor dem Fenster* (No. 21), the piano part sidles or slides rather than strides to the loved one. Here that walking movement is only half-heard, in two bars of left-hand consecutive thirds which never recur, as if the visit is both clandestine and tentative. The untranslatable refrain 'ganz heimelig' conflates the dialect pronunciation of 'heimlich' (secret) with overtones of 'heimelig' (cosy). Brahms seems to favour the former sense, by floating the final phrase in each verse on a high melodic line which sounds separate and shy, like the lover in the first two verses.

NOTES. 1. As in the previous song, the source was the Kretzschmer–Zuccalmaglio *Deutsche Volkslieder* (1840), which sometimes includes so-called folk-song texts of doubtful authenticity. This song might be more effective if the last two verses were omitted; they seem extraneous.

2. But they may have contained a special significance for Brahms. The right hand's A–G–A linked to the left's H–E in bars 7–8 occurs at the last quatrain's '(Herz)allerliebsten mein'. Similarly '(Herz)allerliebsten dein' in the second verse coincides with the piano's A–G–A–D–H. Here too those notes belong to a horn passage in G major (M22), as in No. 21 note 2. In 1858, such a use of M32 would be entirely compatible with an equally deliberate allusion to the Clara-theme M33 at each 'ganz heimelig'.

3. The duetting left-hand thirds of bars 1–2 are M18, here set walking (M1) in tune with the words. The modal harmonies are M27; the top note on each 'heimelig' is M10.

27. (Op. 14, No. 7) Ständchen (Serenade) September 1858
Anon. F major f′–g″

Gut Nacht, gut Nacht, mein liebster Schatz,
Gut Nacht, schlaf wohl, mein Kind!
Dass dich die Engel hüten all,
Die in dem Himmel sind!
Gut Nacht, gut Nacht, mein lieber Schatz,
Schlaf du von nachten lind!

Schlaf wohl, schlaf wohl und träume von mir,
Träum von mir heute Nacht!
Dass, wenn ich auch da schlafen tu,
Mein Herz um dich doch wacht;
Dass es in lauter Liebesglut
An dich der Zeit gedacht.

Es singt im Busch die Nachtigall
Im klaren Mondenschein,
Der Mond scheint in das Fenster dir,
Guckt in dein Kämmerlein;
Der Mond schaut dich im Schlummer da,
Doch ich muss ziehn allein!

Good night, good night, my dearest love, good night, sleep well my child! [Good night, good night, my dearest love, good night, sleep well, my child!] May all the angels in heaven protect you! Good night, good night, my dear love, may you sleep [may you sleep] sweetly the whole night through [sweetly the whole night through]!

Sleep well, sleep well, and dream about me, dream about me this night! [Sleep well, sleep well, and dream about me, dream about me this night!] so that when I too go to sleep my heart will stay awake for love of you, and that it will be thinking about you [about you] in a sheer glow of love all the time [about you all the time].

The nightingale sings on the bush in the clear moonlight [the nightingale sings on the bush in the clear moonlight], the moon shines in your window, peeps into your little bedroom, the moon sees you there asleep, yet I must leave alone [yet I must leave alone].

As the repetitions suggest and the accentuation confirms ('von' on a strong minim downbeat), the words as such were not the primary source of inspiration. Yet the young Brahms is heard singing his heart out in this modest masterpiece of two perfect pages. In the process he discovers and exploits his genius for fine-spun melodic lines, surely spun from his own inner substance by his personal empathy with the excluded lover left lonely outside the bedroom window, on the point of departure, with hints of chill in the air under the bright moon. Hence this lilting love-song waltz from a serenading guitarist, with wistful overtones.

The expansive F major mood soon turns to minor cadences and chromatic uncertainties. Even the ensuing A flat major harmonies, for all their warmth, are related to the main key by its minor mode. There is a further intimation of a sad outcome in the descent of each final vocal phrase from a sustained flattened seventh. But then the beguiling postlude invents a new and charming melody, decorated with accented arpeggios as if in a sprightly dance. The guitar strums and thrums unobtrusively yet incessantly; the invariant rhythm ♩♩♩ is heard in the accompaniment from the first note to the last, as if saying 'ich liebe dich' to itself 136 times, even when moving away alone into the night. This is springtime music; full disillusionment has not yet set in.

NOTES. 1. Brahms took his text from the Kretzschmer–Zuccalmaglio *Deutsche Volkslieder* (1840) with occasional alterations to suit his melodies. But 'Mondenschein' in the third verse may be merely a slip for the original 'Mondesschein'.

2. In the fourth bar of the postlude the left-hand octave overlaps the right-hand chord; but this affords no clear reason why the former should not be arpeggiated like all the others.

3. The last bar's diminuendo exit (which surely needs an explanatory lingering ritenuto, though none is marked) may have inspired Wolf to some of his own far more extended and graphic depictions of a serenading guitarist quitting the stage and leaving the scene, as e.g. in *Ein Ständchen euch zu bringen*.

4. The two wheedling Schubertian echoes of 'mein Kind' in the first verse recall that master's *Ständchen* D957/4. The diminished seventh chords at bars 19 and 21 are M25, providing the pivot for the ensuing flatward modulations (M42); the final long high E♭ is M10, here used with modal folk-song connotations (M27).

28. (Op. 14, No. 8) Sehnsucht (Longing) November 1858
Anon.   E minor e′–g″

Mein Schatz ist nicht da,
Ist weit überm See,

Und so oft dran denk
Tut mirs Herze so weh!

Schön blau ist der See
Und mein Herz tut mir weh,
Und mein Herz wird nicht g'sund,
Bis mein Schatz wieder kommt.

My love isn't here, he's far away across the sea, and every time I think of him my heart aches. The sea is lovely and blue and my heart aches, and my heart won't heal till my love returns. [The sea is lovely and blue and my heart aches, and my heart won't heal till my love returns.]

As in Schumann, the prelude's unadorned minor triad stands as a right-hand signpost to melancholy. Voice and piano cling forlornly together for comfort, on the same melody. At 'schön blau ist der See' (the sea is lovely and blue) the open-air horn-passages and left-hand octaves speak of space and depth, while the modal touches throughout add a fourth dimension of distant past time. Every note sings of sad separation.

NOTES. 1. The source was the Kretzschmer–Zuccalmaglio *Deutsche Volkslieder* (1840). As so often, Brahms chooses a folk-song source yet upgrades much of its dialect, e.g. from 'nit', 'Herzel' and 'mei' to 'nicht', 'Herze' and 'mein'. These readings might be restored; but 'überm' for 'über dem' to suit the melody is irreversible. So is the dialect 'der See' (= lake, in High German), in the sense of 'sea' (= die See).

2. Agathe in her original quasi-literal sextet and churchyard guise (M32; see pp. 21–2) seems to haunt the piano part, often with an added D for Ade (M34), as for example in bars 21–3 to the words '[mein Herz] tut mir weh und mein Herz [wird nicht g'sund]'.

3. The voice–piano unisons or octaves are images of isolation or loneliness (M37). The outdoor horn passages are M22, which say A–G–A–D in this key (cf. No. 26 above), namely G major, here with a sharpened C for the Lydian mode (M27). The top G at 'wird [nicht g'sund]' is M10; the time-change at bar 24 is M26, with an M21 sigh.

4. Even the strict structure has a motivic message of simplicity and restraint. After the two-bar prelude, a four-bar phrase is repeated. In the contrasting eight-bar sequence that follows, the identity between 13–14 and 3–4 or 7–8, and between 17–18 and 5–6, is noteworthy; and those eight bars (11–18) are themselves repeated (19–26) with only slight variations. Thus attention is focused on the central figure's deep feeling, which forms the heart of the music.

5. The occasional changes that Brahms made to the vocal line on his own copy of the first edition are incorporated in the *Gesamtausgabe* (at bars 12, 14, 20 and 22) but not in the Peters edition.

OPUS 19

Five poems for solo voice with pianoforte accompaniment, published in March 1862.

Here Brahms branches out into what was for him yet another new direction; the songs are announced as 'poems', as if each setting was an act of homage to fine literature. The title-page includes the poets' names, for the first time since Op. 6;

and there is a Mörike setting worthy to rank with Wolf's own, of 1888 (which he too included in a set called 'Gedichte') as a musical response to poetic inspiration. The other poems of this opus are not at that exalted level. But the declared intention is there; and it would exert a far greater influence on Brahms's song-writing than he is commonly credited with. From now on, his vocal music is even more often and more overtly devoted to recreating verbal ideas by means of musical symbolism, as well as to reliving (and thus relieving) his own personal feelings.

29. (Op. 19, No. 1) Der Kuss (The kiss) September 1858
Ludwig Hölty, ed. J. Voss   B♭ major f′–a″

Unter Blüten des Mai's spielt ich mit ihrer Hand,
Koste liebend mit ihr, schaute mein schwebendes
   Bild im Auge des Mädchens,
   Raubt ihr bebend den ersten Kuss.

Zuckend fliegt nun der Kuss, wie ein versengend Feur
Mir durch Mark und Gebein. Du, die Unsterblichkeit
   Durch die Lippen mir sprühte,
   Wehe, wehe mir Kühlung zu!

Under Maytime blossoms I fondled her hand, stroked her lovingly [stroked her lovingly], saw my image hovering in the girl's eyes and tremblingly stole the first kiss from her.
   Now that kiss flares like a searing fire through my bone and marrow. You who flashed immortality through my lips, now waft, waft coolness into me [coolness into me].

The outdoor scene is depicted in right-hand bass-clef horn passages over a deep left-hand tonic pedal, suggesting shyness in outdoor shade. Despite that daring kiss, the mood is one of restraint, not passion. This may be a conscious equivalent for the poem's unrhymed classical metre; but it may also reflect Brahms's own nature. The lingering melodic lines suggest a love-song, an effect enhanced by the duetting thirds and sixths throughout. But the song also contains the coolness so essential to the composer and so often craved. And there are many subtle felicities; thus the music from 'schaute' (I saw) onwards, incorporating a momentary quaver rest of hesitation before the stolen kiss, reappears (with the right hand an octave higher) as the final invocation at 'Du' etc, as if to assert that the burning and the cooling are seen to stem from one and the same source.

NOTES. 1. The composer's source, *Gedichte von Ludwig Hölty* ed. Voss (1804), condenses and corrupts the original text beyond repair; but at least 'liebelnd' (caressingly), as in Hölty's original four-stanza poem (given in Friedländer 18) and in Voss's very different two-stanza adaptation, and also in the first edition of this song, could replace the colourless and unauthentic 'liebend' (lovingly) as now printed.
   2. Each stanza, in both versions of the poem, is an asclepiad, as in *Die Mainacht* (see No. 59).

3. This 1858 song may invoke Agathe von Siebold, whose string sextet motto-theme A–G–A–D–H–E (p. 14 above) needs only a change of clef or key to become the pattern (M32) seen in the right hand here at bars 4–6, 9–11.

4. But a Clara-motif (M33) is not thereby ruled out, in 1858; and the persistent and peculiar supertonic pedals, C in the key of B♭ major, seem an apt symbol (M33) for thoughts of the beloved Clara alias Princess Bedur (p. 18 above) whose name means B flat (= B dur in German). Her theme in its C minor form occurs in the right hand at 'zuckend fliegt nun der Kuss'.

5. Within the Schumannian song-style of voice–piano unison the opening tonic pedals are M6 and the duetting thirds and sixths M18. The inner voices (M38) in bars 13–17 and 43–7 underline that duetting effect; so do the top notes at 'mir' and 'ihr' (M10). The right hand's blissful repetitions of lushly harmonised 5–6–5 at bars 51–5 are M19.

30. (Op. 19, No. 2) Scheiden und Meiden (Parting and separation) October 1858

Ludwig Uhland   D minor d'–e''

> So soll ich dich nun meiden,
> Du meines Lebens Lust!
> Du küssest mich zum Scheiden,
> Ich drücke dich an die Brust!
>
> Ach, Liebchen, heisst das meiden,
> Wenn man sich herzt und küsst?
> Ach, Liebchen, heisst das scheiden,
> Wenn man sich fest umschliesst?

And must I now be parted from you, you who are the delight of my life? You give me a farewell kiss, I press you to my heart.

Oh my love, can this be called separation, when we embrace and kiss? Oh my love, can this be called parting, when we clasp each other so close?

The arpeggios may derive from the poem of the next song, *In der Ferne*, where they match the continuous mood of shadowy woodland reverie. Here the vocal melody begins by ranging widely, in leaping fourths or fifths like heartfelt gestures of regret. But, 'Du küssest' induces a mellower mode, introduced by the piano with a new melody in which the voice joins, while the rhythm relaxes into love-song waltz-time. This too is continued and completed by the piano, whose falling third at the end of each verse speaks the fond farewells heard or implied from the outset. The question 'heisst das scheiden . . .?' (can this be called parting . . .?) was always rhetorical; the minor keynote connotes 'yes, alas'.

NOTES. 1. The Uhland source was the *Gedichte* (1815), which Brahms owned in a later edition. Perhaps the poet's reading of 'nun dich' (not 'dich nun') in the first line should now be restored; the change may be a mere slip of the pen, and 'dich' on the high E (M10) instead of the lower A arguably sounds more affecting and effective.

2. The Agathe motif A–G–A–H–E (M32) is recognisable in the right hand at 'ich drücke dich an die Brust' though clothed in clashing chords. The dreamy arpegggios, M9, need a light touch; otherwise the left-hand C# and the voice and piano D in bar 14 for

example can sound disconcertingly dissonant. The 'Ade' (A–D) of farewell, M34, may be deliberate in the opening vocal melody at 'soll ich' and 'meiden'.

3. Cf. the Cornelius duet for soprano and baritone Op. 16 No. 4; and Schoeck Op. 3 No. 5.

31. (Op. 19, No. 3) In der Ferne (Far away) October 1858
Ludwig Uhland   D major d'–e''

Will ruhen unter den Bäumen hier,
Die Vöglein hör ich so gerne.
Wie singet ihr so zum Herzen mir?
Von unsrer Liebe was wisset ihr
In dieser weiten Ferne?

Will ruhen hier an des Baches Rand,
Wo duftige Blümlein spriessen,
Wer hat euch Blümlein hieher gesandt?
Seid ihr ein herzliches Liebespfand
Aus der Ferne von meiner Süssen?

Let me rest here under the trees; I love to hear the birds sing.

How is it that you sing like that, straight into my heart [how do you sing into my heart]? What do you know of our love, here in this far distant land [in this far distant land]?

Let me rest here beside the stream, where fragrant flowers are springing. Who has sent you here, you flowers [who has sent you here]? Are you a heartfelt pledge of love from my sweetheart far away [from my sweetheart far away]?

The song begins with the same sad dreamy music of separation as in No. 30. After 'hör ich so gerne' (I love to hear) the piano's repeated rising thirds wonder what the birds are saying; the dominant sevenths add a question mark; the music moves from minor to major and the parallel intervals sing the answer as a love-duet. After the second 'weiten Ferne' (far distant land) the left hand tolls farewell: 'Ade, Ade'. These notes are taken over by the voice at 'will ruhen' (let me rest), again followed by the interrogative rising thirds. Now the birds' melody is transferred to the flowers. The musical metaphor is one of movement; as the alternating hands in the first verse suggested wings, now the right-hand broken third and sixths depict the play of winds with horn passages to convey the feeling of outdoors and the open air. The postlude repeats 'Ade' insistently; despite the major mode, the music sounds sad, as if permanent parting is its real theme.

NOTES. 1. The manuscript is headed 'An die Ferne', to the girl far away, which helps to confirm the personal feeling of farewell, as in the previous song. The two lyrics are juxtaposed in the poetic source (see No. 30 note 1) and Brahms clinches that connection by motivic links.

2. A–D, as noted above (M34), also occurs in the opening strains (cited from the previous song) and the postlude. By bar 8, C major is a dominant, and at bars 11–12 the harmony is heard as a questioning dominant seventh, M24, which recurs in the piano after

'spriessen'. The parallel thirds and sixths at 'wie singet' are M18, and the alternating hands are the wings of M3. The broken sixths and thirds in triplet quavers are surely a tribute to Schubert, as in the prelude to *Der Lindenbaum*, as if the flowers here were seen stirring in the evening breeze under the lime tree, M4. The birds and flowers are so Schubertian that the minor and major on the same tonic (M39) offer a predictable response.

32. (Op. 19, No. 4) Der Schmied (The blacksmith) May 1859
Ludwig Uhland   B♭ major f'–f''

> Ich hör meinen Schatz,
> Den Hammer er schwinget,
> Das rauschet, das klinget,
> Das dringt in die Weite
> Wie Glockengeläute
> Durch Gassen und Platz,
>
> Am schwarzen Kamin
> Da sitzet mein Lieber,
> Doch geh ich vorüber,
> Die Bälge dann sausen,
> Die Flammen aufbrausen
> Und lodern um ihn.

I can hear my sweetheart, he's swinging his hammer, it sounds and resounds, it peals out afar like the ringing of bells, through streets and market-place.

By the black forge, there my love sits, but when I walk past the bellows puff and the flames roar and shine all around him.

Here, as in *Sonntag* (No. 69), is a lovingly-observed scene in the same idealised and idyllic country town. Such music has so much to offer in its everyday simplicity of charming folk-tune accompanied by basic harmony that there seems no need to search too assiduously for further depth and dimension. Everyone can hear the powerful biceps implied by the left-hand chords, together with the bright sparks, and the ring and rebound of hammer on anvil, suggested by the right hand's snapping dotted rhythms. Nevertheless the poet's added symbolism of adoring and passionate love has not escaped the composer, though it sometimes seems to elude performers of this justly famous song, where there is surely a mutual awareness between the two lovers even before the music begins.

It is no coincidence that the ringing hammer-blows sound to their receptive auditor like church bells that peal upon a wedding; and the fire has blazed up at first sight in the first verse, long before it is mentioned. The left-hand chords are also apt for harmonium or organ tones; the music reads the banns. So the accompaniment, for all its physical vigour, should also sound like a plighted troth. The pianist's two arms embrace the ingratiating vocal melody, which also plays a double part; its own insistence on two alternating notes helps to depict the action, while its bright lilt is that of a love-song. Only in the coda does the piano display the solid blacksmith in a solo character-sketch; and even then he is idealised, not actual. The left hand musingly and amusingly repeats the opening words to itself, 'ich hör meinen Schatz, ich hör meinen Schatz, meinen Schatz' and so on, with the tenderly proud noun always on the key-note; we see and hear only him, because the singer has eyes and ears for no one else. The subdominant–tonic harmony adds an unobtrusive 'Amen', or 'I will'.

NOTES. 1. For the source, see No. 30 note 1.

2. The strict two-strophe structure of 20 + 20 bars, each of twelve with the voice and eight without, is worth analysing; it epitomises Brahms's genius for making the bare bones of music not only live but sing and dance in the flesh. Setting aside transient harmonies, only four chords are employed (I, II, IV, V), and of these the tonic forms the firm foundation for fully half the song; thus the first six bars are tonic pedal. All this implies that the eponymous hero as portrayed by the piano part is a fine sturdy fellow without overmuch sophistication. But the relation between those themes and the girl's vocal melody is perhaps less immediately apparent. The intimacy and indeed identity of that union affords a musical affidavit that the two are already united in thought. His ringing echoes her singing, often on the selfsame notes repeated or inverted (such as F–D or F–E♭ in the first six bars).

3. Some listeners may hear the young Brahms's own biceps embodied here in M2. This right-hand chiming sounds like the bells often rung by Loewe in his ballads; the plainest parallel occurs in his *Tom der Reimer* Op. 135a, which was published (and perhaps written) in 1867, after Op. 19 was printed.

4. Cf Schumann's Op. 145 No. 1 for mixed chorus, with the same key and time-signature.

33. (Op. 19, No. 5) An eine Aeolsharfe (To an Aeolian harp) September 1858

Eduard Mörike   A♭ major e♭'–a♭''

Angelehnt an die Efeuwand
Dieser alten Terrasse,
Du, einer luftgebornen Muse
Geheimnisvolles Saitenspiel,
Fang an,
Fange wieder an
Deine melodische Klage.

Ihr kommet, Winde, fern herüber,
Ach, von des Knaben,
Der mir so lieb war,
Frisch grünendem Hügel.
Und Frühlingsblüten unterweges streifend
Übersättigt mit Wohlgerüchen,
Wie süss bedrängt ihr dies Herz!
Und säuselt her in die Saiten,
Angezogen von wohllautender Wehmut,
Wachsend im Zug meiner Sehnsucht
Und hinsterbend wieder.

Aber auf einmal,
Wie der Wind heftiger herstösst,
Ein holder Schrei der Harfe
Wiederholt mir zu süssem Erschrecken
Meiner Seele plötzlicher Regung,
Und hier – die volle Rose streut geschüttelt
All ihre Blätter vor meine Füsse.

Leaning against the ivied wall of this old terrace, you, mysterious lyre played by a Muse born of air,

begin, begin once again your melodious lament.

You winds have come hither from far away, oh from the fresh-greening mound of the boy who was so dear to me. And brushing against springtime blossoms on your way, surfeited with fragrance, how sweetly [how sweetly] you grieve this heart. And you murmur here into the strings, drawn by their sweet-sounding sorrow, growing in response to my yearning and then dying away again.

But all at once, as the wind gusts more strongly, the harp's lovely cry echoes, to my sweet terror, the sudden stirring of my soul; and here the ripe rose, shaken, strews all its petals at my feet.

Here, for the first time, Brahms finds matching music for a matchless lyric. Poem and song both begin with a solemn invocation. During the initial recitative the semibreve or breve accompaniment suddenly changes, in the middle of the word 'geheimnisvoll' (mysterious), to repeated staccato crotchet triplet chords high in the keyboard. The contrast of register and texture sounds striking and complete; yet the only difference is that the original chords are as it were held up and harped, as if to show the silent instrument what is required of it. Then after 'Klage' (lament) breaths of wind duly steal into the scene and are greeted with 'Ihr kommet, Winde' (You winds have come), as the harp is moved to play its lovely music, in left-hand arpeggios. Here the vocal line is unselfconsciously expressive of the poetic theme; the downward minor chordal melody of the first word, 'Angelehnt', is turned upward and made major, by way of consolation. Similarly the excursions into remote tonalities at 'Wohlgerüchen ... süss' (fragrance ... sweet) and again at 'wohllautender Wehmut' (sweet-sounding sorrow) drift towards far horizons of sensual experience; the harmony sounds momentarily surprised as well as delighted. Apart from a sudden return to recitative at 'Aber auf einmal' (But all at once) the mood of reverie is preserved by constant harp-music in an invariant rhythm and register until the final section, marked poco più lento, where the poem's falling rose-petals are transformed into extra left-hand beats and impulses until the song rejoins the silence whence it arose.

NOTES. 1. The text was first published in Mörike's *Gedichte* (1838), a volume available to Brahms in three later editions. He treats the text without change, apart from occasional variants in punctuation, and almost without repetition.

2. Again exceptionally, the music seems to respond to the poetry as such. But perhaps the inspiration also derived from the icon of the deserted or bereaved girl, if Brahms (as seems likely) was unaware that the poem was a lament for the poet's dead brother.

3. The high repeated chords of the first page would have served Schubert and Wolf as typical symbols of stars, and indeed have affinities with Brahms's own star-motif M11. They are first heard during the word 'geheimnisvolles', and they should surely sound mysterious. The dreamy left-hand arpeggios *passim* are M9; the tense sustained dominant on 'Klage' (M24), is answered by the blissfully consolatory 5–6–5 movement of M19 in the right hand at bars 25–9 etc. The brightening sharp-key notation for 'Wohlgerüchen' is characteristic (M40); the top notes at '*frisch* grünendem' and 'Seele' are M10; the dominant seventh chord after 'herstösst' is an aspect of M24; the quickening left-hand rhythms of the last fourteen bars, with added crotchet triplets, are M16.

OPUS 32

Songs (Lieder und Gesänge) by Aug. v. Platen und G.F. Daumer for solo voice with pianoforte accompaniment, published in February 1865.

This opus was published in 1865 in two parts, with the fine poet Platen and the minor versifier Daumer treated as equals on each title-page and within each volume. Plainly this presented no problem to Brahms, for whom all lyrics were a means to the end of expressive song-writing. But such a priority presupposes that these texts were chosen and arranged for their personal relevance rather than their poetic merit. The result is a song-cycle début in the Schumann tradition, and one well worthy of that master. It begins with regret for lost time and past suffering, which the second song predictably associates with lost love. Hence the tragic isolation of the third, and the yearning nostalgia of the fourth. So the second volume begins with outright revolt and rejection. Next, the hero explicitly confirms that he was once loved but is so no longer. There follow two songs of amorous self-abasement and estrangement, and a grand finale, surely specially selected for its climactic relevance to all these themes. Let me die in your arms, the lover cries; there, even my death-agony would be blissful. The note of unassuageable and indeed almost masochistic self-abnegation is unmistakable; and the music throughout this opus has a sincerity that renders such feelings memorably vivid and true. No doubt it too, like its predecessor *Dichterliebe*, was inspired by a devoted love for Clara Schumann.

34. (Op. 32, No. 1) Wie rafft ich mich auf in der Nacht (I roused and arose in the night), September 1864

August von Platen   F minor c′–g♭″

> Wie rafft ich mich auf in der Nacht, in der Nacht,
> Und fühlte mich fürder gezogen,
> Die Gassen verliess ich, vom Wächter bewacht,
> Durchwandelte sacht
> In der Nacht, in der Nacht
> Das Tor mit dem gotischen Bogen.

Der Mühlbach rauschte durch felsigen Schacht,
Ich lehnte mich über die Brücke,
Tief unter mir nahm ich der Wogen in Acht,
Die wallten so sacht
In der Nacht, in der Nacht,
Doch wallte nicht eine zurücke.

Es drehte sich oben, unzählig entfacht
Melodischer Wandel der Sterne,
Mit ihnen der Mond in beruhigter Pracht,
Sie funkelten sacht
In der Nacht, in der Nacht,
Durch täuschend entlegene Ferne,

Ich blickte hinauf in der Nacht, in der Nacht,
Und blickte hinunter aufs Neue;
O wehe, wie hast du die Tage verbracht,
Nun stille du sacht,
In der Nacht, in der Nacht,
Im pochenden Herzen die Reue!

I roused and arose in the night, in the night, and felt impelled ever onwards [onwards, felt impelled ever onwards]. I left the streets, patrolled by their watchman, and quietly walked in the night, in the night, through the gate with the Gothic arch.

The millstream murmured through its rocky bed; I leaned over the bridge. Far below me I could see the waves flowing so quietly in the night, in the night, yet not one of them ever flowed back [not one of the ever flowed back]. Overhead, like countless kindled fires, the stars wheeled in their melodious courses, and with them the moon in its serene splendour; they shone quietly in the night, in the night, through deceptively remote space.

I looked up in the night, in the night, and looked down [down] again anew [and looked down again anew]. Alas, how have you spent your days? [Alas, how have you spent your days?]. Now in the night, in the night, quietly allay the remorse in your pounding heart.

The homosexual Platen, cruelly mocked by Heine and other contemporaries, lived guilt-ridden and remorseful. The same fate befell A.E. Housman, whose own moving and melancholy verses derived directly from the German Romantic tradition, and on occasion perhaps from this same Platen poem and the human feelings of isolation that it so memorably embodies. Brahms was also responding to the poem's vivid depiction of actual living experience within a real historic German town with its watchman and its great Gothic gateway. The heights and depths of sky and river are reflected in the capacious span of vocal and keyboard compass; this expanse of space, and the irreversible flow of time, form a contrasting frame for the solitary human figure and its despair, as in the Romantic painting of the period. The composer's mind's eye may well also have envisaged the suicidal Schumann on the bridge in Düsseldorf, obsessed with his own guilt and unworthiness.

The one-bar prelude is already up and walking. At 'fühlte mich fürder gezogen' (felt impelled ever onward) the accented semiquavers push the protagonist along. But at 'die Gassen verliess ich' etc. (I left the streets, etc.) the music audibly takes a new turn to one side and almost floats through the gateway on repeated octave triplets, like a sleepwalker. In the interlude these triplets become insistent repeated chords, a paradigm of melancholy, which in turn changes to a more flowing movement at 'der Mühlbach' (the millstream), as the left hand continues its ominous march through the night. After 'zurücke' (back) the gaze lifts and scans the sky. At this exalted pitch of art there is a supreme interfusion of music and metaphor. The higher register for 'Sterne' and 'oben' (stars above), the continuing march rhythm transferred to the right hand over alternating triplets for 'Wandel' (turning), the restrained treble melody made by the first triplet quavers at 'melodisch', the enhanced height and brightness at 'funkelten' (shone), the sudden hollow emptiness of the arpeggios at 'Ferne' (distance); all this is eloquent of a great master of the lied form, the worthy heir and successor of Schubert and Schumann. Such art transcends music and poetry in a new enhanced unity. The reprise maintains this magnificence. At 'o wehe' (alas) the triplet quavers rap out an ominous message which menaces defeat and death at 'stille du sacht' (quietly allay). Then the postlude's harmonies, in what might be called a remorse motif, repeat the earlier interlude between the gateway and the river. This may again remind some listeners of Schumann passing the tollgate and walking to the centre of the bridge, ready to dive and drown in a final dying fall.

NOTES. 1. Perhaps the town was Erlangen in Bavaria, at the confluence of the rivers Regnitz and Schwabach; Platen was living there in 1820, when this poem was written. He has the present tense 'blicke hinunter aufs Neue' (bar 50), according to Max Friedländer; but this is presumably a mere misprint in some issues of the first edition (*Lyrische Blätter*, 1821). Although Brahms owned a copy, he used later collections such as the *Gesammelte Werke* of 1839 for his song settings. There all the verbs stand in the past tense, including 'blickte'. But that word is preceded by 'ich', not 'und'; this slip might well now be corrected in bars 49 and 51.

2. The Housman analogues are mainly in *More Poems*, which has the millstream and bridge at night (XIX), the sight of burning starry beacons on waking from dreams (XLIII) and the constant remorseful threnody for wasted life (e.g. XVI).

3. The suicidal motif adumbrated above, with its movement from minor tonic to flat supertonic, recalls (perhaps deliberately) the analogous progression in the final 'keiner kennt mich mehr hier' etc. at the close of Schumann's *In der Fremde* Op. 39 No. 1. The occasional resemblances to Schubert's *Aufenthalt* D957/5, e.g. in the repeated triplet quaver chords, are also expressive; they too mirror the mood of sombre despair.

4. The walking prelude is M1; the virile dotted rhythms are M31; the ominous unison and octave descent of the passage at 'still du sacht' and earlier at 'durchwandelte sacht' (M37) belongs to the death motif-cluster (pp. 5–6 above); the flowing movement of the river is M5; the emptiness of the omitted third after 'Ferne' is M29; the high keyboard notes for stars before and at 'Sterne' are M11, where the fifth-finger melody should also be brought out with typical staccato for the high points of light, which also suits 'melodisch'. The contrary motion in both hands before and at 'Wandel' is M13; the falling minor second in the right-hand minims at the final 'o wehe' is M20. The flat supertonic at bars 15–16 and in the postlude is M23.

35. (Op. 32, No. 2) Nicht mehr zu dir zu gehen (Never to visit you again) September 1864

Georg Daumer (from the Moldavian)   D minor c′–eb″

Nicht mehr zu dir zu gehen,
Beschloss ich und beschwor ich,
Und gehe jeden Abend,
Denn jede Kraft und jeden Halt verlor ich.

Ich möchte nicht mehr leben,
Möcht Augenblicks verderben,
Und möchte doch auch leben
Für dich, mit dir, und nimmer, nimmer sterben.

Ach rede, sprich ein Wort nur,
Ein einziges, ein klares;
Gib Leben oder Tod mir,
Nur dein Gefühl enthülle mir, dein wahres!

*Never to visit you again, so I decided and so I vowed; and yet I go every evening, for I
have lost all my strength [all my strength] and will-power.*

*I have no more wish to live, I long to perish at this moment [at this moment] and
yet I also long to live for you, with you, and never, never die.*

*Oh, speak to me, say but one word, one single clear word; give me life or death, only
reveal to me your feelings [your feelings], your true feelings.*

The music moves in slow octaves and unisons, as if reluctant yet compelled; and
as it walks, it weeps. The ostensibly immediate and definite verdict 'beschloss ich
und beschwor ich' (so I decided and so I vowed) is pronounced in hesitant phrases
and pauses that reveal the singer's true plight, long before the words confess it; the
vow is broken, and so is the one who made it. This quasi-recitative treatment is
enhanced by interspersed sighs of distress from the piano; thus 'beschloss ich' is
anticipated and echoed in the right hand, with expressive sighs. After 'Abend'
(evening) this sighing motif is heard in every bar, almost in self-mockery, as an
inner voice bemoaning its own martyrdom. The mood recovers somewhat in the
second verse, which begins in the major mode and gains new energy from triplet
crotchets in the accompaniment. Yet the awareness of inevitable self-immolation
prevails over and indeed contradicts the words; thus 'nimmer sterben' (never die)
has a dying fall. The last page, from 'ach, rede', repeats the music of the first, bar
by bar, save for added octaves and off-beat chords to emphasise the urgency of
'Ach, rede' (Oh, speak). In this continuing fatalistic mood we hear the singer's sad
foreknowledge of what the requested word will be, and what the beloved's true
feelings are. The music expects the answer 'no'; the postlude collapses and grovels
in right-hand moans and left-hand falling octaves that stride away into silence
down the keyboard.

Admittedly a description in these terms sounds uninviting. Yet this is a magnificent song in its originality and depth of feeling; it is a requiem for a lifetime of lost love.

NOTES. 1. The text was taken from Daumer's *Hafis* (1846), which Brahms owned. It is chiefly a collection of lyrics modelled on the style of that Persian poet, but with additions from European sources. These verses are called 'Moldavian', i.e. from a province or state west of Romania. They are characterised by the slavish subjection that so appealed to Brahms. He treats their quatrain-structure of alternate rhyming lines (with two extra iambic feet in the fourth) quite cavalierly, making the long lines even longer by verbal repetition.

2. Nevertheless, the poem has plainly affected the composer deeply. Once again the topics are isolation and exclusion; the singer goes out visiting every evening but seems to stand outside on arrival. This time there is no clear indication of Clara (apart from the word 'klares'); but the feeling is no less personal for being generalised.

3. The strong structure is worth special analysis, not only in the basic ABA + coda form but in particular details such as the relation between bars 1 and 4, 2–3 and 5–6, etc.

4. The minor 5–6–5 sighing (M21) is recalled in the right hand at 'wie dies stirbt' in *Denn es gehet* (No. 201), which this song anticipates in other respects, such as key and register. The sad descending semitone is heard again here at 'sterben' and its keyboard echo.

5. The remorseless left-hand octaves are M1. Their depth implies darkness (M6/7), as in *Von ewiger Liebe* (No. 58); here too we know it is evening before any time of day is mentioned, and the final descent declines into dark despair. The rests before and after 'beschloss ich', 'und' etc. are M29; the quickening rhythms after 'Ich möchte' are M16. The inner voice at 'ach, rede' is also motivic (M38).

36. (Op. 32, No. 3) Ich schleich umher (I creep about) September 1864

August von Platen   D minor d'–d''

Ich schleich umher
Betrübt und stumm,
Du fragst, o frage
Mich nicht warum?
Das Herz erschüttert
So manche Pein!
Und könnt ich je
Zu düster sein?

Der Baum verdorrt,
Der Duft vergeht,
Die Blätter liegen
So gelb im Beet,
Es stürmt ein Schauer
Mit Macht herein,
Und könnt ich je
Zu düster sein?

I creep about, troubled and silent. You ask me – oh, ask me not – why? So many a torment shakes my heart! how could I ever be too downcast [be too downcast]?

The tree withers, the fragrance fades, the leaves lie so yellow in the flowerbed. A heavy shower of rain comes storming up; how could I ever be too downcast [be too downcast]?

This fit of Romantic blues is not wholly characteristic, or indeed worthy, of Platen's poetic gifts. But its glum gloominess spoke directly to Brahms's own introversion and isolation, and his own feeling for external nature as a mirror of the soul. The left hand sidles and crawls along, down to the depths of sick-hearted despair. The piano shadows the voice, as in Schumann, and echoes its question 'warum?' (why?) as in Schubert. But the next question, 'zu düster sein?' (too downcast?) is rhetorical, and its reiteration is a statement; there is no choice.

The rhythmic energy increases from regular quavers into triplets in the left hand at 'Das Herz erschüttert' (shakes my heart). The same pattern also suits the corresponding change in the second verse from listless apathy to sudden storm at 'es stürmt ein Schauer'; now the falling phrases sound even more pathetic in association with images of withered trees and blighted hopes, fallen leaves and downcast spirits.

As in the previous song, a description in these terms will no doubt sound discouraging, not to say off-putting; but again the music has a strength and dignity that can offer a rewarding experience in fine performance.

NOTES. 1. The source was no doubt Platen's *Gesammelte Werke* (first published in 1839), as throughout this opus.

2. The key, mood and movement recall the previous song. The creeping left-hand quavers here are M1; the dominant question at 'warum?' is M24, with an instant echo at bars 7–9, where the accompaniment anticipates the rhythmic pattern of *Von ewiger Liebe* (No. 58). The quickening rhythms at bar 10 etc. are also expressive (M16), like the upward arpeggios of storm and stress.

37. (Op. 32, No. 4) Der Strom, der neben mir verrauschte (The river whose sound faded past me) September 1864

August von Platen   C# minor c#'–e''

> Der Strom, der neben mir verrauschte, wo ist er nun?
> Der Vogel, dessen Lied ich lauschte, wo ist er nun?
> Wo ist die Rose, die die Freundin am Herzen trug,
> Und jener Kuss, der mich berauschte, wo ist er nun?
> Und jener Mensch, der ich gewesen, und den ich längst
> Mit einem andern Ich vertauschte, wo ist er nun?

The river whose sound faded past me, where is it now? The bird whose song I listened to, where is it now? Where is the rose that my love wore at her breast, and that kiss which enraptured me, where is [where is, where is] it now? And that man I once was, and whom I long ago exchanged for another self, where is [where is, where is] he now [where is he now]?

The lapidary skill of the verses gives shape and sharpness to elemental emotions.

Again their bitter self-reproach surely struck some deep and resonant chord; this music transforms the past tense into the present. The vanished river reappears in rolling arpeggios, the departed bird flies around in circling thirds. Then the rose-petals sound soft and sweet, *piano e dolce*, far higher in the keyboard than the deep left-hand stream. At the reprise, 'Und jener Mensch' (And that man), the singer's opening melody recurs unchanged. But where's the lost young man? Irretrievably vanished, say the varied melody at 'den ich längst' (whom I long ago) and the varied triplet rhythm at 'vertauschte' (exchanged). Finally all three symbols of transience pass away, never to return, with a long sigh of regret in the postlude. Meanwhile each question – where now? – has been anxiously extended by time-change or repetition and intensified by ending a note higher each time. This is a masterpiece of musico-poetic craftsmanship.

NOTES. 1. The source was again no doubt Platen's *Gesammelte Werke* (first published in 1839), where the poem is among the ghasels. In this oriental verse-form a rhyme is followed by a repeated phrase (here '-auschte, wo ist er nun?') in the first two lines and alternately thereafter, interspersed with unrhymed lines of the same length. Brahms's manuscript has 'wie ist die Rose' instead of the required parallel 'wo ist'; this slip (unlike many others) has sensibly been corrected in published editions.

2. The rolling-river bass octaves and arpeggios are M5; the flying songbird's alternating thirds are M3; the dominant question at bar 4 etc. is M24. The 'Freundin' may be identi-fied by C#–B–A–G#–A at the words 'Freundin am Herzen' (M33). The cross-rhythm at 'vertauschte' is M15; the key of the flattened minor supertonic, D minor in C# minor, at 'wo ist, wo ist er?' in bars 24–5, is also motivic (M23), perhaps with a suggestion of Ade (M34) as the left-hand A–D moves across the bar-line.

3. Schubert's setting of another Platen ghasel, *Du liebst mich nicht*, D756, is worth comparison.

38. (Op. 32, No. 5) Wehe, so willst du mich wieder (Alas, would you once again) September 1864

August von Platen   B minor f#'–g#''

> Wehe, so willst du mich wieder,
> Hemmende Fessel, umfangen?
> Auf, und hinaus in die Luft!
> Ströme der Seele Verlangen,
> Ström es in brausende Lieder,
> Saugend ätherischen Duft!
>
> Strebe dem Wind nur entgegen,
> Dass er die Wange dir kühle,
> Grüsse den Himmel mit Lust!
> Werden sich bange Gefühle
> Im Unermesslichen regen?
> Atme den Feind aus der Brust!

Alas, would you once again enchain me, you hampering fetter? Up and out into the open air [up and out, out into the open air]! Let the soul's yearning flow out, let it flow in resounding songs, and absorb [absorb] ethereal fragrance [absorb, absorb ethereal fragrance]!

Strive against the wind so that it cools your cheek, greet the heavens with joy [greet the heavens, the heavens with joy]! How can anxious feelings arise, confronted with the immensity of the universe? Exhale the enemy from your breast [exhale, exhale the enemy from your breast]!

Perhaps Platen, like Housman, sometimes thought of homosexuality as his fetter and his foe, and sought to escape from those enemy hands. There is ample evidence that Brahms too sometimes sought to escape from his own amorous bonds; indeed, this whole opus is fixed, not to say fixated, in that frame of mind. So this music drives onward and outward remorselessly from its two-bar prelude to its six-bar coda, throughout two strophes, each prolonged and emphasised by the composer's verbal and musical repetitions. A volcanic core of personal feeling is the source of this surging power. Its nine-quaver right-hand rhythm ceaselessly hammers home an urgent message; break out, break away, break free. The prelude's first bar is instantly repeated an octave higher, in accents that seem to sing 'auf und hinaus' (up and out) long before those words actually appear. When they do, the same rhythm recurs in the left hand. Then the music is modified in response to the poet's appeal to external nature; after 'hinaus in die Luft' (out into the open air) the right-hand quavers are grouped in twos instead of threes, like wings in flight. The 9/8 time-signature relaxes into a left-hand 3/4; the harmony softens from sharps to flats in key and notation; the vocal phrases and notes are longer. But on the last word of each verse ('Duft!', 'Brust!') the prelude starts again, bringing the music sharply back to its agonised search for escape and freedom. In the postlude, these are achieved; the duplets instead of triplets, and the marked ritenuto, offer a well-earned rest after so much striving.

NOTES. 1. No doubt the source was again Platen's *Gesammelte Werke* (first published in 1839). His two-strophe structure of dactylic trimeter rhyming abcbac is all but obliterated by Brahms's insistent repetitions. Such treatment implies a personal involvement. No doubt the reference to cooling made a general appeal. But only one commensurate passion is documented; so it is not surprising to find the Clara theme in her B minor guise (M33) at the first five notes of the vocal line:

which is instantly repeated in the left hand.

2. Much the same motif, with optional (yet surely desirable) octaves, provides a piano interlude, in the virtuoso style of Chopin. Indeed, this sounds very like a deliberate allusion to the opening theme of his *Polonaise* Op. 44, bars 9 and 11, which is also extended as a bass line at bars 17–18; that work may well have been in Clara's repertoire at the material time.

3. The insistent dominant harmony of this interlude, bars 6–8, continues the first verse's question at 'umfangen?' (M24). The middle section's flat notation within a sharp key is motivic (M40), like its relaxing duplets; the wing-beats of M3 are apt for a flight into the open air ('hinaus in die Luft'). The top notes and the hammering chords, both *passim*, are M10 and M30 respectively. The postlude's accented hemiola is M14.

39. (Op. 32 No. 6) Du sprichst, dass ich mich täuschte (You say I was mistaken) September 1864

August von Platen   C minor e♭'–a♭''

> Du sprichst, dass ich mich täuschte,
> Beschworst es hoch und hehr,
> Ich weiss ja doch, du Iiebtest,
> Allein du liebst nicht mehr!
>
> Dein schönes Auge brannte,
> Die Küsse brannten sehr,
> Du liebtest mich, bekenn es,
> Allein du liebst nicht mehr!
>
> Ich zähle nicht auf neue,
> Getreue Wiederkehr;
> Gesteh nur, dass du liebtest,
> Und liebe mich nicht mehr!

You say I was mistaken, you swore it by all you hold holy; yet I know you once loved me, though you love me no longer [you love, you love me no longer]!

Your beautiful eyes burned, your kisses burned deep; you once loved me, confess it, though you love me no longer [you love, you love me no longer]!

I do not count on any new faithful return; just admit that you once loved me, and then love me no longer [love, love me no longer]!

The four-bar prelude begins with sad falling phrases, followed by a repeated inner voice that sings reminiscently, as if to itself:

Thus the relationship is succinctly symbolised; the upper right-hand melody laments its lot while the lower asserts its independence. As the voice enters, in the resigned tones of the prelude, the bass octave rhythm swells into chords in both hands; the absence of any beat in the acompaniment, even in mid-bar, speaks eloquently of helplessness in adversity. At 'ich weiss ja doch, du liebtest' (yet I know you once loved me) there is more warmth and animation in the musical movement, with doubled parallel thirds and a freer vocal melody rising to a high distress-signal at the second 'du liebst'. But the piano still maintains its stand-offish silence at the beginning of almost every bar. The prelude returns as interlude, to mirror the unchanging mood; and now, at 'die Küsse brannten sehr' (the kisses burned deep), the lower line briefly emerges in major right-hand warmth. After a reprise of the previous complaints about lost yet enduring love, and its symbolic encapsulation in the piano prelude and interlude, the voice sings of a final sundering: 'ich zähle nicht auf neue getreue Wiederkehr' (I do not count on any new faithful return). The accompaniment echoes that abnegation; in a marvellous matching of mood and music, the lower voice exemplified above disappears down the keyboard and out of earshot, leaving the singer and pianist to remember past love – and indeed to draw some consolation from those memories, to judge by the closing change to the major mode.

NOTES. 1. No doubt the Platen source was the *Gesammelte Werke* (first published in 1839). There, the umlauts are not very distinct; but the second line begins, clearly enough, 'beschwörst', in parallel with the present tense of 'sprichst'. The misreading 'beschworst', as printed in both the *Gesamtausgabe* and Peters, should surely be corrected accordingly.

2. The structure of this deeply-felt song invites close analysis. The prelude's bars 1–4 also occupy 14–17 and 27–30; bars 8–13 recur with variations as 19–24 and 35–40. That leaves 5–8 (which recall, perhaps deliberately, the Schubert song *Rast* from *Winterreise*, D911/10, also an image of resignation) and 31–4 (where the downward departure of the counter-melody is M1). The left hand's broken-octave C is heard some fifty times in the first two pages. This is then varied to six tolling minim Cs, and then six quaver Cs, and then another fourteen quaver Cs, until the prelude returns as a postlude to end the song on its tonic C. So insistent a C pedal is rarely heard in anyone else's music; in Brahms however it is frequent, often in the sense of C for Clara, M33. Note also her melodic outline here at the beginning of each 'allein du liebst nicht mehr'.

3. The duetting thirds and sixths are M18; the crying high notes at 'du liebst' are M10. The inner voice is expressive (M38); so is its Schubertian interpolation of major into minor (M39), ending in its dying and dwindling conclusion on a tierce de Picardie. The keyboard's persistent omission of the first or medial quaver has the helplessness of M29.

40. (Op. 32, No. 7) Bitteres zu sagen denkst du (You mean to say bitter words) September 1864

Georg Daumer (after Hafiz)   F major f'–g''

> Bitteres zu sagen denkst du;
> Aber nun und nimmer kränkst du,
> Ob du noch so böse bist.
> Deine herbe Redetaten
> Scheitern an korallner Klippe,
> Werden all zu reinen Gnaden,
> Denn sie müssen, um zu schaden,
> Schiffen über eine Lippe,
> Die die Süsse selber ist.

You mean to say bitter words; but neither now nor ever can you hurt me, however angry you are.

Your harsh speech-acts founder on a coral reef [founder on a coral reef],
    they all turn to pure benediction, because in order to do damage they must first sail
over lips that are sweetness itself [that are sweetness itself].

Brahms refines the saccharine words into true sweetness. The two-bar prelude is
repeated with a vocal tune distilled from the rhythm of the first line; its falling
tone D–C at 'denkst du' is heard in the left-hand figuration for most of the song,
as if insisting, with due satisfaction, on the thought that the intended harm can
never succeed. The image of sailing on balmy southern seas inspires a dreamy
flow of melody shared by voice and piano, seasoned with occasional clashes
symbolising the woman's ineffectual willingness to wound; but these too are soon
harmlessly averted and absorbed, as the poem explains. There is a Schubertian
echo at 'böse bist' (angry you are) and a wholly Brahmsian anticipation after the
second 'korallner Klippe', where the piano interlude turns aside to sing the notes
which will soon be linked and long drawn out into the final vocal phrase. Thus
the listener learns why the coral reef of the beloved's lips and teeth poses no
real threat; shipwreck will be sweet in that sea. The whole-hearted submission
culminates in an Amen cadence.

NOTES. 1. The Daumer text, from his *Hafis* (1846), which Brahms owned, renders a lyric
by that 14th-century Persian poet, whose own style was so sweet that his contemporaries
aptly nicknamed him 'Sugar-lip'.
    2. There is a hint of regret in the falling tones or semitones, M20 (also heard in the right
hand at 'böse bist', complete with echo) that begin each of the left-hand figurations. Their
missing first quavers are M29, their low pedal notes M6/7, their dreamy arpeggios M9. The
long or short sighs *passim* are M21. The relationship between the interlude melody at bars
18–19 and the vocal line is also expressive; the cadential finality of that melody is typically
Brahmsian. So is the postlude's Amen cadence. The top notes at 'selber' and 'Süsse' are M10.

41. (Op. 32, No. 8) So stehn wir (So here we stand) September 1864
Georg Daumer (after Hafiz)   A♭ major e♭'–f''

            So stehn wir, ich und meine Weide,
            So leider mit einander beide:

            Nie kann ich ihr was tun zu Liebe,
            Nie kann sie mir was tun zu Leide.

            Sie kränket es, wenn ich die Stirn ihr
            Mit einem Diadem bekleide;

            Ich danke selbst, wie für ein Lächeln
            Der Huld, für ihre Zornbescheide.

So here we stand, I and the delight of my eyes, so sadly at odds with each other. All my
attempts to show I love her are in vain; in vain are all her attempts to hurt me.
    It offends her, when I adorn her forehead with a diadem.
    I even thank her, as I would for a smile of grace and favour, for her intimations of
anger.

[So here we stand, I and the delight of my eyes, so sadly at odds with each other, so sadly at odds with each other.]

As in No. 36, there is no prelude; the singer has something to tell us, and is eager to begin. Here we are; together, yet apart. That paradox is made musically manifest; as soon as the sad falling thirds of the opening vocal melody come to an end on 'wir' (we), their canonic counterpart begins in the left hand. There it is instantly restated for further emphasis, though it has vanished from the voice; the two figures are irreconcilably separate and out of phase. The point is graphically made, and then apparently set aside. A new song starts, with new melodies and a new accompaniment of repeated chords. At 'Zornbescheide' (intimations of anger), however, which is where the poem ends, the left hand seems to repeat the opening vocal phrase in descending thirds, C–A♭–F, as if to say, musingly, 'So stehn wir'; this is how we stand, and how things stand with us.

Now Brahms and his own love-life take over, in an explicit and touchingly tender reprise. The voice musingly repeats the opening phrase, and adds further murmurs of affectionate regret. Meanwhile the left hand, that consistent source of Brahmsian subconscious expression, soulfully sighs that same motif, over and over again, first in canon as before and then on its own, eight times all told. This, it says, is how our relationship will always be; so near and yet so far.

NOTES. 1. For the poetic source, see No. 40, note 1. The word 'Weide' (pasture) is short for 'Augenweide', a feast for the eyes. The Daumer text is unchanged apart from the final repetition. But that is so deliberate and so effective as to set listeners searching for some added explanation, e.g. in the consecutive single Cs that introduce it (bars 32–4), the four further Cs that begin it (bars 34–5, as in 1–2), and the Clara-theme (M33) that recurs at the penultimate 'so leider mit einan(der)', after having been even more clearly stated at the outset, beginning on C, at '[lei]der mit einander' in bars 4–5.

2. The falling thirds are motivic (quasi M25) in the sense of rejection (cf. their analogous appearance in the same key and rhythm at 'erst verachtet, nun ein Verächter' in the *Alto Rhapsody* Op. 53). The Schumannian voice–piano octave doubling, here and *passim*, speaks of isolation (M37); the canonic imitations in two separate and apparently irreconcilable voices aptly symbolise the poet's despair (M12). The softening effect obtained by omitting the first piano beat, e.g. in the first bars and the reprise, is M29.

42. (Op. 32, No. 9) Wie bist du, meine Königin (How blissful, my queen) September 1864

Georg Daumer (after Hafiz)   E♭ major d'–f♯"

Wie bist du, meine Königin,
Durch sanfte Güte wonnevoll!
Du lächle nur – Lenzdüfte wehn
Durch mein Gemüte wonnevoll!

Frisch aufgeblühter Rosen Glanz
Vergleich ich ihn dem deinigen?
Ach, über alles was da blüht,
Ist deine Blüte, wonnevoll!

Durch tote Wüsten wandle hin,
Und grüne Schatten breiten sich,
Ob fürchterliche Schwüle dort
Ohn Ende brüte, wonnevoll.

Lass mich vergehn in deinem Arm!
Es ist in ihm ja selbst der Tod,
Ob auch die herbste Todesqual
Die Brust durchwüte, wonnevoll.

How blissful, my queen, your gentle kindness makes you! You have only to smile, and springtime fragrance wafts through my soul, making me blissful [blissful].

The radiance of fresh-flowering roses, shall I compare it to yours? Oh, your blossoming surpasses every flower that blows, it is so blissful [blissful].

If you walked through dead deserts, you would spread green shade, even though fearful sultriness endlessly broods there, you are so blissful [bliss–, blissful].

Let me pass away in your arms; there, even though mortal agony should sear my heart, death itself is blissful [bliss–, blissful].

Again the poem is in ghasel form, as in No. 37, with the rhymes on '–üte, wonnevoll'. Brahms's pauses and repetitions may tend to obscure the verse-form, and even the meaning. He has also been frequently rebuked for slack accentuation of the opening phrase 'wie bist du', in three equal quavers with a strong stress on the first. But '*how* blissful' is exactly what this magisterial music so memorably expresses, by extracting the poetic essence. The prelude sings a dreamy love-duet, into which the voice melts and blends. At the second 'wonnevoll' (blissful) the flowing melodies overlap in piano and voice; at the third, the prelude begins again as if the fullness of emotion had spilt over. The same music is repeated for the second verse.

Now the poem arrives at dead deserts, where the music obediently follows it without question, in a new walking motif and a desolate minor mode. The cruelly oppressive heat elicits gasps and groans of distress from the piano on each first beat from 'fürchterlich' (fearful) to 'brüte' (broods); but the intrepid onward tread never falters until, at the ensuing 'wonnevoll', the arpeggios converge amorously in both hands. The final reprise at 'Lass mich vergehn' (Let me pass away), after the prelude's fourth and last return, again thinks of death and its torment, at 'Todesqual' (mortal agony) etc, which is audibly eased and calmed into bliss by the power of love. Here is a *Liebestod* which, as in all great lieder, raises song to the power of opera.

NOTES. 1. For the poetic source see No. 40 note 1. No doubt the alleviating coolness of green-leaved shade in a hot desert made a special appeal. But Brahms's 'Rosen' instead of 'Rose' in bar 26 might now be corrected.

2. The strict musical structure deserves special study; thus the five-bar prelude begins again, bars 20–24, as the first verse ends, and similarly at bars 39–43 and 60–64 after the second and third.

3. The prelude's duetting right hand, M18, recalls Schumann's postlude to *Intermezzo* Op. 39 No. 2; the dreamy left-hand arpeggios, often reminiscent of *An eine Aeolsharfe*

No. 33, are M9; their amorous convergence at bars 56f is M17. The quasi-canon before 'wonnevoll', at bar 16 etc, is another aspect of the duetting motif M18; the cadential vocal melodies are typical. The top note at 'deinigen' is M10; the musical response to the idea of a journey towards a parched death combines the funereal key of B♭ minor (cf also the left-hand G♭ before 'der Tod' in the reprise) with the added walking movement of M1. The sharp notation in a flat key (M40) adds a touch of colour, here 'grün'; the minor-second groaning at bars 50f is M20; the flat supertonic of M23 falls aptly on 'Todesqual'.

OPUS 33

Romances from L. Tieck's *Magelone* for solo voice and pianoforte. The fifteen songs were published in five volumes (1 and 2 in 1865, 3–5 in 1869) and dedicated to Julius Stockhausen.

This title-page makes no mention of mere accompaniment; the work is integral. Brahms's friend, the baritone Stockhausen, had premièred it with the composer, whose piano parts are demandingly indicative of his own virtuoso talents. But this work's description remains typically laconic. In particular it pays scant respect to its source, the resplendently titled *Die wundersame Liebesgeschichte der schönen Magelone und des Grafen Peter aus der Provence* (*The wondrous love-story of beautiful Magelone and Count Peter from Provence*), in which Ludwig Tieck (1773–1853) sought to create a new poetic language to express the joys and sufferings experienced by the chivalric hero of his Romantic *Novelle*, then (1797) a new art-form. Both the genre in general and this early example proved popular. It was essentially a personal fantasy which nevertheless reflected the universal human experience of all nations and classes, and was intended as a moral lesson as well as a work of art. Hence the title of the collection in which it first appeared, namely *Volksmärchen von Peter Leberecht*, folk- or national tales by Peter Liveright; the meaningful pseudonym, the didactic tone and the global appeal to a common humanity are all entirely characteristic of the Romantic movement. This mélange, and each of its components, made a powerful personal appeal to the young Brahms, who (as we have seen) was already devoted to folk-song or national verse, for example as exemplified in Herder's *Volkslieder*, i.e. poems of different nations, and also to the *Novellen* of Eichendorff, who was Tieck's immediate successor in that form.

There were additional intimate bonds between Brahms and Tieck. The latter's story-telling, as often in such collections of tales, from the *Arabian Nights* onwards, is set against the background of a company of friends who discuss the narratives and discourse on life in general. One of them, as Brahms cannot have failed to notice, is called Clara. Furthermore, the love-story of Peter and Magelone is very much in the *Arabian Nights* vein of inconsequential events and amazing coincidences; and one of those tales, read by Brahms in a copy which Clara Schumann had given him, was represented by him as having a very special meaning for them both (see p. 18 above). Those two tales, moreover, share clear affinities, as if Tieck too had drawn from that same Arabian source, in

German translation; thus both their heroines are robbed in their sleep by a symbolic bird which filches a treasure from each of them and flies off with it. In Tieck's introduction to his own tale, furthermore, his character Clara discourses in musical metaphors of crescendo and decrescendo, and looks forward eagerly to the recreation of a 'Märchenwelt', a world of fairy-tale and folk-legend.

This is no doubt what Brahms too sought to supply. His universal art still speaks to, and for, the whole of humankind. But it surely derived directly from his own autobiographical affinities with Count Peter of Province. Both were Romantic heroes, young men of passionate self-awareness in search of a destiny and an identity. Their adventures and characters are strikingly similar. Both had at least two loves, and both had special musical and metaphorical methods of saying and spelling a woman's name.

This nineteenth-century resonance of picaresque literature within musical minds had already engendered new forms, such as Schumann's lyric pieces for piano inspired by the prose fictions of Jean-Paul Richter[1] and E. T. A. Hoffmann,[2] or Hugo Wolf's *Italian Serenade*[3] for string quartet composed under the comparable influence of Eichendorff's *Aus dem Leben eines Taugenichts*. In all such works the music speaks with a new literary voice whose unprecedented emotive force was not always easy to experience and evaluate. These Brahms songs for example, though masterpieces of that genre, have never enjoyed the esteem they merit. Resistance to them began with Brahms's publishers Breitkopf & Härtel, who in 1864 rejected the first six as too difficult pianistically. He found another publisher, but the initial discouragement no doubt inhibited progress, and it was not until 1869 that the other nine were completed and printed. Their characteristic blend of the intensely personal and the universally valid still poses special problems of interpretation and appreciation; both their literary and their musical language can nowadays easily sound more outmoded than new-minted.

But the effort entailed in assimilating both is richly rewarding. Brahms, for whom Tieck was an admired modern master and mentor, owned and read that writer's collected *Schriften*. (1828–54). Tieck's skills as a critic, historian and translator (notably from Shakespeare) enabled him to adapt ideas and idioms from many sources and centuries, in order to achieve his aim of universality, which Brahms shared. Hence perhaps the corresponding complexity of the piano parts and the difficulty of the cycle as a whole, which goes far beyond a simple picaresque adventure-tale by creating a Franco-German Don Quixote and Dulcinea, the young Count Peter and his beautiful Magelone. The resulting quasi-operatic work for one voice and piano is seriously mispresented by its present-day title, which should surely have named both main protagonists. It might have fared better as *Peter und Magelone*, the only lieder counterpart of its contemporary and comparable masterpiece *Tristan und Isolde*. Because it is a Romantic lied cycle, however, its hero is a single individual here no less than in

---

[1] *Papillons* Op. 2 (ed. E. Sams, unpubd).
[2] *Kreisleriana* Op. 16.
[3] See Sams, 1974b.

Schubert's *Die Schöne Müllerin* and *Winterreise*, or Schumann's *Dichterliebe*. That persona subsumes all the secondary characters. Thus the so-called *Magelone* songs are really all Peter's songs, even those which are actually sung in Tieck's text by Magelone herself (the eleventh song) or by Sulima (the thirteenth).

Perhaps the music needs a verbal framework before it can make its full impact. The original style that Brahms devises for this purpose was strongly influenced, no doubt as a consequence of his his concert tour with Stockhausen, by the Schubert ballad, which builds a coherent musical structure from successive episodes of poetic action or description. Brahms must have composed his music with Tieck's novella in mind, and he set all its lyrics except two. But his modern audiences may not be familiar with that work, which has not worn so well, and in any event its intercalated verses rely on their literary background for their optimum effect. In what follows, therefore, each song is placed in its literary context.

43. (Op. 33, No. 1) Keinen hat es noch gereut (No man has ever rued the day) July 1861

Ludwig Tieck   Eb major d'–ab''

Keinen hat es noch gereut,
Der das Ross bestiegen,
Um in frischer Jugendzeit
Durch die Welt zu fliegen.

Berge und Auen,
Einsamer Wald,
Mädchen und Frauen
Prächtig im Kleide,
Golden Geschmeide,
Alles erfreut ihn mit schöner Gestalt.

Wunderlich fliehen
Gestalten dahin,
Schwärmerisch glühen
Wünsche in jugendlich trunkenem Sinn.

Ruhm streut ihm Rosen
Schnell in die Bahn,
Lieben und Kosen,
Lorbeer und Rosen
Führen ihn höher und höher hinan.

Rund um ihn Freuden,
Feinde beneiden,
Erliegend, den Held,
Dann wählt er bescheiden
Das Fräulein, das ihm nur vor allen gefällt.

Und Berge und Felder
Und einsame Wälder
Misst er zurück.
Die Eltern in Tränen,
Ach alle ihr Sehnen,
Sie alle vereinigt das lieblichste Glück.

Sind Jahre verschwunden,
Erzählt er dem Sohn
In traulichen Stunden,
Und zeigt seine Wunden,
Der Tapferkeit Lohn.
So bleibt das Alter selbst noch jung,
Ein Lichtstrahl in der Dämmerung.

No man has ever rued the day when he mounted his steed to gallop through the world in the fresh flush of youth.

Mountains and meadows, lonely forest, maidens and ladies resplendent in their robes, golden jewellry; everything delights him with its beautiful form.

Visions wondrously pass and fade; intense passions glow among the heady emotions of youth [the heady emotions of youth].

Fame swiftly strews his path with roses; love and caresses, laurel and roses, lead him higher [lead him higher] and ever higher.

He is surrounded by joys [by joys]; his enemies envy the hero even as they fall before him [envy the hero even as they fall before him].

Then he modestly chooses the maiden who alone pleases him above all others [then he modestly chooses the maiden who alone pleases him above all others, above all others].

And he travels back over the mountains and meadows and lonely forests he has left behind him. His parents in tears, and all their yearning – dearest delight reunites them all.

When years have vanished he tells his story to his son, in intimate hours, and shows his scars, the reward of valour [of valour]. So old age [old age] itself remains young, a ray of sunshine [a ray of sunshine] in the twilight [a ray of sunshine in the twilight].

Tieck's hero, the young Count Peter of Provence, is fair-haired and athletic, as the Schumann children remembered the young Brahms. Peter was also a musician, and often silent and withdrawn; Tieck says that his hero was then thought to be in love, a state described in musical terms as a mysterious melody.

Peter is the victor at a grand knightly tournament; but he remains restless until he hears the ballad above sung by an old minstrel and realises that its message is meant for him. He must leave home and seek his fortune. His old parents are distressed, especially his mother; Brahms had left home on a concert tour at nineteen, when his mother was sixty-three. Peter says that he aims to return to his homeland as a known and honoured man; so Brahms returned to Hamburg, publicly hailed as a genius by Schumann. Peter takes a lute, which he could play well, and sings the song he had learned from the old minstrel (after just one hearing);

so this first Magelone romance stands as a personal manifesto from the novel's Romantic hero and also from the cycle's Romantic composer.

The texture of the first Romance (Brahms's own title) is designedly light; its look on the page offers a panorama of breezes and spaces, travel and adventure. In the prelude, a horn fanfare leaps into the saddle; after 'bestiegen' (mounted) the rhythm ♩ ♩ 𝄾 ♪ ♩ canters non-stop throughout more than 100 bars. It can all too easily sound jog-trot if the pianist over-emphasises the first beat or starves the quavers; in capable hands it sounds full of tireless energy. 'Welt' (world) is graphically prolonged and followed by a wide-ranging rise and fall of horn chords hinting at far horizons and hidden dangers. The dactylic cantering becomes subconscious in the bass as the rider dreams along over the regular hoof-beats. But it informs the vocal melodies at every other bar and begins to dominate at 'wunderlich fliehen Gestalten dahin' (visions wondrously pass and fade) and 'jugendlich trunkenem Sinn' (the heady emotions of youth), in time with Tieck's metrical patterns; the prevailing rhythm is promoted to the right hand to indicate increasing awareness of movement through the world. The music of 'Berge und Auen' (mountains and meadows) with its sustained top note at 'erfreut' (delights) resumes at 'Ruhm streut ihm Rosen' (Fame strews roses); the word now selected for this special exalted treatment is 'höher' (higher). Brahms identifies himself and his music with Count Peter and his song so closely as almost to mention by name the maiden 'das ihm nur vor allen gefällt' (the maiden who alone pleases him above all others) with a deliberate key-change and added repetition; each 'Fräulein' is awarded the highest notes yet heard in the song.

Now the music moves into a new and more leisurely phase. The melody of 'Berge und Auen' etc is treated in longer note-values at 'Berge und Felder' (mountains and meadows) as these stretch out behind our returning hero; 'Misst er zurück' and the following phrases move up and away in elated anticipations of the homeward journey. The piano accompaniment has dismounted, leaving only arpeggios of dream and reverie, with an interlude to introduce the new ideas of vanished years ('sind Jahre verschwunden') and the remembrance of youth as a ray of light in gathering gloom ('ein Lichtstrahl in der Dämmerung'). The postlude looks back lingeringly at the glory days of mounted knight-errantry.

NOTES. I. *Pace* Friedländer (1922, 32), Tieck's line 14 (not 15), 'in jugendlich trunkenem Sinn', is taken unchanged from the source Brahms owned, namely the *Schriften* 1828–54. There, the first word is the dative 'keinem'; but the *Gesamtausgabe*'s accusative 'keinen' occurs in an earlier edition of Tieck.

2. The loose rondo structure deserves close study; like the poetic subject, the musical form roams and returns.

3. The modestly-chosen maiden sounds very like Agathe (M32). As that phrase begins ('dann wählt er bescheiden') the music suddenly and surprisingly moves from E♭ major into G major, the key of the second String Sextet (which repeatedly cries her name aloud, see pp. 14–15 above), and can there be seen if not heard to contain the same signature tune, i.e. the notes A–G–A–D–H(= B)–E.

4. The chromatically rising octaves that frame these ideas, recurring before 'dann wählt', are themselves expressive, an aspect of M30; they excitedly line up the candidates, as it were, from whom a choice is to be made.

5. The introductory horn flourishes are M22; the continuous cantering is an aspect of M1; the ominous move towards the tonic (E♭) minor at 'einsame Wälder' may well be motivic in the sense of darkness and danger; all the meaningful sustained high notes are M10. The gradual decline of the vocal line at the first 'in der Dämmerung' signifies the dying of the light into the sad minor supertonic (M23) of old age, before comfort is restored in the tonic major. The melodic sequences heard throughout the song, and this cycle (most clearly here at 'in traulichen Stunden, und zeigt seine Wunden'), often correspond with the rhyme-structure, as in that example.

44. (Op. 33, No. 2) Traun! Bogen und Pfeil (Yes! bow and arrow) July 1861

Ludwig Tieck   C minor e′–g″

> Traun! Bogen und Pfeil
> Sind gut für den Feind,
> Hülflos alleweil
> Der Elende weint;
> Dem Edlen blüht Heil,
> Wo Sonne nur scheint,
> Die Felsen sind steil,
> Doch Glück ist sein Freund.

Yes! bow and arrow are good for the foe; the weak wretch weeps helplessly all the time [the weak wretch weeps helplessly all the time];

but well-being blooms for the noble warrior wherever the sun shines; though the cliffs are steep, fortune is his friend [fortune is his friend. Yes! bow and arrow are good for the foe; the weak wretch weeps helplessly all the time, the weak wretch weeps helplessly all the time;

but well-being blooms for the noble man wherever the sun shines; though the cliffs are steep, fortune is his friend, fortune is his friend. Yes! bow and arrow are good for the foe, the weak wretch weeps helplessly all the time, the weak wretch weeps helplessly all the time].

The long first song served as a general introduction. Now the actual story begins, in Tieck's Chapter 3, entitled 'How the Knight Peter left his parents'. 'The sun had risen in its glory and fresh dew gleamed on the meadows. Peter was in high spirits and spurred his good horse, so that it often reared mettlesomely. An old song came into his head, and he sang it aloud.' The poem that Tieck inserts at this point has only thirty-one words. These forty syllables are set forth in eight lines, rhyming alternately; and those two rhymes (-eil, -eint) share much the same vowel-sound. The poetic thought is comparably compressed into one single contrast, which relies on the same near-homophone; 'der Elende', the wretched man, and 'der Edle', the noble man.

Brahms seems to care little for any such prosodical matters. As before, he obscures them by quasi-operatic reiteration. Critics may complain at this conversion of a brief laconic lyric into a Handelian da capo aria. But the text, while audibly remaining an authentic 'old song', conveys new life and meaning through this added drama. What began as a heraldic motto on a shield or banner becomes the watchword or rallying cry for an extended campaign of arduous action; mental fight, sword in hand. Thus the cowardly caitiff is despised and the exalted hero extolled.

The energy of the opening statement derives from its strong chord-progressions underpinned by falling fifths in the bass line. After the second 'weint', the interlude is almost a scornful parody of unmanly weeping. This is instantly contrasted with the true knight-errant's adventures throughout the wide world, 'wo Sonne nur scheint' (wherever the sun shines), graphically illustrated by a panorama of horn-passages in a wider and freer rhythm. When this idea recurs, after a restatement of the opening theme, it is further embellished with vocal and keyboard flourishes; trumpets are added, as the Romantic hero enters the world arena. The coda's final transition into the major wears a satisfied smile.

NOTES. 1. For the Tieck source see No. 43, note 1. Brahms inflates those thirty-one words into well over a hundred, first by repetitions and then by further repetitions of and within those repetitions. Each of the basic contrasts is elongated into its own twelve-bar building-block and arranged into ABABA musical form, with linking keyboard interludes.

2. The modal harmonies (M27) characterise Tieck's 'old song'; the right hand's stepwise descent after 'weint' in bar 12 illustrates cowardly capitulation, with snivelling semitonal clashes. The open-air horn-passages are M22, again with sequences (at 'dem Edlen blüht Heil' etc.) that respond to the rhymes. In the first of these contrasting B sections the voice also reverts to the opening song's knight-errant rhythm, while the second of them adds high trumpet-calls. The vocal top notes are M10; the final tierce de Picardie confirms that the singer is no poltroon but a true hero.

45. (Op. 33, No. 3) Sind es Schmerzen (Are they sorrows) July 1861
Ludwig Tieck   Ab major c'–gb''

Sind es Schmerzen, sind es Freuden,
Die durch meinen Busen ziehn?
Alle alten Wünsche scheiden,
Tausend neue Blumen blühn.

Durch die Dämmerung der Tränen
Seh ich ferne Sonnen stehn,
Welches Schmachten! Welches Sehnen!
Wag ichs? soll ich näher gehn?

Ach, und fällt die Träne nieder,
Ist es dunkel um mich her;
Dennoch kömmt kein Wunsch mir wieder,
Zukunft ist von Hoffnung leer.

So schlage denn, strebendes Herz,
So fliesset denn, Tränen, herab,
Ach, Lust ist nur tieferer Schmerz,
Leben ist dunkles Grab.

Ohne Verschulden
Soll ich erdulden?
Wie ists, dass mir im Traum
Alle Gedanken
Auf und nieder schwanken!
Ich kenne mich noch kaum.

O hört mich, ihr gütigen Sterne,
O höre mich, grünende Flur,
Du, Liebe, den heiligen Schwur;
Bleib ich ihr ferne,
Sterb ich gerne.
Ach! nur im Licht von ihrem Blick
Wohnt Leben und Hoffnung und Glück!

Are they sorrows, are they joys, these feelings that steal through my heart? All my old desires depart, and a thousand new flowers come into bloom.

Through the twilight of my tears I see distant suns stand. What yearning! What longing! Shall I dare, shall I go nearer?

Alas, and as my tears fall, darkness surrounds me;
yet no desire returns, the future is empty of hope.
So beat then, striving heart; so flow down, teardrops.
Oh, pleasure is only a deeper pain, life is a dark grave.
Must I suffer without deserving to? How is it that in my dreams all my thoughts drift up and down? I hardly know myself any more.

[Must I suffer without deserving to? How is it that in my dreams all my thoughts drift up and down, up and down? I hardly know myself any more.]

Oh, hear me, you kindly stars, oh hear me [hear me], green-growing meadow; and you, Love, hear this sacred vow [you, Love, this sacred vow]. If I must remain far from her I shall gladly die. Oh [oh, oh] only in the light [only in the light] of her gaze dwell life and hope and happiness! [If I must remain far from her I shall gladly die. Oh, only in the light, only in the light of her, of her gaze dwell life and hope and happiness!]

After the previous song Tieck tells how his hero reached Naples, 'having already heard much about its King and his exceptionally beautiful daughter Magelone, whom he was therefore eager to behold face to face'. Peter has his wish at a celebratory feast to which the King invites him as victor ludorum in a local tournament. There is mutual love at first sight, whereupon, as the dazed and dazzled Peter returns to his lodgings, 'an inward music resounded above the whispering of the trees and the plashing of the fountains'. This was soon echoed by the strains of actual music in the vicinity, at which Peter wept and sobbed. He felt that 'the sky had changed and was now showing him its beauty and its paradisal aspect for the first time. And yet this emotion made him so unhappy; among all these joys he felt so completely deserted. The music flowed like a murmuring brook through the quiet garden, and he saw [Magelone's] beauty as if floating high on the silver waves, as the waves of music kissed the hem of her garment and vied to follow her ... the music was now the sole movement, the only activity, in nature, and all its tones slid so sweetly across the grass-tips and tree-tops as if in search of, yet afraid to wake, sleeping love; as if, like the weeping lad, they trembled for fear of being noticed. Now the last notes died away, and the tones faded like a stream of blue light, and the trees began to rustle again, and Peter came to himself and found that his cheeks were wet with tears ...'.

Then he sings Tieck's verses, which at first inspire superlative musical invention. In a long prelude, the poet's waves break into song as arpeggios; then, to the same accompaniment, the melodies flow most memorably from the words. So do the keyboard motifs. In the language of Brahms, the falling mezzo-staccato speaks of tear-drops, while the right-hand alternations sing for joy. After two verses to the same music, the masochistic identity of pleasure and pain is made audible by a movement to the minor mode on the same keynote. But this concentrated lyricism is first tinctured by drama and then watered down by melodrama. The vocal line is interrupted by quaver rests, to show how the striving heart misses a beat; the cadences are ornamented. From 'Ohne Verschulden muss ich erdulden?' (Must I suffer without deserving to?) the music seems to outfly the already highflown words. The suffering is replaced by blustering; ebullient outbursts are mixed with recitative in a style so strongly Schubertian that it seems to elbow Brahms aside.

NOTES. 1. The Tieck source (See No. 43, note 1) has 'dunkeles' not 'dunkles' in line 16, as the prosody requires; but Brahms's turn demands the latter. So that turn should be sung, not bracketed optional as in the Peters edition. In its treatment of the vivace section (at 'O hört mich' etc.) that edition is far preferable to the *Gesamtausgabe*, which gives only the four-bar vocal variant that Brahms communicated to the publisher, Rieter-Biedermann, in 1894 but cancelled in the following year. Peters rightly retains the original version, though it needlessly adds, in small notes, the composer's short-lived preference.

2. The consecutive thirds in the prelude and later (including those in both hands at 'Gedanken auf und nieder') are the love-duet M18; the insistent dominant sevenths at the end of the prelude are M24; the tears splash in staccato drops, M28. The major 5–6–5 joy of M19 resounds *passim* after the double bar and recurs after the first 'kaum' and again after 'Glück'; it changes to minor 6–5 (M20) to introduce the weeping at 'Ach und fällt die Träne'. The flattened supertonics (M23) at 'Zukunft' and 'Leben', followed by the tonic minor, deny those words by foretelling a bleak future and a lack of life. At 'schla-ge' and 'flie-sset' the quaver gaps are vocal gasps, in a quasi-operatic style enhanced by the recitative at each 'Ich kenne mich noch kaum' and the first 'bleib ich ihr ferne' as well as the turn on 'dunkles' and the final grupetto at 'Hoffnung'. At 'Leben' is M23; the horn passages at 'Wie ist's' etc. and 'nur im Licht' etc. are M22.

3. The Schubertian major-minor harmonies mirror the poetic contrast-in-unity of pleasure and pain; M39. Other echoes of Schubert are also reflected from the words. Thus the staccato at 'Ach, und fällt die Träne nieder' is reminiscent of *Letzte Hoffnung* from *Winterreise* D911/16 (where the words 'ach, und fällt das Blatt zu Boden' later occur). The accompaniment at 'O hört mich, ihr gütigen Sterne' (C minor, with repeated G in the right hand, M11, and octave ascent G–A–B–C–D–E♭, in the left, where the alternating hands are M30) is heard in *Kolmas Klage* D217, e.g. just after the words 'erscheinet, ihr nächtlichen Sterne'. The new figuration at 'Flur' begins with the broken G major chords heard in *Der liebliche Stern* D861 (compare also the vocal line at '(Lie)be den heiligen Schwur' here with

bars 9–10 there). The first 'Bleib ich ihr gerne' etc follows the melodic curve of 'nirgends haften dann' etc. in *Grenzen der Menschheit* D716, after the word 'Sterne'. Brahms had performed *Winterreise* and other Schubert lieder with Julius Stockhausen, the dedicatee and first vocal interpreter of Op. 33.

4. Perhaps the notes C–B♭–A♭–G–A♭, introduced into the postlude as yet another new idea constitute a Clara-motif, M33.

5. Cf. Weber's setting, J156.

46. (Op. 33, No. 4) Liebe kam aus fernen Landen (Love came from far-off lands) July 1861

Ludwig Tieck   D♭ major d♭'–f''

Liebe kam aus fernen Landen
Und kein Wesen folgte ihr,
Und die Göttin winkte mir,
Schlang mich ein mit süssen Banden.

Da begann ich Schmerz zu fühlen,
Tränen dämmerten den Blick:
Ach! was ist der Liebe Glück,
Klagt ich, wozu dieses Spielen?

Keinen hab ich weit gefunden,
Sagte lieblich die Gestalt,
Fühle du nun die Gewalt,
Die die Herzen sonst gebunden.

Alle meine Wünsche flogen
In der Lüfte blauen Raum,
Ruhm schien mir ein Morgentraum,
Nur ein Klang der Meereswogen.

Ach! wer löst nun meine Ketten?
Denn gefesselt ist der Arm,
Mich umfleugt der Sorgen Schwarm;
Keiner, keiner will mich retten?

Darf ich in den Spiegel schauen,
Den die Hoffnung vor mir hält?
Ach, wie trügend ist die Welt!
Nein, ich kann ihr nicht vertrauen.

O, und dennoch lass nicht wanken,
Was dir nur noch Stärke gibt,
Wenn die Einzge dich nicht liebt,
Bleibt nur bittrer Tod dem Kranken.

Love came from far-off lands, and no creature followed her, and the goddess beckoned me and enwound me in sweet bonds [enwound me in sweet bonds].

Then I began to feel sorrow, tears dimmed my gaze; 'Oh, what is the joy of love', I lamented, 'why all this dallying? [why all this dallying?]'

'I have found no man far and wide', said the vision lovingly; 'now you must feel the power that once bound heart to heart [that once bound heart to heart]'.

All my desires flew into the blue realm of the breezes. Fame seemed only a morning dream, only a sound of the sea's waves.

Oh, who now will loosen my chains? For my arm is fettered and sorrows swarm around me; will no one, no one, rescue me?

Dare I look into the mirror that hope holds up to me?

Alas, how deceptive the world is; no, I cannot trust it.

Yet do not allow your sole source of strength to waver; if the only one for you does not love you, all that remains for the sufferer is bitter death [all that remains for the sufferer is bitter death].

Magelone loves Peter in return and confides her feelings to her old nurse; 'seek him out, Gertraud, ask about his rank and name'. Peter meets the nurse and gives her one of three costly rings handed to him by his mother as a parting gift, and also a poem of his own, namely the lines above. It moved Magelone deeply, and mirrored her own feelings. In her dreams that night 'she saw herself in a lovely and pleasant garden, where the brightest sunshine shimmered on all the green leaves, and the song of her beloved resounded from the blue sky as if played on harp-strings, and golden-winged birds mounted amazed into the sky and listened to the music; light clouds moved away beneath the melody and became red-rose-coloured and echoed the song …'. When the beloved appears in vision, this heavenly music 'enveloped them both like a golden net, and the bright clouds clothed them about, and they were sundered from the world, dwelling only in themselves and in their love, and she heard nightingales sing and bushes whisper like a distant lament that they were excluded from the bliss of heaven'.

These musical rhapsodies are typical of Tieck; and Brahms provides their lieder equivalent. The 'Love' that begins the poem means Venus, or Frau Minne in the German troubadour tradition. She is suddenly there, as it were at first sight, without prelude or preamble; the music of voice–piano unison, alternating hands and tonic pedal encapsulate her long lone journey from the realms and the times of Minnesang. At the first 'schlang mich ein' (enwound me) there is a recollection of the bliss expressed in the opening strains of the previous song; when those words are repeated, the vocal accents tug and tighten the knots, an effect that recurs at 'gebunden' (bound). Each such context is echoed in an interlude, which begins by clashing chromatically – feeling pain, as the words confirm. Then the piano's quavers shift off the beat, in an image of frustration at having to make do with 'Spielen' (dallying) instead of the true joys of love. That artificiality is empha-sised by an ornament on the repeated 'Spielen'. But the first strains soothingly return, until at 'alle meine Wünsche flogen' (all my desires flew) a new two-handed wing-beat motif of quaver triplets bears a new melody aloft in a new key. Further invention illustrates the poetic ideas of constraint in chains and fetters ('Ketten', 'gefesselt') and distress at a swarm of sorrows ('Sorgen Schwarm'). At the final reprise, Brahms incorporates the quaver triplets of his F major section into the original D flat major music, for no very clear reason except the wish to integrate those contrasts into a musical unity.

NOTES. 1. The Tieck source (No. 43, note 1) has the archaic 'begonn', not 'begann' in its fifth line. Here the *Gesamtausgabe* seems preferable in its treatment of the sung melody at 'Ruhm schien mir', which fits the verbal scansion better than the tune at the later 'Ach, wie trügend ist die Welt'; the Peters edition prints the same vocal line in both passages.

2. The alternating hands and tonic pedal, together with parallel thirds or tenths (M18) and horn passages (M22) form a conglomerate of travelling, steadfastness, love and the great outdoors, to match the poetic idea. At the first 'schlang mich ein' etc. the right hand has the joy of M19, which recurs in the interlude after 'vertrauen'. The ensuing off-beat quavers expressing loss or deprivation (M29) are followed at 'wozu dieses Spielen?' by ominous falling octaves that depict a sad decline. This pattern is repeated with deliberate and meaningful variants (note for example the chordal ascent and higher octave at 'fühle du' etc. and the remodelling of bars 9–10 to make 33–34, again an image of intertwining). The metaphorical flight at 'flogen' is M3. The harsh chromaticism of distress at 'Ketten' etc, notated in sharps (M40), may have influenced the analogous expression in the 1888 *Der Jäger* of Hugo Wolf, despite his overt rejection of Brahms. At 'retten' is the dominant question, followed by the intensified dominant sevenths, of M24. These recur before the final reprise, where the added quaver triplets seem, exceptionally, to lack any special verbal significance.

47. (Op. 33, No. 5) So willst du des Armen (So you'll kindly have pity) May 1862

Ludwig Tieck   F major e♭'–g''

> So willst du des Armen
> Dich gnädig erbarmen?
>   So ist es kein Traum?
> Wie rieseln die Quellen,
> Wie tönen die Wellen,
>   Wie rauschet der Baum!
>
> Tief lag ich in bangen
> Gemäuern gefangen,
>   Nun grüsst mich das Licht,
> Wie spielen die Strahlen!
> Sie blenden und malen
>   Mein schüchtern Gesicht.
>
> Und soll ich es glauben?
> Wird keiner mir rauben
>   Den köstlichen Wahn?
> Doch Träume entschweben,
> Nur lieben heisst leben:
>   Willkommene Bahn!

> Wie frei und wie heiter!
> Nicht eile nun weiter,
>   Den Pilgerstab fort!
> Du hast überwunden,
> Du hast ihn gefunden,
>   Den seligsten Ort!

So you'll kindly have pity on a poor man? so it's no dream? How the streams ripple, how the waves resound, how the tree rustles [how the tree rustles]!

I lay imprisoned in deep dark walls; now daylight greets me. How the sunbeams play! They dazzle and illumine my shy face [my shy face].

And shall I believe it? Will not this exquisite exaltation [this exquisite exaltation] be stolen from me? Yet dreams disappear; only loving is living, a welcome path [a welcome path]!

How free and serene! Now hurry forward no more; away with the pilgrim's staff! You've conquered, you've found it, the most blissful [most blissful] place of all.

Magelone's nurse has met Count Peter once more and told him that her mistress loves him; again he sends her a ring, together with the manuscript of this song, which Magelone sings to herself in her room. In the prelude, the pianist's two arms joyously converge; the music embraces the whole of nature, active and exultant in quaver triplet chords. Unobtrusive left-hand staccato seconds sketch the ripples at 'wie rieseln'; the waves rise in sequential melodies; the treetops rustle on a sustained top note at the first 'rauschet'. The prelude returns as an interlude; then the texture lightens and the tonality brightens, to match the sunbeams, with a chequered chiascuro of dark and bright modulations that reach a climax of diatonic certainty as the right road ('Bahn') is discovered lying open and the reprise goes confidently singing along it.

NOTES. 1. Brahms embellished his Tieck source (No. 43, note 1) by adding 'so' as its first word, for the sake of his melodic up-beat – not, surely (*pace* Friedländer 1922 35), to change the enquiry into a certainty, since all the question marks still stand. The second question, at 'Traum?' even has the interrogatory quality of M24, with the dominant of the relative minor. But the arpeggios are now in left-hand octaves that fall in thirds (echoing the first vocal phrase at 'So willst du …'); thus the dream motif M9 is emphatically negated, and the music proclaims aloud 'this is no dream'.

2. The converging hands of the prelude are M17; the sequences at 'wie rieseln' and 'wie spielen' reflect the rhymes; after 'das Licht' the flat- and sharp-key modulations (M40) supply light-effects, with hints of an induced trance-state in the five falling notes at the second 'schüchtern Gesicht', which serve as a sleep-motif later in the cycle (No. 51). The sustained top notes at 'rauschet' on the first page, 'willkommen' before the reprise and the concluding 'se[ligsten]' are M10. They further emphasise the poet's exclamation marks, as the double dominant-seventh interrogation at each 'Wahn?' (again M24) reinforces the question mark.

48. (Op. 33, No. 6) Wie soll ich die Freude (How then shall I bear all this joy) May 1862

Ludwig Tieck   A major c#'–f#''

> Wie soll ich die Freude,
> Die Wonne denn tragen?

Dass unter dem Schlagen
Des Herzens die Seele nicht scheide?

Und wenn nun die Stunden
Der Liebe verschwunden,
Wozu das Gelüste,
In trauriger Wüste
Noch weiter ein lustleeres Leben zu ziehn
Wenn nirgend dem Ufer mehr Blumen erblühn?

Wie geht mit bleibehangnen Füssen
Die Zeit bedächtig Schritt vor Schritt!
Und wenn ich werde scheiden müssen,
Wie federleicht fliegt dann ihr Tritt!

Schlage, sehnsüchtige Gewalt,
In tiefer treuer Brust!
Wie Lautenton vorüber hallt,
Entflieht des Lebens schönste Lust.
Ach, wie bald
Bin ich der Wonne mir kaum noch bewusst.

Rausche, rausche weiter fort,
Tiefer Strom der Zeit,
Wandelst bald aus Morgen Heut,
Gehst von Ort zu Ort;
Hast du mich bisher getragen,
Lustig bald, dann still,
Will es nun auch weiter wagen,
Wie es werden will.

Darf mich doch nicht elend achten,
Da die Einzge winkt,
Liebe lässt mich nicht verschmachten,
Bis dies Leben sinkt!
Nein, der Strom wird immer breiter,
Himmel bleibt mir immer heiter,
Fröhlichen Ruderschlags fahr ich hinab,
Bring Liebe und Leben zugleich an das Grab.

How then shall I bear this joy, this bliss, so that amidst the beating [the beating] of my heart my soul [my soul] does not depart?

And if the hours of love have now vanished, why should I crave to prolong a life emptied of pleasure, in a dreary desert where no flowers bloom anywhere on the shore?

How time passes by on lead-weighted feet, deliberate stride after stride; but when I must leave, how feather-light its step then flits by [how feather-light its step then flits by]!

Beat, O powerful longing, deep in my faithful heart; as the echo of lute music dies away [dies away], so the sweetest pleasures of life disappear. Oh, how soon [oh, how soon] I shall be scarcely still aware of this bliss [of this bliss, oh how soon I shall be scarcely still aware of this bliss, of this bliss].

Flow, flow ever onward, deep river of time; you soon change tomorrow into today [tomorrow into today] and move from place [from place] to place. You have carried me thus far, now cheerful, now silent; and I shall venture further, come what [come what] may.

Yet I must not count myself wretched, for my only love beckons to me, and love shall never let me languish as long as my life lasts.

No, the stream grows ever broader, the sky stays ever serene for me; with a blithe stroke of the oar I row on down, and bring love and life together [together] to the grave. [No, the stream grows ever broader, the sky stays ever serene for me; with a blithe stroke of the oar I row on down, with a blithe stroke of the oar I row on down, and bring love and life together to the grave, bring love and life together to the grave, bring love and life together to the grave, bring love and life together, together to the grave.]

Peter and the nurse meet for a third time; he declares his intentions honourable and she is impressed by his nobility of lineage and bearing. A tryst with the princess is arranged; while he is waiting, Count Peter performs this song, again to his own lute accompaniment.

Even the prelude is heard singing for joy, over plucked lute-strings. As the voice joins in, the piano trills with pleasure. But then the elation ebbs from words and music; the latter loses its decorations and turns into bare octaves on the barren seashore, at 'wenn nirgend dem Ufer' etc. By the same means, the poet's metaphor of slow time is typically transformed into a physical reality; the walk plods wearily on 'bleibehangnen Füssen' (lead-weighted feet), until the featherlight fleeting of enjoyment resumes before 'federleicht'. At 'Schlage' (Beat) a new key and a steady rhythm over sustained pedal notes depict the passing of earthly pleasures, as if borne away on the current of a deep river – an idea further illustrated in the left hand at 'tiefer Strom' etc. the elation returns at the thought of 'Die Einzge', the only love; and here the voice's muted reminiscence, at 'Liebe lässt mich nicht verschmachten' (love shall never let me languish), of the main theme from *Liebe kam aus fernen Landen* (No. 46) is no doubt deliberate. Now yet another new idea dominates the music, in a mood of abandoned ebullience as the strong rower and the powerful current strike downstream together at 'der Strom'. At the final *animato* the hero again breaks out into a trilling love-song, with an aptly sustained top note on 'Liebe'. Thus the music faithfully maps every moment and every movement of a long journey through life's vicissitudes. For that purpose the words are freely repeated; but the intended incantatory effect can all too easily sound over-insistent in a less than completely committed performance.

NOTES. 1. The Tieck source (No. 43, note 1) has 'entblühn' (shed their bloom) not 'erblühn' (blossom out) in its tenth line. But its twentieth has 'noch', as in Brahms, not 'mehr', so Friedländer's citation of the latter (1922 37) is mistaken. The poet's final words 'an das Grab' mean no more than 'as long as I live', as the sustainedly cheerful A major treatment makes manifest.

2. Perhaps the Schubert song repertory of Brahms and Stockhausen included *Abendröte* D690, also in A major embellished with trills in both hands, as on the first page here.

3. The loving bliss that fades from the poem still glows in the music's memory, as evidenced by the resemblance between bars 47–51 here at 'entflieht des Lebens schönste Lust' and bars 29f at 'Und um sie schweben' etc. of *Ein Sonett* (No. 24).

4. The staccato and trills here suit 'federleicht', in complete contrast with the preceding slow march, M1. The deep F sharp major pedals at 'Schlage' and 'wandelst' are M6, mirroring the depths of the heart before 'tiefer ... Brust' and of time's river after 'tiefer Strom der Zeit', while the joy motif M19 falls pat on the (5–6–5) left-hand triplets at 'Lust' and 'Wonne'. These two ideas combine in the flowing movement at 'tiefer Strom' and the falling octaves that precede and follow it.

49. (Op. 33, No. 7) War es dir (Was it for you) by 1869
Ludwig Tieck   D major e′–g″

> War es dir, dem diese Lippen bebten,
> Dir der dargebotne süsse Kuss?
> Gibt ein irdisch Leben so Genuss?
> Ha! wie Licht und Glanz vor meinen Augen schwebten,
> Alle Sinne nach den Lippen strebten!
>
> In den klaren Augen blinkte
> Sehnsucht, die mir zärtlich winkte,
> Alles klang im Herzen wieder,
> Meine Blicke sanken nieder,
> Und die Lüfte tönten Liebeslieder!
>
> Wie ein Sternenpaar
> Glänzten die Augen, die Wangen
> Wiegten das goldene Haar,
> Blick und Lächeln schwangen
> Flügel, und die süssen Worte gar
> Weckten das tiefste Verlangen;
> O Kuss, wie war dein Mund so brennend rot!
> Da starb ich, fand ein Leben erst im schönsten Tod.

Was it for you that these lips quivered, you to whom that sweet kiss was offered? Can earthly life yield so much joy? Ah, how light [how light] and radiance floated before my eyes, all my senses yearned towards those lips [all my senses yearned towards those lips]! In those clear eyes shone a longing that tenderly [tenderly] beckoned me.

Everything [everything] echoed in my heart, my gaze [my gaze] was lowered, and all the breezes resounded with love-songs [and the breezes resounded with love-songs].

Your eyes shone like twin stars, your cheeks cradled your golden hair, your looks and smiles took wing and your sweet words aroused deepest desire.

[Your looks and your smiles took wing and your sweet words aroused deepest desire.]

O kiss [O kiss], how burning red were your lips! There I died, and found life [found life] for the first time in that most beautiful of deaths [in that most beautiful, most beautiful of deaths].

The lovers have again met; Peter gives Magelone the third and most precious of his rings. In return she places a costly golden chain about his neck and thus declares herself his for ever. They kiss. Peter returns to his room, as if to tell his armour and his lute about his new-found happiness, the like of which he had never known. He kissed his lute-strings, played upon them, and wept. Then he sang, with intense passion, the words above.

At first, the five-bar phrasing sways in waltz-time with Tieck's trochaic pentameter. The vocal melodies parallel the possibly contemporary *Liebeslieder* Op. 52, a word which Brahms chooses to repeat here. The almost timeless and motion-less music at 'in den klaren Augen' (in those clear eyes) embodies that loving gaze and long kiss. The same eyes are invoked in the contrasting G major middle section, beginning 'Wie ein Sternenpaar' (like twin stars), where the piano like the singer's heart repeatedly misses a beat. This music's reverie may incorporate personal reminiscence; hence perhaps its effect of artificiality. It may not be coincidence that the piano part at 'Lächeln' (smiles) and 'und die [süssen Worte]' (and the [sweet words]) both include a possible Agathe allusion in their notes A–G–H–E. But all constraint is swept aside by the serene love-song rhythm of the reprise at 'O Kuss', where the Viennese waltz is dignified and ennobled by great art.

NOTES. 1. For the Tieck source, see No. 43, note 1.

2. The melody at 'wie Licht und Glanz' (repeated at '[Blick]e, meine Blick[e]') is shared with the *Liebeslieder* Op. 52 No. 7, in the same notes, far out of the latter's main key. The ensuing verbal parallel (here 'vor meinen Augen', there 'dicht vorm Auge stehe') is also noteworthy; so perhaps is the occurrence here of the word 'Liebeslieder', which was Brahms's own title for his Op. 52.

2. The left-hand 5–6–5 in bars 2–4 and similarly passim is the joy motif M19. The persistent pedals, especially notable in the seventeen bars after the second 'nach den Lippen', are M8; the consecutive thirds and sixths are the love-motif M18; the absence of a first beat in the G major section is M29; the A–G–H–E arrangements suggest M32; the turns at each 'Verlangen' are quasi-operatic.

3. Friedländer's comment (1922 37) about the unusual 'exact repetition' of twelve whole bars (beginning 'Blick und Lächeln') is misleading. The words are deliberately repeated for emphasis, and their sequential treatment is characteristic of this cycle. Nor is the vocal repetition exact (cf 'tiefste' in each context), while the piano part is carefully varied.

50. (Op. 33, No. 8) Wir müssen uns trennen (We must part) by 1869
Ludwig Tieck   G♭ major d♭'–g''

> Wir müssen uns trennen,
> Geliebtes Saitenspiel,
> Zeit ist es, zu rennen
> Nach dem fernen erwünschten Ziel.
>
> Ich ziehe zum Streite,
> Zum Raube hinaus,
> Und hab ich die Beute,
> Dann flieg ich nach Haus.

Im rötlichen Glanze
Entflieh ich mit ihr,
Es schützt uns die Lanze,
Der Stahlharnisch hier.

Kommt, liebe Waffenstücke,
Zum Scherz oft angetan,
Beschirmet jetzt mein Glücke
Auf dieser neuen Bahn!

Ich werfe mich rasch in die Wogen,
Ich grüsse den herrlichen Lauf,
Schon mancher ward nieder gezogen,
Der tapfere Schwimmer bleibt oben auf.

Ha! Lust zu vergeuden
Das edele Blut!
Zu schützen die Freude,
Mein köstliches Gut!
Nicht Hohn zu erleiden,
Wem fehlt es an Mut?

Senke die Zügel,
Glückliche Nacht!
Spanne die Flügel,
Dass über ferne Hügel
Uns schon der Morgen lacht!

We must part, dear lute, it is time to hasten to the distant desired goal [the distant desired goal]. I am setting out for battle, for spoils, and when I have my booty I shall speed homewards.

In the reddish glow I shall escape with her; this lance [this lance] and this steel armour [this lance, this steel armour] shall protect us.

Come, dear weapons, often donned in sport, now guard my happiness on this new path!

I hurl myself into the waves, I salute their splendid surge; many a man has been dragged under, but the bold swimmer keeps his head above water [the bold swimmer keeps his head above water].

Ha, what pleasure to shed noble blood, to protect my joy, my treasured possession! Who would lack the spirit to fight rather than endure scorn [who would lack the spirit to fight rather than endure scorn]?

Slacken the reins, happy night! spread your wings, so that we shall soon see, over the far hills, the dawn come laughing towards us [dawn, dawn come laughing towards us].

All this time, the princess Magelone has been betrothed to another, for reasons of state. Peter resolves to test her love, and tells her he must return home. She begs to go with him; they plan to escape together. Later in his lodgings he is moved by the sight of his faithful lute 'upon which his fingers had so often expressed the feelings of his heart … He took it up again and sang' the verses above. The prelude tries out lute chords, the accompaniment spreads them staccato (surely throughout those six bars here and in the reprise, though only the first bar is thus marked). Then the voice sings its ingratiating melody, like a serenade to the lute itself. At 'ich ziehe' the music abandons its diffidence and sets out for battle; not in youthful ardour like the minstrel boy, but with a mature deliberate slow march to the sound of the drum. Thus real power and menace are generated; these are no idle boasts. But the following trumpet effects at 'Kommt, liebe Waffen' (come, dear weapons), and the increased energy of waves and surges in crotchet triplets and sequences, may sound somewhat less convincing and indeed perfunctory, especially when culminating in a sustained dominant at 'oben auf' (above water) and continuing into the next section where the poet's taste for blood ('Blut') and distaste for scorn ('Hohn') make no special appeal to the composer.

But with the return of the prelude and the main lute-themes at 'Senke die Zügel' (Slacken the reins) the song again rings true; the lover and the soldier here speak with one voice about their impassioned faith in the future.

NOTES. 1. *Pace* Friedländer (1922 38), Brahms's 'spanne' (not 'spann') on the last page is the word found in the Tieck source (see No. 43, note 1), so the proposed reading of 'eil' is mistaken. But the slip of 'Freude' for its rhyming plural 'Freuden' in bar 56 should surely be corrected in print and performance.

2. The diffident off-beat quavers of the first page are M29; the downward scalar march to the keynote at 'fernen erwünschten Ziel' expresses faith in the future. The demisemi-quaver triplets at 'ich ziehe zum Streite' are clearly expressive, though not heard elsewhere in the songs in any such martial sense; they recall bar 17f of the Adagio of Beethoven's pianoforte sonata Op. 31 No. 2, as if Brahms heard them as a symbol of muffled drums in that context also. The open-air horn passages or trumpet-calls that signal the charge at bar 30 are M22, while the vocal sequences there, at 'ich werfe mich' etc., and later at 'Nicht Hohn zu erleiden' etc., (where the sharp sequences in a flat key are also motivic, M40) are related to the rhyming lines as so often in this cycle. The sustained dominant at 'auf' in bar 41 is M24; the subsequent arpeggios in a new triplet-crotchet rhythm connote waves and surges, M5. The bright top notes at 'tapferer' and 'Morgen' are M10; the postlude's rotating hands in contrary motion (M13) embody a wide panoramic horizon in morning sunlight.

51. (Op. 33, No. 9) Ruhe, Süssliebchen (Rest, sweetheart) by 1869
Ludwig Tieck   A♭ major and A major d'–f#"

> Ruhe, Süssliebchen, im Schatten
>   Der grünen, dämmernden Nacht;
> Es säuselt das Gras auf den Matten,
> Es fächelt und kühlt dich der Schatten,
>   Und treue Liebe wacht.
>   Schlafe, schlaf ein,
>   Leiser rauscht der Hain,
>   Ewig bin ich dein.

Schweigt, ihr versteckten Gesänge,
  Und stört nicht die süsseste Ruh!
Es lauscht der Vögel Gedränge,
Es ruhen die lauten Gesänge,
  Schliess, Liebchen, dein Auge zu.
    Schlafe, schlaf ein,
    Im dämmernden Schein,
    Ich will dein Wächter sein.

Murmelt fort, ihr Melodien,
  Rausche nur, du stiller Bach.
Schöne Liebesphantasien
Sprechen in den Melodien,
  Zarte Träume schwimmen nach.
    Durch den flüsternden Hain
    Schwärmen goldene Bienelein
    Und summen zum Schlummer dich ein.

Rest, sweetheart, in the shade of the green darkling night.
  The grass whispers in the meadows, the shade fans and cools you, and true love keeps
watch. Sleep, go to sleep, the grove rustles ever more softly, I am for ever your own
[I am for ever, for ever your own].
  Hush, you hidden songs, and do not disturb this sweetest rest. The flocks of birds
listen, their loud lays cease; close your eyes, my love. Sleep, go to sleep, in the fading
light, I will watch over you [I will watch over you].
  Murmur on, you melodies, and purl on, you quiet [you quiet] brook. Beautiful
fantasies of love speak in those melodies, tender dreams float after them. Through the
whispering grove golden bees are swarming and humming you to sleep [humming you
to sleep, to sleep].

The lovers elope. On their journey, Peter sings a cheerful song; his voice quivers
through the trees and a distant echo joins in. Every tone goes straight to the lovers'
hearts and fills them with wistful joy. Birdsong, mingled with purling streams,
resounds from the shady woodland; the place is so deserted and echoes arise so
marvellously from the valleys below, that it seems as if spirits are calling and
answering each other through the solitude. So, says the travel-weary Magelone,
'let your sweet voice once again resound through these confused harmonies, to
round off all this lovely music; I'll try to sleep a little . . .'.
  Thereupon Peter sings the verses above, which represent Tieck at his lyric best; and
Brahms effortlessly matches and indeed surpasses them, in a masterpiece of his own.
  The piano prelude anticipates the vocal melody at the words 'schlafe, schlaf ein'
(sleep, go to sleep), with the lullaby effect of singing those words. The off-beat
dominant pedal is hypnotic. But the drowsed senses can still detect and describe
sounds; the first mention of the least noise, at 'säuselt' (whispers) induces the pedal
note's first change of pitch, by one semitone. Meanwhile the vocal melodies
consist of repeated caressing phrases that finally go down to rest at 'treue Liebe

'wacht' (true love keeps watch). The ensuing 'sleep, sleep' is echoed by the overlap-ping piano melody, until the five-note falling phrase already heard recurs at each 'ewig bin ich dein'. By then, only sustained off-beat quavers have been touched by the left hand in any bar, over eighty times all told. And even that repeated pulse is unobtrusive; it belongs inside the music as a heartbeat in the body, an earnest of the constant physical presence explicitly promised in the words.

Now follows a piano interlude that sings a new melody, as if to supply an actual lullaby. At 'Schweigt' (Hush) the voice resumes in small comfortable sequences that stretch out within a cradle of rocking quavers. For the hushed 'Vögel Gedränge' (flocks of birds) and their softening songs, the piano shadows the vocal melody. Now the first strains are repeated down to the slumber-song interlude, with extra quavers to make the music continuous and hence even more hypnotic.

Then comes an animato section, at 'Murmelt fort', with the accompaniment further subdivided into semiquavers. Here all the effects blend and blur into a murmuring buzz of brooklets and bees, until after the first 'summen zum Schlummer dich ein' (humming you to sleep) the left-hand semiquaver arpeggios cease as the dreamer drifts into deep slumber. Finally the lullaby itself drowses off into oblivion.

This fine song sometimes suffers from a break of mood because the animato section is marked by the direction 'forte' as well as a key-shift from dark A flat to bright A major. The contrast must not be too strong or striking, however, whether in colouring or dynamics; even an average forte is often far too loud for either the words or the music, in a context of six surrounding pages marked piano or pianissimo.

NOTES. 1. The Tieck source (see No. 43, note 1) has 'rauschet' not 'rauscht' at bar 30; Brahms prefers to preserve his dotted-crotchet rhythm unruffled.

2. The opening off-beat dominant pedal is a harmonious blend of M6/7 and M24; the five descending notes at 'treue Liebe wacht' and each 'ewig bin ich dein' here constitute a simple slumber motif. The ensuing canon at 'schlafe' etc is M12; the added thirds and sixths at e.g. 'ewig bin ich dein' embody the love-duetting of M18. The final cadence of the slumber-song interlude is remembered at 'Maria' in the opening viola solo of another lullaby, *Geistliches Wiegenlied* (No. 163). The rhythmic impetus that quickens from four sounds per bar up to 'Schweigt', then six quavers up to 'murmelt' and twelve semiquavers thereafter reflects the increasing activity in the background (M16). The major (5–6–5) in the right hand at 'stört nicht' etc is M19; the rhyme-induced sequences at 'Es lauscht' etc. are characteristic of this cycle. The Ab/A key-contrast of dark and bright is also expressive, while the dream-arpeggios for 'Phantasien' and 'Träume' are among the clearest instances of M9. All these are only examples of the deepest correspondences between words and music ever encountered in Brahms, or any lied-composer; and they typify his mature style.

3. Cf. Franz, Op. 1, No. 10; Spohr, Op. 72, No. 2.

52. (Op. 33, No. 10) Verzweiflung (Despair) by 1869
Ludwig Tieck   C minor e♭′–a♭″

> So tönet denn, schäumende Wellen,
> Und windet euch rund um mich her!

Mag Unglück doch laut um mich bellen,
Erbost sein das grausame Meer!

Ich lache den stürmenden Wettern,
Verachte den Zorngrimm der Flut,
O, mögen mich Felsen zerschmettern!
Denn nimmer wird es gut.

Nicht klag ich, und mag ich nun scheitern,
In wässrigen Tiefen vergehn!
Mein Blick werd sich nie mehr erheitern,
Den Stern meiner Liebe zu sehn.

So wälzt euch bergab mit Gewittern,
Und raset, ihr Stürme, mich an,
Dass Felsen an Felsen zersplittern!
Ich bin ein verlorener Mann.

So resound, then, foaming waves, and coil all about me [and coil all about me]! Let misfortune snarl aloud around me [let misfortune snarl aloud around me] and let the cruel sea rage [let the cruel sea rage]!

I laugh at the raging gales, I scorn the fury of the flood. If only the rocks would crush me, for I shall never [shall never] thrive [I shall never thrive].

I shall not lament though I now founder and drown in the watery depths! My gaze will never more be cheered by the sight of my love's star.

So roll down from the mountains in thunder, and rage at me, you storms [rage at me, you storms], so that rock splits upon rock! I am a lost man [a lost man].

As Magelone sleeps, Peter notices her red purse, which he inquisitively opens; it contains his three rings. As he lays it aside a raven flies down and makes off with it. He gives chase, but the bird soars out over the sea. There it drops the purse; Peter finds a rowing boat and puts out in it, but a storm wind blows him out of sight of land. In his desperate plight he sings the lyric above. The piano blusters in harsh semiquavers over an unsteady off-beat bass; the voice cries out in a wide arch of anguish. The word 'Wellen' (waves) is echoed in the keyboard, as if blown away in the storm. Then the music takes up arms against a sea of troubles. The hero's defiance of misfortune elicits a fanfare of horns and trumpets, interrupted by the returning tempest at 'Ich lache' where the mirthless laughter is heard in the left hand.

The mood softens at 'Nicht klag ich' (I shall not lament). But this statement is instantly rejected with both hands by the piano's semitonal moans. Similarly the gaze ('Blick') at love's star ('Stern') is audibly imagined despite the words. Here Brahms deliberately depicts the poem's unspoken hopes, which surface from the depths of despair with an irony worthy of Wolf at his finest, until all such feelings are finally flung aside as the huge drenching surges return, together with an imagined drowning in the depths.

NOTES. 1. In the Tieck source (see No. 43, note 1) the third word is 'dann', not 'denn'. The title is Tieck's, from a later edition of the poems.

2. The arpeggio waves are M5; the off-beat left-hand quavers of M29 express the hero's helplessness. The piano's echoes of 'Wellen' and later at 'nimmer' and 'Gewittern' are Schubertian, like so much else in this cycle; the top notes e.g. at 'grausame' and later 'nimmer' are M10. The vocal sequences at 'Mag Unglück' etc. and 'ich lache', to match the verbal repetition, are also characteristic of this opus. In the latter passage, the hollow left-hand laughter at and after 'lache' (M20) ironically belies the coming assertion 'nicht klag ich', while its major counterpart at 'mein Blick' (M19) also reverses the sense of the words. Meanwhile the virile defiance of 'O, mögen mich Felsen zerschmettern' is embodied in the tonic and dominant interchange of M31, here in F minor and C minor, much as already heard in *Traun! Bogen und Pfeil* (No. 44). The thirds and the converging voices at 'Stern meiner Liebe' are the love-motifs M17/18; in the clearer light of a later star (*Wie froh und frisch* No. 56, note 2) this one may also be seen as an image of Clara, with an analogue of her theme (M33) worn on the right hand at più adagio. The last low note, lost in the depths, is M6.

53. (Op. 33, No. 11) Wie schnell verschwindet (How soon they vanish) by 1869

Ludwig Tieck   F minor c'–f''

Wie schnell verschwindet
So Licht als Glanz,
Der Morgen findet
Verwelkt den Kranz,

Der gestern glühte
In aller Pracht,
Denn er verblühte
In dunkler Nacht.

Es schwimmt die Welle
Des Lebens hin,
Und färbt sich helle,
Hats nicht Gewinn;

Die Sonne neiget,
Die Röte flieht,
Der Schatten steiget
Und Dunkel zieht:

So schwimmt die Liebe
Zu Wüsten ab,
Ach, dass sie bliebe
Bis an das Grab!

Doch wir erwachen
Zu tiefer Qual:
Es bricht der Nachen,
Es löscht der Strahl,

Vom schönen Lande
Weit weggebracht
Zum öden Strande
Wo um uns Nacht.

How soon they vanish, the light and the radiance: morning finds the garland withered that yesterday glowed in splendour, for its flowers faded in the dark night.

The wave of life rolls onward; though brightly coloured, it profits nothing [though brightly coloured, it profits nothing].

The sun sets, the red glow vanishes, shadow arises and darkness comes.

So love drifts away into deserts. Oh, would it endure until the grave! But we awake to deep torment; the ship is wrecked, the sunlight dies.

We are wafted away from our lovely land to a barren shore where night surrounds us.

Meanwhile Magelone wakes and finds herself alone. After many days of wandering she comes to the cottage of an old shepherd and his wife, who ask her to stay with them. 'When the old couple were out, she looked after the house; and then often sang [the verses above] in her loneliness, as she sat at the front door with her spinning-wheel.' Brahms overhears her song and shares her sorrow; he is truly at home in such feelings, and the result is another masterpiece.

The prelude sings a melody which the voice repeats, as if recognising it from olden days, to a full chordal accompaniment which at 'gestern' (yesterday) lends a hand in recalling the tune. Already low octaves have been heard anticipating 'in dunkler Nacht' (in the dark night); wilting chromatics underline the phrase 'verwelkt den Kranz' (the garland withered) and the word 'verblühte' (faded). The melody recurs at 'Es schwimmt die Welle', and after an interlude that echoes the singer's sighs of regret the voice itself declines into its darker register at 'Röte flieht' and 'Dunkel zieht' as the red sunset glow fades and night prevails. Added patterns of falling semiquavers, with thirds in canon followed by arpeggios, show how swiftly love drifts away ('so schwimmt die Liebe'), with gathering momentum. At 'wir erwachen zu tiefer Qual' (we awake to deep torment) the right hand sings out, in eloquent octaves, the melody half heard earlier at 'gestern' etc; then the successive left-hand octave drops into darkness to depict the fate of the wrecked ship and the lost daylight. Finally the piano remodels the opening music with subtle changes of register and emphasis while the voice continues its sweet lamenting.

NOTES. 1. Brahms repeats little and alters nothing in Tieck's text (No. 43, note 1), as if he feels that his main task is to record the sweet sad song that Magelone sang.

2. Given the music's focus on the central figure of a deserted girl, the Clara theme C–B♭–A♭–G–A♭ in the opening bars and the melodic line passim (M33) may not be mere coincidence; nor may the dominant C pedal that often accompanies it, e.g. at bars 25–30. That C pedal is deliberately added at the reprise; it had already appeared alone at the second 'färbt sich helle', where the ensuing interlude, like the matching postlude, anticipates *Da unten im Tale* (No. 185), which is yet another variation on the theme of desertion.

3. The prelude's quasi-vocal mordent confirms that the melody is imagined as a solo song. The low octaves of darkness before 'Nacht', and at sunset ('die Sonne neiget') etc. typify M6; so do the octave drops described above. The sadly flattened sixths in various keys (e.g. at '*ver*blühte') are also motivic (M41), like the vocal sequences at e.g. 'färbt sich helle' etc. The consecutive tenths before and thirds at the reprise are M18; there the canons are M12 and the quickening rhythms M16. This ubiquitous yet unobtrusive motivic intensity is typically Brahmsian.

54. (Op. 33, No. 12) Muss es eine Trennung geben? (Must there be a parting?) by 1869

Ludwig Tieck   C minor f#'–f#''

> Muss es eine Trennung geben,
> Die das treue Herz zerbricht?
> Nein, dies nenne ich nicht leben,
> Sterben ist so bitter nicht.
>
> Hör ich eines Schäfers Flöte,
> Härme ich mich inniglich,
> Seh ich in die Abendröte,
> Denk ich brünstiglich an dich.
>
> Gibt es denn kein wahres Lieben?
> Muss denn Schmerz und Trennung sein?
> Wär ich ungeliebt geblieben
> Hätt ich doch noch Hoffnungsschein.
>
> Aber so muss ich nun klagen:
> Wo ist Hoffnung, als das Grab?
> Fern muss ich mein Elend tragen,
> Heimlich bricht das Herz mir ab.

Must there be a parting, which breaks the faithful heart? No, I cannot call this living; not even dying is so bitter.

When I hear a shepherd's flute, I suffer inward anguish; when I gaze at the sunset, I think ardently of you.

Is there then no real love, must there always be sorrow and separation? Had I remained unloved I should still have a gleam of hope.

But now this must be my lament; where is hope but in the grave? I must endure my misery far away; my heart breaks asunder in silence [my heart breaks asunder in silence].

Count Peter recovers from his despair (No. 52) only to find a great ship manned by Moors bearing down upon him; they take him prisoner as a present for their sultan, who employs him as a servant. 'Peter was generally loved, because the sultan viewed him so favourably. He often walked alone among the flowers of the garden, and thought of his beloved Magelone; in the evening hours too he often took a zither and sang' the verses above.

Perhaps the persistent downward arpeggios derive from Schumann's musing music of a walk among flowers in a garden accompanied by thoughts of the loved one, in *Am leuchtenden Sommermorgen*, Op. 48, No. 12. But the Brahmsian surroundings are far more formal; their main feature is melody, which is plotted in patterns and sequences. It seems to take some precedence over the sense of the words; thus the Schubertian major-mode simplicity at 'ist so bitter nicht' (is not so bitter) sounds unapt for a fate worse than death. The interlude repeats this phrase in augmentation, as if to underline or italicise it, a treatment which becomes finely effective at the words 'Denk ich brünstiglich an dich' (I think ardently of you) at the end of second verse. For the third, the melody is flattened to fit the sentiments of sorrow and separation. Then, for a moment or two, the zither's arpeggios are left in abeyance, while the voice speaks out, quasi parlando, and the piano sings its own especially expressive version of the main theme. The effect, at 'Wär ich ungeliebt geblieben' (Had I remained unloved) etc, is one of a signed statement from the composer made through the persona of Peter.

The main melodies with their cascade of falling arpeggios resume at 'Aber so muss ich nun klagen' (But now this must be my lament) etc; this time, though, the piano's echo of the final phrase is not overt in an interlude but covert in the accompaniment, as the heart breaks in silence. The vocal repetition is changed to the minor mode, which however resolves into the major in voice and piano, as if all sorrow is subsumed in a Schubertian sweetness.

NOTES. 1. For the Tieck source, see No. 43, note 1. Brahms's readings of 'Trennung' for 'Trauer' at bar 20 and 'bricht' (twice) for 'stirbt' in the last line are no doubt revealing; but they seem to be inadvertent slips that call for correction.

2. The downward arpeggios represent the breeze-blown movement of leaves or petals (here M4), as so often in Schumann, as well as a zither accompaniment; the decorative grupetti and portamenti in bars 6, 10, etc. are further evidence that this song, like its predecessor, is imagined as an accompanied solo in accordance with the poetic source. The augmentation of 'ist so bitter nicht' in the following piano interlude is also expressive, like the flattening (M41) of that phrase in the closing vocal line, where the minor–major shifts on the same tonic (M39), together with the piano's final tierce de Picardie, are Schubertian in their ambivalence. Meanwhile the plaintive consecutive thirds, marked espressivo, sigh for lost love at 'Wär ich ungeliebt'; M18.

55. (Op. 33, No. 13) Sulima (Sulima) May 1862
Ludwig Tieck   E major e′–f#″

> Geliebter, wo zaudert
> Dein irrender Fuss?
> Die Nachtigall plaudert
> Von Sehnsucht und Kuss.
>
> Es flüstern die Bäume
> Im goldenen Schein,
> Es schlüpfen mir Träume
> Zum Fenster herein.

Ach! kennst du das Schmachten
Der klopfender Brust?
Dies Sinnen und Trachten
Voll Qual und voll Lust?

Beflügle die Eile
Und rette mich dir,
Bei nächtlicher Weile
Entfliehn wir von hier.

Die Segel, sie schwellen,
Die Furcht ist nur Tand:
Dort, jenseit den Wellen
Ist väterlich Land.

Die Heimat entfliehet,
So fahre sie hin!
Die Liebe, sie ziehet
Gewaltig den Sinn.

Horch! wohllüstig klingen
Die Wellen im Meer,
Sie hüpfen und springen
Mutwillig einher,

Und sollten sie klagen?
Sie rufen nach dir!
Sie wissen, sie tragen
Die Liebe von hier.

Where, my love, do your straying steps tarry? The nightingale is warbling of yearning and kisses [of yearning and kisses].

The trees whisper in golden light, dreams slip in through my window [through my window].

Ah, do you know the longing of my beating heart? this musing and scheming, full of torment and delight? Give wings to your haste and rescue me; under cover of night we can escape from here [under cover of night we can escape from here].

The sails are swelling, your fears are mere folly, there across the waves lies the land of your fathers [there across the waves lies the land of your fathers].

My own homeland is dwindling, so let it go; the power of love draws my thoughts away [the power of love draws my thoughts away].

Listen! how sensual the waves sound in the sea, they leap and skip mischievously around us. And why should they lament? They are calling to you: they know they are taking love away from here [they know they are taking love away from here].

Peter had spent two years among the Moors, in the sultan's palace by the sea-shore, thinking ceaselessly of his parents and his beloved. But he in turn was beloved by the sultan's daughter Sulima, who like Magelone arranges a meeting with him and says she will elope with him. Peter agrees; he believes Magelone dead. But he later reproaches himself for his lack of faith: on the assigned night he again takes a boat and rows away. 'Then he heard the agreed signal; a zither sounded from the garden and a lovely voice sang' the verses above. 'The spirit of love soared through the golden sky; love strove to draw him back, love drove him onwards, the waves murmured melodiously in between, sounding like a song in a foreign language, whose sense could nevertheless be guessed.'

The sense of this music can be guessed from the prelude, which impatiently pirouettes on tip-toe in its eagerness to be off and away. Only a virtuoso pianist can sustain this feathery lightness, which endlessly preens and poises for notional flight. The prelude and the first two interludes have leaping left-hand octaves like conspiratorial heartbeats that illustrate apprehension as well as the 'Schmachten' (longing) that begins verse three; at that signal, these octaves join in with the singing. Here the voice changes its tune for variety's sake; but the new melody is just as eager and ingratiating as ever. The next two verses repeat the first two, and the sixth repeats the third. Here the leaping heart motif is heard as equally apt for the leaping waves; their knowledge that they are taking love away, at 'Sie wissen, sie tragen' etc. is illustrated by a brief left-hand disappearance down the keyboard, a hopeful voyage towards distant horizons. The postlude duly slips its moorings and sails away with brief hints of a pious Amen borne back on the breeze.

NOTES. 1. For the source, see No. 43, note 1. The title is also Tieck's, as in No. 52. The *Gesamtausgabe*'s misprint 'Frucht' at the beginning of verse five is corrected to 'Furcht' in the Peters edition.

2. The Schubert influence is heard here in echoes of his *Romanze des Richard Löwenberz* D907; there too a lover returns from distant captivity among the Moors. There are further manifest affinities with Schubert's *Normanns Gesang* D846, again a song of separated lovers; compare its cry 'Maria, mich wecken' etc. with bars 5–6 etc. here. In both those songs Schubert has the same insistent dotted-note hoof-beat rhythm; like Brahms's lighter flightier version (M3), its impatience is heard from the first bar to the last in a vivid image of swift travel. The upward octave leaps of the heart, and of the waves in the last verse; the vocal sequences at 'das Schmachten' etc to reinforce the rhymes; the final brief disappearing motif at the last 'Sie wissen, sie tragen'; the final Amens: all these are deliberate examples of the Brahmsian *Wortausdruck*. So perhaps the chromatic touches throughout are intended to evoke Moorish modalities.

56. (Op. 33, No. 14) Wie froh und frisch (How glad and fresh)
May 1869
Ludwig Tieck   G major d'–g"

> Wie froh und frisch mein Sinn sich hebt,
> Zurückbleibt alles Bangen,
> Die Brust mit neuem Mute strebt,
> Erwacht ein neu Verlangen.
>
> Die Sterne spiegeln sich im Meer,
> Und golden glänzt die Flut.

Ich rannte taumelnd hin und her,
Und war nicht schlimm, nicht gut.

Doch niedergezogen
Sind Zweifel und wankender Sinn;
O tragt mich, ihr schaukelnden Wogen,
Zur längst ersehnten Heimat hin.

In lieber, dämmernder Ferne,
Dort rufen heimische Lieder,
Aus jeglichem Sterne
Blickt Sie mit sanftem Auge nieder.

Ebne dich, du treue Welle,
Führe mich auf fernen Wegen
Zu der vielgeliebten Schwelle,
Endlich meinem Glück entgegen!

*How glad and fresh my spirits rise, all anxiety is allayed; new courage strives in my
breast, new [new] desire awakens.*

*The stars are mirrored in the sea and the tide shines gold [the tide shines gold]. Once
I rushed reeling this way and that, and was neither bad nor good.*

*But now doubts and hesitancies are laid low; oh, carry me, swaying waves, to the
homeland I have so long yearned for.*

*In the dear darkling distance, there the songs of home are calling; from every star she
looks down with a tender gaze [she looks down with a tender gaze]. Be calm, trusty
waves, lead me on distant paths to the much-loved threshold, at last [at last] towards
my happiness [at last, at last towards my happiness]!*

As Sulima's song dies away in the distance, Peter's boat is seized by the sea-wind.
He sits and sings the verses above. The brief prelude moves immediately to the
dominant, to match the mariner's mood. The gusting accompaniment fills the
sails; the voice exults. Then the music imagines a lull; at 'Die Sterne' (the stars)
etc. the surface of the sea is as serene as the night sky. The first 'golden glänzt die
Flut' (the tide shines gold) continues that relaxed contemplation; the second
extends it, by stretching out the same vocal melody's time-span, as the pianist's
hands, in the same steady rhythm, gradually move further and further apart in a
vivid panorama. Then the previously static right-hand triplets start to stray about,
in a restrained response to 'Ich rannte taumelnd' (I rushed reeling).

Now the winds and waves are reactivated. Again the arpeggios blow the boat
back towards the homeland; and at that word ('Heimat') successive waves billow
up from twelve bass keynotes, like nostalgia striking midnight. There ensues an
exultant vision of home and beauty, until this too is dispersed by the final joyous
reprise of sea and storm.

NOTES. 1. For the Tieck source see No. 43, note 1. There, 'sie' in the fourth strophe is
uncapitalised. *Pace* Friedländer (1922 42), the setting correctly begins the seventh line from
the end 'dort', not 'doch'; but Brahms certainly truncates the following 'einheimische' to

'heimische' (Lieder), whether through inadvertence, or just to suit his melodic line, or because he believed that the latter epithet (which adds the connotation of 'familiar' to the shared meaning of 'local') was better suited to his music and mood. In any event that change is now irreversible.

2. Brahms also seems to have capitalised the simple pronoun 'sie' to show that one She above all others is envisaged here, among the stars; that would explain why the twelve preceding Gs are treated as the dominant of a new key announced with nine bars, totalling twenty-nine beats, of C pedal, embellished with Clara themes (M33) at 'dämmernder Ferne' and 'jeglichem Sterne', in love-duet voice-and-piano thirds (M18).

3. The wind-and-wave accompaniment is M3/4; the left-hand E♭–D at 'Bangen' is M20; the intensified dominants before 'die Sterne' and 'Doch niedergezogen' are M24; the piano's bright high As at 'die Sterne' and the voice's final top Gs on 'Glück', 'endlich' and 'entgegen' are M10/11. After the first 'Flut', the vocal augmentation and the hands in contrary motion (M13) indicate the broad expanses of sky and sea. The quaver triplets that come roaming down the right hand at 'Ich rannte', bar 25, are clearly expressive, though their use is not noted elsewhere.

57. (Op. 33, No. 15) Treue Liebe dauert lange (True love lasts long) May 1869

Ludwig Tieck   E♭ major d'–a♭''

> Treue Liebe dauert lange,
> Überlebet manche Stund,
> Und kein Zweifel macht sie bange,
> Immer bleibt ihr Mut gesund.
>
> Dräuen gleich in dichten Scharen,
> Fordern gleich zum Wankelmut
> Sturm und Tod, setzt den Gefahren
> Lieb entgegen, treues Blut.
>
> Und wie Nebel stürzt zurücke,
> Was den Sinn gefangen hält,
> Und dem heitern Frühlingsblicke
> Öffnet sich die weite Welt.
>
> > Errungen,
> > Bezwungen
> > Von Lieb ist das Glück,
> > Verschwunden
> > Die Stunden,
> > Sie fliehen zurück:
> > Und selige Lust,
> > Sie stillet
> > Erfüllet
> > Die trunkene, wonneklopfende Brust;
> > Sie scheide
> > Von Leide

> Auf immer,
> Und nimmer
> Entschwinde die liebliche, selige, himmlische Lust!

True love lasts long, and outlives many [many] an hour; no doubts can make it anxious, its courage always stays sound [its courage always stays, always stays sound]. Even though it were menaced by close throngs of disaster and death together, calling for inconstancy, love would pit its faithful blood against such dangers.

And then, like mist, all the captors of the spirit [of the spirit] would disperse; and the wide world would open itself [the wide wide world would open itself] to the cheerful gaze of springtime.

Thus happiness is achieved and compelled by love,

the past flies away and vanishes, and blissful delight quietens and fulfils the ecstatic breast that beats for joy; let it part company with sorrow for ever and never [and never, and never] cease from [never cease from] lovely, blissful, heavenly delight

[heavenly delight! let it part company with sorrow for ever and never cease from blissful heavenly delight! True love lasts long; let it part company with sorrow for ever and never cease from lovely blissful heavenly delight]!

Count Peter's parents were desperate for news of their son. Then his mother's three rings were found in a fish being prepared for a feast, and restored to her: this she optimistically interpreted as a sign that he would one day return. He, meanwhile, had landed on an uninhabited island full of flowers, which poignantly reminded him of Magelone. It was as if the wind, moving among the blossoms, seemed to play on lute-strings and speak her sweet name 'which other people cannot recognise, but which I hear loudly and distinctly'. Thereupon 'he recalled a song that he had written years before and now repeated, as follows'; it is about the sweetness of those thoughts that lead one to the beloved. Brahms omits it, whether as too sentimental, or too revealing.

Peter resumes his travels, and eventually comes to the very cottage where Magelone now dwells. 'Before the door sat a beautiful slender girl, at whose feet a lamb played in the grass; and she sang' a long song about the joys of country life, which Brahms also omits from his cycle. Then the lovers gradually recognise each other and are joyously reunited. They journey to Peter's home in Provence and are married there; the King of Naples is reconciled to the union. Now comes the finale of the cycle as of the novella, which Tieck introduces thus: 'On the spot where he had again found his Magelone, Peter commanded a magnificent summer palace to be built . . . In front of it he and his young wife planted a tree; then they sang the following song, which they afterwards repeated at the same place every springtime.'

The prelude seems to say 'Die Liebe', in strong chords which continue, though deferentially shifted off the beat, as the voice enters with its heartening message. At 'Überlebet' (outlives) there is a change of time-signature and added rhythmic impetus in voice and piano, which leads to a quasi-operatic outburst at 'Stund' (hour). This relaxes at the last 'bleibt' (remains) only to break out again at the mention of overt menace ('Dräuen' etc). But the music of staunch defence and defiance sounds somewhat contrived, as if uncongenial to the composer's own nature. He is far more at home when returning to the original themes, now moving more fluently in the new 3/4 time. The adversarial vehemence resumes after 'Was den Sinn gefangen hält' (captors of the spirit) as if resisting arrest, while at the second 'weite Welt' the right-hand octaves range around the horizon. Now the rhythm varies again into crotchet triplets as the voice mounts up triumphantly at 'Errungen' (achieved).

All this has essentially served as a long introduction to the ensuing peroration, beginning at 'Verschwunden' (vanishes) as the sad past is dispelled and dispersed and all is made ready for lovely blissful heavenly delight. Here is the very music of Romantic wish-fulfilment-fantasy, which unfortunately suffers from the innate incoherence of the feelings it so fervently expresses.

NOTES. 1. For the Tieck source, see No. 43, note 1.

2. The ecstatic music overwhelms and submerges the words; hence the manifold repetitions. By the first 'himmlische Lust' Brahms has run out of text altogether; all the rest is da capo, in word and tone. The effort to impose structure on this last song and the whole cycle is only dubiously successful; thus the last bar's descending E♭–B♭–G–F–E♭, though no doubt deliberately intended as the homecoming by inversion of the ascending E♭–F–G–B♭–E♭ horn-passage that symbolises Peter's departure at the beginning of the cycle, is much more readily identifiable by the analytical mind than by the listening ear. Nevertheless this example certainly serves to show what significance Brahms attached to his manipulation of musical motifs and their meanings.

3. The musical structure is deliberately imposed on the poem throughout by arbitrary and copious textual repetition. The result is the most episodic song of the cycle, owing much to the ballad style of Schubert, whose voice is audible passim; thus the top G–A♭ climax at 'Brust' recalls *Du bist die Ruh* D776 at 'erhellt', soon after the word 'Brust'.

3. The omitted first beat in bars 5–8 is M29; the dotted-note left-hand motif of manly resolve heard at and after 'Stund', and after 'Dräuen' etc. is M31. The quickening rhythms throughout are M16. Perhaps Brahms remembered his treatment of 'Lieb (entgegen)' here (with typical sharp-key notation, M40) when he came to compose his last lieder: cf. the B major love-music sections of the fourth *Serious Song* Op. 121 (No. 204). The wide-ranging quaver triplets that roam up and down at 'weite Welt' are analogues of those at 'Ich rannte' etc. in the previous song. The sequences that match the rhyming lines at 'Errungen, bezwungen' etc. are also characteristic of this cycle. The arpeggio reverie at the first 'immer und nimmer' is M9: the alternating hands at 'nimmer entschwinde' etc. are an aspect of M30; the meaningfully expressive top notes at 'Brust' 'Lust' and 'se(lige)' are M10; the intensive dominant before the final 'Treue Liebe' is M24.

OPUS 43

Four songs (Gesänge) for solo voice with pianoforte accompaniment, published December 1868.

The piano has reverted to an accompanying function; only the titles, not the poets, are listed on the cover; and the choice of poems is in large measure personal rather than literary. But here the composer's authentic and individual voice resounds in two masterpieces; with the first two numbers in this set, the world acknowledged a worthy successor to the song-writing of Schubert and Schumann.

58. (Op. 43, No. 1) Von ewiger Liebe (Of love eternal) 1864
Heinrich Hoffmann von Fallersleben (from the Wendish)

B minor a–f#''

Dunkel, wie dunkel in Wald und in Feld!
Abend schon ist es, nun schweiget die Welt.

Nirgend noch Licht und nirgend noch Rauch,
Ja, und die Lerche sie schweiget nun auch.

Kommt aus dem Dorfe der Bursche heraus,
Gibt das Geleit der Geliebten nach Haus,

Führt sie am Weidengebüsche vorbei,
Redet so viel und so mancherlei:

'Leidest du Schmach und betrübest du dich,
Leidest du Schmach von andern um mich,

Werde die Liebe getrennt so geschwind,
Schnell wie wir früher vereiniget sind.

Scheide mit Regen und scheide mit Wind,
Schnell wie wir früher vereiniget sind.'

Spricht das Mägdelein, Mägdelein spricht:
'Unsere Liebe, sie trennet sich nicht!

Fest ist der Stahl und das Eisen gar sehr,
Unsere Liebe ist fester noch mehr.

Eisen und Stahl, man schmiedet sie um,
Unsere Liebe, wer wandelt sie um?

Eisen und Stahl, sie können zergehn,
Unsere Liebe muss ewig bestehn!'

Dark, how dark in forest and field! It is already evening, and now the world is silent. Nowhere a light, nowhere any smoke; yes, and the lark is now silent too.

Out from the village there comes a lad, seeing his sweetheart home; he takes her past the willow-copse, saying so much about so many things.

'If you suffer shame and sorrow, if you suffer shame in others' eyes for my sake, then let our love sunder suddenly, as fast as it once united us; let it depart in the rain and depart in the wind, as fast as it once united us.'

The girl speaks, the girl says: 'Our love will never sunder. Steel is firm, and so is iron, very much so, but our love is even firmer still.

Iron and steel can be reshaped, but who can change our love? Iron and steel can be melted down; our love [our love] must for ever [for ever] abide.'

Dark, how dark, say the first piano notes, anticipating the first words. The left hand of the four-bar prelude sings what will be the opening vocal phrase. Similarly the right-hand melody before 'Nirgend noch Licht' (Nowhere a light) is a predictive pre-echo of those words. Meanwhile the loving pair have become dimly discernible in the music, if only in outline, before they are mentioned in the poem. It is as if Brahms had written 'He' and 'She' (as e.g. in Nos. 148–9) on his piano accompaniment instead of the voice parts. After the finality of the falling fifth at 'schweiget nun auch' (is now silent too), meaning that all nature is stilled, the low notes of the repeated prelude sing in his voice, at 'Kommt aus dem Dorfe' (Out from the village), while her echoing strains are heard at the higher octave in the piano part; thus we are to envisage the poem's 'Bursche' and his 'Geliebte', the lad and his sweetheart, walking along hand in hand. This time his final 'mancherlei' (so many things) is left lingering on the open-ended dominant, as if to illustrate that concept; so much to say, and, as the recurring prelude confirms by breaking in at that moment, so little time to say it in.

Then he sings his heartfelt message, in the left-hand horn passages and strong octaves of virile assurance, further quickened by the triplet quavers of excited utterance, that they should perhaps part. But the music sounds empty and hollow; there are no thirds in the chords, and the tones lack real resolution. In an interlude, the horns abate into loving sixths and the insistent 3/4 rhythm softens into 6/8. Now she replies; and listeners are meant to hear the contrast between the male music of the agitated hunter and her own hushing lullaby tones, the calming and reassuring voice of mother Nature herself. Thus the horn-passages are preserved, but absorbed into the cradle-song. A repeated right-hand note speaks of unshakeable certitude. The metaphors of a strength beyond iron and steel are reinforced by lower repetitions of the lulling motif with added bass octaves. After 'noch mehr' (more still) the interlude muses and murmurs tenderly before the renewed strength of shared love. That sharing is symbolised by a union of his 3/4 and her 6/8 time into a mixture of both; in that strong bond the postlude reaffirms her conclusion that 'our love must for ever abide'.

So indeed it did, if this masterpiece embodies not only a favourite theme but also a deep personal significance. Brahms confided to a friend (as Kalbeck records, ii 300) that when he had played and sung it to Clara Schumann she sat without saying a word, and when he looked at her he saw that she could not speak for tears.

NOTES. 1. The famous text, to which Brahms added his own title, was taken from Hoffmann von Fallersleben's *Gedichte* (1837), already used as a song-source by Schumann. No doubt the composer had access to this same copy from the earliest days of his own enduring love for Clara, and the poem's clear relevance to that plight cannot have escaped him. Consciously or not, he concealed the connection by misattributing this rendering of a lyric from the Wendish (a Slav language still spoken in north-east Germany) to 'Joseph Wentzig' [sic]. These errors remained unrectified for over a century (until Sams 1972b) and have now been further compounded by an otiose ascription to Leopold Haupt (McCorkle 1984 155, followed by Stark 1995 111), whose German version was not only published four years later than Hoffmann's but is textually very different; it cannot have been Brahms's source.

2. Brahms had already set Wenzig translations from Moravian and Czech in 1863 (the two vocal quartets Op. 31 Nos. 2–3). But this song was started much earlier still; the eight-bar melody at 'Eisen und Stahl', even down to the detail of the gruppetto at 'wandelt', is repeated from an unpublished bridal chorus composed for the Hamburg ladies' choir (Kalbeck ii 129). Friedländer (1922, 44) calls this a 'proof' of music's ambiguity; but the fact is that both works are about lasting love; and the Uhland text of the bridal chorus had already been set by Schumann (Op. 146 No. 1). Even the gruppetto itself (here on 'trennet') is meaningful in both contexts; what lasts is music, in the form of a wedding-song.

3. Given the extreme aptness of the words, and Clara's reaction, her theme (M33) might be expected, in some suitable guise; cf. the vocal line at 'Schmach von an(dern) um mich' and again at 'früher vereiniget sind', with its first, third, fourth and fifth notes at the second 'vereiniget sind'.

4. Perhaps it was the element of immediate communication which so pleased the ferociously anti-Brahmsian Hugo Wolf, who found that this song was rightly considered Brahms's masterpiece, and praised its deeply-felt and atmospheric qualities.

5. The dark bass notes are M7; the first three of them, in diminution, are soon transmuted into the arpeggios of dream, M9. The left-hand horn passages at 'leidest du' are M22 and the ensuing dotted-rhythm octaves M31. The quaver triplets (M16) that made an image of motion in the two previous songs here insist upon the same pitch, in accordance with the theme of unchangeability. At the second 'leidest du Schmach' and in the interlude after 'sind' the consecutive tenths or thirds are M18; the succeeding time-change M26, while the final hemiolas at the last 'unsere Liebe' are M14. These latter are sometimes misinterpreted as wrenching the rhythm awry; on the contrary, they make an image of enduring certitude. So do the pedal notes at 'spricht das Mägdelein', M8; the murmuring interlude after 'noch mehr' expresses intimacy.

59. (Op. 43, No. 2) Die Mainacht (The May night) 1866
Ludwig Hölty, ed, J. Voss   E♭ major b♭–f♭''

> Wann der silberne Mond durch die Gesträuche blinkt
> Und sein schlummerndes Licht über den Rasen streut,
>   Und die Nachtigall flötet,
>   Wandl' ich traurig von Busch zu Busch.
>
> Überhüllet vom Laub girret ein Taubenpaar
> Sein Entzücken mir vor; aber ich wende mich,
>   Suche dunklere Schatten,
>   Und die einsame Träne rinnt.
>
> Wann, o lächelndes Bild, welches wie Morgenrot
> Durch die Seele mir strahlt, find ich auf Erden dich?
>   Und die einsame Träne
>   Bebt mir heisser die Wang herab.

When the silver moon gleams through the grove and strews its slumbering light on the lawn, and the nightingale is fluting, I wander sadly from bush to bush.

Covered over by leaves, two doves coo their ecstasy out at me; but I turn away and seek darker shadows, and the lonely tear trickles down.

When, O smiling vision that shines through my soul like sunrise, shall I find you here on earth? And the lonely tear trembles more hotly [hotly] down my cheek.

This song stands out among the brightest Brahmsian visions of the isolated outsider. The low left-hand minim notes or chords are followed by equally quiet right-hand quavers that vividly evoke soft footsteps on greensward at night. At 'die Nachtigall' the left-hand movement is briefly shifted off the beat, as if the music itself were standing still to listen. Then the walking resumes, in the minor, at 'wandl' ich traurig' (I wander sadly). For the second verse, the key and the imagery both change. Lefthand thirds nestle together; the right hand yearns. A climax is reached at 'aber ich wende mich' (I turn away), where the harmony is wrenched back to the tonic minor of sad wandering which returns at 'dunklere Schatten' (darker shadows) with the deep bass note that began the song. Now the lonely tear flows, with a poignant discord on 'Träne' and a brief interlude that culminates on a prolonged dominant seventh chord. Thus the question is posed; when? As the first strains return, the right hand's even quavers are urged into triplets as the tone of enquiry becomes more intense. The alien chords and intervals, departing far from the earlier diatonic harmonies and melodies, cry out 'nevermore'. And the last words and the postlude accept this verdict with a movingly resigned humility.

NOTES. 1. Perhaps the composer was also working on *An die Nachtigall* (No. 66), and felt that one pair of amorous Hölty birds would suffice for his 1860s song-writing; at least he omitted his source's original second strophe (between 'Busch' and 'Überhüllet'), about billing and cooing in the nest. But the topic remained a favourite; cf also *Das Mädchen spricht* (No. 198). Otherwise the Voss edition of Hölty's *Gedichte* (1804) is treated most respectfully, except that it has 'von' not 'vom' [Laub]. In particular the poetic imitation of Greek asclepiads, i.e. one spondee (— —), two choriambi (— ⌣ ⌣ —) and an iambus (⌣ —) reduced by one choriambus in the shorter last line of each strophe, is punctiliously preserved. See also No. 197, note 1.

2. In a conversation reported by George Henschel (1907, 22–3), Brahms selected this setting to illustrate his method of composition; he implies that having found the opening melodic phrase for 'Wann der silberne Mond' he left the song to one side for a considerable time; 'if afterwards I approach the subject again, it is sure to have taken shape'.

3. The initial low note, like that of *Von ewiger Liebe* (No. 58), has the darkness of M7; the rootless second inversions in bars 1–4 are motifs of floating, as in *Immer leiser* (No. 187). The absence of a first beat in the left hand at bars 9–10 is M29: each reference to the sombre tonality of E♭ minor (at bars 11–14 and 23–5) is also motivic. The sighing to illustrate 'girret' is M21; the top E♭s on each 'Träne' and F♭s on 'wende mich' and 'heisser' are M10; the flattened supertonic at 'heisser' (M23) tells of inconsolable despair, later somewhat softened and soothed into resignation by the flattened notes (M41) of the postlude.

3. Cf. Schubert's D194, which uses all four strophes of the Voss source.

60. (Op. 43, No. 3) Ich schell mein Horn ins Jammertal (I sound my horn into the valley of sorrow) by 1860
attrib. Ulrich von Württemburg   B♭ major a'–f''

Ich schell mein Horn ins Jammertal,
Mein Freud ist mir verschwunden,

Ich hab gejagt, muss abelahn,
Das Wild lauft vor den Hunden.
Ein edel Tier in diesem Feld
Hatt ich mir auserkoren,
Das schied von mir, als ich wohl spür,
Mein Jagen ist verloren.

Fahr hin, Gewild, in Waldes Lust!
Ich will dir nimmer schrecken
Mit Jagen dein schneeweisse Brust,
Ein Ander muss dich wecken
Mit Jägers Schrei und Hundebiss,
Dass du nit magst entrinnen;
Halt dich in Hut, mein Tierle gut!
Mit Leid scheid ich von hinnen.

Kein Hochgewild ich fahen kann,
Das muss ich oft entgelten,
Noch halt ich stät auf Jägers Bahn
Wie wohl mir Glück kommt selten.
Mag mir nit g'bührn ein Hochwild schön,
So lass ich mich begnügen
An Hasenfleisch, nit mehr ich heisch,
Das mag mich nit betrügen.

I sound my horn into the valley of sorrow; my joy has escaped me. I have been hunting but must now abandon the chase; the game eludes my hounds. I had chosen a noble beast in this field; it fled from me, as I well see – all my hunting is in vain.

So run away, my prey, into the delight of the forest; I shall never frighten your snow-white breast with my hunting, another will have to rouse you with hunting cries and biting dogs so that you cannot escape; be on your guard, good little doe, with a heavy heart I take my leave.

I cannot catch any noble beast, I must often suffer for that, yet I shall constantly follow the hunter's track, although good fortune seldom comes my way. If no lovely doe will ever fall to my lot, I must learn to relish hare's flesh; I ask no more, that won't deceive me.

Brahms must have spent much time in this same valley of sorrow. The original sixteenth-century poem has been attributed to the keen huntsman and amateur musician Ulrich von Württemburg, who felt constrained to make a loveless marriage for social reasons. But such sentiments would hardly have inspired Brahms, who surely interpreted the poem as a stylised lament for the loss of a high-born love and the consequent need to make do with common flesh. Such topics came disconcertingly close to a composer who both idolised and despised womankind. But the poetry also moved him to provide the perfect tonal equivalent for an elaborate formal allegory of courtly love in the Minnesang or troubadour tradition. As the words insistently stress the poetic themes of hunting, prey and sorrow, so the same chords (tonic, mediant and dominant) constantly reappear. Thus words and music alike are obsessed with a lost deer or dear, in a typical sixteenth-century allegory. No doubt in homage to that same style, each of the piano's sixty-six chords is in root position. The intended effect is one of plain upright rural sincerity, with a consort of hunting-horns; but unless the listener shares Brahms's affinity with early music the result throughout three solemn verses may tend to pall.

NOTES. 1. Brahms's source seems to have been C.F. Becker's anthology *Lieder und Weisen vergangener Jahrhunderte* (1850). 'Abelahn' in the first verse is the modern 'ablassen'; 'fahen' in the third is 'fangen'. Uhland's *Volkslieder* version of this text is entitled 'Herzog Ulrich 1510'. For the rhyme's sake, the last word should be 'betrügen', as in Uhland and Peters, not the *Gesamtausgabe*'s 'betrüben'.

2. The strict AABA' bar-structure 1–11 = 12–22: 23–33: 36–47 is worth noting. There are further internal repetitions (thus in B 23–5 = 26–8) and elaborations (thus A' adds bass notes, and a quasi-coda decorates the penultimate syllable of each verse). In that coda, the pattern D–C–B♭–A–B♭, may well be a Clara-theme (M33), and a date of *c.* 1858 might also suggest the enciphered presence of Agathe, in some unrecoverable transposition. They were both noble women; Brahms chased both and captured neither.

3. The predictable horn passages of M22 recreate the chase; the recurrent minor mediant triads, sometimes with the third omitted (M29), evoke the feelings of hollow frustration as well as an ancient German historic past.

4. Brahms had already set the same text for male voice chorus, as Op. 41 No. 1; its opening words, 'ich schwing' should be 'ich schell', as here.

61. (Op. 43, No. 4) Das Lied vom Herrn von Falkenstein (The song of the lord of Falkenstein) by 1857

Anon.   C minor c'–g''

Es reit der Herr von Falkenstein
Wohl über ein breite Heide,
Was sieht er an dem Wege stehn?
Ein Mädel mit weissem Kleide.

'Gott grüsse euch, Herrn von Falkenstein!
Seid ihr des Lands ein Herre,
Ei so gebt mir wieder den Gefangnen mein
Um aller Jungfrauen Ehre!

'Den Gefangnen mein, den geb ich nicht,
Im Turm muss er verfaulen!
Zu Falkenstein steht ein tiefer Turm,
Wohl zwischen zwei hohen Mauren.'

'Steht zu Falkenstein ein tiefer Turm
Wohl zwischen zwei hohen Mauren,
So will ich an die Mauren stehn
Und will ihm helfen trauren.'

Sie ging den Turm wohl um und wieder um;
'Feinslieb, bist du darinnen?
Und wenn ich dich nicht sehen kann,
So komm ich von meinen Sinnen'.

Sie ging den Turm wohl um und wieder um,
Den Turm wollt sie aufschliessen:
'Und wenn die Nacht ein Jahr lang wär,
Kein Stund tät mich verdriessen!'

Ei, dörft ich scharfe Messer trag'n,
Wie unsers Herrn sein Knechte,
So tät ich mit Dem von Falkenstein
Um meinen Herzliebsten fechten!'

'Mit einer Jungfrau fecht ich nicht,
Das wär mir eine Schande!
Ich will dir deinen Gefangnen gebn,
Zieh mit ihm aus dem Lande.'

'Wohl aus dem Land da zieh ich nicht,
Hab Niemand was gestohlen;
Und wenn ich was hab liegen lahn,
So darf ichs wieder holen.'

The lord of Falkenstein rides over the wide moorland. What does he see standing in his path? A girl in a white dress [yes, dress].

'God be with you, lord of Falkenstein. If you are master of this land, then give me back my prisoner, for the honour of all maidens [yes, honour].'

'I shall not give you my prisoner, he must rot in the tower, the deep tower that stands at Falkenstein between two high walls [yes, walls].'

'If a deep tower stands at Falkenstein between two high walls, then I shall stand by those walls and help him grieve [yes, grieve].'

She went right round the tower and round again: 'Are you there within, my dear love? And if I can't see you I shall go out of my mind.'

She went right round the tower and round again, she wanted to unlock the tower; 'and even though this night was a year long, no hour of it would weary me.

If only I could carry sharp knives, like our lord's servants, then for my dearest sweetheart's sake I'd fight with the lord of Falkenstein [yes, fight].'

'I can't fight with a girl, that would disgrace me! I'll give you your prisoner; leave this land with him [yes, land].'

'I shall not leave this land, I have never stolen anything from anyone, and if I've left anything behind I've every right to go back and fetch it [yes, fetch it].'

Bare detached octaves and unisons in a relentless rhythm tell the story, set the scene and paint the picture, with a wide interval brushstroke at 'breite Haide' (wide moorland), questioning pauses at 'sieht' (sees) and 'stehn' (stand) and a softened seventh for the answer: 'Ein Mädel' (a girl). The listener sees a lone rider confronted by a loving petitioner. She is no mere pleader; she has justice on her side, and unconquerable courage. After 'Kleide' (dress) the leaping left-hand octaves gesture like small but defiant fists brandished upwards at a mounted tyrant. Now the staccato octaves are broken; the solo ride has been interrupted by dialogue. The earlier hint of modulation from C minor into A flat major is briefly broadened into explicit statement at 'aller Jungfrauen Ehre' (the honour of all maidens) before relapsing into the austere home key with repeated gestures. In verse four the melody becomes even more insistent upon tonic and dominant, and the right hand's single notes become chords, to match the heroine's obstinate resistance. But then the music mellows in tune with her mood; a warmly maternal A flat major is confirmed as the key to her character. Without any change in rhythmic urgency, which is indeed reinforced by the direction 'drängend' (pressing), the ballad becomes a love-song. In verse seven however the original defiance returns and continues to the end, with a rather inconsequential last verse and an abrupt ending without postlude, which risks anticlimax save in superlative performance.

NOTES. 1. The text seems to have been conflated from the *Stimmen der Völker* volume of Herder's *Sämtliche Werke* (1827–30), which Brahms owned, together with *Des Knaben Wunderhorn* (1806–8) and the Kretzschmer–Zuccalmaglio *Deutsche Volkslieder* I (1838). Brahms has somewhat bowdlerised the original words, presumably to preserve his idealised white-clad girl from the unrecognised lord's impudent inquiry 'wollt ihr die Nacht mein Schlafbuhle sein?'. In his setting, she knows and and names him from the first, as in the Low German version found in Uhland's *Volkslieder* (1844) 'God gröte ju heren von Falkensten'; so presumably Brahms knew that text too. He also repeats the last word of almost every couplet with an interpolated 'ja', in imitation of the old German ballad style (like Uhland's added 'aber' in Schumann's *Ballade* Op. 139 No. 7).

2. This intense personal involvement is typical, and explicable. From 1856, Brahms lived in Detmold, near Falkenburg; whenever he walked that way he 'always used to declaim [the poem], until one day he composed it' (Kalbeck i 313). Of course its theme of a man's unfair and tragic incarceration and a one-woman campaign for his release would have reminded Brahms of the doomed and demented Schumann in his Endenich asylum *c*. 1856, even without the insistent pedal Cs thirty-six times in bars 11–17 etc. and the Clara-theme (M33) E♭–D–C–B–C concealed as an inner voice at the final 'Ehre' of verse two (and similarly in parallel passages).

3. The trotting staccato octaves are M1; the lifting C octaves are also expressive; the flattened seventh (cf. M41) at 'aller Jungfrauen', anticipates the girl's key of A♭ major at 'Sie ging' etc. The top notes at 'Sinnen' and 'verdriessen' in that section are M10. At the latter word the *Gesamtausgabe* misprints the first left-hand note as C instead of the B♭, correctly given in the Peters edition.

62. (No op. no.) Regenlied (Rain Song) by 1866
Klaus Groth   G minor d'–g''

> Regentropfen aus den Bäumen
> Fallen in das grüne Gras,
> Tränen meiner trüben Augen
> Machen mir die Wange nass.

Scheint die Sonne wieder helle,
Wird der Rasen doppelt grün;
Doppelt wird auf meinen Wangen
Mir die heisse Träne glühn.

*Raindrops are falling from the trees on to the green grass; tears from my sad eyes are
making my cheeks wet [my cheeks wet].*

*When the sun shines out again the grass looks twice as green; on my cheeks the hot
tear will gleam [the hot tear will gleam] twice as bright.*

Groth's lachrymose allegory seems to suggest that love requited is, for some secret
reason, even sadder than love lost. This idea might well have appealed to Brahms
personally; at least he lavishes all his art on these unpromising verses both here and
in *Nachklang*, a later setting of the same poem (No. 103), However, this song
(catalogued as WoO 23, McCorkle 539) never quite comes to life, and the composer left it unpublished among his papers; it was first issued by the Brahms
Gesellschaft in 1908, eleven years after his death. Its melodic and motivic invention sound somewhat contrived; thus the detached tear-drops fall rather too
pat in the right-hand prelude, interlude and postlude. But it is well worth an
occasional hearing.

NOTES. 1. Brahms owned a presentation copy of his friend Groth's *Paraliponema zum
Quickborn* (1854), on which the poet inscribed these verses in May 1856. No doubt the
setting was begun then (the Mendelssohnian overtones of bars 13–16 suggest an early date);
but progress was slow. The later and far more successful setting (No. 103) confirms both
Brahms's dissatisfaction with this one and his personal involvement with the poem.

2. The Clara theme M33, here as it were literally C–B♭–A–G#–A as in Schumann's *Die
Lotosblume*, occurs within the words 'Tränen meiner trüben Augen machen' in this song as
in the otherwise very different *Nachklang*; it also recurs here at 'auf meinen Wangen mir'.

3. Whatever the merits of this setting, much careful thought went into its making, in
such subtle details as the slight brightening of the opening melody from minor to major
(M39) at 'Scheint die Sonne wieder'. The duetting thirds and sixths are M18; their mezzo-
staccato tear-drop minor supertonics are equally motivic (M23). The offbeat semiquavers
after 'Gras' are M29; the meaningful top notes at 'doppelt' (bis) and 'heisse' are M10.

OPUS 46

Four songs (Gesänge) for solo voice with pianoforte accompaniment, published
in October 1868.

Op. 43 was well received; so Brahms felt able to publish almost all the rest of
his completed song-output, as Opp. 46–9, all of which specify the poetic sources.

63. (Op. 46, No. 1) Die Kränze (The Wreaths) *c.* 1864
Georg Daumer (from the Greek)   D♭ major e♭'–g♭''

Hier ob dem Eingang seid befestiget,
Ihr Kränze, so beregnet und benetzt

Von meines Auges schmerzlichem Erguss!
Denn reich zu tränen pflegt das Aug der Liebe,
Dies zarte Nass, ich bitte,
Nicht allzu frühe träufet es herab.
Spart es, bis ihr vernehmet, dass sie sich
Der Schwelle naht mit ihrem Grazienschritte,
Die Teuere, die mir so ungelind.
Mit einem Male dann hernieder sei es
Auf ihres Hauptes goldne Pracht ergossen,
Und sie empfinde, dass es Tränen sind;
Dass es die Tränen sind, die meinem Aug
In dieser kummervollen Nacht entflossen.

Here above the portal shall you be fastened, you wreaths, so rained upon and bedewed by the sorrowful outpouring of my eyes; for the eyes of love are inured to copious weeping.

Do not, I implore you, shed this delicate moisture all too soon. Retain it until you hear her approaching the threshold with her step like the Graces – my adored one, who is so ungentle to me.

Then let it suddenly be showered down on to the golden glory of her head, and let her sense that these are tears [that these are tears] shed by my eyes in this distressful night.

The German text, headed *Hellas* (i.e. ancient Greece) in the 1855 Daumer source, is rather graceless in its diction as well as its booby-trap theme; but its pastiche of the classical pentameter, designed to bring the spirit of ancient Greece and Rome 'a little nearer to the German public', as the poet puts it, is not without its appeal. Daumer's avowed aim was to 'create a truly national work, that is to say, one corresponding to the universality of German spirit and taste'; and in so saying he spoke for the national nineteenth-century movement in song-writing started by Schubert and continued by Schumann,[1] which consciously strove to speak for all mankind. That latter influence is predictably present throughout this song; and Brahms is far more adept than Daumer in showing how German art can absorb and recreate the golden age. At the same time, the skill and sensitivity of this setting surely indicate some powerful personal involvement; and in 1864 the immediate golden age for Brahms was his adoration of the beautiful blonde seventeen-year-old Elisabet von Stockhausen. He had accepted her as a piano pupil in the 1862–3 Vienna season, but suddenly cancelled the lessons in his typical reaction of simultaneous commitment and withdrawal.

His true feelings are indelibly written in his music, here and elsewhere. The piano prelude is a gentle processional march to the temple of Venus; the faithful worshipper brings his votive offering. The repeated motif

[1] E. Sams, *The Songs of Robert Schumann* 3/1993, pp. 5–6 and *passim*.

is deliberately designed to distil tear-drops; but the major key and interval disclose that there is pleasure amid, even perhaps because of, the pain in the poem.

NOTES. I. The source was Daumer's *Polydora* (1855), which Brahms owned. There, the poem is untitled. It emphasises 'sie' in line seven, meaning the one and only; so does the music, if only by placing that word on the first beat (of bar 31).

2. It may not be coincidence that the monogram E. S. (S = Es = E♭) in German, following Schumann's transliteration in *Carnaval* and elsewhere) appears here, as E–D#, in a brief piano solo introduction (bar 28) to the imagined appearance of the beloved with her 'Grazienschritte', and reappears pat in the middle of 'ihres Hauptes goldne Pracht' (bars 41–2). Indeed, the semitonal interval thus formed may even have been the original inspiration, heard in the staccato right-hand notes (M20) before and during the 'schmerzlichem Erguss' at bars 9–13. All the songs of Opp. 46, 47 and 49 were sent as a Christmas present in 1884 to Elisabet and her husband since 1868, the composer Heinrich von Herzogenberg; this one (ii 49) was the first of the few that she singled out for special praise of their 'hidden gold' (sic) mintage.

3. The 'tears of joy' motif illustrated above is a sweet blend of detached tear-droplets (also falling pat in the vocal line at 'träufet es herab') and the major 5–6–5 symbol of delight (M19). These pleasure-and-pain motifs are almost masochistic in their intensity. As the sighs of M21 *passim* suggest, this is passionate music, also embodied in the loving thirds and sixths of M18. The vocal lines at 'Aug der Liebe', 'ungelind' and 'entflossen' at the end of each verse have an assured cadential finality; their top notes are M10. The flattened sevenths and sixths of the postlude are also motivic (M41).

64. (Op. 46, No. 2) Magyarisch (A Magyar song) *c.* 1868 (melody earlier)

Georg Daumer (from the Hungarian)   A major e'–f#''

> Sah dem edlen Bildnis in des Auges
>   Allzu süssen Wunderschein,
> Büsste so des eigenen Auges heitern
>   Schimmer ein.
>
> Herr mein Gott, was hast du doch gebildet
>   Uns zu Jammer und zu Qual
> Solche dunkle Sterne mit so lichtem
>   Zauberstrahl!
>
> Mich geblendet hat für alle Wonnen
>   Dieser Erde jene Pracht;
> All umher, wo meine Blicke forschen,
>   Ist es Nacht.

In gazing at that noble portrait I looked into the all too sweet marvellous radiance of her eyes; and thus I forfeited the serene gleam of my own.

    O Lord God, why did you create, for our woe [for our woe] and torment, such dark stars with so bright a magic ray?

    That glory has blinded me to all the bliss of this world; all around, wherever my gaze goes questing, it is night [all around, wherever my gaze goes questing, it is night, it is night].

Each of the poem's three quatrains has four trochaic lines of five, four, five and two feet respectively. Brahms robustly obliterates that unique metric pattern by pauses and repetitions; but these add real feeling and significance which relax Daumer's typically strained rhetoric into a masterpiece of tenderness and regret, tinged with more than a touch of good-humoured resignation.

The prelude hums its own idea of a Magyar or Hungarian tune, as a tribute to the poet's stated source. The girl looks like a dark-eyed gypsy, and her portrait is perhaps a keepsake in a locket; the gazer opens its cover and instantly falls under her spell, like Tamino in *The Magic Flute*. The opening words are lovingly yet unobtrusively stressed by silence from the piano and a rising sixth, as the voice repeats and the right hand duplicates the opening melody. The parallels and repetitions are in folksong style; so are the hunting horn passages, at 'Herr, mein Gott' (O Lord God) that symbolise not only the open air and the countryside but also the chase with all its thrills, excitements and frustrations. The idea of love's torment ('Jammer … Qual') is tellingly depicted by an excursion into the tonic minor, followed by the flat supertonic of that key with a sad echo from the piano and a top note from the voice. But the immediate return of bright hunting-horns shows that the torment is at least bearable, if not indeed actively pleasurable. After 'Zauberstrahl' (magic ray) there is a new descending theme in the right hand, which will soon be developed into the final drooping melody of 'ist es Nacht'. Thus night falls early; and at the second 'wo meine Blicke forschen' (wherever my gaze goes questing) the vocal line gropes around in the gloom. Finally the bright A major thickens back into the low left-hand octave from which the prelude began. By such apparently artless devices the contrasting visual ideas of the poem, bright eyes and black looks, are mirrored with an enhanced depth of reflection.

NOTES. I. The source was Daumer's *Polydora* (1855), which Brahms owned. There, the text is untitled.

2. Brahms was surely thinking of Clara; note how her theme D–C#–B–A–B (M33) graces the vocal line at the words 'süssen Wunderschein', '(hei)tern Schimmer ein' and 'Erde jene Pracht'. Hence also perhaps the A major of Schumann's equally masterly *Intermezzo* Op. 39, No. 2, on the same theme of portrait-gazing, beginning 'Dein Bildnis' and also clearly addressed to Clara by name. Analysis will disclose further thematic affinities.

3. The accompaniment's parallel thirds or tenths are M18; the diminution of bars 3–6 in 9–10 is also deliberately expressive. The horn-passages (bars 23–6, 31–3, 50–53) are M22; the flat supertonic chord of M23 exemplifies 'Jammer'; the last bar's low octave is M7, to illustrate 'Nacht'; the decorative turn on the last chord is a Schumannian embellishment, an audible tribute to beauty.

4. The careful bar-structure is worth noting: 1–6 = 7–10; 7–14 = 15–22; 23–6 = 50–53; etc.

5. Max Friedländer (50) found it strange that this song should show no Hungarian traits. But other listeners will surely hear the typical strains of the slower and more sedate movements among the *Hungarian Dances* WoO 1 or the *Zigeunerlieder* Op. 103. Indeed, Brahms had included the complete melody, with a figured bass, under the rubric *Ungrische*

Volksweisen in his own MS collection of folksongs *c.* 1854, though it may well be his own invention. Other airs from the same source were used in the *Hungarian Dances* (McCorkle 697–9).

65. (Op. 46, No. 3) Die Schale der Vergessenheit (The chalice of oblivion) by 1868

Ludwig Hölty, ed. J. Voss   E major e♭′–g#″

> Eine Schale des Stroms, welcher Vergessenheit
>   Durch Elysiums Blumen rollt,
> Bring, o Genius, bring deinem Verschmachtenden!
>   Dort, wo Phaon die Sängerin,
> Dort, wo Orpheus vergass seiner Eurydice,
>   Schöpf den silbernen Schlummerquell!
> Ha! dann tauch ich dein Bild, spröde Gebieterin,
>   Und die lächelnde Lippe voll
> Lautenklanges, des Haars schattige Wallungen,
>   Und das Beben der weissen Brust,
> Und den siegenden Blick, der mir im Marke zuckt,
>   Tauch ich tief in den Schlummerquell.

A chalice filled from the stream that rolls oblivion through Elysium's flowers – bring this, O guardian spirit, to him who is languishing for love [him who is languishing for love]. There, where the poetess forgot Phaon, and Orpheus his Eurydice, draw water from the silver springs of sleep. Ah, then shall I immerse your image, my coy mistress, and your smiling lips full of lute music, and the shadowy ripples of your hair, and the heaving of your white breast, and the conquering gaze that shoots through my inmost marrow; all these shall I dip deep in the springs of sleep [dip deep in the springs of sleep].

In classical mythology, a 'genius' or guardian spirit presided over the life of each individual. Phaon was a boatman of Mytilene in Lesbos, who was magically transformed into the handsomest of men; the poetess Sappho is said to have drowned herself for unrequited love of him. No doubt Hölty had been reading Ovid, who tells that story in his *Heroides* 21, and also recounts the far more famous legend of Orpheus and his Eurydice in the *Metamorphoses* 10 and 11. We are to understand that these are examples of a love so enduring that it could be stilled only by a draught of Lethe, a river endowed with the power to make dead souls forget all their earthly experience, so that they could enjoy untroubled felicity in the flower-filled fields of Elysium. There, the waters of Lethe would have to be drunk by poetic licence; that river traditionally ran through hell rather than heaven.

Granted all that foreknowledge, to which Brahms had ready access, the lyric is affecting in its alloy of restrained classical metre and poignant romantic regret, which the music transmutes into pure and noble metal. This rich and beautiful personal statement unites the outward coolness and the inward fire which characterised Brahms as man and musician.

That fire may not be readily recognisable. Max Friedländer (50) quotes and explicitly rejects the comment on this song made by the musicologist and historian Philipp Spitta in a letter to Brahms: 'Ein brennender fieberhafter Schmerz wühlt darin' (a burning feverish pain gnaws within it). But Spitta was close to the composer, and may well have known something of the surrounding circumstances. It is also relevant that Brahms himself had disparaged this work as 'wüst' (barren) in conversation with his friend and admirer Hermann Deiters, and had decided to withhold it from publication. His mind was changed by another close friend, the singer Stockhausen, who performed it memorably and convincingly on a morning visit (Kalbeck ii 300). Very few other songs were the subject of so much recorded discussion; there is surely something very specially personal about this one. It may well embody Brahms's suppressed passion for his young pupil Elisabet von Stockhausen.

Voice and piano begin together, to match the poetic device of apostrophe. At first the longed-for streams trickle in truncated quaver triplets over a low moan in the left hand. But soon they flow free, as Lethe rolls, in a symbolised river of dreams. At the repeated 'bring deinem Verschmachtenden' (bring to him who is languishing for love) the vocal line itself becomes so fluid and wavering as to need a new firm 3/4 rhythm from the accompaniment. This in turn changes at 'Dort' (there) to small moans of regret until the river runs again, in suitably slow and drawn-out tones, at 'schöpf den silbernen Schlummerquell' (draw water from the silver springs of sleep). Now the sighs and the waves converge again, and the opening strains return, diversified with arpeggios as before and a new melody from the piano after (and perhaps meant to imitate) the smiling sound of the lute, at 'Lautenklanges' etc. Finally a new triplet movement and low octaves plumb the desired depths of oblivion.

NOTES. 1. Both the original poem and its adaptation cited above had the genitive Phaons, which Brahms modernised to Phaon. Again the limpid Hölty source (given in Friedländer) was heavily clouded by editorial amendment; but as usual the Voss admixture (first printed in his *Musenalmanach* for 1777, but no doubt set by Brahms from the Hölty–Voss editions of 1782 and later) imparted a special flavour that audibly appealed to the composer and is not without its own poetic merit.

2. Each of the first four bars begins 'E–S' (E–D#) in the left hand, soon echoed at '[Ver]gessen[heit]', before and at the second 'Verschmach[tenden]', and in both hands thereafter, the second time as a modulatory link, F♭–E♭, in the new key of A♭ major. The same motif reappears in the original E major at and after 'dein Bild', before and at the key word '[Ge]biete[rin]', at 'Lauten', '[schatti]ge Wal[lungen]', in the keyboard lute-motif after 'Beben', at 'Brust' and at '[Blick] der mir' and the next bar. Then those notes vanish, as if already steeped in Lethe. This obsessive E–S motif (M35) surely signifies Elisabet von Stockhausen, whom Brahms adored, and with whom he maintained a close friendship once she was safely married. That might at least explain his otherwise puzzling misgivings about this masterwork; he may have feared that its element of artifice was too obtrusive. It was among the songs that Brahms sent to Elisabet in a new edition as his 1884 Christmas present; her specific reaction to it is not recorded.

3. On any hypothesis, the relation of thematic material to structure will repay special study. The integration of successive inventions, and their relevance to the poem, represent Brahms at his finest.

4. The various triplet or duplet quaver wave-motions in the right hand are M5; the left-hand arpeggios of dream at bars 8–14 are M9; the key-change to A♭ major provides a fitting frame for the classical portraits of Phaon and Sappho, Orpheus and Eurydice; the main motif's descending semitonal moan also serves as M20, at bars 27–8, 41–2 etc.; the five-note descent to the tonic, whether minor at '[Ver]schmachtenden' or major at each 'Schlummerquell' is a symbol of slumber; the postlude's final descent into left-hand oblivion has the darkness of M7.

66. (Op. 46, No. 4) An die Nachtigall (To the nightingale) by 1868

Ludwig Hölty, ed. J. Voss   E major d#'–g''

> Geuss nicht so laut der liebentflammten Lieder
>   Tonreichen Schall
> Vom Blütenast des Apfelbaums hernieder,
>   O Nachtigall!
> Du tönest mir mit deiner süssen Kehle
>   Die Liebe wach;
> Denn schon durchbebt die Tiefen meiner Seele
>   Dein schmelzend Ach.
>
> Dann flieht der Schlaf von neuem dieses Lager,
>   Ich starre dann
> Mit nassem Blick und totenbleich und hager
>   Den Himmel an.
> Fleuch, Nachtigall, in grüne Finsternisse,
>   Ins Haingesträuch,
> Und spend im Nest der treuen Gattin Küsse;
>   Entfleuch, entfleuch!

Do not pour the sonorous tones of your love-inflamed songs so loudly down from the blossoming bough of the apple-tree, O nightingale! With your sweet throat you sing love awake in me, for already the depths of my soul are thrilling through and through with your melting lament [your melting lament].

Then sleep flees anew from this couch; then, with moist gaze, pale as death and haggard, I stare at the sky. Fly, nightingale, into the green darkness, into the bushes of the grove, and there in your nest lavish kisses on your faithful bride; fly, fly away.

The words are overwrought. But the intense empathy of this poignant masterpiece makes them serene and sincere. In the prelude, the piano sighs and brings its two hands imploringly together; then the long-drawn-out vocal line and the left hand coincide and converge in four aptly full minims at 'tonreichen Schall' (sonorous tones). Thus the dark stirrings of feathered life among leaves, followed by full-throated bird-song, are subtly symbolised and shared. The sung melody itself has two matching halves, ending at 'O Nachtigall' like slow soft wings, and this symmetry adds its own subliminal effect. So do the left-hand minims that then descend on to the dominant; they are later to become the vocal line of the second 'dein schmelzend Ach' (your melting lament), in the tonic, and will be heard again sung by the right hand in the dominant minor after 'Himmel an' (at the sky). Meanwhile there are sudden sforzando bursts of pain or triumph at 'tönest' (sing), 'süssen' (sweet), 'schon' (already) and 'Tiefen' (depths). Brahms, like Arnold in *Philomela*, had listened carefully to the song of the nightingale.

The opening vocal strains resume at 'dann flieht der Schlaf' (then sleep flees), this time with a sadly flattened sixth on that last word and again on 'Blick' (gaze) as if to show the eyes bleared and blurred with sleeplessness and tears. At the command 'Fleuch, Nachtigall' the wings are explicitly unfolded in the quickening triplets of piano arpeggios, until in the postlude the darkness and distance absorb the singing and the suffering together.

NOTES. 1. As usual, Brahms's Hölty source was the version of Voss (1804), here set unchanged. The original poem is given in Friedländer (51–2). Its six strophes are compressed into four, which concentrate on the nightingale instead of the lost love symbolised thereby. The words are thus made much more settable and singable. Their appeal to Brahms, for whom birds were the supreme symbol of love and sorrow, would also be much enhanced.

2. The prelude's alternating hands are the nature-motifs M3 and M4, as if Brahms imagined the bird from the first as half-hidden among waving foliage. The decrescendo sighing *passim* is M21; the stabbing semiquavers and sforzandi are also deliberately expressive. So are the flat supertonic harmony at the first 'schmelzend ach' (M23), the voice's relaxing five-note descent at the second, the Schubertian change to the minor mode (M39) at 'mit nassem Blick' etc., the quickening quaver triplets (M16) at the reprise, and the finality of the concluding vocal line. The sustained top note at 'Himmel' is M10; the low piano note in the last bar is M6/7.

3. Cf. Schubert's setting D196, also taken from the Voss edition.

OPUS 47

Five songs (Lieder) for a solo voice with pianoforte accompaniment, published in October 1868.

67. (Op, 47, No. 1) Botschaft (A message) by 1868
Georg Daumer (after Hafiz)   D♭ major f'–a♭''

> Wehe, Lüftchen, lind und lieblich
> Um die Wange der Geliebten,
> Spiele zart in ihrer Locke,
> Eile nicht, hinweg zu fliehn!
> Tut sie dann vielleicht die Frage,
> Wie es um mich Armen stehe,
> Sprich: 'Unendlich war sein Wehe,
> Höchst bedenklich seine Lage;
> Aber jetzo kann er hoffen
> Wieder herrlich aufzuleben,
> Denn du, Holde, denkst an ihn.'

Blow, breeze, mildly and charmingly around the cheek of my loved one; play tenderly with her curling hair, make no haste to fly away [make no haste to fly away]!

Then if perchance she should pose the question of how things are with me, her unhappy lover [me, her unhappy lover].

Say; 'his sorrow has been unending, his condition desperate [his condition desperate], but now he can hope for a glorious revival, because you, sweet one, are thinking of him [because you, sweet one, because you, sweet one, are thinking of him].'

The thirteenth-century Persian poet Hafis was popularised in nineteenth-century Germany by free translation, like Omar Khayyam in England. This text is not without humour. But the setting is more serious in its manifest sincerity. So an alleviatingly light touch is needed, as the *grazioso* and *leggiero* instructions acknowledge; otherwise the typically low-lying accompaniment will sound less like a breeze than a thunderstorm.

Given the necessary virtuosity, a zephyr enters in the prelude; and after only a few bars a repeated two-note melody emerges high in the right hand. The notes dwelt upon are those to which 'die Wange' (cheek) will soon be sung; and the small harmonic clash introduces and illustrates the opening word 'wehe', which means not only 'blow' but also 'alas'.

Similarly at 'eile nicht' (make no haste) the quaver triplet movement is slowed down to left-hand duplets, and after 'hinweg' (away) briefly ceases altogether. But the prelude blows back again, stopping at the thought of 'die Wange' as before, this time with no trace of distress. All seems set fair. Even the breeze lies low as if listening, while the voice addresses it in the tenderest of tones. There is a Wolfian felicity in the vocal lift at 'vielleicht' (perchance), ironically insinuating that this very question may indeed be posed. The ensuing piano interlude sounds puzzled, as if waiting to be told what to say. Then comes the answer, suitably sad at first to suit the word 'Wehe' in the unequivocal sense of sorrow but gradually gaining confidence before culminating in a ringing assurance from the voice and a triumphant ascent from the postlude as the breeze obediently flies off to run the required errand.

NOTES. 1. The text was taken from Daumer's *Hafis* (1852). Its verse-structure, somewhat obscured by Brahms's treatment, is worth noting and even stressing in performance. Of its eleven trochaic tetrameters, four (5–8) are highlighted by their rhymes, while 'flieh'n' in line 4 chimes with the final 'ihn'.

2. The parallel thirds, sixths and tenths throughout constitute the love-duetting of M18; as so often in Brahms, they need a specially delicate virtuoso touch throughout. So do all the low notes (also presumably staccato, though not thus marked). The long or small sighs < > are M21; the piano's brief but expressive silence at '(hin)weg' is M29; the unresolved diminished seventh before 'sprich' is M25; the peroration's exultant top notes on 'du' and 'Holde' are M10. The finality of the vocal line in the last three bars is also expressive; the intensifying dominant seventh at the second 'denkst' is M24.

68. (Op. 47, No. 2) Liebesglut (The Fire of Love) by 1868
Georg Daumer (after Hafiz)   F minor and major c♭'–g"

> Die Flamme hier, die wilde, zu verhehlen,
> Die Schmerzen alle, welche mich zerquälen,

Vermag ich es, da alle Winde ringsum
Die Gründe meiner Traurigkeit erzählen?

Dass ich ein Stäubchen deines Weges stäube,
Wie magst du doch, o sprich, wie darfst du schmälen?
Verklage dich, verklage das Verhängnis,
Das waltet über alle Menschenseelen!

Da selbiges verordnete, das ew'ge,
Wie alle sollten ihre Wege wählen,
Da wurde deinem Lockenhaar der Auftrag,
Mir Ehre, Glauben und Vernunft zu stehlen.

*How can I conceal this wild flame, and all the sorrows that torment me, when all the
winds around recount the reason for my grief?*

*Tell me, why should you, how can you, scold me for raising a speck of dust on your
path? Rather complain against yourself, and against the fate that governs all human
souls!*

When that same eternal law decreed that all should choose their own paths,

*then your curling hair was given its orders to steal my rectitude, my religion and my
reason away from me.*

The rhyme-scheme is a ghasel, as defined above (No. 37, note 1), rhyming on
'-ehlen' or '-ählen'. But the effort of finding a rhyme has weakened the sense of the
words, leaving only a feeling of passionate yet prostrate self-abasement. The
setting sounds commensurately convoluted. Perhaps this is another private and
personal confession about Brahms's life and loves; its intense artificiality is
palpable, even in perfect performance.

The flames flicker from the first, in the left hand of the declamatory prelude;
thereafter these figurations flare or fade throughout. At 'die Schmerzen' (sorrows)
the vocal melody recurs a third higher, to show how instantly and painfully the
fire takes hold. It mounts to a top note on 'erzählen' (tell), and the prelude repeats
its wordless expostulation. Then the Persian love-lyric sees its hero as less than the
dust, which briefly whirls about in separate staccato notes at 'Stäubchen' (speak).
To match the philosophical moral about eternal laws the music moves into the
major for a dignified acceptance of fate. The insistent E for 'ew'ge' (eternal) tells
its own story. At 'alle sollten' (all should) the flickering triplet rhythm, which has
so far informed every bar, suddenly disappears, as if the singer has come to terms
with his torment. The rising right-hand figurations sketch a selection of separate
'Wege' (paths), The last page seems to celebrate rather than lament the loss of
honour, faith and reason; well worth it, says the postlude.

NOTES. 1. The textual source was Daumer's *Hafis* (1846), published in the year in which
Brahms became thirteen; he owned a copy, and may well have acquired it then in his native
Hamburg, where it was published. The title here is his own; it embodies his favourite
theme of love as an inward fire that could often benefit from a cooling draught or indeed
a cold douche.

2. Not only the flickering triplets and the opening vocal sequences that match the first
two rhymes are expressive; thus the perplexed questioning of M24 is heard at 'erzählen?',
while the alternating staccato octaves at 'Stäubchen' deliberately if briefly raise the dust.

The date, and the loving major tones of the last page (from 'da wurde'), may suggest Brahms's devotion to the young Elisabeth von Stockhausen, in whose curling blonde locks his own affections were entangled, and whose symbolic presence may be suspected in songs of this period on the subject of love's fires' being extinguished. For what it is worth, the F major music at bar 47f is surprisingly insistent on E octaves, pedal and harmony, and the tonality of E major, for twelve consecutive bars, while the notes E–S (= E flat) appear in the vocal line and right hand at '(Eh)re, Glau(ben)' and again in the right hand after the second 'Ehre' (M35).

69. (Op. 47, No. 3) Sonntag (Sunday) *c.* 1860
Anon., ed. L. Uhland   F major c′–f″

> So hab ich doch die ganze Woche
> Mein feines Liebchen nicht gesehn,
> Ich sah es an einem Sonntag
> Wohl vor der Türe stehn:
> Das tausendschöne Jungfräulein,
> Das tausendschöne Herzelein,
> Wollte Gott, ich wär heute bei ihr!
>
> So will mir doch die ganze Woche
> Das Lachen nicht vergehn,
> Ich sah es an einem Sonntag
> Wohl in die Kirche gehn:
> Das tausendschöne Jungfräulein,
> Das tausendschöne Herzelein,
> Wollte Gott, ich wär heute bei ihr!

So I haven't seen my sweetheart all week. I last saw her of a Sunday, standing at her door, my loveliest darling, my loveliest sweetheart, would to God [would to God] I were with her today [would to God, would to God I were with her today]!

Still, I shan't lose my laughter all week. I saw her of a Sunday, going to church, my loveliest darling, my loveliest sweetheart, would to God [would to God] I were with her today [would to God, would to God I were with her today]!

Here is one of the most perfect pages in lieder history. For all their apparently effortless simplicity, such strains had never been sounded before in German art-song, not even by Schubert, Schumann once complained in a letter to Clara how hard he found it 'für das Volk zu schreiben', to write for the people. Wolf too stood far outside folk-song. But Brahms had no such sense of separation, still less of condescension. He was a man of the people; his temperament and origins were alike humble. So was his musical mind; and he readily and unselfconsciously absorbed and recreated popular music. Here the melody recalls *Soll sich der Mond nicht heller scheinen*, which was well known to Brahms (see No. 21, note 1.) But his own tune is much more direct and memorable. The matching harmonies are plain and homespun up to the very last bars of interlude or postlude, which permit themselves a touch of chromatic adornment like a spruce buttonhole. Even then

the music never ventures out of its home key of F major; it resolves to marry and
settle down, as if sung as a response by the village blacksmith to whom No. 32 was
addressed in the same basic harmonic language. The left hand here, in the
postlude and passim, may hint at a harmonium, or the bombardon bass of a rustic
band; the rhythm is in unchanging ländler or waltz time up to each 'wollte Gott'
(would to God), when the music stops dancing and says 'Amen'. The weekday
thoughts have a Sunday reverence; the peace and contentment of the countryside
and its real as well as idealised innocence make a perfect match to Schumann's
song (his Op, 79 No. 6) in the same key and with the same title.

NOTES. I. Brahms modernised the original Old German as printed in Uhland's *Alte
Hoch- und Niederdeutsche Volkslieder* (1844–5), which decapitalises the text and deletes the
letter h to give such spellings as 'sten', 'ir', 'vergen' and so forth. Kalbeck (ii 322) explicates
that last word as the Middle High German 'verjehn', giving the sense of 'I've lost my
laughter'; but all the known sources print 'g' not 'j' (Friedländer 53) and in any event the
jocund music ought not to be contradicted.

2. In the song's first edition, the refrain 'Wollte Gott' remained unrepeated (out of
modesty, as Brahms explained to his publisher Simrock); its subsequent expansion
completes the balanced structure of this miniature masterpiece.

3. The outdoor horn passages at bars 9–10 are M22; the top notes on 'wollte' are M10;
the brief right-hand staccato at 'heute bei [ihr]' denotes elation. But the music is much less
motivic in the folk-song than in the art-song style.

4. The Schumann *Sonntag*, a setting of very different words, was well known to
Brahms, to judge from its affinities with his own *Komm bald* (No. 184).

70. (Op. 47, No. 4) O liebliche Wangen (O charming cheeks) by 1868
Paul Flemming   D major f#'–a"

O liebliche Wangen,
Ihr macht mir Verlangen,
Dies rote, dies weisse,
Zu schauen mit Fleisse.
Und dies nur alleine
Ists nicht, was ich meine,
Zu schauen, zu grüssen,
Zu rühren, zu küssen,
Ihr macht mir Verlangen,
O liebliche Wangen!

O Sonne der Wonne!
O Wonne der Sonne!
O Augen, so saugen
Das Licht meiner Augen.
O englische Sinnen,
O himmlisch Beginnen!
O Himmel auf Erden!
Magst du mir nicht werden,

O Wonne der Sonne,
O Sonne der Wonne!

O Schönste der Schönen!
Benimm mir dies Sehnen.
Komm, eile, komm, komme,
Du süsse, du fromme;
Ach, Schwester, ich sterbe,
Ich sterb, ich verderbe,
Komm, komme, komm eile,
Komm, komme, komm eile,
Benimm mir dies Sehnen,
O Schönste der Schönen!

O charming cheeks, you fill me with longing to gaze diligently at your red and white. And just this alone is not all I mean; to gaze, to greet, to touch, to kiss, you fill me with longing, o charming cheeks [you fill me with longing, o charming cheeks]!

O sun of bliss! O bliss of the sun! O eyes that absorb the light of my own! O angelic thoughts, O heavenly actions! O heaven on earth! Won't you be mine [O heaven on earth! Won't you be mine]? O bliss of the sun, O sun of bliss?

O fairest of the fair! Cure me of this yearning. Come, hasten, come, come, you sweet, you innocent! Ah, my sister, I die, I die, I perish, come, come, come, hasten, come, come, come, hasten, cure me of this yearning, O fairest of the fair [Cure me of this yearning, O fairest of the fair, of the fair]!

The endless repetitions, and the look of the music on the page, suggest a rousing and rumbustious drinking-song chorus of affectionate trivialities; just sweet nothings over-inflated, small talk writ large. But there is deep feeling here as well as good humour. The musical material is tailored to fit the strophic form; twenty-two bars are thrice restated, and rounded off by a top note which is the all the more effective for having been so long delayed. The style is, no doubt deliberately, Schumannian in its voice-and-piano identity; each sung note is either simultaneously sounded or else instantly echoed in the keyboard, throughout all three verses. This immediacy enhances the eagerness and vigour of the verses, which are further vitalised by many subtler touches. Thus the repeated right-hand quavers after 'zu schauen' (to gaze) begin as thirds, then leap up higher with added octaves in mounting excitement and continue as triads. This cumulative effect is further enhanced, in the same four bars, by the skipping left-hand octaves, which at first just begin the bar, then appear on each beat, and finally perform a tremolando drum-roll. All these effects culminate in enhanced dominants, at the yearning harmonies that reintroduce the opening words of each verse, further emphasised by an expressive ritardando which suggests that the singer has been literally entranced by the sight of all this superabundant beauty and charm. That brief effect is then repeated with such added excitements as broken octaves in the left hand, for just one bar, until the harmonies and tempo relax and hush together, again in quiet contemplation.

Despite appearances, therefore, this song calls for corresponding restraint and seriousness in performance. But the heavy-looking chords, as so often in Brahms (cf. No. 67), need a light touch; and the gushing verses require sincerity and humour in their presentation.

NOTES. I. The poem was taken from Paul Flemming's *Geist- und weltliche Poemata* (Sacred and secular poems) (1660), where the text reads 'nicht, das ich meine' in the first verse, and in the antepenultimate line 'komm tröste, komm heile' (come comfort, come heal), which may well have struck Brahms as sounding too sacred for his unabashedly secular purposes.

2. According to Kalbeck (ii 320) a manuscript is dated June 1868, though this is not confirmed by McCorkle.

3. The opening horn-passages of M22 in a rumbustious 6/8 rhythm suggest a country dance; the stepwise climb started at 'dies rote, dies weisse' in the voice and continued in unison at bars 13–14 denotes mounting excitement; the dreamy arpeggios of M9 at the second and third 'O liebliche Wangen' imply rapt contemplation; the enhanced dominants at bars 18 etc. are M24; the top notes at 'macht' and 'Him(mel)', and above all at the final 'Schö(nen)', are M10.

71. (Op. 47, No. 5) Die Liebende schreibt (Her love-letter) 1858
Johann Wolfgang von Goethe   Eb major f'–ab''

>Ein Blick von deinen Augen in die meinen,
>Ein Kuss von deinem Mund auf meinem Munde,
>Wer davon hat, wie ich, gewisse Kunde,
>Mag dem was anders wohl erfreulich scheinen?
>
>Entfernt von dir, entfremdet von den Meinen,
>Führ ich stets die Gedanken in die Runde,
>Und immer treffen sie auf jene Stunde,
>Die einzige; da fang ich an zu weinen.
>
>Die Träne trocknet wieder unversehens;
>Er liebt ja, denk ich, her in diese Stille,
>Und solltest du nicht in die Ferne reichen?
>
>Vernimm das Lispeln dieses Liebeswehens,
>Mein einzig Glück auf Erden ist dein Wille,
>Dein freundlicher zu mir, gib mir ein Zeichen!

A look from your eyes into mine, a kiss from your lips on my lips, could anything else ever seem joyous to one who had sure knowledge of such things, as I have?

Sundered from you, estranged from my own people, my thoughts ever travel the same track and always return to that same single hour; and then I begin to weep.

My tears dry again, unnoticed. I think to myself 'His love can surely find you here, in this seclusion; and should not you in turn reach out into the distance?'

Hear the whispers of my breaths of love, my sole joy on earth is your good will toward me; give me a sign!

Brahms often felt entirely untrammelled by the poetic form. Here he strictly observes it. Thus he salutes Goethe the formal craftsman as well as the inspired artist; composer and poet had much in common. Seldom has a sonnet been more sensitively set. Its fourteen lines of iambic pentameter are rhymed abba abba cde cde. The octave, or first eight lines, constitute the text of the imagined love-letter, a direct appeal to the intended recipient. The piano wears light quavers and arpeggios; it sighs to itself before 'Blick' (look) and 'Kuss'; it shares close sequences with the voice, like intimate secrets. The sighing resumes after 'entfremdet' (estranged) as the same music is repeated with subtle variants, such as a fleetingly flattened seventh of small-scale sorrow.

The sestet, or last six lines, begins as a soliloquy; the girl's thoughts turn inward to herself and her own innermost emotions. Before and at 'weinen' the right hand sobs in falling seconds, which persist even after the tears have dried ('trocknet'). Then the music gathers strength and purpose. The question at 'reichen' is rhetorical; of course the lover can be reached. But the ensuing piano interlude, in a sensitive character-study, relapses into hesitancy and shyness, expressed in shifting chromaticism. The singer recovers some confidence in a high register further brightened by right-hand octaves, only to end again in uncertain inflexions. The final pleading phrase 'gib mir ein Zeichen' moves out of sung melody into recitative, with a wistful effect of simple direct speech. Please let me hear from you; so says the music, most movingly, until the last notes of the postlude are heard still sighing 'ein Zeichen', searching for a sign.

NOTES. 1. The textual source was no doubt the undated set of *Werke* that Brahms owned. Exceptionally, the inspiration seems to have been as much poetic as personal; although 1858 was the Agathe von Siebold year, and this song of a lonesome girl is no doubt relevant to that experience, there is no obvious use of her theme.

2. The opening vocal sequences correspond with the ab rhyming lines; the sighing is M21; the dominant question (in C minor) at 'scheinen?' is M24; the piano's D flats in bars 11–13 are inflected (M41) to suit the sad 'entfernt' and 'entfremdet'; the weeping seconds at 'weinen' are M20; the ensuing thirds here (and *passim*, e.g. in the left hand for 'Liebewehens', together with the parallel sixths and tenths) are M18; the top notes at 'Ferne' and 'Liebe' etc. are M10. The question at 'reichen' (again M24) and the ensuing canonic imitation (M12) are followed by a piano interlude of shy chromatics that seem to plead for 'ein Zeichen'; its first three notes anticipate those to which that closing phrase will be sung.

3. Wolf, for all his abhorrence of Brahms, must surely have known and profited from this song; the interlude after 'reichen', the brightening octaves on the last page (from 'vernimm'), and the final recitative device all figure among effects which he made very much his own.

4. Cf. Mendelssohn Op. 86 No, 3, which Brahms knew and admired; also Schubert, D673.

OPUS 48

Seven songs (Lieder) for solo voice with pianoforte accompaniment, published in November 1868.

72. (Op. 48, No. 1) Der Gang zum Liebchen (The Walk to the Loved One) by 1868

Anon., Czech (trans, J. Wenzig)   E minor b–e″

Es glänzt der Mond nieder,
Ich sollte doch wieder
Zu meinem Liebchen,
Wie mag es ihr gehn?

Ach weh, sie verzaget
Und klaget, und klaget,
Dass sie mich nimmer
Im Leben wird sehn!

Es ging der Mond unter,
Ich eilte doch munter,
Und eilte dass keiner
Mein Liebchen entführt.

Ihr Täubchen, o girret,
Ihr Lüftchen, o schwirret,
Dass keiner mein Liebchen,
Mein Liebchen entführt!

The moon shines down, so I should visit my love again; how is she, I wonder?
Alas, she'll be in despair and lamenting, lamenting that she'll never see me again in her life!
The moon went down, but I made haste happily, and made haste so that no one could steal my love away.
Keep cooing, you doves, keep whispering, you winds, that no one should ever steal my love away.

'Con grazia' is the composer's direction; he has chosen to transform a folk-song of walking and apprehension into a delectable dance with a spring-heeled rhythm. It is as if Wordsworth's moment of similarly irrational alarm – ' "O mercy!" to myself I cried,/If Lucy should be dead!' – had been set as a love-song ländler. The minor mode with occasional clashes and hesitancies offers an entrancing equivalent to the lover's doubts and fears. The arpeggios waft along instead of walking; after 'zu meinem Liebchen, wie mag es ihr gehn?' (to my love, how is she, I wonder?) the piano interlude's top notes softly sing those words again to itself, in tender concern. Then the rhythm rallies. With the direction *animato*, confidence is restored; the dreamy drifting begins to dance, making light of the girl's despair and lamentation long before those words ('verzaget und klaget') are sung.

The second verse is note for note the same; and the words are again well dressed in matching music. This time the interlude musingly repeats 'eilte, dass keiner mein Liebchen entführt' (made haste so that no one could steal my love away). As before, the elated dance-steps know that she is really safe and waiting; but the mood remains minor and melancholy, as if being in love is no laughing matter.

NOTES. 1. Brahms found the poem in the 'Böhmische Volkslieder' section of *Slawische Volkslieder, übersetzt von Jos. Wenzig* (1830), also the source of No. 75. His different setting of the same text for vocal quartet as Op. 31 No. 3 was written in December 1863; an a cappella version of the present song is earlier still (McCorkle 189). Friedländer's title (1922, 55) for this song, *Der Gang zur Liebsten*, has no authority; it was perhaps a confusion with *Gang zur Liebsten* (No. 26).

2. Brahms recycled the quartet setting, also in 3/4 time, as his piano waltz Op. 39 No. 5; there too he heard the words as a dance.

3. As in No. 69 the folk-song style is much less motivic than usual; but the opening arpeggio reverie is close kin to M9. The *animato* second section needs expressive rubato à la Chopin (cf. his C# minor waltz Op. 64 No. 2 at bars 33f).

73. (Op. 48, No. 2) Der Überläufer (The deserter) *c.* 1853
Anon: from *Des Knaben Wunderhorn*   F# minor b–d″

In den Garten wollen wir gehen,
Wo die schönen Rosen stehen,
Da stehn der Rosen gar zu viel,
Brech ich mir eine, wo ich will:

Wir haben gar öfters beisamm'n gesessen,
Wie ist mir mein Schatz so treu gewesen!
Das hätt ich mir nicht gebildet ein,
Dass mein Schatz so falsch könnt sein.

Hört ihr nicht den Jäger blasen
In dem Wald auf grünem Rasen,
Den Jäger mit dem grünen Hut,
Der meinen Schatz verführen tut.

Let's go into the garden where the lovely roses are. There stand all too many roses, I can pluck one anywhere I will.

We have often sat side by side, how faithful my love was! I never imagined that my love could prove so false.

Don't you hear the huntsman blowing his horn in the forest on the greensward, the huntsman with the green hat who is luring my love away [my love].

The square folk-song melody, beginning with strong stresses on the inessential 'in' and 'wo' (where), the touch of archaic modality in the harmony, the long low octaves which seem to call for sustained string tone, all suggest deliberate devices applied for personal purposes. Brahms must have thought well of this early work, which presumably embodied some special meaning for him. But its attraction for other listeners has perhaps faded, like its symbolic roses.

NOTES. 1. The textual source was the Arnim–Brentano anthology *Des Knaben Wunderhorn* (1806–8). Brahms omitted a fourth verse ('Hört ihr nicht den Trompeter blasen,/In der Stadt auf der Parade?/Den Trompeter mit dem Federbusch/Der mir meinen

Schatz verraten tut') but added the words 'mein'n Schatz' as a sad coda and made other minor changes, such as 'hätt' for 'hat' in line seven.

2. A copy (McCorkle 192) assigns this song to 'Joh. Kreisler/53', i.e. the young Brahms in his Schumannian phase and frame of mind. The manuscript also contains the duet *Klosterfräulein* Op. 61 No. 2, which Brahms himself dated 1852.

3. In 1853, the human situation that obsessed Brahms was Schumann's tragic separation from his wife; hence perhaps the successive Clara themes (M33) in voice and right hand at bars 9–10, echoed and extended by the left hand at bars 13–16, in each verse. The high consecutive thirds at bars 9–11 are M18. The sustained bass octaves are also characteristic; but as usual this folk-song style is not overtly motivic.

74. (Op. 48, No. 3) Liebesklage des Mädchens (The girl's love-lament) *c.* 1854

Anon: from *Des Knaben Wunderhorn*   B major e#′–f#″

> Wer sehen will zween lebendige Brunnen,
> Der soll mein zwei betrübte Augen sehn,
> Die mir vor Weinen schier sind ausgerunnen.
> Wer sehen will viel gross und tiefe Wunden,
> Der soll mein sehr verwundtes Herz besehn,
> So hat mich Liebe verwundt im tiefsten Grunde.

Whoever would see two living fountains should see my two sad eyes that have run quite dry with weeping.

Whoever would see many a wide and deep wound should look at my sorely wounded heart, wounded by love to its inmost depths.

The weeping eyes and wounded heart especially seen and sympathised with by the young Brahms were those of Clara Schumann, whose martyrdom is surely hymned here. The elaborately wrought piano part and the vocal line's casual gap of two crotchets between the verb 'sehen will' (would see) and its object, combine in the first two bars to suggest piano music upon which words have been super-imposed, an impression confirmed by the ensuing scansion. But the inward sorrow is admirably mirrored in the lagging right-hand melody, usually heard a quaver after the voice, and in many poignantly altered chromatic harmonies.

NOTES. 1. The textual source was the Arnim–Brentano anthology *Des Knaben Wunderhorn* (1806–8). Brahms changed 'sehen' to 'sehn', 'besehen' to 'besehn' and 'Lieb' to 'Liebe', presumably for his melody's sake; but his reading of 'Wunden' for 'Wunde' has no such justification, and the right rhyming word might now be restored.

2. There is documentary evidence for 1860 as a *terminus ad quem*; the early date assigned above is inferred from the *Wunderhorn* source shared with No. 73, and the characteristic theme of a woman left lonely.

3. The alternating octaves E–D#–C#–B–C# in bars 1–2, 11–12 and 21, and in the vocal line at the second 'sehen will' are the Clara-theme M33, also heard as D#–C#–B–A#–B at the only voice–piano unisons ('mir vor Weinen schier' and 'hat mich Lieb verwundt') and again in the postlude. For the same weeping eyes and their effect on the composer see *Sapphische Ode* No. 167, note 3.

4. The strict bar-structure 1–10 = 11–20 + coda (21–3) is worth noting; the key of

B major suggests that this music may once have been intended for the early piano trio Op. 8.

5. The parallel left-hand thirds and sixths in bars 1–2 etc. are the love-duet M18, saddened in the postlude's chain of descending thirds; the flattened sixths *passim* are M41; the horn passages of country life in bars 5–7 etc. are M22; the top note on 'sehr' is M10.

75. (Op. 48, No. 4) Gold überwiegt die Liebe (Gold outweighs love) by 1868

Anon., Czech (trans. J. Wenzig)   E minor e′–g″

> Sternchen mit dem trüben Schein,
> Könntest du doch weinen!
> Hättest du ein Herzelein,
> O du goldnes Sternlein mein,
> Möchtest Funken weinen.
>
> Weintest mit mir, weintest laut
> Nächte durch voll Leiden,
> Dass sie mich vom Liebsten traut
> Um das Gold der reichen Braut
> Mich vom Liebsten scheiden.

Little star with the sad light, if only you could weep! If you had a heart, oh my golden star, you'd weep sparks.

You'd weep with me, you'd weep aloud through nights full of sorrow, that they are sundering me from my dear loved one because of a rich bride's gold.

Yet again the chosen theme is a girl's separation and isolation. But the music sounds even more receptive to the idea of a star that weeps sparks. The high vocal and keyboard tessitura of the opening statement turns the listener's attention upwards; then, in a lower register, the right-hand staccato depicts the bright drops, as the singer too comes down to earth at the thought of gold. This downward transition is subtly introduced by added lower octaves at 'Hättest du' (If you had) etc. The same pattern suits the second verse, where the staccato coincides with a notional shower of gold pieces.

NOTES. 1. The German text is not truly folk-like, despite its source, namely Wenzig's work on folklore, the *Westslawischer Märchenschatz* (1857), which Brahms owned. Since the song and the poem both begin 'Sternchen' his substitution of 'Sternlein' for the same word only three lines later is presumably inadvertent; the original text might now be restored.

2. The resemblance between the opening piano parts of this song and *An die Nachtigall* (No. 66) is worth noting. At first glance the poetic ideas have little enough in common; but the star that weeps bright sparks and the bird that sings sad single notes share the same basic audiovisual image.

3. The gasping interruptions of the vocal line after 'mit' in the first bar and 'Schein' in the second are quasi-operatic rather than folk-song in style. The golden staccato dropping of tears or coins at bars 7–8 etc. is M28; there the vocal chain of sadly falling seconds is also motivic (M20), like the especial sadness of the flat supertonic (M23) in a minor key at bars 9, 11, etc., where the heavy sighing is M21. The piano's parallel thirteenths *passim*, like

the tenths of bars 1–2, 5–6, etc., are M18. The high and bright tessitura is suitable for a
star; the top Gs, especially at 'mich' in the second verse, are M10.

76. (Op. 48, No. 5) Trost in Tränen (Comfort for tears) 1858
Johann Wolfgang von Goethe   E major and minor e′–f#″

Wie kommts dass du so traurig bist,
Da alles froh erscheint?
Man sieht dirs an den Augen an,
Gewiss, du hast geweint.

'Und hab ich einsam auch geweint,
So ists mein eigner Schmerz,
Und Tränen fliessen gar so süss,
Erleichtern mir das Herz.'

Die frohen Freunde laden dich,
O komm an unsre Brust!
Und was du auch verloren hast,
Vertraue den Verlust.

'Ihr lärmt und rauscht und ahnet nicht,
Was mich, den Armen, quält.
Ach nein, verloren hab ichs nicht,
So sehr es mir auch fehlt.'

So raffe denn dich eilig auf,
Du bist ein junges Blut.
In deinen Jahren hat man Kraft
Und zum Erwerben Mut.

'Ach nein, erwerben kann ichs nicht,
Es steht mir gar zu fern,
Es weilt so hoch, es blinkt so schön,
Wie droben jener Stern.'

Die Sterne, die begehrt man nicht,
Man freut sich ihrer Pracht,
Und mit Entzücken blickt man auf
In jeder heitern Nacht.

'Und mit Entzücken blick ich auf
So manchen lieben Tag;
Verweinen lasst die Nächte mich,
So lang ich weinen mag.'

*How is that you are so sad, when everyone looks so cheerful? We can see from your eyes
that you've surely been weeping.*

'And if I have been weeping alone, it's my own sorrow, and tears flow so very sweetly, and ease my heart.'

Your happy friends invite you; come to our embrace and confide your loss to us, whatever it is.

'You make so much noise and fuss, and can't guess what torments my poor heart; no, I haven't lost anything, however great my lack.'

Then take heart now; you're young, and at your time of life we have the strength and courage to achieve our aim.

'Alas, I can't achieve it; it stands so far away from me, it dwells as high and gleams as bright as that star above.'

We don't desire stars, we take pleasure in their splendour, gazing upward in delight on every clear night.

'And I look upward in delight on every dear day; let me weep the nights away as long as I care to weep.'

Goethe's poem adapts and refurbishes an old folk-song, with typically lively, clever and moving results. The verses now sing of hopeless love, symbolically envisaged as the desire of the moth for the star; too far above me, out of my sphere. Perhaps this was the composer's own feeling or experience. Certainly the idea of separation by circumstances, with consequent isolation and frustration, made a powerful and profound appeal to him throughout his creative life. This song however is not among his major achievements. It sounds like commissioned work, or the outcome of a challenge.

The first problem is its relation to Schubert's far more famous and successful setting, with which Brahms must have been familiar. The two share the same 6/8 rhythm, the same strict strophic form and the same alternations of major and minor on the same keynote. Here however the friendly prying is far more cheerful and the defensive replies far more melancholy, almost as if to imply that Schubert has misinterpreted the poem.

But the latter's setting arguably sounds much more persuasive, precisely because it mixes and blends both flavours, the sweet and the bitter. The result celebrates love even when hopeless and unreciprocated, whereas Brahms sounds self-pitying in comparison. Perhaps for that reason, the latter's melodic and rhythmic invention fails to flow with comparable freedom. His persistent crotchet–quaver chords remain in effect unvaried despite the extra right-hand notes in the minor section.

NOTES. 1. The Brahms source was no doubt his own undated set of Goethe's *Werke*; he treats his national poet with great respect, almost subservience.

2. The date of 1858 suggests a possible personal involvement. This was the time of Brahms's hapless infatuation with Agathe von Siebold, whom he no doubt regarded as his social superior; and the piano part at the final phrase of each verse (e.g. at the final 'weinen mag') always contains an arrangement of the notes A–G–A–H(=B natural)–E (M32).

3. The piano's consecutive thirds and tenths in the minor section, in which the voice joins at 'fliessen' etc, are M18; the Schubertian major–minor (M39), complete with tierces de Picardie at the end of each verse, symbolises the joys and sorrows of courtly love.

4. A detailed comparison with the Schubert setting D120, published in 1835, is instructive. There are inevitable similarities of detail, for example at 'traurig bist', 'du hast geweint' (with dominant harmony) and 'erleichtern mir das Herz' in the first verse; the

main differences of structure lie in Brahms's longer and more leisurely piano interludes, which render his version of the conversation less direct and immediate than Schubert's.

77. (Op. 48, No. 6) Vergangen ist mir Glück und Heil (Gone are my happiness and wellbeing) by 1859

Anon.   Doric D minor d'–g''

Vergangen ist mir Glück und Heil
Und alle Freud auf Erden;
Elend bin ich, verloren gar,
Mir mag nit besser werden.
Bis in den Tod
Leid ich gross Not,
So ich dich Lieb muss meiden,
Geschieht mir Ach,
O weh der Sach!
Muss ich mich dein verjehen,
Gross Leid wird mir geschehen.

Erbarmen tu ich mich so hart,
Das kommt aus Buhlers Hulde,
Die mich in Angst und Not hat bracht,
Und williglich das dulde.
Um dich allein,
Herzliebste mein,
Ist mir kein Bürd zu schwere,
Wärs noch so viel,
Ich dennoch will
In deinem Dienst ersterben,
Nach fremder Lieb nit werben.

Um Hülf ich ruf, mein höchster Hort,
Erhör mein sehnlich Klagen!
Schaff mir, Herzlieb, dein Botschaft schier,
Ich muss sonst vor Leid verzagen!
Mein traurigs Herz
Leid't grossen Schmerz,
Wie soll ichs überwinden?
Ich sorg dass schier
Der Tod mit mir
Will ringen um das Leben,
Tu mir dein Troste geben.

Gone are my happiness and well-being, and all my joy on earth; I am wretched and quite lost, I shall never recover. Until my dying day I shall endure great distress, if I must lose you, my love; sadness is my lot, alas for my fate, if I must part from you great sorrow will befall me.

I have forced myself to forgive her because as a wooer I must love her; this has brought me to anxiety and distress, which I willingly bear. No burden is too heavy, my dearest love, if borne for you alone; however long it lasts, yet I will die in your service and never seek another love.

I cry for your help, my highest refuge; hear my passionate lament, answer me directly, my fair love, or sorrow will undo me. My sad heart suffers great pain, how shall I overcome it? I fear that death will triumph over me and take my life away; give me your comfort.

As in *Ich schell mein Horn* (No. 60), all the chords are in root position, as direct and uncompromising a stance as this poem's ceaseless outpouring of isolation, sorrow and loss throughout all three verses. But that combined obsessiveness of style and subject-matter can soon pall without special sympathy from the listener. Brahms himself seems to have felt a personal affinity with earlier national music, as if he thought of himself as a Minnesänger as well as a German patriot; and in his hands and voice the tradition rings true. But the performance has to be equally committed, if such work is to be preserved from the reproach of pastichism. It should be sung like a modern lied, with immediacy and intimacy.

NOTES. 1. The source (not given in the *Gesamtausgabe* or Peters) may well have been Franz Mittler's *Deutsche Volkslieder* (1855), which would afford a *terminus a quo*. There the poem is entitled *Klage*, and has 'verlassen' not 'verloren' in the first verse, with 'so schwere' not 'zu schwere' and 'gebracht' not 'hat bracht' in the second.

2. One segment of the vocal melody appears twice in each verse, with different barring (the full bar at 14–15 becomes the half-bar at 19–20). In the first verse, each corresponds to a key verbal phrase: 'so ich dich Lieb muss meiden' and 'muss ich mich dein verjehen'. In the second verse the words include 'in deinem Dienst ersterben'. The only love that Brahms felt forced to forgo, though vowing to die in its service, was for Clara Schumann; so it is no surprise to hear M33, in the form F–E–D–C#–D, six times in all, at the literal high points of the song (also M10).

3. This bar-line shift, together with the modal harmonies of M27 and the horn passages of M22 together characterise the ancient folk- or national-song style.

4. Brahms published his own SATB arrangement of this (surely prior) solo setting as No. 7 of the *Sieben Lieder für gemischte Chor* Op. 62.

78. (Op. 48, No. 7) Herbstgefühl (Autumn feeling) 1867
Adolf von Schack　　　　　　　　　　　　　　　　F# minor d'–e♭''

Wie wenn im frostgen Windhauch tötlich
Des Sommers letzte Blüte krankt,
Und hier und da nur, gelb und rötlich,
Ein einzles Blatt im Windhauch schwankt,

So schauert über mein Leben
Ein nächtig trüber kalter Tag,
Warum noch vor dem Tode beben,
O Herz, mit deinem ewgen Schlag!

Sieh rings entblättert das Gestäude!
Was spielst du, wie der Wind am Strauch,
Noch mit der letzten, welken Freude?
Gib dich zur Ruh, bald stirbt sie auch.

As when the last flower of summer fatally suffers in the freezing breath of wind, and only here and there, yellow and reddish, a single leaf [a single leaf] stirs in that breath of wind; just so there shudders over my life a darkly sad cold day. Why do you still tremble at the thought of death, o heart [o heart], with your eternal beating?

See, all the plants around are stripped of leaves; why do you still toy with your last withered happiness, like the wind in the bushes? Resign yourself to rest; that happiness too will soon die.

Brahms told Clara Schumann (Litzmann i 567) that the poem matched his own mood. Not always, she hoped solicitously. Her diagnosis can be inferred from her proposed therapy; such a genius should get married and settle down. But she added that the song always made her weep. Posterity may agree with her; the false sentiment of the verse is redeemed and ennobled by the music, and the poet's despair is made sadder still by its personal relevance to a great composer. The Brahmsian obsession with icy isolation is epitomised in the only words he chooses to repeat: 'ein einzles Blatt' (a single leaf) and 'O Herz' (O heart).

Meanwhile the two-note chords have crept past in slow motion like the freezing wind. The vocal line moves gradually if at all, to match the wafts of chill air; there are hollow left-hand echoes, e.g. at 'tötlich' (fatally), and the poetic phrases are interrupted, e.g. at 'gelb ... und rötlich' (yellow and reddish), as if breathing is painful. After the second 'Windhauch' (breath of wind) that breeze blows more keenly through the dark sky, in right-hand triplets and bass octaves. The left hand's response to 'Herz mit deinem ewgen Schlag!' (heart with your eternal beating?) ominously rehearses the melody of 'noch vor dem Tode beben' (tremble at the thought of death), which in turn recalls the opening vocal line at 'frostgen' and 'tötlich'. In the last verse, at the words 'Gib dich zur Ruh' (resign yourself to rest), the accompaniment extends the progression heard earlier at 'ein einzles Blatt' into longer note-values and fuller chords, like a requiem for the hopes being buried in those final phrases and concluding chords.

NOTES. 1. The textual source was Schack's *Gedichte* (1867), which has 'vom' not 'im' in the first line and 'über meinem Leben' not the unmetrical 'über mein Leben' in the fifth. Perhaps Brahms made that latter alteration in order to accommodate his Clara-theme M33 as it were literally in the surprising C–B♭–A–G–A melody, D minor within F sharp minor, heard in voice and piano at that moment.

2. In that passage the dark low octaves (M7) illustrate 'nächtlich', while the gusting right-hand triplets (M4) echo *Erstarrung* (Numbness) from *Winterreise*. D911/4. No musician could read Schack's lyric without also recalling the last leaf of *Letzte Hoffnung* D911/16, least of all the devoted Schubertian Brahms, who unobtrusively repeats and prolongs the chordal treatment of his first 'ein einzles Blatt' at the later words 'Gib dich zur Ruh'. Brahms had been on tour accompanying his friend Julius Stockhausen in that master-work; he was also obsessed with icy isolation and standing outside the loved one's home, a topic also touched upon in D911/1. That latter *idée fixe* no doubt also prompted

the final quotation from another late Schubert song, *Der Doppelgänger* D957/13, which was also in Stockhausen's repertory; its '(man)che Nacht in alter Zeit' melody is also heard at the final 'bald stirbt sie auch' here. So deliberate an allusion must rank as not only expressive but intensely personal.

3. Elsewhere, the Schubertian left-hand echoes (e.g. after 'tötlich') may also represent overt homage; the opening thirds, like the tenths at 'einzles', may be associated with lost love, M18; at 'Gib dich zur Ruh' the long chords in and of G major (the flat supertonic, M23) form a funeral chorale, while the ominous silences at each 'stirbt' are M29.

OPUS. 49

Five songs (Lieder) for solo voice with pianoforte accompaniment, published in November 1868.

79. (Op. 49, No. 1) Am Sonntag Morgen (On Sunday morning) by 1868

Anon., Italian (trans. P. Heyse)   E minor e′–a″

> Am Sonntag Morgen zierlich angetan,
> Wohl weiss ich, wo du da bist hingegangen,
> Und manche Leute waren, die dich sahn,
> Und kamen dann zu mir, dich zu verklagen.
> Als sie mirs sagten, hab ich laut gelacht
> Und in der Kammer dann geweint zur Nacht.
> Als sie mirs sagten, fing ich an zu singen,
> Um einsam dann die Hände wund zu ringen.

On Sunday morning, daintily dressed – I know only too well where you were going; and there were many people who saw you and then came to me and denounced you. When they told me about it, I laughed out loud, and then cried in my bedroom at night. When they told me about it I began to sing, and then when I was alone again I wrung my hands sore.

Here is a setting worthy of Wolf in its intensity and subtlety, inspired by the same *Italian Songbook* source, which Brahms was thus the first to discover, by over twenty years.

The first bar's two accented crotchets are accusing gestures, which are continued in the opening words, pointing out the offender. But the voice is already showing signs of stress; there is a break in it. The detached consecutive thirds in both hands are caught trying to sneak off unnoticed. But the defector is soon identified by her finery; the piano echoes the vocal line of 'zierlich angetan' (daintily dressed) as if to draw special attention to the Sunday best, a telling effect repeated at 'hingegangen' (going) and again at 'sahn' (saw you). In between, the thirds sidle surreptitiously past, leaving the singer ostensibly unmoved. But the loud chordal defiance is feigned, the left-hand laughter forced. The confessed weeping 'in der Kammer' (in my bedroom) coincides with a right-hand memory of those finicking steps in consecutive thirds, and where they led; as these ideas are repeated the same responses recur at 'einsam dann' (alone again). The postlude reduces the minor-key thirds to single notes, as if to epitomise the transition from sad love to sadder isolation.

NOTES. 1. The textual source was the *Italienisches Liederbuch* (1860), No. 31 of the *rispetti* or popular love-ditties from Liguria, the Gulf of Genoa region; Heyse has 'zu Nacht', not 'zur Nacht'.

2. Wolf was often vehemently anti-Brahms; but no doubt he knew and even admired this setting. Indeed, his own omission of the poem may well have been an admission of Brahms's success with it.

3. The irregular bar-structure (one of prelude followed by four three-bar and then two five-bar phrases, plus four of postlude) is itself expressive; the ostensible strength soon breaks down. This organisation, as quite often in Brahms, takes precedence over the verbal accentuation; so the strong beats on 'Als', 'und', 'an' and 'um' should be softened, and 'singen' and 'wund' stressed, in accordance with the sense.

4. The music's manifest personal involvement may derive from Brahms's own feelings of betrayal. Perhaps the Clara theme M33 is hidden among the staccato thirds that slip off so unobtrusively throughout; as Malcolm MacDonald notes of this period, 'Possibly, Brahms had divined some hints of Clara [Schumann]'s affair with [Theodor] Kirchner, although this seems to have been one of the best-kept secrets of nineteenth-century music' (1990–138). As in the poem, people would tell.

5. These downward-creeping consecutive thirds are M20 as well as M18; their status as a composite motif of lost love, in the minor, is confirmed by the their reduction to single notes in the last two bars. The semiquaver gaps in bar 2 are quasi-operatic gasps of surprise and distress (M29). The chords of bars 3–4, 6–7 etc also wear a sprightly staccato dress, to illustrate 'zierlich angetan'. The defiant chordal gestures of both hands in bars 14–15 are M30; there the left-hand arpeggios recall the rather forced gaiety of the *Zigeunerlieder*. The ostensibly insouciant leaping left-hand octaves at bars 16–17 and 21–2 are also expressive, like the flat supertonic of M23 at 'geweint' and 'wund'; the top A on 'Hände' is M10.

80. (Op. 49, No. 2) An ein Veilchen (To a violet) by 1868
Ludwig Hölty, ed. J. Voss   E major d#'–g#''

> Birg, o Veilchen, in deinem blauen Kelche,
> Birg die Tränen der Wehmut, bis mein Liebchen
> Diese Quelle besucht! Entpflückt sie lächelnd
> Dich dem Rasen, die Brust mit dir zu schmücken,
> O, dann schmiege dich ihr ans Herz, und sag ihr,
> Dass die Tropfen in deinem blauen Kelche
> Aus der Seele des treusten Jünglings flossen,
> Der sein Leben verweinet, und den Tod wünscht.

Hide, O violet, in your blue calyx, hide the tears of sorrow, until my darling visits this spring. Should she then smilingly pluck you from the grass to adorn her breast with you, oh then nestle close to her heart [then nestle close to her heart, to her heart] and tell her that the drops in your blue calyx were shed from the soul of her most faithful lover, who weeps his life away and longs for death [for death].

No one could guess from this setting that the poem consists of eight smooth unbroken lines, a polished marble surface in imitation of the Greek or Latin

eleven-syllable metre — ∪ / — ∪ ∪ / — ∪ / — ∪ / — ∪ which Tennyson rendered
into English thus:

> 'Look, I come to the test, a tiny poem
> All composed in a metre of Catullus ...' etc.

In earlier and later songs (Nos. 65, 167, 170) Brahms studied prosody; but here he
seems unconcerned with such niceties. He inserts interludes, and repeats phrases.
Thus Hölty's violet is drawn and painted in melodic lines and harmonic
colouring. The resulting art-work is a masterly and original flower-piece ready to
rank with Schubert's *Nachtviolen* (D752) and other such exquisite miniatures.

The piano part appears to take its rise from the spring in the third line, heard
as a soft sweet trickle in some Arcadian scene. This nature-image flows through
both hands in falling or fluttering figurations throughout, signifying a continuous
flow of wave and wind, brook and breeze, long before the word 'Quelle' is
mentioned. But this is its music, as we hear after 'besucht' (visits), and have
already heard in the brief prelude. By the same token, this water-music also tells
of tears. The minor chord and echo after 'lächelnd' (smilingly) reflect and enhance
the girl's unattainable beauty, like the remote harmonies that follow at 'die Brust
mit dir zu schmücken' (to adorn her breast with you). A further change of texture
makes the verbal repetitions nestle and snuggle ('schmiege') insistently, with a
languishing yet exultant outcry on the meaningful top note at 'Herz', the third
and highest repetition of that dying fall. Then comes the peroration. 'Sag ihr' (tell
her) sings the voice, and stops, overcome with emotion. An interlude maintains
the tension. At last we hear the vital message. At this reprise, the flowing and
flowering are firmed into alternating chords as the riverside violet is metamorphosed into a human love-song. Its thirds and sixths make a tender interlude
before the lover's hopeless plight is portrayed at 'der sein Leben verweinet' (who
weeps his life away). The postlude sings the first strains again as if reverting to
violet shyness, guiltily aware of having been overbold in its protestations.

NOTES. 1. The textual source was Hölty's *Gedichte* (1804) in which the original lyrics were
often rewritten by J. H. Voss, whose text Brahms here sets unchanged.

2. The continuous wave-movement is M5; the thirds and sixths at 'mein Liebchen',
intensified by alternation at 'O, dann schmiege', are the duetting love-motif M18. The
intervening Schubertian echoes, e.g. at 'lächelnd', are no doubt a deliberate homage; the
top note reached at the highest 'Herz' is M10; the interlude's use of dominant sevenths to
heighten expectancy is M24; the mournful falling semitone on the middle syllable of
'verweinet' is M20; the flattened supertonic on 'Tod' is M23. The minor sixth on 'den
(Tod)' is also motivic; M41.

81. (Op. 49, No. 3) Sehsucht (Yearning) *c.* 1868

Anon., Czech (trans, J. Wenzig)   A♭ major e♭'–a♭"

> Hinter jenen dichten Wäldern
> Weilst du, meine Süssgeliebte,
> Weit, ach weit! weit, ach weit!

Berstet, ihr Felsen,
Ebnet euch, Täler,
Dass ich ersehe,
Dass ich erspähe,
Meine ferne, süsse Maid!

Behind those dense forests you dwell, my sweet love; far, oh far away, far, oh far away! Splinter, you rocks, lift up, you valleys, so that I may descry, so that I may behold my distant [my distant] sweet maiden [so that I may descry, so that I may behold my distant, my sweet, my distant sweet maiden]!

The melody soars yearningly upwards and away. The accompaniment wishes it had wings too; but it stays deeply earthbound, to point the contrast between dream and reality. The poem's Romantic rhetoric recalls the Magelone style with its grandiose gestures and verbal repetitions. At the fourfold 'weit' (far) the music's yearning, like empty arms outstretched, will be far too ostentatious for some tastes. At 'berstet' (splinter) etc., two melodies converge; as the vocal line falls from its heights the left-hand octaves lift from their depths, in graphic depiction of valleys exalted and mountains and hills made low. But even this average level of inspiration then seems to falter and fade; the Schubertian influence prevails over the authentic Brahmsian voice.

NOTES. 1. The source is regularly cited as the 1830 volume of *Slawische Volkslieder*, translated by Joseph Wenzig. But the same text stands in Wenzig's work on folklore, the *Westslawischer Märchenschatz* (1857), which Brahms owned; there the title is *Seufzer*.

2. The 9/8 effect of repeated quaver triplets recalls Schubert's *Ungeduld* on the same theme of love-longing; but this song's constant reversion to the same verbal ideas, together with the slow tempo, makes the music sound much less impatient, indeed restrained to the point of resignation – an affect enhanced by the postlude's sixfold 'Amen'.

3. The piano's opening triplets are the wing-beats of M3; the dreaming left-hand arpeggios at the second 'weit' are M9; the dominant seventh at the fourth 'weit' is M24. The insistently sequential vocal line at bars 3–4/5–6, 8–9, 16–17/18–19, 20–21/22–3 mirrors the natural repetitions of outcrop and outcry, scene and *Sehnen*; the top notes at 'weit!' 'süss' etc. are M10. The remote sharp-key notation in a flat tonic at the third 'meine ferne' etc. is also motivic (M40), like the postlude's apt image of climbing.

82. (Op. 49 No. 4) Wiegenlied (Lullaby) 1868

First verse Anon; second verse Georg Scherer   E flat major e♭'–e♭''

Guten Abend, gut Nacht,
Mit Rosen bedacht,
Mit Näglein besteckt,
Schlupf unter die Deck.
Morgen früh, wenn Gott will,
Wirst du wieder geweckt.

Guten Abend, gut Nacht,
Von Englein bewacht,
Die zeigen im Traum
Dir Christkindleins Baum:
Schlaf nun selig und süss,
Schau im Traum's Paradies.

Good evening, good night; canopied with roses, adorned with pinks, snuggle under the quilt. Early tomorrow morning, God willing, you'll be woken again.

Good evening, good night, watched over by angels; in your dreams they'll show you the Christ-child's tree. Sleep now, blissful and sweet; in your dreams, peep into paradise.

The quilt is prettily embroidered, like the sentiments. But their tender melody and swaying accompaniment have set this song high if not supreme among the western world's best-loved lullabies. It epitomizes Brahms's genius for turning his own complex personal responses into music of enduring universality. Here that process began in 1859 when the seventeen-year-old Bertha Porubsky from Vienna, on a family visit to Hamburg, joined the ladies' choir, directed there by the young and susceptible Brahms. Among the Austrian popular songs she sang for his delectation was Alexander Baumann's Op. 3 No. 1, with its pleasantly lilting melody (for solo or duet) and teasing words (usually as misquoted by Friedländer (1922 61), but here reproduced from the original publication), thus (Kahler[1] 68)

This was touchingly woven into the piano part of the lullaby that Brahms wrote 'for the happy use' of Mr and Mrs Faber (née Bertha Porubsky), on the birth of their second child. The couple had warmly welcomed the composer when he moved to Vienna in 1862, and the song surely expresses his gratitude to his friends

[1] kindly brought to my attention by Dr Imogen Fellinger.
[2] i.e. Du meinst wohl, du meinst wohl, die Liebe lässt sich zwingen (I suppose you think, I suppose you think that love can be forced)

and his human solicitude for their baby boy. Just as clearly, though, it was inspired by his own penchant for the young mother; and it is that tenderness, enhanced by supreme craftsmanship, that makes this music so admired a masterpiece.

NOTES. 1. Each verse has a different source. The first (originally the only) verse is age-old; there are many possible sources in modern German, including Karl Simrock's *Die Deutschen Volkslieder* (1851) or the Arnim and Brentano anthology *Des Knaben Wunderhorn* (1804), where Simrock may well have found it. But the first edition states that the text was taken from 'Simrocks *Kinderbuch*', i.e. his compilation *Das deutsche Kinderbuch* (1857), which was also on Brahms's shelves. Some Karl Simrock source seems likely, since Brahms set two of his original poems, while his nephew Fritz Simrock was Brahms's main publisher, of this song as of so many other works. It was Fritz Simrock who felt that the song's wide popularity called for the addition of a second verse; and he found a suitable strophe in Georg Scherer's *Die schönsten deutschen Volkslieder* (1868). But its last two lines 'Droben im Paradies/Schlaf nun selig und süss' failed to fit Brahms's melody; so the composer himself supplied the present final couplet. His shortening of 'das Paradies' to ' "s Paradies" is as uncomfortable as his "frohst" ' instead of 'frohste' in *Dort in den Weiden* (No. 183); but he plainly felt, despite his own later reservations (Friedländer 63) that such elisions were allowable in what he took to be the folk-song style.

2. A comparison with the Baumann source excerpted above suggests that Brahms is alluding to the duet version, and interpreting the main voice as a soprano's, at pitch, and the second as a tenor's, sounding an octave lower; the result well exemplifies the shared thirds and sixths of his own love-duet motif M18. His song was originally inscribed 'an B.F. in Wien'; and that monogram may also have been musically handstitched into this splendid sampler (B = B♭ in German). In F major, this idea could readily have resolved into the pious Amen cadences at each 'morgen früh, wenn Gott will'; and in 1875 Brahms instructed his publisher Simrock to use that key. In any key, this may well be the only song to maintain a first-beat tonic pedal unchanged throughout thirty-six bars; there could hardly be a more hypnotically persuasive sleep-motif.

3. Cf. Charles Ives's setting, *c.* 1900.

83. (Op. 49, No. 5) Abenddämmerung (Evening twilight) 1867
Adolf von Schack   E major d#'–f#''

> Sei willkommen, Zwielichtstunde!
> Dich vor allen lieb ich längst,
> Die du, lindernd jede Wunde,
> Unsre Seele mild umfängst.
>
> Hin durch deine Dämmerhelle
> In den Lüften, abendfeucht,
> Schweben Bilder, die der grelle
> Schein des lauten Tags gescheucht.
>
> Träume und Erinnerungen
> Nahen aus der Kinderzeit,
> Flüstern mit den Geisterzungen
> Von vergangner Seligkeit.
>
> Und zu Jugendlust-Genossen
> Kehren wir ins Vaterhaus;

Arme, die uns einst umschlossen,
Breiten neu sich nach uns aus.

Nach dem Trennungsschmerz, dem langen,
Dürfen wir noch einmal nun
Denen, die dahingegangen,
Am geliebten Herzen ruhn,

Und indes zum Augenlide
Sanft der Schlummer niederrinnt,
Sinkt auf uns ein selger Friede
Aus dem Land, wo Jene sind.

Welcome, twilight hour! I have long loved you above all moments, you who soothe every hurt and tenderly enfold our soul.

Through your darkling glow, in the moist evening breezes, hover visions that were frightened away by the garish light of loud day-time.

Dreams and memories draw near from the days of childhood; their ghostly tongues whisper of past bliss.

And we return to the paternal home and the companions of our youthful joys; arms that once embraced us are opened wide to us anew. After the long sorrow of separation we are again allowed to rest on the loved hearts of those who have passed away;

and as sleep softly flows down on to our eyes, a blessed peace descends upon us from the land where our lost loved ones abide.

Themes of soothing coolness and calm, together with nostalgia for a lost childhood, were especially beloved by Brahms. The long prelude's pedal bass and gradually rising consecutive semiquaver thirds evoke the murmur of memories at twilight. The voice now sings through the same strains repeated. After the typically conclusive vocal cadence at 'mild umfängst' (tenderly enfold) new arpeggio figurations anticipate the mention of moist evening breezes ('in den Lüften, abendfeucht'); at 'schweben Bilder' (visions hover) the murmuring semi-quavers resume their ritual of remembrance. The opening statement recurs in the same mood of sweet and sincere recollection of past bliss ('von vergangner Seligkeit'). But now the poet piously aspires to paradise, while the music's attempted evocations of infinite time and space remain obstinately earthbound; and this failure adversely affects the intended heavenly benediction of the reprise.

Indeed, the whole song sounded contrived and false to Brahms's admirer Hermann Levi; and even Clara confessed to feeling that its A major paradisal component lacked the melodic zest and warmth of its E major surroundings (Litzmann i 567). No doubt they both detected notes of insincerity in Brahms's evocation of an afterlife in which he did not believe. Had that charge been made explicit, the composer might have countered that he truly shared the poet's vision of heaven, namely the survival of true love.

NOTES. 1. The textual source was Schack's *Gedichte* (1867), which Brahms owned. Exceptionally, he offers no verbal variants or repetitions, as if the lyric treated truly and sufficiently of subjects sacred to him; soothing comfort, remembered childhood, lasting love.

2. The dark pedal notes are M7; the consecutive thirds combine the loving feelings of M18 with a sidelong movement as twilight creeps across the scene; the breeze-arpeggios for 'Lüfte' are M4. The religiosity of the A major section creates, consciously or not, the sound of a great Amen by the key-changes E–A–E. That section is at least successful in identifying further motifs; thus the division of three-four into 4 x 3 semiquavers is a modest musical equivalent for the timelessness of eternity; cf. Wolf's far more impressive use of the same idea in *Grenzen der Menschheit*. Similarly the distance between the two hands is a small-scale image of great heights and vast spaces, while their contrary motion (M13) and high top notes (M10) aim to turn and shine like the starry heavens, as in *Wie rafft ich mich auf* (No. 34). The prefatory dominant sevenths and sadly descending semitones before the reprise at 'und indes' are M24 and M20 respectively.

OPUS 57

Songs (Lieder und Gesänge) by G.F. Daumer for solo voice with pianoforte accompaniment, in two volumes of four songs each, published in December 1871.

Brahms had already set occasional Daumer poems; here for the first time is a separate set of them, announced as such on the title-page. There is no doubt that they were intended as a personal statement. Brahms had earlier enthused over the stories of the *Thousand and One Nights*, and would later relish the drawings of Max Klinger. He wished to say and indeed to show that erotic art had its human validity. Daumer's deliberate sensuality seems mild enough today, but it often outraged the susceptibilities of nineteenth-century respectability; and a song like No. 8 of this opus, *Unbewegte laue Luft* (No. 91) is still surprisingly frank for its period and genre. But Brahms believed that, as he wrote in the margin of his own copy of one Daumer volume, 'the purely spiritual standpoint, which considers mankind as bodiless beings, is as false as can be'. He left other such annotations in the various source-volumes for this opus. So these songs should be expected to express and explore emotional life, and the Clara-themes that hang and billow out along the vocal lines will hardly be mere coincidence, least of all when they are designed to adorn such phrases as 'es träumte mir, ich sei dir teuer' (I dreamed you loved me) in No. 3, 'wende diesen Blick' (turn away your gaze) in No. 4, 'an deiner Brust' (on your breast) in No. 5, 'aus diesem Angesicht' (from this countenance) in No. 6, and 'eine solche Brust' (such a breast) in No. 7.

84. (Op. 57, No. 1) Von waldbekränzter Höhe (From the forest-crowned height) by 1871

Georg Daumer   G major d'–a''

> Von waldbekränzter Höhe
> Werf ich den heissen Blick
> Der liebefeuchten Sehe
> Zur Flur, die dich umgrünt, zurück.

Ich senk ihn auf die Quelle,
Vermöcht ich, ach, mit ihr
Zu fliessen, eine Welle,
Zurück, o Freund, zu dir, zu dir!

Ich richt ihn auf die Züge
Der Wolken über mir,
Ach, flög ich ihre Flüge,
Zurück, o Freund, zu dir, zu dir!

Wie wollt ich dich umstricken,
Mein Heil und meine Pein,
Mit Lippen und mit Blicken,
Mit Busen, Herz und Seele dein!

From the forest-crowned height I turn the passionate gaze of my love-dimmed eyes back to the meadowland that grows green around you [to the meadowland that grows green around you].

I lower my gaze to the stream. Oh, if only I could flow with it as a wave, back to you [to you], my friend [back to you, to you, my friend].

I lift my gaze to the procession of clouds above; oh, if only I could follow their flights back to you, to you, my friend [back to you, to you, my friend].

How I would enmesh you, my well-being and my suffering [my wellbeing and my suffering] with my lips and looks, with my bosom, heart and soul all yours [with my bosom, heart and soul all yours]!

The Brahmsian nature-music of rustling semiquaver leaves is sustained by urgent and impatient syncopated rhythms; the exalted vocal line inhabits its own crowned heights. After the first ecstatic verse the insistent rhythm relaxes and the music meditates in a melodic interlude whose quiet triplet arpeggios continue into the next section, where they merge into the fluid sound of the mountain spring ('Quelle'), as the voice repeats that same melody. At the wish to flow back with it ('vermöcht ich, ach' – oh, if only I could) the excited impetus returns, together with the opening melody, only to relax again as the earlier interlude recurs. Then the same fluid continuation as before proves equally apt for the depiction of drifting clouds, drawn out in a long high note at 'Züge' to suit their continuous procession. The metaphor of flying back to the beloved at 'flög ich ihre Flüge' (follow their flights) reanimates the rhythm and quickens the quaver triplets into semiquavers, after the final exultant 'zu dir!' (to you!). Then the singer's gaze, having been duly lowered to the spring and lifted to the clouds, looks out again over the forest panorama with another return to the opening strains at 'Wie wollt ich dich umstricken' (How I would enmesh you) and an exultant concluding outcry.

NOTES. 1. The textual source was Daumer's *Frauenbilder und Huldigungen* (1853), which Brahms owned. The titular first phrase was substituted by Brahms for the original coyly unsingable 'Von ***'s schöner Höhe'.

2. This, alone in the opus, is a woman's song; perhaps its favourite theme of lonely love-longing entitled it not only to inclusion but pride of place.

3. The semiquaver or quaver-triplet nature-music of winds or waves is M4/5; their urgent syncopations, and the flats-in-sharps middle section (M40) from 'Ich senk' to 'Züge' are alike motivic. The arpeggios of meditative reverie at the direction 'Ruhiger' are M9. The augmented triads, e.g. D–F#–A# in bar 14, followed by G–B–D#, are rare in Brahms; they seem to signify enhanced intensity. The final climactic top notes at 'Busen' and 'Herz' are M10.

4. That last vocal phrase recalls Schubert's *Auflösung* D807, which has the same key and time-signature, at the concluding phrase 'Chöre, atheri(schen)' in an analogously exultant vein.

85. (Op. 57, No. 2) Wenn du nur zuweilen lächelst (If, just sometimes, you'll smile) by 1867

Georg Daumer (after Hafiz)   E♭ major g'–g''

> Wenn du nur zuweilen lächelst,
> Nur zuweilen Kühle fächelst
> Dieser ungemessnen Glut–
> In Geduld will ich mich fassen
> Und dich alles treiben lassen,
> Was der Liebe wehe tut.

If, just sometimes, you'll smile, and just sometimes fan coolness on to this measureless fire [on to this measureless fire], then in patience [in patience] I'll compose myself and let you do all those things [all, all those things] that cause love pain.

These mildly masochistic feelings must have meant much to Brahms, whose response has a felicity and subtlety worthy of Wolf or Fauré. The musical mood is relaxed and languorous, a barcarolle in a gondola. The contrived verses are transmuted into a tender love-lilt, the essence of wishful thinking in music. The first three notes in voice and piano sing 'wenn du nur' (if only). Then, after the second 'Glut' (fire) and at each 'Geduld' (patience), 'fassen' (compose myself), the first and third 'Alles' and 'lassen', the piano is heard sighing 'if only' to itself, over and over. Meanwhile these same three notes plus the next three in the voice have been subtly folded into a small syncopation to introduce the idea of transient fanning at 'nur zuweilen Kühle fächelst' (just sometimes fan coolness). This 'if only' theme is continued and developed in the right hand, as a rising stairway leading to the first 'Liebe', a culminating moment; then it reappears in its original form at the last sung note, beginning a plaintive postlude that summarises the song; a hurt heart healed.

NOTES. 1. The textual source was Daumer's *Hafis* (1852), which Brahms owned.

2. Note the favourite theme of cooling love's fires, here a metaphor of fulfilment.

3. C–B♭–A–G–A in the top notes of the left hand at 'dieser ungemessnen Glut' and B♭–A♭–G♭–F–G♭ in right-hand octaves at '(was der) Liebe wehe tut' may well exemplify the Clara-theme M33.

4. The brief fanning that changes 2 × 3 quavers into 3 × 2 for the first two beats of bars

3 and 22 is expressive; so is the sadly flattened sixth (E♮♭ in G♭ major, C♭ in E♭ major) at the first 'wehe' and before and at the second (M41). The top note at the first 'Liebe' is M10.

86. (Op. 57, No. 3) Es träumte mir (I dreamed) by 1871
Georg Daumer (from the Spanish)   B major g′–g″

> Es träumte mir,
> Ich sei dir teuer;
> Doch zu erwachen
> Bedurft ich kaum;
> Denn schon im Traume
> Bereits empfand ich,
> Es sei ein Traum.

I dreamed I was dear to you, but I hardly needed to awaken, for already while still dreaming I felt it was only a dream [alas, while still dreaming I felt it was only a dream, only a dream].

The prelude is heard dreaming. From the Brahmsian darkness of the piano's left hand, the characteristic arpeggios slowly float up to the surface of consciousness. The transient disillusion they encounter there, in chromatic chords, is soon resolved; the opening vocal phrase is confident. All seems well. But stress and tension are already present and active within the dream. At 'doch zu erwachen' (but to awaken) the vocal melody itself is floated on the right-hand notes, while accidentals increasingly contradict the feelings of bliss and replace them with confusion and insecurity before fading into daunted silence. As the first strains resume, the chromatic chords are spread out into sad sighs, anticipating 'ach' (alas), which subtly colours the reprise. Now, after 'empfand ich' (I felt) comes an added piano bar of realisation in full chords and low octaves, and the dream-motif itself is tinged with sorrow, in exact accordance with the poetic idea. The postlude seeks solace in ever deeper sleep.

NOTES. 1. The textual source is Daumer's *Polydora* (1855), which Brahms owned; in bar 12, the poet's 'denn, ach,' seems preferable to the composer's 'denn schon', which renders the later 'bereits' otiose.

2. In the prelude, Brahms looks forward to the opening bars of his *Intermezzo* Op. 116 No. 4. But there is a more manifest affinity with, indeed almost a quotation from, the falling fifths and sliding chromatic harmonies of his piano sonata Op. 5, at bars 58–60 of the opening Allegro maestoso. Perhaps that early work (published in 1854) had its own Clara-significance.

3. Her motif M33, in voice and piano at '(träum)te mir, ich sei dir teuer', is instantly echoed in the left-hand canon (M12), as if to underline its meaning. The recurrent arpeggios of dream (deriving from 'im Traume' in bars 12–13 as well as 'es träumte' in bar 4) are M9, and the dark depths from which they rise (deepest of all in the postlude) are M7. The dwindling diminished sevenths at bars 18–20 are M25; the same chords meaningfully interrupt the prelude's duetting love-song thirds (M18) and are made to spread and sigh at the reprise. The top note at the first 'sei' is M10; its sadly flattened sixth is also motivic (M41).

87. (Op. 57, No. 4) Ach, wende diesen Blick (Oh, turn away that gaze) by 1871

Georg Daumer   F minor e♭'–g''

Ach, wende diesen Blick, wende dies Angesicht!
Das Innre mir mit ewig neuer Glut,
Mit ewig neuem Harm erfülle nicht!

Wenn einmal die gequälte Seele ruht,
Und mit so fieberischer Wilde nicht
In meinen Adern rollt das heisse Blut–

Ein Strahl, ein flüchtiger, von deinem Licht,
Er wecket auf des Wehs gesamte Wut,
Das schlangengleich mich in das Herze sticht.

Oh, turn away that gaze, that countenance! Do not fill my inmost being with ever new fire, with ever new grief [fill it not with ever new grief]! When my tormented soul at last finds rest, and my hot blood no longer courses through my veins [through my veins] with such feverish wildness,
  one fleeting ray of your light would reawaken the whole rage of the pain that snake-like stings my heart [that snake-like stings my heart].

Again the music is full of personal feeling. Voice and piano begin together without preamble, to suit the immediacy of the opening address. In the same interest, the vocal line begins as quasi-recitative, with the piano as quasi-continuo. But soon the warm emotions overflow into downward arpeggio gestures that seem to say 'turn away'. Their lower right-hand notes at 'ewig neu(er)' (ever new), and 'Glut' (fire) are a compressed restatement of the 'wende diesen Blick' melody, as if intending to unify cause and effect. At 'Harm' the grief cries out among alien harmonies. The ensuing reference to rest, beginning 'Wenn' is interpreted by Brahms as implying death, which alone could allay love's longing; hence the ensuing heavy chords and inner voices, as if intoned to an organ accompaniment. The last verse then explains, very earnestly, that one of those glances could wake the dead as well as arouse the living. Here the exact reprise of the opening strains repeatedly cries 'look away'. But the singer craves those eyes, that look; this is the very music of hopeless and helpless love.

NOTES. 1. The textual source was Daumer's *Frauenbilder und Huldigungen*, (1853), which Brahms owned. He added another 'wende' in his second bar, for the sake of his melodic line. But his change from 'schlangenhaft' to the repeated 'schlangengleich' may have been mere inadvertence; or perhaps he preferred the enhanced consonantal bite of the latter. In either event it seems too late to restore the original reading.

2. Note the favourite theme of love as a fire from which relief is sought, (cf. No. 105) and the Clara theme M33 at the opening title-phrase 'wende diesen Blick' (and, with the first two notes played together, in the lower right hand at bars 6–7 etc.; bar 5 is similar).

3. The sharps-in-flats notation at 'neuem Harm' and again after 'schlangengleich' is motivic (M40); so are the organ-tones and inner voice (M38) at 'wenn einmal' and the

somnolent five-note descent at 'Seele ruht'. The semitonal moan and prolonged dominant seventh at 'Blut' are M20 and M24 respectively. The symbolism of the downward arpeggio triplets *passim*, and and of the rolled arpeggio at 'rollt', though evidently meaningful, is unique to this song.

88. (Op. 57, No. 5) In meiner Nächte Sehnen (In my nights of yearning) by 1871

Georg Daumer   E minor f#'–g''

> In meiner Nächte Sehnen,
>   So tief allein,
> Mit tausend, tausend Tränen
>   Gedenk ich dein.
>
> Ach, wer dein Antlitz schaute,
>   Wem dein Gemüt
> Die schöne Glut vertraute,
>   Die es durchglüht,
>
> Wem deine Küsse brannten,
>   Wem je vor Lust
> All seine Sinne schwanden
>   An deiner Brust—
>
> Wie rasteten in Frieden
>   Ihm Seel und Leib,
> Wenn er von dir geschieden,
>   Du göttlich Weib!

In my nights of yearning, so deeply alone, with a thousand thousand tears I think of you [I think, I think of you]. Oh, he who beholds your countenance, he to whom your soul has vouchsafed the lovely fire that glows therein, he who has been burned by your kisses, who has ever swooned away for joy on your breast [has ever swooned away for joy, for joy on your breast],
> *how should his soul and body ever find peace when once he has parted from you, you divine woman [you divine, you divine woman]!*

The poem is outspoken for its epoch; the composer's repetitions of selected key phrases enhance its candour. Yet without committed performance the light and fleeting music, for all its excitement, will convey pleasure rather than passion. Both are present here, together with chivalrous grace and discretion, in the high Minnesang tradition. The prelude is poised for flight; then with the entry of the voice it takes wing as a ceaseless surge of emotion, expressed as a powerful rhythmic impulse and a continuous intimate interchange between voice and piano. This is well epitomised in the prelude, where the left hand anticipates the lifting lilt of the opening melody by singing 'in my nights, my nights, my nights of yearning' while the right hand adds the falling phrase 'so tief allein' (so deeply alone). These ideas are extended into a reciprocal duet; thus at the words 'tief allein' the left hand sings the opening melody, while at 'mit tausend, tausend Tränen' the left hand says 'tief allein'. So the melodic lines intertwine and interact throughout. Before and at 'ach, wer dein Antlitz schaute' (oh, he who beholds your countenance), and again at 'die schöne Glut' (the lovely fire) the left hand frolics in octave leaps as if elated at its own memories, while 'an deiner Brust' is saluted with parallel downward plunges, followed by leaps as before. Thus the music should sound just as outspoken as the words, as if expressing passion as well as respect for a woman who was truly divine, identifiable by the copious extant evidence of a lifetime's writing in words and music. Thus considered, the first two bars may be heard as saying, sighing and singing her name; 'ach, Clara', with a variant of her motto-theme M33 at the second repetition of 'deiner Brust'.

NOTES. 1. The textual source was Daumer's *Frauenbilder und Huldigungen* (1853), which Brahms owned.

2. The alternating semiquavers are the wing-music of M3, here a symbol of human love. The convergent melodies of M17 are also a love-motif, like the thirds and sixths of M18. At 'deine Küsse brannten' and elsewhere the piano part recalls the interlude (after 'Schlag') in *Herbstgefühl* (No. 78) depicting past passion. The top notes at 'göttlich' are M10: the sadly flattened sixth at '(ge)schie(den) is motivic (M41), like the Schubertian minor–major transition at "Weib" (M39), smiling through tears at its fond memories.

3. The Clara-motif M33, already adumbrated at the last 'deiner Brust', may be heard again after the final 'Weib' as C–B–A in the treble clef and G#–A in the left, followed by a last interrupted sigh of C–B–A–G#.

89. (Op. 57, No. 6) Strahlt zuweilen auch ein mildes Licht (If a tender light sometimes shines) by 1871

Georg Daumer   E major e'–f#''

> Strahlt zuweilen auch ein mildes Licht
> Auf mich hin aus diesem Angesicht–
> Ach, es können auch wohl Huldgebärden
> Machen, die uns fast das Herze bricht
> Was die Liebe sucht, um froh zu werden,
> Das verraten diese Blicke nicht.

If a tender light sometimes shines out upon me from this countenance, there are also, alas, gracious gestures that can almost break our heart. But that which love seeks for its happiness is not vouchsafed by these glances.

What love seeks, in Daumer's book, is sexual fulfilment. Brahms agrees; and here, as so often, his love-music symbolises frustration, in the mood that Hugo Wolf, in his capacity as outspoken critic, called 'musical impotence'. No doubt Wolf mainly meant the music and its undeniable tendency to relapse into academic device as if to atone for its own bold tunefulness. But this mockery is misconceived; even when left outside in the cold night the Brahmsian inspiration remains tenderly loving, as here. The countenance in question looks readily identifiable; as Brahms once wrote to Clara in an early letter (Litzmann i 18), 'I seem to see a pair of wonderfully beautiful eyes'.

The prelude and the opening strains dream of duetting. After 'aus diesem Angesicht' (from this countenance) left-hand consecutive thirds dominate the music. The insinuating first themes resume at 'Was die Liebe sucht' (that which love seeks); the last word, an emphatic 'nicht', follows the longest chord in the song, a sustained questioning dominant seventh. The postlude reverts, dissatisfied, to the melody of 'was die Liebe sucht' (that which love seeks).

NOTES. I. The textual source was Daumer's *Frauenbilder und Huldigungen* (1853), which Brahms owned.

2. The arpeggios of the prelude and bars 5, 14, 15, 18–19 and 22 are M9; the consecutive thirds and sixths are M18; the long dominant seventh at and after the first 'Blicke' is M24; the falling semitones at that word and at 'das ver(raten)', as in the left hand at the second 'Blicke' are M20. The prelude's and postlude's subdominant harmony is also expressive, in the acquiescent and resigned sense of an Amen cadence; thy will be done.

3. At 'aus diesem Angesicht' is the Clara-theme M33, in the same notes as in Nos. 3 and 7 of this opus, and almost the same as in No. 6; cf. also the melodic curve here at 'Diese Blicke nicht'.

4. This song, like No. 4 of this opus, is about the hypnotic entrancement induced by a woman's face and eyes; there is a thematic link too, in the falling melody at 'wende dies Angesicht' there and 'fast das Herze bricht' here.

90. (Op. 57, No. 7) Die Schnur, die Perl an Perle (The necklace with its rows of pearl) by 1871

Georg Daumer (from the Sanskrit)   B major f#'–a''

> Die Schnur, die Perl an Perle
> Um deinen Hals gereihte,
> Wie wiegt sie sich so fröhlich
> Auf deiner schönen Brust!
> Mit Seel und Sinn begabet,
> Mit Seligkeit berauschet
> Sie, diese Götterlust.
> Was müssen wir erst fühlen,
> In welchen Herzen schlagen,
> So heisse Menschenherzen,
> Wofern es uns gestattet,
> Uns traulich anzuschmiegen
> An eine solche Brust.

The necklace with its rows of pearl on pearl looped about your throat, how happily it lies cradled on your beautiful breast [on your beautiful breast]! Thus it is endowed with soul and feeling, and intoxicated with bliss, by this divine delight.

So what must our own emotions be, in whom hearts are beating, such passionate human hearts, in so far as we ourselves are permitted to nestle so intimately on such a breast [on such a breast].

The verbal repetitions disclose where Brahms's own heartfelt pleasure and emotions lay. His response has its own cradled intimacy. The inner layer of alternating semiquavers between slow vocal line and steady pedal bass seems well designed to symbolise in sight as well as sound, consciously or not, close rows of pearls on a statuesque breathing throat. There is a Schubertian echo after 'gereihte' (looped); then the cradle image at 'wiegt' yields a new dreamy arpeggio figuration until the pearls aptly reappear 'auf deiner schönen Brust'. At 'Seel und Sinn' (soul and feeling), these arpeggios take a new turn from dream to intoxication ('berauschet') and divine delight ('Götterlust').

The pearl-necklace themes return, accompanied by further cradling at 'heisse Menschenherzen' (passionate human hearts) and a renewed ecstasy for 'traulich anzuschmiegen' (nestle so intimately) that relaxes into the final invocation.

NOTES. 1. The textual source was Daumer's *Polydora* (1855), which Brahms owned. The poem, but not the music, stresses the word 'wir' – what must we (human beings) feel?

2. The Clara-figure D#–C#–B–A#–B (M33) appears in the inner voice at bars 1–3, in piano octaves at 18–19, the vocal line at the penultimate 'solche Brust', and piano notes at the last 'solche Brust', as well as piano octaves G–F–E♭–D–E♭ at 14–15.

3. The Schubertian echo of 'gereihte' in bars 6–8 all but quotes the prelude of *An den Mond* D296 – perhaps because that masterpiece (published in 1868 and hence *prima facie* available for citation) also treats the theme of intimate union: 'Selig wer … einen Freund am Busen hält und mit dem geniesst'. Similarly the last vocal line, with its closing suspension unmatched elsewhere in Brahms, may be an equally intentional allusion to Beethoven's passionate love-song *Adelaide*.

4. The thirds and sixths *passim* are M18. The dominant pedal at bars 1–8 is M23; the dreamy arpeggios are M9, transformed at bars 21–8 into the convergent ecstasy of M17. The top A at '(Selig)keit' is M10; the long sighs of M21 are heard throughout. The flat notation in a sharp key at 12–16 is also motivic (M40).

91. (Op. 57, No. 8) Unbewegte laue Luft (Motionless mild air) by 1871

Georg Daumer   E major e'–g#''

> Unbewegte laue Luft,
> Tiefe Ruhe der Natur,
> Durch die stille Gartennacht
> Plätschert die Fontaine nur,
> Aber im Gemüte schwillt
> Heissere Begierde mir,
> Aber in der Ader quillt
> Leben und verlangt nach Leben.
> Sollten nicht auch deine Brust
> Sehnlichere Wünsche heben?
> Sollte meiner Seele Ruf
> Nicht die deine tief durchbeben?
> Leise mit dem Ätherfuss
> Säume nicht daher zu schweben!
> Komm, o komm, damit wir uns
> Himmlische Genüge geben!

Motionless mild air, deep peace of nature [deep peace of nature]. Through the quiet night in the garden only the fountain's splashing is heard [only the fountain's splashing is heard].

But my soul swells with a more ardent desire; in my veins life surges, and yearns for life.

Should not your breast too be filled with more passionate yearnings? Should not my soul's cry thrill your own, through and through? Do not delay to glide gently hither on your ethereal feet! Come, oh come [come, oh come] so that we may bestow heavenly delights on each other [come, oh come] so that we may bestow heavenly delights on each other].

The cycle culminates in the music of explicit sexual fulfilment, a realm in which the liberated Brahms was a follower of Wagner. This song is another *Tristan und Isolde* of the lied.

The prelude dreams and sighs. The long lush harmonies moving solely by semitones, lulled by low left-hand notes, show that there is hardly a breath of wind in all the peaceful nocturnal scene. At the second 'Ruhe', the already slow rhythm is lulled across the bar-line. The pulse quickens, with trills in the right hand as the fountain is heard splashing; then darkness again, and the silence.

Thence suddenly arise the crescendo outcries of ardent desire ('Begierde'), buoyed on an unbroken stream of excited semiquavers. These abate into quaver triplets at each 'Sollte(n) nicht' (Should not), where the harmonies of the prelude and the melody of the opening words return together, as if the loved woman thus addressed is herself imagined as the silent night already described; remote, mysterious, and apparently unmoving, if not unmoved, despite the ingratiating lightness of the appeal to glide hither ('Leise ... schweben'). The same identification reappears at the final invocation 'Komm, o komm'. When those words were first heard, eight bars earlier, they were sung to a confident melody accompanied by a renewed outburst of passionate semiquavers; but all those implorations finally fade and float up to nothingness high in the night air. The passionate appeal was heard and answered off-stage, if at all.

NOTES. 1. The textual source was Daumer's *Frauenbilder und Huldigungen* (1853), which Brahms owned. Its French-sounding 'Fontaine' anticipates the same symbolism at the beginning of *Serenade* (No. 99) addressed to the Spanish-sounding Dolores; perhaps such exotic allusiveness had its own personal appeal for the composer.

2. It would be surprising if Clara were not invoked in this climactic moment, as throughout the cycle; C–B–A–G#–A (M33) resounds high in the treble, with a sforzando on the first note, before the final 'Komm, o komm'.

3. The upsurge of semiquavers again recalls the analogous expressions in Schubert's *Auflösung* D807, symbolising an endless ecstasy as in *Von waldbekränzter Höhe* (No. 84).

4. The dream arpeggios of the prelude etc are M9; there the parallel tenths are M18 and the swelling and fading sighs M21. The hemiolas of 'tiefe Ruhe', recurring in the silence after 'nur', are M14. The fountain's steady quaver movement is water-music, M5, here as in *Serenade* (No. 99), but with trills for 'plätschern' instead of the light staccato evoked by 'niedertropfend'. The dominant question at 'heben?' is M24 and the top G sharps at 'himm(lische)' and 'Genüge' are M10; the left-hand minims' falling semitones at the last 'komm, o komm' etc., M20, may hint at the sadness of frustration. The flats-in-sharps

notation at 'nicht die deine' etc. is more manifestly motivic (M40), like the floating music at 'leise … schweben' and the Amen cadence at the final 'Genüge'.

OPUS 58

Songs (Lieder und Gesänge) for solo voice with pianoforte accompaniment, again in two volumes of four songs each, published in December 1871. The title-page makes no mention of the poets or the sources.

92. (Op. 58, No. 1) Blinde Kuh (Blind Man's Buff) by 1871
Anon., Sicilian (trans. A. Kopisch)   G minor/G major g′–g″

Im Finstern geh ich suchen,
Mein Kind, wo steckst du wohl?
Ach, sie versteckt sich immer,
Dass ich verschmachten soll!

Im Finstern geh ich suchen,
Mein Kind, wo steckst du wohl?
Ich, der den Ort nicht finde,
Ich irr im Kreis umher!

Wer um dich stirbt,
Der hat keine Ruh!
Kindchen, erbarm dich
Und komm herzu!
Ja komm herzu,
Herzu, herzu!

I'm searching in the darkness; my child, where can you be hiding? Alas, she always stays hidden, just to frustrate me [just to frustrate me]!

[I'm searching in the darkness; my child, where can you be hiding?]. I can't find the place, I'm running around in circles … . I'm running around in circles!

He who is dying of love for you can find no rest! Child, have pity [child, have pity] and come out here! [Whoever is dying of love for you can find no rest! Child, have pity, child, have pity and come out here!] Yes, come out here, out here, [come] out here!.

The ceaseless movement in voice and piano, now dashing about in vain pursuit and now turning in frustrated circles, takes its rise from the phrase 'keine Ruh' (no rest). The idea of hands clutching at the air inspires Brahms to a toccata in which nothing is touched. The prelude gives the game away; the scurrying semiquavers begin with a diminution of the man's opening melody, and the two hands are aptly in contrary motion. Within this frame there are further felicities of detail, such as the fleeting suspensions across the bar-line at 'dass ich verschmachten soll' (just to frustrate me). The *animato* interlude gives the game up; the searcher removes his blindfold, and the music lightens into the major mode of truth time. There the charade turns into reality. For all the fun and laughter, listeners learn that playing hard to get has its serious side. Voice and piano combine in one heartfelt appeal; both are heard saying 'Kindchen, erbarm dich' (Child, have pity) and 'herzu' (come here), at different speeds. 'Herzu' in the voice becomes ever more insistent in its upward leaps of a third, a fifth and finally a seventh, punctuated by pauses for breath. The piano adds an Amen chorus. In the 'here I am!' coda the hidden girl comes running gleefully out, ready for a long forgiving embrace on the final sustained chord. The verses bring Brahms out too, at his most vividly visual.

NOTES. 1. The textual source was the 1836 volume of *Gedichte* by Kopisch, Brahms preserves the title (strictly 'Blindekuh', as there printed) but treats the text cavalierly. Thus Kopisch's second verse has lines 7–8 above twice, with 'Und' added to begin line 7. Brahms elects to repeat lines 1–2 instead of his poet's 5–6, thus neatly highlighting and summarising the message of his music, with its typical theme of the frustrated outsider.

2. There is a further personal association. When the young Brahms played hide-and-seek at Göttingen in the summer of 1858 with Otto Grimm, Agathe von Siebold and the Schumann family, Clara had tripped and fallen while running excitedly from her hiding-place. Her daughter Eugenie, then six years old, remembered that moment all her long life (1925 14). Brahms too had good reason to recall that game. So the Clara themes M33 in the voice, and in double diminution in the right hand, at the first 'dass ich verschmachten soll' and similarly at the first 'ich irr im Kreis umher', need not be mere coincidence.

3. The quasi-operatic vocal *fioriture* at 'verschmachten' and 'im Kreis', as an image of circling, and the final rising major seventh, are unique in Brahms; they may offer a tribute to the lyric's Sicilian origin.

4. All the scampering semiquavers, and the equally apt moments of diminution or contrary motion (M13) as a small figure runs off in the opposite direction, are marvellously motivic; so is the Schubertian transition from minor to major on the same tonic, here implying literal or metaphorical enlightenment (M39), and the Amen cadences at each final 'komm her(zu)'. There, as at the accented 'dich' earlier, the top notes are M10.

93. (Op. 58, No. 2) Während des Regens (During the rain) by 1871
August Kopisch   D♭ major f'–a♭''

> Voller, dichter tropft ums Dach da,
> Tropfen süsser Regengüsse;
> Meines Liebchens holde Küsse
> Mehren sich, je mehr ihr tropfet!
> Tropft ihr, darf ich sie umfassen,
> Lasst ihrs, will sie mich entlassen;
> Himmel, werde nur nicht lichter,
> Tropfen, tropfet immer dichter!

Fuller and faster drop around the roof, you drops in the sweet showers of rain; my darling's adorable kisses will increase, the more [the more] you keep on dropping!
While you drop, I'm allowed to embrace her; if you stop she'll dismiss me [she'll

dismiss me]. Sky, please don't brighten; drops, fall ever faster [ever, ever faster, faster, faster]!

The raindrops are equated with kisses; so their keyboard equivalents feel free to remain unaffected by the force of gravity, and splash upwards in their staccato elation. Brahms stresses their erotic relish; thus the accent at 'tropft' (fall) at the top of the keyboard's melodic curve denotes a special smacker, heard again at 'holde Küsse'. In each context the piano's immediate imitation of the opening vocal line also shows the shower's density; the raindrop kisses leave no dry patch anywhere.

Such symbolism is ceaseless and intense. Thus each 'mich entlassen' (unclasp me) is extended by long top notes to show how very protracted and reluctant this process of disengagement would prove to be, at least on the part of the singer. After the second such illustration the bar of silence wryly illustrates empty arms with nothing to embrace. At the first 'immer dichter' (ever faster) the staccato ceases, as the rain obligingly falls more fully, in less separate and distinct drops. So the kisses too are presumably fuller and longer; so much so indeed that when the rain stops neither party takes any notice. After two separate dry pecks from the piano the final sustained chord eloquently unites the happy couple. Such insistent roguishness will not tempt all tastes; but this song will prove nonpareil for some listeners in some moods.

NOTES. 1. The textual source was Kopisch's 1836 *Gedichte*; Brahms again preserves his poet's title.

2. The indifferent vocal accentuation (e.g. the last syllable of 'Regengüsse' on a sustained downbeat in bar 7) shows that the melody takes precedence over the words, even though the music derives directly from the poetic ideas.

3. The tear- and rain-drops are M28, the canonic imitations M12. The joy of M19 is heard at 'tropft ihr'; the top notes at each 'entlassen' etc. are M10, and the bar of silence thereafter is M29, coloured by the questioning dominant seventh of M24. The sharp notation in a flat key is motivic (M40); the final fermata is equally expressive.

94. (Op. 58, No. 3) Die Spröde (The coy girl) by 1871
Anon., from the Calabrese (trans. A. Kopisch, rev. P. Heyse)

A major e'–g''

Ich sahe eine Tigrin
Im dunklen Haine,
Im dunklen Haine,
Und doch mit meinen Tränen
Konnt ich sie zähmen.

Sah auch die harten Steine,
Ja Marmelsteine,
Die harten Steine,
Erweicht vom Fall der Tropfen
Gestalt annehmen.

Und du, so eine zarte
Holdselge Kleine,
Du lachst zu meinem Seufzen
Und bittern Grämen.

*I saw a tigress in the dark grove, in the dark grove, but with my tears I could tame her
[I could tame her].*

*I also saw how hard stones, yes, even marble [such hard stones], softened by dripping
water, could assume new shape.*

*And you, such a tender sweet little girl, you laugh at my sighing and my bitter
grieving [you laugh at my bitter grieving].*

The music is all courtliness and chivalry; like the lover, it reacts to that charming
though cruel laughter by smiling through its tears, The *grazioso* prelude offers its
arm in a sprightly but sedate sequence of steps. The bitter grief is sweetened by
restraint and distance; but there is real regret in the final vocal phrase and the
postlude, where the the prelude's falling sixths become strangely longer and
sadder. Meanwhile a continuous smooth flow of triplet semiquavers runs like a
conduit of tears under the engaging vocal melody. The rococo grace of the dance
is captivating despite the occasional bearish awkwardness of harmony, e.g. in the
flattened notes at the second 'dunklen Haine' (dark grove); both aspects are
equally characteristic.

NOTES. 1. The original textual source was Kopisch's 1836 *Gedichte*, whose title was 'Die
Spröde von Scilla', a town in Calabria, at the toe of Italy. Brahms became dissatisfied with
his poet's forced rhymes at the end of each stanza ('wie wurde zahm sie!/ 'so weich wie
Rahm sie!'/'ja bittern Gram hie'), as printed in this song's first edition; and the lyric was
accordingly rewritten at his request by the truly accomplished translator from Romance
languages Paul Heyse, whose work in that genre had already been admired and set by the
composer (as *Spanisches Lied* No. 9 and *Am Sonntag Morgen* No. 79). Brahms liked the
result, as shown above, and wished he had elicited it before publication. Presumably
Kopisch would have been less impressed; but he had died in 1853.

2. The Schubertian sequences of the prelude recall *Erntelied* D434, which is also about
folksy courtesies. These take a further bow in the interludes. But the piano's semiquaver
triplets are constantly remodelled. They darken with added low octaves (M7) at 'im
dunklen Haine'; at the mention of tears ('doch mit meinen Tränen') they overflow in both
hands (M5). The sighing arpeggios at 'zähmen' are clearly presented as a picture of
soothing or taming, the only identifiable use of such a motif. The patterns at 'Und du, so
eine' and from 'holdselge Kleine' are different again; and new figurations are still being
introduced down to the last bar of the grieving postlude.

3. Surely some personal involvement, rather than any inspiration from admittedly inept
verses later disowned, had liberated this lavish invention; so the E–D# or E–S of Elisabeth
von Stockhausen at 'mit mei(nen) Tränen' may be an embroidered monogram (M35).

4. The top note at 'hold(selge)' is M10; the voice-piano consecutive tenths there, and the
same love-duetting *passim*, are M18. The sad flattenings at 'dunklen' or 'harten' in bars 7 and
9, at 'lachst zu meinem Seufzen' etc. and in the postlude, are motivic (M41), like the
Schubertian major–minor of M39; so is the flat notation in a sharp key (M40). But the
tierce de Picardie, although added as an afterthought to the composer's own copy (and duly
reproduced in the *Gesamtausgabe*), sounds somewhat facile; the unchanged minor mode
over the last twelve bars, as in the Peters edition, seems more aptly predictive of a sad ending.

95. (Op. 58, No. 4) O komme, holde Sommernacht (Oh come, sweet summer night) by 1871

Melchior Grohe   F# major c#'–f#''

> O komme, holde Sommernacht,
>   Verschwiegen;
> Dich hat die Liebe recht gemacht
>   Zum Siegen!
>
> Da brechen manche Knospen los,
>   Verstohlen,
> Da öffnen ihren süssen Schoss
>   Violen;
>
> Da neigt ihr Haupt im Dämmerschein
>   Die Rose,
> Da wird mein Liebchen auch noch mein,
>   Das lose!

O come, sweet summer night, clandestinely; love surely made you for conquest [O come, sweet summer night, clandestinely; love surely made you for conquest]. Now many a bud bursts forth in secret, now violets open their sweet laps, now the rose droops her head in the twilight, and now my love too shall be mine, the wanton [the wanton]!

The composer has chosen his poem for its sensual imagery, which was outspoken for its period; the words are as erotically sweet, full and ripe as a Brueghel de Velours flower-painting. The matching music takes its rise from the word 'Siegen' (conquest). The quaver triplets gallop, the horn calls resound through the countryside, the hunt is up and in full cry. Perhaps the imagined prey is a plump partridge or pigeon; the piano sounds alive with a flutter of wings seeking and taking flight. The opening vocal line well illustrates Brahms's genius for popular song; so buoyantly confident a melody needs to be sung twice over, like a thrush's refrain, just to show that its careless rapture can indeed be recaptured. At 'Da brechen manche Knospen los' (Now many a bud bursts forth) the vocal line becomes more restrained, confidential, quasi-parlando; a plan of campaign is being adumbrated in the twilight. At 'da neigt ihr Haupt' (now the rose droops her head) the opening melody returns a fourth higher and frailer; at that moment of open vulnerability the top note thus far held in reserve is touched, at first tentatively and then with increasing confidence and insistence; 'das lose' (the wanton) in sense as well as sound.

NOTES. 1. The textual source was Grohe's *Reime und Reisen* (1861), which Brahms owned; there, the title is simply 'Sommernacht'.

2. The ubiquitous horn-passages are manifestly motivic (M22), culminating in the long loving embrace of the final sustained chord. The winged triplets are M3; the left hand at bars 6–9 and 30–31, and the right at 14–17 and 33 sings the joy motif M19, restated in left-hand octaves at bars 18–19 (where the *Gesamtausgabe's* octave E# should of course be E natural, as in the Peters editions), 22–3, 32, 34 and in overlapping rising canons (M12) in the postlude. The long sighs in bars 4, 12, 20 and 28 are M21; the final top note is M10.

96. (Op. 58, No. 5) Schwermut (Melancholy) by 1871
Karl Candidus   E♭ minor d'–f''

> Mir ist so weh ums Herz,
> Mir ist, als ob ich weinen möchte
> Vor Schmerz!
> Gedankensatt
> Und lebensmatt
> Möcht ich das Haupt hinlegen in die Nacht der Nächte!

I feel so sore at heart, I feel as if I could weep for pain! Weary of worrying, tired of life,
I'd like to lay down my head in the night of nights [in the night of nights].

Melancholy is putting it mildly. It is almost as if Brahms wished to demonstrate his immense emotional range by juxtaposing this death-wish with the previous song's lusty affirmation of life and love. From the outset the funeral bell tolls in a pedal note so insistent that the opening words are as predictable as the repeated organ-voluntary prelude that accompanies them and also provides an inter-lude after 'Schmerz' (sorrow) which continues after 'Gedankensatt' (weary of worrying). After 'lebensmatt' (tired of life) the cortège arrives at the graveside and is duly interred with solemn minims. In that sleep of death, the dreams that come at 'möcht ich das Haupt hinlegen' (I'd like to lay down my head) hold no terrors at all; they sound benevolent and friendly, and the final major chord promises sound sleep for ever.

This was the Brahms of whom it was said that whenever he felt particularly cheerful he would sing 'The Grave is my Joy' (see *Todessehnen*, No. 161); and the lifeless words here offer the music no real redeeming animation or spirit. Yet the outcome, against heavy odds, can be a noble and memorable song.

NOTES. 1. The textual source was probably the *Vermischte Gedichte* (1869), which Brahms owned. But other Candidus verses had been set prior to their publication by Schumann, who had presumably received them privately; so such manuscript copies may have been Brahms's source, and a form of filial piety may have prompted their selection.

2. Perhaps Schumann is remembered and mourned here; E♭ minor was his own key to death's door. Indeed, all the music is motivic, from the tolling pedal bell-notes of M7, as in *Der Tod, das ist die kühle Nacht* (No. 176), via the sharps-within-flats notation (M40) to the ominous finality of the last vocal cadence and the concluding tierce de Picardie with its special meaning of death as a healing sleep, as so often in Housman. More specifically, the consecutive tenths are M18, as if unhappy love were the cause of all this dejection. The dreaming arpeggios, arranged as in *Es träumte mir* (No. 86), are M9.

3. The careful rhythmic and harmonic structure is worth noting, e.g. in the repeated patterns most evidently exemplified at bars 4–6 and 14–16.

97. (Op. 58, No. 6) In der Gasse (In the lane) by 1871
Friedrich Hebbel   D minor c#'–g♭''

> Ich blicke hinab in die Gasse,
> Dort drüben hat sie gewohnt;

Das öde, verlassene Fenster,
Wie hell bescheints der Mond.

Es gibt so viel zu beleuchten;
O holde Strahlen des Lichts,
Was webt ihr denn gespenstisch
Um jene Stätte des Nichts!

I look down into the lane. She used to live opposite.
   That empty deserted window, how brightly the moon lights it up!
   There is so much else you could light up, you lovely rays of light; why then do you
weave so eerily around that place of nothingness [around that place of nothingness]?

Hebbel was a great dramatist as well as fine lyricist. Here his few lines paint a
scenic backdrop, convene a cast of characters, and enact a tragedy. The words
suggest that the lovers were neighbours, and that the poet still lives in the same
street. But Brahms, the quoter of *Der Doppelgänger* D957/13 (in *Herbstgefühl*, No.
78), seems to see himself as doubly estranged; the direction 'gehend' (walking)
envisages him as a visitor standing outside, as so often, Once there, his inspiration
and his spirits alike seem to flag. The opening vocal melody for 'Ich blicke hinab'
etc. is extrapolated as a prelude, beginning in cold bare minor octaves that set the
scene as Brahms imagines it, even though there is no overt invocation of coldness
in the poem. Then that first theme mellows into the major, as in the second bar
of the prelude, after 'hat sie gewohnt' (used to live) and again at the mention of
moonshine, fleetingly but vividly illustrated in the sustained notes at the second
'hell' (brightly) and 'bescheints' (lights it up). Meanwhile two interludes have
already sighed to themselves 'Ich blicke hinab' (I look down), and a third repeats
that phrase twice. Then the 'blicke hin—' notes become an insistent keyboard
litany, first in both hands and then at 'Lichts' (of light), where they are diminished
in the bass as the treble sequentially intones the second half ('—ab in die') of this
same theme. All this time the voice has been playing and weaving around the
piano music, in quasi-recitative. At 'gespenstisch' (eerily) a new idea makes a
mysterious appearance. The picture and the emotion it portrays are distanced by
being dissolved into a dream, and then obliterated altogether. At the first 'Nichts'
(nothingness) the piano part intersperses its low arpeggios with bars of silence, as
dream alternates with oblivion. On the final word the postlude repeats its 'blicke
hin—' motifs, now rescored to sound like deep groans; the last chords are heard
as a final renunciation. Perhaps the poem's tragedy is overstated; but the effect can
be powerful.

NOTES. 1. The source was Hebbel's *Sämtliche Werke* (1865–7), which Brahms owned.
There the title was 'Spuk'; the composer's change to 'In der Gasse' confirms that his
picture was an exterior.
   2. Note the typical themes of ostracism and exclusion. The rather artificial sound of the
bass octaves A–D at the last two chords suggests a final deep 'Ade' (M34); on that basis, this
would also be an inner meaning of the bare octaves A–D that begin each of the first two
bars in both piano and voice. Further, the end of the postlude and the beginning of the
voice consists of a long-drawn-out Clara-theme (M33) F–E–D–C#–D, soon heard again

in a piano interlude where those same notes are overlaid with duetting consecutive thirds as in the love-motif M18.

3. The bare initial octaves are themselves motivic (M37), like the left-hand diminution at 'Lichts'; and the imagined chill of the night air has exacerbated the feelings of agitated isolation. The alternating minor 5–6–5 at 'öde' etc, and again in the postlude, is M20; the dream-arpeggios at and after 'gespenstisch' are M9; the piano's significant silences after 'Nichts' are M29.

98. (Op. 58, No. 7) Vorüber (Over) by 1871
Friedrich Hebbel   D minor e'–a♭''

> Ich legte mich unter den Lindenbaum,
> In dem die Nachtigall schlug;
> Sie sang mich in den süssesten Traum,
> Der währte auch lange genug.
>
> Denn nun ich erwache, nun ist sie fort,
> Und welk bedeckt mich das Laub;
> Doch leider noch nicht wie am dunklern Ort,
> Verglühte Asche der Staub.

I lay down under the linden-tree, in which the nightingale was trilling; it sang [it sang] me into the sweetest of dreams [it sang me into the sweetest of dreams], which lasted [which lasted] long enough.

For now that I am awake the bird has flown away and I am covered in withered leaves [I am covered in withered leaves] but not yet alas by the dust which in a still darker place [in a still darker place] will cover my burnt-out ashes [my burnt-out ashes].

As in *An die Nachtigall* (No. 66), that bird-song symbolises passionate love; here its departure and the ensuing silence together induces a death-wish. This setting was no doubt intended as a companion-piece to the same poet's *In der Gasse* (No. 97); and Brahms's response is just as ready and real, again as if drawn from some deep personal source. But here he sets the sentiments rather than the lyric as such; and as a result the construction sounds contrived, as if the composer is forcing his musical material to fit the poem, which is itself already rather contorted. Thus the opening melodies are anything but tailor-made for the words; and the required cutting, stretching and stitching, though adroit, can often feel uncomfortable – as in the stressed 'unter' and the dotted minim on 'dem' (which).

But the general mood- and scene-painting are admirable. The repeated bar of prelude depicts the blissful Brahmsian dream-state of trance and bird-song, here with hypnotic repetitions of the words and a sweet full-throated vocal line. The dream arpeggios stop abruptly before 'Denn nun ich erwache' (For now that I am awake), where the surge of new and tragic awareness is expressed by right-hand sextolets and sforzandi that shiver and shake in the cold awakening of a bleak A minor. The accompaniment takes on a drooping tone apt for withered leaves, which suddenly blaze into 'verglühte Asche' (burnt-out ashes). Here the right-hand triplet chords resume, in a funeral march leading down into a final darkness by way of agonized discords that combine both notes of the last anguished cry of 'Asche', as if adding 'ashes to ashes'.

NOTES. 1. The source was Hebbel's *Gesammelte Werke* (1865–7) which Brahms owned. As ever, he responded deeply to the themes of bird-song and dream, isolation and departure; cf. also *Die Mainacht* (No. 59), here with an added dimension of death as in *Der Tod, das ist die kühle Nacht* (No. 176) or *Immer leiser* (No. 187).

2. At 'sie sang', bars 9–10, the nightingale sings a rising minor third, as at the end of *In Waldeseinsamkeit* (No. 155), which is clearly a Clara song. So the repeated Clara-theme here (M33), *molto dolce* and further enhanced by arpeggiation, beginning in the right hand at those words (bars 10–11) comes as no surprise. Perhaps she also appears in the awakening, as in the dream; the piano's top notes at bars 28–31 sing the melody C–B♭–A–G#–A.

3. The preluding [C]–D–C in the left hand, followed by G–A–G in the right at bar 7, is the blissful M19; the left-hand arpeggios of dream (M9) on the first page respond to the word 'Traum' in bars 13 and 16; the top note on 'süsseste' is M10. The falling phrase there and at 'lange genug' symbolises sleep, while the prolonged dominant sevenths at those words are M24. The shivering sextolets at 'erwache' are rarely heard elsewhere; but their motivic sense is manifest. In the postlude's funeral march the right-hand quaver triplets aptly recall Schubert's *Fahrt zum Hades* D526; there the clashing minor 6–5 echo of the second 'Asche' is M20.

99. (Op. 58, No. 8) Serenade: Leise, um dich nicht zu wecken (Serenade: Softly, so as not to wake you) by 1871
Adolf von Schack

A minor e′–b♭″

Leise, um dich nicht zu wecken,
Rauscht der Nachtwind, teure Frau!
Leise in das Marmorbecken
Giesst der Brunnen seinen Tau.

Wie das Wasser, niedertropfend,
Kreise neben Kreise zieht,
Also zittert, leise klopfend,
Mir das Herz bei diesem Lied.

Schwingt euch, Töne meiner Zither,
Schwingt euch aufwärts, flügelleicht;
Durch das rebumkränzte Gitter
In der Schönen Kammer schleicht.

'Ist denn, liebliche Dolores', –
Also singt in ihren Traum –
'In der Muschel deines Ohres
Für kein Perlenwörtchen Raum?

O dem Freund nur eine Stunde,
Wo dein Arm ihn heiss umschlingt,

Und der Kuss von deinem Munde
Feurig bis ans Herz ihm dringt!

Hast du ihn so ganz vergessen?
Einsam harrt er am Balkon,
Überm Wipfel der Zypressen
Bleicht des Mondes Sichel schon.

Wie das Wasser, niedertropfend,
Kreise neben Kreise zieht,
Also zittert, leise klopfend,
Ihm das Herz bei diesem Lied.'

*Softly murmurs the night wind, so as not to wake you, dear lady; softly into the marble
basin the fountain pours its dew. As the water dropping down makes circle after circle,
so my heart [my heart], softly beating, trembles at this song.*

*Soar upward, tones of my lyre, soar upward on light wing; slip through the vine-
covered trellis into my beautiful love's bedroom. 'Is there then, lovely Dolores' (so you
must sing into her dream) 'no room for a little word of pearl in the shell of your ear [no
room for a little word of pearl]? Oh grant your friend just one hour when your arms
embrace him, and the kisses from your sweet lips fierily penetrate his heart [fierily
penetrate his heart, fierily penetrate his heart]!*

*Have you so completely forgotten him? He is waiting all alone by your balcony. Over
the cypress tops the sickle moon is already turning pale. As the water dropping down
makes circle on circle, so his heart [his heart], softly beating, trembles at this song.'*

The intended passion of the inept poem borders on bathos. But Brahms treats its
topics with the utmost seriousness, and the result is a masterpiece of the genre.
The melodic asperities that led Friedländer to dub the song's opening and closing
strains North German, rather than the Spanish style that suits the adorable
Dolores, have surely been softened by time; the music now sounds Mendelssohnian in its grace and charm. The accompaniment is quasi-Aeolian, as if the guitar-
strings are plucked by a passing breeze; the prelude's strumming is soft and sad as
if rather expecting the answer 'no'. The background is deftly delineated; in the
interlude between 'Tau' (dew) and 'Wie das Wasser' (As the water) the guitar's
staccato thirds depicting water-drops, or the beating heart and its hopes, are
suitably tearful in their appeal. After the heart has duly yearned in long left-hand
arpeggios a further interlude enhances the dominant tensions, with a reprise at
'Schwingt euch' (soar upward).

A repeat of the first interlude modulates into the major with a personal appeal
to the beloved Dolores; and here Brahms summons all his melodic resources to
match that directness of speech. Her name is greeted by grace notes that recur in
the same melodic phrase, like a personal touch, at the thought of an enchanted
hour spent whispering in her ear and kissing her lips (at 'liebliche Dolores', 'deines
Ohres', 'eine Stunde', 'deinem Munde'). Meanwhile the guitar sings and sighs in
thirds and sixths like an operatic love-duet; here the idiom of popular music is ele-
vated into high art. There is still room for special effects; the ascending left-hand

octaves symbolise siege and subjugation at 'feurig bis zum Herz' (fierily into his heart).

A final interlude leads to the last reprise; voice and piano combine in a cajoling coda, complete with a passionate outcry including a telling if taxing top note. No fermata is marked there; but lingering is surely permitted.

NOTES. 1. The textual source was Schack's 1867 *Gedichte*. Line six has 'neben Kreisen' not 'neben Kreise', and similarly in the last verse; this slip might now be corrected. But the change from the poet's passionless 'so umschlingt' to 'heiss umschlingt' is less reversible, and arguably an improvement; Brahms is warming to his theme. Yet in the same verse he asks for 'nur eine Stunde' instead of Schack's 'noch eine Stunde'. This may be because the two preceding verses, where the poet presents himself as a regular visitor, have been omitted (after 'Raum?'). But it seems quite Brahmsian, consciously or not, to ask for *only* an hour, instead of yet another hour, as if his passion was limited and this was his début. His main conquest is the poetic form, which he adroitly dresses in the required rondo pattern of A–B–A–C–A plus a coda in which the final dripping fountain will sound like an anticlimax unless declaimed with special intensity. So the song, for all its charm, and despite its overt intention, may nevertheless rank as yet another example of the neglected lover left out in the cold, all too suitably symbolised by the poem's sad cypress and wan moon.

2. The staccato of M28 serves as plucked strings or splashing drops; the latter are specially arpeggiated in bars 15–18 to match 'Wie das Wasser niedertropfend', where the open-air horn-passages are manifestly motivic (M22), like the leaping left-hand arpeggios of the yearning heart at bars 19–22. The duetting thirds and sixths that sing to and with Dolores, e.g. at 'also singt', are M18, tastefully draped in long descending chains at 'Perlenwörtchen' etc. The first 'feurig bis ans Herz ihm dringt' is portrayed in a storming octave ascent; at the second, the reference to the prelude and accompaniment of the passionate love-song *Botschaft* (No. 67) may be intentional. The sadly flat supertonic at the final 'ihn das Herz', M23, is transformed into an ecstatic top note, M10. The hemiolas before the reprise at 'Hast du', and in the antepenultimate bar, are M14.

4. The Mendelssohnian parallels include his *Schilflied* Op. 71 No. 4, which begins with the same figuration as here, though without any serenading connotations, and his *Pagenlied* Op. posth, which shares the same key of A minor and also incorporates its own lute accompaniment.

OPUS 59

Songs (Lieder und Gesänge) for solo voice with pianoforte accompaniment, published in December 1873. As with Op. 58, there are two volumes of four songs each, and the title-page makes no mention of the poets or the sources.

100. (Op. 59, No. 1) Dämmrung senkte sich von oben (Dusk has fallen from above) 1873

Johann Wolfgang von Goethe   G minor g–e″

> Dämmrung senkte sich von oben,
> Schon ist alle Nähe fern,
> Doch zuerst emporgehoben
> Holden Lichts der Abendstern.

Alles schwankt ins Ungewisse,
Nebel schleichen in die Höh,
Schwarzvertiefte Finsternisse
Wiederspiegelnd ruht der See.

Nun am östlichen Bereiche
Ahn ich Mondenglanz und Glut,
Schlanker Weiden Haargezweige
Scherzen auf der nächsten Flut.

Durch bewegter Schatten Spiele
Zittert Lunas Zauberschein
Und durchs Auge schleicht die Kühle
Sänftigend ins Herz hinein.

*Dusk has fallen from above; all nearness is already distant. But first the evening star
stands lifted aloft with its lovely light.*

*Everything blurs into uncertainty, mists creep up on high. Ever blacker depths of
darkness are mirrored in the still lake.*

*Now in the eastern region I become aware of the moon's light and glow; the
branching hair of slender willows dallies with the nearby waters. Through the play of
moving shadows, Luna's [Luna's] magic shine trembles down; and through the eyes
coolness steals soothingly into the heart [through the eyes coolness steals soothingly,
soothingly into the heart].*

This song, uniquely in Brahms's oeuvre, arose from an earlier setting of the same
poem. His friend Hermann Levi wrote (Kalbeck ii 150):

> It was in 1870 or 1871. My song had just been completed, but not yet fair-
> copied, when Brahms spent an evening with me ... in Karlsruhe. The singer
> Johanna Schwartz ... was also present. I wrote out my vocal line in pencil, and
> [she] sang it at sight. Three days later Brahms sent me back my pencilled page,
> which he had taken away without my noticing, and enclosed his own setting of
> the poem, inscribed 'Attempted translation of the attached palimpsest'. He had
> retained four bars of my song, namely the vocal melody at 'Nun am östlichen
> Bereiche'.

There is no record that Levi ever understood why his own setting had been thus
superseded, or why the verses had made so special an appeal to Brahms, whose
Goethe settings are infrequent. The inspiration was hardly the poetry as such,
which is cavalierly treated by repetition. Perhaps Brahms himself was unaware of
his own depth of response to any mention of healing coolness. But the modest
Levi was rightly grateful, just as posterity has been.

The low preluding octaves evoke darkness; an insistent 3/8 rhythm depicts a
continuing process of nightfall, down to the deepest register of voice and piano at
'fern' (distant). Then the music mellows into the major with a sequential melody
over wavering alternate hands, as the 'Abendstern' (evening star) shimmers out
'emporgehoben' (lifted aloft). But that curve contains the lowest vocal note thus

far; the darkness is still pervasive. The prelude's bass line recurs to introduce 'Alles schwankt' (Everything blurs), where the opening melody also returns; the accompaniment's line of semiquavers circumscribes the swirling and rising mists. But an all-enveloping blackness still shrouds the music, as the evening-star melody now delves even deeper than ever, mirrored in the sombre lake; now the lowest note comes at the end of 'Finsternisse' (depths of darkness). Only at the mention of the moonlit east ('am östlichen Bereiche') does the music rise and lighten. At 'schlanker Weiden' the sung sequences wave and sway like the slender willows, trailing in the stream as the left hand rises to meet the falling vocal line. Then the moon's long major melody mirrors the earlier evening star, until new dissonant harmonies are resolved from 'Kühle' (coolness) to 'sänftigend' (soothingly) as they move down into the depths of the heart.

NOTES. I. The poem is No. VIII of the *Chinesisch-Deutsche Jahres-und Iageszeiten*, 1827, published among the *Vermischte Gedichte* of the Nachlass. Brahms owned two sets of Goethe's works (one 1860, another undated); but *prima facie* he drew his text from Levi's setting.

2. Plainly the poem made a deep personal appeal to Brahms; it culminates in his favoured theme, much emphasised here by his own repetitions, of how coolness can soothe and heal the hurt heart. This interpretation imposes a preference for the motivic imagery (M7) of the optional lower and descending vocal line at the final 'Herz hinein'.

3. I am indebted to Graham Johnson for the *aperçu* that the melody here at 'Doch zuerst emporgehoben', etc. is heard again, at pitch, as the first eight notes of the theme that opens the last movement of the clarinet sonata, Op. 120 No. 2 (1894). There will surely be some meaningful verbo-musical connection between the two works.

4. The gradual creeping movement of the opening chords is an image of the descending dark; so are the sidling semiquavers that follow. Both are aspects of the locomotion motif M1. The easy flow of accompanied melody at 'doch zuerst' and later at 'Durch bewegter Schatten' reflects the steady light of the evening star and the moon respectively, while the same music in the minor also serves for the dark mirror of the lake, aptly reaching its lowest level at 'Finsternisse'. The willow-sequences of play and sway, though manifestly expressive in their quickening rhythms (M16), are not noted elsewhere; but they contain the convergence of M17. The Schubertian turn to the major mode of the same tonic on the last page (M39) is here used almost literally in the Goethean sense of more light, while the resolved dissonances at 'Kühle sänftigend' are another audible metaphor.

5. Cf. Schoeck's setting, Op. 19a No, 2.

101. (Op. 59, No. 2) Auf dem See (On the lake) by 1873
Karl Simrock   E major d#'–f#''

Blauer Himmel, blaue Wogen,
Rebenhügel um den See,
Drüber blauer Berge Bogen
Schimmernd weiss im reinen Schnee.

Wie der Kahn uns hebt und wieget,
Leichter Nebel steigt und fällt,
Süsser Himmelsfriede lieget
Über der beglänzten Welt.

Stürmend Herz, tu auf die Augen,
Sieh umher und werde mild;
Glück und Frieden magst du saugen
Aus des Doppelhimmels Bild.

Spiegelnd sieh die Flut erwidern
Turm und Hügel, Busch und Stadt,
Also spiegle du in Liedern
Was die Erde Schönstes hat.

*Blue sky, blue waves, vine-clad hills around the lake [around the lake]; above, an
arc of blue mountains shimmering white in pure snow [shimmering white in pure snow].*

*As the boat lifts and rocks us, light mist rises and falls [rises and falls]; the sweet
peace of heaven lies over the radiant world [over the radiant world].*

*Storming heart, open your eyes, look all around and become mild; you can absorb
happiness and peace from this double image of heaven.*

*See how the waters reflect tower and hill, woodland and town [woodland and
town]; so you should mirror in songs the fairest that earth has to show [the fairest that
earth has to show].*

Brahms loved Switzerland and its scenery. This poem about the lake of Geneva
would have had a special appeal for him even without its clinching moral about
art and nature and their relation in lyric forms, a doctrine to which he would
surely have subscribed and had indeed done much to exemplify. It was his mission
in life to mirror the world in music; and this work may well have been his own
modest and self-effacing way of saying so.

Despite the tempo direction 'Etwas bewegt' (rather brisk) the boat seems to be
riding and swaying at anchor, as if Brahms imagined the poet as seeing the sights
rather than steering a course as in *Mein Liebchen, wir sassen beisammen* (No. 179).
The prelude's pedal points and shifting rhythms resound through most of the
song, like the firm-based rocking of a cradle, as the waves lap contentedly around.
This effect is enhanced by the regular echoing of the poem's line-endings; there
and throughout, the vocal melody is so immediately appealing that its loose fit to
the words should pass unnoticed, despite the need to allocate two notes to every
other syllable, e.g. in the voice's first eight bars.

The second verse uses the same music unchanged; the mood of contented
reverie remains entirely relevant, as encapsulated in the key word 'Himmelsfriede'
(peace of heaven). Then at 'stürmend' (storming) triplet quavers surge up in the
left hand and are gradually absorbed into the accompaniment, as if the wild heart's
shock is being absorbed into the calm waters in both music and poem. But the
listener is told that the artist's life is far from unruffled or untroubled, and that
calmness entails self-control.

This knowledge is embodied in the last verse, where the exact recurrence of the
opening strains is infused with fresh meaning. Simrock was no major poet; yet
here his ingratiating verses are made to convey a Wordsworthian grandeur of
vision. The imagined invocation of nature and humankind together, the works of

God and man, is so splendidly framed and coloured by this music as to make the picture not just presentable but persuasive.

NOTES. 1. The source was Simrock's *Gedichte* (1844), where the verses appear in the section *Schweizerreise 1833* under the title 'Vevay' (sic), on the shores of Lac Léman, the Lake of Geneva, already memorably hymned by Lamartine.

2. Note the unstated yet perceptible theme of passionate turbulence cooled and abated by the healing forces of nature.

3. Brahms demonstrates his melody's dominance by setting the phrase 'steigt und fällt' to the same repeated note.

4. The tonic pedal reflects peace and tranquillity, interrupted only by the equally expressive upsurge of quaver triplets at 'stürmend' etc., The hemiolas at e.g. bars 5–6 are M14; the long dominant seventh before the final reprise at 'Spiegelnd' is M24.

5. The unexpected appearance of E–E♭ within the key of E major at 'Glück und (Frieden)', read in conjunction with note 2 above, may hint at thoughts of Elisabet von Stockhausen (M35).

102. (Op. 59, No. 3) Regenlied (Rain song) 1873
Klaus Groth   F# minor e#'–a''

> Walle, Regen, walle nieder,
> Wecke mir die Träume wieder,
> Die ich in der Kindheit träumte,
> Wenn das Nass im Sande schäumte!
>
> Wenn die matte Sommerschwüle
> Lässig stritt mit frischer Kühle,
> Und die blanken Blätter tauten
> Und die Saaten dunkler blauten,
>
> Welche Wonne, in dem Fliessen
> Dann zu stehn mit nackten Füssen,
> An dem Grase hinzustreifen
> Und den Schaum mit Händen greifen,
>
> Oder mit den heissen Wangen
> Kalte Tropfen aufzufangen,
> Und den neu erwachten Düften
> Seine Kinderbrust zu lüften!
>
> Wie die Kelche, die da troffen,
> Stand die Seele atmend offen,
> Wie die Blumen, düftetrunken,
> In dem Himmelstau versunken.
>
> Schauernd kühlte jeder Tropfen
> Tief bis an des Herzens Klopfen,
> Und der Schöpfung heilig Weben
> Drang bis ins verborgne Leben.

Walle, Regen, walle nieder,
Wecke meine alten Lieder,
Die wir in der Türe sangen,
Wenn die Tropfen draussen klangen!

Möchte ihnen wieder lauschen,
Ihrem süssen, feuchten Rauschen,
Meine Seele sanft betauen
Mit dem frommen Kindergrauen.

*Pour down, rain, pour down; reawaken for me the dreams I dreamed in childhood as
the water foamed in the sand!*

*When the weary sultriness of summer idly strove with cool freshness, and dew shone
bright on the leaves, and the crops turned a darker blue [the crops turned a darker
blue], what bliss it was to stand in the flowing water then with naked feet, or to brush
against the grass, or grasp the foam in my hands, or to feel cold drops on my hot cheeks,
or to bare my boyish breast to the newly-awakened fragrances [to bare my boyish
breast]!*

*Like the dripping flower-cups, my breathing soul stood open, like the flowers
intoxicated with scent, drowned in the dew of heaven,*

*each shuddering drop seeped through to my beating heart, and the holy interweav-
ing of creation penetrated into our secret lives [penetrated into our secret lives].*

*So pour down, rain, pour down; awaken my old songs that we sang in the doorway
while the drops pattered outside. I'd love to listen to them again and their sweet moist
sounds, and softly bedew my soul with innocent childlike awe [with innocent childlike
awe].*

The poem is hectically overwrought; Brahms restores its ideas to health and
healing in one of his finest recreations of boyhood fervour and nostalgia. He could
always echo and respond to such sentiments; and when they were linked with the
restorative effect of cool freshness, another favourite theme, and preserved in
verses penned by a dear North German friend, they would become entirely
irresistible.

The prelude's opening rhythm anticipates the voice's first three notes, as if to
say its own 'Walle, Re[gen]'. But it also seems, as Max Kalbeck says (ii 378f),
to encapsulate some special motivic sense of its own; distant bird-song from
remembered boyhood, or memory tapping at the window-pane. In the right-hand
figuration, dreams duly rise as the rain falls; 'Träume' and 'Regen' belong together
in the music as in the poem. At the mention of leaves ('Blätter') and crops
('Saaten') the vision broadens and brightens, while the rain-fed water flows
('Fliessen') in downward right-hand arpeggios, with staccato single notes in the
left for flakes of foam ('Schaum') turning to chromatic crotchets at 'cold drops'
('Kalte Tropfen'). Thus the scene is vividly recreated and experienced anew. But
the ensuing reflective section lends itself less readily to such depiction. The
staccato chords continue at 'troffen' (dripping) and 'Tropfen' (drops); but the
bright major key-change and the new solemn saraband tempo will sound

contrived without fine performance, especially given the length and stress allotted to the inessential words 'an' (to) and 'ins' (into). However, the reprise of 'Walle, Regen' again recreates the land of lost content, glimpsed through rain and tears and finally shining plain in an unclouded major chord.

NOTES. 1. The text was taken from Groth's *Hundert Blätter: Paralipomena zum Quickborn* (1853), which Brahms owned. There, the poet has 'in den' not 'in dem [Himmelstau versunken]'.

2. Note the favourite theme of heat assuaged by coolness, as Groth's second stanza says.

3. The composer re-worked the main rain-drop theme of this song and the next in the finale of his first violin sonata Op. 78 some five years later. There are traces of its nostalgic mood elsewhere in that same masterpiece; thus the repeated motto-theme that begins the piano and voice parts here also begins the violin part of Op. 78. There however all the musical material is carefully tailored together; here the poetic form has to be suited, which arguably entails too much tucking and pinning.

4. The same-note rhythm ♩ ♪ | ♩, which informs the entire song, is plainly expressive in intent, like the 'kalte Tropfen' accompaniment and the flowing downward arpeggios of the water-music at 'welche Wonne' and the finality of the concluding melodic line at 'Kindergrauen'. The full chordal rain-drop staccato of M28 recurs at 'Wie die Kelche' etc.; the top note at the keyword 'Kinderbrust' is M10.

103. (Op. 59, No. 4) Nachklang (A distant echo) 1873
Klaus Groth   F sharp minor f#'–a''

> Regentropfen aus den Bäumen
> Fallen in das grüne Gras,
> Tränen meiner trüben Augen
> Machen mir die Wange nass.
>
> Wenn die Sonne wieder scheinet,
> Wird der Rasen doppelt grün:
> Doppelt wird auf meinen Wangen
> Mir die heisse Träne glühn.

Raindrops fall from the trees on to the green grass; tears from my sad eyes make my cheek wet [my cheek wet].

When the sun shines out again the grass looks twice as green; twice as bright on my cheeks the hot tear will glow [the hot tear will glow].

This is Brahms's sole re-setting of the same text (see note 1); the words must have meant much to him. Here the emphasis is more on present emotion and less on boyhood reminiscence; so the rain is more metaphorical than real. But it is no less pervasive; again it patters through the piano part as in *Regenlied* (No. 102), with the same rhythmic motif and the same compulsive effect. The rain-drops represent tears of real distress, heard in the plangent discord after 'Wange nass' (cheeks wet). Here the motif is truncated to a repeated ♩ ♪ | ♩. in the right hand at the half-bar, sounding half as long but twice as bright in the piano part at 'Wenn die Sonne' (When the sun) etc. and emerging into a colourful A major after 'doppelt grün' (twice as green). For the next 'doppelt' the same idea is transferred to the left hand, on notes that rise by successive semitones to usher in the final refrain of 'heisse Träne glühn'. The postlude repeats the original rain-song motif, and ends in a more contented and fulfilled frame of mind, as if the tears have afforded real relief.

NOTES. 1. Brahms had already set this poem, from manuscript, by the summer of 1872 under the title *Regenlied* (No. 62). Groth later changed his fifth line 'Scheint die Sonne wieder helle' to the clearer 'Wenn die Sonne wieder scheinet', as above. Brahms reset the poem, thus amended, as a pendant to No. 102, to which his original title *Regenlied* had been transferred. Groth's published version also has the plural 'die Wangen' in line 4, to match line 7.

2. The thematic material again takes precedence over the accentuation; thus bar 5 sets the inexpressive preposition 'in' to a three-crotchet down-beat.

3. The anguished discord that begins bar 17 is instantly followed by the Clara-theme M33 in the left hand. If that usage is intentionally allusive, it might suggest the same significance at the words 'trüben Augen' in bars 10–11. The A major sunshine suits 'die Sonne', and tears gleam (M28) in the postlude's F# major chords.

104. (Op. 59, No. 5) Agnes (Agnes) 1873
Eduard Mörike   G minor g'–g''

Rosenzeit, wie schnell vorbei,
  Schnell vorbei,
Bist du doch gegangen!
Wär mein Lieb nur blieben treu,
  Blieben treu,
Sollte mir nicht bangen.

Um die Ernte wohlgemut,
  Wohlgemut,
Schnitterinnen singen.
Aber, ach! mir krankem Blut,
  Mir krankem Blut,
Will nichts mehr gelingen.

Schleiche so durchs Wiesental,
  So durchs Tal,
Als im Traum verloren,
Nach dem Berg, da tausendmal,
  Tausendmal
Er mir Treu geschworen.

Oben auf des Hügels Rand,
  Abgewandt,
Wein ich bei der Linde;
An dem Hut mein Rosenband
  Von seiner Hand,
Spielet in dem Winde.

Time of roses, alas, how swiftly by, swiftly by, you have passed. If my lover had only kept faith, kept faith, I'd not be so afraid [if my lover had kept faith, kept faith, I'd not be so afraid].

The reaping women sing contentedly, contentedly at the harvest. But I alas am sick at heart, sick at heart, nothing will go right for me any more [sick at heart, sick at heart, nothing will go right for me any more].

So I creep through the meadow vale, so through the vale, as if lost in a dream, up to the hillside where a thousand times, a thousand times, he vowed to be true to me [where a thousand times, a thousand times, he vowed to be true to me].

Up there on the hill's edge, turned away, I weep by the linden tree; in my bonnet the rose-red ribbon, the one he gave me, plays in the wind [the rose-red ribbon, the one he gave me, plays in the wind].

Brahms turns Mörike's beautiful folk-inspired lyric back into the imagined original folk-song by adding further repetitions of his own. Each echo is then treated as it were literally, in matching music, so that the effect becomes rather obtrusive. Perhaps this was intended as an intensified representation of the singer's sad obsession, which Brahms shared; the deserted girl was among his most dearly-cherished themes. For some listeners, such a device will work all too efficiently. But there is no denying its effectiveness; and the composer has devoted much effort to variation and contrast. Examples are the piano's sidelong parallel thirds at 'schleiche' (I creep), the wavering chromatics of the last verse as the ribbon plays in the wind, and the piano's small-scale solo outbursts of grief throughout.

NOTES. 1. The source was either Mörike's *Gedichte*, of which enlarged and revised editions had appeared by 1873, or the novel *Maler Nolten*, which includes the same lyric. Apart from *An eine Aeolsharfe* (No. 33) Brahms drew only once more (in the duet *Die Schwestern* Op. 61 No. 1) on the wealth of that great master; and in each instance it was apparently the supposed plight of unhappy girls that attracted him, rather than the poetry as such.

2. The variable time-signature and modal allusions are M26 and M27 respectively; the canonic imitation at the second 'wär mein Lieb' is M12. Perhaps the imagined arm-movements of the reapers prompted the alternating hands of M2 at 'um die Ernte' etc. The top Gs at 'krank(em)' and 'tau(send)' are M10; the parallel thirds and sixths in the minor tonality are the duetting love-motif M18 as well as a response to 'schleiche'. The piano's drooping chromatics in the last verse are also expressive.

3. Cf. Wolf, No 14 of the Mörike songs; Franz, Op. 27 no. 5; Schoeck WoO 20 (chorus a cappella); Distler, Op. 19 (TB).

105. (Op. 59, No. 6) Eine gute, gute Nacht (A good, good night) 1873
Georg Daumer (from the Russian)   A minor g'–a''

>Eine gute, gute Nacht
>Pflegst du mir zu sagen—
>über dieses eitle Wort
>O wie muss ich klagen!

> Dass du meiner Seele Glut
> Nicht so grausam nährtest;
> Eine gute, gute Nacht,
> Dass du sie gewährtest!

A good, good night, you are accustomed to bid me.
   How I must bewail that idle word! If only you would not so cruelly add fuel to my soul's fire [not so cruelly add to it]; a good, good night, if only you would grant it [if only you would grant it]!

Brahms lived in an age when mere suggestiveness counted as genuine eroticism; and here, as so often, he justifies his poetic choice by his musical treatment. The mood is gently playful and teasing. The prelude is already heard singing the titular key-phrase to itself. Its echoes in left-hand diminution are heard as it were in hiding, safely out of clear earshot. But they peep out rather more boldly in the interlude after 'Nacht' (night), where the right hand semiquavers ironically echo 'eine – gute – gute – Nacht', meaning that the singer knows better. The prelude's motto theme reappears after 'klagen' (bewail), and is shifted into off-beat sighs at 'Seele Glut' (soul's fire). The successively higher top notes at each 'dass' (if only) plead for requited love, which is twice graciously anticipated in the tonic major at 'sie gewährtest' (grant it); the prelude again quotes the title, and all ends happily.

NOTES. 1. The textual source was Daumer's *Polydora* (1855), which Brahms owned. That collection of pastiche national lyrics includes these untitled verses in its Russian section; but perhaps Daumer was rewriting Shelley, whose own poem 'Good night' makes the same point. In *Polydora*, the second 'Eine gute, gute Nacht' is enclosed in inverted commas as if in ironic quasi-quotation; but Brahms presumably felt that his repeated melody was already imitative enough.
   2. No doubt the favourite theme of passion as fire, this time if not cooled then at least not fuelled, made an added appeal to Brahms.
   3. The sentiments seem suitably addressed to Clara, at least covertly in song; so the new ideas B♭–A–G–F#–G and F–E–D–C#–D heard in the postlude may well represent her theme M33.
   4. The many deliberate diminutions create a mood of teasing endearment. The small sighs before and at 'Seele Glut' belong to M21; the top notes on 'dass', giving the sense of 'if only', are M10.

106. (Op. 59, No. 7) Mein wundes Herz (My wounded heart) 1873
Klaus Groth   E minor and major e'–g"

> Mein wundes Herz verlangt nach milder Ruh,
> O hauche sie ihm ein!
> Es fliegt dir weinend, bange schlagend zu –
> O hülle du es ein!
>
> Wie wenn ein Strahl durch schwere Wolken bricht,
> So winkest du ihm zu:
> O lächle fort mit deinem milden Licht!
> Mein Pol, mein Stern bist du!

My wounded heart longs for gentle peace; oh, breathe that peace into it! It flies to you weeping and beating anxiously; oh, enfold it!

As when a ray breaks through heavy clouds, so do you beckon to my heart; oh, keep on smiling with your tender light [with your tender light]! You are my pole and my star [you are my pole, my star, you are my star]!

The prelude sings sadly of the broken heart; its broken sixths continually cry out 'mein wundes Herz'. Meanwhile the left hand twice sharply recalls the wound inflicted; in the ensuing isolated silence the voice enters alone, with a new descending strain for 'mein wundes Herz' that soon roams far upward in a wide range of minor melody, depicting a longing ('verlangt') which the right hand echoes in smaller note-values as if seeking to diminish it. The left hand then sings the same tune in the major, hoping to be held and healed. But the minor tonality returns after 'ihm ein' (into it), and with it the sad 'mein wundes Herz' theme in the left hand. This is instantly inverted in the voice at 'Es fliegt dir weinend' (It flies to you weeping), and is treated more optimistically in the left hand; again the music audibly seeks solace. After an interlude which recalls the prelude, the first strain returns, hopefully as before at 'winkest du ihm zu' (you beckon to my heart). Now the music moves into the tonic major, with a Schubertian felicity. There the 'wundes Herz' melody takes on a far more tender and loving tone; the sixths though still separate are no longer broken but united in a love-duet. That motif thus softened is heard a dozen times, from the voice as well as the piano, in canon and diminution. At the final 'mein Stern bist du', those last words and their left-hand echo also say 'mein wundes Herz', but now in a forgiving major tonality, and in augmentation, with minims instead of crotchets. Thus the heart swells and contracts, in a typical diastole and systole of longing and assuagement, expressed by deliberate artifice as well as unselfconscious artistry, each of the highest order. Only Brahms would thus equate the hurt heart with the contrapuntal brain; but those who relish this blend will find few finer examples in the lied literature.

NOTES. 1. The text was taken from Groth's *Hundert Blätter: Paralipomena zum Quickborn* (1854), which Brahms owned. The choice of this undistinguished lyric, with its weak repetition of 'ein' to finish the second and fourth lines, suggests (as so often) that the composer is expressing a powerful personal feeling, such as his favourite theme of cooling balm for the hurt heart.

2. The prelude's motif

though clearly meaningful in the sense of hurting or wounding is not found elsewhere.

3. The enhanced and prolonged dominant sevenths of bars 4 and 24 are M24; the latter's cadence on E–D# (= S) may perhaps point to Elisabet von Stockhausen, M35. The unaccompanied vocal entry is M29, eloquent of loneliness and isolation; thereafter the minor or major diminutions and inversions are all expressive in the sense of dark despair or brighter hopes. The canonic imitations are M12.

107. (Op. 59, No. 8) Dein blaues Auge (Your blue eyes) 1873
Klaus Groth   E♭ major b♭'–g''

> Dein blaues Auge hält so still,
> Ich blicke bis zum Grund.
> Du fragst mich, was ich sehen will?
> Ich sehe mich gesund.
>
> Es brannte mich ein glühend Paar,
> Noch schmerzt das Nachgefühl:
> Das deine ist wie See so klar
> Und wie ein See so kühl.

Your blue eyes keep such silence, I gaze down into their depths. You ask what I seek to see? I seek to be cured.

A pair of ardent eyes burned me; the after-feeling hurts me [hurts me] still. But your eyes are so clear, like a lake, and like a lake so cool [and like a lake so cool].

Here once again is the favourite theme: healing coolness assuages the fires of passion. The prelude, like the poem, links two lines of sight together. Brahms employs the most effective yet least obtrusive of musical metaphors. As the left hand rises in arpeggio quavers, the right falls in arpeggio crotchets, until they meet and wait expectantly; then they resume and resolve. Thus the gazes mingle. These four bars begin and end in the home key; but as the voice enters, the chromatic chord that created the tension is heard again at 'blaues' (blue). For 'Ich blicke bis zum Grund' (I gaze down into their depths) the vocal melody begins by a gradual crotchet descent, which is then lengthened into left-hand minims; at 'Du fragst mich' the voice joins in the depiction by descending to its lowest note, at the firm asseveration 'gesund' (cured). The interlude laments, which initiates a painful flatward movement at 'es brannte mich' (burned me). But gradually the sorrow ends, and the vision clears, leaving the clear lake-water of an innocent gaze, on which the postlude, mirroring the prelude, lovingly reflects.

NOTES. 1. The text was taken from Groth's *Hundert Blätter: Paralipomena zum Quickborn* (1854), which Brahms owned. Groth was a close personal friend; so the lyric as well as the music may well have been made to fit the composer's favourite theme of healing coolness and his own personal experience of it.

2. These feelings were arguably evoked by, if not voiced to, the young Elisabet von Stockhausen, with Clara also much in mind. They both had beautiful eyes. If so, the key of Es (= E♭) may be significant, M35; and so may the Clara theme D–C–B♭–A–B♭, M33, e.g. in the left hand minims at 'Du fragst mich, was ich sehen will?' and again a minor third higher at the identificatory 'das deine', after which the music regains its cool composure.

3. There is reason to believe that Brahms himself is also present (see pp. 20–21 above) as M36 in the first interlude before 'es brannte mich', with H (= C♭), A, B (= B♭) in the right hand and S (= Es, = E♭) in the left.

4. The prelude's left-hand arpeggios of contemplation are M9; the voice's steady stepwise decline at 'so still, ich blicke' etc is motivic in the sense of sleep, here bordering on hypnosis, while the ensuing left-hand minims there respond to 'still'. The low note on '(ge)sund' recalls 'ich blicke bis zum Grund', down to the depths of M6; the progression

to the questioning dominant at 'sehen will?' is M24. The flatward movement at 'Es brannte' is M42; there, the falling tones and alien harmonies at the word 'schmerzt' symbolise distress, like the ominous glimpses of E♭ minor; similarly the quasi-operatic turn on 'Nachgefühl' confesses that that feeling is still cherished, painful though its recollection may be.

108–112 (No opus numbers) Five Ophelia songs 1873
William Shakespeare, *Hamlet* IV. v., trans. A.W. Schlegel and L. Tieck

No doubt Brahms knew the Schumann setting *Herzeleid* Op. 107 No. 1, on the theme of Ophelia's death by drowning, a fate also sought by Schumann himself. And Brahms had evinced his own special sympathy for sad deserted girls, in many a lied of his own. So he was doubly disposed to grant a favour for his friend, the eminent actor Josef Lewinsky, who was playing Hamlet and had sued for new melodies to be sung by his fiancée Olga Precheisen, as Ophelia. He wrote to her in November 1873 that 'Brahms is a dear chap, he has kept his promise and composed the songs, and also added a piano accompaniment for rehearsal purposes … He thinks that naïve simplicity often makes the greater effect on the stage; but you'll already know about this, and the required folk-song style. Take good care of the manuscript …'. So she did; the score remained unpublished until 1935.

108 Wie erkenn ich dein Treulieb

G minor d'–d''

> Wie erkenn ich dein Treulieb
>   Vor den andern nun?
> An dem Muschelhut und Stab,
>   Und den Sandelschuhn.
>
> Er ist lange tot und hin,
>   Tot und hin, Fräulein!
> Ihm zu Häupten ein Rasen grün,
>   Ihm zu Fuss ein Stein.
>
> *How should I your true love know*
>   *From another one?*
> *By his cockle hat and staff*
>   *And his sandal shoon.*
>
> *He is dead and gone, lady,*
>   *He is dead and gone,*
> *At his head a grass-green turf,*
>   *At his heels a stone.*

The 4/4 3/2 time-signature reflects the run-on rhythm of the first verse, as well as implying a folk-song treatment (M26) also discernible in the modal harmonies (M27). The harmonic movement from dominant (M24) to tonic in the first six bars mirrors the question-and-answer construction. The same easy flow of melody serves for the second verse. This simple framework finds room for unexpected pangs of poignancy at the progressions in bars 2, 5, etc.

109 Sein Leichenhemd weiss wie Schnee

B minor b–d″

> Sein Leichenhemd weiss wie Schnee zu sehn
> Geziert mit Blumensegen,
> Das still betränt zum Grab musst gehn
> Von Liebesregen.

> *White his shroud as mountain snow*
> *Larded with sweet flowers*
> *Which bewept to the grave did not go*
> *With true-love showers.*

The alternation of D major and B minor in two-bar phrases preserves the verbal contrasts inversely, making shroud and grave sound sweeter than flowers and love. But the folk-song style easily absorbs all such anomalies.

Note; printed editions of the Schlegel–Tieck translation replace 'still betränt' (silently bewept) in the third line by the corrected version 'unbetränt' ('not bewept').

110 Auf morgen ist Sankt Valentins Tag

G major d′–d″

> Auf morgen ist Sankt Valentins Tag,
> Wohl an der Zeit noch früh,
> Und ich, 'ne Maid, am Fensterschlag
> Will sein eu'r Valentin.
> Er war bereit, tät an sein Kleid,
> Tät auf die Kammertür,
> Liess ein die Maid, die als 'ne Maid
> Ging nimmer mehr herfür.

> *Tomorrow is Saint Valentine's day,*
> *All in the morn betime,*
> *And I a maid at your window*
> *To be your Valentine*
> *[To be your Valentine, your Valentine].*
> *Then up he rose, and donn'd his clo'es,*
> *And dupp'd the chamber door,*
> *Let in the maid that out a maid*
> *Never departed more*
> *[Never departed, departed more].*

The brief prelude sets the scene and the tone; hunter and prey, with a left-hand tantivy. At 'als 'ne Maid' (out a maid), however, the sequences slide and sidle wheedlingly past, as if the roles were reversed. Either way, the left-hand responses to 'Valentin' and 'herfür' are aptly effective, like distant horn-calls.

111 Sie trugen ihn auf der Bahre bloss

F major d'–e♭''

> Sie trugen ihn auf der Bahre bloss,
> Leider, ach leider!
> Und manche Trän fiel in Grabes Schoss,
> 'Nunter, hinunter! und ruft ihr ihn 'nunter.
> Denn traut lieb Fränzel ist all meine Lust.–
>
> *They bore him bare-faced on the bier,*
> *Hey non nonny;*
> *And in his grave rained many a tear.–*
> *You must sing a-down a-down an you call him a-down-a.*
> *For bonny sweet Robin is all my joy.*

The fourth English line is a spoken aside and the last (which comes several lines later) is surely a snatch of a different ditty; but Brahms sets the words provided, including the interpolation 'Hey non nonny' from the Second Quarto, rendered as 'Leider, ach leider'. The flattened seventh on that first word ('sadly') is motivic. In this song, the manuscript contained only the first six bars of accompaniment; the rest were supplied by Karl Geiringer in the 1935 first edition.

112 Und kommt er nicht mehr zurück?

D minor d'–d''

> Und kommt er nicht mehr zurück?
> Und kommt er nicht mehr zurück?
>   Er ist tot, o weh!
>   In dein Todesbett geh,
> Er kommt ja nimmer zurück.
>
> Sein Bart war so weiss wie Schnee,
> Sein Haupt dem Flachse gleich,
>   Er is hin, ist hin,
>   Und kein Leid bringt Gewinn;
> Gott helf ihm ins Himmelreich!
>
> *And will a not come again?*
> *And will a not come again?*
>   *No, no, he is dead,*
>   *Go to thy death-bed,*

He never [never, never] will come again.

His beard was as white as snow
All flaxen was his poll.
  He is gone, he is gone,
  And we cast away moan.
God a mercy [a mercy] on his soul [on his soul].

Here the harmony derives from the first verse; major for the question, minor for the sad answer. This formula is less relevant to the second verse, where the minor key at the final pious invocation 'Gott helf ihn ins Himmelreich' (literally 'God help him into the kingdom of heaven') might have been construed as ironical comment if used in an art-song; but as usual the folk-song style absorbs any element of contradiction.

OPUS 63

Songs (Lieder und Gesänge) for solo voice with pianoforte accompaniment, published in November–December 1874. The grouping of four Schenkendorf settings, together with generic names for two Felix Schumann and three Groth songs, suggest that Op. 63 was conceived as quasi-cyclical.

113. (Op. 63, No. 1) Frühlingstrost (Springtime comfort) 1874
Max von Schenkendorf   A major e′–a″

Es weht um mich Narzissenduft,
Es spricht zu mir die Frühlingsluft;
Geliebter,
Erwach im roten Morgenglanz,
Dein harrt ein blütenreicher Kranz,
Betrübter!

Nur musst du kämpfen drum und tun
Und länger nicht in Träumen ruhn;
Lass schwinden!
Komm, Lieber, komm aufs Feld hinaus,
Du wirst im grünen Blätterhaus
Ihn finden.

Wir sind dir alle wohlgesinnt,
Du armes, liebebanges Kind,
Wir Düfte;
Warst immer treu uns Spielgesell,
Drum dienen willig dir und schnell
Die Lüfte.

Zur Liebsten tragen wir dein Ach
Und kränzen ihr das Schlafgemach
Mit Blüten.
Wir wollen, wenn du von ihr gehst
Und einsam dann und traurig stehst,
Sie hüten.

Erwach im morgenroten Glanz,
Schon harret dein der Myrtenkranz,
Geliebter!
Der Frühling kündet gute Mär,
Und nun kein Ach, kein Weinen mehr,
Betrübter!

*The scent of narcissus floats around me, the spring breeze speaks to me; you loved one
[you loved one], awake in the red glow of dawn, a wreath rich in blossoms awaits you,
you sad one [you sad one, you sad one]!*

*But you must fight for it and act and no longer repose in dreams; let them vanish
[let them vanish]! Come, dear one, come out into the fields, there in the green house of
leaves you'll find it [find it, find it].*

*We're all well disposed to you, you poor love-sick child, we fragrances [we fragrances];
you were ever our faithful playmate, and so you will be served willingly and briskly by
the breezes [the breezes, the breezes].*

*We'll carry your sighs to your beloved and bedeck her bedchamber with blossoms
[with blossoms]. When you leave her, and stand alone and sorrowful, we'll look after
her [look after her].*

*Awake in the red glow of dawn, the wreath of myrtle already awaits you, you loved
one [you loved one]. Springtime announces glad tidings; so no more sighs and weeping,
you sad one [you sad one, you sad one].*

Again the verses are flowery, not to say florid. In the fourth verse, the much-loved
girl is surprisingly left on her own by her lover. Perhaps this brief allusion appealed
to Brahms, as one of his favourite themes. But he responds with equal eagerness
to each waft of the over-perfumed poem, repeating all its rhyming short lines as if
each held some special significance for him. The virtuoso pianism suggests a cello
sonata, in which the voice plays a quasi-instrumental part.

The prelude's motif almost seems to sing a loved name, as it flies away on
symmetrical wings of lifting and dipping melody. These are then widely separated
and repeated in the left hand, to show from the start how far-flung and long-
sustained the feelings are; fragrance, flight, effort, flowers and so forth, in an
outpouring of springtime ecstasy. The marvel is that the song succeeds so well.
The light 6/4 vocal line is further energised by the 3/2 cross-rhythm of quaver
triplets in the right hand, which is shared by the left at 'Betrübter' (you sad one).
There too a flight of arpeggios anticipates the idea of 'Lüfte' (breezes) in the next
verse. Meanwhile a new double-dotted two-handed sparring appears at 'kämpfen'
(fight). That word in this context surely implies no more than a general ardent

exhortation; but Brahms deliberately adjusts his musical frame to find room for a four-bar image of manly endeavour, as if to remind himself as well as his hearers that faint heart never won fair lady. But all such rhythmic complexities are soon smoothed out in good time for the green arbour ('im grünen Blätterhaus'). The winds themselves take wing as they light-heartedly offer to convey the lover's sighs to his sweetheart, in delicate staccato arpeggios. The initial flying motif briefly re-emerges to illustrate 'von ihr gehst' (leave her). Finally the music of the first verse recurs and flies off to a triumphant and exalted conclusion.

NOTES. 1. The text was taken from Schenkendorf's *Gedichte* (1837), of which Brahms owned the fifth (1878) edition.

2. Perhaps Brahms was thinking of his beloved Elisabet von Stockhausen, as the girl in need of companionship and protection; the prelude seems to sing some such forename, like the left hand later; and E–D# (= E.S.) recurs, in A major, at 'Narzissen(duft)', 'Geliebter', and so forth (M35). The cross-rhythm at 'Kranz', etc., is M15.

3. The motif described above as 'flying' is clearly meaningful, though not heard elsewhere. The virile rhythms at 'kämpfen' are M31. The hemiola at 'Kranz, Betrüb(ter)' etc. is M14; the light upwardly-winging arpeggios there and throughout (most explicitly at 'Lüfte') are M3. The top notes at the first '(er)wach' are M10; the enhanced dominant sevenths at 'ihn finden' and in the interlude after the last 'hüten' are M24. The winds' light sweet staccato (M28) at 'Zur Liebsten' is surely intended to continue throughout that *dolce* passage, though unmarked. There the vocal line at 'kränzen (ihr das) Schlafgemach' is the major 5–6–5 of M19, even though it then contradicts the words 'traurig stehst, (sie)'; in this lively setting, the hours dividing lover from lover will soon pass.

114. (Op. 63, No. 2) Erinnerung (Memories) 1874
Max von Schenkendorf   C major e'–g''

> Ihr wunderschönen Augenblicke,
> Die Lieblichste der ganzen Welt
> Hat euch mit ihrem ewgen Glücke,
> Mit ihrem süssen Licht erhellt.
>
> Ihr Stellen, ihr geweihten Plätze,
> Ihr trugt ja das geliebte Bild,
> Was Wunder habt ihr, was für Schätze
> Vor meinen Augen dort enthüllt!
>
> Ihr Gärten all, ihr grünen Haine,
> Du Weinberg in der süssen Zier,
> Es nahte sich die Hehre, Reine,
> In Züchten gar zu freundlich mir.
>
> Ihr Worte, die sie da gesprochen,
> Du schönstes, halbverhauchtes Wort,
> Dein Zauberbann wird nie gebrochen,
> Du klingst und wirkest fort und fort.

Ihr wunderschönen Augenblicke,
Ihr lacht und lockt in ewgem Reiz.
Ich schaue sehnsuchtsvoll zurücke
Voll Schmerz und Lust und Liebesgeiz.

*You wonderfully beautiful moments, the dearest woman in the whole world has
brightened you with her eternal joy, with her sweet light.*

*You scenes, you sacred places, you received that loved image; what marvels, what
treasures you have unveiled to my eyes there!*

*All you gardens, you green groves, you vineyard in sweet beauty, where my queenly
and pure beloved came to me, demure yet so very friendly.*

*You words that she spoke there, you most beautiful word of all, half breathed away,
your magic spell remains unbroken, you still resound and affect me, on and on.*

*You wonderfully beautiful moments, you laugh and entice in endless allure. I look
back with longing, full of sorrow and joy and covetous love.*

The marvellous music succeeds where the words fail; Brahms has set the haunt-
ingly beautiful poem of fulfilled love and requited longing that Schenkendorf
intended to write.

The broad melody that sings from full chords imagines a wide and long road
winding back to a vanished boyhood. The journey begins without preamble, in
sedate eagerness. Soon the left hand adds dreamy arpeggios of reverie, amid quickening awareness, in the section beginning 'Ihr Stellen' (You scenes), where the new
vocal line audibly flowers from the same stem of memory. First a brief interlude
repeats the four descending notes already sung and played at 'die Lieblichste der
ganzen Welt' (the dearest woman in the whole world); thus her image is again
recalled and beheld. Then the same strains re-emerge a third higher, to show how
the sacred places are still filled with her presence. That picture is again painted
after 'enthüllt' (unveiled) where the interlude sings the melody of 'Licht er(hellt)',
as if that sweet light still brightened the scene.

This is now depicted in greater depth and detail, with alternating chords and
extra quaver movement that stand for the grace of her gait as she approached ('es
nahte sich') and the excitement aroused by the words she spoke ('Ihr Worte, die
sie dort gesprochen'). That magic still works, 'fort und fort' (on and on), as the
long vocal notes and unresolved harmonies also explain before melting into the
final reprise. This too is varied from the opening strain; the left hand is now
shifted back on to the beat, with an effect of utter fulfilled absorption in a love
that will last for ever, as the brief postlude confirms by recalling the 'Lieblichste'
melody and prolonging the final chord.

NOTES. 1. The text was taken from Schenkendorf's *Gedichte* (1837), of which Brahms
owned the fifth (1878) edition.

2. The theme of undying love stood high among Brahms's main sources of inspiration.

3. The omission of the first left-hand beat in the first sixteen bars is M29; the ensuing
upward arpeggios have the reverie of M9; the quickening rhythms at 'Ihr Gärten' and 'Ihr
Worte' etc. are also motivic, M16. So are the flatward modulations for 'das geliebte Bild' and
the 'schönstes … Wort' (M42); the prolonged dominant sevenths at 'fort und fort' are M24.

115. (Op. 63, No. 3) An ein Bild (To a picture) by 1874
Max von Schenkendorf   Ab major d′–ab″

Was schaust du mich so freundlich an,
O Bild aus weiter Ferne,
Und winkest dem verbannten Mann?
Er käme gar zu gerne.

Die ganze Jugend tut sich auf,
Wenn ich an dich gedenke,
Als ob ich noch den alten Lauf
Nach deinem Hause lenke.

Gleich einem, der ins tiefe Meer
Die Blicke lässt versinken,
Nicht sieht, nicht hört, ob um ihn her
Viel tausend Schätze winken.

Gleich einem, der am Firmament
Nach fernem Sterne blicket,
Nur diesen kennt, nur diesen nennt
Und sich an ihm entzücket:

Ist all mein Sehnen, all mein Mut
In dir, o Bild, gegründet,
Und immer noch von gleicher Glut,
Von gleicher Lust entzündet.

*Why are you looking at me with such a friendly expression, you picture from far away,
and beckoning to the banished man? He would come to you all too gladly [he would
come to you all too gladly, all too gladly].*

*All my youth reopens when I think of you, as if I were still treading the old path
towards your home [towards your, your home].*

*Like one who steadfastly gazes down into the deep sea, and neither sees nor hears the
many thousand other treasures all around him [the many thousand other treasures];
like one who looks fixedly at a distant star, and knows and names it alone and delights
therein [and delights therein, therein].*

*So all my yearning and spirit are founded in you, dear picture, and are ever set
ablaze by the same fire and the same joy [set ablaze by the same, the same joy].*

The picture frame is carefully constructed, with conscious artifice; the portrait
itself is a speaking likeness, inscribed with Brahms's famous Agathe theme,
readily recognisable through its thin veil of flats:

A   G   A   H   E

The same notes in augmentation form a solid left-hand easel designed to display the canvas at 'O Bild'; then, in repeated diminutions, they summon the gazer towards them at 'winkest' (beckoning). The same theme extends each hand in acquiescence, first the right then the left, at 'er käme' (he would come). The same music is repeated for the second verse, at 'Die ganze Jugend' (All my youth). Then a dominant pedal and low semibreves announce the accompaniment's absorption in a vision of the deep sea ('ins tiefe Meer') while the vocal line concentrates on the Agathe theme in stepwise sequences. Next, the same treatment is accorded to the left hand, while the same dominant E♭ is lifted three octaves higher in repeated quavers, standing for a bright but distant star ('nach fernem Sterne'). Throughout this middle section, the Agathe theme and its derivates are lovingly developed, to be fully restated as it were *en clair* in the final reprise at 'all mein Sehnen' (all my yearning).

NOTES. I. The textual source was Schenkendorf's *Gedichte* (1837), of which Brahms owned the fifth (1878) edition. He clearly cherished the picture theme, and would also have been especially taken by his favourite images of true love as a durable fire or a deep sea. There had already been a twenty-year cooling-off period since he had parted from Agathe von Siebold, but on this evidence any ashes had remained red-hot. Her name had been burned into the first movement of the 1864 string sextet Op. 36, as well as several early songs, such as *Ein Sonett* (No. 24, in the same key as here); a bridal hymn written for her was woven into the 1864 masterpiece *Von ewiger Liebe* (No. 58). She had married in 1868, at thirty-two, and still lived in Göttingen, like Julius Grimm, the mutual friend from whom Brahms in Vienna would have heard news of her, and perhaps even received a photograph. Her signature-tune cited above, voice and right hand in bars 1–2, 13–14, 46–7, recurs so regularly and in so many guises that it serves as a sure guide to Brahms's compositional methods, e.g

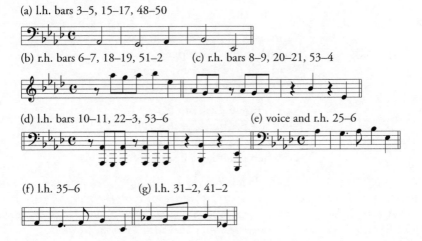

(a) l.h. bars 3–5, 15–17, 48–50

(b) r.h. bars 6–7, 18–19, 51–2   (c) r.h. bars 8–9, 20–21, 53–4

(d) l.h. bars 10–11, 22–3, 53–6   (e) voice and r.h. 25–6

(f) l.h. 35–6   (g) l.h. 31–2, 41–2

while the first three or four notes create a new bass line at bars 29–31, 37–42 and the ascending vocal sequences at 25–32 and 35–42. Typically, the various encipherments differ, often strikingly, in rhythm and texture; thus the motto-theme, symbolising the subject of words and the music together, creates its own new dual unity. For this purpose, it must be distinctly heard, as a portrait must be seen; so both singer and pianist should unobtrusively articulate the unspoken name of Agathe (M32).

2. Perhaps the D♭, also heard in most of these contexts functions as in the string sextet Op. 36 to complete the name A–G–A–D–H–E.

3. Note how the Agathe variations are motivically related to the sense of the words; thus the deep octaves for 'gegründet' at (a) above are M6, with the dominant sevenths of M24 added for 'ins tiefe Meer'; the added thirds and sixths at (c) above are the love-motif M18. Elsewhere, the preluding arpeggio or reverie is M9, and the voice's top A flats are M10. The high repeated right-hand star-notes standing for 'nach fremdem Sterne' are M11; they should surely also be staccato, to signify a point of light.

116. (Op. 63, No. 4) An die Tauben (To the pigeons) 1874

Max von Schenkendorf   C major e′–a♭″

Fliegt nur aus, geliebte Tauben!
Euch als Boten send ich hin;
Sagt ihr, und sie wird euch glauben,
Dass ich krank vor Liebe bin,

Ihr könnt fliegen, ihr könnt eilen,
Tauben, froh bergab und an;
Ich muss in der Fremde weilen,
Ewig ein gequälter Mann.

Auch mein Brieflein soll noch gehen
Heut zu ihr, mein Liebesgruss,
Soll sie suchen auf den Höhen,
An dem schönen, grünen Fluss.

Wird sie von den Bergen steigen
Endlich in das Niederland?
Wird sich mir die Sonne zeigen,
Die zu lange schon verschwand?

Vögel, Briefe, Liebesboten,
Lied und Seufzer, sagt ihrs hell;
Suche ihn im Reich der Toten,
Liebchen, oder komme schnell!

Just fly off now, dear pigeons; I'm sending you as messengers. Tell her, and she's sure to believe you, that I'm love-sick for her [that I'm love-sick for her].

You can fly, you can hasten, pigeons, joyously uphill and down. I must stay here, in a foreign land, an eternally tormented man [an eternally tormented man].

My love-letter too, my loving greeting, should go to her today; it should seek her on the hills, by the beautiful green river [by the beautiful green river].

Will she at last come down from the hills, into the plains? Shall I be shown the sunshine that for too long has vanished from me [too long, too long vanished]?

Birds, letters, messengers of love, song and sighs, tell her this clearly; seek him in the realm of the dead, my darling, or else come soon [darling, or else come soon]!

The pigeons flutter very prettily in quaver triplets, urged on by the syncopated left-hand rhythm. The vocal line's more leisurely arpeggios signify the untrammelled flight itself, with no hint of effort. The music tells the listener not to take the singer's protestations of sickness and torment too seriously. There are brief concessions to the words in the minor harmony at the first 'krank' (sick), a sustained top note at the second, and diminished vocal intervals on each 'gequälter' (tormented). Meanwhile, at 'Ihr könnt fliegen' (You can fly), the triplets have changed direction, like a flock wheeling. The ideas are heard on the wing. At 'Auch mein Brieflein' (My love-letter too) the urgent rhythms are omitted, though this message is equally post-haste; nothing is allowed to interrupt the sweet easy flow of matching musical metaphors, from gliding doves to sliding rivers. In the final reprise at 'Vögel, Briefe' (birds, letters) all the themes journey along together; the opening melody flies high in the right hand and there sings a love-duet with a new vocal line.

NOTES. 1. The textual source was again Schenkendorf's 1837 *Gedichte*, of which Brahms owned the fifth (1878) edition.

2. Perhaps the intended recipient is sufficiently identified by the eleven tonic pedal Cs at 'Auch mein Brieflein' (M33). The diminished interval at 'gequälter Mann' would then be expressive, and the man in question would be Brahms himself, featured in the transposed M36 at that repeated epithet. The flying arpeggios are M3; the top note on 'krank' is M10; the enhanced dominant sevenths before the final reprise are M24; the love-duetting in the last verse is M18.

117. (Op. 63, No. 5) Junge Lieder I: Meine Liebe ist grün (Songs of youth I; My love is green) 1873

Felix Schumann   F# major e#′–a″

> Meine Liebe ist grün wie der Fliederbusch,
> Und mein Lieb ist schön wie die Sonne;
> Die glänzt wohl herab auf den Fliederbusch
> Und füllt ihn mit Duft und mit Wonne.
>
> Meine Seele hat Schwingen der Nachtigall
> Und wiegt sich in blühendem Flieder,
> Und jauchzet und singet vom Duft berauscht
> Viel liebestrunkene Lieder.

My love is green as the lilac bush, and my sweetheart is fair as the sun [my sweetheart is fair as the sun] that shines down on the lilac bush and fills it with fragrance and with bliss [with fragrance and with bliss].

My soul has wings like the nightingale, and sways in the flowering lilac [and sways in the flowering lilac], and exults and sings, enraptured by the fragrance, many a love-intoxicated song [many a love-intoxicated song].

Felix, youngest of the Schumann children, was the godson of Brahms. Felix had yearned to become a musician, but that promising career had been abandoned on medical advice as too taxing. Already at nineteen, in 1873, he was showing symptoms of the tuberculosis to which he would succumb only six years later. But he was still a promising young poet; and his mother sent Brahms some samples, from which this song and the next, as well as No. 160, resulted. 'I'm sending you some of his poems; I'd love you to look through them and make a note of any that please you. Some of them are really pretty; he often has serious thought as well as humour. Tell me frankly what you think of them. Don't suppose that I, as a loving mother, think he's a genius; on the contrary, I have such fear of overestimating the talents of [Robert's] children that I perhaps often set them too high a standard.' Thus wrote his justifiably proud mother in September 1873 (Litzmann ii 25–6). Brahms was also preoccupied with looking through Clara's piano solo arrangements of some thirty Schumann songs, and making suggestions. Later that year we hear of some improvement in Felix's health, despite a persistent cough. On Christmas Eve came the reply; 'Dear Clara, Early this morning the verses fell into my hands and head – probably because I was getting cross at my own inability to provide or think of anything for a festive occasion. Perhaps it could be a little seasonal present for the sisters too, as they're sure to enjoy singing their brother's verses …'.

Clara: 'The song was a lovely surprise, and especially so for Felix. We hadn't told him anything about it. I showed it to Joachim when he arrived that evening, and we started to play it through. Then Felix came in and asked what the words were, and when he saw his own, he turned quite pale. And how beautiful the song is, and its postlude – I could play that on its own, over and over. The G sharp is so marvellous as it leads into the beginning again' (Litzmann ii 37).

The song begins with overt homage to the song-writing of Schumann senior at his most Romantic (*Schöne Fremde* Op. 39 No. 6), as if he had been reborn in his son's poetry and his disciple's music.

Brahms Op. 63, No. 5

Schumann Op. 39, No. 6

Each set of alternating chords expresses a thrilling pantheistic exhilaration generated by natural surroundings. The effect is much enhanced by bright tonality and free vocal melody; for sympathetic listeners, the ripple of sunlight on leaves shines from this music. The interlude conveys mounting excitement culminating on the low left-hand G# octave that Clara especially admired. There follows an exact repetition rare in Brahms; no doubt he felt, rightly, that the slight verses could hardly sustain his usual thoughtful variations. But he had done enough; the song is a masterpiece of its kind.

NOTES. 1. The titles of this song and the next were no doubt Brahms's own, as in Nos. 119–21 and 122–3.

2. Felix Schumann had been travelling in Italy for the sake of his health. His father's setting of the Eichendorff poem *Schöne Fremde* may have intended to evoke Italy as the beautiful foreign land of the title, because of its references to ruined walls, old gods and myrtle trees. Hence perhaps Brahms's quotation of it, given also that Felix's poem too described the effects of light on leaves in conjunction with feelings of intoxicated ecstasy ('Wonne ... liebestrunkene Lieder' here; cf. 'trunken ... grosses Glück' in the Schumann setting). The voice–piano melody in related remote keys confirms the deliberate allusion; analysis discloses many further resemblances, such as the bass-line movement from D# to accidental B# in the opening bars. Even so, the affinity is more notable for its evidence of how Brahms's mind worked than for any clear musico-verbal cross-reference. Here (as often elsewhere, on his own testimony) he speaks in Schumann's language.

3. The interlude's quaver triplets are M3 and its climactic enhanced dominant is M24; the latter's resolution on the low tonic is M8. The finality of the vocal cadences at 'Duft ... Wonne' etc. is motivic; the top As on 'Wonne' and 'Lieder' are M10. The insistent alternate hands throughout are M30.

118. (Op. 63, No. 6) Junge Lieder II (Songs of youth II) 1873–4
Felix Schumann   D major c#'–g''

> Wenn um den Holunder der Abendwind kost
> Und der Falter um den Jasminenstrauch,
> Dann kos ich mit meinem Liebchen auch
> Auf der Steinbank schattig und weich bemoost.
>
> Und wenn vom Dorfe die Glocke erschallt
> Und der Lerche jubelndes Abendgebet,
> Dann schweigen wir auch, und die Seele zergeht
> Vor der Liebe heiliger Gottesgewalt.
>
> Und blickt dann vom Himmel der Sterne Schar
> Und das Glühwürmchen in der Lilie Schoss,
> Dann lasse ich sie aus den Armen los
> Und küsse ihr scheidend das Augenpaar.

When the evening breeze caresses the elder-tree and the moth the jasmine bush, my love and I too exchange caresses on the shady and softly mossy stone bench [on the shady and softly mossy stone bench].

And when the bell sounds from the village, and the exultant evening prayer of the skylark, then we too fall silent and our souls are dissolved by the holy divine power of love [by the holy divine power of love].

And when the host of stars looks down from heaven, and the glow-worm is seen in the lily's lap, then I release her from my arms and kiss both her eyes in farewell [and kiss both her eyes in farewell].

As in No. 117, the setting was more of a chore than a choice; again the marvel is that it succeeds so well. The hectic lyric strives too much for its modest effects; but Brahms sets the essence not the externals. He was always ready to respond to the so-called pathetic fallacy, namely the Romantic identification of human love with external nature, as if their respective beauties and delights were one and the same. All this is further enhanced by the composer's deep affection and sympathy for the doomed young poet, whom he had known and tended from infancy. Melodies and harmonies alike are warm and ingratiating. Chromatic shadows dapple the shining D major surface when the shadiness of the bench ('Steinbank schattig'), the silence of the lovers ('dann schweigen wir auch') and their reluctant parting ('scheidend') are mentioned, which convently occurs at the same place in each verse; otherwise the music moves in an easy natural diatonic flow of breeze and birdsong from first to last, varied only by a soft bass sounding of the evening bell in the second verse.

NOTES. 1. For the text and title, see No. 117. No doubt the two songs were sketched at the same time, at the end of December 1873, but this one, the less inspired of the two, took longer to finish.

2. The lyric ends by bidding farewell to a loved one, as the composer feared he would soon have to say to his godson Felix. In fact, that gifted young poet survived until 1879, when he succumbed to tuberculosis at twenty-five; but his illness had long been diagnosed as fatal and intractable. It may not be coincidence therefore that the music resounds with the notes A–D, which say Ade or farewell in German (M34). That falling fifth is heard thrice in the left hand at the beginning of the first and third strophes (bars 4–5 and 29–30); in the second, it is transformed into the tolling bell, with a deep funereal tone (M6). In the penultimate bar, a low A seems to have been deliberately introduced in the left hand before the final D.

3. Apart from the bell effect, the form is strophically invariant, as in a folk-song. This threefold repetition sounds rather uncharacteristically perfunctory for a lyric which is anything but folk-like in style; but Brahms saw that it was intended as a simple and heartfelt statement and treated it accordingly, with true sympathy.

4. The intensified dominant seventh that ends the prelude is M24; the duetting thirds are the love-song M18; the occasional flatward chromatics are also motivic (M42), like the valedictory vocal line's final farewell at the close of each verse.

119. (Op. 63, No. 7) Heimweh I: Wie traulich war das Fleckchen (Longing for home I: How cosy was the little spot) *c.* 1873

Klaus Groth　　　　　　　　　　　　　　　　　　　　　　G major d'–g''

Wie traulich war das Fleckchen,
Wo meine Wiege ging!
Kein Bäumchen war, kein Heckchen,
Das nicht voll Träume hing.

Wo nur ein Blümchen blühte,
Da blühten gleich sie mit,

Und alles sang und glühte
Mir zu bei jedem Schritt.

Ich wäre nicht gegangen,
Nicht für die ganze Welt!
Mein Sehnen, mein Verlangen,
Hier ruhts in Wald und Feld.

How cosy was the little spot where my cradle rocked [where my cradle rocked]; there was no sapling, no hedge, that wasn't hung about with dreams [that wasn't, wasn't hung about with dreams].

Wherever a flower bloomed, they bloomed too [they bloomed too], and everything sang and shone for me at each step I took [for me at each, each step I took].

I wouldn't ever have gone away, not for the whole world [not for the whole world]! My longing, my yearning, dwells here in forest and field [dwells here, dwells here in forest and field].

The music is meant to mirror the boyhood scenes shared by poet and composer; modest and unpretentious yet completely captivating and unforgettable. The prelude's left hand signs a folk-song stave like a remembered lullaby; its simple theme of four descending semiquavers reappears in the voice at the first 'Wiege' (cradle). The rocking movement in both hands accompanies a cradle song from long ago. At 'kein Bäumchen' (no sapling) the harmony hangs motionless, like the gossamer dreams. In the following interlude the prelude's left-hand melodies audibly bud and blossom in the treble. The same music serves for the second verse, which sings of the same themes. At 'ich wäre nicht gegangen' (I wouldn't ever have left) there are small breaks in the piano part, standing for breaks in the voice; the vocal line itself stays smooth, but is also deployed for expressive ends, such as the long compass of the descending melody that stands for the whole world at 'für die ganze Welt'. In the postlude the folk-song motif is heard in a brief murmured meditation on the opening words: 'wie traulich ... Wiege'.

NOTES. 1. This lyric had been published in *Hundert Blätter: Paralipomena zum Quickborn* (1854) which Brahms owned; like other Groth settings (such as Nos. 120, 121) this song may well have been sketched much earlier. The title *Heimweh* is the composer's own.

2. The extended dominant seventh in the prelude and both interludes is M24; the brief breaks in the accompaniment at 'Ich wäre nicht gegangen' are M29; the top notes at 'meine', 'blühten' and each 'hier' are M10. The flattened chords at 'Heckchen', 'glühte' and 'Verlangen' are also expressive (M41), in the sense of sorrowful yearning.

120. (Op. 63, No. 8) Heimweh II: O wüsst' ich doch den Weg zurück (Longing for home II: Oh if I only knew the way back) 1874
Klaus Groth   E major e'–f#''

O wüsst ich doch den Weg zurück,
Den lieben Weg zum Kinderland!

O warum sucht ich nach dem Glück
Und liess der Mutter Hand?

O wie mich sehnet auszuruhn,
Von keinem Streben aufgeweckt,
Die müden Augen zuzutun,
Von Liebe sanft bedeckt!

Und nichts zu forschen, nichts zu spähn,
Und nur zu träumen leicht und lind,
Der Zeiten Wandel nicht zu sehn,
Zum zweiten Mal ein Kind!

O zeigt mir doch den Weg zurück,
Den lieben Weg zum Kinderland!
Vergebens such ich nach dem Glück,
Ringsum ist öder Strand!

Oh if only I knew the way back, the dear way to the land of childhood! Oh why did I seek my fortune and let go of my mother's hand [my mother's hand]?

Oh how I long to take my rest, not to be woken by any striving, to close my tired eyes, softly covered by love [softly covered by love]! And to seek nothing, to see nothing, and just to dream lightly and gently, not to notice how the times change, a child for the second time [a child for the second time]!

Oh show me the way back, the dear way to the land of childhood! In vain I seek for happiness; all around me is a barren shore [a barren shore].

As in so many of his songs, Brahms metamorphoses an unpromising lyric into a masterpiece, by transmuting its metaphor into music. The catalyst is his own response to a shared North German background, which could be idyllic, as the preceding song among many others had already convincingly claimed. The present poem allusively ends within the sound and sway of the sea, like that Hamburg boyhood itself. There Brahms begins his song, on an imagined strand which was then far from barren; in his memory it still sounds fertile, spacious and full of promise. The prelude creates great waves of nostalgia which continually boom and sigh on the shore of reminiscence. Then the bright tonality moves flatwards at the moment of regret for departure, 'O warum sucht' (Oh, why did I seek) etc. The waves reach a peak of nostalgia at 'O wie mich sehnet' (Oh how I long), where the high octaves briefly yearn before resolving into a new lullaby which sends the left hand to sleep on a two-bar pedal point at 'auszuruhn' (take my rest). This new music is repeated for the third verse, where the symbols of sleep aptly recur at 'der Zeiten Wandel nicht zu sehn' (not seeing the times changing). At 'Vergebens such ich nach dem Glück' (In vain I seek for happiness) the composer is overcome by a personal feeling that goes far deeper than the regretful words, into real tragedy. The descending octaves say a final farewell to the false world, and then depart into austere renunciation. The waves lap emptily, the outlook is bleak; the postlude hopes against hope for better days to come.

NOTES. 1. For the textual source see No. 119.

2. The rising and falling waves that begin the piano part are M5, with the mysterious diminished sevenths of M25 and the deep bass notes of M6. The chromatic yearning at 'sehnet' is characteristic, though uncommon; in the following lullaby at 'Augen zuzutun' the left hand combines the pedal point of sleep with the hemiolas of M14. The latter recur in augmentation at the second '(be)deckt' and the second 'Kind'. The ominous octave descent at 'vergebens' etc, is the Brahmsian death-theme; the flat supertonic there, as earlier at 'warum sucht' ich', is M23.

121. (Op. 63, No. 9) Heimweh III: Ich sah als Knabe (Longing for Home III: Once, as a boy) *c.* 1873

Klaus Groth   A major e'–g''

Ich sah als Knabe Blumen blühn –
Ich weiss nicht mehr, was war es doch?
Ich sah die Sonne drüber glühn –
Mich dünkt, ich seh es noch.

Es war ein Duft, es war ein Glanz,
Die Seele sog ihn durstend ein.
Ich pflückte sie zu einem Kranz –
Wo mag er blieben sein?

Ich such an jedem Blümchen nach
Um jenen Schmelz, um jenes Licht,
Ich forsche jeden Sommertag,
Doch solche find ich nicht.

Ihr wusstet nimmer, was ich trieb?
Ich suchte meinen alten Kranz,
Er war so frisch, so licht, so lieb –
Es war der Jugendglanz.

As a boy, I saw flowers in bloom – I know no more, where were they then? I also saw the sun shining above them – I feel I can see the scene still [I feel I can see it still]. There was a fragrance and a glow that my soul drank in thirstily; I was plucking the flowers for a garland – what can have become of it [what can have become of it]? In every flower I still seek for that lustre, for that [that] light. I search every summer day, but I find no such flowers again. You never knew what I was at? I was looking for my lost garland. It was so fresh, so bright, so dear; it was the gleam of youth [it was the gleam of youth].

The verses seem unrewardingly vague; but again Brahms responds with more than mere nostalgia. There is real regret here, as if he personally shares the poet's predicament; lost love, failed light. The music begins in diatonic brightness, which soon fades and falters amid chromatic confusion and constant key-change. But the recurrent refrains (square-bracketed above) retain and restore the old radiance of fond memories and better days.

NOTES. I. For the textual source see No. 119.

2. Max Friedländer detects the presence of Schubert and identifies *Die Taubenpost* D965A, a song of love-longing, which certainly shows some melodic similarity in the opening vocal line. But there is a much clearer comparison between the refrain here and in *Das Zügenglöcklein* D871; indeed, Brahms seems to quote that song, as if he too wished to sound a passing bell for his own bereavement. If so, it may well be the lost love of Clara that he is mourning here – cf. her threefold theme, M33, in voice and right hand at bar 7 and in the right hand alone at 8–10 (and similarly in bars 33–6).

3. The consecutive sixths and thirds sound like a love-duet, M18; the dreamy arpeggios at 'ich pflückte sie' etc. are M9; the sad minor 6–5, F–E–F–E–F–E, at 'wo mag er blieben sein?' etc. is M20; the top G on 'frisch' is M10.

4. The strict strophic structure bounded by the piano's recurrent two-bar phrase in bars 1–2, 13–14, 39–40, and 52–3 (extended to complete the postlude) deserves detailed analysis. This will show how bars 30–32 have been extended from 5–6 (hence the repetition of the word 'jenes'), and how 46–7 have been altered from 20–21 to match the changed vocal line.

OPUS 69

Nine songs (Gesänge) for solo voice with pianoforte accompaniment, published in two volumes, with named poets, in September 1877.

Brahms twice intimated to his publisher Simrock that this opus should be advertised as 'Mädchenlieder' (Girls' Songs), even though they were not so described on the title-page. Nor in fact are they all girls' songs; thus the third (No. 124) was surely written for a man's voice, in the fashion of the times, since it cries out 'O Mädchen'. But neither Brahms nor his song-writing was sexist in that sense; his art was all-embracing.

122. (Op. 69, No. 1) Klage I: Ach mir fehlt (Lament I: Alas, how I miss) 1877

Anon., Czech (trans. J. Wenzig)   D major d'–f#''

> Ach mir fehlt, nicht ist da,
> Was mich einst süss beglückt;
> Ach mir fehlt, nicht ist da,
> Was mich erfreut!
> Was mich einst süss beglückt
> Ist wie die Well entrückt.
> Ach mir fehlt, nicht ist da,
> Was mich erfreut!
>
> Sagt, wie man ackern kann
> Ohne Pflug, ohne Ross!
> Sagt, wie man ackern kann,
> Wenn das Rad bricht?
> Ach wie solch Ackern ist,

So ist die Liebe auch,
So ist die Liebe auch,
Küsst man sich nicht!

Zwingen mir fort nur auf,
Was mit Qual mich erfüllt;
Zwingen mir fort nur auf,
Was meine Pein:
Geben den Witwer mir
Der kein ganz Herze hat;
Halb ists der ersten Frau,
Halb nur wärs mein!

Alas, how I miss, how I lack, that sweet pleasure I once had; how I miss, how I lack, what gave me such joy! That sweet pleasure I once had has ebbed away like the wave [like the wave]. How I miss, how I lack, what gave me such joy [what gave me such joy]!
    Say, who can till a field without a plough, without a horse? say, who can till a field when the wheel breaks? Alas, such tillage is like love [like love], just like love with no kisses [with no kisses].
    What they keep forcing on me fills me with torment, what they keep forcing on me is agony; they're marrying me off to the widower, whose heart is not whole [not whole]; half belongs to his first wife, only half would be mine [only half would be mine].

And that's not half her luck, or his; she much fears that the old man is impotent into the bargain. The vocal instruction 'unruhig' (restless) seems at first to conflict with the piano's 'grazioso'; but the expressions of continuous defiance are intended to sound almost elegant in their careful control. The prelude is all suppressed but exasperated sighs and restrained but resentful gestures, setting the scene and establishing the mood throughout. The song begins composedly enough on the tonic, but soon announces its distress in chromatic harmonies and varied rhythms. The dramatic pause on the dominant seventh before the voice enters strikes a chord and an attitude; 'just listen to this' is the sense of the music, 'can you credit it?'. Then we learn what the trouble is. The spiky frustrations soften into tender reminiscence at 'Was mich einst süss beglückt' (that sweet pleasure I once had); the metaphor of happiness lapping like a wave prompts a quickened rhythmic impulse at 'die Well, die Well entrückt' (ebbed away like the wave). The piano now improvises in a flow of these semiquavers, anticipating the prelude themes which recur with an audible musical cry of '*how* I miss, *how* I lack'.

It seems that this Wolfian responsiveness of the music to verbal nuance was unconscious, since the same engaging strains are now repeated exactly, though their detailed relevance to the second and third verses is far less clear. But the character-sketch has already come to life, and will bear repetition. The coda adds two bars of cheerful defiance; perhaps all will end happily. Every hearer will hope so.

NOTES. 1. The source was Wenzig's work on folklore, the *Westslawischer Märchenschatz* of 1857, which Brahms owned. His melody constrained him to change 'was mich mit Qual' at the beginning of the third verse to 'was mit Qual mich'.

2. Here a favourite theme is enhanced; the girl is not only deprived of her equally youthful sweetheart but menaced with a literally loveless marriage. Can it be mere coincidence that in this song of final and fatal farewell, the syncopated top notes in bars 5–7 cry out 'A–D–E–A–D–E' (M34) as soon as the voice enters?

3. In this passage only the first four of these semiquaver snaps are marked with an accent in the first verse, and only the first such example in each of the following two verses; but perhaps *simile* is intended in each of these contexts. It would seem consistent to bring out these top notes *passim*, since the basic mood is invariant. Analogous considerations apply e.g. to the left-hand staccato markings in bars 5 or 9, which are not intended to refer solely to those three quavers.

4. The prelude's small sighs are M21; its top line symbolizes separation, as if the odd-numbered quavers are being prised loose and forced further away from the tonic D each time. Then the flattened sixth adds its own distress-signal (M41) and the rhythm quickens for the lapping ebb-tide (M16); the arpeggio wafts of pleasure at 'erfreut' in bars 13–14 are almost like a blush. The prolonged dominant sevenths that introduce each bar are M24.

123. (Op. 69, No. 2) Klage II: O Felsen, lieber Felsen (Lament II: Oh cliff, dear cliff) 1877

Anon., Slovak (trans. J. Wenzig)   A minor d′–f″

O Felsen, lieber Felsen,
Was stürztest du nicht ein,
Als ich mich trennen musste
Von dem Geliebten mein?

Lass dämmern, Gott, lass dämmern,
Dass bald der Abend wink,
Und dass auch bald mein Leben
In Dämmerung versink!

O Nachtigall, du traute,
O sing im grünen Hain,
Erleichtere das Herz mir
Und meines Herzens Pein!

Mein Herz, das liegt erstarret
Zu Stein in meiner Brust,
Es findet hier auf Erden
An nichts, an nichts mehr Lust.

Ich frei wohl einen Andern,
Und lieb ich ihn auch nicht;
Ich tue, was mein Vater
Und meine Mutter spricht.

Ich tue nach des Vaters
Und nach der Mutter Wort,
Doch heisse Tränen weinet
Mein Herz in einem fort.

Oh cliff, dear cliff, why didn't you crash down, when I had to part from my true love? Let twilight fall, God, let twilight fall, so that evening soon beckons and my life also soon [my life also soon] goes down into darkness [goes down into darkness]!

Oh nightingale, you dear bird, oh sing in the green grove; lighten my heart and my heart's pain! My heart lies turned to stone in my breast; it will find here on earth [it will find here on earth] no more joy in anything, in anything [no more joy in anything, in anything].

Now I'm engaged to another, even though I don't love him; I must do what my father and my mother tell me. I obey the orders of my father and mother, yet my heart weeps hot tears [my heart weeps hot tears] all the time [all the time].

The second lament repeats the main poetic themes of the first; separation and coercion. It seems that arranged marriages were as regular among the country folk as the urban gentry. Again Brahms empathises with his heroine's plight, which is now treated much more seriously. She clearly reminds him of a rural Clara; the folksong accompaniment recalls Schumann, almost as if in Brahms's mind that marriage was the misfortune envisaged here. And it had indeed become desperately unhappy, by the time those three first met together; that triangle emitted many a tragic note.

NOTES. 1. The source was Wenzig's work on folklore, the *Westslawischer Märchenschatz* (1857), which Brahms owned. *Pace* Friedländer, it was Wenzig himself, not Brahms, who omitted the second and third verses of an earlier version published in the *Slawische Volkslieder* (1830).

2. The separated and weeping woman is a Brahmsian theme, not to say obsession.

3. Schumann's voice is distinctly if covertly heard here speaking from his *Intermezzo* Op. 4 No. 3, with the same unusual rhythm ♩♪♪♩ on the last beat of the bar, and from his *Armes Waisenkind* (Poor orphan child) Op. 68 No. 6, with the same opening theme in the same 2/4 time-signature; both are also in A minor. Perhaps the C–B–A–G#–A of M33 at '(tren)nen musste von dem (Geliebten)' is no coincidence either.

4. The accompaniment's consecutive tenths are the love-motif M18.

124. (Op. 69, No. 3) Abschied (Departure) 1877

Anon., Czech (trans. J. Wenzig)   B♭ major e♭'–f''

Ach, mich hält der Gram gefangen,
Meinem Herzen ist so weh,
Denn ich soll von hinnen ziehen
Über jenes Berges Höh!

Was einst mein war, ist verloren,
Alle, alle Hoffnung flieht;
Ja, ich fürchte, dass, o Mädchen,
Dich mein Aug nicht wieder sieht.

Dunkel wird mein Weg sich dehnen,
Wenn ich scheiden muss von hier;
Steh ich dann auf jenem Berge,
Seufz ich einmal noch nach dir.

Alas, sorrow holds me captive, my heart is so sore, for I shall have to leave here and go over the top of yonder mountain [over the top of yonder mountain]!

What was once mine is now lost; all, all hope is fled. Yes, I fear, my girl, that my eyes will never see you again [my eyes will never see you again].

My path will stretch out darkly, if I must depart from here; then, when I stand on yonder mountain, I shall sigh for you once again [I shall sigh for you once again].

Here, exceptionally, it is the man who laments; but as in so many other songs the girl is left lonely and lovelorn. The music's marching rhythm and homespun harmonies may be designed to depict a staunch and sturdy countryman, brave in adversity, but still sad under the ostensibly cheerful surface, as the occasional flattened notes testify. The prelude's left hand sets the tone; its four-note phrase will soon be heard beginning the vocal line, which climbs upward from the outset as if already mindful of the mountain. This melody is itself an image of travel; despite the words, it never looks back. No two consecutive notes are ever the same except at 'so weh', which thus stands out like a sore heart; all the rest ceaselessly change position, and shift their ground. The walking accompaniment, which reappears in many other folksong-style compositions and arrangements, is equally graphic and effective. But without superlative performance the major mode will sound out of step with the tragic tale it tries to tell.

NOTES. 1. The source was Wenzig's work on folklore, the *Westslawischer Märchenschatz* (1857), which Brahms owned.

2. Perhaps it was the words 'ich fürchte dass, o Mädchen' etc. (I fear I shall never see you again), and their theme of the deserted girl, that drew Brahms to these verses.

3. The walking semiquavers are M1; the consecutive thirds between voice and right hand in bars 6–7 etc. are M18; the climbing melody is expressive, like the prelude's sadly flattened sevenths (M41).

125. (Op. 69, No. 4). Des Liebsten Schwur (The best-beloved's vow) 1877

Anon., Czech (trans. J. Wenzig)   F major c′–f″

> Ei, schmollte mein Vater nicht wach und im Schlaf,
> So sagt ich ihm, wen ich im Gärtelein traf.
> Und schmolle nur, Vater, und schmolle nur fort,
> Ich traf den Geliebten im Gärtelein dort.
>
> Ei, zankte mein Vater nicht wieder sich ab,
> So sagt ich ihm, was der Geliebte mir gab.
> Und zanke nur, Vater, mein Väterchen du,
> Er gab mir ein Küsschen und eines dazu.
>
> Ei, klänge dem Vater nicht staunend das Ohr,
> So sagt ich ihm, was der Geliebte mir schwor.
> Und staune nur, Vater, und staune noch mehr,
> Du gibst mich doch einmal mit Freuden noch her.

Mir schwor der Geliebte so fest und gewiss,
Bevor er aus meiner Umarmung sich riss:
Ich hätte am längsten zu Hause gesäumt
Bis lustig im Felde die Weizensaat keimt.

Well, if my father would only stop his sulking, awake or asleep, I'd tell him who I met in our little garden. And just sulk, father, sulk away; I met my beloved there, in the little garden [met my beloved there in the little garden].

Well, if my father would stop scolding, I'd tell him what my beloved gave me. And scold away, father, my dear father, he gave me a little kiss and another one to go with it [gave me a little kiss and another one to go with it].

Well, if my father could believe his ears, I'd tell him what my beloved promised me. And be surprised, father, be as surprised as you like, you'll be glad to give me away before long [glad to give me away before long].

My beloved promised me, so firmly and surely, before he tore himself away from my embrace, that I shouldn't have to stay at home any longer than the time when the wheatcrop happily burgeons in the field.

The piano prelude flutters like a bird, in the typical imagery of open-air yearning and exultant dancing; we are meant to see as well as hear a robust country lass in peasant costume. The underlying mazurka-type rhythm that emerges in occasional sforzandos on the third and last beat, e.g. after 'traf' (met) and again at 'Geliebten im Gärtelein' (beloved, in the little garden) should be faintly perceptible *passim*, to accompany the notional elation of off-beat clapping and stamping. As the voice enters, the accompaniment's *sotto voce* is to be taken literally; Brahms must have acquired early, and thereafter taken for granted, the special technique needed for the soft delicate playing of full spread chords. The vocal line is quiet and quasi-conspiratorial; the poem is saying, under its breath, that the girl is expecting a child after that kiss or two, and is just as happy as the wheatfield to prove so fertile. She has reason for looking forward to leaving home. When the lover's vow is revealed in the last verse, at 'Mir schwor der Geliebte', the voice is too excited to wait for the expected piano interlude, and comes bursting in impatiently. Other characteristic subtleties within this deceptively naïve-sounding music include the hidden paternal voice added in the right hand at 'schmolle nur, Vater' (sulk away, father) and similarly at 'zanke' (scold) and 'staune' (be surprised) in the second and third verses; so that when the same music finally recurs at 'ich hätte am längsten' (should have to stay no longer) it takes special satisfaction in thinking that father's tones will soon be heard no more, given any luck, and the left hand frolics accordingly.

NOTES. 1. The source was Wenzig's work on folklore, the *Westslawischer Märchenschatz* (1857), which Brahms owned.

2. The persistent fluttering in both hands is M3; here and elsewhere (e.g. in No. 198) Brahms equates brides with birds. The added paternal voice at the mention of 'Vater' is M37; the rhythmic change and ritenuto that end each verse offer a telling contrast with the lively prelude–postlude that comes dancing on and goes dancing off.

126. (Op. 69, No. 5) Tambourliedchen (Drummer's ditty) 1877
Karl Candidus   A major e'–a''

Den Wirbel schlag ich gar so stark,
Dass euch erzittert Bein und Mark!
Drum denk ich ans schön Schätzelein.
Blaugrau,
Blau,
Blaugrau,
Blau
Ist seiner Augen Schein.

Und denk ich an den Schein so hell,
Von selber dämpft das Trommelfell
Den wilden Ton, klingt hell und rein,
Blaugrau,
Blau,
Blaugrau,
Blau
Sind Liebchens Äugelein.

I play my drum-roll so very hard that it thrills right through you [yes, thrills right through you]! Then I think of my beautiful sweetheart [of my beautiful, beautiful sweetheart]. Blue-grey, blue, blue-grey, blue, so her eyes shine [blue-grey, blue, blue-grey, blue, so her eyes shine].

And when I think of that bright shine, the drumhead of its own accord muffles its fierce tone [muffles its fierce tone] and sounds out bright and clear [sounds out bright, bright and clear]. Blue-grey, blue, blue-grey, blue, are my darling's eyes [blue-grey, blue, blue-grey blue, are my darling's eyes].

Brahms sent this song to his two best-loved lady-friends. But neither Elisabet von Herzogenberg, née Stockhausen, nor Clara Schumann liked it; and the latter austerely added that 'the prelude is very reminiscent of Schubert'. We can hear what she meant; the key and layout suggest one of the piano sonatas then in her repertory, with a touch of Marche Militaire and a typical echo-effect. But Brahms meant it too, perhaps as a deliberate tribute; his song-writing was always sincere, and he was as devoted to Schubert as to the two women, both of whom were pianists. The stiff barrack-square rhythm and left-hand drum-rolls are softened, as the verses require, by singing melodies and wistful chromatics. The young soldier's martial mood is instantly mellowed at 'drum denk ich' (then I think), the first mention of a sweetheart, as the crashing brass band chords are rescored as if for woodwind arpeggios. The colour of her eyes, introduced by a meaningful pause after the second 'Schätzelein' (sweetheart), induces a reverie indicated by an interrupted cadence; the voice's ascending chordal tune, unheard since the prelude, reappears at 'blaugrau, blau', to show that this very subject was in the singer's mind from the first. The verbal repetitions, as so often, are designed to identify and emphasise a general mood; but the song's freshness is preserved by deft touches that vividly delineate a recognisable character and occasion, such as the loud chord that cuts short the day-dreams at the end of each verse. Even the four-square two-verse structure of bar-by-bar identity serves a symbolic purpose; the music is on parade, in open order. Thus the message is drummed home; neither the soldier nor his instrument is as thick-skinned as they seem and sometimes sound. Given suitably sympathetic performance to communicate the tender feelings under the tattoo, this uniformed portrait of the artist (who doted on his own toy soldiers) can be very appealing.

NOTES. 1. The immediate textual source was no doubt the *Vermischte Gedichte* (1869), of Candidus, which Brahms owned. The poet's military vein had earlier been tapped by Schumann in another drum-and-trumpet song, *Husarenabzug* Op. 125 No. 2; perhaps that connection had disposed Brahms favourably to these verses, which he may indeed have inherited, whether in volume form (they also appear in Candidus's *Gedichte eines Elsässers*, 1846) or perhaps in manuscript.

2. The vocal line at 'Drum denk ich ans schön Schätzelein' is among the plainest examples of the joy motif M19; the exultant top A in each verse (M10) is followed by a quiet interlude or postlude ending on a contrastingly loud final chord that anticipates Wolf's drummer-boy in *Der Tambour* (No. 5 of the *Mörike-Lieder*).

3. Perhaps the E. S. of E–D# (in A major, cf. *Frühlingstrost*, No. 113) at 'blau ist' or 'blau sind' was a tonal tribute to Elisabet von Stockhausen, M35. Each such monogram occurs within the motif of Clara, M33; her deeper blue eyes were even more deeply loved (cf. *Dein blaues Auge*, No. 107). The enhanced dominant seventh after the second 'Schätzelein' is M24; the surrounding thirds and sixths are M18; the long descending melody in the piano there and later is symbolic of dreamy reverie.

127. (Op. 69, No. 6) Vom Strande (From the shore) 1877
Anon., Spanish (trans. J. von Eichendorff)   A minor g′–g″

Ich rufe vom Ufer
Verlorenes Glück,
Die Ruder nur schallen
Zum Strande zurück.

Vom Strande, lieb Mutter,
Wo der Wellenschlag geht,
Da fahren die Schiffe,
Mein Liebster drauf steht.
Je mehr ich sie rufe,
Je schneller der Lauf,
Wenn ein Hauch sie entführet
Wer hielte sie auf?
Der Hauch meiner Klagen
Die Segel nur schwellt,
Je mehr mein Verlangen
Zurücke sie hält!
Verhielt ich die Klagen:

Es löst sie der Schmerz,
Und Klagen und Schweigen
Zersprengt mir das Herz.

Ich rufe vom Ufer
Verlorenes Glück,
Die Ruder nur schallen
Zum Strande zurück.
So flüchtige Schlösser,
Wer könnt ihn'n vertraun
Und Liebe, die bliebe,
Mit Freuden drauf baun?
Wie Vögel im Fluge,
Wo ruhen sie aus?
So eilige Wandrer,
Sie finden kein Haus,
Zertrümmern der Wogen
Grünen Kristall,
Und was sie berühren,
Verwandelt sich all.
Es wandeln die Wellen
Und wandelt der Wind,
Meine Schmerzen im Herzen
Beständig nur sind.

Ich rufe vom Ufer
Verlorenes Glück,
Die Ruder nur schallen
Zum Strande zurück.

From the shore I cry out for my lost happiness, but only the sound of the oars comes back to the beach. From the beach, dear mother, where the waves are breaking, the boats sail away and take my lover with them. The more I call them, the faster they fly. If a breeze carries them off, who can hold them back [who can hold them, hold them back]? The breath of my lament merely swells the sail, the more my longing strives to keep them here [to keep them here]! If I suppressed my lamentations, sorrow would release them, and weeping and silence burst my heart between them [weeping and silence burst my heart between them].

From the shore I cry out for my lost happiness, but only the sound of the oars comes back to the beach. Such flimsy foundations, who could rely on them? how could a lasting love be gladly built on them? Like birds in flight, where do they rest? Such hasty travellers, they find no home [they find, they find no home] they shatter the green crystal of the waves, and all they touch is changed [all is changed]. The waves and the wind change ceaselessly; only the sorrow in my heart is constant.

From the shore I cry out for my lost happiness, but only the sound of the oars comes back to the beach.

Exceptionally, there is no prelude; the voice is heard as an actual cry of distress. The piano depicts desolation and its causes; strong winds in the first two bars, high waves in the next two, and the rowlock rattle of pulled oars in the next four. Then, at 'vom Strande' (from the beach), the music is itself sea-borne, on a turbulent barcarolle. Each strophic repetition is rounded off by the refrain as before, with a sustained lamenting top note as the oars recede out of earshot and a prolonged final chord as the girl's gaze continues to yearn seaward after them. Virtuoso performance and interpretation are needed if the song is to make its full effect.

NOTES. I. The Spanish poet, described as anonymous in the translator's source (perhaps the 1832 *Spanisches Lesebuch* of V. Huber) has been identified as Francisco de Borja (1580–1658). His text belongs to a group of traditional lyrics in which a daughter confides her distress to her mother – two favourite Brahmsian themes, which may account for his attraction to these verses. Other examples occur in the 1852 *Spanisches Liederbuch* of Heyse and Geibel, as set by Schumann and Wolf. But Brahms's Eichendorff source (no doubt the *Gedichte* 1843, which he owned) lacks the technical facility and clarity of those who, like Heyse and Geibel, were lesser poets but better translators. Brahms compounded the confusion by three textual errors of his own, all printed in the 1877 issue of Op. 69. Two are rectified by the *Gesamtausgabe*; but the third, 'der Lauf' instead of 'ihr Lauf' in bar 16, is surely also a slip that needs correction.

2. Although Brahms's heart was in his theme, his creative mind was less clearly engaged. The piano part recalls Schumann's *Das ist ein Flöten und Geigen* Op. 48/9, also a song of isolation and love-longing with a sonorous background; and the right-hand sea-music here has evident affinities with Schubert's *Auf dem Wasser zu singen* D774.

3. The right-hand winds and left-hand waves in bars 1–2 etc. are M4/5. The characteristic bass acciaccatura-and-octave click and rattle of oars, repeatedly at 'Ruder' and once in the postlude, which Brahms must often have heard in Hamburg, is an aspect of the virile M31. The hemiola change to 3/4 from 6/8 in the postlude to each verse is M14; the minor 5–6–5 at 'zurü(cke) sie hält' etc. is M20; the dominant there is M24; the top notes are M10.

128. (Op. 69, No. 7) Über die See (Over the sea) 1877
Karl Lemcke   E minor f#'–g''

> Über die See,
> Fern über die See
> Ist mein Schatz gezogen,
> Ist ihm mein Herz
> Voll Ach und Weh,
> Bang ihm nachgeflogen.
>
> Brauset das Meer,
> Wild brauset das Meer,
> Stürme dunkel jagen,
> Sinket die Sonn,
> Die Welt wird leer,
> Muss mein Herz verzagen.

> Bin ich allein,
> Ach, immer allein,
> Meine Kräfte schwinden,
> Muss ich zurück
> In matter Pein,
> Kann dich nimmer finden.

Over the sea, far over the sea, my sweetheart has travelled, and my heart, full of sorrow and pain, has flown anxiously after him.

The ocean roars, the ocean roars fiercely, dark storms are driving on; the sun sinks, the world becomes empty, my heart must despair.

I am left alone, oh ever alone, my strength is failing. I must return, weak with grief; I can never find you.

Here the theme of the girl left lonely finds many of its tenderest and subtlest expressions. The opening vocal line draws a nine-note graph of desolation. The rising melody of 'über die' is inverted and sent falling from the suddenly remote high tone on 'fern' (far), as the thought flies there and back. Each 'die See', like 'das Meer' (the ocean) in the second verse and 'allein' in the third, is set to the same drooping semitone in the same rhythm, a flat-surfaced seascape in miniature. The folk-song notion of 'Wenn ich ein Vöglein wär' (if only I were a bird to fly after my lover), is merely hinted at in the poem, and then only by the last word of the first verse, 'geflogen' (flown), meant as a metaphor. But Brahms with his intense feeling for the flight and song of birds, especially in association with women in all manner of moods and moments, starts his piano chords gently winging at 'ist mein Schatz gezogen' (my love has travelled); the music follows over the sea in imagination, from the instant of departure.

Each 'die See' in the voice is heard over the same sad tonic suspension in the left hand. The voice's falling semitone is then heard as the bass of two further suspensions, now on the dominant, to make two small questioning sighs of sorrow and pain before 'Ach' and at 'Weh'. Then the longing spreads its wings more boldly in both hands, at 'bang' (anxiously) and flies after lost love, singing in a gently rising curve. This flying motif continues in a piano coda, and the same music matches the same mood for two further verses. Thus the effect is enhanced by strophic repetition; the music is heard as the lovelorn girl is seen, standing by the seashore and yearning for wings.

Here Brahms's consummate craftsmanship rivals, in its very different way, the sophisticated art of Wolf. This song, on the page as in performance, is unpretentious and modest; yet it embodies a conscious artifice of structure and design which perfectly expresses the simple sad sincerity that the composer conjures out of a rather unpromising poem.

NOTES. 1. The source was Lemcke's *Lieder und Gedichte* of 1861, which Brahms owned. In each verse, he added an extra syllable to preserve his basic 3/4 rhythm; the poet's 'ist mein' becomes 'ist ihm mein', 'sinkt die' 'sinket die' and 'muss zurück' 'muss ich zurück'.

2. The desertion-theme and bird-metaphor are alike typical. The wings are M3; their climbing vocal progression culminating on 'geflogen' is also expressive, like the suspensions

in bars 9–10 and 11–12 with their questioning dominants (M24). The voice's top G (which suits 'wild' and 'ach' as well as 'fern') is M10.

3. E minor is a convenient Agathe key, as in the four-part Heyse setting Op. 44 No. 10; her memory may be embodied and her name embroidered (as an anagram, in bars 1–2 and again in 3–4) within this music; M32.

129. (Op. 69, No. 8) Salome (Salome) 1877
Gottfried Keller   C major g'–g''

>Singt mein Schatz wie ein Fink,
>Sing ich Nachtigallensang;
>Ist mein Liebster ein Luchs,
>O so bin ich eine Schlang.
>
>O ihr Jungfraun im Land,
>Von dem Berg und über See!
>Überlasst mir den Schönsten,
>Sonst tut ihr mir weh!
>
>Er soll sich unterwerfen
>Zum Ruhm uns und Preis!
>Und er soll sich nicht rühren,
>Nicht laut und nicht leis!
>
>O ihr teuren Gespielen!
>Überlasst mir den teuren Mann!
>Er soll sehn, wie die Liebe
>Ein feurig Schwert werden kann!

If my sweetheart sings like a finch, I'll sing a nightingale's song; if he's a lynx then I'm a snake. Oh you maidens in the country, from the mountains and over the sea! leave that handsomest of men to me, or you'll cause me pain [leave that handsomest of men to me, or you'll cause me pain]!

He must surrender, to our glory and our praise, and he must not stir, whether loudly or softly! Oh you dear playmates, leave that dear man to me! He shall see how love can become a fiery sword [how love can become a fiery sword]!

Keller's typical blend of simplicity and complexity engenders matching music. When Wolf had finished *Alte Weisen*, his own Keller settings, he looked through Brahms's two treatments of the same texts (the other was *Therese*, No. 156) and expressed outrage at what he found. As he wrote to his mistress Melanie Köchert on 20 August 1890: 'What a master Brahms is, after all, – of the bagpipes and the concertina! ... I can't refrain from quoting one passage, noteworthy for its quite especially original declamation [namely this song's seven-bar vocal line from 'O ihr Jungfraun' (Oh you maidens) to 'See'] ... and so it goes yodelling on to the end in its well-known noble popular-song style' (Wolf, 1964, pp. 119–120). Many listeners will sympathise with these strictures. The unremarkable vocal melody is forced and foisted on to the words, which audibly resist and resent such treatment.

But if the hearer is content to consider the poem as frame or background for a portrait, its subject comes to life. Thus interpreted, Wolf's scathing critique is helpful. He surely hears the country instruments and song-style with total accuracy; bagpipes in the left hand, concertina in the right, with a local or country accent in the voice throughout, which does indeed seem to yodel, perhaps in deliberate tribute to Keller's Swiss background. The resulting one-woman band was what Theodor Billroth claimed to detect in this music; a dark-eyed sixteen-year-old full of mischief and fun. Other devotees of Brahms will savour the same colourful character-sketch, given a suitably fast and light performance.

NOTES. 1. The textual source was no doubt Keller's *Neuere Gedichte* (1851), which Brahms owned. Each of the poems in the series *Von Weibern* has a woman's name for title; no special significance attaches to 'Salome'.

2. But perhaps the poet pictured her less lovingly than the composer – who was similarly indulgent to her lover, to judge from his replacement of Keller's 'stolzen' (proud) by his own 'teuren' (dear) in the last verse. On any analysis, the last line was the source of the right-hand sword-motifs that flash out and leap up in octave salutes at 'ein feurig Schwert'; they lack such relevance at their first appearance. Conversely the concertina's sharp snapping rhythms are apter for the first verse's finches than anything in the second. The protracted dominant seventh and long pause, like a shout awaiting an answer, as the distant maidens are called for at 'See' is M24.

3. Cf. Pfitzner Op. 33 No. 5, and Wolf's own setting, No. 2 of his 1890 Keller songs.

130. (Op. 69, No. 9) Mädchenfluch (A girl's curse) 1877
Anon, Serbian (trans. S. Kapper)   A minor and major e'–a''

> Ruft die Mutter, ruft der Tochter
>   Über drei Gebirge;
> 'Ist, o Mara, liebe Tochter,
>   Ist gebleicht das Linnen?'
> Ihr zurück die junge Tochter
>   Über neun Gebirge;
> 'Nicht ins Wasser, liebe Mutter,
>   Taucht ich noch das Linnen,
> Denn, o sieh, es hat das Wasser
>   Jawo mir getrübet,
> Wie dann erst, o liebe Mutter,
>   Hätt ich es gebleicht schon!
> Fluch ihm, Mutter, liebe Mutter,
>   Ich auch will ihm fluchen!
> Gäbe Gott im hellen Himmel,
>   Dass er sich erhänge –
> An ein böses Bäumchen hänge,
>   An den weissen Hals mir!
> Gäbe Gott im hellen Himmel,
>   Dass er lieg gefangen –
> Lieg gefangen tief im Kerker,
>   An der weissen Brust mir!

Gäbe Gott, der Herr im Himmel,
  Dass er Ketten trage –
Ketten trage, festgeschlungen,
  Meine weissen Arme!
Gäbe Gott im hellen Himmel,
  Dass ihn nähm das Wasser,
Dass ihm nähm das wilde Wasser,
  Mir ins Haus ihn bringe!'

The mother calls, calls to her daughter across three mountain ranges: 'O Mara, dear daughter, is the linen bleached [is the linen bleached]?'

The young daughter calls back to her, over nine mountain ranges; 'I haven't yet dipped the linen into water [not yet dipped the linen], for, just look, Jawo came and troubled the water, so how could I have done the bleaching yet?

Curse him, mother, dear mother; I'll curse him too [curse him, mother, dear mother, and I'll curse him too]!

May God in the bright heavens grant that he hangs himself, hangs himself on a bad tree – on my white neck [on my white, white neck]!

May God in the bright heavens grant that he lies imprisoned, lies imprisoned in a deep dungeon – on my white breast [on my white, white breast]!

May God, the Lord in heaven, grant that he is put in chains, put in firmly-clasping chains – in my white arms [my white, white arms]!

May God in the bright heavens grant that the waters take him, the wild waters take him, and bring him to me in my house [bring him to me in my house, that the wild waters take him and bring him to me in my house, bring him to me here into my house, my house]!'

Jawo may have been in really deep trouble; it was Judas who traditionally hanged himself on a bad tree. The prelude splashes and trickles in fluid triplet octaves, setting the scene; all is ready for the bleaching. But that process never begins, despite a further attempt following maternal enquiries about the linen. From the outset, the water-supply, like the girl's mood, is troubled and turned off. Instead there is a flow of musical ideas, such as the copious reappearance of the opening vocal motif of calling ('Ruft die Mutter') in the piano part as the water is troubled ('Wasser … getrübet').

The semi-serious appeals to the Almighty are couched in terms of nature-music, like wing-beats or waves of passion, as if Jawo himself had taken refuge behind the mountains and had to be flown or flowed to in spirit, as in many another song on the same favourite themes.

NOTES. 1. The textual source was Siegfried Kapper's *Gesänge der Serben* (1852). In bars 28 and 31 respectively, Brahms has the name 'Jawo' instead of 'Jowo', with 'dann' instead of 'denn' in the next line.

2. The composer's fascination with mother–daughter colloquies, and the theme of the yearning unhappy girl, may have prompted his preoccupation with this rather unprepossessing poem.

3. As so often, the country characters are depicted in terms of rural song and dance, here the Balkan equivalents of mazurka and galop.

4. Vocal and keyboard accents are stipulated at each 'an den weissen (Hals)', but not at 'Brust' or 'Arme'. Perhaps Brahms felt that the meaning 'the tree, *namely* my neck' needed no further underlining after its first mention. But there is comparable inconsistency elsewhere; thus the postlude to that passage is all *ben marcato* the first time but only accented thereafter.

5. The fluid prelude is M5; the dominant question at each 'Linnen?' is M24; the wing-beats are M3; the conclusive vocal cadences at 'weissen Hals mir' etc. are also expressive, with M10 top notes.

OPUS 70

Four songs (Gesänge) for solo voice with pianoforte accompaniment, with named poets, published in September 1877.

131. (Op. 70, No. 1) Im Garten am Seegestade (In the seaside garden) 1877

Karl Lemcke   G minor d'–g''

Im Garten am Seegestade
Uralte Bäume stehn,
In ihren hohen Kronen
Sind kaum die Vögel zu sehn.

Die Bäume mit hohen Kronen,
Die rauschen Tag und Nacht,
Die Wellen schlagen zum Strande,
Die Vöglein singen sacht.

Das gibt ein Musizieren
So süss, so traurig bang,
Als wie verlorner Liebe
Und ewiger Sehnsucht Sang.

In the seaside garden the ancient trees stand; in their high tops the birds can hardly be seen [can hardly be seen].

The trees with high tops, they rustle day and night, the waves beat on the shore, the birds sing softly.

That music-making is so sweet, so forebodingly sad, like a song of lost love and endless longing [a song of endless longing].

The prelude's ascending left-hand arpeggios and descending minor thirds begin the dream of lost love that this modest masterpiece so intensely experiences and conveys. Listeners are invited to imagine the sea-mists that the poem conjures up but does not name directly; each successive picture appears as if through a haze of sound, in anticipation of Debussyan impressionism. The accompaniment imper-

ceptibly changes, literally in line with the vocal melody, into small stirring movements as of folding wings that gradually settle down into inaudibility, a typical
tonal image of invisibility, at 'sind kaum die Vögel zu sehn' (the birds can scarcely
be seen); as those words are repeated the figuration itself half disappears. The
prelude's long lamentation returns; the left-hand quavers extend into triplets as
the high foliage stirs in the wind at 'Bäume' (trees), or the waves ('Wellen') break
on the shore. Deep bass notes sigh as the rustling darkens into night at 'Rauschen
… Nacht'; a repeated piping tone in the treble confirms the voice's assurance that
'die Vöglein singen sacht' (the birds sing softly). Then these off-beat right-hand
notes imperceptibly drift back into the prelude's descending-third theme of lost
love, to match the poetic concept of sorrowful feelings aroused by soft sounds. In
the reprise, birds and trees and waves all sing in sad chorus at the mention of
'Musizieren' (music-making). The postlude is resigned; all over, long ago. But the
remaining memories could hardly be more compellingly poignant and tender. As
Clara Schumann herself confided to the composer in May 1877; 'marvellous; this
is a song one can dream in'.

NOTES. 1. The textual source was Karl Lemcke's *Lieder und Gedichte* (1861); Brahms
changed the poet's 'Vöglein' into 'Vögel' (bars 9 and 12), but not in bar 21; the original text
might be preferred, for the sake of consistency as well as fidelity.

2. The descending thirds are expressive (as at 'unser Liebe' in *Geheimnis*. No. 137); the
same applies to the continuous light quavers that suggest a soft rustling here (and gossamer
in *Sommerfäden*, No. 171). The dreamily-rising arpeggios are M9; the nestling wings are
M3, and the interspersed silences in the piano part at 'kaum die Vögel zu sehn' are M29.
The darkening bass notes are M6/7, and at 'rauschen Tag and Nacht' (which may be meant
to say A–D, M34) they anticipate, for no very clear thematic reason, *O Tod* No. 203 at
'noch wohl essen mag'. The wave-music at 'die Wellen schlagen' etc. is M5; the piping
right-hand treble of soft bird-song after 'singen sacht', and the long-drawn-out augmentation at the final vocal phrase are also symbolic.

3. Unsurprisingly, the Clara motif M33 appears twice in successive sequences, in voice
and piano at 'als wie verlorene Liebe und ewiger Sehnsucht Sang'; the thirds and sixths
there are M18.

4. The musical structure and its relation to the text will repay close analysis. The
impression of unity and simplicity among ceaseless change and diversity is effected by
superlative technique placed at the service of the verses; one figuration or melody blends
imperceptibly into the next, as in a haze or a dream, yet each of the many separate
expressive meanings remains vivid and memorable.

132. (Op. 70, No. 2) Lerchengesang (Larks' song) by 1877

Karl Candidus   B major f#'–g#''

>   Ätherische ferne Stimmen,
>   Der Lerchen himmlische Grüsse,
>   Wie regt ihr mir so süsse
>   Die Brust, ihr lieblichen Stimmen!
>   Ich schliesse leis mein Auge,
>   Da ziehn Erinnerungen

> In sänften Dämmerungen
> Durchweht vom Frühlingshauche.

Ethereal distant voices of the larks' heavenly greetings, how sweetly you move my heart,
you dear voices [my heart, you dear voices]!
   I gently close my eyes, and memories pass by in soft half-lights [memories pass by in
soft half-lights] pervaded by the breath of springtime.

Brahms distills the essence of these verses into the fine music of his new-found
neo-impressionist phase (as in No. 131 above). In the prelude, the arpeggios of
reverie start in the treble clef from a high pedal B, a waking dream at dawn; the
right hand reaches lark-like heights in the keyboard. Having thus set the scene,
amid sighs, the piano is suddenly silent, leaving the vocal melody free to float and
sing alone over wide open space, literally as well as figuratively, in a new relaxed
rhythm. At 'wie regt ihr mir so süsse' (how sweetly you stir my heart) the piano's
four-quaver arpeggios come down to earth and drift in a rhythmic vagueness
among the voice's crotchet triplets; thus the sleeper rouses and dreams become a
mere memory. The opening strains recur at 'ich schliesse leis mein Auge' (I gently
close my eyes), listening to larks in imagination, and the rhythmical blurring
effects recur as the recollections steal softly past. They still have their poignant
moments, the harmonies suggest, but are now softened into blissfulness by the
effluxion of time.

NOTES. 1. The Candidus text was taken from the *Vermischte Gedichte* (1869), which
Brahms owned.
   2. No doubt Clara was in mind, as in so many other songs of reverie and nostalgia; but
any such allusion (perhaps M33 in the D#–C#–B–A#–[C#]–B of 'Ich schliesse leis mein
Auge', and the opening vocal melody) appears veiled here.
   3. There is a clearer echo, from this song into the high treble flights of the Andante in
the second piano concerto (Op. 83, 1881).
   4. The tonic pedal notes of the opening piano bars are motivic (M8), like the
unaccompanied vocal recitatives (with a bird-song decoration on 'himmlische'), and the
transient discords including the sadly flattened sixth on the first 'Däm(merungen)' (M41).
The dream arpeggios are M9, the silences M29.
   5. The deceptively simple ABA structure is worth special study; A: 1–10 (5, 8)= 18 etc,
with (27), 28–9 interpolated; B: 11–17 = 30 etc. with 33–6 heightened from 14–17; A
(=postlude) 37–40 (= 18–21= 1–4) with 41–2 added. The bracketed bars are piano silences.

133. (Op. 70, No. 3) Serenade: Liebliches Kind (Serenade: Dear child) 1876

Johann Wolfgang von Goethe   B major f#'–g#''

> Liebliches Kind,
> Kannst du mir sagen,
> Sagen warum
> Einsam und stumm
> Zärtliche Seelen
> Immer sich quälen,

Selbst sich betrüben
Und ihr Vergnügen
Immer nur ahnen
Da, wo sie nicht sind;
Kannst du mirs sagen,
Liebliches Kind?

*Dear child, can you tell me, tell me why it is that sensitive souls always fret in silence
by themselves, always grieve and feel they'd be happier anywhere than where they
actually are [than where they are]? Can you tell me this [can you tell me this], dear
child [dear, dear child]?*

Goethe's lyric is a song allotted to his character Rugantino in the Singspiel
Claudina von Villa Bella. The verses insinuatingly chide and wheedle; Brahms
turns them into a love-song to a young girl, whose touchingly childlike littleness
is whimsically symbolised by diminutions. After a two-chord prelude, each vocal
phrase is instantly echoed in canon at the half-bar in such a way that its first three
notes are twice repeated in halved note-values, thus:

voice   piano

Lieblich - es

and this pattern is strictly maintained, with an effect of deliberate yet unobtrusive
teasing, throughout the first half of the song. At the same time the continuous
left-hand arpeggios sound dreamily reflective. The mood is thus deftly designed
to be both musing and amusing. At the repeated 'kannst du mirs sagen' (can you
tell me) the canonic imitation between voice and piano become more manifest
and intense, in the same note-values, with an effect of enhanced enquiry and
earnest reflection. There follows a long-drawn-out 'liebliches Kind' with further
instrumental echoes and repetitions; the song is almost a trio for singer, girl and
guitar.

NOTES. 1. Brahms owned two sets of Goethe's *Werke*, and also knew Christian Neefe's
setting of this poem (as may be inferred from the fact that he retains its title). The text
should run '… Sagen, warum/Zärtliche Seelen/ Einsam und stumm/ Immer sich quälen?'.
This cannot now be amended; but the mistake 'betrüben' (trouble) instead of the required
rhyme 'betrügen' (betray) should surely be corrected.
   2. In Goethe's charming Singspiel *Claudina von Villa Bella* the hero Rugantino, who
has gained entry as a guest in the villa by a ruse, is asked for a quiet good-night song, which
he performs to his own zither accompaniment. His audience consists of two girls who are
disconcerted by his presence. One is Lucinde, with whom he had fallen in love at first sight
during a brief chance meeting, and the other is Claudina herself, to whom he is unknown.
The song is intended to have teasing overtones for both.

3. The consecutive thirds at each 'nicht sind' are the love-motif M18, as in another so-called serenade *Leise um dich nicht zu wecken* (No. 99). The diminutions and canons (M12) are also expressive.

4. The close-knit structure repays study. Thus the one-bar prelude seems a mere tonic–dominant appendage until compared with the last bar but three ('liebliches'); then the relationship becomes apparent.

5. The correct text was set not only by Neefe, in his collection called *Serenades*, but also by Reichardt (twice), Schubert (the vocal line of D239 No. 9, where it is perplexingly allotted to a different character, Pedro), Bruch, Op. 49, No. 1 and Metner Op. 6 No. 5.

134. (Op. 70, No. 4) Abendregen (Evening rain) 1875
Gottfried Keller   A minor–C major c′–g″(a″)

Langsam und schimmernd fiel ein Regen,
In den die Abendsonne schien;
Der Wandrer schritt auf engen Wegen
Mit düstrer Seele drunter hin.

Er sah die grossen Tropfen blinken
Im Fallen durch den goldnen Strahl;
Er fühlt es kühl aufs Haupt ihm sinken
Und sprach mit schauernd süsser Qual:

Nun weiss ich, dass ein Regenbogen
Sich hoch um meine Stirne zieht,
Den auf dem Pfad, so ich gezogen,
Die heitre Ferne spielen sieht.

Und die mir hier am nächsten stehen,
Und wer mich scharf zu kennen meint,
Sie können selber doch nicht sehen,
Wie er versöhnend ob mir scheint.

So wird, wenn andre Tage kamen,
Die sonnig auf dies Heute sehn,
Ob meinem fernen, bleichen Namen
Der Ehre Regenbogen stehn.

Slowly and gleaming fell the shower, shone through by the evening sun; the traveller trudged down narrow paths, sombre in his soul. He saw the large drops shine as they fell through the golden ray; he felt them splashing cold on his head, and he spoke, shuddering in sweet torment:

Now I know that a rainbow is rising high around my brow, visible all along the path I have taken, throughout the serene distance [throughout the serene distance].

And those who stand closest to me here, and whoever reckons to know me in detail [know me in detail], not even they can see how redeemingly [redeemingly] this rainbow shines above me. So, in future times which will look back sunnily upon today, above my distant pale name the rainbow of honour will stand [the rainbow of honour will stand, the rainbow of honour will stand].

Keller typically twists his lovely opening lines into knotty thoughts. His verses avoid vainglory by their patent sincerity; he knows posterity will look up to his achievement, and that is his consolation for personal unhappiness. Such symbolic rainbows are all the agnostic knows of heaven. By selecting this poem for musical setting, Brahms implies that he agrees; he too knew his real worth, for all his genuine modesty. But, as the song says, such recognition would take time. Meanwhile those who stood closest remained aloof; Clara Schumann criticised Keller's poem for its bombast (Litzmann ii 97) while Elisabet von Herzogenberg (i 69) teased the composer about his own.

Over a century later, this song stands self-justifyingly secure. At first the music too walks through the sunlit rain; bright separate drops fall and splash through the prelude and opening vocal melody. They return at 'die grossen Tropfen' after having changed, at 'der Wandrer schritt' (the traveller trudged), into a linked chain of movement which in turn recurs when the wanderer reappears, as if rounding a bluff, at 'er fühlt' (he felt). Here he speaks his inmost thoughts; and the previous brief interlude is developed into a new prelude that culminates in a prolonged dominant seventh, as if the wandering minstrel has tuned, lifted and struck his harp. That instrument, in left-hand triplets, now accompanies a solemn aria, at 'Nun weiss ich' (Now I know). Voice and piano exult at the thought of a rainbow's extensive visibility; the keyboard texture changes at every bar or two, like a shifting spectrum. At the mention of future days ('wenn andre Tage kamen') the aria resumes, apparently da capo; but the vocal melody is still subjected to ceaseless change, though the harp figurations continue and round off the song. In the postlude, an inner voice sings the rainbow melody of 'Nun weiss ich', with an inner certitude of posthumous renown.

As Max Kalbeck points out (iii 60), it was in the summer of 1875 that Brahms had felt his honour grievously impugned by Wagner because of their controversy (ibid., ii 121f) about the ownership of the manuscript of *Tannhäuser*, which Brahms had acquired in good faith. His composition of this song during the same period, and its unprecedented separate publication that October in the publisher Fritzsche's *Blätter für Hausmusik* (Journal of Domestic Music) must have helped to heal a deep and painful hurt. This affords further compelling evidence for the sensitively personal nature and cathartic function of the Brahmsian lied.

NOTES. 1. The textual source was the first edition of Keller's *Neuere Gedichte* (1851), which Brahms owned. Perhaps the poet was more susceptible than the composer to accusations of bombast; in later issues the last two lines were changed to the comparatively modest 'Um meinen fernen blassen Namen/Des Friedens heller Bogen stehn'. In the Peters edition the last word of the poem's seventeenth line reads 'kommen' instead of the rhyming 'kamen', which should surely be reinstated.

2. The raindrop mezzo-staccato (M28) should surely continue through each shower, though marked thus only in the prelude. Typically, the accentuation (e.g. at the very first word, 'lang*sam*') is subordinated to this motivic writing. But the top A on 'und', designed to extend the equally motivic chain of descending thirds, arguably goes too far;

the rising sixth from the lower A to the higher note on 'schim(mernd)' sounds more persuasive.

3. The quasi-operatic quaver rests in the first vocal bar are M29. The walking movement at bars 7–10 and its chromatic enhancement and prolongation at bars 16–20 may be compared with the same motif (here M1) in Schubert's *Der Wanderer* D649, a recollection perhaps prompted by the words 'der Wandrer' in bars 6–7 here. The dreamy arpeggio of M9 at bars 10–11 leads into the reverie induced by the raindrops at 'Ich sah die grossen Tropfen ...'; its culmination in the rather portentous dominant seventh at bars 21–4 (cf. also 48–9) is M24. The harp-music accompaniment at 'leise und feierlich' is expressive; so, more explicitly, is its modification into the joyous 5–6–5–6–5 alternation (M19) to illustrate 'heitre'. The insistent changes of accompaniment figuration (bars 32–49) serve as a metaphor of gradual yet perceptible change, like the colours of the rainbow (as harmonic progressions are used in Wolf's *Phänomen*, No. 32 of the *Goethe-Lieder*). The postlude's inner voice (M38) is the musical equivalent of a meditation on the aforementioned rainbow, whose melody (bar 25) it quotes.

5. Within so thoroughly and deliberately motivic a context, the resemblance in voice and piano at bars 44–7 to Schumann's *Er, der herrlichste von allen* at the words 'wandle, wandle deine Bahnen' (go your ways), complete with meaningful canon (here M12) will hardly be mere coincidence; at this point in each song, the words describe loneliness and isolation redeemed and ennobled by a sense of high mission and destiny.

OPUS 71

Five songs (Gesänge) for solo voice with pianoforte accompaniment, with named poets, published in September 1877.

135. (Op. 71, No. 1) Es liebt sich so lieblich im Lenze (How lovely to love in the springtime) 1877

Heinrich Heine   D major d′–g#″

> Die Wellen blinken und fliessen dahin –
> Es liebt sich so lieblich im Lenze!
> Am Flusse sitzet die Schäferin
> Und windet die zärtlichsten Kränze.
>
> Das knospet und quillt und duftet und blüht –
> Es liebt sich so lieblich im Lenze!
> Die Schäferin seufzt aus tiefer Brust;
> 'Wem geb ich meine Kränze?'
>
> Ein Reiter reitet den Fluss entlang;
> Er grüsset so blühenden Mutes!
> Die Schäferin schaut ihm nach so bang,
> Fern flattert die Feder des Hutes.
>
> Sie weinet und wirft in den gleitenden Fluss
> Die schönen Blumenkränze.
> Die Nachtigall singt von Lieb und Kuss –
> Es liebt sich so lieblich im Lenze!

The waves shine and flow past – how lovely to love in the springtime! By the river sits the shepherdess and weaves the tenderest [weaves the tenderest] of garlands.

There's budding, burgeoning, fragrance and bloom – how lovely to love in the springtime! The shepherdess sighs from the fullness of her feelings: 'To whom shall I give my garlands [to whom shall I give my garlands]?'

A horseman comes riding along by the river; he greets her with such youthful élan [with such youthful, such youthful elan]! The shepherdess looks anxiously after him, the plume in his bonnet [the plume in his bonnet] flutters afar. She weeps and throws her pretty flower-garlands into the flowing river. The nightingale sings of loving and kissing – how lovely to love in the springtime!

Not always, not for everyone; indeed, rather rarely, says the ironic Heine. At first, Brahms sounds far more ebullient. His piano quaver octaves flow sweetly past singing the tune of 'fliessen dahin' (flow past) and turn into a love-duet at 'Lenze' (springtime). The shepherdess's wreaths are woven with left-hand countermelodies. Then the river runs as before, to the same high climax at 'Lenze'; but the wreaths are now intertwined with sighs to suit 'seufzt'. The rider arrives on a new cantering theme; after its departure the left hand takes a long lingering look, at 'Die Schäferin schaut'. The river resumes with new quickening rhythms, and after 'wirft' the two hands hurl away 'die schönen Blumenkränze' (her pretty flower-garlands). Thus far, the musical invention has been ceaseless in its flow of varied verbal equivalence. Yet there are further fresh and delightful ideas still left in reserve, like the lifting piano octaves and top note at 'Die Nachtigall singt von Lieb and Kuss', followed by a sudden sustained outburst of keyboard semiquavers, at first with a new syncopated rhythm and then with a new two-note right-hand motif in the postlude which sings to itself 'dahin' (past) as in the first line. But this now means 'past and gone'; and the postlude's fleetingly flattened sixth signals a cloud that will briefly dim the music's springtime brightness before the last sustained arpeggiated chord.

NOTES. 1. Brahms owned Heine's *Sämtliche Werke* (1861–3), where the fifth line ended 'mit duftender Lust' and the seventh 'aus tiefer Brust'. But the composer knew, preferred and used Heine's earlier version of the fifth line, heedless of the lost rhyme. Brahms also changed Heine's 'sitzt' and 'grüsst' to 'sitzet' and 'grüsset', to suit his melody, and the mock-archaic 'Reuter' and 'reutet' to 'Reiter' and 'reitet'; he also preferred to use the repeated refrain as a title, rather than the poet's laconic heading *Frühling*.

2. Note the favourite theme of the girl left lonely, despite the surface cheerfulness of the music. The higher alternative note is surely preferable at the second '*wem* geb ich', as if to say: 'to whom, indeed?'.

3. The flowing quavers are M5, the consecutive thirds M18, the long sighs M21; the top G on 'Lenze' and 'Nachtigall' and 'Kuss' is M10. The cantering triplets are M1, the throwing gestures M2; the sustained dominant seventh before 'Die Nachtigall' is M24. The quickening rhythms, and the postlude's falling seconds (6–5, 2–1, etc.) are also motivic (M16 and M20); so is the sadly flattened sixth there (M41).

4. The fluttering-plume triplets at 'Hutes' etc. after 'fern' recall the twinkling-star triplets, also watched through 'entlegene Ferne', of *Wie rafft ich*, No. 34.

5. The irruption of the galloping rider into the rural scene recalls Schubert's *Der Schäfer*

und der Reiter D517 and looks forward to Mahler's full-scale orchestral treatment of the same idea in the fourth section of *Das Lied von der Erde*. There too the riders are followed by the girls' long yearning looks.

136. (Op. 71, No. 2) An den Mond (To the Moon) 1877
Karl Simrock   B minor e#′–g″

> Silbermond, mit bleichen Strahlen
> Pflegst du Wald und Feld zu malen,
> Gibst den Bergen, gibst den Talen
> Der Empfindung Seufzer ein.
> Sei Vertrauter meiner Schmerzen,
> Segler in der Lüfte See;
> Sag ihr, die ich trag im Herzen,
> Wie mich tötet Liebesweh.
>
> Sag ihr, über tausend Meilen
> Sehne sich mein Herz nach ihr.
> 'Keine Ferne kann es heilen,
> Nur ein holder Blick von dir.'
> Sag ihr, dass zu Tod getroffen
> Diese Hülle bald zerfällt;
> Nur ein schmeichlerisches Hoffen
> Sei's, das sie zusammenhält.

Silver moon, you always paint forest and field with your pale rays; into mountains and valleys you instil sighs of longing.
Let me confide my sorrows to you,
as you sail over the seas of space. Tell her whom I hold in my heart how the pangs of love are killing me. Tell her that my heart yearns for her across a thousand miles. Say: 'No distance can heal it, only a loving look from you'.
Tell her that this mortal shell, stricken to death, will soon decay; a flattering hope is all that holds it together [a flattering hope is all that holds it together].

Brahms treats the pedestrian poem as a walking song. This may indeed have been Simrock's intention. The triple feminine rhymes of his first three lines (a scheme thereafter abandoned), and the trudging metrical feet of his trochaic quadrimeter, emphasise the poet's weariness on his journey as well as his sorrow at parting. Some listeners may find the matching music over-insistent. Yet given sympathetic interpretation and attention this neglected song can be heard as a masterpiece of the highest order, transcending and redeeming the words. The first inspiration is the prelude's idea that the way-worn wanderer goes singing as well as sighing on his way. The three-bar melody with added triplets and spread left-hand guitar-chords is deliberately separated from the intercalated marching rhythms, and thus softened into a strolling and strumming serenade to the moon, whose light enters with the voice at 'Silbermond', to the same melody. Thus the scene is set and illuminated with that word's first long syllable.

We learn at the outset that word-setting is not to be our chief concern; thus 'gibst' is given two quite different treatments in consecutive bars. Sense-setting and mood-painting are paramount. As the piano part travels, a right-hand or vocal melody shines over it and lights its path. This division symbolises the song's two components as Brahms visualises them in his music; the nocturnal movement and exalted glowing of man and moon. The singer continues to walk in the night, with typical deep left-hand octaves. At the word 'Seufzer' (sigh) and again at 'Schmerzen' (sorrow) the preluding melody recurs higher in the stave, like an upturned gaze at the moon.

At 'Sag ihr' (tell her) the thematic material unobtrusively undergoes a complete change in both voice and piano. The new music is inspired by the thought of direct communication with the distant beloved; and the horn passages with their shifting major and minor thirds, first heard at 'Liebesweh' (pangs of love), marvellously evoke the open countryside dappled in moonshine and shadow and the endless distances dividing lover from lover. Instead of walking, the accompaniment now glides serenely, as if in immediate response to the image of the moon as a 'Segler in der Lüfte See', sailing on seas of air; Brahms makes it a stately galleon. After 'Blick von dir' the prelude returns and the sad trudging resumes, in the contrasting reality of separation and sorrow, only to dissolve again into the dreamy wide-ranging music of the the moonlit landscape, which in turn is linked to the serenading motifs that end the song in a still reverie. It is as if the loving and healing look requested at 'ein holder Blick von dir' has been granted in imagination. The postlude sustains that moment of major-key optimism; all may yet be well. But we are to understand that, requited or not, the love thus conveyed will never fail or falter.

NOTES. 1. Brahms owned Simrock's *Gedichte: Neue Auswahl* (1863); but the source may well have been the *Gedichte* (1844) (which also contains 'Vevay', see No. 101). There the second word of the last line is 'dass' not 'das', with a consequent slight change of meaning. As in other songs (such as No. 24) Brahms would also have decapitalised the loved one from 'Her' to 'her'.

2. Throughout the song, in voice and piano, the plaintive Clara-motif M33 recurs in its B minor form, e.g. at 'Vertrauter meiner Schmerzen'; the prelude's first five melody notes are a tonal anagram. Brahms asked his publisher to transpose this song a tone down, which would have turned this motif into C–B–A–G#–A; but nothing came of that request.

3. The alternation of major and minor thirds on the same keynote, with tonic-and-dominant bass, recurs in *Nachtwandler* (No. 158), another song about walking in a moonlit night. This homage to Schubert (M39), here closely akin to the G major horn passages at e.g. bar 51f in the second movement of the D major piano sonata D850, is most manifest in the resemblance between this song's accompaniment and that of *Rast* in *Winterreise* D911/10, which trudges in the same 2/4 rhythm and texture.

4. The walking movement is M1. The duetting sixths and thirds are M18, the dark depths of the left hand M6/7, the open air horn passages M22. The major postlude is an extended tierce de Picardie, signifying unfailing love.

137. (Op. 71, No. 3) Geheimnis (The secret) 1877
Karl Candidus   G major f'–a''

> O Frühlingsabenddämmerung!
> O laues, lindes Wehn!
> Ihr Blütenbäume, sprecht, was tut
> Ihr so zusammenstehn?
>
> Vertraut ihr das Geheimnis euch
> Von unsrer Liebe süss?
> Was flüstert ihr einander zu
> Von unsrer Liebe süss?

O spring evening twilight! O mild soft breeze [o mild soft breeze]! You flowering trees, speak [speak], why do you stand so close together [why do you stand so close together]? Are you confiding to each other the secret of our sweet love [of our sweet love]? What are you whispering to each other about our love [our love, about our sweet love]?

Again a lame poem is healed by music. The sighing prelude sets up a secret leafy murmur, with hidden voices among its arpeggios, hinting at a love-duet in consecutive sixths among the implied four-part harmony. These two piano bars are repeated as the voice enters singing the higher melody, painting the composite image in music; leaves and feelings alike are seen to be stirred. When the words 'O laues lindes Wehn' (O mild soft breeze) are echoed, the piano is lower and quieter, as if the natural surroundings had incorporated human emotions.

The trees make a rather wooden love-symbol in the verses, but a Brahmsian touch sets them flowering. As they are apostrophized at 'Ihr Blütenbäume' (You flowering trees) the left-hand horn passages are eloquent of open-air vistas in woodland scenery; and the vocal melody is later metamorphosed into a right-hand love-motif, immediately after the first mention of 'unsre Liebe süss' (our sweet love), which is then echoed and developed afresh with each further allusion. Meanwhile the texture has been subtly varied. Added chromatic inflexions in voice and piano match the mysteriousness of 'Geheimnis' (secret). Then the small choir of leaves is softly reinforced by octave doublings as extra voices are added at 'flüstert ... einander' (whispering to each other); and the off-beat dominant pedal-point holds the music strangely still despite its intense and insistent questioning. Here again Brahms has little help from the words, which offer only yet another repetition of the question. But the song's last five bars attempt a tonic answer. They repeat the opening strains in shifting harmonies that hint at doubts and uncertainties until the postlude deftly sketches a tall tree of lasting love, from root to top.

NOTES. I. The Candidus text is taken from his *Vermischte Gedichte* (1869), which Brahms owned.

2. There are certain parallels with the previous song. Again the tempo may present difficulties, because the feelings and details are so intense; they will be lost or blurred except in suitably careful performance, which for most artists will entail a slower rather than a faster tempo. When the Herzogenbergs tried through this song (i 22–3) they had lingered with especial sentiment on the left-hand chromatics, and were later mortified to notice the

injunction 'very lively'. The composer obligingly deleted 'very', and also drew attention to the later injunctions 'immer langsamer, Adagio', and a whole-bar fermata. These readings were later changed to the present 'allmählich langsamer' at bar 21, with 'langsam' at bar 29. In the Peters edition (but not the *Gesamtausgabe*), bar 30 has a fermata over a sustained note in the voice part, not the whole bar. On any interpretation, the Herzogenbergs were fine musicians, and their intuition compels respect. The tempo should surely never sound unduly hurried.

2. Perhaps Schumann's *Der Nussbaum*, also in compound duple time in the same key, on a comparable theme, and also illustrated with leafy arpeggios, provides a parallel in tempo, though the prevailing mood here is far more tense and uncertain.

3. The duetting thirds and sixths passim are M18; the left-hand horn passages at bars 11–12 are M22. The prolonged dominant seventh at bar 16 is M24. Especially noteworthy is the transformation of the 'Blütenbäume' melody in the right hand at bars 20 and 22, later further modified into sad descending minor thirds at bars 26 and 28. Equally motivic is the tolling dominant pedal (M8) in that passage, which may suggest that 'unsre Liebe' is less mutual than the singer would wish, and has even remained unrequited.

138. (Op. 71 No. 4) Willst du, dass ich geh? (Do you want me to go?) 1877

Karl Lemcke   D minor d'–a''

Auf der Heide weht der Wind –
Herzig Kind, herzig Kind –
Willst du, dass trotz Sturm und Graus
In die Nacht ich muss hinaus –
    Willst du, dass ich geh?

Auf der Heid zu Bergeshöh
Treibt der Schnee, treibt der Schnee;
Feget Strassen, Schlucht und Teich
Mit den weissen Flügeln gleich.
    Willst du, dass ich geh?

Horch, wie klingts herauf vom See
Wild und weh, wild und weh!
An den Weiden sitzt die Fei,
Und mein Weg geht dort vorbei –
    Willst du, dass ich geh?

Wie ists hier in deinem Arm
Traut und warm, traut und warm:
Ach, wie oft hab ich gedacht;
So bei dir nur eine Nacht –
    Willst du, dass ich geh?

Over the moorland blows the wind, sweet child, sweet child; is it your will that despite all that storm and horror I must go out into the night [I must, I must go out]? Do you want me to go [do you want, do you want me to go]?

Over the moorland, mountain-high, the snow drives, the snow drives; it winnows pathways, ravine and tarn together, with its white wings [together, with its white wings]. Do you want me to go [do you want, do you want me to go]?

Hark how the storm soughs up from the lake, wild and harsh, wild and harsh! By the willows sits the witch, and my road leads past her [my road leads past her]! Do you want me to go [do you want, do you want me to go]?

Here in your arms how cosy and warm it is, how cosy and warm. Oh, how often I have thought – just one night thus with you [just one, one night with you] – Do you want me to go [do you want, do you want me to go]?

The question openly expects the answer 'no'; the verbal repetitions and other depictions of urgent insistence, such as the piano's hammering alternations and pedal notes, and the wheedling or hectoring vocal line, seek to impose that response. It is inherent in the poem that only one voice is heard; and a very powerful and persuasive monologue it makes. But the patrician Elisabet von Herzogenberg felt (i 27) that such situations could only be treated 'in the folksong style'. This provoked a sarcastic riposte from Brahms, himself a man of the people. His much-loved Elisabet was rather offended. She protested, with some justice (i 39), that she was no prude; she had often defended his even more overtly sensual songs, such as *Unbewegte laue Luft* (No. 91). Truly beautiful music, she explained (such as the Andante of the C minor piano quartet Op. 60, which Brahms had just sent in manuscript) might ask any question it would, with no offence in the world. Nor had she any objection in principle to the question 'May he stay?'; she just felt that Karl Lemcke, whose trivially erotic verses she detested (as also in *Salamander*, No. 197) was not the man to ask it. Such solecisms, in her judgement, devalued the songs.

She may well also have noted and resented the implications of the verse about the witch in the willows, with its barely-veiled threat that the thwarted suitor can easily fall prey to alternative allurements; if free love is refused, it may have to be purchased. Here too Brahms might well have sympathised with the poetic plight and plea; he himself was not unknown to the prostitutes of Vienna (cf. Schauffler 1933, 224f; MacDonald 1990, 397–8).

However the poem is assessed, the music surely refines and redeems it. The alternating octaves of the prelude blow down like chill winds, setting the scene and the tone together. The minor key is minatory; the rather threatening declamation takes precedence over the vocal melody (in such rough accentuations as 'in die Nacht'). In the third verse, beginning 'Horch' (Hark) the piano part sighs and soughs in canon, as the wild winds blow.

Finally, at 'hier in deinem Arm' (here in your arms) the major mode on the same tonic announces a change of tone, as if permission to stay had already been granted harmonically. The cold winds are still heard, in alternating staccato, but there is a cosy glow about the music; at 'so bei dir nur eine Nacht' (just one night thus with you) the voice yodels with joy and attains its top note. The last long vocal tone celebrating the singer's triumphs, now and to come, is accompanied by full chords first high and detached and then low and sustained in a tableau vivant of lively anticipation and fulfilment.

NOTES. 1. The textual source, as with No. 128, was Karl Lemcke's *Lieder und Gedichte* (1861), which Brahms owned. In the poet's first line, which might now be restored, the wind whistles ('saust') instead of just blowing ('weht') as in the song.

2. The contretemps with Elisabeth von Herzogenberg née Stockhausen may have been exacerbated by the composer's own thoughts of her, in his E–D# (= E. S.) motif 35, thus, at each of the first three refrains:

3. The winds' alternating octaves in the prelude etc. symbolize sudden sforzando gusts; the Schubertian minor–major changes, signify pleasure and pain stemming from the same source (M39), The thirds and sixths *passim* are M18. The yodelling effect at 'so bei dir' is the joy of M19; the top A at the second 'eine' is M10; the intensely questioning dominant sevenths at the last 'geh' are M24; the final chords and fermata say 'I'm staying'.

4. Wolf may have remembered this song for his own gale- or breeze-motif in *Begegnung*, No. 8 of the *Mörike-Lieder*; compare that accompaniment *passim* with e.g. the first half of bar 10 here.

139. (Op. 71, No. 5) Minnelied (Love song) 1877
Ludwig Hölty, ed. J. Voss   C major d'–g''

Holder klingt der Vogelsang,
Wenn die Engelreine,
Die mein Jünglingsherz bezwang
Wandelt durch die Haine.

Röter blühen Tal und Au,
Grüner wird der Wasen,
Wo die Finger meiner Frau
Maienblumen lasen.

Ohne sie ist alles tot,
Welk sind Blüt und Kräuter;
Und kein Frühlingsabendrot
Dünkt mir schön und heiter.

Traute, minnigliche Frau,
Wollest nimmer fliehen,
Dass mein Herz, gleich dieser Au,
Mög in Wonne blühen!

Sweeter sounds the bird-song when the girl, pure as an angel, who won my young heart, walks through the groves.

Valley and meadow bloom redder, the grass grows greener, where my lady's fingers have plucked Maytime flowers.

Without her, all is dead, blossoms and plants are withered, and no spring sunset looks radiant and serene to me.

Gentle and charming lady, never leave me, so that my heart like this meadow may bloom in bliss [may bloom in bliss]!

The poem's title evokes an entire epoch of mediaeval love-lyrics from the time of the troubadours. The music is comparably courtly; its stately dance-measure is the fixed warp through which the bright and flexible vocal line is memorably tapestried. The right hand even finds room for added hidden melodies in thirds, like birds within leaves (after 'Vogelsang', birdsong) to accompany 'die Engelreine' (the girl, pure as an angel). Not only are the birds singing sweeter and the flowers and grass looking brighter at the sights and thoughts described; so is the lover. We are not told that the girl herself sings as she walks; but Brahms achieves that effect also. The natural scene, and human love as part of that scene, make an age-old sweet chorus of song and duet. All this is achieved without a hint of exaggeration or sentimentality. On the contrary, all is restraint and decorum, as befits the Minnelied and its courtly conventions.

The vocal syncopations imply a Wolfian subtlety and felicity of word-setting. But this song is not really concerned with verbal detail; otherwise the composer would surely have stressed 'holder' (sweeter) not 'klingt' (sounds) in the opening phrase, and used the same note-values for 'grüner' (greener) as for 'röter' (redder) in the second verse. The techniques of absolute music are placed at the service of emotive expression, as in the unobtrusive canonic imitations with which the piano echoes 'alles tot' (all is dead), '-abendrot' (sunset), etc, and the final embellishment of the vocal melody with a leaping phrase and shining top note at the final 'Wonne' to show how a heart blossoms in bliss. For the right hearer in the right mood, this is among the major masterpieces of the lied.

NOTES. I. As usual, Brahms's source was the Voss edition (1804) of the *Gedichte*. Friedländer gives the original Hölty poem, which shares with the shorter Voss version 'wann' not 'wenn' in the first quatrain and 'blühet' not 'blühen' in the second.

2. Friedländer (100) was told by Mandyczewski, who spoke with authority, that Brahms much regretted having permitted the publication in C major of a song originally written in D major and transposed to accommodate a singer friend. Nevertheless, the dozens of insistent C pedals may evoke the ideal of Clara, as in the first symphony. Of the song's 54 bars, no fewer than 41 are pedal-points, whose basic tonic–tonic–dominant–tonic pattern corresponds with the A–A–B–A structure, rounded off by an eight-bar coda.

3. Kalbeck (iii 141) draws attention to the popular Upper Austrian dance-tune attributed to Joseph Gungl (1810–89) and perhaps deliberately borrowed by Brahms here (cf. *Wiegenlied*, No. 82 above):

But it would also be Brahmsian to allude, if to any Gungl, then to the set of waltzes called *Minnelieder* Op. 283; and No. 3 indeed has more than a passing resemblance.

4. The duetting thirds and sixths *passim* are M18; the inner melodies in bars 7–8 (19–20, 38–9) are M38 and the canons in bars 28–35 are M12. The alternative notes

provided at the last 'Wonne' are otiose; of course the top notes should be taken, Mio. The final vocal cadence is a Brahmsian signature-tune.

5. The complex 3/4 syncopations may be compared with the straightforward 6/8 simplicity of the Schubert and Mendelssohn settings, D429 and Op. 8 No. 1 respectively, which conform far more closely to the verbal cadences.

6. Cf. also Charles Ives's setting (?1892).

OPUS 72

Five songs (Gesänge) for solo voice and pianoforte accompaniment. with named poets, published in September 1877.

140. (Op. 72, No. 1) Alte Liebe (Old love) *c.* 1876
Karl Candidus   G minor d'–f"

Es kehrt die dunkle Schwalbe
Aus fernem Land zurück,
Die frommen Störche kehren
Und bringen neues Glück.

An diesem Frühlingsmorgen,
So trüb verhängt und warm,
Ist mir, als fänd ich wieder
Den alten Liebesharm.

Es ist als ob mich leise
Wer auf die Schulter schlug,
Also ob ich säuseln hörte,
Wie einer Taube Flug.

Es klopft an meine Türe
Und ist doch niemand draus;
Ich atme Jasmindüfte,
Und habe keinen Strauss.

Es ruft mir aus der Ferne,
Ein Auge sieht mich an,
Ein alter Traum erfasst mich
Und führt mich seine Bahn.

The dark swallow returns from a distant land; the pious storks return and bring new luck [new luck].

On this spring morning, so dimly veiled and warm, I seem to find love's old grief again [love's old grief].

It is as if someone touched me on the shoulder, as if I heard rustling, like a dove's wings. There is a knock at my door, yet no one is outside; I breathe the scent of jasmine, yet I have no bouquet. Someone is calling me from afar, eyes are gazing at me. An old dream seizes me and takes me along with it [an old dream seizes me and takes me along, along with it].

The air is full of wings and dreams as the long-flighted vocal line floats among upward piano arpeggios. 'Neues Glück' (new luck) sounds sad, as if intentionally ironic. Yet there is new hope; the 'Frühlingsmorgen' (spring morning) is greeted by new keyboard figurations and wider vocal intervals. This mood too is evanescent; for 'verhängt' (veiled) the voice twice falls through the wide interval of a seventh; and after the second 'alten Liebesharm' (love's old grief) the arpeggios of dream darken ominously into the minor mode. Now separate pieces of the musical material are tacked together to make new patterns and pictures. In the song as in the poem, new notes of personal feeling are struck. At 'Es ist, als ob' (It is as if) the dreaming arpeggios are heard higher in the keyboard; the voice moves by slow step, as if in a trance. For the imagined knocking ('Es klopft') long low bass notes reverberate in the mind. Syncopations and left-hand octaves or chords conjure up a personal presence, with its own new voice. At the reprise the key word 'Traum' reappears and bears the singer off with it on long flights of nostalgic arpeggios from both voice and piano. The music itself is beautifully elusive, like the poetic experience it recreates and indeed transcends.

NOTES. 1. The Candidus text was taken from his *Vermischte Gedichte* (1869), which Brahms owned. As he guardedly explained to Elisabet von Herzogenberg (i 31), German storks are 'fromm' (pious) because they bring babies and return in December, i.e. in good time for Christmas.

2. The first piano bar is motivic in its melancholy. The persistent dreamy arpeggios of M9 enter with the voice; these dominate the musical expression. At the last 'ein alter Traum', as the dream departs and disappears into the past taking the singer with it, the arpeggios in contrary motion (M13) anticipate the final 9/4 section of *Mein Herz ist schwer* (No. 166), on the same subject in the same key. At bar 23 the dream motif M9 is heard in the tragic tonality of E flat minor. The quasi-recitative passages thus introduced may hint at the Clara motif (M33) with a new sad semitone included (D–C–C♭–B♭–A–B♭, C–B–A–A♭–G–F#–G, left hand, bars 24–30). A name is called out in octaves at bars 40–41; the ensuing emphasis on the dominant seventh at 'Auge sieht mich (an)' is M24. The hemiolas there are M14; the falling A–D fifths of the postlude may be motifs of farewell, M34.

4. The subtle structure is worth special study. Throughout, the musical texture is ceaselessly rewoven in a typically Brahmsian song style. Thus the opening four-bar vocal melody is deftly cut and restitched to make new material; its first phrase becomes an answer at bars 34–5 and 38–9, while its second reappears at bars 26–7 and 30–31. Again, the piano figuration at 'verhängt und' briefly reappears before 'Es (ruft)' before becoming the main motif at the second 'ein alter Traum'; this motif of sad dreaming, repeated upward arpeggios ending in a falling second (M9 + M20) may be compared with the passage at 'oft im Traume' in *Immer leiser* (No. 187).

141. (Op. 72, No. 2) Sommerfäden (Gossamer) 1876
Karl Candidus   C minor d'–f''

> Sommerfäden hin und wieder
> Fliegen von den Himmeln nieder;

Sind den Menschen Hirngespinste,
Fetzen goldner Liebesträume.
An die Stauden, an die Bäume
Haben sie sich dort verfangen;
Hochselbsteigene Gewinnste
Sehen wir darunter hangen.

Gossamer threads, this way and that, waft down from the skies; they are the cobwebs of human thought, the remnants of golden love-dreams [the remnants of golden love-dreams].

On the bushes and trees, there they are caught; there we see our very own personal fate hanging by a thread [see it hanging by a thread].

Here is another fine example of the unobtrusive yet persistent audio-visual symbolism that characterises Brahms's best song-writing. The first two bars of prelude spin out one single line of quavers in each hand; in the next two bars, that movement is halted and left hanging. Both those images are presented in a sad C minor. Thus the poet's rather maladroit ideas and expressions, and their feeling-tones, are clearly and deftly delineated. At 'fliegen' (waft down) the right-hand notes descend all the way down the scale, an effect recalled in the interlude after 'Liebesträume' and again in the voice at 'hochselbsteigenes Gewinnste' (our very own personal fate), expressing a gradual but continuous decline. Then we also hear what the prelude's (and interlude's) second half means; the word 'hangen' is spread over the sonorous surface of the music, and its first syllable is sustained along four Andante crotchets, by far the longest note in the song until that same effect recurs on the last word, with the same sad sigh.

NOTES. 1. The Candidus text was taken from his *Vermischte Gedichte* (1869), which Brahms owned. It has 'der Menschen' (bar 10), not 'den Menschen', which though it stands thus in every printed edition is just a mistake in need of correction in print and performance.

2. The falling minor seconds in bars 3–4 etc, like their later prolongation at each 'hangen', are M20. The scale passages at bars 8 etc are also expressive in their downward drift; so are the off-beat quavers (M29) at 'Liebesträume', which illustrate separate remnants or 'Fetzen'. The last low octave minor keynote denotes an ultimate descent, M6/7.

3. The lines of single quavers in both hands are analogous with the running semi-quavers of *Blinde Kuh* (No. 92); despite the difference in depiction, each accompaniment shares the same idea of continuous motion.

3. Perhaps C minor is Clara's key here, as in the first Symphony. If so, the last long octave and the C–B♭–A–G–A♭ at 'Liebesträume' may both exemplify M33.

142. (Op. 72, No. 3) O kühler Wald (O cool forest) *c.* 1877
Clemens Brentano   A♭ major d′–e♭″ (f″)

O kühler Wald,
Wo rauschest du,
In dem mein Liebchen geht?

O Widerhall,
Wo lauschest du,
Der gern mein Lied versteht?

Im Herzen tief,
Da rauscht der Wald,
In dem mein Liebchen geht,
In Schmerzen schlief
Der Widerhall,
Die Lieder sind verweht.

O cool forest in which my love goes walking, where are you murmuring? Where are you
hiding, O echo that loves to understand my song [my song]?
    Deep in my heart, there the forest is murmuring [there the forest is murmuring] in
which my love goes walking. The echo has fallen asleep in sorrow, the songs have wafted
away [the songs have wafted, wafted away].

The solemn crotchet chords walk along sedately, accompanying the vocal melody.
A rising fourth, as at 'Widerhall' (echo), is half-heard hidden in the left hand at
'wo lauschest du?' (where are you hiding?). The questioning harmonies after
'versteht?' (understand) remain unresolved; at 'im Herzen tief' (deep in my heart)
the left hand expresses deep feelings, in a remote region of tonality. The home key
resumes at 'rauscht der Wald' (the forest is murmuring), where a new quaver
movement continuously stirs among the symbolic foliage of regret and memory
until the final repeated 'verweht' wafts the vocal line away, and the initial
imagined woodland walk returns to end the song with a sad sigh.

NOTES. I. No doubt the textual source was Brentano's *Gedichte in neuer Auswahl* (1861),
which Brahms owned. He must have relied on an earlier publication, perhaps the
Gesammelte Werke (1852–5), for his other Brentano setting *Abendständchen* Op. 42 No. 1,
for six-part chorus *a cappella*, written in 1859. But that source also includes *O schöner Wald*,
so this song may date from that year.
    2. Brahms set the poem's first and third verses, omitting the second and fourth, thus
combining condensation with criticism. The missing twelve lines are not especially
inspired. Even so, such treatment seems cavalier. In particular it rejects Brentano's hope for
a renewal of love and the lyrics thus induced; for Brahms, those days are over. The choice
of poem may have been motivated by the favourite theme of cooling; the setting sounds
intensely personal.
    3. Clara Schumann preserved an album of pressed leaves and flowers plucked on
woodland walks with the 22-year-old Brahms during their stay in Switzerland, July 1855.
Her theme (M33) appears in the voice part here, as E♭–D♭–C♭–B♭–C♭, at 'in Schmerzen
schlief der Widerhall'; see also *In Waldeseinsamkeit* (No. 155).
    4. The walking chords are M1; the sustained dominant sevenths at 'versteht?' are M24;
the deep octaves for 'tief' are M6, with the flatward movement of M42; the silences that
precede them and recur in the last bar but two are M29; the surprising excursion to (in
effect) E major at 'Herzen tief' anticipates the key and progression of 'O Tod' in the third
Serious Song, No. 202. The enhanced rhythmic interest at 'da rauscht der Wald' is also
motivic (M16), and adds the rustling-foliage implications of M4. The last phrase's chromatic rise to the mediant, though heard only in this song, is clearly motivic in the sense of
'verweht', like the sighs of M21 in the previous bar and the postlude.

5. The alternative small note f″ on 'gern' in bar 8, though authentic, is rarely performed and has little to recommend it.

143. (Op. 72, No. 4) Verzagen (Despair) 1877
Karl Lemcke   F# minor c#′–f#″

> Ich sitz am Strande der rauschenden See
> Und suche dort nach Ruh,
> Ich schaue dem Treiben der Wogen
> Mit dumpfer Ergebung zu.
>
> Die Wogen rauschen zum Strande hin,
> Sie schäumen und vergehn,
> Die Wolken, die Winde darüber,
> Die kommen und verwehn.
>
> Du ungestümes Herz sei still
> Und gib dich doch zur Ruh,
> Du sollst mit Winden und Wogen
> Dich trösten, – was weinest du?

I sit by the shore of the raging sea, and there I seek rest [there I seek rest]; I gaze at the motion of the waves in numb submission [in numb submission].

The waves crash on the shore, they foam and vanish [they foam and vanish]; the clouds, the winds above, they arrive and disperse [they arrive and disperse].

You unruly heart, be silent and take your rest [and take your rest]; you should find comfort in winds and waves; why are you weeping [weeping, why are you weeping]?

The piano's stormy demisemiquavers demand virtuoso yet self-effacing performance, like a subdued concerto. The low left-hand notes depict the depths of the sea, and of despair. At 'ich schaue' (I gaze) the figuration changes from confusion to collision in sudden splashes of sound. A long stepwise vocal descent by tone and semitone offers an equally vivid image of 'dumpfer Ergebung' (numb submission). Thus the character and the scene are delineated together, each in the same distress and turmoil. The same music serves for the second verse. In the third, the central figure is thrown into relief. The prelude's theme is again repeated, and then sung, with a higher climax, to the words 'Du ungestümes Herz' (You unruly heart), before being reabsorbed into the wild clamour of wind and wave; we are to understand that the singer is at one, perhaps literally, with the stormy sea.

NOTES. 1. The text was taken from Lemcke's *Lieder und Gedichte* (1861), which Brahms owned.

2. This setting may again illustrate the favourite themes of the deserted girl and the sad sea-shore. Perhaps she is united with her lost sweetheart here too, in the musical imagination, as more overtly in *Treue Liebe* (No. 15), written 23 years earlier. The two songs share the same musical theme in the same notes and key, e.g. in the prelude here and the

opening vocal melody there. Perhaps Clara's tragedy is remembered here too, with 'doch zur Ruh' in the third verse sung to M33. Compare also the arpeggio water-music of *Vom Strande* (No. 127).

3. The arpeggios of wind and wave are M4 and M5; the semitonal clashes and splashes at 'Ich schaue' etc. are also expressive, like the long stepwise descent of 'dumpfer Ergebung' also heard in *Sommerfäden* (No. 141) and *Geistliches Wiegenlied* (No. 163). Note 1 above may suggest that the last low left-hand F sharps form a funeral knell, M7.

4. The Peters low-key edition (though not the *Gesamtausgabe*) prints an alternative lower note on the first 'dich' of the third verse; but the higher note, which is M10 here and *passim*, should surely be sung.

144. (Op. 72, No. 5) Unüberwindlich (Unconquerable) 1876
Johann Wolfgang von Goethe   A major g#–f#"

> Hab ich tausendmal geschworen
> Dieser Flasche nicht zu trauen,
> Bin ich doch wie neugeboren,
> Lässt mein Schenke fern sie schauen,
> Alles ist an ihr zu loben,
> Glaskristall und Purpurwein;
> Wird der Pfropf herausgehoben
> Sie ist leer und ich nicht mein.

> Hab ich tausendmal geschworen
> Dieser Falschen nicht zu trauen,
> Und doch bin ich neugeboren,
> Lässt sie sich ins Auge schauen,
> Mag sie doch mit mir verfahren
> Wies dem stärksten Mann geschah,
> Deine Scher in meinen Haaren,
> Allerliebste Delila!

I've vowed a thousand times not to trust this bottle [not to trust this bottle], yet I feel as if new born, when my cup-bearer shows it to me from a distance [when my cup-bearer shows it to me from a distance].

Everything about it is praiseworthy, crystal glass and crimson wine; no sooner is the cork taken out [no sooner is the cork taken out] than it's empty and I'm not my own master [it's empty and I'm not my own master, it's empty and I'm not my own master].

I've vowed a thousand times not to trust this traitress, and yet I'm as if new-born, as soon as I'm allowed a sight of her [as soon as I'm allowed a sight of her].

Let her deal with me as it befell the strongest of men; set your shears to my hair [set your shears to my hair], my dearest Delilah [my dearest Delilah, my dearest Delilah]!

On abundant evidence, Brahms shared Schumann's delight in puns and word-play; the musical ear often enjoys verbal echoes. So this racy poem about the impotence inflicted by a 'Flasche' (bottle) alias 'Falsche' (traitress) may well have made an immediate and powerful appeal. But why begin by quoting Domenico Scarlatti? In German, as in English, wine and women may both be scarlet; but (as so often) Schumann affords a far clearer clue (Sams 1972b). In his 1839 critique of the 'Complete Piano Works' of Scarlatti (Kreisig i 400) Schumann says that not too many should be taken together; but they would have an exhilarating effect if sampled in moderation and at the right time. Just so. No doubt Brahms had both read the review and studied (and perhaps inherited) the Scarlatti volume in question. His quotation comes from No. 133 of the 200 it contains. And when he later sent some Scarlatti works to his friend Billroth (8 May 1885) he explained that 'they're sure to please you, so long as you don't tackle them on a massive scale but just take modest portions', thus following if not indeed citing Schumann's opinion. Hence the hidden relevance of Scarlatti to the sexist Brahms (MacDonald 397–8); beware of wine and women, and use them both in moderation.

Similarly, this motto-theme permeates the music. It provides the preluding octaves duly labelled 'D. Scarlatti'. Then it becomes the bass line. As the words begin, Brahms starts to compose in earnest, at first in a frank drinking-song with a hiccuping staccato accompaniment, finishing at the wrong chord on 'trauen' (trust) to indicate distrust as well as inebriation. There follows an orotund unison at the second 'dieser Flasche nicht zu trauen' [not to trust this bottle], with the same wrong chord. Now the melodic flow becomes mellower in voice and piano, with an echoing interlude. After 'Alles' (Everything) Scarlatti is reborn at the keyboard; his descending quaver arpeggio takes over the right hand

and his main theme is repeated in the left

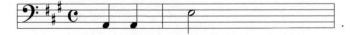

As the cork pops out on a forte chord at 'Pfropf' the bibulous staccato resumes. A brief interlude applauds the extraction and prepares for another swig. But the music now feels the need for a bar's rest; and as the voice resumes at 'Hab ich tausendmal geschworen' (I've vowed a thousand times) its gait is still decidedly unsteady. The two hands stumble after each other in canon, unable to recollect their own main theme. 'Falschen' (false one, or traitress) falls on a lugubriously disapproving minor chord; at 'nicht zu trauen' (not to trust) the long notes of recitative are enunciated with an effort. From this flat tonality, however, the cheerful music of renewal bubbles up again, culminating in a masochistically maudlin tonic outburst of self-surrender to the dearest of Delilas, where the key-phrase 'Deine Scher in meinen Haaren' (set your shears to my hair) enthusiastically sings the opening Scarlatti melody.

This masterpiece testifies to its composer's rarely-used comic gift, which

challenges comparison with the good-humoured drinking songs in Wolf's own
Goethe settings from the *Westöstlicher Diwan*, or Ravel's *Chanson à boire*.

NOTES. 1. Brahms owned two sets of Goethe's *Werke*; this lyric is found in both, The
Gesamtausgabe's 'Propf' in its seventh line is corrected in the Peters edition.

2. Both poet and composer were devoted if not devout Bible-readers. Each may well
have known that Samson (Judges 16–17) was born a Nazarite, a member of a strict sect who
abjured strong drink and let their hair grow (Numbers 6, 1–21). The infatuated Samson
rashly confided to his adored Delilah that 'if I be shaven then my strength will go from me';
she promptly 'called for a man and caused him to shave off the seven locks of his head'. It
is Goethe who makes her intervene personally, equipped with shears like the Fate Atropos.

3. An essay could be written about the subtle skills deployed in weaving the Scarlatti
theme across the Brahmsian texture. Thus the kinship of bars 1–3 with 5–7 is not audibly
apparent; yet they could be performed simultaneously without discord.

4. The tittuping or hiccuping staccati are expressive, like the vocal augmentation and
piano diminution at 'Alles ist …' and 'Glaskristall …' and the canonic exchange (M12)
between the two hands at 'Hab ich doch …' etc. The expectant dominant seventh in the
interlude after the last 'nicht mein' is M24, the ensuing silent bar is M29. The croaking
melody at the culminating distrust of women ('dieser Falschen nicht zu trauen' on the
penultimate page) may well speak with the voice of Brahms himself (M36).

OPUS 84

Songs (Romanzen und Lieder) for one or two voices with pianoforte accompaniment, with named poets or sources, published in July 1882.

145. (Op. 84, No. 1) Sommerabend (Summer evening) *c.* 1881
Hans Schmidt   D minor and major b♭–d''

(Die Mutter)	Geh schlafen, Tochter, schlafen! Schon fällt der Tau aufs Gras, Und wen die Tropfen trafen, Weint bald die Augen nass!
(Die Tochter)	Lass weinen, Mutter, weinen! Das Mondlicht leuchtet hell, Und wem die Strahlen scheinen, Dem trocknen Tränen schnell!
(Die Mutter)	Geh schlafen, Tochter, schlafen! Schon ruft der Kauz im Wald, Und wen die Töne trafen, Muss mit ihm klagen bald!
(Die Tochter)	Lass klagen, Mutter, klagen! Die Nachtigall singt hell, Und wem die Lieder schlagen, Dem schwindet Trauer schnell!

(Mother): Go to sleep, daughter, go to sleep; already the dew is falling on the grass, and whoever is touched by those drops will soon weep their eyes wet [will soon weep their eyes wet]!

(Daughter): Enough of weeping, mother, enough of weeping; the moonlight shines bright, and whoever is shone on by those rays, their tears will soon dry [their tears will soon dry]!

(Mother): Go to sleep, daughter, go to sleep, already the screech owl is hooting in the forest, and whoever hears that cry will soon be mourning too [will soon be mourning too]!

(Daughter): Enough of mourning, mother, enough of mourning, the nightingale sings clear, and whoever heeds that song will soon forget their sorrow [will soon forget their sorrow]!

The voice of experience advises against dew and owls in the minor, the voice of innocence rhapsodises about moonlight and nightingales in the major. Thus the mother may be warning her daughter about unwanted pregnancies, in a discreetly symbolic sex-talk. The former's dew-drops, at 'wen die Tropfen trafen' etc., with their alternating thirds, are almost a satire on love-duets; the latter's cheerful acceptance of nature in all its aspects begins with added triplets. The composer's sympathies audibly lie with the latter; mother sounds torpid and negative compared with her livelier and more responsive offspring, as their contrasting piano figures suggest, with e.g. ♩ and ♩

in their respective opening bars.

NOTES. 1. The text was taken from Schmidt's undated *Gedichte und Übersetzungen*, which Brahms owned; the song's headings 'Mother' and 'Daughter' were added by the composer, here and in the next two songs, as if to confirm one of his favourite themes.

2. The broken thirds at 'Tropfen' (M18?) should surely be rendered with the typical dew-drop or tears mezzo-staccato of M28, an effect which falls less pat but remains arguably apt in the mother's second verse. Meanwhile the daughter's added quaver triplets are expressive (M16) in the sense of a springier step, a sprightlier dance, like her exultantly ascending left hand octaves for 'Strahlen' and 'Lieder'. The Schubertian minor–major change is M39; the fleeting minor inflexions in the major interlude and postlude are M41.

3. The engaging middle-European folk-song melodies and strong rhythmic impulse recall the *Ungarische Tänze* WoO 1 and anticipate the *Zigeunerlieder* Op. 103.

146. (Op. 84, No. 2) Der Kranz (The Wreath) *c.* 1881
Hans Schmidt   G minor and major a–g″

> (Die Tochter)   Mutter, hilf mir armen Tochter,
>   Sieh nur, was ein Knabe tat;
>   Einen Kranz von Rosen flocht er,
>   Den er mich zu tragen bat!

> (Die Mutter)   Ei, sei deshalb unerschrocken,
>   Helfen lässt sich dir gewiss!

Nimm den Kranz nur aus den Locken,
Und den Knaben, den vergiss!

(Die Tochter)   Dornen hat der Kranz, o Mutter,
Und die halten fest das Haar!
Worte sprach der Knabe, Mutter,
An die denk ich immerdar!

(Daughter): Mother, help your poor daughter, just see what a boy has done, he wove a wreath of roses and asked me to wear it [asked me to wear it]!
   (Mother): Oh, don't let that scare you, of course I can help you! Just take the wreath out of your tresses and forget the boy [forget the boy]!
   (Daughter): But the wreath has thorns, mother, and they've caught on my hair!
   And the boy spoke words to me, mother [mother], that I think about all the time [that I think about all the time]!

As in No. 145, the vocal line takes precedence over the poetic metre; hence 'aus' and 'und' fall on strong beats. But here the melodies are less ingratiating and the accompaniment figures more complex. This is the music of thorns and entanglement, in accordance with the allegorical verses, and the result can hardly be ingratiating, despite the optimistic direction Allegro grazioso. The two-bar prelude comprises four increasing cries for help, set to the same little moans with which the voice begins ('Mutter, hilf') over a light twining of repeated semiquavers. Thus the girl displays her wreath. But at that idea, which connotes marriages as well as funerals, the music first softens into simpler melodies and then weaves a two-hand pattern (at 'flocht').

Mother needs only a brief pause for thought; she is familiar with such problems. Her opening melody, now in the major, is bright and broad like a smile. The thorny wreath is to be disposed of. But the audience (and mother) must understand that it's not so easy. The girl herself, in the allegory, is perhaps already a mother-to-be. She has much to think about, now and in the future. So the music, from the sustained 'Worte' (words) onwards is at first full of plaintive sighs but then brightens into a final exultant acceptance.

NOTES. I. The text was taken from Schmidt's undated *Gedichte und Übersetzungen*, which Brahms owned; here, as in Nos. 145 and 147, the composer added the song's headings 'Mother' and 'Daughter'. The theme of the deserted girl was always dear to his heart.

   2. The prelude depicts painful entanglement, with the interwoven leaves of M4 and the gaps of M29. The sad 5-6-5-6-5 at 'Mutter, hilf mir' etc. is M20; the voice and right-hand duetting is M18, and the piano hemiola at the second 'tragen' is M14. Perhaps 'Ade' is meant by the mother's dismissive A-D at each 'vergiss', M34. After the motivic Schubertian change from G minor to G major on the last page (M39), the girl's top Gs at 'Wort(e)' and 'die' are M10 and the keyboard's gusty sighs there and *passim* are M21.

   3. The typical patchwork structure is worth close analysis. The keyboard texture varies thus: A = 1–2, B = 3–5, C = 6–7, D = 8–9, E = 10–12, F = 13–14, G (interlude) = 15–16, H = 17–21, I = 22–3, J = 24–6, K = 27–8, L = 29–30, where each patch has a different colouring and texture. But there are continuous connecting threads; thus the left-hand figure in A begins B, the right-hand arpeggios of C transfer to the left at D, and so on. The

reprise at the daughter's response is again deceptive; its first few bars (31–5) from 'Dornen' repeat and reinforce her initial appeal at 'Mutter, hilf mir', but then, just as deliberately, they dress up again in further swathes of new material. By these means Brahms says that his song's ostensible simplicity is deceptive; here is real emotional life in all its manifold complexity.

147. (Op. 84, No. 3) In den Beeren (Among the berries) c. 1881
Hans Schmidt   E♭ major (B major) f#'–g''

(Die Mutter)   Singe, Mädchen, hell und klar,
                Sing aus voller Kehle,
                Dass uns nicht die Spatzenschar
                Alle Beeren stehle!

(Die Tochter)   Mutter, mag auch weit der Spatz
                Fliehn vor meinem Singen,
                Fürcht ich doch, es wird den Schatz
                Um so näher bringen.

(Die Mutter)   Freilich, für so dreisten Gauch
                Braucht es einer Scheuche,
                Warte nur, ich komme auch
                In die Beerensträuche!

(Die Tochter)   Mutter, nein, das hat nicht Not:
                Beeren, schau, sind teuer,
                Doch die Küsse, reif und rot
                Gibt es viele heuer!

(Mother): Sing, my girl, bright and clear, sing full-throated, so that the flock of sparrows doesn't steal all our berries!

(Daughter): Mother, however far my singing may make the sparrow fly, I fear it will bring my sweetheart all the nearer [bring him all the nearer].

(Mother): Well, we certainly need some way of scaring off that bold bird; just wait, and I'll come into the berry bushes too!

(Daughter): No, mother, we don't need that; look, berries are dear, but ripe red kisses [ripe red kisses] are plentiful this year [are plentiful this year]!

Again the symbolism is overt. The prelude's two alternating hands converge as if to protect the berries. These gestures continue as the mother's voice enters in folksong style, cheerful and knowing. The piano part pecks in repeated diminuendos, and then accompanies the full-throated singing ('aus voller Kehle'); the pecking resumes to illustrate the 'Spatzenschar' (flock of sparrows) and snaps in a resentful staccato at the thought of their daring depredations. The interlude sighs soulfully. At the daughter's reply the tonality brightens and the pecking is tender; the girl is already reminded of her lover, who comes sidling up in her imagination (or perhaps in reality) at 'fürcht ich' (I fear). Mother resumes in the home key. Then the music sighs and brightens as before, and the sidling strains recur at 'Küsse' with a long lingering on an expressive top note at 'viele' (plentiful) and a final clinching comment from the piano.

NOTES. 1. The text was taken from Schmidt's undated *Gedichte und Übersetzungen*, which Brahms owned; as in the two previous songs, the headings 'Mother' and 'Daughter' were added by the composer.

2. The convergence of hands is M17, the pecking or kissing thirds are M18, the sighing interlude exemplifies M21; the sidling movement at 'fürcht ich doch' etc. is analogous with the sidelong semiquavers or quavers of Nos. 92 and 141 respectively; the sustained top note at 'viele' is M10.

148. (Op. 84, No. 4) Vergebliches Ständchen (A Serenade in vain) c. 1878

Anon.   A major and minor e'–f#''

(Er)   Guten Abend, mein Schatz,
       Guten Abend, mein Kind!
       Ich komm aus Lieb zu dir,
       Ach, mach mir auf die Tür,
       Mach mir auf die Tür!

(Sie) Mein Tür ist verschlossen,
       Ich lass dich nicht ein;
       Mutter, die rät mir klug,
       Wärst du herein mit Fug,
       Wärs mit mir vorbei!

(Er)   So kalt ist die Nacht,
       So eisig der Wind,
       Dass mir das Herz erfriert,
       Mein Lieb erlöschen wird;
       Öffne mir, mein Kind!

(Sie) Löschet dein Lieb,
       Lass sie löschen nur!
       Löschet sie immerzu,
       Geh heim zu Bett, zur Ruh,
       Gute Nacht, mein Knab!

(He): Good evening, my dear, good evening, my child [good evening, my child]! I'm here because I love you, oh, open your door to me, open your door to me [open, open, open your door to me]!

(She): My door's locked and I won't let you in [I won't let you in]; Mother gives me wise advice; if you were allowed in, it would be all up with me [all up, all up, all up with me]!

(He): So cold is the night, so icy the wind [so icy the wind] that my heart is freezing, my love will go out, open to me, my child [open to me, open to me, open to me, my child]!

(She): If your love will go out, then just let it go out [just let it go out]; if it keeps going out then go home to bed and take your rest. Good night, my lad [goodnight, goodnight, goodnight my lad]!

The direction 'lively and good-humoured' well describes this much-loved masterpiece. Exceptionally, the composer himself was more than content with his work; in his entirely understandable elation he even told a friend that he would trade all his other songs for this one (Kalbeck iii 337).

Two rising phrases in the brief prelude signal the naïve suitor's arrival. He trolls out his simple sequences, heedless of verbal accentuation ('guten' first on two quavers, then on two crotchets), in unison with the piano octaves. No utterance could be more forthright or direct; this is a village wooing in tones. A hearty piano interlude repeats the wooer's invocation; then so does he. The pleading becomes more insistent, punctuated by chordal gestures; at 'mach mir auf' (open ... to me) the vocal line reaffirms what the prelude was saying. Now the girl sings, in the same strain. Like many a Brahms heroine, she has had a chat with her mother. So the interlude between each 'lass dich nicht ein' (won't let you in) is now as it were feminized in the musical imagination, from strong chords to frail notes frilled with extra quavers. Now the same music is turned into tones of self-pity, blowing and moaning in the bleak tonic minor of cold night and icy wind ('so kalt ist die Nacht, so eisig der Wind'), with gusty off-beat accents. The girl mocks these misfortunes, this time with stronger chords in her interlude, while at 'löschet' (going out) the piano part breaks into outright laughter. The postlude parodistically restates the prelude's application for admission, ending on a two-handed sforzando as the door is metaphorically (or perhaps the window is literally) slammed tight shut, with a final shout of 'Gute Nacht!' in the postlude. But all concerned, including the audience, will understand that this is not to be the singer's last word on the subject.

NOTES. 1. Brahms found this lyric in his cherished copy of the Kretzschmer–Zuccalmaglio *Deutsche Volkslieder* (ii 1840), where it is called a folk-song from the lower Rhine. But the composer's insistence on the duet form (it was he who added the speech-prefixes 'Er' und 'Sie'), and his other invocations of the folk-song style as he conceived it, have suffused this song with memorable melody and character. It is nowadays rarely performed as a duet; but the title-page sanctions that presentation.

2. Two favourite themes are united here; icy isolation of the lover, and maternal advice to a daughter.

3. The love-duetting thirds and sixths are M18; the missing first beat at bars 11, 13, etc., is M29; the postlude's first two bars of hemiola are M14. The Schubertian major/minor is M39; and the gusting accented minim off-beats from 'erfriert' onwards are also expressive, like the leggiero laughter.

149. (Op. 84, No. 5) Spannung (Tenseness) *c.* 1878
Anon.   A minor and major e'–g'' (a'')

> (Er)   Gut'n Abend, gut'n Abend, mein tausiger Schatz,
>   Ich sag dir guten Abend;

Komm du zu mir, ich komme zu dir,
Du sollst mir Antwort geben, mein Engel!

(Sie) Ich kommen zu dir, du kommen zu mir?
Das wär mir gar keine Ehre;
Du gehst von mir zu andern Jungfraun,
Das hab ich wohl vernommen, mein Engel!

(Er) Ach nein, mein Schatz, und glaub es nur nicht,
Was falsche Zungen reden,
Es geben so viele gottlose Leut,
Die dir und mir nichts gönnen, mein Engel!

(Sie) Und gibt es so viele gottlose Leut,
Die dir und mir nichts gönnen,
So solltest du selber bewahren die Treu
Und machen zu Schanden ihr Reden, mein Engel!

(Er) Leb wohl, mein Schatz, ich hör es wohl,
Du hast einen Anderen lieber,
So will ich meiner Wege gehn,
Gott möge dich wohl behüten, mein Engel!

(Sie) Ach nein, ich habe kein Anderen lieb,
Ich glaub nicht gottlosen Leuten,
Komm du zu mir, ich komme zu dir,
Wir bleiben uns beide getreue, mein Engel!

(He): Good evening, good evening, my dearest love, I bid you good evening; come you to me and I'll come to you, and you must give me an answer, my angel!

(She): If I came to you, and you to me, that would do me no honour at all; you go from me to other girls, so I'm reliably told, my angel!

(He): Oh no, my love, just don't believe what false tongues tell, there are so many ungodly folk with a grudge against us, my angel!

(She): And if there are so many ungodly folk with a grudge against us, then you above all should keep faith and shame their slanders, my angel!

(He): Farewell, my love, I understand that you love another more, so I shall go my ways, and may God protect you, my angel!

(She): Oh no, I don't love anyone else, I don't believe ungodly folk, come you to me and I'll come to you, we'll both stay true to each other, my angel [come you to me and I'll come to you, we'll both stay true to each other, my angel]!

The meeting is tense and moody. The young man presents his credentials and other polite civilities; but we soon hear that all is not well. After some melancholy minor-key duetting in a brief prelude, the accompaniment is spiky and edgy for each of the first two verses, with emphatic pedal-notes; the lover sings 'I bid you good evening' with descending chromatic intervals at 'sag' (bid) and 'gut'. His sweetheart's rejoinder adds its own verbal reservations; and her final phrase is heavy with irony, as if 'Engel' were in inverted commas. In her estimation, he's no angel. So when his ensuing protestations are somewhat smoothed and sweetened by flowing right-hand semiquavers, the vocal line stays uneasy, maintaining the tension with four further drooping intervals, exacerbated by harsher harmonies. All this is repeated in her reply. Now he bids farewell, in unison with the piano's reprise of the opening melody; and at 'so will ich meiner Wege gehn' (so I shall go my ways) the left hand walks briskly away. This is too much; the music cries aloud for reconciliation in a Schubertian change to the major key on the same tonic, at the girl's cry of 'Ach nein'. And now the listener learns that the first five verses have served solely as preparation and prelude for this moving moment. All is forgiven; there will be a happy ending and a fresh start, in an exultant outpouring of mutual love. A cynic might wonder how long this will last. But Brahms has no doubt; the final love-duet singing, whether metaphorical in the musical imagery or literal with the two voices intertwined (an optional version which deserves an occasional hearing) will never be done.

NOTES. 1. As in No. 148, the source was the Kretzschmer–Zuccalmaglio collection *Deutsche Volkslieder* (ii 1840). Brahms adds 'He' and 'She', and supplies an optional duet ending at the final 'Komm du zu mir'. He also somewhat softens the text by substituting 'das hab ich wohl vernommen' in verse two for the original livelier phrase 'das kann ich an dir wohl spüren', I can tell that just by being with you; and he added 'und' between 'Schatz' and 'glaub' in verse three to bridge a melodic gap.

2. As the happy ending implies, the true theme is lasting love.

3. The duetting thirds and sixths, major or minor, are M18; the semiquaver walking away is M1. The tonic pedals in the first two verses are also motivic (M8), like the Schubertian key-change in the last verse (M39).

OPUS 85

Six songs (Lieder) for solo voice with pianoforte accompaniment, with named poets or translator, published in July 1882.

150. (Op. 85, No. 1) Sommerabend (Summer evening) 1878
Heinrich Heine   Eb major d'–d''

> Dämmernd liegt der Sommerabend
> Über Wald und grünen Wiesen;
> Goldner Mond im blauen Himmel
> Strahlt herunter, duftig labend.
>
> An dem Bache zirpt die Grille,
> Und es regt sich in dem Wasser,

Und der Wandrer hört ein Plätschern
Und ein Atmen in der Stille.

Dorten, an dem Bach alleine,
Badet sich die schöne Elfe;
Arm und Nacken, weiss und lieblich,
Schimmern in dem Mondencheine.

Darkling, the summer evening lies over forest and green meadows; the golden moon shines down from the blue sky, tenderly soothing.
By the brook the cricket chirps and the waters stir, and the wayfarer hears a splashing and a breathing in the stillness.
There, alone by the brook, a fair water-nymph is bathing; arms and neck, white and lovely, gleam in the moonlight.

Heine's poem happens to sound a special chord in the composer's mind; the response is profound. The music shared by this song and the next (see note 1) symbolises feelings of release and relaxation, attributed in each poem to the idea of being bathed in cooling water by healing moonlight. Here the sense of soothing tenderness is closely associated with womanly beauty. This is surely a love song.

Two long solemn chords intone an incantation. The falling vocal arpeggios at 'Dämmernd liegt' (Darkling lies) and 'über Wald' (over forest) are inverted to make bass counter-melodies, in a picture of moon and man. At the first 'An dem Bache' (by the brook) the music is mysteriously metamorphosed to match the slight sounds and movements described, as if the wayfarer stands still and says 'listen … what was that?'. At 'ein Atmen' (a breathing) the harmonies become even more tense and perplexed. The prelude's slow semibreves recur, and anticipation is further increased as the song and the singer hold their breath.

At this magic moment the foliage parts and the moon emerges; the scene is brightened and bared. The voice recalls its first descriptive strains, the right-hand counter-melody sings more clearly in the higher octave, the left-hand arpeggios announce a vision. 'Dorten' (there) the beauty of nature stands revealed. The poem is the apotheosis of Romanticism, for whose devotees this setting is a major masterpiece.

NOTES. 1. The textual source was Heine's *Sämtliche Werke*, (1861–6), which Brahms owned. This poem and the next (set as No. 151) were first written and published as separate lyrics but then juxtaposed as Nos. 85 and 86 of the collection called *Die Heimkehr*, where Brahms found them. Their musical unification, and their titles, are his own invention; his song-writing had a quasi-linguistic significance of its own.
    2. This takes precedence over the word-setting; so the first and third beats of the middle verse (on 'an', 'in', 'und' etc.) should not be overstressed, despite their intentional correspondence with Heine's trochaic metre.
    3. The naked naiad embodies a poetic ideal (cf. No. 205 note 3). Brahms worshipped Elisabet von Stockhausen, who may well have been translated into music as E. S. (= Es = E flat) as contained in the prelude's semibreves, which reappear before the reprise. Those two notes (M35) are the distilled essence of the song (e.g. in the left hand at 'blauer

Himmel' and the right at 'weiss und lieblich'). They belong to successive dominant sevenths, heard in the prelude and repeated in the interlude after 'Stille', which in the context of nocturnal wayfaring ('Mond' … 'der Wandrer') cannot fail to recall the second bar and the last two bars of Schubert's *Wandrers Nachtlied* D768 in the same key and time. The second song is called *Wanderlied* in the Heine source. All such personal allusions are highly Brahmsian.

3. The inverse relation and convergence between bass and voice at bars 3 and 5 (M17) may have been motivated by the poetic idea of relative position, earth and sky, forest and moon. The consecutive sixths at 'labend', like the thirds at 'An dem Bache', etc., are M18; the sustained dominant sevenths in the prelude and before the reprise at 'Dorten' are M24; the dreamy left-hand arpeggios thereafter are M9. The quickening rhythms there are also motivic (M16); so are the pedal points *passim* (M8) and the yearningly chromatic harmony in the postlude.

4. Cf. Schoeck's setting, Op. 4 No. 1.

151. (Op. 85, No. 2) Mondenschein (Moonlight) 1878
Heinrich Heine   Eb major d'–g''

> Nacht liegt auf den fremden Wegen,
> Krankes Herz und müde Glieder, –
> Ach, da fliesst, wie stiller Segen,
> Süsser Mond, dein Licht hernieder;
>
> Süsser Mond, mit deinen Strahlen
> Scheuchest du das nächtge Grauen;
> Es zerrinnen meine Qualen
> Und die Augen übertauen.

Night lies over the unknown pathways; sick heart and tired limbs –
Ah then, like a silent blessing, sweet moon, your radiance comes flooding down.
With your beams, sweet moon, you dispel night-time terrors. My troubles melt away,
my eyes brim over.

This sequel ends with the same chords that began its predecessor; the two are thus envisaged as a unity. They should perhaps always be performed together, because each musical invocation of the moon sheds light on the other. Here the wayfarer is far gone, as the ominous opening octaves announce in their sombre descent down the keyboard. The sick heart and the tired limbs are alike in longing for their last rest. At that second phrase, 'müde Glieder', the previous song's interlude is modified and extended; this time the feelings are even more stressful and intense. So the voice's invocation of moonlight flows out even more consolingly. The piano's counter-melody, heard successively higher in the keyboard during the first song, now emerges an octave higher still over deep bass notes and syncopations, as if the moon is imagined moving brightly through the dark night, dispelling night-time terrors ('scheuchest du das nächtge Grauen'). All the tensions dissolve, leaving only one single repeated keynote, in a marvellous moment of redeeming self-acceptance as the initial suicidal mood lightens back into life. While the voice sings its final incantation at 'es zerrinnen' (melt away) the piano's arpeggios crest in long minims, first in rising fourths and then in falling fifths, making an image of open space and the healing power of nature that brings renewal and hope.

NOTES. 1. For the textual source, see No. 150 notes 1 and 3; for a possible inspirational source see its note 3. Heine has an exclamation mark at 'Ach!' in line 3; its sense of quiet wonderment is beautifully conveyed by the right-hand melody, marked *dolcissimo*.

2. The unstated unifying theme of healing coolness suffuses the music.

3. The ominous descending octaves are M7, wearing black E♭ minor armbands. The consecutive thirds, M18, suggest that the singer is suffering the agonies of unrequited love as well as physical distress; the semitonal groaning is M20/21. The top notes at 'krankes Herz' are thematic, M10, and should certainly be preferred to the tame alternatives provided. At 'Ach, da fliegt' the left-hand syncopations are motivic, like the quickening rhythms (M16) and the flatward modulation (M42) after 'zerrinnen'; the hypnotised arpeggios there and in the postlude are M9.

152. (Op. 85, No. 3) Mädchenlied (Girl's song) 1878
Anon., Serbian (trans. S. Kapper)   A minor g′–g″

> Ach, und du mein kühles Wasser!
> Ach, und du mein rotes Röslein!
> Was erblühst du mir so frühe?
> Hab ja nicht, für wen dich pflücken!
> Pflück ich dich für meine Mutter?
> Keine Mutter hab ich Waise!
> Pflück ich dich für meine Schwester?
> Ei doch, längst vermählet ist sie!
> Pflück ich dich für meinen Bruder?
> Ist gezogen in die Feldschlacht!
> Pflück ich dich für den Geliebten?
> Fern, ach, weilet der Geliebte!
> Jenseit dreier grünen Berge,
> Jenseit dreier kühlen Wasser!

Alas, and you my cool river! Alas, and you my red rose! Why do you bloom so early? I have no-one to pluck you for.

Shall I pluck you for my mother? I the orphan have no mother! Shall I pluck you for my sister? But no, she has long since married.

Shall I pluck you for my brother? He has gone to the wars! Shall I pluck you for my lover? Alas, my lover tarries far away! Across three green mountains and across three cool rivers [across three cool rivers].

The rural rhythm notated in 5/4 time (though in fact three plus two crotchets throughout) emulates the rather flat-footed trochees of the verse, with its deliberately awkward diction. The music too has a country accent. But that ambiance and these topics spoke with a special appeal to Brahms. The prelude and interlude convey his message by anticipating the melodic line to which 'jenseit' (across) etc. is first sung, and it quotes verbatim the piano accompaniment to the final repetition. Here is a song of keeping one's distance. But the concomitant coolness and detachment of water and rose, as mirrored in the alternation of separate hands, and the independence of melody and bass, are deceptive. The real feeling is deferred until the sustained high vocal line at the end of the song, which strives to stretch into the distance; in vain, according to the one-bar minor-chord postlude.

NOTES. 1. The textual source was the *Gesänge der Serben* (1862), of Siegfried Kapper, whose last lines were 'jenseits dreier grüner Berge, jenseits dreier kühler Wasser'.

2. Note the favourite themes in combination; erotic symbolism, cool water and a love-lorn orphan country girl.

3. The touches of modal harmony and the composite time-signature are folk-song indicators, M26/27; the consecutive sixths of prelude, interlude and last four bars but one sing a sad love-duet, M18.

4. The left-hand pattern varies to suit the structure: prelude = the final bars of accompaniment; interlude = the two previous bars.

153. (Op. 85, No. 4) Ade! (Farewell!) 1882
Anon,. Czech (trans. S. Kapper)   B minor and major f#'–f#''

> Wie schienen die Sternlein so hell, so hell
> Herab von der Himmelshöh!
> Zwei Liebende standen auf der Schwell,
> Ach, Hand in Hand: 'Ade!'

> Die Blümlein weinten auf Flur und Steg,
> Sie fühlten der Liebenden Weh,
> Die standen traurig am Scheideweg,
> Ach, Herz an Herz: 'Ade!'

> Die Lüfte durchrauschen die Waldesruh,
> Aus dem Tal und von der Höh
> Wehn zwei weisse Tücher einander zu:
> 'Ade, ade, ade!'

How the stars shone so bright, so bright, down from the heights of heaven! Two lovers stood on the threshold, alas, hand in hand; 'Farewell' [alas, hand in hand, 'Farewell']!

The flowers wept on meadow and pathway, they shared the sorrow of the lovers, who stood sadly at the parting of the ways, alas, heart to heart, 'Farewell' [alas, heart to heart, 'Farewell']!

The breezes rustled through the quiet forest; out of the valley and from the height two white kerchiefs waved at each other, 'Farewell, farewell, farewell [farewell, farewell, farewell]'!

The quick unceasing rhythms of the piano part place a virtuoso technique at the service of background scene-painting; nature itself murmurs words of sad sympathy. The weight of expression is thus thrown on to the vocal line, which is not among the composer's strongest or most memorable; and three identical verses impose a further strain on its resources. But there is a reward; the Schubertian major key on the same tonic for the end of each verse and its final 'Ade!' makes that wistful hope of reunion one day all the more moving for the disappointment predicted by the prevailing minor mood.

NOTES. 1. The textual source was the *Slawische Melodien* (1844), of Siegfried Kapper, who has 'von des Himmels Höh' in bars 5–7.

2. Note the favourite themes of isolation and separation by a wide panorama.

3. The 6–5–3 major melody within the relative minor key, at 'hell, so hell' etc. is rather rare in Brahms; it recalls another song of separation *Der Überläufer* (No. 73) at 'wollen wir gehen'.

4. The background piano part is M4/5, for the waving of breezes and kerchiefs. Its hemiolas, e.g. at 'standen' in each of the first two verses, and as the lovers stand and wave in the third, indicate a change from motion to stasis; M14. There, predictably for a song called 'Ade', the 'A–D' motif M34 occurs eight consecutive times. The Schubertian mode-change from B minor to major (M39) is also motivic; there, the last 'Ade' in each verse should surely be sung (despite the rather surprising provision of alternative notes) to the lifting third d#"–f#". This recalls the 'ferne' interval of the distant nightingale in *Waldeseinsamkeit* (No. 155) in the same key and the same notes, and perhaps with the same protagonists in mind.

5. Cf. Franz Op. 11 No. 1, under the title *Abschied*, which is well worth comparison and performance.

154. (Op. 85, No. 5) Frühlingslied (Spring song) 1878
Emanuel Geibel   G major g'–g"

> Mit geheimnisvollen Düften
> Grüsst vom Hang der Wald mich schon,
> Über mir in hohen Lüften
> Schwebt der erste Lerchenton.
>
> In den süssen Laut versunken
> Wall ich hin durchs Saatgefild,
> Das noch halb von Schlummer trunken
> Sanft dem Licht entgegenschwillt.
>
> Welch ein Sehnen! welch ein Träumen!
> Ach, du möchtest vorm Verglühn,
> Mit den Blumen, mit den Bäumen,
> Altes Herz, noch einmal blühn.

With mysterious fragrances the forest already greets me from the hillside; above me in the high breezes floats the first call of the lark.

Absorbed in that sweet sound I walk through the cornfield which, still half dazed with sleep, softly swells up towards the light.

Such a yearning, such a dreaming! Oh, before you burn out, old heart, you would love to blossom again with the flowers and trees [to blossom again, old heart].

Brahms, though twenty years younger than his poet, sincerely shared the same sentiments. It was in 1878, at 45, that he grew 'the bushy and patriarchal beard that completely transformed his looks – accentuating his dignity, but also his appearance of age, the more so as it rapidly went grey' (MacDonald 234). The note of regret for lost youth sounded in this song is equally deliberate, yet effective. The music belongs in both realms; its recollections of springtime are still vivid, which makes its autumnal mood all the more melancholy and moving. The brief prelude starts to sigh; its rhythmic complexities of two against three quavers are typical images of maturity and its depth of experience. The voice's rising major seventh, unique in Brahms, stands for the feeling embodied in the words 'geheimnis(voll)' (mysterious) and 'Sehnen' (yearning) with which Geibel artfully begins his first and third verses. Even on the printed page they look like a statement and a reprise, and that formal pattern imposes a correspondence of meaning; the mystery of nature is equated with the renewal of love-longing.

The erotic content latent in the poetic imagery is musically embodied in the duetting sixths at 'Lüften schwebt der erste ... (Lerchenton)', the first call of the lark on high. Already at 'über mir' the alternating notes of Brahms's joy motif begin a blithe carolling that links the soaring bird-song with its uplifting effect on the listener; and that delight is prolonged throughout the morning walk in the 'Saatgefild' (cornfield). There the left hand turns downwards in a progression of sequential quaver triplets; at 'halb von Schlummer trunken' (half dazed with sleep) the piano's syncopations and dynamics go surging and sighing along in the brightening dawn-shine. In the ensuing reprise, at 'Blumen' and 'Bäume' (flowers ... trees) extra quavers are unobtrusively added to hint at blossoming. The postlude swells and exults in an image of new springtime.

NOTES. 1. The textual source was no doubt the *Spätherbstblätter* (1877), which Geibel (also the poet of No. 166) put forth in his own late autumn.

2. The sighing crescendi and descrescendi are M21; the right-hand quaver rests at the first beat and half-bar are M29; the dreamy arpeggios, e.g. at 'halb von Schlummer trunken', are M9; the V–VI–V joy motif beginning at bar 5, and its continuance through changing harmonies, is M19; the top notes of the left-hand triplets signifying 'wall' ich hin' are M1; the long dominant seventh preparing the reprise (bar 19) is M24. The top tonic notes at 'Lüften' and 'Blumen' are M10; the mysterious rising seventh at 'geheimnis–' etc. is also expressive.

3. Even at this pitch of motivic invention there is still room for extra allusive subtleties, such as the continuous cross-grained rhythms (M15) and the added quavers illustrative of blossoming (M16) as shown by a comparison between bar 7 and bar 26.

155. (Op. 85, No. 6) In Waldeseinsamkeit (In woodland solitude) 1878
Karl Lemcke   B major e#'–g''

> Ich sass zu deinen Füssen
> In Waldeseinsamkeit;
> Windesatmen, Sehnen
> Ging durch die Wipfel breit.
>
> In stummem Ringen senkt ich
> Das Haupt in deinen Schoss,

Und meine bebenden Hände
Um deine Knie ich schloss.

Die Sonne ging hinunter,
Der Tag verglühte all,
Ferne, ferne, ferne
Sang eine Nachtigall.

I sat at your feet in woodland solitude. A breath of wind, a yearning, passed through the broad treetops. In speechless turmoil I bowed my head in your lap, and I closed my trembling hands around your knee [and I closed my trembling hands around your knee]. The sun went down, all the daylight faded. Far, far, far away a nightingale sang [a nightingale sang].

This fine song confirms that the composer saw nothing unduly erotic or sentimental in the verses; for him, on the contrary, they record a moment of pure feeling in every sense, like Daumer's *Wir Wandelten* (No. 177). The matching music here is Keatsian in its intensity; it unites 'the holiness of the heart's affections and the truth of imagination'.

The brief prelude is already darkling towards nightfall. After 'Waldeseinsamkeit' (woodland solitude) the right hand echoes that word's melody with minor inflexions, while the left hand repeats its accompaniment line an octave lower. Thus there are two figures, at two levels, within the wide woodland. Already there is a hint of sadness; and the minor mediant turns into the tonic minor key at 'Windesatmen' (A breath of wind). Here the sighing is regretful and mutual, as the voice's later left-hand shadowing shows.

These bars now become the broken heart of the music, every beat a pang; the insistence of its sighing and suing is imaged in the reiterated right-hand rhythms. The prelude and the first vocal melodies recur with regained serenity at 'Die Sonne ging herunter' (The sun went down). Then, in a memorable last page, the distant nightingale is heard in dream, singing softly and sadly of what might have been, in a passionate requiem for lost or unrequited love.

NOTES. 1. The source was Lemcke's *Lieder und Gedichte* (1861), which Brahms owned. He marked the first line, 'Ich sass zu deinen Füssen', in blue pencil; in a letter to him, his close friend Elisabet von Herzogenberg (i 188) singles out this song as 'born from a deep inward experience', as if she knew its source. The profound emotions it embowers surely recall one magical moment from the Swiss holiday with Clara in 1856, of which she treasured her own memories and souvenirs (such as pressed flowers labelled 'plucked on a woodland walk with Johannes') all her long life. Her voice is heard in the opening D#–C#–B–A#–B, which is among the clearest of Clara motifs, M33. Brahms sits adoringly at her feet – perhaps also in letters as well as music, since the notes B (=B♭=A#), A, H (=B) and S (=Es=D#) also occur in both bar 5 and bar 6, among the 'Waldeseinsamkeit' (M36). It was he who chose that word for his song's title, to encapsulate a mood and moment that he too cherished all his life.

2. The isolation and the symbolic nightingale are among Brahms's favourite themes; thus the falling vocal phrase on the first 'Nachtigall' anticipates the last 'Widerhall' of the later *Nachtigall* (No. 180).

3. From the prelude's deep bass notes (M6/7), which later presage the setting sun, to the

dreaming left-hand arpeggios at 'ferne' etc. (M9) every aspect of the music is typically motivic, including the Schubertian alternations of major and minor (M39), the canonic imitations (M12) in bars 5–8 and the falling tones and semitones throughout the following piano part. In particular the semitones on 'atmen', 'Sehnen', 'Ringen' are M20; the top G on 'sang' (as earlier on 'Seh[nen]') is M10.

4. The higher F#s should be sung at the end; there seems no good reason to offer, still less accept, the lower octave as in the *Gesamtausgabe* and Peters.

OPUS 86

Six songs (Lieder) for low voice with pianoforte accompaniment, with named poets, published in July 1882.

The tessitura is indeed notably lower in this group than elsewhere; the voice never ranges above e#''. Perhaps the composer's own voice was deepening, in his fiftieth year.

156. (Op. 86, No. 1) Therese (Teresa) 1878
Gottfried Keller   D major b–d''

> Du milchjunger Knabe,
> Wie schaust du mich an?
> Was haben deine Augen
> Für eine Frage getan!
>
> Alle Ratsherrn in der Stadt
> Und alle Weisen der Welt
> Bleiben stumm auf die Frage,
> Die deine Augen gestellt!
>
> Eine Meermuschel liegt
> Auf dem Schrank meiner Bas;
> Da halte dein Ohr dran,
> Dann hörst du etwas!

You baby boy, how is it you're looking at me? What a question your eyes have asked!
All the councillors in the city and all the wise men in the world remain dumb at the question your eyes have posed!
There's a sea-shell lying on my cousin's cabinet; just put your ear against it and you'll hear something!

The 'milchjung' or immature young man, perhaps with a hint of the milksop about him, will hear a secret murmur; the fathomless sound of the deep sea, the mystery of nature. In the mind of Brahms, who was himself a late developer (MacDonald 1990, 398–9), Teresa is a mature woman, as avouched by her inclusion among these songs for low voice. Her beardless admirer is being teasingly fobbed off as too uninstructed (at least for the time being) in the ways of the world. So the Countess might have sung to Cherubino. The poem is typically Kellerian in its symbolic sophistication; but Brahms treats it in a popular style, as if he envisaged the buxom Teresa in peasant costume at the door of her country cottage. Perhaps this effect, like the yodelling in *Salome* (No. 129), was an acknowledgement of Keller's Swiss antecedents. Indeed, the composer contemplated a comparable effect in this song too; he told Elisabet von Herzogenberg (i 180) that he was having second thoughts about the melodic line, and 'it would be a special pleasure for me if you could say "yes" to the following reading, and find it just right':

Du   milchjung - er   Knabe,   wie schaust du   mich   an

(and similarly with the parallel line about the city councillors, rhythmically adapted as necessary). Brahms also asked his copyist to make the same amendments. Fortunately, his valued adviser far preferred the simpler and smoother original version, which accordingly still stands.

The prelude seems to sing its heroine's name four times to the insistent 3/4 rhythm ♩ | ♩ ♩, with a blush of harmonic uncertainty and a final wheedling 'The – re – se'. She, in response to these overtures, rejoins in what sounds like recitativo secco, with a detached rhetorical question of her own. Its opening notes recur at 'Frage getan' (asked a question), again with a further prolongation from the piano; the answer is left hanging in the air. At 'alle Ratsherrn' (all the councillors) the rhythm becomes more playful, with added quavers to suggest an animated discussion of this tricky topic; but the melodic outline remains the same down to the extended final signature tune, again followed by the same searching question, this time asked by the boy's eyes ('deine Augen gestellt'). For the sea-shell ('eine Meermuschel') the alternating quavers resound from the depths of the keyboard, while the Teresa melodies shift across the barline in a new sensuous swing and sway. Then at 'halte dein Ohr dran' (put your ear against it) the left-hand octaves boom like breakers on the shore, while for 'dann hörst du etwas' (you'll hear something) we hear yet again the Teresa theme, still as undulating and mysterious as the sea, a Brahmsian evocation of the eternal feminine.

NOTES. 1. As Hugo Wolf tendentiously put it, Brahms used 'an earlier edition of Keller's poems for his criminal purposes', i.e. the *Neuere Gedichte* (1851). No doubt 'auf dem Schrank meiner Bas' ', i.e. on the cabinet of my (female) cousin, seemed rather too obviously designed as a rhyme for 'hörst du etwas'. But the empty snail-shell in the grass that Keller later substituted loses the traditional hollow sea-shell sound and its mystical associations, arguably to the detriment of the poem and hence of its matching music. There was much of the peasant in Brahms, whose setting here is a sedate but sensual ländler or country dance.

2. It may be that Clara was in mind; cf. her theme D–C#–B–A#–B (M33) hidden away here in the right hand at 'Frage getan!', and similarly at 'Augen gestellt!'.

3. This B minor mode fits the dominant questioning at those moments, M24; the

effects of added rhythmic interest in verses two and three are M16. The booming sound of the deep sea at the low left-hand E after 'Meer–' (cf. also the same note at 'ge(tan)' and 'ge(stellt))') is M6; the same idea informs the left-hand octaves that rise and fall by semitones for five bars at 'Bas', and again in the supremely expressive postlude.

4. Brahms seems to recall this postlude at the close of *Ich wandte mich* (No. 203), in the same mood of sad but serene acquiescence.

5. Cf. Hugo Wolf, No. 3 of the Keller songs; Pfitzner Op. 33, No. 3, also to the later text.

157. (Op. 86, No. 2) Feldeinsamkeit (Alone in the fields) *c.* 1879
Hermann Allmers   F major b–e♭''

> Ich ruhe still im hohen grünen Gras
> Und sende lange meinen Blick nach oben,
> Von Grillen rings umschwirrt ohn Unterlass,
> Von Himmelsbläue wundersam umwoben.
>
> Die schönen weissen Wolken ziehn dahin
> Durchs tiefe Blau, wie schöne stille Träume;
> Mir ist, als ob ich längst gestorben bin
> Und ziehe selig mit durch ew'ge Räume.

I rest at peace in the tall green grass and slowly turn my gaze on high [on high]; all around me, crickets chirp endlessly, and I am wondrously interwoven with the blueness of the sky [wondrously interwoven with the blueness of the sky].

The lovely white clouds sail away through the deep blue like lovely silent dreams [like lovely silent dreams]. I feel as if I have long since died and am drifting blissfully with them through eternal space [and am drifting blissfully with them through eternal space].

The poet invokes incantatory repetitions to induce and convey his trance-state; blueness, lovely, blue, lovely, as if gazing rapturously into the eyes of mother nature herself. Brahms adds his own hypnotic effects by repeating words and phrases: on high, wondrous weaving, silent dreams, eternal space. After the prelude's skyward lift the right hand chords change and drift like cloud-shapes. But much of the music stays on the ground, and even seems to take root there, in the sustained bass octaves. These two levels, feet on the ground of reality and head in the clouds of imagination, are linked by long flights of vocal melody. The spacious panorama leaves room for detailed depiction; thus the right thumb's undersong at the first words 'ich ruhe still' recurs two octaves lower at 'Himmelsbläue' (blueness of the sky) and is then interwoven in other registers as if to illustrate the idea of being 'umwoben'.

The prelude recurs as an interlude; and now the music is sent audibly flatward at the word 'Blau', which is painted with accidentals at 'schöne stille Träume' (lovely silent dreams) as if seen through a deep purple haze. Brahms could have made a further fortune as a popular song-writer, as indeed he was in his day; and this passage also affords an added clue to his colour-coding. At 'mir ist, als ob' (I feel as if) we hear another of his intensely personal expressions. The alternating octaves in both hands almost envisage a cortège, as if 'gestorben' (passed away) led inexorably down to a deep grave. The music remains earth-bound until the postlude, when the preluding themes are again heard striving to soar upwards and follow the clouds.

NOTES. I. The textual source was the *Dichtungen* (1860) of Allmers, which Brahms owned. The poet is now remembered mainly for his reaction to a gift of the song (perhaps in its manuscript version, now lost) and a performance arranged for him by the composer, who was understandably delighted with the work's success. Allmers was much less impressed (Kalbeck iii 341). As he later wrote (Friedländer 116): 'Of course I must acknowledge that the master's work was worthy and magisterial in itself ... but how does this almost artificial melody reflect my feelings, my mood, of being lost in space and time and becoming one with the miracle of nature?'. Ears better attuned to lieder imagery would surely have heard exactly such reflections; but the poet had a point. His precious text had been altered; thus his second verse begins 'Und schöne' not 'Die schönen' [Wolken]. Even his first words 'ich liege' were changed to 'ich ruhe', with immediate overtones of R. I. P.. In the verses, the individual dissolves and vanishes; in the music, the Romantic creative persona transcends space and time, anticipating a Straussian *Tod und Verklärung*.

2. The death and burial motif of alternate descending octaves in thirds, M7, embodies the composer's own personal obsessions. But these might have been enhanced by acquaintance with Schubert's *Totengräbers Heimwehe* D842, in the same key, where a grave digger finally attains the heaven of his dreams in entirely analogous tones. Brahms was certainly also familiar with *The Magic Flute*, and the kinship between his falling phrase at 'gestorben bin' here and Mozart's 'in ewiger Nacht', whence his dark spirits finally depart on the very same notes, may well also entail unconscious reminiscence as well as a shared use of the German motivic tradition.

3. The pedal points are M8. The rising M9 arpeggios of dream are, unusually, heard in the voice-part, at 'hohen grünen Gras', 'meinen', 'Wolken ziehn dahin' and 'schönen' in bars 4, 6, 20 and 22. Also motivic are the darkening tonalities for 'tiefe Blau' (M42) and the quasi-operatic turns at 'umwoben' and 'Räume'.

4. The strong structure, framed by the same two bars of prelude, interlude and postlude at 1–2, 17–18 and 34–5, is well worth close analysis.

5. Cf. Charles Ives's setting (1897).

158. (Op. 86, No. 3) Nachtwandler (Sleepwalker) *c.* 1877
Max Kalbeck   C major c'–e''

Störe nicht den leisen Schlummer
Dess, den lind ein Traum umfangen!
Lass ihm seinen süssen Kummer!
Ihm sein schmerzliches Verlangen!

Sorgen und Gefahren drohen,
Aber keine wird ihn schrecken,
Kommst du nicht, den Schlafesfrohen
Durch ein hartes Wort zu wecken.

Still in seinen Traum versunken
Geht er über Abgrundtiefen
Wie vom Licht des Vollmonds trunken,
Weh den Lippen, die ihn riefen!

Do not disturb the quiet slumber of him who is softly enfolded in a dream! Leave him his sweet grief, his painful yearning [his painful yearning]!

Cares and dangers menace him, but none of them will affright him unless you come to wake him, happy in his sleep, with a harsh word [wake him with a harsh word].

Silently immersed in his dream he walks over the depths of abysses as if drunk with the light of the full moon [as if drunk with the light of the full moon]; woe to the lips that called him [the lips that called him]!

Max Kalbeck was the composer's friend and first biographer. He says, and he was well placed to know, that the emotional content of his verses was in close accord with Brahms's frame of mind in 1876 and 1877; perhaps it was actually written and submitted for setting with that rapport in mind. Nowadays, its coded message may need a key, which Kalbeck himself sought to supply (iii 342): 'Only ethical tightrope walkers or unworldly dreamers, who fail to understand the perils of their path, and remain unaware of them, can safely negotiate the knife-edge between two abysses, our passions and our duties.' But even that ostensibly candid account is a bowdlerised circumlocution. Physical frustration and fulfilment are the contrasting themes of these verses, which say do not arouse me or I shall fall and it will be your fault. Elisabet von Herzogenberg was perceptive, according to her own ethos, in her assessment of them as 'far from edifying' (ii 164).

But the music is deeply-felt, and sympathetic listeners will find this song most appealing and moving. The prelude glides like a sleep walker, safe and secure unless interfered with, in a dreamy major–minor chiaroscuro of full moon and clouds. The voice–piano unison at the opening words 'störe nicht' hangs out a recurring sign: Do not disturb. This broadens into duetting thirds at 'dess, den lind' (him who is softly [enfolded]); thus isolation is alleviated. The rest is a longing love-song waltz, full of hidden melodies; thus the left-hand phrase C–B–A–A♭–G, itself an extension of the opening melody, is heard in voice and left hand at 'ihm sein schmerzliches Verlangen' (his painful yearning) and echoed in off-beat right-hand quavers when those words are repeated. In the last verse the dark abysses become deep pedal points over which the vocal melody glides serene and unscathed; their lowest note coincides with the first syllable of 'Abgrundtiefen' (depths of abysses). In the postlude the original prelude figure reappears in its entirety, as if to prove that it has survived all its past perils; and in the final long chord it settles down to the undisturbed repose and dreamless sleep it longs for.

Elisabet von Herzogenberg, though cool about the words, had warmed to the music's endearing tenderness. 'I especially enjoy the ending, from 'wie vom Licht des Vollmonds trunken' (as if drunk with the light of the full moon) ... and how the excitement at 'weh den Lippen die ihn riefen' (woe to the lips that called him) subsides ... into unstilled longing which seems specially created for this haunting song – all this, in its richness and at the same time in its great simplicity, gives me much joy' (i 187).

Those two contrasting elements, chromatic richness and diatonic simplicity, corresponding to the poetic symbolism of fulfilment and abstinence; these are indeed the keys that unlock the human meanings of this modest masterpiece.

NOTES. 1. Max Kalbeck writes (iii 333):

When I first met Brahms in Breslau in 1874 he was good enough to take an interest in my attempts at poetry, and asked me to send him some samples in Vienna. I wrote out some half-dozen of my pieces for him, including *Nachtwandler*, which I included in *Nächte*, a collection of my poems published in 1878 ... During a visit I paid him in Vienna early in 1877 he confessed with some embarrassment that he had set 'all sorts' of things of mine; but he could not be persuaded to show me any of them; the results weren't quite to his satisfaction, and needed further detailed revision. This song was finally finished in the winter of 1881/2 ...

2. No doubt Elisabet, née Stockhausen, understood its special significance and knew that it might have been written to, for and about her; she was, second only to Clara, the great love of Brahms's life. The repeated C–B–A–A♭(G#), in the key of C, suggests an unfulfilled Clara theme (M33); the overt version G–F–E–D#–E at 'Verlangen' etc. also embraces E.S. (=D#) (M35).

3. The thirds and sixths *passim* are the love-duetting M18. Equally motivic are the Schubertian major–minor contrasts on the same tonic, M39 (which also appear in e.g. *An den Mond*, No. 136, painting the same moonscape of light and shadow), the sadly flattened sixth (M41) at bar 6 etc. and the pedal notes (M8) and syncopations *passim*.

159. (Op. 86, No. 4) Über die Heide (Over the heath) *c.* 1877
Theodor Storm   G minor c#'–e♭''

> Über die Heide hallet mein Schritt;
> Dumpf aus der Erde wandert es mit.
>
> Herbst ist gekommen, Frühling ist weit,
> Gab es denn einmal selige Zeit?
>
> Brauende Nebel geisten umher,
> Schwarz ist das Kraut und der Himmel so leer.
>
> Wär ich nur hier nicht gegangen im Mai!
> Leben und Liebe – wie flog es vorbei!

Over the heath my tread resounds, accompanied by a dull echo from the earth.
   Autumn has come, spring is far away; was there really once a time of bliss?
   Brewing mists go ghosting about, the foliage is black and the sky so empty [the foliage is black and the sky so empty].
   If only I'd never walked here in Maytime! Life and love – how they flew past!

The fine poem dictates the music, almost literally. The prelude trudges along, leaving a silence in the last two quavers through which the vocal melody chimes like a hollow echo that lies at the heart of words and music alike, symbolising lost love and the resulting emptiness of life. This is the only answer to the voice's anguished questions. The melodic curve for 'dumpf aus der Erde' (dully from the earth), which rises and falls back to ground level, is extrapolated as the left-hand motto-theme in the one-bar prelude and throughout the song. That image is further enhanced by depth, octaves and off-beat right-hand chords, with hidden melodies and canons and sighing phrases in the brief interludes. At 'Brauende

Nebel' (brewing mists) continuous off-beat chords are sketched and shaded in by the right hand, while the persistent 6/8 rhythmic figure ♪♪♪ ♪ ⅄ ⅄ goes on walking under that mist as if in a trance. After the second 'leer' (empty) the piano's quaver rhythm is accented, like an attempt to quicken the step and leave the scene. Then silence supervenes, as if the singer has stopped in his tracks, struck by a sudden vivid recollection. At the ensuing reprise, the second half of each bar is now filled with added off-beat chords, as the moments of remembered regret and remorse accumulate. The word 'Liebe' is stressed by prolongation; then the postlude declines into nightfall, with broken echoes of the final vocal phrase and its tragic significance. All this and much more is achieved unobtrusively, with consummate self-effacing art.

NOTES. 1. The source was surely Storm's *Gedichte* (1852), which Brahms owned (rather than the *Gesammelte Schriften* vol. 7 cited by McCorkle 356). The composer's reversal 'Wär ich nur hier' in the final couplet looks like a slip which requires correction to Storm's 'Wär ich hier nur'.

2. Note the typical topics of the revisitant Doppelgänger and the lost lover left outside in the cold autumn mists.

3. The octaves plus space and silence are paralleled in No. 168, on the same theme of isolation; the right-hand mists at 'Nebel' etc. recall the figuration from the fourth bar after 'Nebel' in *Dämmrung senkte sich* (No. 100); the vocal line at 'Liebe' etc. recalls *Wehe, so willst du mich wieder* (No. 38), which has clear Clara affiliations.

4. The basic walking movement is MI; the silences in bars 1–4 and 20 are M29; the deep bass notes are M6. The strong structure repays analysis; note for example the correspondence between bars 1–6 and 7–12, overlapping at 'Herbst' etc., and the rhythmic conflation of each such sentence into the last, from 'wär ich' onwards.

160. (Op. 86, No. 5) Versunken (Overwhelmed) *c.* 1878
Felix Schumann   F# major b–e#″

> Es brausen der Liebe Wogen
> Und schäumen mir um das Herz;
> Zwei tiefe Augen zogen
> Mich mächtig niederwärts.
>
> Mich lockte der Nixen Gemunkel,
> Die wunderliebliche Mär,
> Als ob die Erde dunkel
> Und leuchtend die Tiefe wär.
>
> Als würde die seligste Ferne
> Dort unten reizende Näh,
> Als könnt ich des Himmels Sterne
> Dort greifen in blauer See.
>
> Nun brausen und schäumen die Wogen
> Und hüllen mich allwärts ein,
> Es schimmert in Regenbogen
> Die Welt von ferne herein.

The waves of love roar and foam around my heart; two deep eyes drew me irresistibly downwards. I was enticed by tales of nixies, those wondrously lovely legends, as if the earth were dark and the sea-bed bright [the earth dark and the sea-bed bright]! As if the most heavenly of distant places became entrancingly close, there below, as if I could touch all the stars of heaven in the blue sea [as if I could touch all the stars of heaven in the blue sea]. Now the waves roar and foam and engulf me all around; the world shimmers in rainbows from afar.

Clara's tragically short-lived son (1854–79) is still largely unhonoured, but, thanks to Brahms, not unsung. As before, he sets Felix in the style of Robert, no doubt as a deliberate tribute to both together. This poem shows real promise; the dark earth and the bright sea make a memorable reversal. After preluding chords, the waves roar and foam in semiquaver arpeggios; among them, the far-flung vocal line of the vacillating lover is tossed wildly up and down, this way and that. At 'Herz' (heart) the left hand's dive in octaves anticipates 'niederwärts' (downwards). For 'mich lockte der Nixen Gemunkel' (I was enticed by tales of nixies) the music seems to recall an old ballad of long ago and far away, which recurs at 'die seligste Ferne' (the most heavenly of distant places); around these diversions the waves sing their own siren song. After the reprise the postlude breaks up the wave-arpeggios between the two hands, in a hectic attempt to match the enhanced poetic image; but this needs bravura performance if it is not to sound somewhat perfunctory.

NOTES. 1. For the genesis of two other Felix Schumann settings see Nos. 117 and 118. But Max Kalbeck (*pace* McCorkle 356) need not have been mistaken in his claim (ii 483) that this song was already written in 1873.

2. Brahms would always have felt a special affinity for a lyric about deep gazes (as in *Dein blaues Auge*, No. 107), water-nymphs (*Sommerabend* No. 150 above) and the cooling effects of waves (*passim*).

3. The postlude's broken octaves are somewhat in the style of those in Schumann's song *Sehnsucht* of 1840, again perhaps in deliberate tribute to Felix's father. His mother may also be remembered, in this setting about the magnetic power of deep eyes; cf. her five-note theme M33 in voice or piano, *passim*.

4. The wave-arpeggios are M5; the thirds at 'mich lockte', later extended into full chords, are a love-song duet, M18. The dream-arpeggios, e.g. after 'Mär', are M9. The modulation into E♭ (D#) major at 'als würde' is equally motivic (M40) in its flat–sharp notation.

161. (Op. 86, No. 6) Todessehnen (Yearning for death) 1878

Max von Schenkendorf   F# minor and major a#–d#"

Ach, wer nimmt von meiner Seele
Die geheime, schwere Last,
Die, je mehr ich sie verhehle,
Immer mächtiger mich fasst?

Möchtest du nur endlich brechen,
Mein gequältes, banges Herz!

Findest hier mit deinen Schwächen,
Deiner Liebe, nichts als Schmerz.

Dort nur wirst du ganz genesen,
Wo der Sehnsucht nichts mehr fehlt,
Wo das schwesterliche Wesen
Deinem Wesen sich vermählt.

Hör es, Vater in der Höhe,
Aus der Fremde fleht dein Kind:
Gib, dass er mich bald umwehe,
Deines Todes Lebenswind.

Dass er zu dem Stern mich hebe,
Wo man keine Trennung kennt,
Wo die Geistersprache Leben
Mit der Liebe Namen nennt.

Ah, who will take from my soul this secret heavy burden which, the more I conceal it, seizes me ever more powerfully [seizes me ever more powerfully]? If only you could break at last, my tormented anxious heart! All you find here, with your weaknesses and your love, is nothing but grief [nothing but grief].

There alone will you completely recover, where your yearning lacks nothing, where a sister-being is united with your own being.

Hear me, Father on high, your child pleads from this alien land; grant that your life-giving wind of death may soon blow around me.

Grant that it may lift me to the star where parting is unknown, where the language of spirits calls life by the name of Love [calls life by the name of Love].

Brahms not only overcomes his innate distaste for morbid religiosity but makes these maudlin verses ring true. The depths of his own death wish may often have been profound. As he told Elisabet von Herzogenberg in 1879 (i 106), his art had been criticised by his café acquaintance Mosenthal for its excessive solemnity; and his protest that he often felt cheerful had been met by the rejoinder: 'Yes, … and then you sing "Das Grab ist meine Freude" ' ('The Grave is my Joy'). So it is, in this song; the yearning for release transcends all else.

There is no prelude; the emotion can no longer be suppressed. The voice and right hand speak in unison for extra emphasis; the left-hand octaves are ominous and sombre. At 'Die, je mehr ich sie verhehle' (The more I conceal it) the walking sequences rise slowly as if painfully hefting a heavy burden, and then collapse, crushed, into the depths of the keyboard. The second verse strives to start again; but now, at 'Findest hier' (You find here) the journeying sequences turn downwards from the start, as if destined to end in grief ('Schmerz'), which a plaintive interlude echoes in two sad sighs. Now the broad vocal melody travels in imagination to a happy land far far away, which is suddenly radiant in a new serene rhythm and long-flighted melody accompanied by high arpeggios and chords in a Biblical instrumentation of harp and psaltery. The agnostic Brahms must have meant all this metaphorically; but its effect of exaltation can be real and lasting.

NOTES. 1. The textual source was Schenkendorff's *Gedichte* (1837), the fifth edition of which (1878) Brahms owned. The poet died young.

2. This song's special significance for its composer can be heard in the first clarinet's quotation of its 'Vater in der Höhe' melody, at pitch, in the first 'Più Adagio' section of the second piano concerto, Op. 83, completed three years later. There the piano part itself also relates to an earlier song, *Lerchengesang* (No. 132), with its music of bird-song in the high wide heavens. This symbolism of spiritual transcendence is as deliberate as it is typical.

3. The walking music of bars 5–10 and 15–20 is M1; each passage ends in the moaning minor second of M20 with the dominant questioning of M24. The expressive interlude at bars 20–22 can be compared with its counterpart at bars 16–18 of *Nachklang* (No. 103); the sighs here are M21. The dreamy harp music in the last section, M9, conveys a vision of the artist's heaven on earth, namely union with the beloved. This ideal is expressed in the apparent syncopations from 'die Geistersprache' onwards; these hemiolas, M14, meant absolute certitude to Brahms, as in the culmination of *Von ewiger Liebe* (No. 58), on the same theme in every sense.

4. So personal and compelling a declaration of sad and secret yet eternal love might be expected to cry 'Clara', however cryptically; cf. the opening right-hand chords' half hidden notes A–G#/F#–E#–F# in bars 1–2 (M33).

OPUS 91

Two songs (Gesänge) for contralto with viola and pianoforte, published in November 1884. The title-page names neither of the textual sources, almost as if the voice parts were imagined as wordless.

162. (Op. 91, No. 1) Gestillte Sehnsucht (Assuaged longing) *c.* 1884
Friedrich Rückert   D major/minor a–e″

> In goldnen Abendschein getauchet,
> Wie feierlich die Wälder stehn!
> In leise Stimmen der Vöglein hauchet
> Des Abendwindes leises Wehn.
> Was lispeln die Winde, die Vögelein?
> Sie lispeln die Welt in Schlummer ein.
>
> Ihr Wünsche, die ihr stets euch reget
> Im Herzen sonder Rast und Ruh!
> Du Sehnen, das die Brust beweget,
> Wann ruhest du, wann schlummerst du?
> Beim Lispeln der Winde, der Vögelein,
> Ihr sehnenden Wünsche, wann schlaft ihr ein?
>
> Ach, wenn nicht mehr in goldne Fernen
> Mein Geist auf Traumgefieder eilt,
> Nicht mehr an ewig fernen Sternen
> Mit sehnendem Blick mein Auge weilt;

Dann lispeln die Winde, die Vögelein,
Mit meinem Sehnen mein Leben ein.

*Bathed in the golden light of evening, how solemnly the forests stand! Into the soft voices
of the birds breathes the soft wafting of the evening winds. What are the winds and the
birds whispering? They are whispering the world to sleep [to sleep].*

*But you, my desires, ever stirring in my heart without rest or repose, you, my
yearning that animates my breast – when will you rest, when will you sleep? The winds
and birds whisper; but you, my yearning desires, when will you fall asleep [when will
you fall asleep]?*

*Oh, when my spirit no longer wings into golden distances on its pinions of dream,
when my eyes no longer dwell yearningly on eternally remote stars, then the winds and
the birds will whisper my life away, with my longing.*

I shall go on yearning, says the poet, until the day I die. But he is in no hurry to
depart; on the contrary, his longings are his life. Brahms begins in a blessed state
of Nirvana. His concept of perfect bliss, here as in the next song, is a warm
maternal lullaby from a solo viola whose alto clef symbolises the alto register. Its
honeyed melody sings through the prelude and is then joined by a duetting voice,
which drops to its lowest note at 'stehn' (stand) followed by a long bass octave on
a mysterious flattened seventh, a single-note image of the solemn forest. At 'was
lispeln' (what are they whispering?) the viola lullaby floats and hovers in
light-breathed semiquaver-triplet arpeggios before sending itself to sleep, after 'im
Schlummer ein', in a dreamy extension of the vocal melody just heard in answer
to that question. Then all three performers fall silent too, in sympathy.

But they are instantly recalled to reality. Brahms interprets Rückert's restless
longing as his own; intense, turbulent, frustrated, minor in mode and chromatic
in texture. At 'Du Sehnen, das die Brust beweget' (You, my yearning that animates
my breast) piano and viola utter great sighs of complex syncopations and
subdivisions, in a brief but revealing glimpse beneath the sweet serene surface.
Thus 'wann schlaft ihr ein' becomes less a question than a heartfelt appeal for relief
from tormenting thoughts and desires, so that the major reprise sounds like the
answer to a prayer. There is no finer or more assuaging music of relief and release
in the lied form.

NOTES. 1. The textual source was Rückert's *Gedichte* in their third edition (1836–8),
which Brahms owned. After 'schlaft ihr ein', a third verse, which further emphasises the
poet's longing, is omitted, thus preserving the desired ABA form.

2. The viola is the mellow voice of autumn itself, singing of warm sunshine or cold
winds in the Schubertian contrast of major and minor modes on the same tonic (M39).

3. The piano's descending arpeggios (M4) and deep bass octaves (M8) form an image
of the solemn forests; the right-hand melody at bars 2–4, high A–D–F#–E–low A,
anticipates the vocal line at 'die Wälder stehn'. The left-hand flattened-seventh octave after
that last word is also motivic (M41), like the viola's flights at 'lispeln' that drift with the
winds and wings (M3/4), the questioningly enhanced dominant seventh for 'schlummerst
du?' (M24), the notation of D major in D minor (M40) at 'Beim Lispeln', leading into the
flats of 'sehnenden' etc. (again M41).

163. (Op. 91, No. 2) Geistliches Wiegenlied (A holy cradle-song) 1863
Lope de Vega (trans. E. Geibel)   F major and minor c′–e″

Die ihr schwebet
Um diese Palmen
In Nacht und Wind,
Ihr heilgen Engel,
Stillet die Wipfel!
Es schlummert mein Kind.

Ihr Palmen von Bethlehem
Im Windesbrausen,
Wie mögt ihr heute
So zornig sausen!
O rauscht nicht also!
Schweiget, neiget
Euch leis und lind;
Stillet die Wipfel!
Es schlummert mein Kind.

Der Himmelsknabe
Duldet Beschwerde;
Ach wie so müd er ward
Vom Leid der Erde.
Ach, nun im Schlaf ihm
Leise gesänftigt
Die Qual zerrinnt,
Stillet die Wipfel!
Es schlummert mein Kind!

Grimmige Kälte
Sauset hernieder,
Womit nur deck ich
Des Kindleins Glieder!
O, all ihr Engel
Die ihr geflügelt
Wandelt im Wind,
Stillet die Wipfel!
Es schlummert mein Kind.

You who hover around these palm-trees in night and wind, you holy angels, hush the tree-tops! My child is asleep [my child is asleep].

You palm-trees of Bethlehem in the raging wind – how can you thresh so angrily tonight? Oh roar not so! Be silent, lean down calmly and gently; hush the tree-tops [hush the tree-tops]! My child is asleep [my child is asleep].

The heavenly babe suffers distress; oh how weary he has grown with all the sorrows of the world [oh how weary, how weary he has grown with all the sorrows of the world]. Oh now that in sleep his pains are gently eased, hush the tree-tops [hush the tree-tops]!

My child is asleep [my child is asleep].

A fierce coldness comes roaring down; with what shall I cover my baby's limbs? Oh all you angels that wander winged in the wind, hush the tree-tops [hush the tree-tops]! My child is asleep [my child is asleep].

'Before long I'll be sending you a marvellous old Catholic song for household use; you'll never discover a lovelier lullaby!' So Brahms wrote to his good friend the great violinist Joseph Joachim in April 1863, shortly before the latter's marriage to the contralto Amalie Schneeweiss. Brahms meant the 16th-century lullaby folk-song carol 'Joseph, lieber Joseph mein'. He was very fond of Amalie, as of many other singers (especially contraltos); he would later insist on her innocence when her jealous husband accused her of infidelity, which caused a long quarrel with Joachim; and he saw nothing incongruous about combining a cradle-song for a child with a love-song for its mother (as in *Wiegenlied*, No. 82). When he found a later Virgin's Cradle-Song in Geibel's deft translation, the associations of Amalie's maiden name (white as snow) and a child born to Joseph and baptised through Johannes would surely have inspired in him the feelings of tender reverence and love that resound throughout this masterpiece. It begins with a low voice, symbolised by a solo viola, singing the old carol melody, the German words of which are included for reference in the score. They say: 'Josef, lieber Josef mein,/Hilf mir wieg'n mein Kindlein fein,/Gott, der wird dein Lohner sein,/Im Himmelreich, Der Jungfrau Sohn, Maria [Maria].' (Joseph, my dear Joseph, help me to cradle my sweet child; God will reward you in the kingdom of heaven, the son of the Virgin Mary [Mary]).

The piano sketches a light accompaniment drawn from this cradle-song. Nothing disturbs the diatonic serenity of the scene or the singing or the rhythmic rocking; the winds are hushed and still, as if the prayer had already been heard and answered. The viola shines out in long quiet notes. Even the sustained flattened mediant in voice and piano at 'Nacht' (night) casts a warm shadow; the climate is clement. At the first 'Es schlummert mein Kind', voice and instruments unite in a long falling chain of drowsy thirds, like unbroken slumber. The viola's carolling returns. But now, at 'Ihr Palmen' (You palm-trees), the wind becomes as it were visible in the leaves and audible in the right hand, while voice and viola share small moans of distress. The breeze briefly intensifies, but is soon lulled back into abatement as the slumber themes and the lullaby melody recur.

At 'Der Himmelsknabe' (the heavenly babe) the tempo and the temperature both change. The child's sorrow is reflected in the wind-swept sky, as the accompaniment ascends and chills in the minor mode; at 'ach, wie so müd' the viola sighs in sympathy. But then listeners hear, as before, how all these pains (here that word, 'Qual', aptly recurs on the flattened note of the earlier 'Nacht') are softened into sleep. Once again the winds blow and are duly rebuked and hushed, until the viola's solo singing resumes and ends.

NOTES. 1. The textual source was the *Spanisches Liederbuch* (1852), the translations by Emanuel Geibel and Paul Heyse already used by Schumann, whose copy Brahms may well have inherited.

2. The complex compositional history is well summarised in McCorkle 374–5.

3. The incorporated musical allusion is a typically Brahmsian procedure, like the equation of a solo viola with a maternal voice, as in the previous song.

4. The quoted carol and the opening vocal line both share the 5–6–5 elation of M19. The former's thirds recur *passim*, e.g. in the left-hand sequences at bars 13–15. These are close kin to the doubled parallel thirds at the first 'Es schlummert', etc.; this lullaby use of the love-motif M18 recalls the same dual significance at bars 33f of *Ruhe, Süssliebchen* (No. 51). The Schubertian major and minor on the same key-note (M39), meeting in the flattened thirds at 'Nacht' und 'Qual', are also motivic; so are the viola's widespread arpeggios, M3, especially after 'geflügelt'.

5. The same text was set by Wolf in 1889, as No. 4 of the sacred songs in his *Spanisches Liederbuch*.

OPUS 94

Five songs (Lieder) for low voice with pianoforte accompaniment, with named poets, published in November 1884.

Again the tessitura is indeed lower than usual; here the top notes are in much the same range as Op. 86, but the low notes are somewhat deeper.

164. (Op. 94, No. 1) Mit vierzig Jahren (At forty years old) *c.* 1883
Friedrich Rückert

B minor F#–d'

> Mit vierzig Jahren ist der Berg erstiegen,
> Wir stehen still und schaun zurück;
> Dort sehen wir der Kindheit stilles liegen
> Und dort der Jugend lautes Glück.
>
> Noch einmal schau, und dann gekräftigt weiter
> Erhebe deinen Wanderstab!
> Hindehnt ein Bergesrücken sich, ein breiter,
> Und hier nicht, drüben gehts hinab.
>
> Nicht atmend aufwärts brauchst du mehr zu steigen,
> Die Eb'ne zieht von selbst dich fort;
> Dann wird sie sich mit dir unmerklich neigen,
> Und eh du's denkst, bist du im Port.

At forty years old, the mountain has been climbed. We stand in silence and look back. There we see the quiet joys of childhood, and there the noisy joys of youth [the noisy joys of youth].

Take one more look and then, with renewed vigour, raise your walking-staff! A broad mountain ridge stretches into the distance; and not here, but on the other side, the way leads downhill.

There is no more need to climb panting upwards, the plain draws you onward of its

own accord; then it will imperceptibly descend with you, and before you realise, you
will be in port [before you realise, you will be in port].

In effect, life ends at forty. Perhaps that was unduly pessimistic; but the average
life-span was less then than now, and the song's regretful retrospection was
irresistibly moving. 'Brahms told me himself, contentedly, that [his friend the
baritone Julius] Stockhausen, when they were rehearsing this song together, was
so overcome by emotion that he was unable to finish it' (Kalbeck i 277).

The walking prelude slows down with a sigh, as if out of breath. The voice
enters with a marching rhythm, which also soon peters out; the mountain has
been climbed. Then a broad panorama unfolds, in long minims and octaves, as we
look back ('dort sehen wir'). After the second 'lautes Glück' (noisy joys) the
walking resumes, first effortful and then striding; the octave panorama returns as
the scene is again surveyed; 'hindehnt ein Bergesrücken' (a mountain ridge
stretches). Ominously, the road then goes downhill all the way – to death and
extinction, the music admonishes. But stoic resignation supervenes, to the same
strains as before, embellished as ever by the Brahmsian response to words; thus
the vocal line itself imperceptibly descends with the singer's path at 'mit dir
unmerklich neigen'. Then comes the peroration that so unmanned Stockhausen,
who was some seven years older than Brahms and hence in his late fifties at the
time. Here a new figuration appears in rolling arpeggios that surely derive from
the poet's rather incongruous final 'Port' which cannot fail to imply the end of
a voyage, more home from sea than from the hill. To Max Kalbeck (iii 522)
the modulation to the tonic major sounded more like a warm welcome into
heaven's haven than consignment to the cold grave. But the idea of death could be
a comfort to Brahms, as in his selection and setting of several other texts (such as
O Tod, No. 203). And all such critiques, however just, are silenced by this masterly
music.

NOTES. 1. The poem was published in the journal *Deutscher Musen-Almanach* (1883),
where Brahms may have found it; hence the composition date allocated by Friedländer
(122) and McCorkle (386). But the song may have been written earlier; the poem had
already appeared in Rückert's own selection of *Gedichte* (1846).
   2. Friedländer (loc. cit.) draws attention to six falling fifths, a–d, differently harmonised
each time. He means the vocal line at 'Mit vier(zig)', 'dort se(hen)', 'Noch ein(mal)',
'Hindehnt', 'nicht at(mend)', 'dann wird'; and this pattern is indeed noteworthy in
occurring at the beginning of each odd-numbered line of the poem. The notes are in fact
f#–B; but there is every likelihood that a–d (= 'Ade', a farewell to youth and life) was indeed
intended; M34.
   3. The offbeat quavers of bars 3–4 and 15–16 are the effortful walking motif M1
(cf. 'gekräftigt' in bar 15). As usual, the alternative vocal notes at bar 6 should be avoided.
The doom-laden bare-octave descent ending 'hinab' is M7; the triplet wave-motion in
peroration and postlude is M5. The flattened supertonic at the second 'eh du's denkst' is
M23; the last vocal notes anticipate, also perhaps in the sense of sleep, '(O Tod) wie wohl
tust du' in No. 203.
   4. The Schubertian B minor/major transition (M39) prompts a comparison with
another song of old age, *Greisengesang* D778 in the same keys. There too the poet was
Rückert; perhaps the allusion was deliberate.

165. (Op. 94, No. 2) Steig' auf, geliebter Schatten (Arise, beloved shade) 1883/4

Friedrich Halm   E♭ minor b♭'–e♭''

> Steig auf, geliebter Schatten,
> Vor mir in toter Nacht,
> Und lab mich Todesmatten
> Mit deiner Nähe Macht!
>
> Du hasts gekonnt im Leben,
> Du kannst es auch im Tod,
> Sich nicht dem Schmerz ergeben,
> War immer dein Gebot.
>
> So komm! Still meine Tränen,
> Gib meiner Seele Schwung
> Und Kraft den welken Sehnen
> Und mach mich wieder jung.

Arise before me, beloved shade, in the dead of night and revive me, in my deathly weariness, with the power of your presence [with the power of your presence]!

So you could in life; so you can still, even in death. Do not succumb to sorrow, that was always your command [that was always your command].

So come! Dry my tears, give zest to my soul and strength to my withered sinews, and make me young again [and make me young again].

Here is a powerful evocation of the *Requiem* mood, in Brahms's most funereal key. That work was said by Clara Schumann to have been written in memory of his mother, who had died in 1865. Her loss had affected him deeply; she was the most beloved of all his dead dear ones, and had no doubt often encouraged and exhorted him.

The introductory spread chords suggest a minstrel's harp, with an effect of solemn incantation. The spirit thus addressed instantly appears as a dark left-hand figure whose falling thirds are echoed in the vocal line. That figure falls silent as if listening sympathetically while the voice bewails its weariness to death, at 'Todesmatten', to a much more restrained melody and drooping chromatic chords. But it reappears as soon as the apparition is again invoked, at the repeated 'deiner Nähe Macht' (the power of your presence), where the thirds fall to a new depth. Then the rhythm suddenly quickens into quaver triplets at the recollection of past vigorous life ('Du hasts gekonnt im Leben') and the resolve never to succumb. In the poem, this brings new hope. Not so in the music, which now repeats the opening strains note for note, while the postlude plumbs the depths of despair. This treatment is undeniably effective in its no doubt deliberate contrast with the words; there will be no comfort, no rejuvenation, nothing but the night.

NOTES. 1. The textual source was Vol. 9 of Halm's *Gesammelte Werke* (1856–72), which Brahms owned. The poem's sixth line has 'noch' not 'auch'; this should surely be corrected.

2. The quickening rhythm at bars 16–17 and 22–3 is motivic (M16). So, for Brahms as

for Schumann, is the tonality of E flat minor; its doleful finality is further indicated here by the absence of any tierce de Picardie in the postlude, despite the ostensibly hopeful words. The descending thirds *passim* are M7; the quasi-hemiola rhythm at bars 6–8 and 31–4 is M14.

166. (Op. 94, No. 3) Mein Herz ist schwer (My heart is heavy) 1883/4
Emanuel Geibel   G minor d'–e''

> Mein Herz ist schwer, mein Auge wacht,
> Der Wind fährt seufzend durch die Nacht;
> Die Wipfel rauschen weit und breit,
> Sie rauschen von vergangner Zeit.
>
> Sie rauschen von vergangner Zeit,
> Von grossem Glück und Herzeleid,
> Vom Schloss und von der Jungfrau drin–
> Wo ist das alles, alles hin?
>
> Wo ist das alles, alles hin,
> Leid, Lieb und Lust und Jugendsinn?
> Der Wind fährt seufzend durch die Nacht,
> Mein Herz ist schwer, mein Auge wacht.

My heart is heavy, my eyes are wide awake, the wind fares sighing through the night. The tree-tops murmur far and wide, they murmur of times long past. They murmur of times long past, of great joy and heartbreak, of the castle and the maiden within it – where has all this, all this fled? Where has all this, all this fled – grief, love and joy and the spirit of youth? The wind fares sighing through the night, my heart is heavy, my eyes are wide awake [my heart is heavy, my eyes are wide awake].

Brahms respects the verbal structure, where the last line of each quatrain is the first of the next and the poem ends as it began; these repetitions are treated with matching music. In the prelude the wind sighs in alternating octaves that touch the tree-tops and set them sighing in their turn. Those two components are then separately developed. Brahms seeks to show that his own youth and loves, like his poet's, have gone with the wind, which is heard sighing as it blows by. But the tree-tops must stay in place, however much they thresh and ply; so 'Die Wipfel' are depicted as deep-rooted (though off-beat and sighing) chords. At 'Sie rauschen' (they murmur) both ideas combine; the tree-top chords are set shaking in the wind of alternate hands. At the second 'Wo ist' (where is) the lighter texture recalls bright memories; after 'Jugendsinn' (spirit of youth) the piano quotes the melody just sung at 'Leid, Lieb and Lust' (grief, love and joy), a suitable title for a Brahmsian love-song waltz. But soon the wind blows all this away, and the song ends in the chordal contemplation of tree-tops as the storm subsides.

NOTES. 1. The textual source was Geibel's *Spätherbstblätter* (1877). Brahms respectfully recalls Schumann's setting of Geibel's *Sehnsucht* Op. 51 No. 1, which is analogously nostalgic and also begins with virtuoso broken octaves, here depicting high winds at night (the small-type optional notes should certainly be played, despite the technical difficulties imposed by the direction *pianissimo*).

2. The sighing tree-top chords at 'Wipfel' combine the dominant seventh questioning of M24 (what are they saying?) with the regretful sighing of M21 (they are lamenting lost love); their missing first crotchets (M29) recur after 'Jugendsinn' and at the last 'Auge'. The right-hand pangs of regret at the second 'wo ist' and 'Alles' are M20; the Schubertian piano echo of 'Leid, Lieb und Lust' is also expressive.

167. (Op. 94, No. 4) Sapphische Ode (Sapphic Ode) 1883/4
Hans Schmidt   D major a–d''

> Rosen brach ich nachts mir am dunklen Hage,
> Süsser hauchten Duft sie, als je am Tage;
> Doch verstreuten reich die bewegten Äste
>   Tau, der mich nässte.
>
> Auch der Küsse Duft mich wie nie berückte,
> Die ich nachts vom Strauch deiner Lippen pflückte;
> Doch auch dir, bewegt im Gemüt gleich jenen,
>   Tauten die Tränen.

I plucked roses by night from the dark hedgerow; they breathed a sweeter fragrance than ever by day; yet the branches, as they moved, freely showered me with dew.

The fragrance of those kisses too enchanted me as never before, when I plucked them by night from the rose-bush of your lips; yet you too, moved in your inmost feelings like the roses, were bedewed with tears.

The poem unites classical metre with Romantic rhyme and imagery. Brahms loved all three, and responded whole-heartedly; the result is rightly renowned for its beauty and restraint.

The song begins with off-beat chords that stand motionless as if listening to the voice's broad arpeggio melody, amid the dark night of long low bass notes. Then voice and piano move stealthily forward, soft step by step. After 'hauchten' (breathed) two gentle sighs are heard from the keyboard. The music attains a higher register and thence moves downward as it were among the branches, while the right-hand off-beat chords are made staccato to suggest the splashing of full dew-drops. In the second verse, this staccato arrives earlier, to heighten the kissing image at 'Strauch deiner Lippen' (rose-bush of your lips) etc. It continues through the following comparison at 'Doch auch dir' (Yet you too) only to cease before 'gleich jenen' (like the roses). Here the vocal line is deepened and extended, like the inmost feelings it encompasses. Words and music say together that the roses are but symbols of human love, which were never more sweetly distilled.

NOTES. I. The textual source was Schmidt's undated *Gedichte und Übersetzungen*, which Brahms owned.

2. Of course this song could well be sung (as the poem was written) by a man, despite its omission from Fischer-Dieskau's otherwise complete account of male-voice Brahms lieder (EMI SLS 5002, 1974); the title refers only to the verse-form used by the Greek

poetess Sappho of Lesbos (mentioned in the Hölty lyric of *Die Schale der Vergessenheit*, No. 65) who flourished *c.* 600 BC. Schmidt adroitly adds rhymes, aabb, to the unrhymed quatrain form named after her, i.e. three pentameters and a dimeter patterned thus: — ◡ / — ◡ / — ◡ ◡ / — ◡ (thrice) followed by — ◡ ◡ / — ◡. Brahms pencilled these symbols for long and short (or heavy and light) syllables in the margin of this poem; his melody faithfully follows those patterns. The form has often been imitated in English (as in Swinburne's *Sapphics*).

3. The craftsmanship here is worth close analysis. The Schumannian device of voice–piano unison is followed down to the last detail, as shown by a comparison between bars 10–11 and 25–6. The Schumann affinities seem to go deeper still, in the Clara motif M33, C–B♭–A–G#–A in voice and piano octaves at bars 8–9 and 23–4. This in turn may explain why the final cadence is so very redolent of Schubert's *Am Meer*, a source also quoted by Brahms in the slow movement of his B major piano trio Op. 8. Brahms and Clara had been together in his native Hamburg, which was the scene of the Heine lyric set by Schubert; the parallelism between the passages at 'Tau, der mich nässte' and 'tauten die Tränen' here and at 'vergiftet mit ihren Tränen', anticipated by 'fielen die Tränen nieder' in D957/12 is so plain as to imply deliberate allusion.

4. The low minims and semibreves are M6 ('dunklen'); the continuous love-duetting is M18, with M21 sighs; the tear-drop staccato is M28.

5. The interlude at bars 13–14 is an analogue of bars 27–8 in *An die Nachtigall* (No. 66), where the situation is similar.

168. (Op. 94, No. 5) Kein Haus, keine Heimat (No house, no homeland) 1883 or 1884

Friedrich Halm♭   D minor d'–d''

> Kein Haus, keine Heimat,
> Kein Weib und kein Kind,
> So wirbl ich, ein Strohhalm,
> In Wetter und Wind!
>
> Well' auf und Well' nieder,
> Bald dort und bald hier;
> Welt, fragst du nach mir nicht,
> Was frag ich nach dir?

No house, no homeland, no wife and no child; so I am whirled like a wisp of straw in storm and wind. Up with one wave, down with the next, now here and now there; if you do not ask about me, world, why should I ask about you?

The words suggest a Miller of the Dee, or D minor, who cares for nobody, no not he, if nobody cares for him. In the poetic source, this nihilistic lyric is sung by an outcast before his self-sacrificial death. But the poet was more notable for the expression of feeling than for characterisation; and Halm's description 'Strohhalm' (wisp of straw) is surely a punning personalised monogram.

Brahms is equally allusive in this, the shortest of all his songs. He had long left his native North German Hamburg for alien Austrian Vienna, where he rented an apartment; he would never have a wife or a child. In the preluding octaves and after the initial statement in each verse he deliberately fans and winnows his music down to the merest wisps of melody and harmony here and there among blank windblown spaces. The opening figure is basic Brahmsian shorthand for a puff of wind, slight in itself but sufficient to disperse a man of straw, a nobody whose musical equivalent is the silence pointedly maintained by the piano at 'wirbl ich' (I am whirled) and 'Strohhalm', and again at 'fragst du (nach) mir nicht' (if you do not ask about me), where no one is heard asking. But the last long note and massive sustained major chord serve to disclose a real personality relishing its final defiance of fate.

NOTES. I. The textual source was Halm's dramatic poem *In der Südsee* in Vol. 7 of the *Gesammelte Werke* (1856–72), which Brahms owned. Even without personal significance, the theme of bidding farewell to the world may well have prompted the use of a symbolic A–D motif (M34), for example at the key word 'Strohhalm'.

2. The tentative rhythm may be remembered from *Über die Heide* (No. 159) which also moves and pauses, impelled yet reluctant.

3. The puffing motifs are M21; the dry-as-dust staccato is M28; the silences within the bar-lines are M29. The final tierce de Picardie and fermata are also expressive, in the sense of 'Frei aber Froh' (see p. 13).

OPUS 95

Seven songs (Lieder) for solo voice with pianoforte accompaniment, with named poets or translator, published in November 1884.

The volume was also issued in a transposed edition for low voice; but the manuscripts are no longer extant, so the original keys cannot be positively identified.

169. (Op. 95, No. 1) Das Mädchen (The girl) 1883

Anon., Serbian (trans, S. Kapper)   B minor and major e′–g#″

Stand das Mädchen, stand am Bergesabhang,
Widerschien der Berg von ihrem Antlitz,
Und das Mädchen sprach zu ihrem Antlitz;
'Wahrlich, Antlitz, o du meine Sorge,
Wenn ich wüsste, du mein weisses Antilitz,
Dass dereinst ein Alter dich wird küssen,
Ging hinaus ich zu den grünen Bergen,
Pflückte allen Wermut in den Bergen,
Presste bittres Wasser aus dem Wermut,
Wüsche dich, o Antlitz, mit dem Wasser,
Dass du bitter, wenn dich küsst der Alte!
Wüsst ich aber, du mein weisses Antlitz,
Dass dereinst ein Junger dich wird küssen,
Ging hinaus ich in den grünen Garten,
Pflückte alle Rosen in dem Garten,
Presste duftend Wasser aus den Rosen,

Wüsche dich, o Antlitz, mit dem Wasser,
Dass du duftest, wenn dich küsst der Junge!

The girl stood, she stood by the cliff face, which reflected her own, and the girl spoke to her face: 'Truly, my face, oh you my sorrow,

if I knew, oh you my white face, that one day an old man will kiss you [that one day an old man will kiss you] I'd go out into the green mountains, I'd gather all the wormwood in the mountains, I'd press the bitter juice from the wormwood, I'd wash you, oh my face, in that juice, so that you'll taste bitter when the old man kisses you [bitter when the old man kisses you].

But if I knew, oh my white face, that one day a young man will kiss you [that one day a young man will kiss you], I'd go out into the green garden, I'd pluck all the roses in the garden, I'd press fragrant water from the roses, I'd wash you, oh my face, in that water, so that you'll smell sweet when the young man kisses you [smell sweet when the young man kisses you]!

The song, like its heroine, begins by confronting its own reflected features in a rustic square-dance. The first two bars are mirrored by the second two, the next pair is echoed by the succeeding pair. Each time, the girl's 3/4 ländler beat of 'stand das Mädchen', is followed by a male march embodying a dotted rhythm; thus the girl and her imagined partner, young or old, are symbolised in sound. At 'wahrlich, Antlitz' (Truly, my face) her melody frowns in a flattened third, anticipating 'Sorge' (sorrow), as if her face is her misfortune. Perhaps she has been promised to an old man. But soon the music's mood mellows optimistically, in a new major mode, as a much younger lover is made most welcome. He induces a dreamy swoon at the second 'Dass dereinst ein Junger dich wird küssen' (that one day a young man will kiss you), at which thought the piano part preens and pirouettes with a sweet gaiety in complete contrast with the earlier bass notes and accented chords that went grubbing for wormwood throughout a whole mountain range. Instead, voice and accompaniment ease out into regular six-bar phrases of cheerful song and dance before the three- and four-crotchet girl–boy patterns reappear at 'dass du duftest' (so that you'll smell sweet) and prance off to an elated embrace.

NOTES. 1. The textual source was *Die Gesänge der Serben* (1852) by Siegfried Kapper, whose 'nach' in line seven appears as 'zu' in the song.

2. Again a Brahms girl agonises at the mere thought of an old man, as in No. 122. The composer was fifty when this song was written.

3. The varied three- or four-crotchet bars are M26; the latter's virile dotted rhythm is M31. The sadly flattened thirds are also motivic (M41), like the Schubertian major/minor of M39. The low left-hand notes in bars 17–20 stand for the firm-rooted mountains, M8; the tranced and entranced arpeggios at 'dass dereinst' are M9; the top G# at the final 'Jun(ge)' is M10.

4. Brahms arranged this song, also in 1883, for mixed voice quartet a cappella. Op. 93a No. 2.

170. (Op. 95, No. 2) Bei dir sind meine Gedanken (All my thoughts are with you) c. 1883

Friedrich Halm   A major e′–f#″

Bei dir sind meine Gedanken
Und flattern um dich her;
Sie sagen, sie hätten Heimweh,
Hier litt es sie nicht mehr.

Bei dir sind meine Gedanken
Und wollen von dir nicht fort;
Sie sagen, das wär auf Erden
Der allerschönste Ort.

Sie sagen, unlösbar hielte
Dein Zauber sie festgebannt;
Sie hätten an deinen Blicken
Die Flügel sich verbrannt.

My thoughts are with you, and flutter [flutter] around you; they say they were homesick, they were no longer wanted here [they were no longer wanted here].

My thoughts are with you, and they don't want [don't want] to leave you; they say that would be the loveliest place on earth [the loveliest place on earth].

They say that your magic holds them inescapably in thrall; that in the fire of your gaze they have scorched their wings [they have scorched their wings].

The poetic thoughts are metaphorical moths. As in *Botschaft* (No. 67), Brahms often makes his ideas sound rather substantial; here they resemble the birds whose song and flight he so loved. Their wing-beats fill the air from the first; the word 'flattern' (flutter) is repeated for emphasis, on a wide-ranging dotted melody. Then their complaints are voiced, first in the querulous chromatics of exile and then in the tonic major of happy homecoming. The same pattern suits the second verse, with chromatic reluctance to leave and diatonic satisfaction at staying. In the last verse, the music is slightly but effectively varied; the fluttering melody is replaced by a long note on '*fest*gebannt' (inescapably in thrall) to show how enduring their subjection will be. Now the flatward chromatic movement evokes singed wings, while the following bright A major depicts the adored flame.

NOTES. 1. The textual source was Vol. 7 of Halm's *Gesammelte Werke* (1856–72), which Brahms owned.

2. Perhaps the Schumann reminiscences are subconscious. It may be that Brahms was also working on another A major song of the same period, also full of wing-motifs (*Auf dem Schiffe*, No. 181) which begins by mentioning the Rhine; hence his audible indebtedness here to Schumann's *Berg' und Burgen* Op. 24 No. 7, also in A major, about 'den Rhein', 'mein Schiffchen' and a deep but unhappy love. On any interpretation, the Clara-themes of M33 ought surely to be expected in this song; but if they are present, they are disguised (e.g. as G#–A–C–B♭–A in the voice at the first '(all)erschönste Ort' instead of the usual C–B♭–A–G#–A).

3. The strong strophic structure is interestingly varied to suit the sense: prelude 1–6 = interlude 29–34, varied as postlude 57–62; first and second verses 7–29, third verse = 35–7 + two-bar coda, except for the long vocal note at 'fest' and the lowering of pitch in the piano from 23–9 to 51–7, as if the singed wings had sagged.

4. The wing-beats are M3; the flatward movement of discontent is also motivic (M42), to suit 'Heimweh' etc.

171. (Op. 95, Nos. 3a, 3b) Beim Abschied (At parting) 1883/4
Friedrich Halm   D major f#'–f#"

> Ich müh mich ab und kanns nicht verschmerzen,
> Und kanns nicht verwinden in meinem Herzen,
> Dass ich den und jenen soll sehen
> Im Kreis um mich herum sich drehen,
> Der mich nicht machte froh noch trübe,
> Ob er nun ging oder bliebe,
> Und nur die Eine soll von mir wandern
> Für die ich ertragen all die Andern.

For all my efforts, I can't get over my distress, I can't overcome it in my heart, at seeing this or that person circling around me who couldn't make me happy or sad whether they went or stayed [whether they went or stayed], while only she is now going to leave me, for whose sake alone I have endured all those others [while only she is now going to leave me, she for whose sake alone I have endured all those others].

The *Gesamtausgabe* prints two versions; in the second, the composer's own revision of his first published setting, the 3/8 vocal part has a 2/4 piano accompaniment not just from 'und nur die Eine' (while only *she*) but from the first words onward. The effect is even more stressfully busy and agitated, the very music of unwelcome attention. Thus Brahms lavished love and skill on this obscure lyric, with the irresistible inference that it had made some special personal appeal to him and indeed exactly described his own situation and feelings. If so, 'she' could only have been Clara Schumann, for whose dear sake Brahms indeed endured much uncongenial company without overt complaint. She never deserted him; but their relationship was often strained and sometimes estranged; the composition of this song (the date of which is uncertain) may confidently be assigned to one such period.

NOTES. 1. The textual source was Vol. 1 of Halm's *Gesammelte Werke* (1856–72), which Brahms owned, He changed 'ginge' (line six) into 'ging' to suit his vocal line. The predictable Clara motif M33 would be expected to occur at the first appearance of the key phrase 'nur die Eine soll von mir wandern' (bars 41–5; cf. also 6–9 and 16–19); there the sung melody is heard to contain F#–E–D–C#–D.

2. The complex rhythms are M15; the prelude's enhanced dominant seventh is M24; the occasional sad flats are M41.

172. (Op. 95, No. 4) Der Jäger (The huntsman) *c.* 1883

Friedrich Halm   F major e′–f″

Mein Lieb ist ein Jäger,
Und grün ist sein Kleid,
Und blau ist sein Auge,
Nur sein Herz ist zu weit.

Mein Lieb ist ein Jäger,
Trifft immer ins Ziel,
Und Mädchen berückt er,
So viel er nur will.

Mein Lieb ist ein Jäger,
Kennt Wege und Spur,
Zu mir aber kommt er
Durch die Kirchtüre nur.

My love's a huntsman; his garb is green
  and his eyes are blue, but his heart is too open [his heart is too open].
My love's a huntsman, never misses his aim,
  and he charms the girls, as many as he will [as many as he will].
My love's a huntsman, knows trails and tracks,
  but his only way to me is through the church door [only through the church door].

Here are the same key and time-signature as *Sonntag* No. 69. This country character has replaced their innocence with innuendo, matched by knowing music that flirts and winks as it pirouettes; yet her song, in its very different way, is just as loving and lively. The prelude, which also serves as two interludes and a postlude, enters with a laugh and a ländler-like leap. The voice begins unaccompanied, to show the girl's independence; the piano joins in at 'ein Jäger' (a huntsman) each time, and as it were adds an exclamation mark. The falling triad of the first three vocal notes and the rising fourth of the next two are then discreetly imitated and echoed in the left hand, to hammer the point home. The melodic keyboard echo after 'grün ist sein Kleid' (his garb is green) announces a further joke, which becomes more apparent with each verse; our blue-eyed Lothario ('blau ist sein Auge') is always bang on target ('trifft immer ins Ziel') and can find his way anywhere ('kennt Wege und Spur'). Those three key phrases, with falling vocal sequences, are embellished with laughing off-beat staccato quavers and followed by a spirited rising phrase as the singer asserts her rights and conditions, the first of which is legal matrimony. All this paints a colourful picture of the versatile huntsman and the girl who is a match for him, and more. The music is sure that they will live happy ever after.

NOTES. 1. The textual source was the dramatic poem *Wildfeuer* in Vol. 7 of Halm's *Gesammelte Werke* (1856–72), which Brahms owned. There the poem is one of a pair called *Margots Lieder*; hence perhaps the detailed musical characterisation.

2. The prelude's repeated major 5–6–5 is the joy motif M19; the Schubertian echoes of 'grün ist sein Kleid' etc. are also expressive, like the laughing off-beat left-hand quavers.

3. The last two bars of the prelude–interludes–postlude may be compared with the equally sprightly conclusion of *Vergebliches Ständchen* (No. 148).

173. (Op. 95, No. 5) Vorschneller Schwur (Overhasty vow) *c.* 1883
Anon., Serbian (trans. S. Kapper)   D minor and major d′–a″

> Schwor ein junges Mädchen:
> Blumen nie zu tragen,
> Blumen nie zu tragen,
> Niemals Wein zu trinken,
> Niemals Wein zu trinken,
> Knaben nie zu küssen.
>
> Gestern schwor das Mädchen –
> Heute schon bereut es:
> 'Wenn ich Blumen trüge,
> Wär ich doch noch schöner!
> Wenn ich Rotwein tränke,
> Wär ich doch noch froher!
> Wenn den Liebsten küsste,
> Wär mir doch noch wohler!'

A young girl vowed never to wear flowers, never to wear flowers, never to drink wine, never to drink wine, never to kiss boys. That's what she vowed yesterday – and today she's already regretting it.

'If I wore flowers, I'd be even prettier! If I drank red wine, I'd be even merrier! If I kissed my best beloved, I'd be even happier [if I kissed my best beloved, I'd be even happier]!'

Even the minor-key opening has a little melodic lilt of its own. Cheerfulness keeps breaking in. The vow was never entirely serious; and the very thought of its unnatural absurdity makes the peasant girl dance with delight, as she sings her folk-song strains to a simple accompaniment. After 'küssen' (kiss) and again after the second 'Mädchen' (girl) Brahms inserts meaningful meditative pauses over the barline to show that this is the real stumbling-block, in his estimation. Flowers and wine might just possibly be dispensed with; but not kissing. At 'heute schon' (today already) the harmonies become briefly perturbed and puzzled, as if to ask 'what am I saying?', But even before 'bereut es' (regretting it) these mild per-plexities are readily resolved. The following major section adds a springier step to the dance and preserves many of the voice part's previous melodies and rhythms to show that this is just the same girl as before who has now come to her senses. The postlude chuckles the opening tune of 'Schwor ein jung(es) …' to confirm that she remains an unreformed character.

NOTES. 1. The textual source was Kapper's *Die Gesänge der Serben* (1852).

2. The melodies might well have found a place in the *Hungarian Dances*. The major section adds a quasi-orchestral accompaniment with busier rhythms (M16), bass notes and string chords.

3. The threefold D″–F″–A′ in voice and piano (bars 1–2, 9–10, 17–18) which later becomes a threefold D″–F#″–A′ no doubt deliberately mirrors the triple vow thrice recanted, much as Kalbeck suggests (iii 529).

4. The voice's falling fifth A–D at 'küssen', and again pedalled in the left hand after 'bereut es' is already bidding the vow adieu, M34; the top As in the Animato section are M10. The Schubertian transition from minor to major is also motivic (M39).

174. (Op. 95, No. 6) Mädchenlied (Girl's song) c. 1883
Anon., Italian (trans. P. Heyse)   F major f′–g″

> Am jüngsten Tag ich aufersteh
> Und gleich nach meinem Liebsten seh,
> Und wenn ich ihn nicht finden kann
> Leg wieder mich zum Schlafen dann.
>
> O Herzeleid, du Ewigkeit!
> Selbander nur ist Seligkeit!
> Und kommt mein Liebster nicht hinein,
> Mag nicht im Paradiese sein!

On judgement day I'll rise up and straightaway I'll go looking for my best beloved, and if I can't find him I'll lie down and go to sleep again [lie down and go to sleep again].
    Oh heartache, you're eternal! To be with another is the only bliss! So if my beloved doesn't arrive, I'd rather not be in paradise [rather not be in paradise]!

The three-note prelude's arpeggio descent is sequentially extended; so, quite independently, is the vocal line of two falling phrases. This subtly mirrors the poetic image; the music as it were tentatively gets out of bed, still half asleep, as the village girl envisages her resurrection. But once up, she takes more purposeful steps; before and at 'wenn ich ihn nicht finden kann' (if I can't find him) the alternating staccato chords and rising left-hand octave go searching about, only to lapse into a legato at the first 'leg wieder mich zum Schlafen dann' (lie down and go to sleep again). At the second, the pace slows down; then the interlude droops accordingly, in the same falling phrases as before. At 'O Herzeleid' (Oh heartache) the vocal sequences are accompanied by duetting thirds in both hands, imagining the desired companionship. The walking and searching are resumed; and this time the repeated final phrase is drawn out from two bars to four, with lengthened notes to show how tedious eternity will become for those on their own. The postlude signifies assent by going to sleep again.

NOTES. 1. The text (which has 'du Ewigkeit' as in the *Gesamtausgabe*, not 'die Ewigkeit' as in Peters) was taken from Heyse's *Gedichte*. There this poem had four verses; the setting omits the first two, which describe the poor 15-year-old washergirl who sings this song at dawn, still sleepy-eyed.

2. The theme of rejecting paradise if on one's own is treated with even greater insouciance in Schubert's *Seligkeit* D433. Brahms's setting, despite his direction 'behaglich' (contentedly), is sober and earnest; the song is another aspect of his predilection for the plight of girls left lonely.

3. The staccato steps are M1; the low Fs for 'Schlafen', and again in the postlude, are

M7; the duetting thirds are M18. The augmentation in the last vocal phrase is also expressive.

175. (Op. 95, No. 7) Schön war, das ich dir weihte (Beautiful gifts) *c.* 1883

Georg Daumer (from the Turkish)   F minor e′–g″

> Schön war, das ich dir weihte,
> Das goldene Geschmeide;
> Süss war der Laute Ton,
> Die ich dir auserlesen;
> Das Herze, das sie beide
> Darbrachte, wert gewesen
> Wärs zu empfangen einen bessern Lohn.

Beautiful was the golden jewellery I consecrated to you; sweet was the sound of the lute I selected for you; the heart that offered up both those gifts would have been worthy to receive a better reward [would have been worthy, would have been worthy to receive a better reward].

The setting, like the jewellery, is highly-wrought and artificial, as attested by the weak last syllables of 'goldene' and 'Geschmeide' (jewellery) set on strong downbeats. But its genuine warmth adds dignity and lovingness to the poetic tone of self-regarding reproach, as if the words were chosen for some special personal appeal to which the music responds. A dominant pedal introduces an adornment of the quasi-parlando vocal line in thirds and sixths; at 'süss war der Laute Ton' (sweet was the sound of the lute) the vocal line is repeated over a piano accompaniment now much mellower in the lower octave. At 'das Herze', the same vocal melody recurs, itself a third lower than before and with major harmonies, as if to stress that both the jewel and the lute were sacrificial symbols of a loving and suffering heart. But the unfulfilled feelings of the frustrated lover seem to lack a clear and compelling musical equivalent, and the inspiration seems to flag until the reprise at the final 'wärs zu empfangen' (would have been [worthy] to receive).

NOTES. 1. The textual source was Georg Daumer's *Polydora* (1855), which Brahms owned. It has 'wars' not 'wärs', i.e. the more definite reproach 'had been', not 'would have been', at bars 13 and 19.

2. Analogous complaints about being unloved, from the same collection, had already been set as *Es träumte mir* and *Eine gute, gute Nacht* (Nos. 86 and 105); the present song may well have been started at the same time and retained many years for further painstaking revision.

3. A song on such a theme makes a covert musical reference to Clara almost mandatory; note the repeated pedal C of M33 at the outset (bars 1–3), soon followed by C–B♭–A♭–G–A♭ in voice and piano (3–4, 7–8) and then in the piano alone (r.h. 20–21 and l.h. 22–3).

4. The thirds and sixths are M18, the sighs in bars 16–17 are M21. The offbeat syncopations are also expressive.

5. The A A1 B A2 structure has been carefully crafted: the thematic material at bars 2–5 and 6–9 is varied at 12–18 and recurs at 19–22, with one bar of introduction and two of coda.

OPUS 96

Four songs (Lieder) for solo voice with pianoforte accompaniment, published in February 1886. Three of the songs are drawn from Heine and one from Daumer, as if those poets were equal in accomplishment (cf. Op. 32); but neither is named on the title-page.

This issue is remarkable for the announcement, in English, of an 'English text by Mrs. John P. Morgan, New-York', followed by the stern warning that 'Mrs. Morgan's translation is the only translation authorized by the Composer', and was 'Copyright 1886 by G. Schirmer'. No doubt the arrangement was lucrative; Mrs. Morgan was the wife of Pierpoint Morgan, the American multi-millionaire. And it must have been sanctioned by the German publisher Simrock; Brahms himself spoke no English (otherwise he could hardly have sanctioned these laboured renditions, even by proxy). But he offered no recorded objection; so here is some evidence of his feelings about the song-form. He saw no need to rely solely on the original German words, as if he felt that his music's *Wortausdruck* had already sufficiently embodied their emotive content.

176. (Op. 96, No. 1) Der Tod, das ist die kühle Nacht (Death is the cool night) *c.* 1884

Heinrich Heine   C major c′–a″

> Der Tod, das ist die kühle Nacht,
> Das Leben ist der schwüle Tag.
> Es dunkelt schon, mich schläfert,
> Der Tag hat mich müd gemacht.
>
> Über mein Bett erhebt sich ein Baum,
> Drin singt die junge Nachtigall;
> Sie singt von lauter Liebe,
> Ich hör es sogar im Traum.

Death is the cool night, life is the sultry day. It is growing dark already; I feel drowsy; the day has wearied me. Over my bed rises a tree wherein the young nightingale is singing; she sings of sheer love [of sheer love], I hear it [I hear it] even in my dreams [even in my dreams].

From this fine lyric Brahms fashions a great song of death and undying love. The vocal line too spans an extensive compass, from the day's dark ending on the tonic C of 'Tag' to the bright high A of 'Liebe'. The pervasive 6/8 rhythm ♪ ♩ ♪ ♩ tolls and pulses throughout, half death and half life. As the voice intones its opening phrase the left hand descends deep into darkness; warmer life returns in added rhythms and closer harmonies to match the sultry day. Left-hand octaves hang across the barline like falling shadows around 'es dunkelt schon' (it is growing dark already) etc., where the verb is briefly heard governing the remote E flat minor realm of death. At the second mention of day ('der Tag') the wrenching rinforzando chords remember the wretchedness of waking. The close harmonies return, and 'Über mein Bett' (over my bed) brings a magical change of pitch and texture as though the music has taken the text literally and moved out into the open air. The arpeggios, spread chords and pedal points are set dreaming, to convey the vision of sheer love. Finally, after the first 'Traum' (dreams) the deep C pedal note strikes midnight at the half-bar. Such eternal yearnings, the music claims, will outlive death itself.

NOTES. 1. The text is the untitled No. 87 of *Die Heimkehr*, which Brahms must surely have seen in his copy of Heine's *Buch der Lieder* when he set its Nos 85–6 as the first two songs of his Op. 85, Nos. 150–1. The poetic contrast between cool night and sultry day would have made an especially deep appeal to him; so perhaps this setting also was written or begun *c.* 1878. The theme of everlasting love may suggest that the C pedal stands for Clara, M33, as in the C minor symphony Op. 68, finalised *c.* 1876.

2. The pattern of rhymes in the first and fourth line in each quatrain ('Nacht ... gemacht', 'Baum ... Traum' is unique in Heine; but it is sensitively significant of world-weariness.

3. The descending left-hand line at the beginning is M6/7; the consecutive thirds in both hands at bars 4–6 and 11–13 (heard again at 23f) foretell that this is to be a love song, M18. The E flat minor chord of death at 'dunkelt', and the offbeat octaves, are also expressive. So are the ensuing rinforzando chords, which recall the bright day. However, these should not be exaggerated, because they represent only reminiscence not actuality, and the background whence they emerge is pianissimo. The high tessitura in voice and piano at bar 14f is M10, with the visionary quality of M9 in the left-hand arpeggios; note here how the vocal line at bars 18–19 matches the opening melody an octave higher, as if to identify love with death in a miniature *Liebestod*.

4. The tolling deep Cs of midnight in bars 25–31 suggests that Brahms may have been impressed by the close of Schumann's *Davidsbündlertänze* Op. 6, also written in homage to Clara, and by Schubert's *Der Gondelfahrer* D808 (with other resemblances including key- and time-signature).

177. (Op. 96, No. 2) Wir wandelten (We were walking) *c.* 1884
Georg Daumer (from the Magyar)   Db major d#′–g♭″

Wir wandelten, wir zwei zusammen,
Ich war so still und du so stille;
Ich gäbe viel, um zu erfahren,
Was du gedacht in jenem Fall.

Was ich gedacht – unausgesprochen
Verbleibe das! Nur Eines sag ich:
So schön war Alles, was ich dachte,
So himmlisch heiter war es all.

In meinem Haupte die Gedanken,
Sie läuteten wie goldne Glöckchen:
So wundersüss, so wunderlieblich
Ist in der Welt kein andrer Hall.

We were walking, we two together. I was so silent and you so silent; I would give much to know what you were thinking at that time. As to what I thought, let that remain unspoken! I shall say only one thing [say only one thing]. Everything I thought was so beautiful, so heavenly and serene. The thoughts in my mind, they chimed like golden bells; so wondrously sweet, so wondrously lovely, like no other sound in the world [so wondrously sweet, so wondrously lovely, like no other sound in the world].

Such thoughts are so atypical of the erotic poet Daumer that the gold might have rung false. But the music makes it sound valid and valuable; this is the song of songs for all devoted Platonic lovers. Elisabet von Herzogenberg, who deprecated the sensuous suggestiveness she heard in other Brahms songs, such as *Willst du, dass ich geh?* (No. 138), instantly recognised and saluted here the tonal equivalent of ideal adoration. 'It must be one of the most glorious songs in the world'. So she wrote (ii 61) to its composer, who idealised and idolised her; and so it still is, over a century later.

It owes that eminence to its intensity. Every note of every bar is a heartfelt response to the poem. The bells are already chiming in the prelude, as the two melodies walk together hand in hand at a respectful half-bar's distance. They are not church or wedding bells; they are all tuned to the same sweet soft yet distinct dominant note, to symbolise enduring unity, and they ring true. Even the two separate melodies are soon heard to be one and the same. As the voice enters, the left hand again echoes its first three notes; after 'zusammen' (together) the piano sings the same song twice, in diminution, while echoing that vocal phrase. All the thematic material, whether in repeated notes, arpeggio or canon, is woven from these same simple strands. The voice at 'ich gäbe viel' (I would give much) etc, and again at 'nur Eines sag ich' (I shall say only one thing) responds to that latter hint of recitative and speaks those phrases in music; indeed the fusion of word and tone throughout, by technique as well as inspiration, is a striking feature of this masterpiece.

NOTES. I. The text is taken from Daumer's *Polydora* (1855), which Brahms owned. There the word set in bars 33–4 is 'lauteten' (sounded) not 'läuteten' (rang). The poet also emphasised the first 'du', which Brahms correspondingly placed on the first beat (of bar 12).

2. The thirds and sixths are the love-duetting M18. Another love-motif, M17, often found in Wolf songs, is heard at 'in jenem Fall', bars 16–17, where the right-hand chords and the vocal melody as written are drawn together; perhaps Brahms heard a woman's voice in this song. The canonic imitations (M12) and the flatward change (M42) to E major (= F♭ major) are also motivic; the Schubertian echoes and the bell-notes throughout are also expressive. The top G♭s are M10, and the bliss of the postlude is expressed in the tonic or dominant 5–6–5 of M19.

3. The structure is worth special study, e.g. the identity of bars 18–19 with 7–8 and 21 with 14. The barring is fluid throughout; there should be no stress on the final syllable '-men' in bar 9 or '-chen' in bar 20.

178. (Op. 96, No. 3) Es schauen die Blumen (All the flowers look up)
c. 1884

Heinrich Heine   B minor f#'–g#''

    Es schauen die Blumen alle
    Zur leuchtenden Sonne hinauf;

Es nehmen die Ströme alle
Zum leuchtenden Meere den Lauf.

Es flattern die Lieder alle
Zu meinem leuchtenden Lieb;
Nehmt mit meine Tränen und Seufzer,
Ihr Lieder wehmütig und trüb!

All the flowers look up at the radiant sun, all the rivers run their course to the radiant sea. All my songs [all] flutter to my radiant love; take my tears and sighs with you, you wistful and cheerless songs [you wistful and cheerless songs].

The highly Heinesque theme of thoughts winging to the beloved had already been treated in *Bei dir sind meine Gedanken* (No. 170); it meant much to Brahms. Here the upward look of flowers and the onward flow of rivers are subsumed in the same urgent flights of semiquaver triplets that symbolise the wings of song throughout. The irresistible forces of nature are thus economically depicted in this miniature frame, which still finds room for such deft and subtle touches as the deep left-hand note for 'Meere' (sea), the piano syncopations at 'Es flattern die Lieder' (songs flutter) and the off-beat semiquaver bass for the message of tears and sighs, to show how deep the hurt goes, and how insistently yet unobtrusively it makes its presence felt. The final 'trüb' (cheerless), as the wing-beats falter and fail, echoes (perhaps deliberately) the sad song of the nightingale in *In Waldeseinsamkeit* (No. 155). But the final major chord suggests that there may still be hope.

NOTES. 1. The unfamiliar text (a posthumous addition to the *Lyrisches Intermezzo*) is taken from Heine's *Werke* (1861), which Brahms owned.

2. Clara was surely in mind here as in Nos. 155 and 170, though her musical themes remain unstated.

3. The continuous wings are M3; their parallel thirds or sixths are M18; the deep bass note for 'Meer' is M6; the minor 6–5 at the first 'trüb' is M20. The left hand's canonic imitations at bars 10 and 14, and the insistent offbeat semiquavers at 'nehmt mit meine Tränen' etc. are also expressive.

179. (Op. 96, No. 4) Meerfahrt (A voyage) *c.* 1884
Heinrich Heine   A minor e'–g″ (a♭″)

Mein Liebchen, wir sassen beisammen
Traulich im leichten Kahn.
Die Nacht war still und wir schwammen
Auf weiter Wasserbahn.

Die Geisterinsel, die schöne,
Lag dämmrig im Mondenglanz;
Dort klangen liebe Töne
Und wogte der Nebeltanz.

Dort klang es lieb und lieber
Und wogt es hin und her;

Wir aber schwammen vorüber
Trostlos auf weitem Meer.

My darling, we sat lovingly side by side in the light skiff. The night was silent, and we
floated along on a wide waterway [on a wide, wide waterway].

The beautiful haunted island lay glimmering in the moonlight; there sweet music
resounded and the dancing mists swirled. The sounds grew ever sweeter, the mists
swirled this way and that; but we floated past, forlorn on the wide sea [forlorn on the
wide sea, on the wide, wide sea].

In this fine strange song, as in *Botschaft* (No. 67) and elsewhere, Brahms makes
difficult technical demands; this skiff, like those breezes, will sound anything but
light without virtuoso performance. The prelude is a barcarolle, the vocal melody
a gondolier's serenade, remote from the native Hamburg of both poet and
composer. But the low bass notes speak of the great sea itself, no mere lagoon. The
music depicts the depths of despair; love is doomed to drown and die without ever
savouring the enchantments of Heine's imaginary island, a Cythera sacred to
Venus. Those alluring strains are no doubt embodied in the prelude's sustained
melody, which is never heard again save for a shortened reprise after the second
'Wasserbahn' (waterway) and a brief outcry at the first 'trostlos' (forlorn);
otherwise the music like the lyric sails straight past, borne on a ceaseless 6/8
wave-motion. The pulse quickens at the sound of sweet music ('klangen liebe
Töne'); the dancing mists evoke cloudy chromatics and key-change at 'Nebeltanz'.
Their confused climax at 'wogte hin und her' (swirled this way and that) is
plangently discordant; at least one of the voyagers is culpably indifferent to the
delights of that magic island. Finally their boat dwindles down to one low
motionless note, a speck on the horizon.

NOTES. 1. The text is taken from Heine's *Lyrisches Intermezzo*, no doubt found in the
Werke (1861) that Brahms owned.

2. Again Clara was presumably in mind; they had met at Brahms's (and Heine's) native
Hamburg in the early days of their relationship (see No. 167 note 3). But here her theme
is inconspicuous if not absent, or indeed suppressed.

3. The accompaniment's staccato (not meant to be confined to those few bars where it
is specifically marked) expresses the lightness and indeed the frailty of the 'leichter Kahn'
(M28); cf. the floating staccatos of another 'Schifflein', the 'schwimmend Eden' of *Auf dem
See* (No. 192).

4. The deep bass notes in bar 7 etc. are M6; the melodic turn in bar 10 is also
expressive, like the flatward chromatics of M42 at 'Dort klang'.

5. The optional top A♭ seems, exceptionally, to have no special significance, whereas the
alternative F suggests the apt pleasure motif M19, suiting 'lieb und lieber'; so perhaps the
F is to be preferred.

6. Cf. Franz Op. 18 No. 4; Hugo Wolf 1878.

OPUS 97

Six songs (Lieder) for solo voice with pianoforte accompaniment, with named
poets or sources, published in February 1886.

The first edition carried the same English notice about translation as in Op. 96.

180. (Op. 97, No. 1) Nachtigall (Nightingale) *c.* 1885
Christian Reinhold   F minor d♭′–a″

> O Nachtigall,
> Dein süsser Schall,
> Er dringet mir durch Mark und Bein.
> Nein, trauter Vogel, nein!
> Was in mir schafft so süsse Pein,
> Das ist nicht dein,
> Das ist von andern, himmelschönen,
> Nun längst für mich verklungnen Tönen,
> In deinem Lied ein leiser Widerhall!

O nightingale, your sweet tones pierce me to the marrow.
No, dear bird, no! what causes me such sweet pain is not your notes but others, of heavenly beauty, which have long died away for me, leaving a wistful echo in your song [a wistful echo]!

This endearingly wistful song is no less successful for being in some sense manufactured (see note 1); Brahms's craftsmanship is hardly less inspiring than his creative artistry. The treble-clef prelude has a fluting melody adorned with acciaccature over single staccato notes, followed by floating octave lifts over syncopated chords, with a liquid effect of bird song amid rainy leaves. The same music is then rearranged as accompaniment while the voice repeats its affecting melody. A brief interlude echoes the end of the prelude. Thus the present scene is set, only to be immediately replaced by another from the past. At 'Nein, trauter Vogel' (No, dear bird) voice and piano move into an accompanied recitative, which movingly culminates in full-throated melody at 'Das ist von andern, himmel-schönen' (not your notes but others, of heavenly beauty). Then the voice is in effect left alone, like the singer, in a high but falling chromatic phrase that epitomises a sad decline from past happiness. The bird-song accompaniment recurs to grace the words 'in deinem Lied' (in your song) and the voice slowly adds the sweet lovesong thus wistfully echoed from far away and long ago. 'Inspired', said Elisabet von Herzogenberg (ii 63); and posterity has endorsed that judgement.

NOTES. 1. The textual source was Reinhold's *Gedichte* (1853), which Brahms owned. It has 'dringt', not 'dringet' in line three; the vocal melody, already composed for the same poet's *Ein Wanderer* (No. 195), required extra syllables. Both songs also share the same key and time-signature; and Brahms told the Herzogenbergs in May 1885 (ii 59), that the pair 'came into the world as twins, so to speak'. But they are far from identical. And whatever its origin, this song's opening melody when arranged as a piano prelude achieves a re-creation of sensual bird song that is hardly conveyed so vividly anywhere else in the lied repertoire.

2. The left-hand staccato is akin to M28; the parallel thirds, tenths, etc. are M18; the left-hand dream arpeggios of M9 are heard in bars 20–21 (followed by the intensified dominant seventh of M24) and again at the final 'Widerhall'. The top A on 'längst' is M10; the falling minor second on 'Tönen' is M20; the four-part secco accompaniment at bars 12–17 and the gruppetto on the last 'lei(ser)' are also expressive.

181. (Op. 97, No. 2) Auf dem Schiffe (On the ship) by May 1885
Christian Reinhold   A major g′–a″

> Ein Vögelein
> Fliegt über den Rhein
> Und wiegt die Flügel
> Im Sonnenschein,
> Sieht Rebenhügel
> Und grüne Flut
> In goldner Glut, –
> Wie wohl das tut,
> So hoch erhoben
> Im Morgenhauch!
> Beim Völein droben
> O wär ich auch!

A little bird flies over the Rhine and cradles its wings in the sunshine; it sees vine-clad hills and green waves in a golden glow [in a golden glow];
    how fine it feels [how fine it feels] to be borne so high aloft in the morning breeze! If only I too could fly high above with that bird [if only I could, if only I could]!

The poet's title unobtrusively tells us that flying even surpasses floating; so the music sets out to brighten and heighten that former feeling still further. The repeated figure ♩♪ ⁷ on each 3/8 quaver twitters like bird-song and flutters like a wing-beat. At 'wie wohl das tut' (how fine it feels) the music changes its tune from depiction to empathy, in accordance with the words. At 'so hoch erhoben' (borne so high aloft) the arpeggios dreamily imagine what flying must be like. The bird-music briefly reappears at 'Beim Vöglein', followed by further flights of fancy. At the repeated 'wär ich auch' the romantic metaphor is made musically vivid. First the low tonic pedal brings the singer down to earth, or rather the deck-level of a ship-board vantage-point; then the rising or falling thirds of the original flying motif are lowered in pitch and evened out in rhythm to reinforce the unspoken moral; alas, we lack wings. But we can float; and we can fly in spirit, the postlude reassuringly adds.

NOTES. 1. The textual source was Reinhold's *Gedichte* (1853), which Brahms owned. The melodic pattern requires that the poem's second 'Vögelein' is elided to 'Vöglein' at bars 46–7.

    2. The right hand's opening 5–6–5 is the joy motif M19; the fluttering *passim* is M3; the top As at 'Son(nenschein)' and 'gold(ner)' are M10 (with Schubertian piano echoes that are also expressive). The long dominant seventh at 'wohl' etc. is M24, and the dreamy arpeggios there are M9. The low notes at the first 'o wär ich auch' are M6; the piano's bar of silence at the last 'O' is M29.

    3. At bars 5–7 the fluttering rhythm assumes the descending-sixth form found in the prelude of another bird song, *Das Mädchen spricht* (No. 198), also in the brightness of A major.

182. (Op. 97, No. 3) Entführung (Abduction) by May 1885
Willibald[1] Alexis   D minor d'–f''

> O Lady Judith, spröder Schatz,
>   Drückt dich zu fest mein Arm?
> Je zwei zu Pferd haben schlechten Platz
>   Und Winternacht weht nicht warm.
>
> Hart ist der Sitz und knapp und schmal,
>   Und kalt mein Kleid von Erz,
> Doch kälter und härter als Sattel und Stahl
>   War gegen mich dein Herz.
>
> Sechs Nächte lag ich in Sumpf und Moor
>   Und hab um dich gewacht,
> Doch weicher, bei Sankt Görg ichs schwor,
>   Schlaf ich die siebente Nacht!

O Lady Judith, my coy love, does my arm press you too close? Two on a horse isn't comfortable, and the winter night-wind isn't warm [the winter night-wind isn't warm].

The saddle is hard, short and narrow, and my coat of mail is cold, yet colder and harder than saddle or steel was your heart to me [was your heart to me].

Six nights I lay in marsh and moor, sleepless for your sake, but I swore by Saint George that I'd sleep more softly on the seventh night [I'd sleep more softly on the seventh night]!

Elisabet von Herzogenberg, who found the knowing innuendo of *Willst du dass ich geh* and *Nachtwandler* (Nos. 138 and 158) decidedly distasteful, felt (ii 65) that this ballad fell well within the bounds of acceptability. She thought 'the words splendid and the music delectable'. Perhaps the poem's pretended English-historical source distanced it from the forcible abduction it recounts with such relish.

However, the piping treble octaves of the prelude sound anything but villainous or virile. Even considered merely as a tally-ho horn-call motif they seem decidedly unimpressive; and they remain undeveloped. But the fierce stride and speed of the marauder once mounted are irresistible. The hoofbeats of the quaver triplet accompaniment pound and rebound with springing vigour, to depict the abductor triumphantly galloping off with his prize.

NOTES. 1. The textual source was the *Balladen* (1836) of Willibald Alexis, the pen-name of Wilhelm Häring; Brahms drew his duet *Walpurgisnacht* Op. 75 No. 4, from the same collection.

2. It seems from Elisabet von Herzogenberg's letter (loc. cit.) that the strophic form was originally invariant. But then the song was 'too soon over'; couldn't the composer at least

---

[1] not (*pace* the *Gesamtausgabe*) 'Wilibald'.

extend the last verse somewhat? He apparently did so (*pace* Friedländer 132), since the last verse in fact prolongs the last line from the previous two bars to three and adds a wider-ranging piano part. And this is no doubt an improvement, like the repetitions added, on second thoughts, to *Sonntag* (No. 69).

3. The prelude's horn-call, though clearly motivic in the sense of M22, is not noted elsewhere; the insistently urgent hoof-beats are M1 with the virile rhythms of M31 and expressive jolting syncopations. Perhaps the final A–D (M34) bids a soldier's farewell to Lady Judith's earlier existence.

183. (Op. 97, No. 4) Dort in den Weiden (There in the willows) c. 1884

Anon.   D major a′–a″

> Dort in den Weiden steht ein Haus,
> Da schaut die Magd zum Fenster naus!
> Sie schaut stromauf, sie schaut stromab:
> Ist noch nicht da mein Herzensknab?
> Der schönste Bursch am ganzen Rhein,
> Den nenn ich mein!
>
> Des Morgens fährt er auf dem Fluss
> Und singt herüber seinen Gruss,
> Des Abends, wenns Glühwürmchen fliegt,
> Sein Nachen an das Ufer wiegt,
> Da kann ich mit dem Burschen mein
> Beisammen sein!
>
> Die Nachtigall im Fliederstrauch,
> Was sie da singt, versteh ich auch,
> Sie saget: Übers Jahr ist Fest,
> Hab ich, mein Lieber, auch ein Nest,
> Wo ich dann mit dem Burschen mein
> Die Frohst am Rhein!

There in the willows stands a house, with a girl looking out of the window! She looks upstream, she looks downstream: hasn't my sweetheart arrived yet? The handsomest lad on all the Rhine, him I name mine [him I name mine, him I name mine]!

Each morning he rows on the river and sings his song; in the evening, when the fireflies dance and his boat rocks by the riverbank, then I can be together with my young man [together with my young man, together with my young man]!

I too understand what the nightingale sings in the lilac bush; she says that in a year's time there'll be a wedding feast, and then, my dear, I'll have a nest too, where I'll live with my lad and be the happiest girl on all the Rhine [the happiest girl on all the Rhine, the happiest girl on all the Rhine]!

Despite the original sub-title 'Niederrheinisches Volkslied' this purely Brahmsian music flows far from the lower Rhine (note 1). Indeed, the left hand's staccato chords suggest one of the *Zigeunerlieder* from the same late period, with a vigorously gypsyish effect of offbeat hand-claps and stamping. As so often, the girl's lover is absent, leaving her as the sole and central figure. This time, however, the cheerful major key and untroubled harmonies look forward to an atypically happy ending.

The voice sings in sixths or thirds with the piano, like a love-duet. The quaver rhythm slackens and softens at 'Fenster naus' (out of the window) and 'Herzensknab' (sweetheart) and instantly turns into skipping semiquavers at the thought of 'der schönste Bursch' (the handsomest lad). The interlude augments the opening vocal melody into a solo dance. The same music serves for the second verse. In the third, the right hand octave after 'Fliederstrauch' (lilac bush) and 'Fest' (wedding feast) is playfully arpeggiated, while after 'Nest' the accompaniment bursts out into delighted semiquaver triplets. The interlude reappears as postlude, with a triumphant flamenco-like finality of posture and gesture.

NOTES. 1. The textual source was the Kretschmer–Zuccalmaglio *Deutsche Volkslieder* (ii 1840). The authenticity of the lyric and its appended melody have been disputed; but Brahms accepted both (though he bowdlerised the racy 'Glühärschlein' into 'Glühwürmchen') and used them in other so-called folk-song versions, notably No. 31 of his *49 Deutsche Volkslieder*. Here however he writes his own far superior melody, which wholly justifies the opus number's implicit claim that this is his own original work.

2. The duetting thirds and sixths are M18, the changing time-signatures M26. The waiting dominant seventh at bar 18, intensified still further at bar 31, is M24; the top note on 'Frohst' is M10. The offbeat staccato is also motivic, perhaps depicting the fireflies (M28) as points of light; so are the quickening rhythms (M16). It is worth noting how all the semiquaver chords and notes of bars 9–10 and the right-hand chords of 11–12 are as it were tripletised with extra excitement at 27–30.

184. (Op. 97, No. 5) Komm bald (Come soon) 1885
Klaus Groth   A major d#'–g''

> Warum denn warten
> Von Tag zu Tag?
> Es blüht im Garten
> Was blühen mag.
>
> Wer kommt und zählt es,
> Was blüht so schön?
> An Augen fehlt es,
> Es anzusehn.
>
> Die meinen wandern
> Vom Strauch zum Baum;
> Mir scheint, auch Andern
> Wärs wie ein Traum.
>
> Und von den Lieben,
> Die mir getreu
> Und mir geblieben,
> Wärst du dabei!

Why then wait from day to day? Everything in the garden that wants to flower is doing so.

 But who comes and counts all that lovely flowering? It lacks eyes to look at it.

 My eyes stray from bush to tree; I think others too would find it like a dream [like a dream].

 And among all the dear friends who still love me and are left to me, I wish that you were here [that you, that you were here]!

The words seem to amount only to a naïve holiday postcard; wish you were here. But Groth was an accomplished artist, and the message he sends is moving in its immediacy; you above all. The riot of blossom ('blüht' twice, and 'blühen') is a feast for the eyes ('an Augen', 'die meinen') to take stock of and look at. But the heart lacks the one friend without whom the flowers waste their sweetness. There is also an elegiac tinge; to any Brahms-lover the title 'Komm bald' recalls the pathos of the dying girl in *Immer leiser* (No. 187) who, with those words, implores her lover to visit her soon if he wants to see her alive.

The music enhances those messages and transmits them to other close and dear friends. It too seems to be standing in the garden, in a warm summertime A major; the piano prelude contains a hidden intertwined melody, which soon unobtrusively flowers and chimes into octaves and further repetitions at the key words 'warten', 'Tag' and 'Garten', only to relapse wistfully into single notes as the appeal is apparently unanswered. The second verse renews the same plea. There follows a direct personal address. At 'Die meinen' (My eyes) the melody emerges from its concealment and speaks out, in the rhymes 'wandern' (stray) and 'Andern' (others); the piano's offbeat chords accompany this impassioned recitative, which moves disconsolately flatwards down to the last 'wie ein Traum'. Here the minor mode says sadly that no one will come, and the garden will fade for yet another summer. But then the reprise adds, with compelling conviction, that what really matters is the abiding love of old and dear friends; and all who feel thus will find this song a perpetual joy.

NOTES. 1. The North German Groth, who was 66 at the time, sent these verses to his dear friend and fellow-countryman Brahms as a 52nd birthday greeting in May 1885. The composer in turn soon sent his setting to the young singer Hermine Spies, whom they both much admired.

2. The melody takes precedence; there should be no vocal stress on 'von', 'an', 'vom' or 'und' in bars 7, 9, 18 and 32 respectively despite the downbeats. In bar 18 the Peters 'von' needs correction to 'vom'.

3. The sigh of M21 and the loving thirds of M18 are both contained in the hidden inner voice heard in the first two verses, which is itself motivic (M38); at the moment when it speaks out loud in the piano part, the voice is singing its heartfelt first 'wärst du dabei'. In the third verse the omitted downbeats are M29 and the hemiola at the second 'wärs wie ein Traum' is M14. The top G on 'mir' is M10.

4. The inner voice that sings almost throughout this song is heard at 'heiter' and 'geschmücket' in Schumann's solo song *Sonntag*, with the same 3/4 time-signature, as if in expressive remembrance.

5. There are also affinities with Brahms's own *Ein Sonett* (No. 24), which suggest that he also thought of *Komm bald* as a love-song.

6. The strong rhythmic and harmonic kinship between bars 5–6 here and the opening of the violin sonata Op. 100 (1886) serves to confirm the fact established by that work's later quasi-quotation of *Wie Melodien* (No. 186), that this sonata-movement was inspired by Brahms's Groth settings.

7. The *Gesamtausgabe* right-hand chords after the second 'wärs' need an F natural.

185. (Op. 97, No. 6) Trennung (Separation) by 1885
Anon.: Swabian   F major e'–f"

> Da unten im Tale
> Läufts Wasser so trüb,
> Und i kann dirs net sagen,
> I hab di so lieb.
>
> Sprichst allweil von Liebe,
> Sprichst allweil von Treu,
> Und a bissele Falschheit
> Is auch wohl dabei.
>
> Und wenn i dirs zehnmal sag,
> Dass i di lieb und mag,
> Und du willst nit verstehn, muss i
> Halt weiter gehn.
>
> Für die Zeit, wo du g'liebt mi hast,
> Da dank i dir schön,
> Und i wünsch, dass dirs anderswo
> Besser mag gehn.

Down there in the valley the stream is so troubled [the stream is so troubled], and I can't tell you how much I love you [how much I love you].

You always talk about love, you always talk about being true [you always talk about being true], but there's a bit of falseness in you as well [in you as well].

And when I tell you ten times how much I love you and care about you [love you and care about you] and you refuse to understand, I'll just have to go my ways [just have to go my ways].

For the time when you loved me, I thank you kindly; and I hope you fare better elsewhere [yes, fare better elsewhere].

The prelude's falling phrases perfectly express the prevailing mood of loving valediction. Thereafter the gentle keyboard flow of even quavers takes its rise from the sadly troubled stream, itself an image of tears. The tinges of bitterness or asperity are also limpidly mirrored by the accompaniment, notably in the passing sharp at the second 'läufts Wasser' (the stream runs) and the apt hint of false relations at 'i hab di so lieb' (I love you so). The interludes echo the prelude in diminution, as if waving goodbye. The refined revision of the original melody and the skilled and subtle accompaniment elevate this work to one of the finest folk-inspired art-songs ever composed.

NOTES. I. Brahms drew this text, like No. 183, from the Kretzschmer–Zuccalmaglio *Deutsche Volkslieder* (ii 1840). According to Friedländer (133–4), the original Swabian folk-song was regularly performed in a chirpy and cheeky vein; but this claim seems to be founded solely on one performance put on specially for him. His complaint that Brahms added a 'sentimental strain, as if the separation had deeper and more painful causes' is accordingly baseless. Of course the song was always sad and serious, as its text confirms. Brahms treated it thus in his own folk-song arrangements, notably as No. 6 of the *49 Deutsche Volkslieder*. It represents his own much-cherished theme of the girl left lonely.

2. The flow of even quavers is M5; the duetting thirds and sixths are M18. The sighs of M21 need to be brought out, even though the marked dynamic level never rises above *p* and *pp*. The diminutions are also expressive.

OPUS 105

Five songs (Lieder) for a lower voice with pianoforte accompaniment, with named poets or sources, published in October 1888.

These are presumably the original keys, since the higher voice edition is described as 'transposed'.

186. (Op. 105, No. 1) Wie Melodien (Like melodies) 1886
Klaus Groth   A major a–e″

Wie Melodien zieht es
Mir leise durch den Sinn,
Wie Frühlingsblumen blüht es
Und schwebt wie Duft dahin.

Doch kommt das Wort und fasst es
Und führt es vor das Aug,
Wie Nebelgrau erblasst es
Und schwindet wie ein Hauch.

Und dennoch ruht im Reime
Verborgen wohl ein Duft,
Den mild aus stillem Keime
Ein feuchtes Auge ruft.

Like melodies, thoughts are passing quietly through my mind; like spring flowers they blossom and then drift away like a fragrance [away like a fragrance].

Yet when words come and capture them and bring them into my view, they turn pale like grey mist and vanish like a breath [and vanish like a breath].

But there surely remains hidden within the rhyme a certain fragrance that has been gently summoned out of the silent blossom by a tearful eye [that has been gently summoned out of the silent blossom by a tearful, a tearful eye].

The poem sows a packet of mixed metaphor to say what Karl Kraus would later elegantly formulate thus: 'Was leicht mir in den Schoss fiel,/Wie schwer muss ich's erwerben/Bang vor des Worts Verderben;/Ach, dass mir dieses Los fiel.' (Ideas that came unsought-for, how hard I had to polish them – anxious lest words demolish them. Art must, alas, be fought for.) This theme of creative difficulty may seem unpromising; but Brahms was above all adept at the art of painting subtle pastel shades of meaning in the medium of music. The song's melodies, like the poem's, are metaphors for memories. The vivid vocal line is like a violin singing a forlorn love-song from long ago; the words selected for repetition tell of departure and tears. But, as the changing harmonies wistfully explain, all this has been blurred and mellowed by time into a mood of smiling nostalgia, tinged only here and there with moments of regret. Thus the evanescent fragrance of the verses is distilled and preserved in this memorable masterpiece.

NOTES. 1. The textual source was Klaus Groth's *Hundert Blätter: Paralipomena zum Quickborn*, which Brahms owned. The main theme here reappears, somewhat expanded, in the opening Allegro amabile of the A major Violin Sonata Op. 100 (notably at bars 51–4, 67–70, 188–91, 204–7), also composed in the summer of 1886.

2. The rising arpeggios are M9; the right-hand thirds at bars 7–10, 22–4, 36–40 are M18. The descending melody at 'schwindet wie ein Hauch' and the postlude's Amen cadence are also expressive, like the flattened sixths at bar 19 and the downward left-hand octaves at bars 34–5 (in the sense of 'greyness, pallor' or 'summoning, beckoning' respectively).

3. The meaningfulness of those last two examples can also be inferred from their departure from the the basic strophic structure (e.g. exact repetition in bars 1–6 and 28–33). But why bars 17–18 should differ from 4–5 or 31–2 is less clear.

4. The progression at bars 8–9 recurs in *Immer leiser* (No. 187) at bars 14–15, with the same significance of half-heard sounds.

5. Cf. Charles Ives's setting (?1898).

187. (Op. 105, No. 2) Immer leiser wird mein Schlummer (My sleep grows ever quieter) 1886.

Hermann Lingg   C# minor a–f′

> Immer leiser wird mein Schlummer,
> Nur wie Schleier liegt mein Kummer
>   Zitternd über mir.
> Oft im Traume hör ich dich
> Rufen draus vor meiner Tür,
> Niemand wacht und öffnet dir,
>   Ich erwach und weine bitterlich.
>
> Ja, ich werde sterben müssen,
> Eine Andre wirst du küssen,
>   Wenn ich bleich und kalt.
> Eh die Maienlüfte wehn,
> Eh die Drossel singt im Wald:
> Willst du mich noch einmal sehn,
>   Komm, o komme bald!

My sleep grows ever quieter; only my grief, like a veil, lies trembling over me [over me]. I often hear you in my dreams calling outside my door. No one wakes and lets you in; I awake and weep bitterly [weep bitterly].

Yes, I shall have to die; you will kiss another when I am pale and cold [pale and cold], before the May breezes blow, before the thrush sings in the wood: if you would see me once again, come, oh come soon [come, oh come soon].

Voice and accompaniment begin together, pianissimo, without preamble. The melody is shared, but the vocal phrases are interrupted as if consumptively short of breath; the right hand duets with itself in thirds and sixths. Thus the listener knows from the first that the girl though sick is insistent, her message though weak is urgent, and both are full of love. The bass has broken octaves that move downwards into sleep ('Schlummer'); the minor key is melancholy, but the tonal equivalent of grief ('Kummer') is deferred until the falling tones or semitones of each 'über mir' (over me). As the voice sings of its dreams, these faint moans are repeated in the right hand over weak dreamy left-hand arpeggios deprived of their first quaver beat. Thus the music's pulse is already thin. Then its expression becomes disembodied. The left hand's spread chords are rootless and floating; their successive harmonies are disconnected. Words and tones weep together at the repeated 'weine bitterlich' (weep bitterly).

The opening strains resume, this time voiceless; but the piano is heard singing the opening melody, 'immer leiser wird Schlummer', as if to itself. The bass notes are sepulchral at 'bleich und kalt' (pale and cold)). But there is no hint of self-pity or reproach, and hence no trace of sentimentality, even though the end is imminent and there will be no visit. The disembodiment resumes, again in unrelated and rootless harmonic progressions that float free from suffering, until the sighing postlude breathes a final farewell to the world. Here is the Brahmsian motivic language at its most movingly expressive.

NOTES. 1. The text was taken from Lingg's *Gedichte* (1855).

2. As so often, the theme of the deserted girl touched the deepest of responses.

3. The duetting thirds and sixths are M18; the left-hand arpeggios of dream after 'Traum' are M9; the bass notes at 'bleich und kalt' are M6/7. The dying fall of tones and semitones at each 'über mir' is M20; cf. also the minor 6–5 moaning on the second 'weine'. The omission of the first beat at bars 10–16 etc. is M29. The disembodied second inversion arpeggios on the alien chords of G, F, and C at 'niemand wacht' etc. are also manifestly expressive; they recur to symbolise final disappearance in the even remoter regions of G, B♭, and D♭ . This last chord however comes full circle; D♭ or C♯ is also the tonic major, in a Schubertian resolution (M39) which may make the ending even sadder, as if death has already come to claim the maiden.

4. The rising thirds in the last movement of the A major violin sonata Op. 100 may allude to the vocal line at bars 15–20 here; if so, the likeliest link is Hermine Spies, who sang this song so feelingly, and in expectation of whose arrival the sonata was written (Kalbeck iv 16); see also No. 184, note 1.

5. Cf. Pfitzner Op. 2 No. 6.

188. (Op. 105, No. 3) Klage (Lament) *c.* 1888
Anon.: Lower Rhine   F major d'–d''

> Feins Liebchen, trau du nicht,
> Dass er dein Herz nicht bricht!

Schön Worte will er geben,
Es kostet dein jung Leben,
Glaubs sicherlich!

Ich werde nimmer froh,
Denn mir ging es also:
Die Blätter vom Baum gefallen
Mit den schönen Worten allen,
Ist Winterzeit!

Es ist jetzt Winterzeit,
Die Vögelein sind weit,
Die mir im Lenz gesungen,
Mein Herz ist mir gesprungen
Vor Liebesleid.

Dear girl, don't trust him; then he won't break your heart. He'll give you fine words,
but they'll cost your young life, never doubt it [never doubt it].
*   I'll never be happy again, the same fate befell me; the leaves have fallen from the tree*
with all the fine words, and it's wintertime [it's wintertime].
*   Now it's wintertime, the birds are far away that sang to me in the spring, my heart*
is broken with the sorrow of love [with the sorrow of love].

The girl advises a friend and then reveals her own sorrows. Here is Brahms too at
his most sympathetic and confiding. The opening melody is as it were dictated by
the first words, 'Feins Liebchen, trau du nicht'. The same strain recurs, followed
by simple sequences and a cadential phrase with typical verbal repetition for
enhanced effect and a further echo from the piano at the end of each verse; the
successive postludes sigh 'sicherlich … Winterzeit … Liebesleid' in a cumulative
summary of the music's melancholy message. This perfect page says much in a
small compass; but it looks (and can easily sound) tame, even trivial. It calls for
finely-judged performance if all its art-song subtleties and folk-song simplicities
are to be elicited and expressed.

NOTES. I. As in No. 183, which may date from the same period, the textual source was
the Kretzschmer–Zuccalmaglio *Deutsche Volkslieder* (ii 1840), which has 'zersprungen' not
'gesprungen' in verse three.
   2. Note Brahms's favourite theme of the deserted girl.
   3. The newly-invented vocal line has the plaintive expressive inflections of true
folksong. But the piano's equally typical mix of four bars in four-part harmony and four
of accompanied recitative followed by three in a different style again plus a six-bar postlude
of entirely novel material, is entirely typical of the Brahms art-song and quite unlike
any genuine folksong. The harmony also fluctuates from modal in the first three bars to
chromatic at each vocal cadence.
   4. The modal inflexions are M27; the absence of a first beat in bars 5–8 is M29; the
consecutive right-hand thirds or sixths in bars 9–14 are M18; the postlude's long sigh is
M21.

189. (Op. 105, No. 4) Auf dem Kirchhofe (In the churchyard) *c.* 1888
Detlev von Liliencron   C minor and major b–e♭″

> Der Tag ging regenschwer und sturmbewegt,
> Ich war an manch vergessnem Grab gewesen,
> Verwittert Stein und Kreuz, die Kränze alt,
> Die Namen überwachsen, kaum zu lesen.
>
> Der Tag ging sturmbewegt und regenschwer,
> Auf allen Gräbern fror das Wort: Gewesen.
> Wie sturmestot die Särge schlummerten,
> Auf allen Gräbern taute still: Genesen.

The day passed heavy with rain and blown by storm. I had stood by many a forgotten grave, where stone and cross were weather-beaten, the wreaths old, the names overgrown and hardly readable.

The day passed blown by storm and heavy with rain. On all the graves froze the word: Departed. How still amid the storm the coffins slumbered. On all the graves the word silently thawed into: Healed.

The word-play on 'gewesen' (departed) and 'genesen' (healed) cannot be precisely preserved. Nor is its sense notably clear or consolatory; there is no poetic assurance of posthumous achievement as in other songs (such as *Abendregen*, No. 134), still less any hint of a life to come (as in *Todessehnen*, No. 161). At most Liliencron predicts a peace as profound as Duncan's in *Macbeth*: 'After life's fitful fever he sleeps well'. But this thought inspired Brahms, together (as Max Kalbeck reports, iv 134) with a visit to a Swiss churchyard. Thus the music, like the poem, records an actual lived experience. The prelude's long organ-chords and deep pedal notes, interspersed by sweeping arpeggios, peal out into a rain-lashed graveyard, where the voice begins by describing the day. Then the sequences in voice and piano move reminiscently among the headstones at 'ich war an manch vergessnem Grab gewesen' (I had stood by many a forgotten grave), pausing to peer at the inscriptions. After 'kaum zu lesen' (hardly readable) a sombre discord and a chain of descending minor thirds envisage oblivion. The opening strains return; the minor thirds descend again at 'Gewesen' (Departed). Then comes the music of healing, in the Schubertian comfort of the major mode. As in *Abendregen*, the final chord is lifted from the dark earth to shine out like a rainbow, until the fermata finally fades; the same chord in the same key with the same significance. No song ever came closer to the restrained, almost rationalist, melancholy of the *German Requiem*.

NOTES. 1. The textual source was Liliencron's *Adjutantenritte und andere Gedichte* (1883), which Brahms owned.

2. It is said (following Kalbeck, loc. cit.) that the C major section quotes the melody by Leo Hassler harmonised as 'O Haupt voll Blut und Wunden' in Bach's *St. Matthew Passion*. But that tune is in D minor, a fourth higher than here; and the composer's allusion was surely personal and secular. Bach used that melody again in the same work, in the same notes as 'Wie sturmestot die Sär(ge)', in the chorale 'Wenn ich einmal soll

scheiden'; so those (as the harmony also confirms) will be the words that Brahms seeks to evoke. He says, in his own special idiom, that he craves a comforting presence at his own demise. The next lines are 'So scheide nicht von mir/Wenn ich den Tod soll leiden/so tritt du dann herfür'. Perhaps the C major and minor keys and pedal-points here are covert appeals to Clara (M33).

3. The three-quaver-plus-crotchet sequences in bars 9–11 reflect, deliberately or not, the transition from walking along (M1) to standing still and looking more closely; the G minor piano line at 'kaum zu lesen' returns in C major at '(ge)nesen' and the following bar, again with a motivic significance which (like the storm-arpeggios) is not encountered elsewhere.

4. The Schubertian key-change is M39. The descending minor thirds after 'lesen', the final vocal line at 'Genesen' and the postlude's Amen cadence, together with the many suggestions of church-organ voluntary, are also expressive.

190. (Op. 105, No. 5) Verrat (Betrayal) 1886
Karl Lemcke   B minor/B♭ minor F#–d#'

Ich stand in einer lauen Nacht
An einer grünen Linde,
Der Mond schien hell, der Wind ging sacht,
Der Giessbach floss geschwinde.

Die Linde stand vor Liebchens Haus,
Die Türe hört ich knarren,
Mein Schatz liess sacht ein Mannsbild raus:
'Lass morgen mich nicht harren;

Lass mich nicht harren, süsser Mann,
Wie hab ich dich so gerne!
Ans Fenster klopfe leise an,
Mein Schatz ist in der Ferne!'

Lass ab von Druck und Kuss, Feinslieb,
Du Schöner im Sammetkleide,
Nun spute dich, du feiner Dieb,
Ein Mann harrt auf der Heide.

Der Mond scheint hell, der Rasen grün
Ist gut zu unsrem Begegnen,
Du trägst ein Schwert und nickst so kühn,
Dein Liebschaft will ich segnen!

Und als erschien der lichte Tag,
Was fand er auf der Heide?
Ein Toter in den Blumen lag
Zu einer Falschen Leide.

In a mild night I stood by a green linden-tree, the moon shone brightly, the wind moved softly, the mountain stream flowed swiftly [swiftly].
   The linden stood in front of my darling's house, I heard the door creak. My love was

stealthily letting a man out: 'Don't keep me waiting tomorrow, don't keep me waiting, sweet man, how I love you! Tap gently at the window, my sweetheart is far away [yes, far away].

Leave that cuddling and kissing, my dear, and you too, handsome lad dressed in velvet; make haste, you cunning thief, a man is waiting for you on the moor, [yes, on the moor].

The moon shines bright, the green turf is fit for our meeting; you wear a sword and you nod so boldly, I want to bless your wooing [your wooing, I want to bless your wooing, your wooing, yes, to bless it]!

And when the light of dawn appeared, what did it find on the moor? A dead man lay among the flowers, to a false woman's sorrow [yes, sorrow].

The prelude to this ballad of infidelity and retribution sardonically cites Brahms's own hymn to undying love (No. 58); here too the singer is watching in the night, and the resemblance is at its most manifest just before the voice begins;

Verrat   Von ewiger Liebe

Then the story is told, at first in quasi-recitative, with piano punctuation. The menace and all its motives are vividly conveyed. At 'Linde' (linden-tree) the dark outline of the leaning figure becomes visible, as the piano reiterates the opening vocal melody; at 'der Giessbach floss geschwinde' (the mountain stream flowed swiftly) the accompaniment briefly fills with rushing movement and sound, symbolic of a murderous two-handed attack.

This idea recurs in the major, at 'Lass morgen mich nicht harren' (Don't keep me waiting tomorrow), like a caressing and embracing of the 'süsser Mann' (sweet man) thus addressed; the vocal line cruelly parodies the girl's tones. At 'Lass ab' (Leave) the wronged watcher's voice bursts out in menace; the sforzandi draw and wield a sword of their own to match that of the interloper, duly recorded later in the same symbolism at 'du trägst ein Schwert'. At the repeated 'segnen' the duel begins; after eight accented crotchet chords of thrust and and parry the death blow is dealt on a grinding and groaning dissonance. An interlude recalls the assassin's theme and adds a long echo of exhausted satisfaction. At 'und als erschien' (and when appeared) the first vocal strains recur, with an accompaniment changed from the original unobtrusive lurking rhythms into the broad brightness of 'der lichte Tag', as the day breaks. The final full minor chord, marked with a decrescendo sign, signifies triumph and tragedy together.

NOTES. I. The text was taken from Lemcke's *Lieder und Gedichte* (1861), which Brahms owned. The composer added 'ja' before his repetitions, in ballad-style, no doubt under the influence of his own folksong setting *Es reit ein Herr und auch sein Knecht* (WoO 33/28), also about jealousy and murder, and in the death-key of E♭ minor, also used here in the *più mosso* section.

2. Perhaps Clara was still in mind, as in *Von ewiger Liebe*, despite the absence here of any overt reference to her motifs. She had taken her friend and champion Theodor Kirchner (1823–1903) as a lover (Reich 209); and the waiting watcher outside the house in the cold night is a typical Brahms theme. On this interpretation, the fourfold 'A–D' at bars 26–8 might well be bidding goodbye, M34.

3. The brief interlude after the first repeated 'Heide' is surely expressive in the sense of vigorous activity, but its use is not noted elsewhere.

4. The absence of a first beat in bars 3–5 is M29; the parallel tenths in bar 7 etc. are M18. The virile horn passages at the first 'segnen' are also motivic (M22). The diminished-seventh death-blow is M25. The decrescendo sign on the final chord suggests that the accompaniment was instrumentally conceived and might well prove viable in an orchestral arrangement.

5. The cruelly guyed tones at 'Lass morgen mich nicht harren' may have provided Wolf with a pointer to his own parallel parody at 'O lieber Pate' in No. 14 of his *Italian Songbook*.

OPUS 106

Five songs (Lieder) for solo voice with pianoforte accompaniment, with named poets or sources (though Christian Reinhold is wrongly called 'Carl'), published in October 1888.

This was a higher-voice yet original-key issue; the lower-voice counterpart was called 'transposed edition'.

191. (Op. 106, No. 1) Ständchen (Serenade) *c.* 1888
Franz Kugler   G major d'–g#''

> Der Mond steht über dem Berge,
> So recht für verliebte Leut;
> Im Garten rieselt ein Brunnen,
> Sonst Stille weit und breit.
>
> Neben der Mauer im Schatten,
> Da stehn der Studenten drei
> Mit Flöt und Geig und Zither
> Und singen und spielen dabei.
>
> Die Klänge schleichen der Schönsten
> Sacht in den Traum hinein,
> Sie schaut den blonden Geliebten
> Und lispelt: 'Vergiss nicht mein!'

The moon stands over the mountain, just right for people in love; in the garden a fountain is playing, otherwise there's silence all around.

By the wall, in shadow, stand three students with flute and fiddle and zither, and sing and play [sing and play].

The sounds steal softly into the dreams of the loveliest of girls; she sees her fair-haired lover and whispers 'don't forget me!'

Even if the blonde lover was one of the serenaders, he is seen by his sweetheart only in her dreams. The music too is full of amused ironic detachment, as if in loving memory of old times. In the prelude, alternate spread chords suggest soft water-drops as well as fluting and strumming, while the right hand's alternations introduce the three young musicians with a carefree student song. This trio takes a brief bow before the voice begins with its masterly and unforgettable melody which is presented as the actual serenade. Thus the scene and the stage are set, and the miniature drama unfolds. In the music as in the poem there are two main characters surrounded by serenading. Two themes lovingly coincide yet keep their decorous distance, as the notes steal gently into a dreaming head. At 'im Garten rieselt ein Brunnen' (in the garden a fountain is playing) the vocal line as it were looks down from the window while the piano melody rises up singing the opening words about the moon over the mountains. The breadth of 'Stille' (silence) is indicated by long vocal notes.

Then the serenaders are introduced. The violin and flute play in duetting sixths; after 'drei' (three) the third instrument is introduced in alternating spread chords which recur at 'Zither' and 'spielen' (play). Meanwhile the harmonies have blurred into remote regions of music and moonlight, while the piano part adds a new excitement with wide quickening arpeggios. The student song recurs; the serenaders return to their opening strains. All ends happily, the postlude confides with its echo of the sung melody for 'vergiss nicht mein'. The final unexpected staccato chord may even indicate that the sleeping girl awakes and will recognise her lover. There is no fear that she or any other listener can ever forget this music and its amorous message.

NOTES. 1. The source was Kugler's *Gedichte* (1840), which Brahms owned. The theme of the unfulfilled lover standing outside among potential rivals may well have made a special appeal to Brahms.

2. The prelude's staccato zither chords also suggest water-music as in the duet 'Es rauschet das Wasser' Op. 28, No. 3; the right-hand student song at bars 2–3 (as at 25–6) is M19. The preparatory dominant seventh at bars 4 and 27 is M24. The intertwining counter-melodies are also motivic, like the excitedly quickening rhythms after each 'dabei' (M16) and the dream-arpeggios of M9. The key-changes from G to E at bars 8 and 31 foreshadow the new perspective in each passage (from horizon to garden in the former and from dream to vision in the latter). The final top G#, which derives its expressive quality from the word 'Geliebten' rather than the earlier 'Brunnen', is M10.

3. The careful structure is worth detailed study. Thus the first bar's implied theme

recurs at bar 13 and a tone lower in 23 before being stated in full, a third higher, at the reprise (bar 24) and repeated in its original form at bar 36. A slight variant, with an altered fifth note, is heard in the right hand at bars 4–5 (27–8) and in the voice, a third lower, at bars 8–9 (31–2), simultaneously with its corresponding inversion in voice or piano. On a smaller scale the vocal notes of 'Berge' and 'verliebte' (and later at 'Schönsten' and 'Traum hin(ein)' are inverted in the accompaniment. More generally, the ABA form is arranged thus: the prelude and first or third verse, bars 5–14 or 24–36, constrast with the second verse, bars 15–23, in which 15 is sequentially modified into 19 and 21, and 18 into 20 and (less recognisably) 22.

192. (Op. 106, No. 2) Auf dem See (On the lake) 1885
Christian Reinhold   E major d#'–g#'' (a'')

> An dies Schifflein schmiege,
> Holder See, dich sacht!
> Frommer Liebe Wiege,
> Nimm sie wohl in Acht!
>
> Deine Wellen rauschen;
> Rede nicht so laut!
> Lass mich ihr nur lauschen,
> Die mir viel vertraut!
>
> Deine Wellen zittern
> Von der Sonne Glut;
> Ob sies heimlich wittern,
> Wie die Liebe tut?
>
> Weit und weiter immer
> Rück den Strand hinaus!
> Aus dem Himmel nimmer
> Lass uns steigen aus!
>
> Fern von Menschenreden
> Und von Menschensinn,
> Als ein schwimmend Eden
> Trag dies Schifflein hin!

Nestle quietly up to our boat, lovely lake; it is a cradle of pious love, so take good care of if [take good care of it].

Your waves are resounding; speak not so loud; let me listen only to her who is confiding so much to me.

Your waves shimmer under the sun's heat; perhaps they secretly sense what love can do?

Leave the shore further and further away; from this paradise let us never land [from this paradise let us never land].

Far from the talk and the thoughts of this world, like a floating Eden carry this boat along [like a floating Eden carry it, carry this boat, carry this boat along].

Those who can accept the text on its own terms, as Brahms did, will find this setting as masterly as its self-description is exact: 'Anmutig bewegt und ausdrucksvoll' (con moto grazioso ed espressivo). The floating barcarolle prelude is buoyed on waves of dream. As the voice enters, the rowing rhythm is eased along on ripples of downward arpeggios, as it were in time with the oars. At 'Deine Wellen rauschen' and again at 'Deine Wellen zittern' (your waves resound … your waves shimmer) the music briefly swells and falls in vivid elemental images of splashing water or pulsating light; otherwise the playing arpeggios surround and protect the singing melody, as the poet implores. There is a subtle hint of extra physical effort on 'Weit und weiter' (further and further) as the left hand crotchets are shortened to quavers and the arpeggios are shared between the two hands. At 'als ein schwimmend Eden' the music grants the poet's prayer; the lake is stilled and silent. As the wave-motion abates and ceases, a long sustained right-hand note together with a time-change create an effect of effortless floating in eternity, until the barcarolle is recalled in a two-bar postlude.

NOTES. 1. The textual source was Reinhold's *Gedichte* (1853). Brahms omitted the poem's third verse, after 'vertraut'.

2. The dreamy arpeggios of the prelude and postlude are M9; they can also signify love-songs, as in the lute-accompaniment of *Serenade* (No. 99) and the wave-music of *O wüsst ich doch* (No. 120). The piano's Schubertian echo of 'holder See' after 'sacht' is also expressive. The alternative top A (which should be preferred) on 'Himmel' is M10. The final hemiolas (already anticipated at bars 4, 19 and 43) are M14.

4. Elisabet von Herzogenberg heard (ii 207) an instrumental quality in this song, which she assessed as sounding 'charming on the fiddle – better than sung, I almost think'; and she criticised the concluding harmonies as discordant with her concept of a floating Eden. But these harmonies, however surprising, arise mainly from the parallel sixths of the love-motif M18, and require interpretation in that sense.

193. (Op. 106, No. 3) Es hing der Reif (Hoarfrost was hanging) 1888
Klaus Groth   A minor d'–a''

Es hing der Reif im Lindenbaum,
Wodurch das Licht wie Silber floss.
Ich sah dein Haus, wie hell im Traum
Ein blitzend Feenschloss.

Und offen stand das Fenster dein,
Ich konnte dir ins Zimmer sehn –
Da tratst du in den Sonnenschein,
Du dunkelste der Feen!

Ich bebt, in seligem Genuss,
So frühlingswarm und wunderbar:
Da merkt ich gleich an deinem Gruss,
Dass Frost und Winter war.

Hoarfrost was hanging in the linden-tree, through which the light flowed like silver. I saw your house as, bright in a dream, a sparkling fairy castle [a sparkling fairy castle].

And your window stood open, I could see into your room –
then you stepped into the sunshine, you the darkest of fairies!
I trembled in blissful pleasure, filled with springtime warmth and wonder; but
I instantly gathered from your greeting that it was frost and winter time [that it was
frost and winter time].

'Dreamily' is the direction; and the poem describes a dream. So left-hand arpeggios in a persistent lullaby rhythm come drifting upwards throughout the song, save when at the word 'offen' the accompaniment stands still to look through the open window. There the melody is moulded into recitative; elsewhere the vocal line has a folk-song simplicity which is lost if the tempo is too slow.

NOTES. 1. The source was Groth's *Hundert Blätter: Paralipomena zum Quickborn* (1854), which Brahms owned. Brahms always responded with especial empathy to the theme of standing outside in the cold, which he felt was his own fate. His own adored dark lady, also quite unlike the traditionally golden-haired good luck fairy, was Clara; so the piano's ominous statement of her theme's last four notes, B♭–A–G#–A (M33), at the final 'Frost und Winter war', may be no coincidence.

2. The ubiquitous arpeggios of dream are M9; the moaning minor seconds in the vocal entry, the interludes that follow 'sehn' and frame 'ich bebt', and the four-bar postlude, are M20; the silences in the recitative section are M29; the top notes, e.g. at the second 'blitzend' and on 'dir', are M10. The flattened supertonic is also motivic in the sense of 'Frost' (M23) in the final vocal phrase.

194. (Op. 106, No. 4) Meine Lieder (My songs) 1888
Adolf Frey   F# minor e#'–f#''

> Wenn mein Herz beginnt zu klingen
> Und den Tönen löst die Schwingen,
> Schweben vor mir her und wieder
> Bleiche Wonnen, unvergessen
> Und die Schatten von Zypressen.
> Dunkel klingen meine Lieder!

When my heart begins to make music, when it unfolds the wings of melody
*   then I see hovering back and forth before me pale joys, unforgotten, and the*
shadows of cypress trees. My songs sound dark [my songs sound dark]!

The final phrase might serve as an epigraph for many a Brahms song; far too many, his detractors will say. As so often, the lyric seems specially selected to reflect his own private griefs and grievances. But only its general mood and imagery are matched in the music, which floats free yet seems sombre, like a bird at twilight. Again the expression sounds more instrumental than vocal, like an excerpt from a violin sonata, as Elisabet von Herzogenberg had suggested about *Auf dem See* (No. 92, note 4); and she also described this one, her favourite, in terms of absolute music. The words are indeed pegged and stretched out along the melodic line, as if they really belonged elsewhere, e.g. at 'und die Schatten von Zypressen' (and the shadows of cypress trees).

But the musical craftsmanship is as impeccable as ever. In typically Brahmsian fashion, a different song seems to begin after every few bars; yet the total effect is seamless. The four-bar prelude also serves as postlude, but with an added inner melody, as if the thoughts of love had turned a solo into a duet. The prelude is repeated as the voice strikes in. After 'löst die Schwingen' (unfolds the wings) the right hand sounds out high in the treble, before the vocal line continues in canon, again symbolising a duality. This second presence within the music is the source of those ghostly memories that haunt the singer anew, but also of the darkness in which they dwell. At the repeated 'dunkel klingen meine Lieder' (my songs sound dark) the voice is shadowed in unison and then drifts down into the depths of the keyboard – a passage especially admired by Elisabet von Herzogenberg, who was well placed to fathom its underlying significance.

NOTES. 1. The text is taken from Frey's *Gedichte* (1886), which Brahms owned.

2. The melody at 'löst die Schwingen', heard again in augmentation before and at the next words, is a Clara-theme (M33) which links on to yet another, all in voice and piano together, as the heart flies free on wings of song.

3. The flights of falling arpeggios are M3; the left-hand ascending arpeggios are M9; the canon is M12; the sad minor 6–5, D–C#, deliberately inserted into the penultimate bar, is M20, and the inner voice is M38.

195. (Op. 106, No. 5) Ein Wanderer (A Traveller) 1885
Christian Reinhold   F minor e'–a♭"

> Hier, wo sich die Strassen scheiden,
> Wo nun gehn die Wege hin?
> Meiner ist der Weg der Leiden,
> Dess ich immer sicher bin.
>
> Wandrer, die des Weges gehen,
> Fragen freundlich: wo hinaus?
> Keiner wird mich doch verstehen,
> Sag ich ihn, wo ich zu Haus.
>
> Reiche Erde, arme Erde,
> Hast du keinen Raum für mich?
> Wo ich einst begraben werde,
> An der Stelle lieb ich dich.

Here, where the roads divide – where do the paths now lead?
  Mine is the path of suffering; of that I can always be certain [be certain].
  Other travellers on the path ask affably 'whither bound?'. But none of them will understand me if I tell him where I am at home [where I am at home].
  Rich earth, poor earth, have you no place for me? Where I shall be buried one day, in that place I shall love you [I shall love you]!

The music corresponds closely with the verbal ideas. First the brief prelude serves as a signpost to melancholy, whatever route is taken. Then the two hands audibly go their separate ways in contrary motion, just as 'die Strassen scheiden' (the roads divide):

At 'meiner ist der Weg der Leiden' (mine is the path of suffering) the falling bass line submits to its inevitable fate and disappears downhill into darkness. The sighing semiquavers at each 'sicher bin' (be certain) suggest that unrequited love lies at the centre of all this suffering. But now the music becomes rather barren, in the absence of verbal inspiration. The other travellers are treated rather perfunctorily, with spikily stand-offish rhythms at 'Keiner wird mich … verstehen' (no one will understand me). But the despair and doom of the last verse are aptly introduced by a musical death-wish of descending octaves and rounded off by a final reference to the same falling theme.

NOTES. 1. The textual source was Reinhold's *Gedichte* (1853), which Brahms owned.

2. The prelude's Schumannian image for melancholy is designedly expressive, as confirmed by its brief reappearance in low thirds as if from afar, at bar 13. When this idea recurs before the last verse it wears the mourning octaves of M6/7, already heard in single notes at bars 7–8, before a final repetition in the last three bars. The contrary motion is M13. Also expressive are the piano echoes of the vocal questions after 'Wege hin?' and 'wo hinaus?'. The minor 6–5 in bar 4, left hand, and again at the beginning of bars 10 and 11, right hand, is M20; the top G on 'ich' is M10; the intensified dominant seventh after 'zu Haus' is M24; the dream arpeggio of M9, often associated with death, is heard in the last two bars.

OPUS 107

Five songs (Lieder) for solo voice with pianoforte accompaniment, with named poets, published in November 1888. Like Op. 106, this was a higher-voice yet original-key issue; the lower-voice version was called a 'transposed edition'.

196. (Op. 107, No. 1) An die Stolze (To the proud one) 1886
Paul Flemming   A major e′–a″

> Und gleichwohl kann ich anders nicht,
> Ich muss ihr günstig sein,
> Obgleich der Augen stolzes Licht
> Mir missgönnt seinen Schein.
> Ich will, ich soll, ich muss dich lieben,
> Dadurch wir beid uns nur betrüben,

Weil mein Wunsch doch nicht gilt
Und du nicht hören wilt.

Wie manchen Tag, wie manche Nacht,
Wie manche liebe Zeit
Hab ich mit Klagen durchgebracht,
Und du verlachst mein Leid!
Du weisst, du hörst, du siehst die Schmerzen
Und nimmst der keinen doch zu Herzen,
So dass ich zweifle fast
Ob du ein Herze hast.

And yet I can do no other, I must be lovingly disposed towards her, even though the proud light of her eyes denies me its shine. I will, I shall [I shall], I must love you, which brings only sorrow to us both because my wishes are unregarded and you will not listen [and you will not listen].

How many a day, how many a night, how much dear time,
have I spent in lamenting, yet you mock my distress! You know, you hear [you hear], you see my pains, yet you take none of them to heart, so that I almost doubt whether you have a heart at all [whether you have a heart at all].

The poem and its setting have already begun as it were off-stage, like many a Shakespeare scene. The singer continues his fast and expressive train of thought. The accompaniment too sets off in a flash of immediacy; the pulse is already racing, and there is no time for preliminaries. But the first hearers were puzzled; the music is all too audibly forced to fit the poem by pointless repetition and other devices. Elisabet von Herzogenberg (who may well have been the undeclared subject; see note 1) thought that Flemming's 'proud one' was not the same as the composer's; she discerned a rift between text and music (ii 206). Many will share that impression, but not everyone will demur; irreconcilable disparity is after all the main theme, as often in Wolf. But the typical Brahms style is far more direct and personal; and the underlying idea in this song, marked 'very lively and expressive', is surely the tone of loving yet exasperated despair occasionally heard in his letters to Elisabet as well as often in those to Clara.

On any interpretation the bitter words contrast sharply with the sweet music. Even the chromatics at 'Ich will' etc sound more resigned than anguished, while the ensuing quasi-operatic declamation and sequential melody are cheerfully high-spirited. The professed plight is not taken too tragically after all.

NOTES. 1. The text, from which Brahms omitted two more verses in the same vein, is taken from Flemming's posthumous *Geistliche und Weltliche Poemata* (1660). That volume was not found in Brahms's library; and the only other settings he made from it (the four-part *Geistliches Lied* Op. 30 and *O Liebliche Wangen*, No. 70) both date from about 1860, when he was in love with the young Elisabet, née Stockhausen. There are certain affinities of key and style with No. 70; so perhaps this song also began as an early homage. For what it is worth, her musical initials E–S (=D#) appear in the voice at bars 4–5 and 34–5 (M35).

2. The strict strophic structure deserves special study. The first 30 bars are laid out thus: six (1–6) + four (7–10) + three (11–13) + two (14–15) + two (16–17) + four (18–21) + six

(22–7) + three (28–30). This pattern is repeated for the second verse, except that 31–4 is
an octave higher than 1–4, for no very clear reason. Each group contains new material,
except 7–10 (37–40), which are 1–4 as it were reorchestrated with treble chords instead of
bass notes.

3. The long left-hand quasi-cello tune, though manifestly motivic in intent, is not
noted in the same form elsewhere. The arpeggios after 'günstig sein' (be lovingly disposed),
are akin to M9. The missing crotchets and recitative mode at 'dadurch' are M29. At the
preceding word (bars 16–17) the enhanced dominant is M24, and the long minor moan
F–E is M20, which is apt for both 'Lieben' in the first verse and 'Schmerzen' in the second,
since these are equated. Similarly a poignant augmented chord effectively introduces both
'betrüben' and 'Herzen'. But perhaps the vocal line was dictated by each verse independently; thus the the long high five-crotchet F natural (M10) is far apter for the stressed
'muss' than for the neutral 'siehst', whereas the vocal leap to the top A at 'verlachst' (M10)
suits that idea well, but sounds ungainly at the earlier 'seinen'. The alternating thirds at bars
21–9 etc. and the augmentation are alike expressive; the rhythmic change there (hemiola)
is M14.

197. (Op. 107, No. 2) Salamander (Salamander) 1888
Karl Lemcke   A minor and major e′–g″

> Es sass ein Salamander
> Auf einem kühlen Stein,
> Da warf ein böses Mädchen
> Ins Feuer ihn hinein.
>
> Sie meint, er soll verbrennen,
> Ihm war erst wohl zu Mut,
> Wohl wie mir kühlem Teufel
> Die heisse Liebe tut.

*A salamander was sitting on a cool stone. Then a bad girl flung it right into the fire
[right into the fire].*

  *She thought it would burn up, but it was in its element as never before – just as hot
love suits a cool devil like me [how well hot love suits a cool devil like me].*

The playful arpeggios frisk to and fro, as if the composer were imagining the
lizard's earlier activity before settling down. At 'da warf ein böses Mädchen' (a bad
girl flung) the quavers aptly assume a contrary motion. Then the piano's right
hand flicks 'ins Feuer', disdainfully yet effectively (as shown on p. 7) in gestures
which are then deftly fashioned into a more powerful image of throwing. The
interlude briefly recalls the opening melody's salamander theme, which then duly
tails off. What happened next? asks the music anxiously, still in the minor. The
answer arrives in the major, with Schubertian ease and assurance. Now the falling
and rising arpeggios amusingly depict the salamander frolicking amid the flames,
unscathed. The equally Schubertian right hand echo of enquiry after 'verbrennen'
adds further meaning. Burnt up? Me? Never. On the contrary, 'ihm ward erst
wohl zu Mut' (it was in its element as never before), again with contrary motion
and repeated throwing gestures to show that the idea turned out unexpectedly

well. The postlude sounds ambiguous, first elated then gloomy; but the final broad chords beam beatifically.

NOTES. 1. The source was Lemcke's *Lieder und Gedichte* (1861), which Brahms owned. According to Pliny (*Historia Naturalis* x, 86; xxix, 23), the salamander was a lizard-like monster enabled, by its own bodily coolness, to live in fire. The name and the legend were later applied to the harmless newt-like amphibians now so called. Their symbolism of imperviousness to physical passion appealed to erotic poets; Brahms was no doubt also familiar with his favourite Daumer's treatment of the same theme 'Ich bin ein Salamander', in *Hafis*, 1846. The autobiographical aspects are manifest; Brahms often selected themes of passion and coolness. He might even have been pointing to one girl in particular, namely Elisabet von Stockhausen, as his own tormentor; note E–S (E♭, as D#) in the right hand at 'ins Feuer ihn' and in the vocal melody at 'wie mir' or '(hei)sse Liebe'. Such allusions would be entirely typical; and so is the 20-year time-lag between feeling and song.

   2. The moving arpeggios are M1; the throwing motif is M2; the dominant and pause before the key-change are M24. The Schubertian key-changes are M39; the contrary motion is M13; the postlude's ruefully flattened seventh and sixth are M41. The Schubertian echoes are also expressive.

198. (Op. 107, No. 3) Das Mädchen spricht (The girl speaks) 1886
Otto Gruppe   A major e'–f#"

> Schwalbe, sag mir an,
> Ists dein alter Mann,
> Mit dem du's Nest gebaut?
> Oder hast du jüngst erst
> Dich ihm vertraut?
>
> Sag, was zwischert ihr,
> Sag, was flüstert ihr
> Des Morgens so vertraut?
> Gelt, du bist wohl auch noch
> Nicht lange Braut?

Tell me, swallow, is it your last year's mate that you're building a nest with [building a nest with]?
   Or are you but newly betrothed to him [betrothed to him]?
   Say, what are you both twittering, say, what are you both whispering so intimately each morning [so intimately each morning]?
   I know; you haven't long been a bride either, have you [haven't long been a bride]?

The music's sprightly responsiveness to the verses suggests that their identification of bird and bride had made a special appeal to Brahms. Such locutions as 'alter Mann' (last year's mate, literally 'old man') and 'flüstert' (whispering) are designed to evoke human marriage and newly-wed pillow-talk. The former colloquialism antagonised Elisabet von Herzogenberg (ii 206); perhaps she also felt that the bird's implied possible change of partner was too flighty. But time disperses all such objections, and the dancingly delightful music dispels them altogether.

In the prelude the light wings rustle and snuggle together. As the voice enters, the right hand anticipates and echoes the newly-wed girl's inquisitive questionings. The piano muses to itself in new arpeggio themes, reverting at 'dich ihn vertraut' (betrothed to him) to the love-themes of the prelude, now heard in due solemnity much lower in the keyboard, like organ-tones. To start the second verse, the right-hand bird-music is aptly embellished with extra twitterings; then the music reverts to its original form with the prelude repeated as postlude and cheerfully resolved. The questions are definitively answered.

NOTES. 1. The text was taken from Gruppe's *Gedichte* (1835), which Brahms owned.

2. *Dort in den Weiden* (No. 183) provides a pleasant parallel; there too the girl understands the nightingale's song because she also ('auch' in both contexts) is about to be married. The occasional affinities between the present song and *Spanisches Lied* (No. 9) may suggest that Brahms sensed a similar newly-betrothed and flirtatious mood in that text too.

3. The prelude's winnowing wings are M3; its expectant dominant seventh in bar 4 is M24; all the duet-music, such as the sixths at 'Nest gebaut', is M18. The arpeggios before and during 'oder hast du', though clearly expressive in the sense of musing and wondering, are not noted in the same context elsewhere.

199. (Op. 107, No. 4) Maienkätzchen (May Catkins) *c.* 1887
Detlev von Liliencron   B♭ major f'–g''

> Maienkätzchen, erster Gruss,
> Ich breche euch und stecke euch
> An meinen alten Hut.
>
> Maienkätzchen, erster Gruss,
> Einst brach ich euch und steckte euch
> Der Liebsten an den Hut.

May catkins, first greeting, I pluck you and pin you on my old hat.
   May catkins, first greeting [first greeting], once I plucked you and pinned you on my sweetheart's hat [once I plucked you and pinned you on my sweetheart's hat].

Springtime's first greeting is ironically transformed into an omen of parting, a sign of lost love. From this rather unpromising lyric Brahms fashions a memorable garland of wistful nostalgia, on his favourite themes of separation and sadness. But here the singer is male; the wound is less painful and the music less poignant. A two-bar prelude anticipates the vocal line at 'einst brach ich euch' (once I plucked you) etc.; thus the sad outcome is foreseen long before the situation is described, and the song begins as it were in the past tense. And the story itself is designedly old hat. Its musical equivalent, as the voice enters, is a sedate formal ländler with thirds and sixths in the right hand and a drone in the left like the village band with fiddles and a string bass, varied with fuller woodwind chords, on some forgotten market day in a bygone springtime.

The preluding dotted rhythm recurs in an interlude. Now the first insouciant vocal melody is again flattened and prolonged by extended time-values (as at the double 'erster Gruss', first greeting) and also by verbal repetition, to suggest the lapse of time since that sad separation. In the postlude a falling sigh dwindles and departs with real regret before the strong final cadence recovers composure.

NOTES. 1. The text, like that of No. 189, is taken from Liliencron's *Adjutantenritte und andere Gedichte* (1883), which Brahms owned; its blend of art-lyric and folk-song styles is finely recreated here.

2. Perhaps the shared hat-decoration, for the hand of a lost lover, and the faded flowers, reminded Brahms of his own *Agnes* music, in No. 104 above; here too the folk-song strains seem to take the floor as a country dance, in a rhythm that recalls his setting of Mörike's first line 'Rosenzeit, wie schnell vorbei'. The motto-theme here may also recall Agathe (M32), with the characteristic pattern

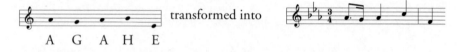

A   G   A   H   E   transformed into

and variants, in bars 1–2, 9–10, 11–12, 17–18, etc.

3. The thirds and sixths are M18; the top G on 'einst' is M10; the postlude's falling phrase in single notes is a long regretful sigh, as in *Mädchenlied* (No. 200). In bars 15–16, the flattened seventh is motivic (M41); the augmentation there, at 'erster Gruss', is expressive, and so are the postlude's dwindling single-note descent and its last two forte chords. But these should not be overstated; they merely mean that a chapter is closed, not that the book of remembrance itself is slammed shut.

200. (Op. 107, No. 5) Mädchenlied (Girl's song) *c.* 1887
Paul Heyse   B minor f#'–f#''

> Auf die Nacht in den Spinnstub'n,
> Da singen die Mädchen,
> Da lachen die Dorfbub'n,
> Wie flink gehn die Rädchen!
>
> Spinnt Jedes am Brautschatz,
> Das der Liebste sich freut.
> Nicht lange, so gibt es
> Ein Hochzeitgeläut.
>
> Kein Mensch, der mir gut ist,
> Will nach mir fragen;
> Wie bang mir zu Mut ist,
> Wem soll ichs klagen?
>
> Die Tränen rinnen
> Mir übers Gesicht –
> Wofür soll ich spinnen?
> Ich weiss es nicht!

At night in the spinning-room, the girls sing, the village lads laugh, how briskly the wheels turn!

Every girl is spinning for her trousseau, to please her beloved; before long, there'll be wedding-bells.

Nobody who loves me wants to ask for me; how sick at heart I feel, to whom can I tell my sorrow?

The tears trickle down my face. What am I spinning for? I don't know [I don't know, I don't know]!

Heyse's poem is typically well-turned; the music transforms it into true pathos. The wheel spins in semiquaver arpeggios; the vocal line interweaves ascending sequences which are extended by the right hand to a tense climax whence successive staccato thirds fall like tears. The third verse varies; the sequences are heard in canon, like a conversation with a longed-for but imaginary lover. At 'die Tränen rinnen' (the tears trickle) the wheel stops and the tonic pedal tolls tragically, with a sighing echo of 'übers Gesicht' (down my face) from the piano. The descending thirds in the voice at 'wofür soll ich spinnen' (what am I spinning for?) confirm the tearful plaint of the earlier interludes, which recur in the postlude.

NOTES. 1. The textual source was Heyse's 1885 *Gedichte*, which has 'Spinnstuben' and 'Dorfbuben' in the first quatrain, 'Hochzeitsgeläut' in the second and 'Wofür ich soll spinnen,/Ich weiss es nicht!' in the last. Deliberately or not, the composer's changes add the locutions and the immediacy of folk-song.

2. The poet was an admirer of Brahms and Schumann (who had also set his lyrics), and the theme of the love-lorn and lonely girl must also have made a special appeal. It may not be by coincidence that each verse begins with the Clara theme M33, in its characteristic B minor mode.

3. The descending thirds at bars 9–11 etc. are expressive, as in the postlude to *Maienkätzchen* (No. 199); the tear-drop staccato here is M28.

4. Cf. Schumann Op. 107, No. 4.

OPUS 121

Four serious songs (Gesänge) for a bass voice with pianoforte accompaniment, dedicated to Max Klinger, published in July 1896. The title-page makes no mention of the Biblical sources.

Self-deprecatory as ever, Brahms affected to make light of these serious songs, even going so far as to call them 'gottlose Schnaderhüpfeln' in writing to Elisabet von Herzogenberg (ii 275). They are certainly godless in that their texts, though Biblical, are (as the same source explains, 272) 'not only antidogmatic but also in part unbelieving'.[1] The untranslatable 'Schnaderhüpfeln' is a South German expression meaning haymakers' lively songs and dances at harvest-time. As usual, there was a vein of deep earnestness within the Brahmsian irony; he was contemplating his own lifetime's harvest of accomplishment, and surely with real celebration. In these great songs the unbeliever recreates his own credo. He would

[1] i.e. 'ungläubig', which the unreliable English translation of 1909 wrongly renders as 'incredible', no doubt by confusion with 'unglaubhaft'.

die as he had lived, proclaiming the supremacy of work and love, yet welcoming extinction and non-existence once the end had come. He finds these unfamiliar and indeed unChristian sentiments in Luther's translation of the Bible, which distils the heady grandeur of Old Testament (or Apocryphal) Hebrew and New Testament Greek into plain German. This can lead to difficulties of interpretation among English audiences; the directness of the music makes a marvellous match for the German texts, but sounds less concordant with the familiar words of the King James Bible. Hence the policy adopted here of rendering Luther's prose by direct literal translation. The Authorised Version texts are supplied in the Notes, for purposes of comparison.

In expressing his own eschatology, the doctrine of last and final things, in these last and final songs, Brahms was brave; for he stood in the shadow of death – his own, as well as Clara Schumann's. He was to share his father's fate and die slowly of a liver cancer, in April 1897. And that affliction had already begun when he composed or completed Op. 121, early in May 1896. In the same month Clara died, at 77, having rallied sufficiently to scribble a few touchingly illegible lines for his birthday on 7 May. In July he wrote to her daughters Marie and Eugenie; 'Such texts have long preoccupied me; and although I did not expect having to receive worse news about your mother, something often speaks and works within the human being, almost unknown to us, and this may well sometimes resound as poetry or music'. Those words well describe the genesis of these four enduring masterpieces.

201. (Op. 121, No. 1) Denn es gehet dem Menschen (Man and beast) 1896

Ecclesiastes (Der Prediger Salomo) 3. 19–22[1]   D minor A–f′

Denn es gehet dem Menschen wie dem Vieh, wie dies stirbt, so stirbt er auch, und haben alle einerlei Odem; und der Mensch hat nichts mehr denn das Vieh; denn es ist alles eitel.

Es fährt alles an einen Ort; es ist alles von Staub gemacht, und wird wieder zu Staub.

Wer weiss, ob der Geist des Menschen aufwärts fahre, und der Odem des Viehes unterwärts unter die Erde fahre?

Darum sahe ich, dass nichts bessers ist, denn dass der Mensch fröhlich sei in seiner Arbeit; denn das ist sein Teil. Denn wer will ihn dahin bringen, dass er sehe, was nach ihm geschehen wird?

19. For it goes with the man as with the beast; as the one dies, so dies the other [as the one dies, so dies the other];

*   and they all have but one breath [and they all have but one breath], and the man has no more than the beast; for all is vain [for all is vain].*

*   20. All goes to one place, all is made of dust, and becomes dust again.*

---

[1] Not 18–22, as in the *Gesamtausgabe*.

21. Who knows whether the spirit of man travels upward [travels upward, travels upward]

*   and the breath of the beast travels downwards, under the earth [downwards, under the earth]?*

22. So I saw that there is nothing better than that a man should rejoice in his work, for that is his lot.

*   For who shall bring him to see what shall happen after him [what shall happen after him]?*

The prelude is a cortège, in which the voice joins; the repeated piano notes toll a knell. The high crying melody at the second 'wie dies stirbt' is a double lament, for our mortality and for its apparent unfairness, as if humanity deserved better. The interlude insists on these tragic themes. As the funeral bell continues to toll, inner voices intone the initial stepwise vocal lines at 'Denn es' and 'Menschen wie dem (Vieh)' (with the man as with the (beast))[1], each repeated in different pitches with the latter in canon like a procession of chanting monks. This rejoins and swells the cortège at 'und der Mensch' (and the man), with another anguished outcry at the second 'es ist alles eitel' (all is vain). Before that last syllable has ended, the dust begins to fly about in a desolating sound-picture of swirling specks over a dry staccato ground, ending on the repeated key word 'Staub' (dust) with a profound and prolonged dominant asking anxiously whether this can indeed be so. Even as the dust gradually subsides, the voice is heard crying out 'Who knows?' ('Wer weiss'). Its octave drop is echoed by the piano in the same dying fall, as if the question is already subconsciously settled before it is posed. The great right-hand chords offer gestures of farewell; in the interlude after the last 'aufwärts fahre' (travels upwards) the dust drifts ominously downwards, as if in denial. The gestures resume at 'und der Odem des Viehes' (and the breath of the beast) and reintroduce the procession at 'Darum sahe ich' (So I saw); after 'Teil' (lot) the dust whirls around once more. On the last page, the ominous pedal points and slow trills toll and boom like funeral bells and muffled drums. The last two chords recall the earlier 'Wer weiss?', as if even the consolation of bequeathing good works to posterity is itself uncertain or indeed delusory.

NOTES. 1. The Authorised Version runs: 19. For that which befalleth the sons of men befalleth beasts; even one thing befalleth them; as the one dieth, so dieth the other; yea, they have all one breath; so that a man hath no pre-eminence above a beast; for all is vanity. 20. All go unto one place; all are of the dust, and all turn to dust again. 21. Who knoweth the spirit of man that goeth upward and the spirit of the beast that goeth downward to the earth? 22. Wherefore I perceive that there is nothing better, than that a man should rejoice in his own works, for that is his portion; for who shall bring him to see what shall be after him?

2. This text for all its impressive orotundity seems less clear than Luther's (whose 'whether' is surely an improvement) and also more wordy (the phrase 'even one thing befalleth them', which has no German equivalent, is otiose).

3. The higher line at the second 'denn es ist alles eitel', with its echo of 'wie dies stirbt' should certainly be sung.

4. As ever, the textual repetitions emphasise the composer's personal concerns. Everything dies and returns to dust; all is vanity, except one's duty to one's own work,

which offers the only possible survival and salvation; and even that is unsure. This ideal, already optimistically adumbrated in *Abendregen* (No. 134), made a double appeal to Brahms the painstaking craftsman no less than the inspired artist.

5. Brahms recalls his own *Requiem* Op. 45. Thus the opening vocal melody here runs parallel to that of the equally processional 'Denn alles Fleisch'. Compare also the baritone solo 'Herr, lehre doch mich', in the same key as here and with much the same message of tragic transience. When all humanity is dispersed and dismissed at 'Ach, wie gar nichts' the same motif of broken diminished sevenths (M25) is heard as when the dust whirls here.

6. Perhaps the insistent A–D chords and notes are also meaningful in both works, M34. The opening vocal octaves or unisons with the keyboard's inner voice combine M37 and M38. The later dominant questions at 'aufwärts fahre' and 'unter die Erde fahre?' are M24, like the prolonged dominant interlude after the latter. Meanwhile the effortful two-handed chords are also expressive, with the omitted first beat as in M29, which recurs, after the final fermata, further enhanced by the addition of a dotted minim rest, i. e. in peace. Meanwhile the penultimate chord is also motivic in its syncopation for surprise effect, as shown by its unexpected accented appearance on the eighth beat of a 9/4 bar.

202. (Op. 121, No. 2) Ich wandte mich (Evil under the sun) 1896
Ecclesiastes (Der Prediger Salomo) 4. 1–3.   G minor and major G–e'

Ich wandte mich, und sahe an alle, die Unrecht leiden unter der Sonne; und siehe, da waren Tränen derer, die Unrecht litten und hatten keinen Tröster, und die ihnen Unrecht täten, waren zu mächtig, dass sie keinen Tröster haben konnten.

Da lobte ich die Toten, die schon gestorben waren, mehr als die Lebendigen, die noch das Leben hatten;

Und der noch nicht ist, ist besser als alle beide, und des Bösen nicht inne wird, das unter der Sonne geschieht.

1. I turned and looked at all who suffer wrong under the sun [who suffer wrong under the sun]; and behold [behold] there were tears [tears] of those who suffered wrong and had no comforter, and they who wronged them were too mighty, so that they could have no [no] comforter.

2. So I praised the dead who had already died more than the living who still had life.

3. And whoever does not yet exist is better than both, and is not aware of the evil that happens under the sun.

The prelude's downward movement in broken octaves already yearns for death, long before that theme is mentioned. The voice enters to the same music shrouded in chords, as if 'Ich wandte mich' (I turned) takes a last look back at suffering humanity from the very brink of the grave. At first, the prospect is bleak but bearable. The brief right-hand interlude theme after 'Sonne' is first echoed in sequential augmentation at 'siehe' (behold), then repeated verbatim by the voice at 'da waren Tränen' and again echoed in augmentation a tone higher at the second 'Tränen'. The same ideas recur at 'dass sie keinen, keinen' (that they ... no, no). The words are repeated to underline the musical imagery of close and detailed scrutiny. The scene, though sad, is not set as tragedy. Brahms feels, with his chosen text, that this is how life must be; the strong oppress the weak. At 'Da lobte ich die Toten' (So I praised the dead) the prelude's broken octaves descend into darkness again, with a right-hand chordal reiteration of that last word. The same idea serves to stress each accented syllable of 'schon gestorben waren' (who had already died); the words and ideas are again underlined in the music as in the text. The preacher illustrates the sermon with powerful gestures of movement and stillness, departure and rest. At 'Und der noch nicht ist' (And whoever does not yet exist) the broken octaves change from the tonic minor into a diminished seventh arpeggio; the previous song's image of dust is now slowed and changed to nothingness, followed by a bar's silence in homage to non-existence. The emphatic gestures recur at 'besser als alle beide' (better than both). Nothing could be surer. Yet the music, for all its weight of grief continuously depicted in falling thirds, now becomes blissful in the tonic major. Here at last comes the comfort, which is maternally warm. The absence of tyranny turns into tenderness itself; the preacher's peroration, which is negative in the Biblical text, here suddenly sings out in positive praise of that mixture of triumph and tragedy which constitutes human existence. Perhaps this conclusion is inconsistent with the nihilistic despair in the words; but this fine music transcends them by being true to life.

NOTES. 1. The Authorised Version runs: 1. So I returned, and considered all the oppressions that are done under the sun; and behold the tears of such as were oppressed, and they had no comforter; and on the side of their oppressors there was power; but they had no comforter. 2. Wherefore I praised the dead which are already dead more than the living which are yet alive. 3. Yea, better is he than both they, which hath not yet been, who hath not seen the evil work that is done under the sun.

2. As ever, the repetitions embody the composer's personal concerns; he asks all his listeners to share the plight of the oppressed, to behold it, weep for it, and deplore the absence of a comforter. But his music offers a surrogate. As the verse he chose for the *Requiem* says: 'As one whom his mother comforteth, so will I comfort you' (Isaiah 66. 13); and there is often a close kinship of key and mood between the two works, e.g. treble D–D#–E followed by bass C#–D at the penultimate choral 'ich will euch trösten' in the Requiem V and in the piano at 'Sonne geschieht' here.

3. The preluding broken-octave descent, continued at the voice's entry and repeated at 'da lobte ich die Toten' is M6/7; so is the related treatment at 'der noch nicht ist', where the diminished-seventh harmony is M25 and the descending thirds are also expressive, like the augmentations and diminutions *passim* and the Schubertian change to the tonic major (M39) at 'und des Bösen'. Those falling left-hand thirds, a late motif of desolation (as in Nos. 199 and 200) will recur verbatim on the opening words of the next song. The ensuing bar of silence is M29. The falling semitone on the first 'leiden' and at 'könnten' is M20, heard again in the postlude after the long sigh of M21 at the last words. Then the postlude's repeated left-hand octave key-notes are M6. Earlier, the accompaniment's hemiolas at bars 15–16, 19–20 and 31–32 are M14. Especial motivic significance is expressed by the subtle equation of the first 'siehe' and the second 'Tränen' where the same chord and melody are differently distributed.

203. (Op. 121, No. 3) O Tod (O death) 1896
Ecclesiasticus (Apocrypha) 41, 1–2.   E minor and major B–f#'

O Tod, wie bitter bist du, wenn an dich gedenkt ein Mensch, der gute Tage und genug hat und ohne Sorge lebet; und dem es wohl geht in allen Dingen und noch wohl essen mag!

O Tod, wie wohl tust du dem Dürftigen, der da schwach und alt ist, der in allen Sorgen steckt, und nichts Bessers zu hoffen, noch zu erwarten hat!

1. O death [O death] how bitter [how bitter] you are when anyone thinks of you who has good days and enough and lives without troubles, and with whom all things go well and who can still eat heartily! [O death, O death, how bitter, how bitter you are.]

2. O death [O death], how kind you are to the needy man who is weak and old, who suffers all troubles and has nothing better to hope for or expect. [O death, how kind you are, how kind, how kind you are!]

As ever, Brahms's repetitions embody his own feelings. He had always yearned for release from life's fever, in many another song. Here, at sixty-three and already ailing, he imagines extinction as a healing process, like Socrates. The result is a love-song to death that stands high among the finest ever composed in the lied tradition. Death comes as a bitter menace to some, yet a sweet comfort to others; and the master of musical expression shows that these two apparently constrasting features belong to one and the same face, thus:

The song abounds in such subtle felicities. At 'wenn an dich gedenket ein Mensch' (when anyone thinks of you) the frequent yet unobtrusive canonic interchanges between voice and right-hand are thoughtfully reflective. At 'gute Tage und genug hat' (has good days and enough) the alternating hands ply greedily as their wielder eats well. At that idea, after 'essen mag', this assertive music breaks off, as if such enjoyment is too good to last, and resumes the opening outcry. Then comes a new and loving visitation. Death is all major melody in wide rising or falling intervals and tenderness in the soothing gestures of the right-hand descending note by repeated note as if slowly stroking a tired brow into sleep. The brief staccato at 'schwach und (alt)' (weak and old) touches upon the thought of failing strength. The final invocation is unforgettable; no better or more peaceful end could be imagined.

NOTES. I. In the Authorised Version (which included the Apocrypha) the text runs: I. O death, how bitter is the remembrance of thee to a man that liveth at rest in his possessions, unto the man that hath nothing to vex him, and that hath prosperity in all things; yea, unto him that is yet able to receive meat! 2. O death, acceptable is thy sentence unto the needy and unto him whose strength faileth, that is now in the last age, and is vexed with all things, and to him that despaireth, and hath lost patience!

2. The expressive falling thirds that characterised Brahms in his later years, heard for example in the previous song at the beginning of its G major section, start this song in the minor key, in the left hand as well as the voice, and are later equated with vocal rising sixths in the major key on the same tonic, as illustrated above. The canonic imitations for 'gedenket' are also motivic (M12), and the solemn A–D descent at the second 'gedenket ein Mensch' may represent the final farewell of M34. The alternating hands there are also motivic, like the soothing inner voice (M38) in the right hand in the E major section, and the frail staccato for 'schwach'. The enhanced dominant seventh at 'hat' is M24.

204. (Op. 121, No. 4) Wenn ich mit Menschen- (Love) 1896
I Corinthians (I Korinther) 13, 1–3, 12–13   E♭ major and B major A♭–g′

Wenn ich mit Menschen- und mit Engelzungen redete, und hätte der Liebe nicht, so wär ich ein tönend Erz, oder eine klingende Schelle.

Und wenn ich weissagen könnte und wüsste alle Geheimnisse und alle Erkenntnis, und hätte allen Glauben, also, dass ich Berge versetzte, und hätte der Liebe nicht, so wäre ich nichts.

Und wenn ich alle meine Habe den Armen gäbe, und liesse meinen Leib brennen, und hätte der Liebe nicht, so wäre mirs nichts nütze.

Wir sehen jetzt durch einen Spiegel in einem dunkeln Worte, dann aber von Angesicht zu Angesichte. Jetzt erkenne ichs stückweise, dann aber werd ichs erkennen, gleichwie ich erkennet bin.

Nun aber bleibet Glaube, Hoffnung, Liebe, diese drei; aber die Liebe ist die grösseste unter ihnen.

1. If I spoke with the tongues of men and of angels, and had not love, I'd be sounding bronze or a tinkling bell.

2. And if I could prophesy and knew all mysteries and all knowledge, and had all faith, so that I could remove mountains, and had not love, then I'd be nothing [then I'd be, I'd be nothing].

3. And though I gave all my goods to the poor, and let my body be burned [my body be burned], it would be no use to me.

12. We see now through a mirror, in a dark saying, but then face to face. Now I know in part, but then I shall know just as I am known.

13. Now there remains faith, hope, love, these three, but love is the greatest among them [love is the greatest among them].

As always, the textual repetitions are revealing; so, in this famous passage, are the omissions. Brahms drew no inspiration from St Paul's reflections (verse II) about putting away childish things on attaining man's estate. On the contrary; Brahms preserved his boyhood preoccupations (including his cherished set of toy soldiers) and relived them in his music. He also felt free to take for granted the apostle's eulogy of love (as long-suffering, kind, modest and so forth, verses 4–8). The words he retained sufficed to pay a supreme musical homage to that virtue, which had always constituted his own experience and practice, and hence became another main theme of his music, especially in the song form. But his interpretation of love is equally personal; and there is no surprise or incongruity in Kalbeck's inference from the textual facts (note 3 below) that parts of this song expresses the composer's much earlier love for Elisabet von Stockhausen.

The opening strains, with their vigorous left-hand leaps and jerky recurrent rhythm ♪ ♩., and their wide-ranging vocal lines, seem to suggest bodily vigour. The underlying idea, which may also derive from a discontinued song-setting (note 4), remains relevant here; in our journey through life, all our many endeavours and exertions will prove in vain without love. So whenever that latter concept is about to be mentioned, throughout the song, the piano falls silent in reverential anticipation; and the word 'Liebe' is lovingly prolonged among a contrastingly gentle flow of even quavers. At 'also, dass ich Berge versetzte' (so that I could remove mountains), the basic physical imagery emerges unmistakably; the piano's octaves and chords in contrary motion audibly (and visibly) mime grasping and displacing with both hands. The comparably dismissive gestures of the two hands in alternation (M30) are equally apt for both the 'klingende Schelle' (tinkling bell) and the later 'nichts' (nothing); for the second 'nichts nütze' (no use) both ideas combine. After the first, the descending minor thirds in octaves repeat the 'klingende Schelle' motif.

Then the song offers a complete change of key, time and mood, in order to hymn the love it has so ceaselessly celebrated thus far. The slow 3/4 crotchet melody with repeated right-hand triplet accompaniment sounds like reverential organ music in some sublime ceremony. At 'dann aber von Angesicht zu Angesichte' the triplet quavers move upward in vision, until the interlude recalls the listener to reality by quoting the melody that opened this section, and hence recalling its words 'Wir sehen jetzt durch einen Spiegel' (we see now through a mirror). Conversely the sadly falling vocal line at 'stückweise' (in part) is instantly echoed in the piano. Thus the dimness and distance of the human condition is acknowledged. But the thought of bright nearness brings back the face-to-face music of 'von Angesicht zu Angesichte', which is as close as the agnostic Brahms ever came to a communion with deity. As the pious aria ends, the humanist moral returns. But now the thought is that love reigns supreme not only among faith, hope and love, these three, but always and everywhere. Amor vincit omnia, love is lord of all; that is the humanist message now conveyed via those massive arches of melody that span the bridge passage leading on to the final repeated reassurance about 'the greatest of these'. As the high notes explain, the culminating 'Liebe' is not only the strongest but the tenderest, and indeed that its strength lies in its tenderness.

Nun aber blei - bet Glau - be, Hoff - nung,

Lie - - be, die - se drei -

NOTES. 1. Brahms makes a number of slight changes to Luther's text (such as 'Worte' for 'Wort') to suit his vocal line; and he omits 'and have not charity' after 'burned'. The *Gesamtausgabe*'s 'Engelzungen' in bar 5 should however be preferred to the Peters edition's 'Engels=zungen'.

2. The Authorised Version runs: 1. Though I speak with the tongues of men and of angels, and have not charity. I am become as sounding brass or a tinkling cymbal. 2. And though I have the gift of prophecy, and understand all mysteries, and all knowledge; and though I have all faith, so that I could remove mountains, and have not charity, I am nothing. 3. And though I bestow all my goods to feed the poor, and though I give my body to be burned, it profiteth me nothing ... 12. For now we see through a glass, darkly; but then face to face: now I know in part, but then shall I know even as also I am known. 13. And now abideth faith, hope, charity, these three; but the greatest of these is charity.

3. The sketches for this work (Kalbeck iv 449–51, McCorkle 485) contain a version of bars 44–66, at the transition into B major, which includes lines from the lyric 'Water-sprite in the valley-spring' that Keller had included in his sequence called 'First Love' – as if that music had originated in a setting of those verses. No such song has survived. But the Keller poem begins with the favourite Brahmsian theme of drowning sorrow in the clear lake, and ends with a bathing golden-haired water-sprite; and both those passages are quoted on the sketch. Further, an extant pair of Heine songs, thematically linked by Brahms (Nos. 150 and 151) contain the same favourite image of assuaged suffering and the same picture of a bathing nymph, identifiable among the composer's best-loved beauties by her gleaming white skin (Heine) as well as her golden hair (Keller). Her maiden name of Stockhausen had long been changed to Herzogenberg, so there may perhaps be some added personal significance in the modulation here from E♭ major (Es = S in German) to B major (H in German).

4. Kalbeck also noted that the sketches for this song include the first two lines of a Rückert poem, thus 'On my journey through my life I travelled towards the shimmering light of happiness' – a will o' the wisp or deceptive ideal in comparison with love.

5. The snap rhythm exemplified above is stated more clearly in the physical exertion of M2 at bars 20–22, which recur at 'Leib brennen', as if the body itself is carted off and flung in the fire. The dismissively alternating hands at bars 9–12, and again at 26–9 (as in the previous song at 'gute Tage' etc.) are also motivic, like the flatward movement at 'meine Habe' (M42) where the shift to a remote key assorts well with the verbal hyperbole. Both ideas combine to illustrate 'nichts nütze' (no use). The diminished-seventh octave descent in minor thirds in bars 10–11, repeated in 42–3, is expressive, like the half-bar of silence (M29) before each of the first three 'Liebe's (the third of which, bars 38–9, was inserted by the composer for special emphasis). The minor seconds on 'stückweise' are M20, with a Schubertian echo; the turn on 'ich er(kennet)' indicates that the voice is paramount, as if in an operatic aria. The enhanced dominant seventh before the modulation to B major is M24. In that key, the upward arpeggios of dream or vision are M9. The large alternative

intervals for 'Glaube' and 'Hoffnung' quoted above should certainly be sung; so should the top G, which illustrates M10. The vocal line's final cadence is typically conclusive; the postlude's hemiolas (already heard at 'erkennen gleich wie') are M14.

Annex

205–212 Op. 103 Nos. 1–8, from the *Zigeunerlieder* (Gypsy songs, Nos. 1–7, 11) 1887–8

The *Zigeunerlieder* for vocal quartet and piano were first published in October 1888. Brahms spoke of them deprecatingly; thus he had told Elisabet von Herzogenberg earlier that year (ii 173) that he had refrained from sending her some 'cheerful and high-spirited nonsense' that had been performed and well received among his friends in Vienna. That description aroused her curiosity, as the composer no doubt intended. In March he sent her the manuscript, with further disparagement (ibid. 180): 'I should be glad if this provides you with an hour of amusement. But I fear it's more as if I had intruded with some bad joke into your quiet and sober room. In any event, the story will surely displease you?'. Heinrich von Herzogenberg was ill at the time, and the household was depressed; but Brahms clearly thought of Elisabet as rather teasably prudish at the best of times, and of his *Gypsy Songs* as frankly erotic, as indeed they are. Perhaps race and raciness were associated in his mind; and he would not have failed to notice that the *Hafis* versions by his favourite love-poet, Georg Daumer, contained a section headed *Zigeunerisch*. But whatever the antecedents of these *Zigeunerlieder*, Brahms had no reason to be ashamed of them; quite the contrary. The melodies are occasionally indebted to his textual source, namely Hugo Conrat's undated *Ungarische Liebeslieder: 25 ungarische Volkslieder für mittlere Stimme*. But Op. 103 mainly contains original settings of Conrat's adroit translations from the Hungarian. Nos. 1–7 and 11, in Brahms's own versions for solo voice and piano, were published in April and May 1889; and the work has become so well known in these arrangements (which may indeed have constituted the original inspirations in some instances) that they are included here for convenience as a heterogeneous group of lieder. They may even be interpreted as a quasi-cycle, as Brahms's own indication of 'a story' suggests. He had long cherished the gypsy idiom, as attested by the melodies included in his early pseudonymous four-hand piano pot-pourri *Souvenirs de la Russie* (*c.* 1850; McCorkle 689). And Elisabet warmed to his mature *Gypsy Songs*, as she told him in October 1888. 'They rush and pound and stamp along and then resume their sweet ingratiating flow'. She especially relished 'the glowing life in the first two, the charming humour in No. 6, and the adorable melancholy inwardness of [No. 7], the second part of which moves me to tears'. As so often, she speaks for posterity.

205. (Op. 103, No. 1) He, Zigeuner (Hey, gypsy)

A minor d#'–g''

He, Zigeuner, greife in die Saiten ein!

Spiel das Lied vom ungetreuen Mägdelein!
Lass die Saiten weinen, klagen, traurig bange,
Bis die heisse Träne netzet diese Wange!

Hey, gypsy, strike your fiddle-strings! Play the song of the faithless girl! [bis]
Let the strings weep and moan in sad despair, until the hot tear moistens this cheek!
[bis]

We are to understand that the singer is himself the betrayed lover. The prelude
instructs the violinist in performance praxis, as it were borrowing the instrument
and slashing at it with a cry of 'like this!', in four two-handed stabs of rage. As the
voice enters with its beguiling melody the stabbing theme continues in the left
hand, while the right thrums in broken triplet chords, turning the basic 2/4 into
6/8. Even the time-signatures are at odds. The voice breaks into a wild leap at
each 'vom ungetreuen' (of the faithless); the wound is still painful to the touch.
Meanwhile the end of one couplet and the beginning of the next (Saiten ein! Spiel
das Lied vom – Strike the strings! Play the song) share the same melody, implying
that this is the very song in question, well known to singer and gypsy fiddler alike.
The same four notes, now in the major, begin the second verse, where the left
hand halts for a moment of reflection and relaxation at 'traurig bange' (in sad
despair). Then the masochistically induced scalding tear-drops recur, to the
opening tune. The thought of that relief inspires a major tonic close for the first
and only time in the song; but this soon reverts to the minor in two staccato
chords with a sustained soft twang as the violin is notionally abandoned and
packed away, leaving the singer to muse on his wrongs.

NOTES. 1. The Conrat source has the unmetrical 'die Wange' in its last line; Brahms's
'diese Wange' is an improvement.

2. The top notes at 'Zigeuner', 'ungetreue' and 'heisse' are M10; the teardrop staccato of
M28 is implicit throughout and explicit in the postlude. The cadential vocal line at bars
12–14, and the A minor open-string violin chords without mediants, are also expressive.

206. (Op. 103, No. 2) Hochgetürmte Rimaflut (Towering tide of the Rima)

D minor d'–g''

Hochgetürmte Rimaflut, wie bist du so trüb,
An dem Ufer klag ich laut nach dir mein Lieb!
Wellen fliehen, Wellen strömen,
Rauschen an den Strand heran zu mir;
An dem Rimaufer lasst mich ewig weinen nach ihr!

Towering tide of the Rima, how troubled you are; on the bank I lament aloud for you,
my love! [bis]
Waves rush by, waves stream past, roaring up to me on the shore; here on the bank
of the Rima let me mourn her loss for ever! [bis]

The series continues in the same melancholy mood of regret, and reproach. To start each phrase, at 'Hochgetürmte' (towering) and 'An dem Ufer' (on the bank), two big minor chords crash and staccato octaves splash, as if depicting quarrels and tears as rough waves and spray. After the double bar, at 'Wellen fliehen' (waves rush by), the towering waves are heard rushing by in the left hand, which twice quotes the vocal melody for the opening epithet 'hochgetürmte'. But the major ending suggests a sudden change of mood, softening into the next song.

NOTES. I. Conrat's first line has 'Rimafluten, wie seid ihr', while his last reads 'An dem Ufer lasst mich klagen nach dir, mein Lieb'.

2. The staccato octaves are expressive, like the acciaccature in voice and piano and the final tierce de Picardie.

3. An effective performance would save Brahms's alternative high notes (M10) for the last verse, in a crying climax on his second 'weinen nach ihr'.

207. (Op, 103, No. 3) Wisst ihr (Do you know)

D major f#' (c#')–g''

Wisst ihr, wenn mein Kindchen
Am allerschönsten ist?
Wenn ihr süsses Mündchen
Scherzt und lacht und küsst.
Mägdelein,
Du bist mein,
Inniglich
Küss ich dich,
Dich erschuf der liebe Himmel
Einzig nur für mich!

Wisst ihr wann mein Liebster
Am besten mir gefällt?
Wenn in seinen Armen
Er mich umschlungen hält.
Schätzelein,
Du bist mein,
Inniglich
Küss ich dich,
Dich erschuf der liebe Himmel
Einzig nur für mich!

Do you know when my little girl is loveliest of all? When her sweet little mouth is jesting and laughing and kissing.

Sweetheart, you're mine, I kiss you passionately; dear heaven created you for me alone. [bis]

Do you know when my dearest pleases me most? When he holds me tight in his arms.

Darling, you're mine, I kiss you passionately; dear heaven created you for me alone! [bis]

If these songs are performed as a cycle, the sadness of the first two casts some shadow over the ensuing sunshine; so Nos. 3–6 will be all the more poignant for that, especially if they are performed as it were in the past tense. But the actual presentation is immediacy itself, as the canonic echoes here are designed to tell us. Each protagonist appears in person, only a dance step apart. The opening vocal melody instantly recurs low in the left hand at 'Kindchen' (little girl) and in high bright octaves at 'Mündchen' (little mouth), while the tune for 'allerschönsten' (loveliest of all) recurs low in the left hand at the next word, 'ist', each time with an initial accent; and similarly in the second verse – as if to say yes, that's how she looked, that's how he held me, just like that. And to focus and enhance that telling image, the contours of the two main figures snugly correspond, thus

uniting passionately in both hands at 'küsst' and 'hält' for a further illustration of kissing and holding. Similarly the optional second voice in the refrains at 'Mägdelein' (sweetheart) etc. makes a notional love-duet. Meanwhile the gypsy band plays its own special instruments, in the running left-hand quasi-dulcimer semiquavers that turn into accented crotchets at 'dich erschuf der liebe Himmel' (dear heaven created you) and gypsy-fiddle octaves and chords (borrowed from the first song) after each final 'für mich!'. The whole work is fashioned with unobtrusive deftness by a cunning miniaturising hand, like a complex watch mechanism enclosed in its own polished case; and it chimes delightfully.

NOTES. 1. For his melody's sake, Brahms added 'einzig' to the last line of each verse.

2. The figures quoted above are typically Brahmsian in their sex-symbolism; technically speaking, each is the other's retrograde inversion.

3. The canons are M12, and the duetting sixths M18; the two questioning dominants, at 'ist?' and 'gefällt?', are M24, while the flattened left-hand seventh at *dolce*, bar 5, is M41.

208. (Op. 103, No. 4) Lieber Gott (Dear Lord)

F major f'–f''

Lieber Gott, du weisst, wie oft bereut ich hab
Dass ich meinem Liebsten einst ein Küsschen gab.
Herzgebot, dass ich ihm küssen muss,
Denk so lang ich leb an diesen ersten Kuss.

Lieber Gott, du weisst, wie oft in stiller Nacht
Ich in Lust und Leid an meinen Schatz gedacht,
Lieb ist süss, wenn bitter auch die Reu,
Armes Herze bleibt ihm ewig, ewig treu.

Dear Lord, you know how often I've repented that little kiss I once gave my dearest man.

My heart commanded me to kiss him, and as long as I live I'll think of that first kiss.
[bis]

Dear Lord, you know how often in the silent night I've thought in joy and sorrow about my sweetheart.

Love is sweet, though repentance is bitter; this poor heart will always, always stay true to him. [bis]

Here is another miniature masterpiece of insouciance and charm, far from the solemnity the words imply but no less true and affecting on that account. The character is drawn in the first bar, *vivace grazioso* in general and *piano leggiero* in the keyboard's toe-tapping dance-measure, all flounce and frolic. At 'oft bereut ich hab' (often I've repented) the first bar's right hand is inverted, as if to deny or withdraw that repentance. There is a slight flirting with A minor, but the right hand's staccato upper or lower voice, whether overt or hidden, keeps on making a direct appeal to the deity by singing the opening words of each verse, 'Lieber Gott, du weisst'. In the second repeated section, delight bursts out unrestrained in top notes, arpeggios and broken chords that absorb any lingering traces of bitterness or sorrow.

NOTES. I. The last line has 'bleibt ihm', not 'bleibt mir' as given by Ophüls.

2. The top notes are MIO; the dominant seventh followed by a silent bar before the Da Capo is M24 followed by M29.

209. (Op. 103, No. 5) Brauner Bursche (The swarthy lad)

D major d'–g''

> Brauner Bursche führt zum Tanze
> Sein blauäugig schönes Kind,
> Schlägt die Sporen keck zusammen,
> Czardas-Melodie beginnt,
> Küsst und herzt sein süsses Täubchen,
> Dreht sie, führt sie, jauchzt und springt;
> Wirft drei blanke Silbergulden
> Auf das Cimbal, dass es klingt.

The swarthy lad takes his blue-eyed beautiful girl to the dance,
*   he clashes his spurs boldly together, a csardas melody begins,*
*   he kisses and hugs his sweet little dove, turns her, leads her, shouts and leaps;*
*   he throws three bright silver coins on the cimbalom so that it jangles [all bis].*

Perhaps the glimpse of a gypsy lad and his blue-eyed girl together was designed to create a special 19th-century erotic frisson. The piano's high-booted dance music twirls its macho mustachios in the exultant stamping rhythms of an authentic csardas, complete with duple time, cross-bar syncopations, expressive pauses and rhythmic variation, all compressed into one perfect page. The piano echoes after 'blauäugig schönes Kind' (blue-eyed beautiful girl) and 'Melodie beginnt' are meant to sound like love-song strains, as if the gypsy band is playing their tune. The vocal line at 'Silbergulden auf das Cimbal' (silver coins on the cimbalom) imitates the prelude and postlude, as if this dashing gesture has sparked off the music again, by demanding an encore.

NOTES. 1. The cimbalom is the gypsy dulcimer; but the practice of throwing coins on to that instrument would be rightly discouraged.

2. The prelude's pause after a strong dominant seventh is M24 followed by M29. M24 can be heard again, asking 'what happened next?' at the word 'springt'; the varied dance-rhythms are M15/16. The Schubertian echoes are also expressive.

210. (Op. 103, No. 6) Röslein dreie (Three little roses)
G major e♭′–g″

Röslein dreie in der Reihe blühn so rot,
Dass der Bursch zum Mädel geht ist kein Verbot!
Lieber Gott, wenn das verboten wär,
Ständ die schöne weite Welt schon längst nicht mehr,
Ledig bleiben Sünde wär!

Schönstes Städtchen in Alföld ist Ketschkemet,
Dort gibt es gar viele Mädchen schmuck und nett!
Freunde, sucht euch dort ein Bräutchen aus,
Freit um ihre Hand und gründet euer Haus,
Freudenbecher leeret aus!

Three little roses in a row bloom so red; for a lad to go courting a girl is not forbidden! [bis]
Dear Lord, if that were forbidden the fair wide world would long ago have ceased to exist, and staying a bachelor would be a sin! [bis]
The finest town in Alföld is Kecskemét, there lives many a kind handsome girl! [bis]
Friends, find yourselves a young bride there, sue for her hand and set up house; quaff beakers of joy! [bis]

Brahms must have paid special attention to this text; he was a confirmed bachelor, a fact he overtly regretted yet often jested about, as in his favourite aphorism on the subject: 'I'm sorry to say I've never married, and have had to remain a bachelor, thank God'. Both strains are clearly heard in this engaging song, which treats the topic lightly yet with a trace of lingering regret for the lost dynasty and destiny. After two small sighs in the prelude the cimbalom or gypsy dulcimer chords are played with a zestfully two-handed downward movement that breaks out into frank hilarity at the falling semiquavers after the second 'blühn so rot' (bloom so red) and 'kein Verbot' (not forbidden).

NOTE. The prelude's minor chords are expressive of mild melancholy here as in Schumann; so is the flattened sixth (M41) at 'nicht (mehr)', which also casts a slight shadow. But these clouds are soon dispelled by the piano's required xylophonic effects with their dry almost wooden quality of hammer-striking staccato; and the equally symbolic semiquaver laughter at 'rot', 'Verbot' etc., also has a Wolfian quality. The top notes at 'Lie[ber]' and 'le[dig]' are M10; the pause after a strong dominant at the Da Capo, as in Nos. 3 and 4 of this set, is M24 followed by M29.

211. (Op. 103, No. 7) Kommt dir manchmal in den Sinn (Do you sometimes recall)

E major d#'–g#''

Kommt dir manchmal in den Sinn,
Mein süsses Lieb,
Was du einst mit heilgem Eide
Mir gelobt?
Täusch mich nicht, verlass mich nicht,
Du weisst nicht wie lieb ich dich hab,
Lieb du mich, wie ich dich,
Dann strömt Gottes Huld auf dich herab!

Do you sometimes recall, my sweet love, what you once promised me with a holy vow?
[bis]
  Don't deceive me, don't leave me, you don't know how much I love you, love me as
I love you and then God's grace will pour down upon you! [bis]

The words do not define the sex of the singer; but in a Brahms song, as in the Romantic lieder tradition in general (and often in real life) it is the woman who is left lamenting – as in *Agnes* Op. 59/5 (No. 104). Here the lyric, for all its lovingness, bodes ill; the singer is doomed to be deserted. The result is a small masterpiece of tender vulnerability. The vocal melody, doubled in the right hand, rises while the left hand falls in single notes; thus the two voices are heard separating as the song begins, in an explicit musical metaphor. The falling fifth of 'süsses Lieb' is repeated with quiet insistence in the keyboard; similarly the rising interval of 'mir gelobt' is successively extended into gentle but reproachful reminders: 'you *promised* me'. In the reprise, the keyboard staccato touches on the same points, as if saying 'remember' softly to itself. Similarly the canonic right-hand echoes in diminution after the falling vocal phrases 'täusch mich nicht, verlass mich nicht' (don't deceive me, don't leave me) and so on are like loving and linking gestures loth to let go. The postlude's hopefulness enhances the poignancy of a real-life ending that will not be so happy.

NOTES. 1. In this voice and piano version, the original E♭ major was changed to E major.
  2. The deserted girl was sure to evoke the composer's special sympathy.
  3. The diverging voices are Wolfian in their motivic expressiveness; the staccato here, and more manifestly in bars 9–11, is another image of detachment or separation. So are the canonical echoes (M12) at bars 17–18 etc., enhanced by the sighing of M21, and the right hand's Schubertian echoes of 'süsses Lieb'. The love-song thirds and sixths in the postlude and earlier are M18; the IV-I Amens at bars 6–8 etc. suit the holy vow, and so do the top notes of M10 at the second 'heilgem', and again at 'lieb' und 'Gottes'.

212. (Op. 103, No. 8) Rote Abendwolken (Red evening clouds)

D♭ major e♭'–a♭''

Rote Abendwolken ziehn
Am Firmament,

Sehnsuchtvoll nach dir, mein Lieb,
Das Herze brennt;
Himmel strahlt in glühnder Pracht
Und ich träum bei Tag und Nacht
Nur allein von dem süssen Liebchen mein.

Red evening clouds sail past in the firmament.
  How yearningly my heart burns for you, my love. [bis]
   The sky is aflame in glowing glory, and I dream by day and night only of my sweet
love.

The tonality mirrors the moods and colours of a hectic skyscape and its metaphorical meaning. First comes the remoteness of five flats, which melt into four
sharps and back again like changing cloud-shapes. At 'sehnsuchtsvoll' (yearningly)
the rhythm is blurred and softened by syncopation as the two melodic lines in
voice and keyboard drift towards each other across the bar-lines. In the second
section the vocal sequences rise on high before resuming their first strains in the
culminating last line. There could be no stronger declaration of undying love. Yet
in a finished performance the earlier melancholy will continue to dapple that
shining certitude with shadows of doubt. Brahms stayed unmarried and lived
alone, fulfilled in his art but not in his life; the fine yet unpretentious music of
these gypsy songs reflects something of that ambivalence.

NOTES. 1. The song corresponds to No. 11 of the original Op. 103 for vocal quartet.
   2. Undying love is a favourite Brahmsian theme.
   3. The two converging melodic lines are the love motif M17; the top notes at
'sehnsuchtsvoll', 'Tag und Nacht' and 'süssen' are M10; the deep bass notes at 'mein' are
M8.

APPENDIX: THE POETS

(*denotes a translation or adaptation into German)

'**Alexis, Willibald**', pseudonym of Wilhelm Häring, 1798–1871: *Entführung* Op. 97/3 (No. 182). As Brahms had no doubt been told, the young Schumann had met Häring, whose pen-name combined two saints. This may well have inspired Schumann's own interest in the comparable conjunction of Clara, Eusebius, and Florus (a forerunner of Florestan), as suggested in Sams 1967. Brahms was well aware of those interlinkages, and embellished them with special symbolic (perhaps musical) significances of his own, as he informed Clara soon after their first meeting (Litzmann i 16). For his earliest historical novels, Häring had hit on the even more telling pseudonym 'Sir Walter Scott'; but he soon found and displayed his own original talent for narrative invention, which also enlivens his occasional ballads. Brahms set another, *Walpurgisnacht* (also drawn from the *Balladen* 1836), as a duet for sopranos, Op. 75/4.

Allmers, Hermann, 1821–1902: *Feldeinsamkeit* Op. 86/2 (No. 157). Allmers was a nature poet, as in this song and in the vocal quartet *Spätherbst* Op. 92/2 (also drawn from his *Dichtungen* 1860). He was highly regarded in his own day, but is now remembered mainly if not solely for his spirited rejection of Brahms's otherwise universally admired solo setting (as detailed in Kalbeck iii 341f). That reputation is rather unfair; poets (like Housman in English) are often deaf to musical equivalence, however masterly.

The Bible *see* Luther, Martin.

Bodenstedt, Friedrich von, 1819–92: *Lied aus 'Ivan'* Op. 3/4 (No. 4). Like Geibel, Heyse and Schack, Bodenstedt belonged to the literary coterie assembled by Maximilian II of Bavaria at Munich in the mid-1850s. His *Lieder des Mirza Schaffy* (1851) featured undemanding renderings of oriental poetry, which attained cult status in their day; they were among the earliest such pastiches. The idea of translation, genuine or not, made a special appeal to Brahms, no doubt because of his Romantic devotion to the ideal of a universal lyricism transcending the constraints of nation and class, as in Herder (q.v.).

Borja, Francisco de, 1580–1658: wrote the poem translated by Eichendorff and set by Brahms as *Vom Strande** Op. 69/6 (No. 127).

Brentano, Clemens, 1778–1842: *O kühler Wald* Op. 72/3 (No. 142). Brentano was a powerful force in German Romanticism, as a poet and novelist. His father was Italian, and he himself (as Brahms no doubt knew) wrote and thought in musical terms. His lyrics are often simple and singable in the Goethe tradition; his *Abendständchen*, also drawn from the *Gesammelte Werke* 1852–5, was set by Brahms for unaccompanied six-part chorus, Op. 42/1. In collaboration with Achim von Arnim (1781–1831) Brentano collected, edited, and sometimes invented (as in the well-known *Es ist ein Schnitter, der heisst Tod*, treated by Mendelssohn as a folk-song, Op. 8/4, or by Schumann as a folk-chorus, Op. 75/1) the contents of the famous anonymous anthology *Des Knaben Wunderhorn* (see Volkslieder). In his youth, Brahms had met and been much impressed by Brentano's sister Sophie, who was also Arnim's widow, together with her daughter Gisela (whose name Brahms typically turned into musical notes, see p. 14).

Candidus, Karl, 1817–72: *Schwermut* Op. 58/5 (No. 96), *Tambourliedchen* Op. 69/5 (No. 126), *Lerchengesang* Op. 70/2 (No. 132), *Geheimnis* Op. 71/3 (No. 137), *Alte Liebe* Op. 72/1 (No. 140), *Sommerfäden* Op. 72/2 (No. 141). Candidus was a versifying clergyman, of little account as an independent poet but with a lyric gift that called for, and called forth, music. His work had induced tunefulness in the sick Schumann. Brahms's interest may have derived from his quasi-filial piety; but he too was moved into melody in his own much more masterly solo settings. His duet *Jägerlied* Op. 66/4, also drawn from the *Gedichte* of 1869, is also well worth a hearing.

Chamisso, Adalbert von, 1781–1838: *Die Müllerin* no Op. number (No. 8). The poem made a personal appeal to Brahms, as attested by its second and quite different setting as Op. 44/5 (also found in the *Gedichte* of 1839) for unaccompanied four-part women's chorus. No doubt he would have made more use of this fine poet, the laureate of women and work, had it not been for Schumann's priority in *Frauenliebe und -leben* and other Chamisso songs.

Conrat, Hugo: *Zigeunerlieder** Op. 103/1–8 (Nos. 205–12). Brahms often visited the Vienna home of this music- and poetry-loving merchant whose translations from the Hungarian (made with the help of his Hungarian-born children's nurse Fräulein Witzl) also figure in the *Vier Zigeunerlieder* Op. 112/3–6 for vocal quartet SATB. The acquaintance had begun because Conrat had thoughtfully tried out his translations on the composer of the *Hungarian Dances*; Brahms found them, and him, congenial, and their collaboration developed into friendship (Kalbeck iv 96 etc.).

Daumer, Georg, 1800–75; *Nicht mehr zu dir zu gehen** Op. 32/2 (No. 35), *Bitteres zu sagen** Op. 32/7 (No. 40), *So stehn wir** Op. 32/8 (No. 41), *Wie bist du, meine Königin** Op. 32/9 (No. 42), *Die Kränze** Op. 46/1 (No. 63), *Magyarisch** Op. 46/2 (No. 64), *Botschaft** Op. 47/1 (No. 67), *Liebesglut** Op. 47/2 (No. 68), *Von waldbekränzter Höhe* Op. 57/1 (No. 84), *Wenn du nur zuweilen lächelst** Op. 57/2 (No. 85), *Es träumte mir** Op. 57/3 (No. 86), *Ach, wende diesen Blick* Op. 57/4 (No. 87), *In meiner Nächte Sehnen* Op. 57/5 (No. 88), *Strahlt zuweilen auch* Op. 57/6 (No. 89), *Die Schnur, die Perl' an Perle** Op. 57/7 (No. 90), *Unbewegte laue Luft*

Op. 57/8 (No. 91), *Eine gute, gute Nacht** Op. 59/6 (No. 105), *Schön war** Op. 95/7
(No. 175), *Wir wandelten** Op. 96/2 (No. 177). Daumer was Brahms's favourite
lyricist, whose attractions lay mainly in a submissive eroticism, bordering on
masochism, which seems mild enough now though controversial then. On
another Daumer poetic anthology, *Mahomed und sein Werk*, which Brahms also
owned, the composer wrote the revealing words: 'der rein geistige Standpunkt, der
den Menschen als körperloses Wesen betrachtet, sei der unwahrste' (the purely
spiritual viewpoint, which considers the human being as bodiless, is entirely
untrue). Daumer also appealed as a universalist authority on the whole world's
kinship. In addition to practising as a homeopathic doctor, he studied comparative religion and languages world-wide, and became a teacher eminent
enough to be called upon to undertake the earliest education of the child of nature
Kasper Hauser, who in 1828 was discovered abandoned near Daumer's home in
Nuremberg. So he could be seen as a healing guru, who wrote and taught for the
benefit of humankind in all its aspects, whether physical or spiritual, thus amply
fulfilling the Brahmsian ideal defined under Herder below. Brahms, for his own
part, rated Daumer fully worthy to rank alongside the true poet Platen, in Op. 32.
In addition to the 19 solo settings listed above, Daumer's love-lyrics inspired the
masterly *Liebeslieder** Op. 52 and *Neue Liebeslieder** Op. 65, both originally for
vocal quartet (SATB, with duets and solos) and piano four hands, which appeared
in many arrangements and brought Brahms further fame and fortune. Daumer
texts are also the source of the vocal quartets *Fragen** Op. 64/3, *O schöne Nacht*
Op. 92/1 and WoO 26* (a separate canonic setting to the same text as Op. 52/10).
That considerable oeuvre has long outlived its verses, yet still revivifies them. A
relevant and touching anecdote is told by Max Kalbeck (ii 137–8): 'For Brahms,
Daumer's anthologies were a true treasure-trove of song-texts. Even in Daumer's
rather coy and clumsy original verses, which to their cost are readily distinguish-
able from his rifacimenti and free translations, Brahms was able to discern the
hidden sparks of spirit and fan them into bright flame; and he felt bound to his
poet by the liveliest gratitude. To show him his true feelings, he sought to make
the personal acquaintance of his poet. So when, at the beginning of May 1872, he
happened to be en route from Nuremberg to Karlsruhe, he made a detour via
Würzburg, where Daumer lived (and in 1875 died), found the street and house
after much trouble, and was astonished when a little shrivelled old man introduced himself as the German Hafis [i.e. the great Persian love-poet]. Brahms, to
whom it became clear in the course of conversation that Daumer knew nothing
of him and his songs, teasingly inquired after the poet's many loves, meaning the
women he had hymned so glowingly. Then the old man silently smiled to himself
and called in from the adjoining room an equally old, small and wizened little
woman, saying 'I've never loved anyone but this – my wife'. Brahms too was
faithful, also for a long lifetime, to the homely charms of Daumer's poetry,
which the spirited music preserves and enhances. Of the 19 solo songs, only five
(Nos. 84, 87–9, 91) derive from original verse; but the rest are free renderings,
rather than translations, from their world-wide sources. So Daumer deserves
full credit and further attention, and has received very little of either. His

achievements, indeed his existence, remain largely unmentioned in literary manuals.

Eichendorff, Joseph, Freiherr von, 1788–1857: *In der Fremde* Op. 3/5 (No. 5), *Lied* Op. 3/6 (No. 6), *Mondnacht*, WoO 21 (No. 7), *Parole* Op. 7/2 (No. 16), *Anklänge* Op. 7/3 (No. 17), *Vom Strande** Op. 69/6 (No. 127). Among all other Romantic novelists and lyricists Eichendorff was the supreme poet of the so-called pathetic fallacy, the interlinking of nature with human feelings. Brahms mentions these writings with evident relish in one of his earliest letters to Clara Schumann (Litzmann i 9); forty years later he was enthusing to the Herzogenbergs about that youthful idolatry. His Eichendorff settings were indeed mainly confined to the same early period – not only the solo songs, but *Der Gärtner* Op. 17/3 and *Der Bräutigam* Op. 44/2, both for women's chorus (the former with two horns and harp, the latter a cappella), the duet *Die Nonne und der Ritter* Op. 28/1, and the canons for women's voices *Wenn die Klänge* and *Ein Gems auf dem Stein*, Op. 113 Nos. 7–8) all date from *c.* 1860 or earlier. Only the neglected *Tafellied* Op. 93b for six-part mixed chorus and piano is a middle-period work; and its lines are atypical of Eichendorff in their salon *galanterie*. No doubt Brahms sensed the daunting shadow of Schumann's superlative settings; but he had also grown somewhat out of sympathy with Eichendorff's natural Christian piety and its reliance on divine guidance.

'**Ferrand, Eduard**', pseudonym of Eduard Schulz, 1813–42: *Treue Liebe* Op. 7/1 (No. 15). Schulz was a minor poet who died young. But he was not without talent or promise, and a volume of his *Gedichte* had been published in 1843. Schumann had sketched a setting of one its lyrics, *Ein Gedanke*, and Brahms may have inherited that source-book. But he made no other use of it; and the lyric he chose is better evidence for his interest in its theme (the deserted and desperate girl) than for Schulz's literary merit.

Flemming or Fleming, Paul, 1609–40: *O liebliche Wangen* Op. 47/4 (No. 70), *An die Stolze* Op. 107/1 (No. 196). The Saxon Flemming introduced a new note of virile vigour into early German verse; he was also a traveller and a musician. Hence his triple appeal to Brahms, not unlike that of Daumer two centuries later. But he also wrote pietistic verse which appealed to the young Brahms, as in the willing acceptance of fate's decree hymned in the agreeable youthful setting of *Geistliches Lied* for mixed chorus with organ, Op. 30.

Frey, Adolf, 1855–1920: *Meine Lieder* Op. 106/4 (No. 194). The Swiss minor poet and novelist Frey was also a professor of literary history at Zürich. This reflective lyric, like Klaus Groth's *Wie Melodien* Op. 105/1 (No. 186), is about the nature of the poetic impulse. It says much for Brahms's own preoccupations that he should find and set two (perhaps the only two) singable lyrics on that somewhat intractable topic.

Geibel, Emanuel, 1815–84: *Frühlingslied* Op. 85/5 (No. 154), *Geistliches Wiegenlied** Op. 91/2 (No. 163), *Mein Herz ist schwer* Op. 94/3 (No. 166). Brahms also sketched, but abandoned, two other Geibel spring songs (McCorkle 664); posterity is the poorer. But he had been anticipated, and perhaps inhibited, by Schumann's many Geibel settings. That fine poet and dramatist had been the leading member of the Munich coterie patronised by the King of Bavaria; his early lyrics had earned him a lifelong pension from the King of Prussia, whose service he later entered. In an age of revolutionary turmoil, he remained predictably conciliatory, even apolitical, while strongly sympathising with the ideal of the national Germany that he helped to create and lived to see. His art, though disciplined and restrained, is self-expressive and full of personal feeling. In all those respects he much resembled Brahms, who (as Max Kalbeck relates, iv 386f) also delighted in Geibel's dramas and translations, such as *Brunhild* and the *Klassiches Liederbuch.* Together the two friends joined in enthusiastic praise of the great artist in form and language, who was a troubadour, poetic philosopher and translator, and yet today, as [Brahms] said, 'is eyed askance by wretches who had no feeling for such things'. Geibel's easy fluency of style accounts for both his wide popularity in his day and his comparative neglect now. But he has the flair and the discipline of the born translator, as witness his renderings of Spanish popular or national lyrics in collaboration with his younger friend Paul Heyse (q.v.).

Goethe, Johann Wolfgang von, 1749–1842: *Die Liebende schreibt* Op. 47/5 (No. 71), *Trost in Tränen* Op. 48/5 (No. 76), *Dämm'rung senkte sich von oben* Op. 59/1 (No. 100), *Serenade* Op. 70/3 (No. 133), *Unüberwindlich* Op. 72/5 (No. 144). Goethe is the greatest of all German writers, as supreme in lyric as in dramatic and other forms. His poetry seeded the lied genre with Mozart's *Das Veilchen*, which heralded the most profuse and varied flowering ever sown by any poet in any musical field, with contributions from the greatest masters as well as specialist song-writers. Brahms was a comparative latecomer, and his Goethe lieder though impressive were correspondingly restricted. There was perhaps another limiting factor, namely that the song form was itself too constraining for so towering a presence; hence the many other settings of Goethe by Brahms in a variety of forms and forces ranging from the full orchestra (as in the cantata *Rinaldo* Op. 50 for tenor solo, the *Rhapsodie* Op. 53 for alto, both with male voice chorus, and the *Gesang der Parzen* Op. 89 for six-part mixed chorus) via the piano, whether with four hands (as in the finale to the *Neue Liebeslieder* Op. 65/15 for SATB) or two (the duets *Es rauschet das Wasser* Op. 28/3 and *Phänomen*[1] Op. 61/3), the SATB quartets (*Wechsellied zum Tanze* Op. 31/1 and *Warum?* Op. 92/4) or a cappella (the SATB chorus *Beherzigung*[2] Op. 93a/6), or the canons for women's voices (*Göttlicher Morpheus* and *Grausam erweiset sich* Op. 113/1–2; the latter recomposed for four women's voices as WoO 24). Only in the light of this complete list can Brahms's knowledge of and response to Goethe's manifold greatness become fully visible; it is almost as if the composer had deliberately sought to match that wide range.

[1,2] Cf. the Wolf settings at, respectively, No. 32 of the Goethe song-book and No. 4 of the six early songs for male voice.

Grohe, Melchior, 1829–1906: *O Komme, holde Sommernacht* Op. 58/4 (No. 95). Grohe was a minor poet who wrote on erotic themes and had travelled in Europe and the Middle and Far East; what appealed to Brahms was no doubt what he took to be the typical tones of the cosmopolitan adventurer, in every sense.

Groth, Klaus, 1819–99: *Regenlied* WoO 23 (No. 62), *Regenlied* Op. 59/3 (No. 102), *Nachklang* Op. 59/4 (No. 103), *Mein Wundes Herz* Op. 59/7 (No. 106), *Dein blaues Auge* Op. 59/8 (No. 107), *Heimweh I* ('Wie traulich') Op. 63/7 (No. 119), *Heimweh II* ('O wüsst ich') Op. 63/8 (No. 120), *Heimweh* III ('Ich sah') Op. 63/9 (No. 121), *Komm bald* Op. 97/5 (No. 184), *Wie Melodien* Op. 105/1 (No. 186), *Es hing der Reif* Op. 106/3 (No. 193). Klaus Groth has always occupied a place, however modest and marginal, in German literary history, because he was the first writer to explore in any depth the poetic potential of Plattdeutsch, or Low German. And now, with an increasing regional hegemony within the European frame, his work is enjoying something of a renaissance. His occasional tales and copious verses, written in a dialect akin to Dutch, evince both tenderness and humour; their readership, though restricted, included Groth's influential friend and North German countryman Brahms; and their main themes reflect the composer's own moods of melancholy and nostalgia. Further (like the two duets for soprano and alto *Klänge* I and II Op. 66/1–2, and *Im Herbst* for unaccompanied mixed chorus Op. 104/5) they could readily be written in or rendered into High German, for singing purposes, and thus made more universal.

Gruppe, Otto, 1804–76: *Das Mädchen spricht* Op. 107/3 (No. 198). Gruppe was a literary critic and classical scholar, whose works on the tragic art of the Greeks and allied topics were also owned and studied by Brahms.

'**Hafiz**' was the pseudonym of the fourteenth-century Persian poet Shams ed-Din Muhammed. He was celebrated for the sensuous sweetness of his love-lyrics, which were much imported or imitated in 19th-century Germany. But Brahms was setting Daumer (Opp. 32/7–9, 47/1–2, 57/1, 65/2) or Rückert (the women's canon Op. 113/3), not Hafiz.

'**Halm, Friedrich**' was the self-effacing pseudonym (Halm = straw) of Eligius von Münch-Bellinghausen, 1806–71: *Steig' auf, geliebter Schatten* Op. 94/2 (No. 165), *Kein Haus, keine Heimat* Op. 94/5 (No. 168), *Bei dir sind meine Gedanken* Op. 95/2 (No. 170), *Beim Abschied* Op. 95/3 (No. 171), *Der Jäger* Op. 95/4 (No. 172). Halm stands on the margins of literature as a dramatist and poet popular in his day for his effusive national and poetic sentiment. As a Viennese theatre manager he may have been personally known to Brahms, who may also have inherited some of the texts from his mentor Schumann (whose *Geisternähe* Op. 77/3 is a Halm setting). Another Brahms setting, apparently of the poem 'Schneegestöber' (Flurry of Snow) found at 1/228 of the 1872 *Werke* was suppressed by the composer after (and perhaps because) the poem had been deprecated by Elisabet von Herzogenberg as unworthy of his music.

Häring *see* Alexis.

Hebbel, Friedrich, 1813–63: *In der Gasse* Op. 58/6 (No. 97), *Vorüber* Op. 58/7 (No. 98). Hebbel possessed the dramatic and lyric genius to which Halm and others aspired. As a playwright, he brought history, psychology and myth into the theatre, thus prefiguring the problem plays of Ibsen and Shaw; as a poet, he inspired not only Brahms (who also set the delectable *Abendlied* Op. 92/3, SATB with piano) but a wide diversity of other composers. Thus Schumann based his only opera, *Genoveva*, (much admired, and personally interpreted, by Brahms; see Sams 1971a) on Hebbel's play of that name; and both Schumann and his wife Clara thought themselves highly honoured when Hebbel visited their home. Further, Hebbel shared with Brahms the unusual progression from boyhood poverty in Hamburg to fame and fortune in Vienna; there the two masters met in 1863, the last year of Hebbel's life. They shared a pervasive sense of melancholy, a penchant for autumn and twilight, a high-minded seriousness of artistic purpose. Such poetic sentiments assort well with Romantic music; Hebbel deserves a special citation for his services to lieder.

Heine, Heinrich, 1797–1856: *Es liebt sich so lieblich* Op. 71/1 (No. 135), *Sommerabend* Op. 85/1 (No. 150), *Mondenschein* Op. 85/2 (No. 151), *Der Tod, das ist die kühle Nacht* Op. 96/1 (No. 176), *Es schauen die Blumen* Op. 96/3 (No. 178), *Meerfahrt* Op. 96/4 (No. 179). Heine ranks next to Goethe as the greatest lied-lyricist of all time, most memorably set to music from Schubert, Mendelssohn and Schumann onwards. His best-known collection of poems is aptly titled *Buch der Lieder* (1827); no other single volume ever written approaches its success as a source-book for song-writers. Heine's detractors have stigmatized this early love-poetry as journalistic, even trivial; and it may sometimes seem to have a certain hollowness at its heart. But when filled with music such art-work becomes complete and perfect. There are additional reasons for his appeal to Brahms, notably a cosmopolitan universality. In political terms, that quality was expressed as a ceaseless and brave campaign for individual liberty of thought, including freethought; in lyric forms, Heine's style at its best was Goethean in its blend of folk-song simplicity with a new boldness of imagery. But perhaps even Brahms came to feel somewhat inhibited by the musical masterpieces of his exalted predecessors; another Heine setting (of the poem 'Wie der Mond sich leuchtend drängend') was criticized – no doubt justifiably – by Elisabet von Herzogenberg and destroyed by the composer.

Herder, Johann, 1744–1803: *Murrays Ermordung** Op. 14/3 (No. 23), *Ein Sonett** Op. 14/4 (No. 24). Herder was the first historian of cultural evolution, and has thus influenced every aspect of modern human endeavour including aesthetics and politics as well as literature and music. Brahms owned the complete works, in ten closely-printed volumes. At twenty-three, he wrote his name and the year, 1856, on the fly-leaf of the essay *Zur Religion und Philosophie*. He also pencilled especially frequent underlinings on the volume that contained Herder's German versions of European lyrics and ballads, characteristically called *Stimmen der Völker in Liedern* (Voices of the Nations in Songs). Those translations had already helped to create the lied, both by providing early singable texts (e.g. for Beethoven and Loewe) and also by introducing the young Goethe to European lyrics, including Shakespeare and folk-poetry (the source of *Erlkönig* as set by both Schubert, D328, and Loewe, Op. 1/3). Herder's influence on Brahms went deeper still. Both were men of the people, and both had experienced personal deprivation. In his passionate internationalism, Herder was a prime founder of the German Romantic movement. Hence, surely, his appeal to Brahms, who also loved the literature of all ages and nations, which transcended the boundaries of class, race and language by skilled translation, which in turn is raised to a higher power by the art of song. Here too Brahms was continuing the Romantic musical tradition of Schumann, whose song-texts embody the same ideals of universality. And Brahms extended the same themes still further, from such Herder sources as the Ossian *Gesang aus Fingal** for women's chorus with two horns and harp, Op. 17/4 and *Darthulas Grabesgesang** for six-part chorus Op. 42/3, the two *Weg der Liebe** duets from Percy's *Reliques of Ancient English Poetry* Op. 20/1–2, and the *Edward** duet Op. 75/1. That last text had already served as the notional underlay for the pianoforte *Ballade* Op. 10/1, which had manifestly begun as a setting of it. And Herder sources again surface in the solo piano music many years later; thus two lines from his translation of 'Lady Anne Bothwell's Lament' from Percy's *Reliques* are superscribed over the Intermezzo Op. 117/1, the opening melody of which audibly sings those words, while Op. 117/3 (though the score does not say so) derives from the Herder translation of the Scottish lyric 'O waly, waly' (Kalbeck iv 280).

Heyse, Paul, 1830–1914: *Spanisches Lied** Op. 6/1 (No. 9), *Am Sonntag Morgen** Op. 49/1 (No. 79), *Mädchenlied** ('Am jüngsten Tag') Op. 95/6 (No. 174), *Mädchenlied* ('Auf die Nacht') Op. 107/5 (No. 200); amendments to *Die Spröde** Op. 58/3 (No. 94 q.v.). Heyse, like Geibel (q.v.), was a leading member of the Munich school; and he stayed in that entourage for the last sixty years of his long life, receiving the Nobel prize for literature in 1910. His novellas have lost much of their lustre; but his occasional lyrics are well cut and polished, and his translations from Romance languages have retained all their pristine shine. Brahms must have been among the very first purchasers of the Heyse and Geibel *Spanisches Liederbuch** 1852, the source of his Op. 6/1 setting dated the following year. No doubt he had been drawn to Heyse's early lyrics by Schumann's Opp. 107/4 and 125/5, Brahms's own treatments of the same texts appear as his Op. 107/5 (perhaps not by coincidence) and the first of the *Vier Lieder aus dem Jungbrunnen*[1] Op. 44/7–10, for four-part women's chorus. The former is a late song; Brahms maintained his penchant for Heyse for much of his life. The appeal was partly personal. It was to Heyse that Brahms turned (by way of his friend and correspondent Hermann Levi) for improvements to the Kopisch text of *Die Spröde*; Brahms was pleased with the result and announced his intention of visiting Heyse in Munich at the next opportunity to offer his gratitude and to discuss other matters (Kalbeck ii 376). These included the possible composition of an opera to a Heyse libretto. Nothing came of that project; but the planned visit duly took place, and Brahms always remembered it. He said that in all his life he had never met a nicer man than Heyse, who knew how to enliven and lighten any gathering; even when he came into the room it was as if the sun had suddenly shone out (Kalbeck ii 439). Four other *Jungbrunnen*[1] settings for mixed chorus Op. 62/3–6 may well represent earlier work *c.* 1860, like the different version of No. 4 catalogued as WoO 19; but a setting of the Heyse *Brautlied,* later destroyed as unsuccessful, dates from 1885 (McCorkle 665).

Hoffmann von Fallersleben, 1798–1874; *Liebe und Frühling I/II* Op. 3/2–3 (Nos. 2–3), *Wie die Wolke* Op. 6/5 (No. 13). *Nachtigallen schwingen* Op. 6/6 (No. 14), *Von ewiger Liebe** Op. 43/1 (No. 58). August Heinrich Hoffmann added his birthplace to his surname, so as to be more readily recognisable. In the result, posterity has been uncertain what to call him; nor is he now much mentioned by any name. Even his supreme achievement in the lieder field, as the source of the text that Brahms used for his masterly *Von ewiger Liebe*, was overlooked for more than a century (until Sams 1972a) and is still confused by other accreditations (McCorkle 155). But the poet of 'Deutschland über alles' has always had his own special distinction, and his work warrants a revival of interest. Like most German artists of his generation, he was an active supporter of personal freedom and German unity; and in an age of repression and petty principalities he suffered for those beliefs, for example by being relieved of his Breslau professorship of literature and philology and subjected to decades of official persecution. But his creed and his talent have triumphed, because he spoke and wrote for a whole nation in its own voice. He was a musically gifted collector and editor of folk-songs, and in his simple singable verses the *Volkslied* lived again. No wonder therefore that he appealed so strongly, both as polemicist and lyricist, to Schumann, whose tuneful settings of Hoffmann's songs for children (*Soldatenlied c.* 1845, Opp. 79/1–6, 12, 15, 20) and lovers (Op. 77/2) deserve to be better known. Hoffmann's poetry was also known to and composed by the 14-year-old Brahms (McCorkle 663); the two later met in in Göttingen (Kalbeck i 97), and enjoyed a real rapport. In addition to the solo songs, the duet Op. 28/2 derives from a Hoffmann anthology, while the voice–viola canon WoO 27 sets his own original text and the womens' canon Op. 113/6 uses his translation.

Hölty, Ludwig, 1748–76: *Der Kuss* Op. 19/1 (No. 29), *Die Mainacht* Op. 43/2 (No. 59), *Die Schale der Vergessenheit* Op. 46/3 (No. 65), *An die Nachtigall* Op. 46/4 (No. 66), *An ein Veilchen* Op. 49/2 (No. 80), *Minnelied* Op. 71/5 (No. 139). Next to Goethe, the sadly sickly and short-lived Hölty was the most gifted lyricist of the German 18th century: his verse, though deep-rooted in the metres and subject-matter of the classical tradition, diffuses a sweet dreamy aroma of Romantic melancholy. He is thus close kin to Brahms himself, as the latter explicitly acknowledged in a letter to Adolph Schubring of February 1869 (*Briefwechsel* viii 214). There Brahms indignantly defended his song-writing against the charge of setting indifferent verses: 'Which are my "fustian" texts? I hope you don't mean my beloved Hölty, for whose lovely warm words I find that my music isn't strong

---

[1] The title of a novel with interspersed lyrics in the German Romantic tradition.

enough, otherwise you'd find me setting more of them. Another volume will appear soon, from Rieter, which contains – another Hölty setting. Please read it seriously and tell me whether it and the poet himself aren't delightful.' The setting in question is difficult to identify; but at least the fellow-feeling is manifest. However, Brahms actually used the early edition of Hölty brought out by the latter's friend and contemporary J. H. Voss, which contains many unauthorised amendments; the admired words, though also set in all good faith by both Mendelssohn and Schubert, are often unauthentic, as exemplified in the notes to each song above. *An die Nachtigall,* for example, is much more Voss than Hölty (both versions are conveniently set forth in Schochow i 172–3). Those extensive alterations are not now reversible. Essentially, they update the original classical diction into new romantic terms; and this very process may have rendered the lyrics more congenial to nineteenth-century song-writers. In any event, Voss deserves special recognition, and is hence separately listed below.

Kalbeck, Max, 1850–1921: *Nachtwandler* Op. 86/3 (No. 158). The music critic Kalbeck, who also had genuine if limited poetic talent, was a friend of Brahms and hence well placed to write relevant verses that would make their own personal appeal, as arguably in this song. His eight-volume biography of Brahms remains essential reading. However, his work has been criticised and indeed rejected as inaccurate, often on no very clear or verifiable grounds. It is certainly true that his romanticised style and approach are no longer fashionable. However, the same might be said about Brahms himself, who also set Kalbeck's poem *Letztes Glück* (for mixed chorus, Op. 104/3), again presumably selected for its congenial Romantic theme of remembered fulfilment during deprivation.

Kapper, Siegfried, 1821–79; *Mädchenfluch** Op. 69/9 (No. 130), *Mädchenlied** Op. 85/3 (No. 152), *Ade!** Op. 85/4 (No. 153), *Das Mädchen** Op. 95/1 (No. 169), *Vorschneller Schwur** Op. 95/5 (No. 173). Kapper was a gifted and much-travelled linguist who turned Serbian verse into Czech (set by Dvořák Op. 6/1–4) and Slavonic verse into German (set by Brahms as above). According to Max Kalbeck (iii 328, 519), the latter genre was difficult to match in musical metre, with the implication that the versification was rather rough. But that was typical of the folk-verse genre which Brahms found so attractive. He arranged *Das Mädchen* for four-part mixed chorus, and added another setting from the same source (*Gesänge der Serben* (1852)) as Opp. 93a/2 and 5.

Keller, Gottfried, 1819–90: *Salome* Op. 69/8 (No. 129), *Abendregen* Op. 70/4 (No. 134), *Therese* Op. 86/1 (No. 156). Keller began as a painter, in oil and water-colour. Then he turned to authorship, and found his true métier. At first he was influenced by the Pan-German politics of Heine, Hoffmann and other lesser figures who could breathe the bracing air of freedom in Keller's Swiss homeland. But later he matured and mellowed into the greatest of Swiss writers, noted for the heights and breadth of his world-view and cherished for the sharp-sighted humour and endearing tenderness of his novels and short stories and above all his lyrics, which are musical in form yet often visual in imagery and philosophical in content. This caused a clash of stylistic response. Thus the settings by Wolf or Pfitzner of the first and third texts above (as Nos. 2 and 6, or as Op. 33/5 and 3, respectively, among their own Keller collections) permit instructive comparisons among the three composers. There is also special evidence of Brahms's personal involvement with Keller's poetry (see No. 204, note 2). Further, the two artists knew and respected each other, and rejoiced in each other's company (Kalbeck iii 27ff) from the 1870s onward. It was at the writer's wish that Brahms (rather reluctantly) set Keller's *Kleine Hochzeitskantate* in 1874 for SATB and piano, as the rarely heard but engaging WoO 16.

Kopisch, August, 1799–1853; *Blinde Kuh** Op. 58/1 (No. 92), *Während des Regens* Op. 58/2 (No. 93), *Die Spröde** Op. 58/3 (No. 94). Kopisch was a painter, writer and traveller who translated folk-poems (as in the first and third songs above) and wrote agreeable if undemanding verses derived from folklore and legend.

Köstlin *see* Reinhold.

Kugler, Franz, 1808–58: *Ständchen* Op. 106/1 (No. 191). Kugler was an artist, art historian, musician and poet who began his career as assistant editor to Chamisso on the journal *Musenalmanach*. Like Kopisch, he was a skilled versifier of legends. Many of his early lyrics were published in the so-called *Skizzenbuch* of 1830, which was lent to Brahms by Kugler's son, whom he had met on holiday in Switzerland (Kalbeck iv 105). In returning it, Brahms intimated that he had put it to good purpose. He later acquired the *Gedichte* of 1840, which contained the two lyrics he set for mixed voice quartet Op. 112/1–2, *Sehnsucht* and *Nächtens*.

Lemcke, Karl, 1831–1913: *Über die See* Op. 69/7 (No. 128), *Im Garten am Seegestade* Op. 70/1 (No. 131), *Willst du, dass ich geh?* Op. 71/4 (No. 138), *Verzagen* Op. 72/4 (No. 143), *In Waldeseinsamkeit* Op. 85/6 (No. 155), *Verrat* Op. 105/5 (No. 190), *Salamander* Op. 107/2 (No. 197). Lemcke was a poet and critic who lectured on literature and art. His volume of *Lieder und Gedichte* (1861) was published in Brahms's home town of Hamburg. Perhaps it had a restricted circulation; despite the racy musicality of the poems, there are few or no other Lemcke settings. But Brahms instantly seized on them, partly perhaps out of local loyalty, or other personal reasons such as their applicability to his own circumstances, and also their overt eroticism (adjudged excessive by the stern Elisabet von Herzogenberg; see No. 138). By 1862 he had set four of Lemcke's patriotic military lyrics for four-part male chorus (Op. 41/2–5), so some of the solo songs from the same source may have been sketched at the same time though not completed until much later.

Liliencron, Detlev von, 1844–1909: *Auf dem Kirchhofe* Op. 105/4 (No. 189), *Maienkätzchen* Op. 107/4 (No. 199). Liliencron, in his day, was a strong influence on German writers and a significant poet in his own right, who was rightly revered by his successor Rilke. His predictable patriotic and folk-song themes have an unromantic touch of realism, as befits a Prussian cavalry officer, together with an engaging originality (which disposed him to espouse the cause of Hugo Wolf, for example) and an admixture of internationalism (his mother was born in America, and he travelled there in later life).

Lingg, Hermann, 1820–1905: *Immer leiser wird mein Schlummer* Op. 105/2 (No. 187). Lingg was another member of the Munich circle. He wrote the epic poem *Die Völkerwanderung* and several dramas, but is mainly remembered for his lyrics, published in three volumes 1854–70. These are sometimes dark and ominous as in the Brahms setting, and they derive from Lingg's experience of disease and death as a professional physician; but they also have their own musicality.

Luther, Martin, 1483–1546: the Biblical texts of the *Vier Ernste Gesänge (Four Serious Songs** Op. 121/1–4 (Nos. 201–4). Luther founded the Reformation by protesting against the Roman Catholic faith in which he had been reared and ordained. In literary terms, he was also a chief precursor of the Romantic movement, in two respects. First, he was devoted to songs both sacred and secular (he wrote the hymn 'Ein' feste Burg ist unser Gott', and the drinking-chorus extolling 'Wein, Weib und Gesang' is attributed to him); secondly, his famous oration at the Diet of Worms in 1521 is among the earliest manifestos in favour of individual feeling. There he breathed a Promethean defiance, famously enshrined in his self-extenuatory yet self-laudatory phrases 'Here stand I. I can do no other, God help me.', thus invoking himself thrice in eleven words (or ten in the original German 'Hier stehe ich. Ich kann nicht anders. Gott helfe mir'). In matters of religion, his stance is the same; thus his *Large Catechism* claims that 'Whatever your heart clings to and confides in, that is really your God'. All this would captivate and inspire the Romantic Brahms; and Luther's translation of the scriptures had the same powerful appeal, with the added attraction of distilling the spirit of Oriental poetry, as Daumer had done for Hafiz. It is no accident that Middle Eastern writings in translation, and German Volkslieder (see below), were Brahms's main lifelong sources of verbo-musical inspiration. In addition to the texts of Op. 121/1–4, as translated and identified in the notes to those songs (Nos. 201–204) the following passages of Luther's Bible (arranged in that order) were set by Brahms in a variety of genres and forces: Exodus* 34.6–7 (Op. 110/1); Deuteronomy* 4.9 (Op. 109/3); Job* 3.20–23 (Op. 74/1): Psalms* 13 (Op. 27), 22. 5–6 (Op. 109/1), 29.11 (Op. 109/1), 39.5–8 (Op. 45/3), 51.12–14 (Op. 29/2), 69.30 (Op. 110/1), 84.2–3, 5 (Op. 45/4), 126.5–6 (Op. 45/1); Isaiah* 35.10, 51.11 (Op. 45/2), 66.13 (Op. 45/5); Lamentations* 3.41 (Op. 74/1); Matthew* 5.4 (Op. 45/1); Luke* 11.21, 17 (Op. 109/2); John* 16.22 (Op. 45/5); I Corinthians* 13.1–2, 12–13 (Op. 121/4), 15.51–5 (Op. 45/6); Hebrews* 13.14 (Op. 45/6); James* 5.7 (Op. 45/2), 5.11 (Op. 74/1); I Peter* 1.24–5 (Op. 45/2); Ecclesiastes* 3, 19–22 (Op. 121/1), 4.1–3 (Op. 121/2); Revelations* 4.11 and 14.13 (Op. 45/6, 7), 19.1–2, 2.5–7, 11.15–16 (Op. 55); Ecclesiasticus* (Apocrypha) 41. 1–4 (Op. 121/3), 51. 35 (Op. 45/5); Wisdom of Solomon* (Apocrypha) 3.1 (Op. 45/3). In addition, the first verse of a hymn by Luther is used in the motet Op. 74/1. So comprehensive a selection might at first seem to imply that Brahms was notable for his orthodox Christian piety. But in fact these are mostly short excerpts, sometimes cited out of order, and chosen to express passionate individual feelings, rather than the coherent thought-content of Holy Writ. Brahms, like many another freethinker, knew and loved the Bible as literature combining esoteric imagery with direct diction, as in German Romantic poetry of the period, whether as original verse or as translation. Brahms's biblical Latin deserves a special mention. In the autograph of his first piano concerto Op. 15 the slow movement is headed 'Benedictus qui venit in nomine Domini', blessed is he that cometh in the name of the Lord, as in Matthew 21.9 and the Roman liturgy. Brahms, who called Schumann 'Domine', clearly applied those words to Clara, heedless of their meaning or gender. 'The very day [Brahms] arrived [at the Schumann home in Düsseldorf] Clara had discovered she was pregnant . . .' (MacDonald 1990, 17). So it is not surprising, though it may be disconcerting, to discover that his F major *Ave Maria* Op. 12 (Vulgate Luke* 1.28, 42) ends its setting of 'Benedicta tu in mulieribus' (blessed art thou among women) with C–B–A–G#–A (bars 47–9; cf. also the alto line at bars 56–9) and its repeated invocation of 'Maria' with E♭–D–C–B–C (bars 5–7, 26–8); see also pp. 15–17 above.

Meissner, Alfred von, 1822–85: *Nachwirkung* Op. 6/3 (No. 11). Meissner, critic, traveller and versifier, was a friend of Siegfried Kapper in Prague, and personally known to Brahms (Kalbeck ii 426). His *Gedichte*, first published in 1845, were regularly reprinted; Brahms's choice is typical in its easy rhyming and light eroticism. His critical and other writings were also popular because of their journalistic readability.

Mörike, Eduard, 1804–75: *An eine Äolsharfe* Op. 19/5 (No. 33), *Agnes* Op. 59/5 (No. 104). Mörike in Germany, like Baudelaire (1821–67) in France, counts as the first and ranks among the greatest of his nation's symbolist poets. He was also notable for his skills at sketching and colouring (his novel *Maler Nolten* is about a painter) and his love and knowledge of music (exemplified in his short story *Mozart auf der Reise nach Prag*) and classical languages (from which he was a gifted translator). Like Brahms, he was modest and shy (he made a living as a pastor, and later as a lecturer); and he too was inspired by folk-song, as in *Agnes*. Brahms also set his poem *Die Schwestern* as the duet Op. 61/1, His lovely lyrics had been set as solo songs from Schumann onwards (Opp. 64/1–2, 79/24, 107/3, 125/3), notably by Wolf (57 settings all told, culminating in the 53 contained in the Mörike songbook of 1888). There is ample further material (see also Lesle 1975, Sams 1975 and 1980) for many a commemoration of this great poet in 2004, his bicentenary birth-year.

Münch-Bellinghausen *see* 'Halm'.

Platen (-Hallermünde), August, Graf von, 1796–1835: *Wie rafft' ich mich auf* Op. 32/1 (No. 34), *Ich schleich umher* Op. 32/3 (No. 36), *Der Strom* Op. 32/4 (No. 37), *Wehe, so willst du mich wieder* Op. 32/5 (No. 38), *Du sprichst* Op. 32/6 (No. 39). Platen was a distinguished and fastidious stylist, who wrote satirical drama as well as emotive lyrics. But he was thrice an outsider; as a nobleman and a homosexual, living in Italy, he remained aloof from any Pan-German movement in politics or Romanticism in literature. Nevertheless his predilection for non-German verse-forms such as the ghasel and the sonnet (of which he created some of the very finest examples, in his *Ghaselen* (1821) and *Sonette aus Venedig* (1825)) aligned him with the Romantic movement's centrifugal striving towards other worlds and lands and times. Further, his unfeigned isolation sounded a new note of genuine deprivation. As Platen said in a sonnet, he stamped his personal seal on language. The same seal was also applied to the language of music, through such deeply responsive settings as those of Schubert, D751 and 756, and the matching minor-key motifs of Brahms Op. 32.

Reinhold, Christian (pseudonym of Christian Köstlin), 1813–56: *Nachtigall* Op. 97/1 (No. 180), *Auf dem Schiffe* Op. 97/2 (No. 181), *Auf dem See* Op. 106/2 (No. 192), *Ein Wanderer* Op. 106/5 (No. 195). Brahms was friendly with the Fellinger family, especially Richard and his wife Maria née Köstlin. She was an artist and sculptor who also took many of the famous photographs of the composer in his later years. Her father had been a professor of law, and an accomplished amateur poet; she brought his verses to the composer's attention (Kalbeck iii 531).

Reinick, Robert, 1805–52: *Liebestreu* Op. 3/1 (No. 1), *Juchhe!* Op. 6/4 (No. 12). Reinick was popular with song-writers as well as the general public, because of his verses' singable simplicity and visual quality. Like Brahms, he loved and wrote for children; he was also an artist and engraver, whose best-known volume of poetry was the *Lieder eines Malers* (Songs of a Painter) (1838). Its envoy is addressed to Reinick's close friend Franz Kugler (q.v.), another artist–poet set by Brahms. But a third such poet, far greater than either, seems to have taken a very different view; Eduard Mörike (q.v.), who knew some English, assigned bogus bird-song doggerel to a Wendehals, or wryneck,[1] in an ironic parody of German Romanticism. But Reinick at least exemplifies music's uncritical absorption of inferior texts; such settings as Schumann's Op. 36/1–6 can readily rise far above poetic flatness.

Rousseau, Johann, 1802–67: *Der Frühling* Op. 6/2 (No. 10). Rousseau was a prolific Catholic journalist and popular versifier. In the fourth (1866) edition of his poems he added proudly 'set to music by Reissiger and Julius Weiss', quite unaware of this Brahms song (Friedländer 6).

Rückert, Friedrich, 1788–1866; *Gestillte Sehnsucht* Op. 91/1 (No. 162), *Mit vierzig Jahren* Op. 94/1 (No. 164). Rückert was a professor of oriental languages and also a major poet. Some of the evidence for that latter claim lies in the music that his verses inspired in the great masters of German song. In 1822, Schubert had distilled the essence of Platen (q.v.) in two lieder; in 1823, he rendered the same homage and service to five Rückert lyrics (D741, 775–8), thus creating yet another new style, shone through by poetic warmth like an eastern sunrise. Rückert, like Platen, had begun with adaptations of oriental lyrics (including ghasels) that extended the boundaries of German lyricism into new realms of imagery and

[1] in his poem *Zur Warnung*, set by Wolf as No. 49 of the *Mörike-Lieder*.

diction. This movement, already discernible in the Biblical translations of Luther (q.v.), and established by Goethe's *Westöstlicher Diwan*, was much admired by Brahms for its universalism (see also Bodenstedt, Daumer, Herder, etc.) as well as its poetic merits. Rückert had many more strings to his lyre. He was an accomplished master of philosophy, translation, drama, ballads and above all love-poetry; and this too had made a new music in Schumann's many settings, notably his *Liebesfrühling* Op. 37 and *Minnespiel* Op. 101. Brahms's two settings are typically older, and hence more melancholy and meditative; but he too turns the Rückert style into matching music.

Schack, Adolf Friedrich von, 1815–94: *Herbstgefühl* Op. 48/7 (No. 78), *Abend-dämmerung* Op. 49/5 (No. 83). *Serenade* Op. 58/8 (No. 99). Schack was a gifted art critic and translator (who collaborated with Geibel, q.v., on the renderings from the Spanish known as *Romanzero*) and a prolific poet and playwright. He was much admired in his own day for the strength of his commitment to creative internationalism as well as for the euphony of his style. At his best, he can combine genuine feeling with competent craftsmanship, as in the terza rima *An Mendelssohn*; and his devotion to painting and music helped to create colourful imagery and singable rhythms. His collected literary works were published in six volumes (1884–8) of which the second contains the complete poems, first printed in 1866. The three that Brahms selected for setting are widely spaced within that collection, which he owned and had no doubt studied extensively; the same applies to Schack's three-volume history of the art and literature of Spain. Schack's name will live as the poet of Strauss's *Ständchen* Op. 17/2 and other songs, as well as Brahms's *Serenade* Op. 58/8; even if he had no enduring lyric voice of his own, such works give him one.

Schenkendorf, Max, 1783–1817: *Frühlingstrost* Op. 63/1 (No. 113), *Erinnerung* Op. 63/2 (No. 114), *An ein Bild* Op. 63/3 (No. 115), *An die Tauben* Op. 63/4 (No. 116), *Todessehnen* Op. 86/6 (No. 161). More than a century after Schenkendorf's death he was still being hailed, even in an English history of German literature, as the 'most gifted poet' of national revolt. This assessment related to his 'persistent belief that one day the old German empire will be revived' (Robertson 436–7). It is certainly true that his *Gedichte* (1815) were reissued with plentiful supplement-ation up to 1913. Brahms is known to have owned the 1878 fifth edition, which he had no doubt studied devotedly; but all his five settings date from earlier years. As a devoted follower of Bismarck, he would have found Schenkendorf's reputation as a popular soldier-poet entirely congenial; but in fact the bulk of the latter's published lyrics consist of personal Romantic effusions of which Brahms's settings are entirely representative. They made no such appeal to any other great song-writer, which confirms the assessment of Brahms himself as a thorough-paced Romantic.

Scherer, Georg, 1828–1909: *Wiegenlied* Op. 49/4 (No. 82), verse two. Scherer compiled such collections as the *Illustriertes Deutsches Kinderbuch* (1849), *Deutsche Volkslieder* (1851) and *Die schönsten deutschen Volkslieder* (1868). Like most anthologists of the period, he rewrote or invented some of his own so-called folk-song texts, such as the second verse he added to the traditional strophe that Brahms had set in the first edition of his *Wiegenlied*. So this addition appears in later issues of that song, at the suggestion of Brahms's publisher Fritz Simrock, with a further amendment by Brahms himself (see No. 82 note 1).

Schlegel, August, 1767–1845; *Ophelia-Lieder** WoO 22/1–5 (Nos. 108–112). August Schegel and his brother Friedrich were the co-founders of Romantic theory (Robertson 411ff), and the former's translation of Shakespeare was his 'most significant achievement, and, in some ways, the most significant of the whole Romantic School' (ibid., 413). Brahms also drew on the Schlegel translation for his setting of 'Komm herbei, komm herbei, Tod'* (Come away, come away, death') for women's chorus with horn and harp Op. 17/2.

Schmidt, Hans, 1856–?: *Sommerabend* Op. 84/1 (No. 145), *Der Kranz* Op. 84/2 (No. 146), *In den Beeren* Op. 84/3 (No. 147), *Sapphische Ode* Op. 94/4 (No. 167). The young Hans Schmidt had musical as well as poetical talent. He studied music in Vienna with Brahms's friend Nottebohm, and was made welcome in their circle. In 1881, he sent Brahms a copy of his (undated but presumably recent) *Gedichte und Übersetzungen* and received a warm reply about the love and respect in which his music and poetry were held (Kalbeck iii 299–300). Perhaps he knew of Brahms's fascination with the mother–daughter theme (the subject of the first three songs) and with classical metrics (the essence of the fourth), and had penned the poems especially.

Schulz, Eduard; see 'Ferrand, Eduard'.

Schumann, Felix, 1854–79; *Junge Lieder I/II* Op. 63/5–6 (Nos. 117–18), *Versunken* Op. 86/5 (No. 160). Felix, named in memory of Mendelssohn, was the youngest child of Robert and Clara Schumann. His remarkable talents remained unripe, and were gravely inhibited by his severe illness. But he found time and energy to study Italian, Spanish and English, make translations from Moore and Burns, write poems of his own, play the violin and the piano, become an adept mountain-climber and fell-walker and (like his father before him) take up the study of law at Heidelberg, until he fell victim to tuberculosis at only twenty years old. As Brahms said to Clara 'I don't know how I could contain myself for joy if I had such a son'. The three Brahms settings form a fitting memorial for the unfortunate Felix; some touching reminiscences and poems were recorded by his sister Eugenie in her *Erinnerungen* (1927).

Shakespeare, William, 1564–1616; *Ophelia-Lieder** WoO 22/1–5 (Nos. 108–112). As the letters to Billroth, for example, amply illustrate, Brahms was a well-informed Shakespearean, who had studied the plays in the Schlegel and Tieck translation; cf. also Litzmann i 124 and Avins 204. But the *Ophelia* songs represent the fulfilment of a personal promise rather than the expression of feeling, even though Brahms himself so often chose to depict abandoned and distraught women.

Simrock, Karl, 1802–76; *Auf dem See* Op. 59/2 (No. 101), *An den Mond* Op. 71/2 (No. 136). Karl Simrock was the son of the Bonn music publisher Nicolaus and the uncle of Brahms's own lifelong publisher and friend Fritz Simrock. Karl was a prolific writer and translator (especially from the old German of the *Nibelungenlied* and Walther von der Vogelweide) as well as an active political reformer far in advance of his time, for example in combining a powerful German patriotism with fervent Francophile sympathies. His aspirations for a unified Germany, reflected in his lifelong preoccupation with folk-song collection (also used by Brahms: see Volkslieder below), were shared by the composer.

Storm, Theodor, 1817–88; *Über die Heide* Op. 86/4 (No. 159). The North German Storm lived a quiet life as a local civil servant. Like his admired Eichendorff, he was a story-teller as well as a poet; but Storm's sense of coherent form and structure, as well as his determinedly secularist outlook, render his Novellen (from *Immensee*, 1850 to *Der Schimmelreiter*, 1888) far more realistic if more mundane than his idol's. His poetry, similarly, is rather less magical, though still most appealing in its kindliness and humour and its sensitivity to scene and mood. As Brahms would have known, he dedicated a dialect poem to their fellow-countryman Klaus Groth (q.v.); and Mörike, who was well placed to know, said of it (as he might have said of Storm's lyric gift in general) that even in perusal it sounded sung.

Thibault IV, 1201–53: *Ein Sonett** Op. 14/4 (No. 24). Thibault de Champagne, King of Navarre, wrote the original French lyric that Herder translated. Brahms surely found the Gallic quasi-troubadour derivation attractive in its affinity with his own native Minnesang.

Tieck, Ludwig, 1773–1853: *Romanzen aus 'Magelone'* Op. 33/1–15 (Nos. 43–57). Tieck has already been discussed as the poet of these *Magelone-Lieder*, which exemplify a deep and sustained interlinkage between music and literature. The initial musical inspiration might have derived from Mendelssohn, whose charming Tieck setting *Minnelied* Op. 47/1 has something of the same Franco-German troubadour tradition.

Uhland, Ludwig, 1787–1862: *Heimkehr* Op. 7/6 (No. 20), *Scheiden und Meiden* Op. 19/2 (No. 30), *In der Ferne* Op. 19/3 (No. 31), *Der Schmied* Op. 19/4 (No. 32). From his earliest years, Uhland was the embodiment of German Romanticism in all its varied aspects; a fine poet in both ballad and lyric forms, a distinguished jurist and civil servant, a historian and archivist who collected and edited folk-songs, and a dauntless campaigner for personal liberty and national unity. His hallmarks are powerful personal feeling combined with careful craftsmanship. He was thus a born Brahmsian; and that affinity appears in other works, notably the choral Op. 44/6 and 12, and the early sketches for the unpublished *Brautgesang* (McCorkle 679) as well as the engaging canon WoO 29, Uhland's folk-song anthology was also a favourite source for Brahms (see Volkslieder below).

Vega, Lope de, 1562–1635: *Geistliches Wiegenlied** Op. 91/2 (No. 163). Lope de Vega, the world's most prolific dramatist, also wrote the original poem that Geibel translated.

Volkslieder, i.e. German folk-song sources. It is not now always possible to identify the sources, let alone authenticate the texts, of the German folk-songs that Brahms held so dear and set so often, whether as solo songs or choruses, anew or arranged. The entire topic is systematically analysed and charted in McCorkle 552–609. But the anthologies and compilers partly or wholly responsible for the texts used by Brahms for his own original work deserve to be named and listed, as follows:

Arnim–Brentano, *Des Knaben Wunderhorn* (see Sams 1974a): Op. 43/4 (No. 61). Op. 48/2–3 (Nos. 73–4), Op. 49/4 (verse 1) (No. 82); cf. also the duets Opp. 66/5, 75/2 and the choruses Op. 62/1–2.

Becker, C., *Lieder und Weisen vergangener Jahrhunderte*: Op. 43/3 (No. 60).

Herder, J., *Stimmen der Völker*: Opp. 14/2, 43/4 (Nos. 22, 61).

Hoffmann von Fallersleben, H., *Die Deutschen Gesellschaftslieder des 16. und 17. Jahrhunderts*: the duet Op. 28/2.

Kretzschmer–Zuccalmaglio, *Deutsche Volkslieder mit ihren Original-Weisen*: Op. 14/5–8 (Nos. 25–8), Op. 43/4 (No. 61), Op. 84/4–5 (Nos. 148–9) Op. 97/4, 6 (Nos. 183, 185), Op. 105/3 (No. 188); cf. also the choral Opp. 22/1–3, 7, 93a/1, and the canons Op. 113/3–5.

Mittler, F., *Deutsche Volkslieder*: Op. 14/1 (No. 21), Op. 48/6 (No. 77), arranged for chorus Op. 62/7.

Scherer, G., *Deutsche Volkslieder*: Op. 7/4–5 (Nos. 18–19), Op. 49/4 (verse 2) (No. 82).

Simrock, K., *Die deutschen Volkslieder*: Op. 14/1 (No. 21).

Uhland, L., *Alte hoch- und nieder-deutsche Volkslieder*: Op. 43/4 (No. 61), Op. 47/3 (No. 69), and the choruses Opp. 22/4–6, 41/1.

Voss, Johann, 1751–1826: Voss is worth recording in his own right as the editor of Hölty (q.v.) in versions that composers accepted and might even have preferred. Voss was a teacher and a classicist, whose translation of Homer has been placed (Robertson 304) on the same exalted level as Schlegel's of Shakespeare. He also has his own modest but enduring place in lied history as the poet of Loewe's Op. 9 v/i 1 (a text also set by Brahms as the choral Op. 44/1), or Mendelssohn's Opp. 8/9 and 11, 9/1 and 6.

Wenzig, Joseph, 1807–76: *Der Gang zum Liebsten** Op. 48/1 (No. 72), *Gold überwiegt die Liebe** Op. 48/4 (No. 75), *Sehnsucht†** Op. 49/3 (No. 81), *Klage I/II** Op. 69/1–2 (Nos. 122–3), *Abschied** Op. 69/3 (No. 124), *Des Liebsten Schwur** Op. 69/4 (No. 125). The bilingual Wenzig helped to found the Bohemian national movement. He not only translated Czech folk-poetry into German but also wrote the original Czech libretti of Smetana's operas *Dalibor* and *Libusse.*

Württemberg, Ulrich von (attrib.); Op. 43/3 (No. 60), also set for chorus as Op. 41/1.

SELECT BIBLIOGRAPHY

ML	Music and Letters
MQ	Music Quarterly
MT	Musical Times
NZfM	Neue Zeitschrift für Musik
ÖMZ	Österreichische Musikzeitschrift
TLS	Times Literary Supplement

Avins, S. *Johannes Brahms: Life and Letters*, 1997

'Babel'. 'Music in the Foreign Press' (on Reger's musical cryptography and Brahms' veiled autobiography), *MT* June 1953, 267–8

Biba, O. Hofmann R. & K., eds. '. . . *in meinen Tönen spreche ich': Für Johannes Brahms 1833–1897*, 1997

Botstein, L., ed. *The Compleat Brahms*, 1999

Bozarth, G. 'Synthesizing word and tone: Brahms's setting of Hebbel's "Vorüber" ', in Pascall 1983, 77–98

—— 'The Origins of Brahms's *In stiller Nacht*, *MLA Notes*, liii/2 (Dec. 1996), 363–80.

Brahms, J. *Briefwechsel* i–xvi, 1907–22; see also separate correspondents e.g. Herzogenbergs, Simrocks and (for Clara Schumann) Litzmann

—— *Des Jungen Kreislers Schatzkästlein*, ed. C. Krebs, 1909

—— *Gesamtausgabe*: i.e. the *Sämtliche Werke: Ausgabe der Gesellschaft der Musikfreunde*, ed. E. Mandyczewski *et al.*, 26 vols, 1926–8, repr. Dover Press, 1968–91

—— *Ophelia-Lieder*. see Geiringer

—— *Die Müllerin*, see Draheim

Draheim, J., ed. *Die Müllerin*, 1983

Franken, F. 'Robert Schumann in der Irrenanstalt Endenich', Archiv-Blätter 1, Stiftung Archiv der Akademischen Künste, 1994, 7–16

Frenzel, H. *Daten deutscher Dichtung*, 1952

Friedländer, M. *Brahms Lieder*, 1922 (Eng. trans., 1928); and see Peters edition

Frisch, W., ed. *Brahms and His World*, 1990

Geiringer, K., ed. *Ophelia-Lieder*, 1935

Gesamtausgabe, see under Brahms

Goedeke, K. *Grundriss zur Geschichte der deutschen Dichtung* vol. 3, 1881

Haight, G. 'George Eliot's Bastards', in *George Eliot: A Centenary Tribute*, ed. Haight and VanArsdel 1982, 5

Hallmark, R., ed. *German Lieder in the Nineteenth Century*, 1996

Hancock, V. *Brahms's Choral Compositions and His Library of Early Music*, 1983

—— 'The growth of Brahms's interest in early choral music, and its effect on his own choral compositions', in Pascall 1983, 27–40

—— 'Brahms's links with German Renaissance music: a Discussion of Selected Choral Works', in Musgrave 1987, 95–110

—— 'Brahms: Volkslied/Kunstlied', in Hallmark 1996, 119–52

Henderson, F. 'The Hidden Hand of William Clarke', in *Worcester College Record*, 1998, 72

Henschel, G. *Personal Recollections of Johannes Brahms*, 1907

—— *Musings and Memories of a Musician*, 1918

Herzogenbergs *Johannes Brahms im Briefwechsel mit Heinrich und Elisabet von Herzogenberg*, two vols., ed. M. Kalbeck, 1907; Eng. trans., 1909/*R* 1986

Hofmann, K. *Die Bibliothek von Joh. Brahms*, 1974

—— *Die Erstdrucke der Werke von Johannes Brahms*, 1975

—— *Die Erstdrucke der Werke von Robert Schumann*, 1979

Holde, A. 'Suppressed Passages in the Brahms–Joachim Correspondence, Published for the First Time', *MQ*, xlv (1959), 312

Jenner, G. *Brahms als Mensch, Lehrer und Künstler*, 1905

Joachim, J. *Briefe* v–vi, 1911–13

Johnson, G. in notes to vol. 20 of the Hyperion CD (CDJ 33020) complete Schubert edition, 12

Kahler, O.-H. 'Brahms' Wiegenlied und die Gebirgs-Bleamln des Alexander Baumann', in *Brahms-Studien* vi, ed. K. Hofmann and K. Wagner, 1985

Kalbeck, M. *Johannes Brahms*, 1904–14

Keys, I. *Brahms*, 1989

Kluge, H. *Geschichte der deutschen National-Litteratur*, 1897

Kreisig, M. *Robert Schumann: Gesammelte Schriften über Musik und Musiker*, 1914

Kühn, D. *Clara Schumann, Klavier: Ein Lebensbuch*, 1996

Lesle, L. *Eduard Mörike im Lied*, 1975

Litzmann, B., ed. *Clara Schumann, Johannes Brahms: Briefe aus den Jahren 1853–96*, 1927; Eng. trans., 1927, 2/1971

MacDonald, M. *Brahms*, 1990

McCorkle, M. *Johannes Brahms: Thematisch-Bibliographisches Verzeichnis*, 1984

Michelmann, E. *Agathe von Siebold*, 1930

Minchin, L. *Brahms Songs in English*, 1995

Mörike, E. *Mozart's Journey to Prague and Selected Poems*, transl. by David Luke, 1997

Musgrave, M. 'Brahms's First Symphony: Thematic Coherence and its Secret Origin' *Music Analysis* ii, 1983

—— ed. *Brahms 2: Biographical, Documentary and Analytical Studies*, 1987

Nietzsche, F. *Der Fall Wagners*, 1888

Oehlmann, W. *Reclams Liedführer* 1973

Ophüls, G. *Brahms-Texte*, 1897, 2/1908, 3/1923

Pascall, R., ed. *Brahms: Biographical, Documentary and Analytical Studies*, 1983

—— ' "My Love of Schubert – No Fleeting Fancy": Brahms's Response To Schubert', *Schubert Durch Die Brille*, Mitteilungen 21, June 1998, 39–55

Peters edition: Lieder in four volumes, edited by Max Friedländer

Potter, L. *Royalist Literature 1641–1660*. 1989, 58

Quigley, T. *Johannes Brahms: An Annotated Bibliography of the Literature through 1982* (1990)

—— *Johannes Brahms: An Annotated Bibliography of the Literature from 1982 to 1996* (1990)

Reich, N. *Clara Schumann, the Artist and the Woman*, 1985

Richarz, F. 'Auszüge aus Dr. Franz Richarz' Verlaufsbericht', Archiv-Blätter 1, Stiftung

Archiv der Akademischen Künste, 1994, 17–24

Robertson, J. *A History of German Literature*, 1939

Roy, I. 'Les Puissances Européennes et la Chute de Charles Ier, in *Revue d'Histoire diplomatique*, 1978, 10

Sams, E. *The Songs of Hugo Wolf*, 1961, 2/1983, 3/1992

—— 'Did Schumann use Ciphers?' *MT*, vol. 106, 1965, 584–91 (trans. *NZfM* Jg. 127, 1966)

—— 'The Schumann ciphers', *MT*, vol. 107, 1966, 392–400

—— 'The Schumann ciphers: a coda', *MT*, vol. 107, 1966, 1050–1

—— 'Why Florestan and Eusebius', *MT*, vol. 108, 1967, 131–4

—— 'Politics, Literature and People', *MT*, vol. 109, 1968, 25–7

—— *The Songs of Robert Schumann*, 1969, 2/1975, 3/1993

—— 'The Tonal Analogue in Schumann's Music', *Proceedings of the Royal Musical Association* 96 (1969–70), 103–17

—— 'Elgar's cipher letter to Dorabella', *MT*, vol. 111, 1970, 151–4

—— 'Variations on an original theme (Enigma)', *MT*, vol. 111, 1970, 258–62

—— 'Elgar's Enigmas', *MT*, vol. 111, 1970, 692–4

—— 'A Schumann Primer', *MT*, vol. 111, 1970, 1096–7

—— (1971a) 'Brahms and his Musical Love-Letters', *MT*, vol. 112, 1971, 329–30

—— (1971b) 'Brahms and his Clara Themes', *MT*, vol. 112, 1971, 432–4

—— (1971c) 'Schumann's Hand Injury' *MT*, vol. 112, 1971, 1156–9; vol. 113, 1972, 456

—— (1972a) *Brahms Songs*, 1972 (Fr. trans. *Les Lieder de Brahms* 1989)

—— (1972b) 'Zwei Brahms-Rätsel', in *ÖMZ* 27/2 (2, 1972), 83–4

—— (1972c) 'Von ewiger Liebe', in *NZfM* 133 (5. 1972), 257

—— (1972d) 'The Songs' in *Schumann: A Symposium* ed. A. Walker, 1972

—— (1972e) 'The Tonal Analogue etc.' in *Schumann: A Symposium*, ed. A. Walker. 1972, reprinted from 1969–70 item above

—— Solutions to unsolved cipher in Thurloe (State Papers) filed in the Bodleian Library with Clarendon MS 94 (1973)

—— (1974a) 'Notes on a Magic Horn', *MT*, vol. 115, 1974, 556–8

—— (1974b) 'Literary Sources of Hugo Wolf's String Quartets', *Musical Newsletter* iv (1974)

—— 'Homage to Eduard Mörike', *MT*, vol. 116, 1975, 532–3

—— with Moore, J.: 'Cryptanalysis and historical research', *TLS* 4 March 1977, 253

—— v. Roy, 1978

—— *Sir William Clarke MSS*, Harvester Microform 1979, 23–34

—— (1980a) article, 'Cryptography, Musical' in *New Grove*, 1980 and in the forthcoming 7th edition; also published in *Cryptologia* vol. 3 no. 4, October 1979

—— (1980b) article 'Mörike, Eduard', in *New Grove*, 1980

—— (1980c) Schubert work-list, *New Grove*, 1980

—— (1980d) Schumann work-list, *New Grove*, 1980

—— (1980e) Wolf article and work-list, *New Grove* 1980

—— (1980f) 'Cracking the historical codes', *TLS* 8 February 1980, 154

—— v. Haight, 1982

—— *The New Grove Schubert* (with Maurice Brown), 1982

—— Review of Brahms, *Die Müllerin*, ed. Draheim, *MT*, vol. 125, 1984, 509

—— Review of McCorkle, 1984, *MT*, vol. 126, 1985, 406

—— v. Waite, 1985

—— Review of Keys, 1989, *MT*, vol. 131, 1990, 146–7

—— 'Cryptanalysis and Historical Research', *Archivaria* (1985–6), 87–97

—— Script and presentation for Central TV film on Code and Cipher in Music, produced by Jim Berrow and directed by Simon Target, 1989

—— v. Potter, 1989

—— Review of MacDonald, 1990, *MT*, vol. 131, 1990, 428

—— v. Spalding 1990, xii

—— v. Woolrych 1992

—— 'Elgar's Enigmas', *Music and Letters*, vol. 78, 1997, 410–15

—— v. Henderson 1998

—— edition of Schumann *Papillons* Op. 2 (unpubd)

Schauffler, R. *The Unknown Brahms*, 1933

Schochow, M. *Schuberts Liedertexte*, 1974

Schumann, C., see Litzmann

Schumann, E. *Erinnerungen*, 1925

Simrocks *Briefe* ix–x, an P. und F. Simrock, 1917; xi–xii, an F. Simrock, 1919

Spalding, R. *The Diary of Bulstrode Whitelocke*, 1990, xii

Stark, L. *A Guide to the Solo Songs of Johannes Brahms*, 1995

Stein, F. *Verzeichnis deutscher Lieder seit Haydn*, 1967

Swafford, J. *Johannes Brahms*, 1997

Trautwein, W. *Robert Schumanns letzte Lebensjahre*, Archiv-Blätter 1, Stiftung Archiv der Akademischen Künste, 1994, 4–6

Waite, P. *The Man from Halifax: Sir John Thompson. Prime Minister*, 1985, ix

Wolf, H. *Kritiken*, 1911

—— *The Music Criticism of Hugo Wolf*, trans. H. Pleasants, 1979

—— *Briefe an Melanie Köchert*, 1964

Woolrych, A. new preface to *The Clarke Papers*, ed. C. Firth, 1992

INDEX TO THE SONGS:
TITLES AND/OR FIRST WORDS

The serial number allotted to each song is shown in parenthesis; all other numbers refer to pages, with the main reference shown in bold type. Songs and other settings mentioned in Appendix; the Poets are not separately indexed.

GENERAL INDEX